THE LAW OF
TERMINATION OF EMPLOYMENT

THE LAW OF
TERMINATION OF EMPLOYMENT

Sixth Edition

Robert Upex MA, LLM

of the Middle Temple, Barrister;
Professor of Law at the University of Surrey

Chapter 13 on Insolvency of the Employer
Nick Humphreys
Solicitor, Richards Butler

JORDANS
2001

Published by
Jordan Publishing Limited
21 St Thomas Street
Bristol BS1 6JS

British Library Cataloguing-in-Publication Data

A catalogue record for this book is available from the British Library.

ISBN 0 85308 731 8

Typeset in house
Printed by MPG Books Ltd, Bodmin, Cornwall

PREFACE

The first edition of this book was published in 1983, soon after I had been appointed to a post at the University of Surrey. This, the sixth, edition comes just after my return to a Chair there. When I cast my mind over the last 18 years, I am struck by how extensively the law has changed. In many ways the issues remain the same, though perhaps the emphases have changed. Just to take one example: the question of whether a person is employed or self-employed continues to pose problems, as is shown by the recent cases relating to casual workers. But, in addition to that, the recent tendency to extend rights to workers raises further questions relating to the meaning of the definition of 'worker'.

The last edition of this book was published in 1997. In the four years that have since elapsed, there has been a constant flow of significant cases and, as a result, there is scarcely a chapter of this book which has not been affected. Even the law relating to unfair dismissal, which celebrates the thirtieth anniversary, in 2002, of its introduction, continues to see new decisions, though it is fair to say that it is generally more settled now.

At the time of the publication of the last edition, legislative change had not been particularly significant, though there had been a consolidation measure in 1996, the Employment Rights Act. Since then, industrial tribunals have become employment tribunals, thanks to the Employment Rights (Dispute Resolution) Act 1998. New legislation has introduced new categories of automatically unfair dismissal, for example dismissals in connection with the Working Time Regulations, dismissals for whistleblowing, and dismissals in connection with taking leave for family reasons. It has added to the types of dismissal for which the remedy of interim relief is available, eg dismissals for whistleblowing, dismissals for reasons connected with trade recognition, and dismissals of employees for performing the functions of an employee representative. The rules governing compensation have been changed in relation to cases involving an employee's failure to use, or an employer's failure to give access to, an internal appeals procedure. The Employment Relations Act 1999 raised substantially the maximum compensatory award a tribunal may award in an unfair dismissal case, so that it now stands at £51,700; it also provided for the indexation of that limit, together with the limit of a week's pay. It removed the limit on the compensatory award in cases of dismissal in health and safety cases and dismissals for whistleblowing. Apart from these changes, the Act also introduced the right for workers to be accompanied at a grievance or disciplinary hearing, together with the right not to be unfairly dismissed for exercising that right.

There has also been a welter of decisions to absorb. These have necessitated recasting a number of chapters. Chapter 2 has had to be substantially revised to take account of the case-law on the Acquired Rights Directive and the Transfers of Undertakings Regulations. This includes decisions of the European Court of Justice in *Allen v Amalgamated Construction Co Ltd, Francisco Hernández Vidal SA v Gomez Perez* and *Oy Liikenne AB v Liskojärvi and Juntunen* and the Court of Appeal in *ECM (Vehicle Delivery Service) Ltd v Cox* and *ADI (UK) Ltd v Willer*. There have been significant decisions of the House of Lords in relation to casual workers, the definition of redundancy and the question of compensation for injury to feelings as a head of damages in wrongful dismissal cases: see *Carmichael v National Power plc, Murray v Foyle Meats Ltd* and *Johnson v Unisys Ltd*. This last decision raises the possibility of tribunals making awards of compensation in respect of injury to feelings in unfair dismissal cases, which would be a significant development. Important Court of Appeal decisions include *Bottrill v Secretary of State for Trade and Industry* and *Sellars Arenascene Ltd v Connolly* (which considers the circumstances in which directors or sole shareholders may be employees), *Montgomery v Johnson Underwood Ltd* (agency workers), *Foley v Post Office* (the test of fairness in unfair dismissal cases, following on from the Employment Appeal Tribunal (EAT) decision in *Haddon v Van den Bergh Foods Ltd*), *Post Office v Liddiard* (dismissal of employees for offences unconnected with their work), *Cerberus Software Ltd v Rowley* (and other cases involving PILON (pay in lieu of notice) clauses) and *Bartholomew v London Borough of Hackney* (on negligence in giving references for employees). There have also been many significant decisions in the EAT.

All these important developments amply justify the decision to publish a new edition of the book. The aim of this edition, as of previous editions, is to consider the main causes of action available to employees whose employment is terminated and to present the law and the relevant issues in a way which will be of value to those practising in this field. This edition, like its predecessors, covers the statutory rights given by the Employment Rights 1996 and the rights given by the common law to employees whose employment has ended. The law of wrongful dismissal, which derives exclusively from the common law and was developed in a series of nineteenth and early twentieth century cases, remains of importance, particularly as employment tribunals now have jurisdiction to hear wrongful dismissal cases.

In this edition, I have followed the method of treatment I adopted in previous editions and have treated the rights separately. Thus, the statutory rights are considered in Part I and the common law rights in Part II. Procedural considerations are dealt with in Part III. Chapter 13, which deals with insolvency, was written by my then colleague Fiona Tolmie for the previous edition. It has been updated by Nick Humphreys, of Richards Butler, to whom I am grateful for relieving me of the worry of wrestling with this complex area. Part IV contains chapters dealing with the main problems which may arise after the termination of an employee's employment – competition and references. In the Appendices, the

Employment Tribunals (Constitution and Rules of Procedure) Regulations 2001 have been included. I hope that the book will thus remain a *vade mecum* for legal advisers, whether advising employers or employees, and will enable them to decide what claims a dismissed employee may have, what the remedies are, and what levels of compensation are likely to be awarded. I hope that this process will be assisted by the use of worked examples.

It is a great pleasure to be able again to acknowledge my indebtedness to my colleagues in chambers, particularly Peter Mitchell, who updated those parts of Chapters 10 and 14 which deal with the procedural aspects of injunctions. I would also like to express my gratitude to Professor Ian Smith, of the University of East Anglia, for so generously giving up time to discuss with me issues relating to the order of calculating compensation in the context of contributory fault by the employee and the payment of *ex gratia* payments and other payments made upon termination.

I wish to express my gratitude to my publishers for undertaking the compilation of the Tables and Index.

I have based my exposition of the law on my understanding of the materials available to me as at 31 August 2001.

Robert Upex
29 Bedford Row Chambers
September 2001

CONTENTS

TABLE OF CASES

References are to paragraph numbers.

TABLE OF STATUTES

References are to paragraph numbers.

TABLE OF STATUTORY INSTRUMENTS

References are to paragraph numbers and Appendices (App).

TABLE OF INTERNATIONAL MATERIALS

References are to paragraph numbers.

TABLE OF ABBREVIATIONS

ACAS	Advisory Conciliation and Arbitration Service
COET	Central Office of Employment Tribunals
CPR	Civil Procedure Rules 1998
EAT	Employment Appeal Tribunal
ECJ	European Court of Justice
EPCA 1978	Employment Protection (Consolidation) Act 1978
ERA 1996	Employment Rights Act 1996
ERA 1999	Employment Relations Act 1999
ETA 1996	Employment Tribunals Act 1996
IA 1986	Insolvency Act 1986
PILON	Pay in Lieu of Notice
TULRCA	Trade Union and Labour Relations (Consolidation) Act 1992
TUPE	Transfer of Undertakings (Protection of Employment) Regulations 1981

INTRODUCTION

The purpose of this introduction is to indicate the possible causes of action a dismissed employee may have against an employer and the considerations which should determine the cause of action to pursue. The choice is most likely to be between complaining of unfair dismissal in the employment tribunal or of suing for wrongful dismissal in the High Court or county court; additional jurisdiction in wrongful dismissal cases has also been conferred on employment tribunals. In the restricted number of cases in which the employee's relationship with the employer is governed by public law, it may also be possible to pursue a public law remedy.[1]

An employee is employed by the employer under a contract of employment; the relationship is governed by the rules of the law of contract which have been adapted to the specific form of contractual relationship involved. This applies particularly to the termination of the contract: if either party wishes to terminate the contract, he or she must do so according to the terms of the contract (express or implied) governing notice. A failure to do so leaves that party open to an action by the other for breach of contract. An employee who wrongfully terminates the contract is most likely to be liable in damages, since the courts do not readily grant to employers other forms of relief such as specific performance and injunctions.[2] An employer who wrongfully terminates the contract is liable to an action for wrongful dismissal (if he or she has actually dismissed the employee) or breach of contract (if he or she has committed a breach of a term in the contract which has caused the employee to resign and, in effect, accept the repudiation). The rules governing these forms of action are rules developed by the common law, particularly over the last hundred or so years.

An *unfair dismissal* occurs, on the other hand, when the employer's method of terminating the contract is unfair. An unfair dismissal need not be wrongful; a dismissal with the correct notice may still be unfair if the employer uses an unfair procedure, for example by dismissing the employee without any warning and without giving an opportunity to put his or her side of the story. So wrongful dismissal is essentially a common law claim for breach of contract, whereas unfair dismissal is a totally statutory right, originally created by the Industrial Relations Act 1971, and now continued in the Employment Rights Act 1996. The two claims are not mutually exclusive and may be pursued at the same time.

---

[1]   See Chapter 11.
[2]   See Chapter 10.

The main determining factor is the amount of compensation the employee is likely to receive. Generally, an employee who is entitled to a fairly short period of notice, eg one month, is unlikely to be awarded higher damages in the High Court than the compensation he or she would receive in the employment tribunal. Further, if he or she is given the correct notice, no wrongful dismissal action will lie, since there is no breach of contract. On the other hand, a highly paid employee, who is entitled to a long period of notice (eg 12 months) and is dismissed without any notice, or who has a five-year fixed-term contract which is brought to a premature end by the employer, is more likely to obtain higher compensation from the High Court than the employment tribunal has jurisdiction to award. The amount of compensation that a tribunal may award is subject to a statutory limit. The limit is £25,000 for wrongful dismissal claims; in the case of unfair dismissal claims, the limit is £58,900. In two cases, there is no limit to the amount of compensation that may be awarded: dismissals in health and safety cases and dismissals for making a 'protected disclosure'. Thus an employee who stands to be awarded damages in excess of the statutory limit for unfair dismissal compensation is better advised to sue for wrongful dismissal. If he or she does so, and also complains of unfair dismissal, there will be a set-off between the two types of compensation.

There are other determining factors apart from the level of possible compensation, however. Perhaps the most important for an adviser to have in mind is the qualifications and exclusions to which the unfair dismissal right is subject. These are considered fully in Chapter 1. For example, employees do not qualify for their statutory rights until they have been 'continuously employed' for one year; once they have reached pensionable age, they are generally excluded from the statutory rights. So an employee who is outside the 1996 Act will only be able to pursue common-law remedies.

The most important factors affecting the choice of cause of action are, therefore, the following:

(a)   the length of the employee's employment;
(b)   the amount of notice entitlement;
(c)   whether the notice received corresponded with the notice entitlement;
(d)   the level of earnings; and
(e)   if he or she was employed under a fixed-term contract, the length of the unexpired part of the contract.

A further point to note in wrongful dismissal cases is that the existence of jurisdiction in employment tribunals in respect of damages for breach of contract means that decisions have to be made as to whether to pursue such a claim in the county court or the employment tribunal. This jurisdiction arises by virtue of section 3 of the Employment Tribunals Act

1996[1] and the Employment Tribunals Extension of Jurisdiction (England and Wales) Order 1994,[2] and is considered more fully in Chapter 9.

The division of this book follows the basic division between the common law and the statutory rights. The statutory rights, together with their remedies, are considered first, in Part I (Chapters 1–8). The common-law rights and remedies are dealt with in Part II (Chapters 9–11); there also the effect of public law is discussed. Part III deals with procedural considerations; limitation periods and the insolvency of the employer. Part IV considers two particular types of problem which may arise after termination of the employment relationship: competition by ex-employees and references.

---

[1] Formerly s 131 of the Employment Protection (Consolidation) Act 1978, as amended.
[2] SI 1994 No 1623.

Part I:

THE STATUTORY RIGHTS

Chapter 1

PRELIMINARY CONSIDERATIONS

1. PERSONS ENTITLED

(a) Employee or not?

(i) The definition of employee

1.01   The rights discussed in Part I, Chapters 4, 5 and 6 are available only to 'employees'. An employee is employed under a 'contract of service' or a 'contract of employment' and is distinguished from an independent contractor or self-employed person, who works under a 'contract for services'. In essence the distinction between them lies in the nature of the obligation undertaken. Both may be engaged to achieve a particular result, but the independent contractor may have far greater latitude than the employee in the way he or she achieves that result, for example in hours of work and use of sub-contractors.

1.02   Section 230(1) of the Employment Rights Act 1996 defines an 'employee' as 'an individual who has entered into or works under … a contract of employment'. 'Contract of employment' means 'a contract of service or apprenticeship, whether express or implied, and (if it is express) whether it is oral or in writing'.[1] There is no definition of 'self-employed person', 'independent contractor' or 'contract for services' in the Act.

1.03   Much recent legislation has given rights to 'workers', a term defined in section 230(3) of the 1996 Act, although the statutory rights considered in this book are conferred only upon 'employees'. Because of the growing importance of the concept of a 'worker' and because there are some noticeable anomalies in the statutory provisions, the concept is examined at the end of this section (see para 1.50).

1.04   Two other points are worthy of note here. First, section 23 of the Employment Relations Act 1999 contains a provision which gives the Secretary of State power to extend employment protection rights to groups who currently do not enjoy them, including individuals expressly excluded from the rights.[2] The order made may confer the rights on individuals who are of a 'specified description'.[3] It may also provide that individuals are to be treated as parties to workers' contracts or contracts of employment and make provision as to who are to be regarded as the employers of individuals. The order may also modify the operation of any rights as

---

[1]   See s 230(2).
[2]   ERA 1999, s 23(3).
[3]   ERA 1999, s 23(2).

conferred on individuals by the order.[1] It is not clear what steps are intended to be taken under this provision. It may be that specific groups who are currently treated as excluded from the legislation will be included within the order, for example clergy. Equally, there is no reason why the order should not be a general provision extending the relevant legislation to workers instead of employees, for example. In the latter case, the effect would be considerable and would, at least to some extent, reduce the problems involved in making a distinction between employees and self-employed persons.

1.05   The second matter worthy of note here is what is called IR35. This results from a provision in the Finance Act 2000[2] relating to 'personal service companies'. The legislation applies to a 'worker' who provides services to another person ('the client') under arrangements involving an intermediary (for example, a company or partnership) in circumstances such that, if the contract had been made directly, the worker would have been an employee of the client. If the legislation applies, then tax and national insurance contributions must be paid on a minimum amount of salary, which may be either in the form of actual payments during the year or as a notional payment deemed to have been paid to the worker by the intermediary. The effect of the legislation will be to make these sorts of arrangements less attractive to those who provide their services in this way, since their tax position will be less favourable. For a more detailed consideration of these matters, reference should be made to the standard works on tax law. Finally, it should be noted that an attempt has been made to seek judicial review of the legislation on the basis that the provisions were incompatible with European Community law and the Human Rights Act 1998. The High Court refused to grant judicial review.[3]

(ii) The definition in practice

1.06   Because of the generality of the statutory definitions set out above, the courts have laid down tests to enable a distinction to be made between employees and self-employed and contracts of service and contracts for services. The tests originally derived from the cases on vicarious liability, but have been refined over the last 30 years or so. Many of the older cases used what is called the 'control' test, and some used the 'organisation' or 'integration' test. The test currently used is the 'multiple' test, of which there are numerous variants.

1.07   The 'multiple' test was formulated in *Ready Mixed Concrete (South East) Ltd v Minister of Pensions and National Insurance*,[4] where MacKenna J said:

---

[1]   ERA 1999, s 23(4)(a)–(c).

[2]   Sch 12; see also the Social Security Contributions (Intermediaries) Regulations 2000, SI 2000 No 727.

[3]   See *R v Commissioners of Inland Revenue ex parte Professional Contractors Group Ltd* (2001) IDS Brief B685/13. The report of the case helpfully summarises the main provisions of the legislation.

[4]   [1968] 2 QB 497.

'A contract of service exists if the following three conditions are fulfilled:

> (i)   The servant agrees that in consideration of a wage or other remuneration he will provide his own work and skill in the performance of some service for his master.
> (ii)   He agrees expressly or impliedly that in the performance of that service he will be subject to the other's control in sufficient degree to make that other master.
> (iii) The other provisions of the contract are consistent with its being a contract of service.'[1]

The judge formulated his conclusion in terms of whether the person in question was in business on his own account, a formulation which has been recurrent ever since. Despite the fact that a number of factors in the case suggested the conclusion that the person concerned was an employee, the judge based his conclusion that he was self-employed on what he called 'the ownership of the instrumentalities', ie the tools of the trade.

1.08   This case was followed soon after by *Market Investigations Ltd v Minister of Social Security*.[2] Cooke J's approach was similar to that of MacKenna J, but he refined the third part of that judge's test. He said that the fundamental test was: 'Is the person who has engaged himself to perform these services performing them as a person in business on his own account?'. He went on:

> 'No exhaustive list has been compiled and perhaps no exhaustive list can be compiled of considerations which are relevant in determining that question, nor can strict rules be laid down as to the relative weight which the various considerations should carry in particular cases. The most that can be said is that control will no doubt always have to be considered, although it can no longer be regarded as the sole determining factor; and that factors, which may be of importance, are such matters as whether the man performing the services provides his own equipment, whether he hires his own helpers, what degree of financial risk he takes, what degree of responsibility for investment and management he has, and whether and how far he has an opportunity of profiting from sound management in the performance of his task.'[3]

This test was applied by the Privy Council, which cited the above passage with approval, in *Lee Ting Sang v Chung Chi-Keung*[4] to a mason

---

[1]   [1968] 2 QB 497 at p 515.

[2]   [1969] 2 QB 173.

[3]   *Ibid* at pp 184–185.

[4]   [1990] ICR 409. The passage in the text was also quoted with approval by Sir Nicolas Browne-Wilkinson V-C in *Andrews v King* [1991] ICR 846 at p 850. The case involved the assessment to tax of a farm worker who organised a number of men together for picking or grading potatoes as and when they were required by potato merchants who operated near Spalding. The farm worker, Andrews, was assessed to tax on the basis that he was a self-employed gang-master who employed the members of the gang. He was therefore assessed to tax as a self-employed person and served with PAYE determinations of tax payable by an employer. The Vice-Chancellor held that he was not carrying on business on his own account and that all the members of the gang, including Andrews, were employed by the potato merchants.

working mainly for a sub-contractor who was paid either a piece rate or a daily rate for his work, depending upon the nature of the work.[1]

1.09   The most recent case in which the Court of Appeal has considered this issue is *Express & Echo Publications Ltd v Tanton*.[2] The facts of the case are reminiscent of those of *Ready Mixed Concrete*. They involved a driver who was made redundant from his employment and who was later re-engaged under a contract which the company intended, and the driver agreed, should be a contract for services. Clause 3.3 of the agreement provided that should the driver be 'unable or unwilling to perform the services personally he shall arrange at his own expense entirely for another suitable person to perform the services'. The driver applied to the employment tribunal for a declaration that his status was that of employee and an order that he should be supplied with a written contract of employment in similar terms to those enjoyed by the company's employees. The tribunal determined that he was an employee and the Employment Appeal Tribunal (EAT) dismissed the company's appeal. The Court of Appeal, however, allowed the company's appeal, saying that as a matter of law where a person is not required to perform the contract personally the relationship is not one of employee and employer. Thus, clause 3.3 was wholly inconsistent with the contract being one of service. Peter Gibson LJ, with whom the other members of the Court agreed, said:[3]

> '... [I]t is necessary for a contract of employment to contain an obligation on the part of the employee to provide his services personally. Without such an irreducible minimum of obligation, it cannot be said that the contract is one of service ... [I]t is established on the authorities that, where, as here, a person who works for another is not required to perform his services personally, then as a matter of law the relationship between the worker and the person for whom he works is not that of employee and employer.'

1.10   This case was distinguished by the EAT in the later case of *MacFarlane v Glasgow City Council*,[4] which involved qualified gymnastic instructors working at sports centres operated by the council. If an instructor could not take a class, she would arrange for a replacement from a register of coaches maintained by the council. The replacements were paid by the council, not by the applicant. Lindsay J, President of the EAT, said that the clause in *Tanton* was extreme and that that case was distinguishable on the grounds, amongst others, that the applicant could not simply choose not to work in person and that she was not free to

---

[1]   The findings of fact, as summarised by the Hong Kong Court of Appeal, are set out at pp 412–413 of the report. At pp 413–414, the Privy Council's judgment goes on to say that, had it been sitting as a court of first instance, it would have concluded that the mason was an employee. This leads on to a discussion of the circumstances in which an appellate court is entitled to interfere with the decision of a lower court. This aspect of the case is considered at para 1.45.

[2]   [1999] ICR 693.

[3]   *Ibid* at pp 699–700.

[4]   [2001] IRLR 7.

provide any substitute, but only someone from the council's own register. Further, the council paid the substitute direct. Of *Tanton* the EAT said:[1]

> 'The individual there, at his own choice, need never turn up for work. He could, moreover, profit from his absence if he could find a cheaper substitute. He could choose the substitute and then in effect he would be the master. Properly regarded, *Tanton* does not oblige the tribunal to conclude that under a contract of service the individual has, always and in every event, however exceptional, personally to provide his services.'

1.11   An alternative test to the tests considered above is to ask: 'Was his contract of service within the meaning which an ordinary person would give to the words?'. This approach has been taken in a number of cases.[2] In *Withers v Flackwell Heath Football Supporters Club*,[3] the EAT reformulated it by saying that the question to ask of the applicant, while he was doing his job, was 'Are you your own boss?'. This 'elementary lay approach' has not been much favoured in recent years and cannot be regarded as helpful in dealing with the difficulties posed by cases of this kind.

1.12   The process of deciding whether a person carries on business on his or her own account has been described by Mummery J in *Hall v Lorimer*,[4] in the following terms:

> '[I]t is necessary to consider many different aspects of that person's work activity. This is not a mechanical exercise of running through items on a checklist to see whether they are present in, or absent from, a given situation. The object of the exercise is to paint a picture from the accumulation of detail. The overall effect can only be appreciated by standing back from the detailed picture which has been painted, by viewing it from a distance and by making an informed, considered, qualitative appreciation of the whole. It is a matter of evaluation of the overall effect of the detail, which is not necessarily the same as the sum total of the individual details. Not all details are of equal weight or importance in any given situation. The details may also vary in importance from one situation to another ... The process involves painting a picture in each individual case.'

The case was a tax case, but it is to be noted that the judge accepted, as was common ground between the parties, that the question whether or not there is a contract of employment is to be determined by reference to the general law of employment, as applied to all the facts of the particular case.[5]

---

[1]   [2001] IRLR 7 at p 11.
[2]   See *Argent v Ministry of Social Security* [1968] 1 WLR 1749, *Challinor v Taylor* [1972] ICR 129 and *Thames Television Ltd v Wallis* [1979] IRLR 136.
[3]   [1981] IRLR 307. A bar steward at a club was held to be an employee, although it was agreed that he should be taken on 'on a self-employed basis'.
[4]   [1992] ICR 739 at pp 744–745. The Court of Appeal upheld his decision that the taxpayer was not an employee: see [1994] ICR 218. See also *Lee Ting Sang v Chung Chi-Keung*, above, [1990] ICR 409 at p 414, where the Privy Council used similar language.
[5]   *Ibid* at p 743.

1.13   It should also be noted that a person may be both an employee and self-employed; the two types of status are not mutually exclusive. In *Sidey v Phillips*,[1] for example, a barrister also held a position as a part-time lecturer. It was held that his fees from part-time lecturing were properly assessed to income tax as an employee, as his lecturing was done under a contract of employment.

1.14   A recurrent problem concerns the weight to be attached to a declaration by the parties that the person in question is to be treated as an independent contractor. MacKenna J, in the *Ready Mixed Concrete* case, stated it to be a question of law, irrespective of what the parties have declared it to be, although he went on to say that in cases of doubt, a declaration might help in resolving the doubt one way or the other.[2] Subsequently, however, the Court of Appeal has taken the view that the label should be disregarded, even in cases of doubt.[3]

1.15   In *Young & Woods Ltd v West*,[4] for example, a man who joined the company as a skilled sheet metal worker under an oral contract was offered alternative methods of payment; he could go on the company's books as an employee or be treated as self-employed. He opted for the latter (having been self-employed for about 10 years before he joined the company), and obtained the agreement of the Inland Revenue. His working conditions were no different from those workers who were treated as employees. On his dismissal, the question arose whether he was an employee or not. The Court of Appeal upheld his argument that he was; applying the *Market Investigations* test, Stephenson LJ said: 'I am satisfied that the parties can resile from the position which they have deliberately and openly chosen to take up and that to reach any other conclusion would be, in effect, to permit the parties to contract out of the Act …'.[5] Statements such as this suggest the thought that this might be an appropriate area in which to apply section 203(1) (considered in more detail below), since an agreement to provide work as a self-employed person is arguably an agreement which 'purports … to exclude or limit the operation of any provision of' the 1996 Act.

1.16   The facts of the *Ready Mixed Concrete* and *Market Investigations* cases show the application of the multiple test and those decisions are generally used when a court or tribunal has to decide whether a person is an employee or not, irrespective of the context in which the question arises. The *Ready Mixed Concrete* case itself probably forms the basis upon which various 'employers' deal with their staff, eg fast-food chains and driving schools.[6] In a considerable number of cases, however, people taken on as

---

[1]   (1986) 59 TC 458. See also *Fall v Hitchen* [1973] 1 WLR 286.

[2]   [1968] 2 QB 497 at p 513.

[3]   *Ferguson v John Dawson and Partners (Contractors) Ltd* [1976] IRLR 346 and *Young & Woods Ltd v West* [1980] IRLR 201; contrast *Massey v Crown Life Assurance Co* [1978] ICR 590.

[4]   [1980] IRLR 201.

[5]   *Ibid* at p 207.

[6]   *BSM (1257) Ltd v Secretary of State for Social Services* [1978] ICR 894.

self-employed have been held by the courts to be employees. The following are the more important:

1. 'lump labourer';[1]
2. television reporter;[2]
3. sales representative;[3]
4. bar steward;[4]
5. holiday camp entertainers;[5]
6. lecturer for weight-watchers classes.[6]

It is worth bearing in mind, however, the words of Vinelott J in *Walls v Sinnett*:[7]

> 'It is ... quite impossible in a field where a very large number of factors have to be weighed to gain any real assistance by looking at the facts of another case and comparing them one by one to see what facts are common, what are different and what particular weight is given by another tribunal to the common facts. The facts as a whole must be looked at, and what may be compelling in one case in the light of all the facts may not be compelling in the context of another case.'

1.17 A decision that one person is or is not an employee is, therefore, not to be regarded as determinative of the status of others in that position. Thus, the conclusion in one case that a barristers' senior clerk[8] or a vision mixer[9] is self-employed does not mean that all barristers' senior clerks or vision mixers should be regarded as self-employed. All the facts of each case need to be looked at.

1.18 The following factors are the most important to evaluate in painting a picture of a person's work activity:

1. the contractual provisions;
2. the degree of control exercised by the 'employer';
3. the obligation of the 'employer' to provide work;
4. the obligation on the person to do the work;
5. the provision of tools, equipment, instruments and the like;
6. the arrangements made for tax, National Insurance contributions, sick pay and VAT;

---

[1] *Ferguson v John Dawson and Partners (Contractors) Ltd* [1976] IRLR 346. Those employed as lump labourers will be given form SC60, which is a Sub-Contractor Income Tax Deduction Certificate.

[2] *Thames Television Ltd v Wallis* [1979] IRLR 136.

[3] *Tyne & Clyde Warehouses Ltd v Hamerton* [1978] ICR 661.

[4] *Withers v Flackwell Heath Football Supporters' Club* [1981] IRLR 307.

[5] *Warner Holidays Ltd v Secretary of State for Social Services* [1983] ICR 440.

[6] *Narich Ltd v Commissioner of Payroll Tax* [1984] ICR 286 (New South Wales, Australia).

[7] (1986) 60 TC 150 at p 164. See also Mummery J's remarks in *Hall v Lorimer* [1992] ICR 739 at p 745.

[8] *McMenamin v Diggles* [1991] ICR 641.

[9] *Hall v Lorimer* [1992] ICR 739. The Court of Appeal dismissed the Inland Revenue's appeal against the decision that the taxpayer was self-employed: see [1994] ICR 218.

7.   the opportunity to work for other employers;
8.   other contractual provisions, such as fees, expenses, and holiday pay;
9.   whether the relationship by which the person is a self-employed independent contractor is genuine or whether it is designed to avoid the employment protection legislation.

1.19   So far as the statutory provisions to be considered in this book are concerned, there is a clear divide between employees and self-employed: the former enjoy the benefit of the rights not to be unfairly dismissed and to receive a redundancy payment, whereas the latter do not. It may be noted, however, that, when the issue concerns health and safety rather than employment protection, particularly when a person has sustained injuries, the courts tend to treat as employees persons who might not be regarded otherwise as employees. This may be done in two ways: either by classifying the injured person as an employee, so that he or she is covered by the employer's common law duties, or by treating section 3 of the Health and Safety at Work Act 1974 as extending the employer's obligations so as to embrace the employees of sub-contractors. Examples of the first approach are to be found in *Ferguson v John Dawson and Partners (Contractors) Ltd*[1] and *Lane v Shire Roofing Company (Oxford) Ltd.*[2] In both cases, persons who were effectively working 'on the lump' and who suffered serious personal injuries were classified as employees and were awarded large sums of damages, to which they would not have been entitled had they been classified as self-employed persons, since they would have been outside the employer's common law duty of care. Examples of the second approach are to be found in a series of cases involving injuries to employees of sub-contractors working on an 'employer's' site. In *R v Rhone-Poulenc Rorer Ltd,*[3] for example, three people were carrying out repairs at factory premises belonging to the company, two of whom were employees of a sub-contractor and one an employee of the company. One of the sub-contractor's employees fell and died. The Court of Appeal upheld the company's conviction under section 3 of the 1974 Act, saying that the proper discharge of an employer's obligations under that provision might well make it necessary to take the same precautions for the safety of a sub-contractor's employees as for that employer's own employees, if the sub-contractor's employees were under the employer's direction and control. The decision of the House of Lords in *R v Associated Octel Co Ltd*[4] makes it clear, however, that for the purposes of section 3 it is necessary to determine whether the activity in question is part of the employer's undertaking.

---

[1]   [1976] IRLR 346.
[2]   [1995] IRLR 493. See also *Lee Ting Sang v Chung Chi-Keung* [1990] ICR 409, considered above.
[3]   [1996] ICR 1054. See also *R v British Steel plc* [1995] ICR 586, a decision to similar effect, and *R v Gateway Foodmarkets Ltd* [1997] IRLR 189.
[4]   [1996] ICR 972.

(iii) Application to specific working relationships

1.20   The following groups of people are specifically considered here:

1.   directors;
2.   partners;
3.   homeworkers and casual workers;
4.   part-time workers;
5.   musicians;
6.   sub-postmasters;
7.   temporary workers;
8.   church ministers and priests;
9.   apprentices;
10.   barristers' clerks; and
11.   office-holders.

When considering the status of the persons in these groups, it should be remembered that in any particular case much depends upon the facts of the case. The observations which follow should be treated, therefore, as no more than indications of the approach likely to be taken by a court or tribunal.

1.21   **Directors** A director *qua* director is not an employee, and there need be no contract of employment between a director and the company. Where no contract exists, removal of the director by the company will cause no liability under employment law. Directors of public companies will almost invariably be employees and will have a 'service contract' or 'service agreement'. In most cases, this is merely a different name for a contract of employment, although it is likely to contain a more extensive array of terms than the contracts of other employees. The question of whether a director is an employee usually only arises in the context of small companies, more often than not family companies. The existence of a contract of employment will be presumed if the director is required to work full-time in return for a salary.[1]

1.22   The Companies Acts make specific provision for directors' service contracts. For example, section 318 of the 1985 Act requires directors' service contracts (or a memorandum of them) to be open to inspection by the company's members and section 319 requires a company to obtain the approval of a general meeting if it is proposed to employ a director under a fixed-term contract of more than five years' duration during which the contract cannot be terminated by notice or can only be terminated in specified circumstances. A company is free to alter its Articles, under section 9. If, in doing so, it breaks an agreement with a director, it will be liable for breach of contract. This will also be the position if the new Articles merely give power to end an agreement which would not otherwise have been terminable and it is then brought to an end.[2]

---

[1]   *Trussed Steel Concrete Co Ltd v Green* [1946] 1 Ch 115. See, particularly at p 121.
[2]   See *Southern Foundries (1926) Ltd v Shirlaw* [1940] AC 701.

1.23   A director without an express service contract may have an implied contract, the contract being inferred from the nature of the work done in the business.[1] In *Folami v Nigerline (UK) Ltd*, the EAT said:

> '... Where it is established that a person has been appointed managing director of a company, that his duties include effective management of the affairs of the company in all its aspects, that he has discharged those duties, and that he has been remunerated by that company in the sense that he has received a salary from the hands of that company, the prima facie conclusion to be drawn is that he is an employee of the company ... It seems now to be established that a director appointed managing director, with duties of this kind, even though he has no separate contract, is in contractual relationship with the company, and is, for some purposes at least, to be considered an employee of the company ...'[2]

1.24   A director of a small private company is unlikely to be held to be an employee, unless the work done is consistent only with work done under a service contract. In *Parsons v Albert J Parsons & Sons Ltd*,[3] the Court of Appeal held that a director who worked full-time for the company was not an employee. There was no express contract or memorandum of an oral contract of service, as required by the Companies Act 1985, section 318; his remuneration (which did not depend upon the specific services rendered by him during the year, but depended upon the funds available) was entered separately in the accounts as 'directors' fees and emoluments'; and he (together with his fellow directors) was treated as self-employed for National Insurance purposes. The Court of Appeal said that the fact that all the directors worked full-time for the company was not enough for a contract to be implied. In the later case of *Eaton v Robert Eaton Ltd*,[4] the EAT stressed that the question in such cases is essentially one of fact and refused to interfere with the decision of the employment tribunal that the person in question was not an employee. The tribunal had reached its decision on the grounds, first, that there was nothing in writing and no board minute or memorandum to indicate that he was an employee and, secondly, that he was not paid any remuneration from 1981.

1.25   In recent years there has been a regular flow of cases involving the directors of small private companies. *Buchan v Secretary of State for Employment* and *Ivey v Secretary of State for Employment*[5] involved claims that a person who was both a director and major shareholder in two different small private companies which became insolvent were employees of the companies for the purpose of recovering redundancy and other payments from the National Insurance Fund. In the *Buchan* case the claimant was a director and 50% shareholder who worked for the company full-time and

---

[1]   *James v Thomas H Kent & Co Ltd* [1951] 1 KB 551.

[2]   [1978] ICR 277 at p 280.

[3]   [1979] ICR 271. *Cf European Processing Ltd v Nimmo* (EAT 732/91) IDS Brief 481, in which the EAT upheld the tribunal's decision that the employee/director did not cease to be an employee during a period of 10 months when he did not draw a salary in order to obtain tax advantages.

[4]   [1988] ICR 302.

[5]   [1997] IRLR 80.

was treated as an employee for tax and National Insurance purposes; in the *Ivey* case, the claimant owned 99% of the shares of the company and was also managing director. Like Mr Buchan, he was treated as an employee. In both cases, the EAT refused to interfere with the employment tribunal's decisions that the two men were not employees and were not therefore entitled to make a claim. Although the technical issue involved in these cases was whether the EAT could interfere with the tribunal's decisions on the grounds that they contained an error of law, it is clear from these and other cases[1] that, under the presidency of Mummery J, the EAT's view was that in most cases directors with majority shareholdings in private companies should not be treated as employees, largely on the grounds that the ability of the shareholder to prevent his or her dismissal is crucial. By contrast, the Court of Session in Scotland refused to apply *Buchan* and took the view that a controlling shareholder could be an employee.[2]

1.26 The Court of Appeal considered this area of the law in *Secretary of State for Trade and Industry v Bottrill*.[3] In this case, the facts were that the employee became managing director and sole shareholder of a United Kingdom company on the understanding that a company in the United States would at a future date acquire 80% of the equity. He entered into a contract of employment with the United Kingdom company under which he was paid a salary from which tax and National Insurance contributions were deducted. He was not paid any director's fees. The company later went into liquidation and he made a claim for a redundancy payment from the Secretary of State under section 182 of the ERA 1996. On the question whether he was an employee (and thus entitled to claim) or not, the Court of Appeal held that he was. The Court rejected the approach taken by Mummery J and said that whether a shareholder or director of a company is an employee or not can only be determined by having regard to all the relevant facts. Whilst a controlling shareholding in a company is significant, it is not, on its own, determinative of the issue. The Court concluded that it was open to the tribunal to decide that the applicant was an employee. The Court of Appeal reached a similar conclusion in *Sellars Arenascene Ltd v Connolly*,[4] which involved a majority shareholder in a company (EGP). He entered into a service agreement with EGP, which was prepared by solicitors and in a standard form. When the question arose as to whether he became an employee of the company, the tribunal decided that the agreement did not give rise to an employer/employee relationship. The Court of Appeal said that the tribunal had erred, by attaching significance to that factor to the exclusion of all other relevant factors. As a

---

[1] See *Dalton v Secretary of State for Employment* (EAT 721/94), *Grimwood v Secretary of State for Employment* (EAT 375/95), *Culver v Secretary of State for Employment* (EAT 744/95), *Rowden v Secretary of State for Employment* (EAT 1228/95) and *McQuisten v Secretary of State for Employment* (EAT 1298/95).

[2] *Fleming v Secretary of State for Trade and Industry* [1997] IRLR 682.

[3] [1999] ICR 592. The EAT subsequently applied *Bottrill* to a similar situation where the applicant was sole director and controlling shareholder of a company and entered into a contract of employment with the company: see *Smith v Secretary of State for Trade and Industry* [2000] ICR 69.

[4] [2001] IRLR 222.

result, it had nullified its finding that the service agreement was not a sham and that the applicant had 'behaved as an employee'. It said that the only legitimate conclusion that the tribunal could have drawn was that Mr Connolly was an employee.

1.27   Partners In general, a person running a business in his or her own name or with partners will be self-employed, although it should be noted that section 2(3)(b) of the Partnership Act 1890 declares that if an employee, employed by a person engaged in a business, is to be remunerated by a share of the profits of the business, that does not of itself make the employee a partner in the business. Thus, equity partners are not employees of the partnership in which they are partners; a view upheld by the Court of Appeal in *Cowell v Quilter Goodison Co Ltd and QG Management Services Ltd.*[1] Depending on the circumstances, a salaried partner may be no more than an employee.[2]

1.28   Homeworkers and casual workers Those who work for a person but do the work away from the premises are outworkers, and, if they do the work in their own domestic environment, are called homeworkers. Whether such persons are employees will depend upon the facts of any given case, as the cases have stressed. In *Airfix Footwear Ltd v Cope,*[3] for example, the decision that the homeworker in question was an employee was due to the fact that she had been working for Airfix Footwear five days a week for seven years. In *Nethermere (St Neots) Ltd v Taverna and Gardiner*[4] both the homeworkers involved worked under flexible arrangements; they took as much work as they wanted and did not work when they wanted. They were held to be employees. The Court of Appeal stressed that the question is essentially one of fact and that an appellate court should be slow to interfere with the decision of the employment tribunal.

1.29   In *O'Kelly v Trusthouse Forte plc,*[5] which involved the question whether 'regular casuals' called in to work at banquets were employees, the decision of the employment tribunal was that they were not. The determinant factor was that there was no mutuality of obligation as they were effectively on 'standby' unless and until they were asked to come in and assist with a particular banquet. The Court of Appeal said that, as the tribunal had correctly weighed up all the factors involved in the case, there

---

[1] [1989] IRLR 392. See also *Thompson Brothers & Co v Amis* [1917] 2 Ch 211, *Ross v Parkyns* (1875) LR 2 Eq 331 and *Easdown v Cobb* [1941] 1 All ER 49.

[2] *Stekel v Ellice* [1973] 1 All ER 465.

[3] [1978] ICR 1210.

[4] [1984] ICR 612.

[5] [1983] ICR 728. See also *Mailway (Southern) Ltd v Willsher* [1978] ICR 511, in which the EAT held that a person who registered as a part-time packer with the employers was not an employee. The employers called upon her to work as and when they needed her and she was not obliged to work, when asked, if she did not want to. The EAT took the view that the arrangements in question did not amount to a contract of employment in accordance with which she was normally required to work. It should be noted, however, that this case arose under the guarantee payments provisions of the legislation.

were no grounds for interfering with its decision. This case is considered more fully at para 1.45.

1.30 The status of casual employee has received attention from both the Court of Appeal and House of Lords in recent years. In *Clark v Oxfordshire Health Authority*,[1] the issue was whether a nurse retained by a health authority on a casual basis to fill temporary vacancies in hospitals was an employee. She worked for the authority's 'nurse bank'; she had no fixed or regular hours of work but was offered work as and when a vacancy occurred at one of the authority's hospitals. When she did not work, she had no entitlement to pay, or to holiday pay or sick leave. She worked on this basis for some three years, from January 1991 to January 1994; during that period, however, there were various gaps, during 1992 and 1993. The only issue decided by the employment tribunal, and thus the subject of appeal, was whether there was a 'global contract of employment' between the parties. This was described by Sir Christopher Slade in the case under discussion as 'a continuing overriding arrangement which governed the whole of [the parties'] relationship and itself amounted to a contract of employment ...'.[2] If a global contract of employment existed, the gaps in employment during the time she was on the nurse bank would have counted towards her length of employment and she would have had sufficient continuity; if there was not, each gap would have broken continuity and she would not accumulate sufficient continuity.[3] Following its previous decisions in *Nethermere (St Neots) Ltd v Taverna and Gardiner*[4] and *McLeod v Hellyer Brothers Ltd*,[5] the Court of Appeal said that a contract of employment cannot exist in the absence of mutual obligations subsisting over the entire duration of the relevant period. It said that, although the mutual obligations required to found a global contract of employment need not necessarily consist of obligations to provide and perform work, some mutuality of obligation is required. In the present case, there was no mutuality of obligation: the authority was under no obligation to offer work nor was Ms Clark under any obligation to accept it. She had no entitlement to any pay when she did not work and no entitlement to holiday pay or sick leave. There was thus no global contract of employment. The Court of Appeal remitted the case, however, to the employment tribunal to consider other issues, such as whether there existed a specific engagement which could amount to a contract of employment and provide the basis for an unfair dismissal claim.

---

[1]   [1998] IRLR 125. See also *Stevedoring & Haulage Services Ltd v Fuller* [2001] IRLR 627.

[2]   *Ibid* at p 127, para 15.

[3]   It should be remembered that this case arose at a time when the qualifying period of employment for employees claiming the right not to be unfairly dismissed was two years. For a discussion of continuity of employment, see para 1.114.

[4]   *Loc cit.*

[5]   [1987] IRLR 232.

1.31   The issue of casual staff was again considered by the House of Lords, in *Carmichael v National Power plc.*[1] The case involved tour guides who were taken on by means of an exchange of letters on a 'casual as required basis' to act as guides taking parties on tours of power stations operated by the predecessor of the respondent company. As in the *Clark* case, they were not obliged to take work and the company did not guarantee that work would be available. They were paid only for the hours they worked. The employment tribunal and the EAT held that they were not employees, but the Court of Appeal allowed their appeal on the ground that the exchange of letters gave rise to a contract of employment. The majority of the Court of Appeal avoided the issue of absence of mutuality by implying terms relating to the performance of the guides' duties. The House of Lords rejected this approach and allowed the company's appeal. Lord Irvine of Lairg LC said that, had the appeal turned exclusively on the construction of the exchange of letters, he would have had no hesitation in holding, as a matter of construction, that there was no obligation on the company to provide work or on the guides to accept it. He said that it was clear that the parties did not intend the letters to 'constitute an exclusive memorial of their relationship' and that, in looking at the documents, the surrounding circumstances and how the parties conducted themselves, the tribunal was correct to conclude that they did not intend that their relationship should be regulated by contract.[2]

1.32   Whilst it is important to stress that each case turned on its own particular facts, the significance of both is that those who have informal arrangements with their 'employers' are unlikely to be held to have a contract of employment and that the point on which their argument is likely to founder is the absence of mutuality of obligation. Even if it is held that a particular engagement does give rise to a contract of employment, the gaps between the engagements may lead to the consequence that each time an engagement ends there is a break in continuity of employment, so that at the start of the next engagement the employee has to start accumulating continuity again. The termination of an engagement would only give rise to an unfair dismissal claim in such circumstances if the engagement had lasted more than a year, so as to give the person concerned sufficient qualifying employment to present a complaint.

1.33   Part-time workers Similar questions arise when considering whether part-time workers are employees as arose when considering the status of homeworkers and casual workers. It may be that a person may work for five different employers on five different days of the week, doing a full day's work for each employer. If that is so, then, if the factors set out above point to employment, such a person's status is properly to be regarded as that of an employee. Equally, however, the very fact that such

---

[1]   [1999] ICR 1226. See also *Stevedoring & Haulage Services Ltd v Fuller* [2001] IRLR 627, in which the Court of Appeal decided that a person who worked for an employer expressly on the basis that no mutual obligations as to the provision and acceptance of work existed, was not an employee.

[2]   See pp 1230G–1231F.

a person does work for five different 'employers' on five different days of the week must also raise the question whether he or she is more properly to be regarded as self-employed.

As with casual workers and homeworkers, this question is very much a question of fact. All that can be said is that it should not be too readily assumed that the status of those who work for a number of different 'employers' is that of an employee. All the factors relevant to their work should be considered.

1.34   Musicians Musicians who play in orchestras are likely to be held to be self-employed.[1] In *Midland Sinfonia Concert Society Ltd v Secretary of State for Social Services*[2] (which involved three musicians who were employed to play in an orchestra by separate invitation and at irregular intervals, and who were remunerated solely in respect of each occasion on which they played), Glidewell J took the view that the amount of control exercised was no more than was necessary to ensure that the various musicians assembled in the right place at the right time in order to form an orchestra, and that the control exercised by the conductor was clearly a fundamental part of orchestral playing.

On the other hand, those who have a regular engagement are probably employees, even if their regular engagement only lasts for a short period, such as a summer season.[3]

1.35   Sub-postmasters In *Hitchcock v Post Office*,[4] the EAT applied the *Ready Mixed Concrete* and *Market Investigations* tests and held a sub-postmaster to be self-employed. He was under a substantial measure of control in relation to the conduct of Post Office business, but the other circumstances, particularly the facts that he provided the premises and part of the equipment at his own expense, that he was able to delegate his duties and that he employed other people, pointed to the conclusion that he was in business on his own account.

1.36   Temporary workers Those covered here are 'temporary' workers whose services are supplied by an intermediary (the labour supplier[5]) for the benefit of a third party (the hirer) for a limited period of time. Two

---

[1]   *Winfield v London Philharmonic Orchestra Ltd* [1979] ICR 726 (principal oboist), *Addison v London Philharmonic Orchestra Ltd* [1981] ICR 261 (associate player and three additional or extra players) and *Midland Sinfonia Concert Society Ltd v Secretary of State for Social Services* [1981] ICR 454 (guest musicians employed irregularly by invitation).

[2]   [1981] ICR 454.

[3]   *Warner Holidays Ltd v Secretary of State for Social Services* [1983] ICR 440.

[4]   [1980] ICR 100. See also *Tanna v Post Office* [1981] ICR 374, a decision under the Race Relations Act 1976.

[5]   The activities of fee-charging labour suppliers were regulated by the Employment Agencies Act 1973, which applied to 'employment businesses' which supplied the services of employees employed by them, and 'employment agencies' which supply workers for placement with employers. Both required a licence under s 1(1) and (4). These statutory provisions have now been repealed by the Deregulation and Contracting Out Act 1994, ss 35 and 81(1), and Sch 10, para 1(1) and (2) and Sch 17.

relationships are involved – that between the worker and the agency and that between the worker and the hirer.

1.37   In *Construction Industry Training Board v Labour Force Ltd*,[1] the Divisional Court expressed the view that the contractual relationship between the supplier/agency and the worker was not one of service, but one *sui generis*. A similar decision was arrived at in *Wickens v Champion Employment*,[2] where temporaries were employed by an agency under a contract of service. Nevertheless, the court held that the other provisions of the contract were inconsistent with a contract of employment. The question involved in that case was whether the general terms of engagement of the agency's temporary workers gave rise to an employment relationship. In *McMeechan v Secretary of State for Employment*,[3] on the other hand, the employee's claim, as reformulated in the Court of Appeal, was that he was entitled to be treated as an employee of the agency in respect of a single engagement with a particular client in respect of which the money he was claiming on the agency's insolvency had been earned. The Court of Appeal held that he was. Waite LJ, with whom the other members of the Court agreed, said:[4]

> 'There is nothing inherently repugnant ... about a state of affairs under which, in an employment agency case, the status of employee of the agency is allocated to a temporary worker in respect of each assignment actually worked, notwithstanding that the same worker may not be entitled to employee status under his general terms of engagement ... Whether or not employment status should, or should not, be so allocated in any particular case will of course need to be resolved as a question of fact according to the particular circumstances of each case ... The force of [the preceding statements] is not lost in cases where ... the agency and the temporary worker have committed themselves to standard terms and conditions which are intended to apply both to the general engagement and to the individual stints worked under it. The only result of that fusion is that the same conditions will have to be interpreted from a different perspective, according to whether they are being considered in the context of the general engagement or in the context of a single engagement ...'

This case should be regarded as turning on its particular facts and on the way in which the Court of Appeal re-formulated his claim. In the later case of *Montgomery v Johnson Underwood Ltd*,[5] the tribunal decided that the applicant became an employee of the agency, following the *McMeechan* case. It considered all aspects of the relationship between her and the agency, including mutuality of obligation and control, and concluded that, on balance, those factors pointing to the existence of an employment contract outweighed those against. Included in the list of factors pointing against a contract of employment was the finding that there was 'little or

---

[1]   [1970] 3 All ER 220. See also *Ironmonger v Movefield Ltd t/a Deering Appointments* [1988] IRLR 461 and *Pertemps Group Ltd v Nixon* (EAT 496/91) IDS Brief 506.

[2]   [1984] ICR 365. See also *Knight v Anglian Industrial Services* (EAT 640/96) IDS Brief 586.

[3]   [19971 ICR 549.

[4]   *Ibid* at pp 563–564.

[5]   [2001] IRLR 269.

no control, direction or supervision'; the tribunal also took the view, following *McMeechan*, that the absence of mutuality of obligation was irrelevant. The Court of Appeal held that it had erred in reaching this decision. It said that mutuality of obligation and control are the irreducible minimum legal requirements for the existence of a contract of employment and that the tribunal should have followed the guidance of MacKenna J in the *Ready Mixed Concrete* case (see para 1.07).

1.38   In general, it is unlikely that a worker placed by an agency will become an employee of the hirer, although application of the tests set out above may lead to the conclusion that an employment relationship has arisen. Recent examples of this general proposition are *Serco Ltd v Blair*[1] and *Costain Building & Civil Engineering Ltd v Smith and Chanton Group plc*.[2] In both cases, employees were supplied by an employment agency to a customer of the agency in circumstances such that the EAT held that no employment relationship arose. In the second case, an engineer was supplied by an agency to Costain. There was an agreement between the agency and Costain for the supply of services by the engineer and the agreement stated that he would be under the strict supervision of Costain. There was no agreement between him and Costain, however, and he did not receive any disciplinary or grievance documentation, nor did he expect to receive sick pay or holiday pay, and there was no clause providing for notice of termination. The engineer raised a number of health and safety issues and eventually was appointed a health and safety representative for the site. After he had produced a number of reports critical of Costain's management of the site, Costain informed the agency that they did not want him to continue to work on the site. He claimed that he had been unfairly dismissed by Costain contrary to ERA 1996, section 100(1)(b). The EAT held that he did not become an employee of Costain and that therefore he could not complain of unfair dismissal. It followed that his appointment as a health and safety representative was ineffective. The EAT pointed out that when a health and safety representative is appointed, he or she should already be an employee. It rejected the argument that the appointment of the engineer as a representative had the effect of altering his status.

1.39   The issue arose again in *Motorola Ltd v Davidson and Melville Craig Group Ltd*.[3] Mr Davidson responded to an advertisement for jobs as analysers to repair mobile telephones with Motorola. The recruitment process was carried out by Melville Craig, which had an agreement with Motorola for the supply of temporary workers. He was taken on; under the terms of his contract he was bound to comply with all reasonable instructions and requests made by Motorola. He was later suspended by Motorola's regional service manager, following a disciplinary hearing. The manager then decided to terminate his assignment with Motorola. He presented a complaint of unfair dismissal and the tribunal decided that he was an employee of Motorola. His appeal to the EAT was confined to the

---

[1]   EAT unreported, 31 August 1998.
[2]   [2000] ICR 215.
[3]   [2001] IRLR 4.

issue whether as between Motorola and Mr Davidson there existed a right of control sufficient to make Motorola his employer. The EAT held that there was.

This last case illustrates the point made above – that application of the tests for determining whether a person is an employee may lead to the conclusion that he or she was an employee. The difference between the *Serco* case and the *Motorola* case lies essentially in the degree of control exercised by the client of the agency. It is worthy of note, however, that in both the *Serco* case and the *Costain* case, the client asked the agency to withdraw the person concerned, whereas in the *Motorola* case the client itself undertook the disciplinary action.

1.40   Church ministers and priests[1] The tendency of courts and tribunals in all the cases which have come before them in recent years has been effectively to remove from church ministers and priests the temporal jurisdiction of the courts, by holding, irrespective of religious denomination, that they are not employed under a contract of employment.[2] The preferred approach is that of the Court of Appeal in *President of the Methodist Conference v Parfitt*,[3] which is to ask, first, whether the applicant had a contract with the religious organisation in question, and, if there was a contract, whether the contract was a contract of employment. In that case, May LJ cited with approval[4] the dissenting judgment of Waterhouse J in the EAT. He said:

'I consider that the starting point for any consideration of the relationship between the Methodist Church and its ministers must be an examination of the faith and doctrine to which they subscribe and they seek to further ... I am unable to accept that either party [in that case] intended to create a contractual relationship. Moreover the elaborate code of practice and discipline of the Methodist Church, containing a wide spectrum of rules, recommendation and exhortations addressed to a variety of subsidiary organisations and persons, does not seem to me to be capable of formulation in terms of a contract between identifiable parties.'

Dillon LJ said: '... I have no hesitation in concluding that the relationship between a church and a minister of religion is not apt, in the absence of clear indications of a contrary intention in the document, to be

---

[1]   For a detailed analysis of the status of priests in the Church of England see Brodin, 'The Employment Status of Ministers of Religion' (1996) 25 ILJ 211. The thrust of her argument is that Church of England priests should not all be treated alike and that unbeneficed clergy should be treated as employees, thus giving them access to employment rights.

[2]   See, for example, *Barthorpe v Exeter Diocesan Board of Finance* [1979] ICR 900, *President of the Methodist Conference v Parfitt* [1984] ICR 176 and *Davies v Presbyterian Church of Wales* [1986] ICR 280.

[3]   [1984] ICR 176.

[4]   *Ibid* at p 441.

regulated by a contract of service'.[1] The Court of Appeal's approach in the *Parfitt* case has been followed in cases involving other religions.[2] In *Diocese of Southwark v Coker*,[3] which involved a priest of the Anglican Church who was an assistant curate in the diocese of Southwark, Mummery LJ, in the Court of Appeal, said that there was no contract at all, on the footing that there was no intention to create a contractual relationship of any kind.

In cases of this kind, therefore, it is likely that the court or tribunal will conclude that there was no contract between the person concerned and the religious authority, thus rendering it unnecessary to consider whether the contract was a contract of employment.

1.41   Apprentices The definition of 'contract of employment' in section 230(2) of the 1996 Act includes a contract of apprenticeship. Although apprenticeships are not very common these days, Sedley J observed in *Wallace v CA Roofing Services Ltd*[4] that 'the announcement of the demise of apprenticeship is exaggerated'. He held that an oral agreement under which the employee was employed by the company, as supplemented by a statutory written statement giving his job title as 'apprentice sheet metalworker', was a contract of apprenticeship. Accordingly, he was entitled to damages for the premature termination of the contract for redundancy before the end of the apprenticeship.

1.42   Barristers' clerks In *McMenamin v Diggles*,[5] a tax case, Scott J held that the assumption by the taxpayer, Diggles, of the duties of senior clerk under an arrangement entered into with a set of barristers' chambers did not amount to the holding of an office within the relevant tax legislation. The agreement with the members of the chambers contemplated that he could either act as head clerk himself or provide some other suitably qualified or experienced person to do so. Thus, the element of personal services was absent from the agreement.[6]

---

[1]   [1984] ICR 176 at p 442. See also *Davies v Presbyterian Church of Wales* [1986] ICR 280 at p 289, *per* Lord Templeman: '… [I]t is possible for a man to be employed as a servant or as an independent contractor to carry out duties which are exclusively spiritual'. He went on to say, however, that in that case the applicant could not point to any contract between himself and the church.

[2]   See *Santokh Singh v Guru Nanak Gurdwara* [1990] ICR 309, which concerned a Sikh priest who was dismissed by his temple. The EAT refused to interfere with the employment tribunal's decision that he was not an employee of the temple. In *Birmingham Mosque Trust v Alavi* [1992] ICR 435, which involved a Professor of Islamic Studies who was appointed director and khateeb of the Birmingham Central Mosque, the EAT allowed the applicant's appeal on the grounds that the tribunal failed to make any findings as to whether the applicant had a contract and, if he did, whether the contract was a contract of employment. The case was remitted to a differently constituted tribunal.

[3]   [1999] ICR 140.

[4]   [1996] IRLR 435.

[5]   [1991] ICR 641.

[6]   *Ibid* at p 644E.

1.43   Office holders As Morison J pointed out in *Johnson v Ryan*,[1] 'there are three categories of office holder: an office holder whose rights and duties are defined by the office they hold and not by any contract, such as a police officer; secondly, there are also office holders who retain the title "office holder" but are in reality employees with a contract of service … ; and, thirdly, there are also workers who are both office holders and employees, such as company directors'.

1.44   In *Johnson v Ryan*, the issue was whether an employee who was promoted to the post of rent officer thereby became an office holder and lost her protection as an employee. The EAT held that she was an employee. It said that, in determining whether an office holder is an employee, the factual circumstances are relevant; in particular whether there was a payment of salary and whether it was fixed, and whether the worker's duties were subject to close control by the employer or whether he or she worked independently. It went on to say that the provisions of the Rent Act 1977, section 63 do not exclude the possibility of a rent officer being also an employee. Adopting a purposive approach in relation to the protection of employees, since it would be inequitable for the applicant to lose the statutory protection to which she had been entitled in her previous positions with the local authority when she was promoted to rent officer, it concluded that, on the facts, she was both an office holder and an employee. It also held that the applicant's employer was the local authority, not the Secretary of State for the Environment or the chief rent officer.

(iv) Question of law or fact?

1.45   The approach of the appellate courts to the question whether a person is an employee or not depends upon whether or not the construction of a written contract or document is involved. If, exceptionally, the relationship is dependent solely upon the true construction of a written document, the question will be one of law, upon which an appeal will lie.[2] In other cases, it has generally been regarded as a mixed question of fact and law.[3] In *O'Kelly v Trusthouse Forte plc*,[4] the Court of Appeal affirmed that a question of law is involved. A majority, however, also held that the answer to the question whether a person is an employee or not involves questions of degree and fact which it is for the employment tribunal to determine. An appellate tribunal may not interfere with the employment tribunal's decision unless the employment tribunal has misdirected itself in law or its decision is one which no tribunal, properly

---

[1]   [2000] ICR 236 at p 242.

[2]   *Davies v Presbyterian Church of Wales* [1986] ICR 280, *Lee Ting Sang v Chung Chi-Keung* [1990] ICR 409 at p 414, and *McMeechan v Secretary of State for Employment* [1997] ICR 549. For a discussion of the historical basis for this rule, see Lord Hoffmann's speech in *Carmichael v National Power plc* [1999] ICR 1226 at pp 1232–1233.

[3]   *Global Plant Ltd v Secretary of State for Social Services* [1972] 1 QB 139 and *Maurice Graham Ltd v Brunswick* (1974) 16 KIR 158.

[4]   [1983] ICR 728, followed by the Court of Appeal in *Nethermere (St Neots) Ltd v Taverna and Gardiner* [1984] ICR 612. See also *Lee Ting Sang v Chung Chi-Keung* [1990] ICR 409.

directing itself on the relevant facts, could have reached. The effect is to place a heavy burden on an applicant who disagrees with a tribunal's decision and to restrict the scope for appeals to the EAT and the Court of Appeal.

1.46 This approach, which derives from the House of Lords' decision in *Edwards v Bairstow*[1] (a tax case), was approved by the Privy Council in *Lee Ting Sang v Chung Chi-Keung*.[2] Lord Griffiths, who delivered the opinion, said:

'The decision [whether or not a person is employed under a contract of employment] will depend upon the evaluation of many facts and there will be many borderline cases in which similarly instructed minds may come to different conclusions. It is in such situations that an appeal court must not interfere and it is in this sense that the decision is said to be one of fact.'[3]

He went on to emphasise Lord Radcliffe's remarks in *Edwards v Bairstow*:[4]

'... [T]he reason why the courts do not interfere with commissioners' findings ... when they really do involve nothing but questions of fact ... is simply that by the system that has been set up the commissioners are the first tribunal to try an appeal, and in the interests of the efficient administration of justice their decisions can only be upset on appeal if they have been positively wrong in law. The court [sc EAT] is not a second opinion, where there is reasonable ground for the first ... Their [sc the court's] duty is no more than to examine those facts with a decent respect for the tribunal appealed from and if they think that the only reasonable conclusion on the facts found is inconsistent with the determination come to, to say so without more ado.'

In the instant case, the Privy Council concluded that the first instance judge's reliance upon two dicta culled from cases of a dissimilar character might have misled him in his assessment of the facts of the case and amounted to an error of law.

1.47 In *Hall v Lorimer*,[5] Mummery J applied the *Lee Ting Sang* case and said:

'The appellate court will not interfere with the conclusion of the fact finding tribunal where the decision ... comes within what has been described as the "band of possible reasonable decisions". The appellate court realises that there are borderline or grey areas in which tribunals, properly instructed on the law and facts, can legitimately and reasonably arrive at different conclusions ...'

1.48 More recently, the Court of Appeal appears to have modified the approach to dealing with appeals set out above. In *Express & Echo*

[1]   [1956] AC 14.
[2]   [1990] ICR 409 at p 414. See also *Andrews v King* [1991] ICR 846 at p 849.
[3]   *Ibid* at p 415.
[4]   [1956] AC 14 at pp 38–39.
[5]   [1992] ICR 739 at p 744. The Court of Appeal upheld his decision: see [1994] ICR 218.

Publications Ltd v Tanton,[1] Peter Gibson LJ said that he accepted that the correct approach to the determination of the question whether or not an applicant is an employee is as follows:[2]

'(1)   The tribunal should establish what were the terms of the agreement between the parties. That is a question of fact.
(2)   The tribunal should then consider whether any of the terms of the contract are inherently inconsistent with the existence of a contract of employment. That is plainly a question of law, and although this court, as indeed the Employment Appeal Tribunal before us, has no power to interfere with findings of fact (an appeal only lies on a point of law), if there were a term of the contract inherently inconsistent with a contract of employment and that has not been recognised by the tribunal's chairman, that would be a point of law on which this court, like the Employment Appeal Tribunal before us, would be entitled to interfere with the conclusion of the chairman.
(3)   If there are no such inherently inconsistent terms, the tribunal should determine whether the contract is a contract of service or a contract for services, having regard to all the terms. That is a mixed question of law and fact.'

In that case, the Court of Appeal treated as an error of law falling within the second part of the approach set out above the decision of the chairman of the employment tribunal that the relevant clause of the contract was one of many factors to be taken into account and did not preclude the relationship of employer and employee coming into existence. It is submitted that the Court of Appeal's view in *Tanton* is at variance with the approach taken by that Court in *O'Kelly v Trusthouse Forte plc*[3] and subsequent cases in its suggestion that the approach of a tribunal to individual terms rather than to the whole contract may be characterised as an error of law. In other words, the second stage of the three-stage approach accepted by Peter Gibson LJ appears to be an additional and arguably supernumerary gloss on the previous approach.

1.49   In exceptional cases where the relationship between the parties depends solely upon the true construction of a written contract or document, the question will be one of law. This was made clear by the House of Lords in *Davies v Presbyterian Church of Wales*.[4] Lord Templeman, with whom the other Lords agreed, said:[5] 'The question to be determined is a question of law, namely whether upon the true construction of the book of rules a pastor of the church is employed and is under a contract of service'. This was followed by the EAT in *Santokh Singh v Guru Nanak Gurdwara*,[6] which involved the construction of the relevant constitutions of a Sikh temple, and by the Court of Appeal in *McMeechan v Secretary of State*

---

[1]   [1999] ICR 693.
[2]   *Ibid* at p 697.
[3]   [1983] ICR 728.
[4]   [1986] ICR 280.
[5]   *Ibid* at p 288.
[6]   [1990] ICR 309.

for Employment,[1] which involved the construction of a written contract entered into by an employment agency with a 'temp'.

(v) The concept of 'worker'

1.50   Much of the legislation enacted in recent years has been expressly applied to a 'worker'. Before 1997, the only legislation to refer expressly to a worker was the Wages Act 1986, subsequently consolidated into Part II of the Employment Rights Act 1996. It may be noted, however, that the definition of 'employment' to be found in the Sex Discrimination Act 1975 and the Race Relations Act 1976 is wide enough to embrace self-employed persons and thus goes wider than the definition of employee in the 1996 Act.[2]

1.51   The 1996 Act defines 'worker' as:

'an individual who has entered into or works under ... —

(a)   a contract of employment; or
(b)   any other contract, whether express or implied and (if it is express) whether oral or in writing, whereby the individual undertakes to do or perform personally any work or services for another party to the contract whose status is not by virtue of the contract that of a client or customer of any profession or business undertaking carried on by the individual ...'[3]

Clearly the definition embraces all employees; it also seems to be wide enough to embrace self-employed persons who offer consultancy services and thus are effectively sole traders.

1.52   One of the apparent oddities of the legislation is that many of the recently introduced rights, for example under the Working Time Regulations (as amended)[4] or the National Minimum Wage Act 1998, apply to 'workers' but if such persons are dismissed for a reason connected with the Regulations or the Act they may only complain of unfair dismissal if they are employees. This seems to be completely anomalous.

(b) Excluded employees

1.53   It should be noted that if there is a dispute as to whether an employee is in one of the groups of excluded employees, that question will be dealt with by the employment tribunal at a preliminary hearing. It should also be noted that the 1996 Act applies to a period of employment even where the employee was excluded 'by or under this Act' from any right conferred by the Act.[5] But the provision expressly applies only to exclusion 'by or under this Act' and so would not embrace an employee

---

[1]   [1997] ICR 549.
[2]   See SDA 1975, s 82(1) and RRA 1976, s 78(1).
[3]   ERA 1996, s 230(3).
[4]   SI 1998 No 1833, as amended by the Working Time Regulations 1999, SI 1999 No 3372.
[5]   Section 215(1)(b).

excluded because he or she was employed under an illegal contract of employment, for example.

(i) Illegal contracts of employment

1.54   A contract of employment is illegal either if it is prohibited by statute or if its objects are forbidden by the common law on the grounds of public policy. The most significant impact which the doctrine of illegality has had upon this area of the law is in relation to contracts which involve the commission of a fraud on the Inland Revenue, and which may be made void at common law as being contrary to public policy. An example is *Miller v Karlinski*,[1] where the employee was employed under a contract which provided that he should receive a salary of £10 per week and should also recover from the employer the amount of income tax payable on that salary, by including it in an account for travelling expenses. Du Parcq LJ said:[2] 'I find it impossible to say that, where a man agrees to work and to be paid according to a scheme devised ... so as to defraud the revenue, the whole agreement is not an illegal agreement which the courts will not enforce'. A similar view was taken by the Court of Appeal in *Napier v National Business Agency Ltd*,[3] where a secretary was engaged for £13 a week plus £5 a week as 'expenses', the payments being made in this way to mislead the Inland Revenue. The Court of Appeal held that that part of the agreement was not severable from the rest of the contract and the whole contract was unenforceable.

1.55   Illegal contracts fall into two distinct categories. In the first category are contracts which are illegal *per se*, or which cannot be performed by one or both of the parties otherwise than illegally, for example where employer and employee agree to defraud the Revenue. In such cases the state of knowledge of the parties is irrelevant and their ignorance of the illegality will not save them from the consequences.[4] In these cases, as Lord Coulsfield explained in *Salvesen v Simons*,[5] the principle is that 'if a party knew what was being done, it is irrelevant that he did not know that it was illegal'. In this last case, the arrangement between the employee and his employer was that part of his wages should be paid as a management fee to a business operated by him and his wife in partnership. The EAT held that this arrangement involved a misrepresentation to the Inland Revenue in that there was no proper basis for the payment of a management fee to the partnership, since the payment was not for services provided but was a diversion of the employee's remuneration; to that extent it was a fraud on the Revenue. The employee's contract was therefore unenforceable. On the other hand, if the payments in question are

---

[1] (1945) 62 TLR 85.
[2] *Ibid* at p 86.
[3] [1951] 2 All ER 264.
[4] See *Miller v Karlinski* (1945) 62 TLR 85, *Corby v Morrison* [1980] ICR 564 and *Newland v Simons & Willer (Hairdressers) Ltd* [1981] ICR 521 at p 527. All these cases involved arrangements which amounted to frauds on the Inland Revenue.
[5] [1994] ICR 409.

irregular the employee's contract will not necessarily be rendered illegal.[1] It should be noted, however, that an arrangement will not necessarily be illegal if it is entered into in good faith and is a proper method of reducing tax, which is open and above board and either has been or will be disclosed to the Inland Revenue.[2]

1.56 In the second category are contracts which are *ex facie* legal but illegally performed: for example where the employer defrauds the Revenue by failure to deduct tax from the employee's wages, or where performance of the contract by the employee involves acts for sexually immoral purposes.[3] In such cases, the employee's state of mind will be decisive. In *Newland v Simons and Willer (Hairdressers) Ltd,*[4] May J said:

> '... [W]here both employer and employee knowingly commit an illegality by way of a fraud on the revenue in the payment and receipt of remuneration ..., which is an essential part of such a contract, ... there can be doubt that this does turn it into a contract that is prohibited by statute or common law, and consequently the employee is precluded from enforcing any rights [he or] she might otherwise have against [the] employer.'[5]

1.57 In *Coral Leisure Group Ltd v Barnet,*[6] Browne-Wilkinson J drew a distinction between '(a) cases in which there is a contractual obligation to do an act which is unlawful and (b) cases where the contractual obligations are capable of being performed lawfully and were initially intended so to be performed, but which have in fact been performed by unlawful means'. In the former case, if it is possible to sever or separate the tainted contractual obligations from the untainted, the whole contract will not be unenforceable. In the latter case, the fact that the employee in the course of his or her employment has committed an unlawful or immoral act will not by itself prevent him or her from enforcing the contract, unless the contract is entered into for the purpose of doing the unlawful or immoral act or the contract itself (as opposed to the mode of its performance) is prohibited by law.[7] The later Court of Appeal decision in *Hewcastle Catering Ltd v Ahmed*[8] took this approach in dealing with unfair dismissal claims by employees who assisted in their employer's scheme to evade the payment of VAT and contains a valuable review of the decisions in this area.

1.58 These common-law principles of illegality have been applied by the EAT to employees' statutory rights, with consequences which may be

---

[1] *Annandale Engineering v Samson* [1994] IRLR 59.
[2] *Lightfoot v D & J Sporting Ltd* [1996] IRLR 64.
[3] As in *Coral Leisure Group Ltd v Barnet* [1981] ICR 503. The employee's contract involved him in obtaining prostitutes for customers of his employers.
[4] [1981] ICR 521.
[5] *Ibid* at p 530.
[6] [1981] ICR 503.
[7] *Ibid* at p 509.
[8] [1992] ICR 626.

disproportionate to the wrong done by them.[1] In *Corby v Morrison*,[2] for example, the illegality arose from the fact that the employee was paid an extra £5 a week without any deduction being made in respect of income tax or social security liability. The EAT held that the contract was illegal *per se*, and added, *obiter*, that if the contract had been one which was *ex facie* legal and knowledge had become relevant, the test was subjective, not objective.[3] An example of a contract *ex facie* legal is *Newland v Simons & Willer (Hairdressers) Ltd*, where the EAT emphasised that the actual state of the employee's knowledge was what mattered and it was not enough that she ought to have known but in fact did not know, whether through stupidity, misunderstanding or inexperience.[4]

1.59   As can be seen from this discussion of the case-law, most of the cases in which illegality has been contended for have been cases which involved a method of payment of wages to an employee involving a fraud on the Inland Revenue. Another type of case which should be considered, however, is one where the employee enters employment whilst an illegal immigrant. Few cases have considered this question and those that have, have done so fairly cursorily. In *Sharma v Hindu Temple*,[5] the facts were that the employee was employed by the temple at a time when he had no visa relating to his stay or employment in the United Kingdom. The employment tribunal dismissed his complaint on the ground of illegality. The EAT held that the tribunal had made insufficient findings of fact, particularly as to whether the employee was knowingly in breach of the conditions of his leave to enter the country, and remitted the case for a rehearing. In the course of the judgment, Wood J quoted from the judgment of Devlin J in *St John Shipping Corporation v Joseph Rank Ltd*:[6]

> '[A] contract which is entered into with the object of committing an illegal act is unenforceable. The application of this principle depends upon proof of the intent, at the time when the contract was made, to break the law; if the intent is mutual the contract is not enforceable at all, and, if unilateral, it is unenforceable at the suit of the party who is proved to have it.'

Wood J went on to say that if the employee was held knowingly to be in breach of the condition of his leave, the contract would be illegal in its formation.

1.60   This approach was followed by the EAT in the later case of *Bamgbose v The Royal Star and Garter Home*.[7] The facts were that the employee, a Nigerian, entered this country in 1989 when his passport was stamped 'Leave to enter for six months/Employment prohibited'. His application for leave to remain after the expiry of the six months was

---

[1] See *Tomlinson v Dick Evans 'U' Drive Ltd* [1978] ICR 639.

[2] [1980] ICR 564. See also *Davidson v Pillay* [1979] IRLR 275.

[3] [1980] ICR 564 at p 570.

[4] [1981] ICR 521 at pp 531–532. See also *McConnell v Bolik* [1979] IRLR 422.

[5] EAT 253/90.

[6] [1957] 1 QB 267 at p 283.

[7] (EAT 841/95) IDS Brief 585.

refused, but he remained and worked between June 1990 and February 1991. He married in 1991 and applied for leave to remain as a foreign spouse; the application was granted with effect from 27 January 1993. It was accepted by the employee that when he entered the employment of the employers in November 1991 he knew that he was not permitted to work in the United Kingdom and was in breach of the Immigration Act 1971. He was dismissed within two years of permission being granted to remain and work in the United Kingdom. The EAT upheld the tribunal's decision that his contract was tainted with illegality from the time he started employment with the employers until permission was granted and that, consequently, he did not have two years' qualifying employment which was necessary at that time for the purposes of an unfair dismissal complaint. The EAT noted that, because he knew he did not have the right to take up employment, the contract was illegal from its inception, and applied Devlin J's dictum, quoted above.

1.61   The final question to consider in cases involving illegality is whether the objectionable part of an agreement may be severed. This has generally arisen in the context of arrangements involving a fraud on the Inland Revenue. In that context, the argument that severance should be permitted has been rejected on the grounds that an agreement to defraud the Inland Revenue is as a whole illegal and unenforceable.[1] Another possibility, that if a person seeking to enforce his rights is not in *pari delicto* with (ie is less blameworthy than) the employer, he should be allowed to enforce the contract to a limited extent, appears to have found little favour.[2] It has also been argued that, since it is now public policy that employees should be entitled to the employment protection rights given them by the ERA 1996, an employment tribunal should weigh the public policy of protecting the Revenue against the public policy of protecting the employee and decide to which claims of public policy to give precedence. This view was rejected by the EAT in *Newland v Simons & Willer (Hairdresser) Ltd*.[3] On the other hand, if the illegality does not consist of a fraud on the Inland Revenue, the contract may be severable. This is in effect what happened in the *Bamgbose* case, considered above. After permission to work in the United Kingdom was granted, the illegality ceased and the taint was removed. Had the employee been continuously employed for two years (as was then the period necessary to qualify for the right not to be unfairly dismissed), he would have been able to enforce his right not to be unfairly dismissed, based on the length of employment after the grant of permission.

1.62   It follows from the present state of the law that, if an employee is employed under a contract of employment tainted with illegality, no week of employment under that contract will count in computing continuous employment (see para 1.114). The illegality or otherwise of a contract does

---

[1]   *Miller v Karlinski* (1945) 62 TLR 85 at p 86, followed in *Corby v Morrison* [1980] ICR 564. It is worth noting that both cases involved contracts which were illegal *per se*.

[2]   *Attridge v Jaydees Newsagents Ltd* (1980) (EAT 603/79) IDS Brief 185.

[3]   [1981] ICR 521 at p 533.

not, however, affect the employment tribunal's jurisdiction to hear a case, but only concerns the parties' right to enforce the contract.[1]

(ii) Diplomatic and state immunity

1.63   The question of diplomatic and State immunity is governed by the State Immunity Act 1978, which limits the immunity of sovereign States. Section 1 of the Act makes general provision for the immunity of a State from the jurisdiction of the courts of the United Kingdom 'except as provided' by the provisions of the Act. Section 1(2)[2] requires a court and, by implication, an employment tribunal to give effect to this immunity even though the State does not appear in the proceedings. Foreign Heads of State, members of their family forming part of their household and their private servants are also immune.[3]

1.64   Section 2 deals with the question whether a State has submitted to the jurisdiction of the courts and tribunals of the United Kingdom. Section 2(1) provides that a State is not immune as respects proceedings in respect of which it has submitted to the jurisdiction. A State will be deemed to have submitted either if it has instituted proceedings or if it has 'intervened or taken any step in the proceedings'.[4] In the latter case, it will not be deemed to have submitted if the intervention or step taken is for the purpose of claiming immunity or 'asserting an interest in property in circumstances such that the State would have been entitled to immunity if the proceedings had been brought against it'.[5] Section 2(5) of the Act provides that a State will not be deemed to have submitted to the jurisdiction if it takes any step in the proceedings 'in ignorance of facts entitling it to immunity if those facts could not reasonably have been ascertained and immunity is claimed as soon as reasonably practicable'. A submission to the jurisdiction under a misapprehension induced by wrong advice will amount to a mistake of law and will not be covered by section 2(5).[6]

1.65   A further question may arise as to whether the person who purports to submit to the jurisdiction has authority to do so within section 2(7).[7] This provision states that the head of a State's diplomatic mission, or the person for the time being performing his or her functions, is to be deemed to have authority to submit on behalf of the State. It also provides that 'any person who has entered into a contract on behalf of and with the authority of a State shall be deemed to have authority to submit on

---

[1]   *Wilkinson v Lugg* [1990] ICR 599.

[2]   See *Sengupta v Republic of India* [1983] ICR 221 and *United Arab Emirates v Abdelghafar* [1995] ICR 65.

[3]   State Immunity Act 1978, s 20.

[4]   Section 2(3).

[5]   Section 2(4).

[6]   See *Malaysian Industrial Development Authority v Jeyasingham* [1998] ICR 307.

[7]   For an example of a case in which the question arose as to whether a High Commission had submitted to the jurisdiction, see *London Branch of the Nigerian Universities Commission Bastians* [1995] ICR 358.

its behalf in respect of proceedings arising out of the contract'. In *Malaysian Industrial Development Authority v Jeyasingham*,[1] the complaint of unfair dismissal was brought against an investment authority which was part of a Department of State of Malaysia. The director of the authority entered a notice of appearance but subsequently sought to claim immunity. The EAT held that under section 2(7) the High Commissioner was the only person who could waive sovereign immunity and, unless it could be shown that he had done so, the employment tribunal was bound to hold that the authority was entitled to immunity. In *Arab Republic of Egypt v Gamal-Eldin*,[2] one of the issues was whether letters from the medical counsellor at the embassy amounted to steps in the employee's unfair dismissal proceedings. The EAT said that, since the counsellor was not head of the mission and was not the person who had entered into the contract of employment with either of the applicants, he was not deemed to have authority to submit to the jurisdiction on behalf of his State under section 2(7). It also said that, on the evidence, the letters written by him did not constitute the taking of steps in the proceedings or a submission to the jurisdiction.

1.66 Section 4 restricts the immunity of a State from proceedings relating to a contract of employment; section 16(1)(a) excludes the application of section 4 to proceedings concerning the employment of members of a diplomatic mission[3] or the members of a consular post.[4] In *Sengupta v Republic of India*,[5] Browne-Wilkinson J said of section 16(l)(a): '[It] operates to exclude jurisdiction over claims relating to the employment not only of diplomatic staff but also of lower grade administrative, technical and domestic staff irrespective of their nationality'. This dictum was applied by the Court of Appeal in dismissing a claim by a British national employed as a secretary in the Saudi Arabian embassy in London.[6]

1.67 A State is not immune as respects proceedings relating to a contract of employment between the State and an individual where the contract was made in the United Kingdom or the work is to be wholly or partly performed here.[7] This rule does not apply in the following circumstances:

---

[1] [1998] ICR 307.

[2] [1996] ICR 13. See also *Ahmed v Government of the Kingdom of Saudi Arabia* [1996] ICR 25.

[3] Within the meaning of the Vienna Convention on Diplomatic Relations (Vienna, 18 April 1961; TS 19 (1965); Cmnd 2565), which is contained in the Diplomatic Privileges Act 1964, Sch 1; see, in particular, art 1. In *Arab Republic of Egypt v Gamal-Eldin* [1996] ICR 13, the EAT held that members of an embassy staff employed in the administrative and technical service of the mission were 'members of a mission' for the purposes of s 16.

[4] Within the meaning of the Vienna Convention on Consular Relations (Vienna, 24 April 1963; TS 14 (1973); Cmnd 5219), which is contained in the Consular Relations Act 1968, Sch 1; see, in particular, art 1.

[5] [1983] ICR 221 at p 225.

[6] In *Ahmed v Government of the Kingdom of Saudi Arabia* [1996] ICR 25.

[7] Section 4(1). Section 4(6) makes it clear that the statutory rights and duties of employers and employees are included.

1.   where, at the time when the proceedings are brought, the individual
        is a national of the state concerned;

2.   where, at the time when the contract was made, the individual was
        neither a national of the United Kingdom[1] nor habitually resident
        here; and

3.   where the parties have otherwise agreed in writing.[2]

The first two exceptions do not apply where the work is for an office,
agency or establishment maintained by the State in the United Kingdom for
commercial purposes unless the individual was, when the contract was
made, habitually resident in that State.[3] In the third case, the parties may
not exclude the jurisdiction of the courts of the United Kingdom where
United Kingdom law requires the proceedings to be brought before the
United Kingdom courts.[4]

(iii) Employees of international organisations[5] and the Commonwealth Secretariat

1.68   Numerous international arrangements, to which the United
Kingdom is a party, provide for the legal status, privileges and immunities
of international organisations and persons connected with them. The
United Kingdom has also entered into headquarters agreements with
certain international organisations which have their headquarters here. The
International Organisations Act 1968[6] makes it possible for an organisation
to be declared by Order in Council to be one of which the United Kingdom
or its government and one or more foreign sovereign States are members;
in such a case, to the extent specified by the Order, the legal capacities of a
body corporate and certain immunities and privileges may be conferred
upon the organisation.[7] The only reported case to consider the Act is
Mukoro v European Bank for Reconstruction and Development,[8] in which the

---

[1]   Section 4(5) defines 'national of the United Kingdom'. It has been amended subsequently
        by the British Nationality Act 1981 and the Hong Kong (British Nationality) Order 1986.

[2]   Section 4(2).

[3]   Section 4(3). For the meaning of 'commercial purposes', see ss 17(1) and 3(3). In *Arab
        Republic of Egypt v Gamal-Eldin* [1996] ICR 13, the EAT held that on the evidence the
        purposes of the medical office of the embassy were not 'commercial purposes'.

[4]   Section 4(4). This includes proceedings before an employment tribunal: see s 22(l).

[5]   For detailed consideration of this topic, reference should be made to Halsbury's *Laws of
        England*, Vol 18(2), paras 913–928, and Bowett's *The Law of International Institutions*,
        5th edn, 2001, Sands and Klein.

[6]   The predecessors of this Act were the Diplomatic Privileges (Extension) Acts 1944–1950
        and the International Organisations (Immunities and Privileges) Act 1950. Orders made
        under those Acts were continued by the 1968 Act.

[7]   For a list of organisations in relation to which orders have been made, reference should be
        made to Halsbury's *Statutory Instruments* Vol 5, pp 128–129. The organisations listed
        include the African Development Bank, the European Bank for Reconstruction and
        Development, the International Jute Organisation and the International Tin Council.

[8]   [1994] ICR 897.

EAT held that the relevant Order[1] granted immunity in respect of a claim of racial discrimination.

It should be noted that the Commonwealth Secretariat is immune from any suit or legal process.[2] So an employee of the Commonwealth Secretariat will have no remedy before an employment tribunal or before the High Court or a county court.[3]

(iv) Crown employees

1.69 Statutory rights are generally made expressly applicable to Crown employees, with the significant exception of the right to receive a redundancy payment. Section 191(3) of the ERA 1996 Act defines Crown employment as 'employment under or for the purposes of a government department or any officer or body exercising on behalf of the Crown functions conferred by a statutory provision'. So Crown employees enjoy most of the employment protection rights conferred by the 1996 Act, except those relating to minimum periods of notice and redundancy payments.[4]

1.70 Members of the armed forces and reserve forces[5] are eligible to be treated as Crown employees and thus to be protected by many of the statutory rights, but this will only take effect when section 192 of the Employment Rights Act 1996 and the Armed Forces Act 1996 are brought into effect. At the time of going to press, these provisions were not operational. Until then, the position is governed by Schedule 2, paragraphs 16 and 17 of the Employment Rights Act 1996,[6] whose effect is to exclude members of the armed forces from the statutory rights. Once section 192 comes into effect, the ERA will apply to service as a member of the armed services, but only in accordance with its provisions. Section 192(2) includes the right not to be unfairly dismissed, but excludes sections 100 to 103 and 134 from its operation.[7] Section 192(3) enables modifications to be made to the unfair dismissal provisions in their application to service as a member of the armed forces. These modifications may include provisions which preclude complaints or references being made to an employment tribunal unless the aggrieved persons have made a complaint to an officer under the 'service procedures for the redress of complaints' applicable to him or her and has submitted the complaint to the Defence Council, and the Defence Council have made a determination

---

[1] The European Bank for Reconstruction and Development (Immunities and Privileges) Order 1991, SI 1991 No 757.

[2] By virtue of the Commonwealth Secretariat Act 1966.

[3] See *Gadhok v Commonwealth Secretariat* (1977) 12 ITR 440.

[4] Section 191(2). Note also ss 159 and 160, in relation to redundancy payments.

[5] Note the Reserve Forces Act 1996.

[6] These provisions were formerly contained in EPCA 1978, s 138(3).

[7] Section 100 relates to dismissal in health and safety cases, s 101 to dismissals of shop workers and betting workers, s 101A to working time cases, s 102 to dismissals of trustees of occupational pension schemes, and s 103 to dismissals of employee representatives and are considered in Chapter 5. Section 134 applies to teachers in aided schools.

with respect to the complaint.[1] An order modifying the unfair dismissal provisions must provide for these procedures to result in a determination to be made in sufficient time for a complaint or reference to be made within a specified period of no longer than six months.[2]

In the context of members of the reserve forces, the provisions of the Reserve Forces (Safeguard of Employment) Act 1985 should be noted.

The provision by which the protection given to Crown employees might be removed from them, where a certificate issued by a Minister of the Crown stated that the employment should be excepted from the statutory provisions on the grounds of national security, has now been repealed.[3]

(v) Parliamentary staff

1.71   House of Commons staff are expressly protected by section 195 of the ERA 1996 and section 278 of the 1992 Act, which apply to any person appointed by the House of Commons Commission or employed in the refreshment department and members of the Speaker's personal staff.[4] The Commission is treated as the employer of staff appointed by it; the Speaker is the employer of his personal staff and those employed in the refreshment department and not employed by the Commission.[5] But both may designate another person who will then be deemed to be the employer of any staff so designated; this does not apply to the Speaker's personal staff.[6]

House of Lords staff are also protected, by virtue of section 194 of the ERA 1996. The protection extends to those who are a 'relevant member of the House of Lords staff', a term defined[7] as any person employed under a contract of employment with the Corporate Officer of the House of Lords.

(vi) Employees over retirement age

1.72   The relevant provisions governing the exclusion from the statutory rights of employees over retirement age are sections 109 (for unfair dismissal cases) and 156 (for redundancy payments claims).

An employee is excluded from the *right not to be unfairly dismissed* if he or she:

---

[1]   Section 192(4), as amended by s 26 of the Armed Forces Act 1996, as from a day to be appointed. The service redress procedures are the procedures referred to in s 180 of the Army Act 1955, s 180 of the Air Force Act 1955 and s 130 of the Naval Discipline Act 1957, as substituted by s 20 of the Armed Forces Act 1996: see s 192(6), as amended by s 26 of the Armed Forces Act 1996.

[2]   Section 192(7) and (8).

[3]   Section 193(1). It should be noted that a new section 193 has been substituted for the former section 193 by the Employment Relations Act 1999, s 41 and Sch 8, para 1, with effect from 18 April 2001. The new provision is of much more restricted scope than the previous provision.

[4]   See s 195(5) and TULRCA 1992, s 278(3).

[5]   Section 195(6).

[6]   Section 195(7). Note also s 195(8).

[7]   By s 194(6) and TULRCA 1992, s 277(3).

'attained the following age on or before the effective date of termination,[1] that is to say—

> (i)   if in the undertaking in which he was employed there was a normal retiring age for an employee holding the position which he held and the age was the same whether the employee holding that position was a man or a woman, that normal retiring age; and
> (ii)   in any other case, the age of sixty-five.'

1.73   The exclusion relating to retiring age does not apply to employees dismissed, or selected for dismissal for redundancy, for reasons related to trade union membership or activities[2] or for reasons related to trade union recognition.[3] In addition, section 109(2) (as amended) provides that the age exclusion set out in section 109(1) is not to apply in the case of certain types of dismissal. These are:

1.   dismissal of an employee in connection with leave for family reasons;
2.   dismissal for reasons connected with health and safety;
3.   dismissal of a shop or betting worker for refusing Sunday work;
4.   dismissal in connection with an employee's rights under the Working Time Regulations;
5.   dismissal for reasons relating to an employee's performance of his or her duties as an occupational pension fund trustee;
6.   dismissal for reasons relating to an employee's performance of his or her duties as an employee representative;
7.   dismissal for making a 'protected disclosure';[4]
8.   dismissal for assertion of a statutory right;
9.   dismissal of an employee in connection with the national minimum wage legislation;
10.   dismissal in connection with an employee's rights under the Tax Credits Act 1999;
11.   dismissal for participation in official industrial action;[5]
12.   dismissals of employees arising under paragraph 28 of the Transnational Information and Consultation of Employees Regulations 1999;
13.   dismissals arising under regulation 7 of the Part-time Workers (Prevention of Less Favourable Treatment) Regulations 2000;
14.   selection for dismissal for redundancy in situations 2–13 above.

---

[1]   This phrase is defined in s 97: see Chapter 3.
[2]   TULRCA 1992, s 154(2), inserted by the Trade Union Reform and Employment Rights Act 1993, s 49(1) and Sch 7, para 1(b).
[3]   TULRCA 1992, Sch A1, para 164, inserted by the Employment Relations Act 1999, s 1(1) and (3) and Sch 1.
[4]   Defined in ERA, ss 235(1) and 43A.
[5]   TULRCA 1992, s 239(1).

In cases where section 109(2) is alleged to apply, the burden will be on the employee to satisfy the tribunal that the reason for the dismissal is one of those which avoids the operation of the age exclusion rule.

1.74   Section 156(1) excludes an employee from the *right to receive a redundancy payment* and is worded as follows:

> 'An employee does not have any right to a redundancy payment if before the relevant date[1] he has attained—
>
> (a)   in a case where—
>> (i)   in the business for the purposes of which the employee was employed there was a normal retiring age of less than sixty-five for an employee holding the position held by the employee, and
>> (ii)   the age was the same whether the employee holding that position was a man or a woman,
>
> that normal retiring age; and
>
> (b)   in any other case, the age of sixty-five.'

Although the provisions of what is now sections 109 and 156 are worded differently, both should be interpreted in the same way. The case-law has considered only what is now section 109, but there is no reason to suppose that it is not also equally applicable to section 156. It should be noted that the phrase 'normal retiring age' is not synonymous with 'pensionable age'.[2]

1.75   In *Nothman v Barnet London Borough Council*,[3] the House of Lords held, by a majority, that section 109(1):[4]

> 'sets up only one barrier to be overcome by the class of employee whose conditions of employment specify a normal retiring age, and another and entirely different barrier to be overcome by the class of employee whose conditions of employment specify no retiring age.'

So it is necessary to determine first whether there is a normal retiring age; if there is, the second barrier will not apply; if, on the other hand, there is no normal retiring age, the second barrier will then operate.[5]

1.76   The House of Lords, however, did not specifically discuss what is meant by the phrase 'normal retiring age', although Lord Salmon indicated

---

[1]   'Relevant date' is defined in s 145: see Chapter 3.
[2]   See *Ord v Maidstone and District Hospital Management Committee* [1979] ICR 369 and *Stepney Cast Stone Co Ltd v MacArthur* [1979] IRLR 181.
[3]   [1979] ICR 111. See at p 116, *per* Lord Salmon at pp 118–119, *per* Lord Edmund-Davies and at p 121, *per* Lord Russell of Killowen.
[4]   Previously section 64(1)(b) of the Employment Protection (Consolidation) Act 1978.
[5]   For an example of this type of case, see *Patel v Nagesan* [1995] ICR 988. In that case, the Court of Appeal said that there was no evidence that there was a normal retiring age for an employee holding the employee's position, since all that the evidence showed was an employer trying to impose a contract with a term that the employee should retire at 60, which she resisted.

that it will be necessary to look at the conditions of employment to see if they specify a normal retiring age.[1] After differences of opinion in the Court of Appeal[2] about the meaning of the phrase, the House of Lords decided, in *Waite v Government Communications HQ*,[3] that it means the retiring age laid down in the terms and conditions upon which the employee was employed ('the contractual retiring age'). The presumption that the contractual retiring age is the normal retiring age may be displaced by evidence that there is in practice some higher age at which employees holding the position are regularly retired, and which they have reasonably come to regard as their normal retiring age. Lord Fraser of Tullybelton said:

'The proper test is ... not merely statistical. It is to ascertain what would be the reasonable expectation or understanding of the employees holding that position at the relevant time. The contractual retiring age will prima facie be displaced by evidence that it is regularly departed from in practice. The evidence may show that the contractual retirement age has been superseded by some definite higher age, and, if so, that will have become the normal retiring age. Or the evidence may show merely that the contractual retirement age has been abandoned and that employees retire at a variety of higher ages. In that case there will be no normal retiring age and the statutory alternatives of 65 for a man and 60 for a woman will apply.'[4]

1.77 This test was applied in *Hughes and Coy v DHSS*,[5] in the context of retirement policy in the civil service. When the employees in question were recruited, the policy was to allow them to remain until 65, subject to continued efficiency. This policy was changed in 1981, when both employees were over 60. They were both compulsorily retired in accordance with the policy. The House of Lords rejected their claims to present complaints to the employment tribunal. Applying the *Waite* test, Lord Diplock said that the presumption that the contractual retiring age is the normal retiring age is rebutted only as long as the policy in question remains in force. He said:

'When a change in administrative policy takes place and is communicated in a departmental circular to ... those employees in the category whose age at which they would be compulsorily retired was stated in a previous circular to be a higher age than 60 years, any reasonable expectations that may have been aroused in them by any previous circular are destroyed and are replaced by such other expectations as to the earliest date at which they can be compelled to retire if the administrative policy announced in the new circular is applied to them.'[6]

---

[1] [1979] ICR 111 at p 116.
[2] *Howard v Department for National Savings* [1981] ICR 208, *Department of Health and Social Security v Randalls* [1981] ICR 100 and *Secretary of State for Trade v Douglas* [1983] IRLR 63. Contrast *Post Office v Wallser* [1981] IRLR 37.
[3] [1983] ICR 653. See also *Swaine v Health and Safety Executive* [1986] IRLR 205.
[4] [1983] ICR 653 at pp 662–663.
[5] [1985] ICR 419.
[6] *Ibid* at p 430.

1.78   In *Brooks v British Telecommunications plc*,[1] the EAT had to consider the test stated above in the context of British Telecom's retirement policy. This was stated in an operating instruction dating from 1972, under which employees could be compulsorily retired at 60 but might be retained after that age if they were fit, efficient and willing and there was a business need for their retention. The employees were over the age of 60 when they were dismissed. The EAT said that the test of what was the normal retiring age required a tribunal to ascertain what would be the reasonable expectation of employees at the relevant time and referred to the age at which employees of all groups could reasonably expect to retire. It said that the reasonable expectation of employees was to be found by asking what actually happened to employees reaching 60, having regard to statistics and any policy announcements of the employers or consultation during counselling sessions. It added that the employment tribunal must be satisfied that the employers' policy of normal retiring age was genuine and had not been displaced or abandoned. The EAT said that the tribunal should first satisfy itself that the employer's policy of normal retiring age is genuine and existing and is not a sham and has not been abandoned. The normal retiring age may be a 'contractual retiring age', a normal retirement age established by practice, or a 'policy retiring age', one established by a statement of policy. The policy may be unconditional or discretionary; for example, the continued employment or re-employment of those who are fit and efficient and for whom the employer has a need. The age established by this inquiry will be the normal retiring age unless displaced by evidence that it has been regularly departed from in practice, so that it amounts to an abandonment. The EAT said that, when considering whether a normal retiring age has been displaced, an employment tribunal may use statistical evidence, but that it is a matter for it to decide. It followed the earlier decision of *Denham and Todd v British Telecommunications plc* (unreported), which emphasised that:

> 'when the facts show that retention beyond [the normal retiring age] is not simply left to the volition of the employee but depends on the discretion of the employer applying genuine criteria which are strictly applied, ... it is open to the tribunal to find that the normal retiring age is the contractual retiring age, notwithstanding that a not insignificant number of employees are allowed to remain beyond that age.'

1.79   The Court of Appeal upheld the decision of the EAT.[2] It emphasised that the employment tribunal has to consider what, at the effective date of termination of the employee's employment, and on the basis of the facts known at that time, was the age at which employees of all age groups in the employee's position could reasonably regard as the normal age of retirement applicable to that group. It said that the employment tribunal was right to reject the inclusion into the test of the

---

[1]   [1991] ICR 286. See also *Whittle v Manpower Services Commission* [1987] IRLR 441 and *Mauldon v British Telecommunications plc* [1987] ICR 450.
[2]   [1992] ICR 414.

reasonable expectations of members of the group of what would happen to those approaching 60 at the dates of the dismissed employees' dismissals. It said that the definition of 'position' (discussed further below) does not include the element of age and, in effect, that the employees holding a 'position' cannot be divided into a sub-group of those who are approaching 60, since to do so would introduce the element of age which is not present in the statutory definition. The authorities in this area have subsequently been reviewed by the Court of Appeal in *Barclays Bank plc v O'Brien*.[1]

1.80 A further question is whether the normal retiring age may be below the contractual retiring age. In *Bratko v Beloit Walmsley Ltd*,[2] the EAT said that the employer cannot reduce the normal retiring age below the contractual age of retirement, without going through the normal steps necessary to change a contractual term. It said that the decision of the House of Lords in the *Waite* case contemplates only the possibility of a normal retiring age higher than the contractual retiring age, and not lower. An employee who agrees to a change in the terms of the pension scheme applicable to him or her, involving a reduction of the pension age, is not automatically taken to have agreed to a change in the normal retiring age. The employment tribunal must ascertain whether the contractual position between the parties has altered, and see whether the employee has understood the change and generally agreed to it.[3]

1.81 An employee who is taken on after the age of 65 may be held to have a normal retiring age which is later than 65, but it remains necessary to look at the terms of the contract. The fact that an employee is taken on when over 65 does not mean that there must be implied a later retiring age.[4]

1.82 A further point to note is the meaning of the word 'position' in section 109; it is defined in section 235(1). The statute refers to a normal retiring age for an employee holding the position the employee in question held. In *Brooks v British Telecommunications plc*,[5] the EAT held that the statutory definition of 'position' included consideration of the nature of an employee's work, which of necessity related to the work actually done and not merely to the employee's grade. It upheld the employment tribunal's conclusion that it was necessary to look and see whether, as a matter of common sense and practicality, the work done by two people was sufficiently similar for it to be sensible to treat them as holding the same position. The Court of Appeal in the same case said that 'age is not an element to be taken into account under the definition of position'.[6] In *Barber v Thames Television plc*,[7] the Court of Appeal said that in applying the

---

[1] [1994] ICR 865.

[2] [1996] ICR 76.

[3] *Stepney Cast Stone Co Ltd v MacArthur* [1979] IRLR 181 and *BP Chemicals Ltd v Joseph* [1980] IRLR 55.

[4] See *Dixon v London Production Tools Ltd and Phildon Instrumentation (London) Ltd* [1980] IRLR 385.

[5] [1992] ICR 414.

[6] [1992] ICR 414 at p 422.

[7] [1992] ICR 661.

definition of 'position' the matters to be taken into account include terms, whether contractual or by virtue of the expectation of the person concerned, which fall within the phrase 'terms and conditions of the employee's employment' as used in the definition of 'position' in section 235(1). It is thus possible to have employees who have the same job title, but who occupy different positions. The fact that employees have different retirement ages as terms of their contracts may be taken into account in determining whether the employees are in the same 'position'. In the case in question, the Court of Appeal said, in effect, that there were two groups of senior supervisors: those employed before January 1978 (when there was a variety of arrangements as to retiring age) and those who joined after that date, who had a compulsory retirement age of 60. The employee in question fell within the first group, and the Court of Appeal held in respect of that group that from 26 October 1987 (when he was informed of a change of policy) there was a normal retirement age of 64. The employee was therefore excluded from the statutory provisions.

1.83 Finally, there is the question of how employment tribunals should deal with issues relating to the normal retiring age. The question whether there is a normal retiring age is a question of fact.[1] The tribunal will therefore need to consider all the circumstances to enable it to determine the question and will have to make relevant findings of fact. The President of the EAT has suggested that in cases such as this it is not appropriate to proceed by way of preliminary hearing and on the basis of assumed facts, separately from the rest of the case. In such cases it is often better to hear all the facts first and then resolve the issues.[2]

(vii) Short-term and casual employees

1.84 Section 108(1) (as amended)[3] sets out the general rule that an employee must have been continuously employed[4] for one year before qualifying for the right not to be unfairly dismissed. (The qualifying period remains two years in the case of the right to receive a redundancy payment.[5]) This means that short-term, seasonal and casual workers are likely to be excluded, as are employees taken on as temporary replacements for employees absent on maternity leave (or for other reasons).

1.85 The one-year qualifying period does not apply, however, to employees dismissed, or selected for dismissal for redundancy, for reasons

---

[1] *Barclays Bank plc v O'Brien* [1994] ICR 865 and *Secretary of State for Education v Birchall* [1994] IRLR 630.

[2] See *Secretary of State for Education v Birchall* [1994] IRLR 630.

[3] By the Unfair Dismissal and Statement of Reasons for Dismissal (Variation of Qualifying Period) Order 1999, SI 1999 No 1436. The Order affects employees whose effective date of termination falls on or after 1 June 1999.

[4] Continuity of employment is discussed later in this chapter.

[5] ERA 1996, s 155.

related to trade union membership or activities[1] or trade union recognition.[2] In addition, section 108(3) (as amended) provides that the requirement for a qualifying period of employment set out in section 108(1) is not to apply in the case of certain types of dismissal. These are:

1. dismissal of an employee in connection with leave for family reasons;
2. dismissal for reasons connected with health and safety;
3. dismissal of a shop or betting worker for refusing Sunday work;
4. dismissal in connection with an employee's rights under the Working Time Regulations;
5. dismissal for reasons relating to an employee's performance of his or her duties as an occupational pension fund trustee;
6. dismissal for reasons relating to an employee's performance of his or her duties as an employee representative;
7. dismissal for making a 'protected disclosure';[3]
8. dismissal for assertion of a statutory right;
9. dismissal of an employee in connection with the national minimum wage legislation;
10. dismissal in connection with an employee's rights under the Tax Credits Act 1999;
11. dismissal for participation in official industrial action;[4]
12. dismissals of employees arising under paragraph 28 of the Transnational Information and Consultation of Employees Regulations 1999;
13. dismissals arising under regulation 7 of the Part-time Workers (Prevention of Less Favourable Treatment) Regulations 2000;
14. selection for dismissal for redundancy in situations 2–13 above.

In cases where section 108(3) is alleged to apply, the burden will be on the employee to satisfy the tribunal that the reason for the dismissal is one of those which avoids the operation of the one-year rule.

(viii) Employment outside Great Britain

1.86   Until 25 October 1999, the effect of section 196(3) of the ERA 1996 was to exclude an employee who 'under his contract of employment ... ordinarily works outside Great Britain' from the right not to be unfairly dismissed. The whole of section 196 was repealed with effect from that date, however. This means that the cases considered in previous editions of this book are now irrelevant.

---

[1] TULRCA 1992, s 154(2), inserted by the Trade Union Reform and Employment Rights Act 1993, s 49(1) and Sch 7, para 1(b),
[2] TULRCA 1992, Sch A1, para 164, inserted by the Employment Relations Act 1999, s 1(1) and (3) and Sch 1.
[3] Defined in ERA, ss 235(1) and 43A.
[4] TULRCA 1992, s 239(1).

1.87   It should be noted that an important effect of this repeal will be to extend the employment protection rights in the legislation of the United Kingdom to employees from other countries who come to work here. Provided that they have sufficient continuity of employment to qualify for the relevant right, the fact that they might previously have been treated as 'ordinarily' working outside the United Kingdom is irrelevant.

1.88   For the purpose of computing an employee's period of employment, the provisions of sections 210–219 apply to a period of employment during which the employee was engaged in work wholly or mainly outside Great Britain.[1] In the context of redundancy payments, however, a week will not count in the case of an employee who, during the whole or part of it, was employed outside Great Britain and was not an employed earner, in respect of whom an employer's contribution was payable, during that week; the fact that the week does not count will not break continuity.[2]

(ix) National security

1.89   Until 18 April 2001, section 10(4) of the Employment Tribunals Act 1996 provided that a complaint of unfair dismissal must be dismissed if the action complained of was for the purpose of safeguarding national security. A certificate issued by or on behalf of a Minister of the Crown, certifying that the action specified in the certificate was take for the purpose of safeguarding national security, was conclusive of the fact that the action was taken for that purpose. This did not apply where the complaint was that the dismissal was unfair by virtue of sections 99, 100, 101A(d), 103 or 105(1).[3] These types of unfair dismissal are considered in Chapter 5.

1.90   The Employment Relations Act 1999[4] has substituted new sections 10, 10A and 10B, with effect from 18 April 2001. Section 10(1) is in similar terms to the former section 10(4) above. The remaining provisions of the new section 10 enable procedure regulations to be made governing procedure in 'Crown employment proceedings'.[5] The regulations may make provision enabling a Minister 'if he considers it expedient in the interests of national security' to take a number of actions, including directing the tribunal to exclude the applicant or the applicant's representative from all or part of the proceedings; the tribunal may also take similar steps of its own motion. In such cases, the regulations may make provision for the applicant's interests to be represented by the

---

[1]   Section 215(1).

[2]   Section 215(2)–(6), as amended by the Social Security Contributions (Transfer of Functions) Act 1999, s 18 and Sch 7, para 21(1)–(3), as from 1 April 1999.

[3]   Employment Tribunals Act 1996, s 10(5). Note also s 10(6).

[4]   See s 41 and Sch 8, para 3.

[5]   Proceedings will be Crown employment proceedings if the employment to which the unfair dismissal complaint relates is Crown employment or is connected with the performance of functions on behalf of the Crown: see s 10(8).

Attorney General (or, in Scotland, the Advocate General).[1] The new section 10A provides for procedure regulations to be made dealing with the hearing of evidence in relation to confidential information; section 10B makes provision for restriction of publicity in cases involving national security and makes it an offence to publish anything likely to lead to the identification of a witness whose identity was directed to be kept secret, or the reasons for the tribunal's decision where the tribunal has been directed or has decided to keep secret all or part of the reasons for its decision. The relevant regulation is regulation 8 of the Employment Tribunals (Constitution and Rules of Procedure) Regulations 2001,[2] which came into effect on 16 July 2001.

(x) Miscellaneous exclusions

1.91 Share fishermen, ie masters or crew members of fishing vessels remunerated 'by a share in the profits or gross earnings of the vessel', are excluded from the rights not to be unfairly dismissed and to receive a redundancy payment.[3] Section 161 excludes a domestic servant who is a close relation of the employer from the right to receive a redundancy payment.

1.92 Those employed in police service[4] are expressly excluded from all the provisions relating to the right not to be unfairly dismissed, with the exception of section 100.[5] Being office-holders, they are also impliedly excluded from the right to receive a redundancy payment. This statutory exclusion has been held to apply to the British Transport Police Force.[6] A police cadet has been held not to be the employee of the police authority, or indeed, an employee at all,[7] and prison officers have also been held to be excluded.[8] The position of those who are serving as members of the armed forces has been considered earlier, in the context of Crown employment (see para 1.70).

---

[1] See s 10(5)–(7).

[2] SI 2001 No 1171.

[3] Section 199(2). See also *Goodeve v Gilsons* [1985] ICR 401.

[4] 'Police service' is defined in s 200(2) as service '(a) as a member of a constabulary maintained by virtue of an enactment, or (b) subject to section 126 of the Criminal Justice and Public Order Act 1994 [which stipulates that prison staff are not to be regarded as in police service], service in any other capacity by virtue of which a person has the powers or privileges of a constable'.

[5] Section 200(1), as amended by the Police (Health and Safety) Act 1997, s 6(2), with effect from 1 July 1998. Section 4 of that Act inserted a new section 134A into the 1996 Act which states that, for the purposes of section 100, the holding of the office of constable or an appointment as police cadet is to be treated as employment by the relevant officer under a contract of employment. 'The relevant officer' is defined in s 134A(2).

[6] *Spence v British Railways Board* [2001] ICR 232.

[7] *Wiltshire Police Authority v Wynn* [1981] QB 95.

[8] *Home Office v Robinson and The Prison Officers' Association* [1982] ICR 31.

1.93   Employees with pension rights are subject to regulations[1] made by the Secretary of State under what is now section 158 of the ERA 1996 which may exclude their right to a redundancy payment or reduce the amount of any redundancy payment. Holders of certain public offices are excluded from the right to receive a redundancy payment[2] since special schemes exist for them which are more beneficial than the statutory scheme. An example of such a scheme is the Whitley Council Agreement, which provides for redundancy payments. Such schemes may include a provision for referring disputes to an employment tribunal, as does the Whitley Council Agreement. In that case, they are governed by section 177, which does not provide a limitation period for the bringing of claims. References under section 177 are, therefore, governed by the ordinary limitation rules and must be brought within six years.[3]

1.94   Crown employees, House of Commons staff and House of Lords staff are excluded from the right to receive a redundancy payment,[4] as are those employed in any capacity under the government of an overseas territory.[5]

1.95   Section 171 gives the Secretary of State power to make regulations providing for specified office-holders to be embraced by the coverage of the redundancy provisions;[6] section 172 gives the Secretary of State power to make regulations treating the termination of certain employments by statute as equivalent to dismissal. Regulations made under this section have extended the redundancy provisions to chief constables and chief officers of fire brigades.[7]

(c) Contracting out of the statutory rights

1.96   Employees may be excluded by contracting out in two types of circumstances. First, they may enter into an agreement with their employer, as a result of which the employment tribunal decides that the employment has been terminated by mutual agreement and not dismissal. In such a case, the fact that there has been no dismissal means that a complaint of unfair dismissal or a claim for a redundancy payment will fail. To be within the legislative protection, an employee must be able to show a dismissal. In such cases, it is arguable that section 203(1) of the ERA

---

[1]   The Redundancy Payments Pensions Regulations 1965, SI 1965 No 1932, particularly reg 3. See *Stowe-Woodward BTR Ltd v Beynon* [1978] ICR 609, *British Telecommunications plc v Burwell* [1986] ICR 35 and *Royal Ordnance plc v Pilkington* [1989] ICR 737.

[2]   Section 159.

[3]   *Greenwich Health Authority v Skinner* [1989] ICR 220 and *Stevens v Bexley Health Authority* [1989] ICR 224.

[4]   Sections 191(1) and (2), 194(1) and (2) and 195(1) and (2).

[5]   Section 160(1); see s 160(2) and (3) for the definition of 'Government of an overseas territory'.

[6]   See the Redundancy Payments Office Holders Regulations 1965, SI 1965 No 2007, the Redundancy Payments (Office Holders) (Scotland) Regulations 1966, SI 1966 No 1436 and the Redundancy Payments (Share Fishermen) Regulations 1966, SI 1966 No 145.

[7]   See the Redundancy Payments Termination of Employment Regulations 1965, SI 1965 No 2022.

1996 should apply, but, as the cases discussed below demonstrate, this has generally not been an approach which has commended itself to the employment tribunals and the EAT, despite dicta in some of the cases that section 203(1)[1] should be given a broad construction.

Secondly, employees may also be excluded by contracting out where they make an agreement with their employer which is covered by the provisions of section 203(2) of the ERA 1996. These are also considered in this section.

(i) Bilateral termination agreements

1.97 In the context of the statutory rights,[2] the courts and tribunals tend to show themselves to be reluctant to find that there is a genuine bilateral agreement between employer and employee providing for the termination of the employee's employment, as opposed to an apparent agreement engineered by the employer. Cases in which the employee has been given notice by the employer, but has agreed to bring forward the date of departure at the request of the employer, will not be treated as cases of bilateral termination, but of dismissal; similar considerations apply to postponement of the date of departure.[3] If, however, the date of departure is brought forward by the employer at the employee's request, that may be treated as a case of bilateral termination,[4] although it is probably better to regard it as a case of termination by the employer. The EAT has held that a resignation on agreed terms will not amount to a dismissal, even if preceded by difficulties between the parties.[5] In *Birch v University of Liverpool*,[6] the question was whether an employee who responded to the employer's invitation to apply for early retirement and whose application was approved could claim to have been dismissed for the purposes of a redundancy payments claim. One of the important factors of the early retirement scheme was that an employee's application was subject to final approval by the employer. The Court of Appeal held that the contract had been terminated by the parties by mutual agreement. The facts that the employee's application was subject to the approval of the employer and that there might have been a redundancy situation did not mean that the final approval, if given, amounted to a dismissal within the statutory definition.

The expiry of a fixed-term contract may be treated as a termination by agreement if the contract contemplated the termination of the contract in certain specified circumstances and those circumstances occur.[7]

---

[1]   Formerly, s 140(1) of the EPCA 1978.

[2]   This is different from the position at common law. See Chapter 9.

[3]   See *McAlwane v Boughton Estates Ltd* [1973] ICR 470, *Lees v Arthur Greaves (Lees) Ltd* [1974] ICR 510 and *Mowlem Northern Ltd v Watson* [1990] ICR 751.

[4]   As in *L Lipton Ltd v Marlborough* [1979] IRLR 178.

[5]   See *Sheffield v Oxford Controls Ltd* [1979] ICR 396, *Staffordshire County Council v Donovan* [1981] IRLR 108 and *Logan Salton v Durham County Council* [1989] IRLR 99.

[6]   [1985] ICR 470. See also *Scott v Coalite Fuels and Chemicals Ltd* [1988] ICR 355.

[7]   *Brown v Knowsley Borough Council* [1986] IRLR 102.

Some of the decided cases[1] in this area have been decided without reference to what is now section 203 of the ERA 1996 and its predecessor,[2] and questions must arise as to whether they would have been decided differently had that provision been considered.

(ii) The statutory rules

1.98   The general rule on contracting out is to be found in section 203. This states that any provision in an agreement (whether or not it is a contract of employment) will be void:

> 'in so far as it purports—
>
> (a)   to exclude or limit the operation of any provision of this Act; or
> (b)   to preclude any person from presenting a complaint to, or bringing any proceedings under this Act before, an employment tribunal.'

There are various exceptions to the general rule, which are set out in section 203(2). The three most important for present purposes are:

1.   agreements reached under the auspices of a conciliation officer;
2.   compromise agreements reached after advice from a 'relevant independent adviser'; and
3.   waiver clauses in relation to fixed-term contracts.

These are considered in turn below.

1.99   The general rule In *Council of Engineering Institutions v Maddison*,[3] the EAT said that any agreement purporting to deprive employees of their rights under the legislation must be clearly established and that any uncertainty should be resolved in their favour. It added that section 203 (formerly section 140) should be construed broadly, but that such agreements, however carefully drawn up, cannot be enforced, so that it will be open to either party to resile. In *Courage Take Home Trade Ltd v Keys*,[4] the EAT applied what is now section 203 to an agreement to accept a sum of money by way of full and final settlement of an employee's claim after the tribunal had upheld his complaint as unfair and adjourned the question of remedy. The EAT said that the provisions of section 203 do not cease to have effect after proceedings have been started or after liability, as opposed to remedy, has been determined. It held that the agreement was void, but also held that it was just and equitable to award no compensation to the employee.[5] Section 203 does not apply, however, to an agreement to take

---

[1]   For example, *Sheffield v Oxford Controls Ltd*, above. See, however, *Hanson v Fashion Industries (Hartlepool) Ltd* [1981] ICR 35 and *Tocher v General Motors Scotland Ltd* [1981] IRLR 55.
[2]   Section 140 of the EPCA 1978.
[3]   [1977] ICR 30. See also *Naqvi v Stephens Jewellers Ltd* [1978] ICR 631, where the EAT applied what is now s 203 to an agreement to withdraw a complaint of unfair dismissal.
[4]   [1986] ICR 874. See also *Carter v Reiner Moritz Associates Ltd* [1997] ICR 881.
[5]   See Chapter 8 which sets out the rules for calculating compensation.

voluntary retirement, even if the agreement supersedes a notice of dismissal.[1] In *Sutherland v Network Appliance Ltd*,[2] the agreement (to which it was conceded the statutory provisions relating to compromise agreements set out below did not apply) was made 'in full and final settlement of any claims you may have against the company arising out of your employment or its termination'. The employee later presented a complaint to the employment tribunal claiming, amongst other things, unfair dismissal and damages for breach of contract. The tribunal held that he had compromised any claim he might have for damages for breach of contract and held, therefore, that it had no jurisdiction to consider that part of the claim. The employee appealed on the footing that the entire agreement was void. The EAT dismissed his appeal, saying that section 203(1) of the 1996 Act only makes void a provision in an agreement 'insofar as it purports' to exclude or limit the operation of any provision of the Act; the statute does not state that the provision is void 'if' it purports to exclude or limit the operation of a provision. The contractual claim thus remained compromised. It is not possible, however, to compromise a claim which the parties could not have contemplated at the time when they signed the agreement. The House of Lords so decided in *Bank of Credit and Commerce International SA v Ali*,[3] a case arising from the decision of the House of Lords in the previous case of *Malik v Bank of Credit and Commerce International SA*,[4] which held that in appropriate cases so-called 'stigma damages' may be awarded. The House of Lords said that, in the absence of clear language, the courts will be slow to infer that a party intended to surrender rights and claims of which he or she was unaware and could not have been aware.

1.100   In recent years, a number of cases have considered the effect of an agreement by employees that if they fail to return from leave or holiday on a specified date, the contract will terminate or they will be assumed to have terminated their employment. In *Igbo v Johnson Matthey Chemicals Ltd*,[5] the facts were that the employee wished to visit some of her family in Nigeria. Her employers agreed to extended leave of absence, but it was explained to her that she must return to work on 28 September 1983. She was given a document, which she and the employers' personnel officer signed. The document ended: '... you have agreed to return to work on 28 September 1983. If you fail to do this your contract will automatically terminate on that date'. She did not return on that date because, although she had returned from Nigeria, she was ill. She sent a medical certificate to the employers, who wrote to her to tell her that by reason of her failure to attend, her employment was terminated in accordance with the terms of the agreement. She complained of unfair dismissal. The Court of Appeal

---

[1]   *Scott v Coalite Fuels and Chemicals Ltd* [1988] ICR 355. Cf *Birch v University of Liverpool* [1985] ICR 470.

[2]   [2001] IRLR 12.

[3]   [2001] IRLR 292.

[4]   [1997] ICR 606.

[5]   [1986] ICR 505. The Court of Appeal overruled *British Leyland (UK) Ltd v Ashraf* [1978] ICR 979. See also *Midland Electric Manufacturing Co Ltd v Kanji* [1980] IRLR 185 and *Tracey v Zest Equipment Co Ltd* [1982] ICR 481.

held that the agreement had the effect of limiting the operation of sections 94 and 95 of the ERA 1996[1] in that it converted a right not to be unfairly dismissed into a conditional right not to be dismissed, and that it was therefore void by virtue of section 203. The significance of this decision is that it gives the employment tribunal jurisdiction to examine the circumstances of such agreements.[2]

1.101   The question of termination of employment by mutual agreement and the effect of section 203 was considered by the EAT in *Logan Salton v Durham County Council*.[3] The employee was in dispute with the council; matters came to a head when he was given notice of a disciplinary hearing. He subsequently received a letter about the hearing, enclosing a copy of a statement which was to be considered at the hearing. The statement set out a number of complaints against him and concluded with a recommendation that he should be summarily dismissed. He decided to resign and discussed the matter with his union representative, who negotiated terms with his employers. As a result, a written agreement was drawn up and signed by both parties. It was agreed that his employment would end by mutual agreement and financial arrangements were also agreed with regard to an outstanding car loan. The employee subsequently complained of unfair dismissal. He argued that the agreement had been entered into under duress and was therefore void and also that it was rendered void by what is now section 203 of the ERA 1996. The EAT refused to interfere with the employment tribunal's decision that the agreement was freely entered into and was not made under duress; it also decided that there was a mutual agreement to terminate the contract and, therefore, that there was no dismissal, relying on the earlier decision in *Sheffield v Oxford Controls Ltd*.[4] It also upheld the tribunal's decision that the agreement was not rendered void by section 203. It distinguished *Igbo v Johnson Matthey Chemicals Ltd* on the grounds that the agreement entered into by Mr Logan Salton was not a contract of employment but was a separate agreement entered into willingly, without duress and for good consideration and that the termination of the employment did not depend upon the happening of a future event. The EAT stressed its view that:

> 'in the resolution of industrial disputes it is in the best interests of all concerned that a contract made without duress, for good consideration, preferably after proper and sufficient advice, and which has the effect of terminating a contract of employment by mutual agreement ... should be effective between the contracting parties ...'

1.102   The three most important exceptions to the general rule set out in section 203(1) above are agreements reached under the auspices of a

---

[1]   Formerly, ss 54 and 55 of the EPCA 1978.
[2]   As happened in *Ali v Joseph Dawson Ltd* (EAT 43/89). The dismissal was held by the EAT to be fair.
[3]   [1989] IRLR 99.
[4]   [1979] ICR 396.

conciliation officer, compromise agreements reached after advice from a 'relevant independent adviser' and waiver clauses in fixed-term contracts.

1.103   Agreements reached with the help of a conciliation officer Agreements reached under the auspices of a conciliation officer are not affected by section 203. Section 203(2) excludes agreements reached both before and after a complaint has been presented to an employment tribunal. Section 18 of the Employment Tribunals Act 1996 sets out the duties of the conciliation officer. These, together with the relevant case-law, are discussed at the end of this chapter.

1.104   Compromise agreements There is an exception to section 203(1) in the case of compromise agreements reached after advice from a 'relevant independent adviser'.[1] Its effect is that employees who make compromise agreements will be excluded by section 203(2) from pursuing their statutory rights, provided that the compromise agreement complies with the conditions set out in section 203(3), (3A), (3B) and (4). It should be noted that these requirements only affect employees who are party to compromise agreements and who receive advice from a 'relevant independent adviser'.

1.105   The conditions set out in section 203(3)[2] are:

1.   the agreement must be in writing;
2.   the agreement must relate to the 'particular proceedings';
3.   the employee must have received 'advice from a relevant independent adviser[3] as to the terms and effect of the proposed agreement and in particular its effect on his [or her] ability to pursue his [or her] rights before an employment tribunal';
4.   when the adviser gives the advice, a contract of insurance or an indemnity provided by a professional body must be in force covering the risk of a claim by the employee in respect of loss arising in consequence of the advice;
5.   the agreement must identify the adviser; and
6.   the agreement must state that the conditions regulating compromise agreements under the 1996 Act are satisfied.

1.106   It is not clear what the phrase 'the particular proceedings' means. Until section 203(3)(b) was amended by the Employment Rights (Dispute Resolution) Act 1998, the phrase was 'the particular complaint'. The substituted phrase would tend to suggest, for example, that an employee who brings or threatens proceedings in respect of unfair dismissal and compromises those proceedings will not be precluded from subsequently bringing proceedings in respect of the alleged infringement of another statutory right. Thus, a compromise agreement which referred to an

---

[1]   See s 203(2)(f).
[2]   As amended by the Employment Rights (Dispute Resolution) Act 1998.
[3]   Defined in s 203(3A) and (3B).

agreement not to take any proceedings 'arising out of the termination of your employment' is probably too general. This kind of issue was considered by the EAT in *Lunt v Merseyside TEC Ltd,*[1] but it should be noted that the case was decided when section 203(3) was in its unamended form. In that case, the employee wrote a letter to her employers claiming that she was suffering from a stress-related illness caused by conduct of her employers which she considered to amount to harassment, victimisation and sex discrimination. She later entered into a compromise agreement by which the employers agreed to terminate her employment by reason of ill-health and to make specified payments in respect of all claims for unfair dismissal, redundancy and breach of contract. The employee subsequently presented complaints of sex discrimination, unfair dismissal and breach of contract; the employers relied upon the compromise agreement to argue that the jurisdiction of the employment tribunal was excluded. The EAT upheld the decision of the tribunal chairman to dismiss her complaints relating to the claims which had been compromised and to sever the claim relating to sex discrimination, which was allowed to proceed. The EAT said that section 203(3)(b) does not permit a 'blanket' agreement compromising claims of which there has been no indication. It quoted with approval from *Harvey on Industrial Relations and Employment Law:*[2]

> 'A compromise agreement cannot … seek to exclude potential complaints that have not yet arisen on the off-chance that they might be raised … However, where a number of different tribunal claims … have been raised by the employee, whether in an originating application or in correspondence prior to the issue of proceedings, there does not seem to be any good reason why these should not all be disposed of in the one compromise agreement. The alternative approach, that there should be a separate agreement for each and every complaint raised, would seem to be supererogatory in such circumstances.'

1.107   This case may be contrasted with the decision of the Court of Appeal in *Sheriff v Klyne Tugs (Lowestoft) Ltd,*[3] although it appears from the report of the decision that the compromise agreement involved was not one falling within section 203(3). The employee launched a complaint of racial discrimination against his employers. He claimed that he had suffered racial abuse, intimidation and bullying and that this had caused a nervous breakdown. During the hearing he entered into a settlement agreement with his employers, one of whose terms stated: 'The applicant accepts the terms of this agreement in full and final settlement of all claims which he has or may have against the respondent arising out of his employment or the termination thereof being claims in respect of which an industrial tribunal has jurisdiction'. The employment tribunal then issued a formal decision dismissing the application on withdrawal by the applicant. He subsequently brought an action against the employers in the county court, claiming damages for personal injury in respect of the treatment he

---

[1]   [1999] ICR 17. The view taken by the EAT in this case is consistent with the approach taken in *Livingstone v Hepworth Refractories Ltd* [1992] ICR 287.

[2]   Paragraph T[729].

[3]   [1999] IRLR 481.

had received; the particulars of claim were almost identical to the allegations involved in the previous racial discrimination claim. The Court of Appeal upheld the decision of the county court to strike out the claim as being an abuse of the process of the court. The Court's decision was based on two grounds: (i) that the county court claim fell within the terms of the compromise agreement because it was a claim for compensation for injury sustained by the appellant arising out of his employment with the respondents, and in respect of which the employment tribunal had jurisdiction; and (ii) that the action fell within the public policy principle enunciated in *Henderson v Henderson*[1] that claims that have been or could have been litigated in one tribunal should not be allowed to be litigated in another. The same issue of the conduct of the ship's master lay at the heart of both the proceedings in the employment tribunal and the county court action, and the appellant could have brought forward his whole claim for compensation in the employment tribunal.

The difference between the two above cases arguably lies in the fact that in the last case the employee was effectively trying to resuscitate the same litigation he had compromised in another tribunal. That is different from compromising one claim and then embarking on another, although it is clear that it will not always be easy to draw the line between the two types of case.

1.108 Section 203(3A) defines as a 'relevant independent adviser' the following categories:

(a)   a qualified lawyer;[2]

(b)   an officer, official, employee or member of an independent trade union who has been certified in writing by the trade union as competent to give advice and as authorised to do so on behalf of the trade union;

(c)   a person who works at an advice centre (whether as an employee or volunteer) and has been certified in writing by the centre as competent to give advice and authorised to do so on behalf of the centre;

(d)   a person 'of a description specified in an order made by the Secretary of State'.[3]

Section 203(3B) excludes the following categories from the definition:

(a)   a person employed by or acting in the matter for the employer or an associated employer;

---

[1]   (1843) 3 Hare 100.

[2]   Defined in s 203(4). In England and Wales a 'qualified lawyer' is a barrister, whether in practice or employed to give legal advice or a solicitor of the Supreme Court who holds a practising certificate. In Scotland, the equivalents are advocates, whether in practice or employed to give legal advice, and solicitors who hold a practising certificate. This definition means that trainee solicitors and legal executives, for example, cannot give advice as qualified lawyers.

[3]   No order had been made at the time of going to press.

(b)   in the case of a person within (b) or (c) above, if the trade union or
        advice centre is the employer or an associated employer;
(c)   in the case of a person within (c) above, if the employee or worker
        makes a payment for the advice received from him or her;
(d)   in the case of a person of a description specified by an order made by
        the Secretary of State, if any condition specified in the order in
        relation to the giving of advice by persons of that description is not
        satisfied.

1.109   It should be noted that an employee may sue in the employment
tribunal an employer who fails to make a payment due under a
compromise agreement.[1] What is not clear, however, is what steps are
available to an employee where the employer breaches a clause in the
compromise agreement which does not relate to money, for example an
agreement to provide an appropriately worded reference. Such a breach of
the agreement would not be enforceable in the tribunal. It is suggested,
therefore, that in such circumstances the agreement would be invalidated
by the employer's breach, thus enabling the employee to resurrect the
tribunal proceedings.

1.110   Waiver clauses in fixed-term contracts Waiver clauses in relation
to fixed-term contracts are excluded from the operation of section 203,[2] if
the provisions of section 197(3) are complied with. It should be noted that
the provisions relating to waivers of an employee's unfair dismissal rights[3]
were repealed by the Employment Relations Act 1999[4] and thus the waiver
provisions only apply now to the waiver of an employee's entitlement to a
redundancy payment. It is likely that the continuing existence of these
provisions will also need to be reviewed when implementation of the
Council Directive relating to fixed-term work comes to be considered.[5]

1.111   Section 197(3) provides that an employee employed under a
contract for a fixed term of two years or more is not entitled to a *redundancy
payment* in respect of the expiry of the fixed term without its being renewed
(whether by the employer or by an associated employer).[6] The employee
must have agreed in writing, before the fixed term expires, to exclude any
claim to a redundancy payment in the event of the non-renewal of the fixed
term. The agreement may be in the contract itself or a separate agreement.[7]

---

[1]   See *Rock-It Cargo Ltd v Green* [1997] IRLR 581. The EAT held that a compromise agreement
      is a 'contract connected with employment' within s 3(2) of the Employment Tribunals Act
      1996.
[2]   By s 203(2)(d).
[3]   Section 197(1) and (2).
[4]   Sections 18(1) and 44 and Sch 9(3)
[5]   Council Directive 99/70/EC concerning the framework agreement on fixed-term work
      concluded by ETUC, UNICE and CEEP. The directive should have been implemented by
      the Member States by 10 July 2001 but the United Kingdom intends to implement the
      Directive by 10 July 2002, on the basis of a provision in the Directive permitting a year's
      delay if there are 'special difficulties'.
[6]   Section 197(3).
[7]   Section 197(4).

If the agreement is made during the currency of a fixed term and the term is renewed, the agreement will not apply to the term as renewed.[1]

1.112 The most recent case to consider the provisions of section 197 is *Housing Services Agency v Cragg*.[2] The EAT said that the following requirements must be met:[3]

1.   There must be a fixed-term contract.
2.   The contract must in the first instance be for a term of two years or more. It is not permissible to aggregate successive fixed terms so as to amount to two years or more.
3.   Before the expiry of the fixed term the parties must enter into a waiver agreement as defined in section 197(4).
4.   If dismissal, consisting of the expiry of the fixed term without its being renewed, occurs, the employee is excluded from the right to bring a claim for a redundancy payment.
5.   If there is no dismissal under 4, because either the contract is renewed or the employee is re-engaged on different agreed terms, then, if the original fixed term is renewed for a further fixed term, whether for a period of two years or less, and during that extended term the parties enter into a section 197(4) waiver agreement, then dismissal arising out of the expiry of the original fixed term as extended will not give rise to a claim for a redundancy payment.

1.113 The expiry of a fixed-term contract will also be treated as a dismissal for the purposes of the statutory rights.[4] The meaning of 'fixed-term' contract is considered in Chapter 3.

2. CONTINUITY OF EMPLOYMENT

1.114 Continuity of employment is important in the present context because the statutory rights considered in Part I are available only to employees who have been 'continuously employed' for the requisite period of time. In the case of the unfair dismissal rights, that period is one year;[5] in the case of the entitlement to a redundancy payment, it is two years.[6] Continuity of employment is also used to compute the amount of a redundancy payment and of a basic award of compensation for unfair dismissal: see Chapter 8. The main rules for determining continuity are in sections 210–219. The effect of changes of employer upon continuity is considered in the next chapter. It should be noted that any week during which the employee has a contract of employment with the employer

---

[1] Section 197(5).
[2] [1997] IRLR 380. See also *London Underground Ltd v Fitzgerald* [1997] ICR 271.
[3] [1997] IRLR 380 at p 385.
[4] Section 136(1)(b): see Chapter 2.
[5] Section 108(1), as amended by Unfair Dismissal and Statement of Reasons for Dismissal (Variation of Qualifying Period) Order 1999, SI 1999 No 1436.
[6] Section 155.

counts towards the period of continuous employment, *irrespective of his or her weekly hours of work.*

(a) The general rules

1.115 Continuity of employment involves two elements: first, the existence of a continuous (ie unbroken) relationship between employer and employee; and secondly, an unbroken relationship which lasts the requisite length of time.

1.116 The length of the employee's period of employment is computed in months and years of 12 months, but if there is any question whether continuity has been broken, the employment must be looked at week by week in accordance with the statutory provisions.[1] The date at which the employee must have the minimum period of employment is the 'effective date of termination' (in the case of unfair dismissal complaints) or the 'relevant date' (in redundancy payments cases).[2] The starting date for the calculation is the day on which he or she started work.[3] That means the day on which the employment under the contract began, not the day on which the employee started to perform the duties. In *General of the Salvation Army v Dewsbury,*[4] the employee's contract started on 1 May 1982, a Saturday. Because the following Monday was a bank holiday, she actually started teaching on 4 May. The EAT held that her period of employment was to be calculated from 1 May 1982.

1.117 The effect of these rules is that the tribunal should decide the starting date of the employment and the effective date of termination (or relevant date). If the effective date of termination is less than one year after the starting date (two years in the case of a redundancy payments claim), the employee will have insufficient continuity. Thus, an employee whose contract starts on 1 September 2000 and whose effective date of termination is 26 August 2001 will not qualify for the right not to be unfairly dismissed. The provisions of sections 97(2) and 145(5) should be noted in this context, however. Their effect is to postpone the effective date or termination or relevant date in cases where the employer gives less notice than the employee is entitled to under section 86. The effect is that, if an employee on the verge of qualifying for the statutory rights is dismissed summarily, the effective date of termination or relevant date may be extended by one week, which may be sufficient to carry him or her over the threshold of the qualifying period. These provisions are considered in Chapter 3.

1.118 Sections 210–219 set out the rules for determining whether a week counts. The general rule is that a week which does not count under these provisions will break continuity.[5] If continuity is broken, the employee's period of previous employment will be destroyed, and the qualification

---

[1] Section 210(3). 'Week' is defined in s 235(1) as 'a week ending with Saturday'.
[2] Sections 97 and 145. For the meaning of these terms, see Chapter 3.
[3] Section 211(1).
[4] [1984] ICR 498.
[5] Section 210(4).

process will have to start all over again. There are, however, specific provisions which prevent this result occurring, particularly in the case of strikes and lockouts (see para 1.149). If a period (a week or longer) does not count but does not break continuity (eg because the employee is on strike during that period), the beginning of the period of continuous employment will be treated as postponed by the length of the period which does not count; thus a month's strike will mean that the start of continuous employment will be taken to have been a month later.[1]

1.119 The one-year qualifying period does not apply, however, to employees dismissed, or selected for dismissal for redundancy, for reasons related to trade union membership or activities[2] or trade union recognition.[3] In addition, section 108(3) (as amended) provides that the requirement for a qualifying period of employment set out in section 108(1) is not to apply in the case of certain types of dismissal. These are:

1.   dismissal of an employee in connection with leave for family reasons;
2.   dismissal for reasons connected with health and safety;
3.   dismissal of a shop or betting worker for refusing Sunday work;
4.   dismissal in connection with an employee's rights under the Working Time Regulations;
5.   dismissal for reasons relating to an employee's performance of his or her duties as an occupational pension fund trustee;
6.   dismissal for reasons relating to an employee's performance of his or her duties as an employee representative;
7.   dismissal for making a 'protected disclosure';[4]
8.   dismissal for assertion of a statutory right;
9.   dismissal of an employee in connection with the national minimum wage legislation;
10. dismissal in connection with an employee's rights under the Tax Credits Act 1999;
11. dismissal for participation in official industrial action;[5]
12. dismissals of employees arising under paragraph 28 of the Transnational Information and Consultation of Employees Regulations 1999;
13. dismissals arising under regulation 7 of the Part-time Workers (Prevention of Less Favourable Treatment) Regulations 2000;
14. selection for dismissal for redundancy in situations 2–13 above.

---

[1]   Section 211(3).
[2]   TULRCA 1992, s 154(2), inserted by the Trade Union Reform and Employment Rights Act 1993, s 49(1) and Sch 7, para 1(b),
[3]   TULRCA 1992, Sch A1, para 164, inserted by the Employment Relations Act 1999, s 1(1) and (3) and Sch 1.
[4]   Defined in ERA, ss 235(1) and 43A.
[5]   TULRCA 1992, s 239(1).

1.120   There is no qualifying period of employment for employees whose dismissal is made unlawful by the provisions of the Sex Discrimination Act 1975, the Race Relations Act 1976 or the Disability Discrimination Act 1995.

Provided that the employee is employed by the same employer, continuity of employment is not affected by the fact that he or she may have a number of consecutive contracts of employment with that employer involving different types of work or different terms of working in different places.[1]

1.121   Continuity of employment has been held not to be preserved in two types of case involving employees who are dismissed by their employers and then taken back after a short period of time. In *Roach v CSB (Moulds) Ltd,*[2] the EAT decided that there was insufficient continuity of employment in the case of an employee who was dismissed by his employers, went to work for another employer for about 12 days, and then returned to his previous employers at a lower grade for some seven months before being finally dismissed by them. The EAT reached a similar conclusion in *Ryan v Shipboard Maintenance Ltd*[3] in the case of an employee who was employed on a series of jobs with the same employer and at the end of each was paid off, drawing social security until the next job. It is arguable that in this last case the gaps between the jobs would be covered by the temporary cessation of work provisions in what is now section 212(3)(b) (see paras 1.131 *et seq*).

1.122   On the other hand, in *Carrington v Harwich Dock Co Ltd,*[4] the EAT held that an employee's continuity of employment was not broken where he resigned from his employers one Friday and was re-engaged the following Monday. In *Sweeney v J & S Henderson (Concession) Ltd,*[5] the EAT went further and held *Roach v CSB Mould Ltd* to have been wrongly decided. The employee resigned one Saturday and immediately took up employment with a different employer. He regretted that decision, however, and applied to be taken back by his previous employer. He was accepted and resumed work with them the following Friday. The EAT held that section 212(1) applies where, during any part of successive weeks, the employee works for the employer under a contract of employment, even if there is a gap in the employment created by the employee obtaining alternative employment. Section 212(1) will apply so long as there is at least one day in each week with the employer. On its facts, *Roach* is perfectly consistent with the decision in *Sweeney* and it would seem unnecessary to say that it was incorrectly decided.

---

[1]   *Re Mack Trucks (Britain) Ltd* [1967] 1 WLR 780, *Wood v York City Council* [1978] ICR 840 and *Bradford Metropolitan District Council v Dawson* [1999] ICR 312. See also *Tipper v Roofdec Ltd* [1989] IRLR 419.

[2]   [1991] ICR 349.

[3]   [1980] ICR 88. See also *Hellyer Brothers Ltd v McLeod* [1986] ICR 122.

[4]   [1998] ICR 1112.

[5]   [1999] IRLR 306.

1.123   There is a presumption of continuous employment.[1] So, in the case of a dispute about continuity, the burden is on the employer to show that it was broken at some stage. It should be noted, however, that the presumption only applies to employment by one employer;[2] it cannot be applied to employment with different employers.[3] In *Secretary of State for Employment v Cohen and Beaupress Ltd*,[4] the EAT held that an employment tribunal had erred in applying the presumption of continuity to an employee's employment with three successive employers. It said that the presumption only applies to employment with the one employer, unless the case can be brought within section 218(1)–(6).[5] This means that in a case where there are successive employers, the employment tribunal must make findings as to whether there have been transfers falling within the appropriate provisions. Section 218 is discussed in the next chapter.

1.124   The following points should also be noted:

1.   The employee's statutory rights in respect of continuity cannot be increased by agreement or estoppel.[6] So an agreement between employer and employee that employment will be treated as continuous cannot affect the employee's statutory rights, although it may give rise to an action for breach of contract.

2.   An employer cannot enter into an agreement with an employee whose effect is to exclude or limit the operation of the continuity rules. Any attempt to do so will be contrary to section 203(1)(a) and, therefore, void.[7]

3.   The continuity provisions generally apply to a period of employment during which the employee is engaged in work wholly or mainly outside Great Britain or is excluded from a right conferred by the 1996 Act.[8] However, in relation to redundancy payments, a week (or part of a week) of employment outside Great Britain will not count if the employee was not an employed earner in respect of whom an employer's contribution was payable, during that week. The fact that the week does not count will not break continuity.[9]

4.   If an employee is employed under a contract which is void for illegality, no period of employment under such a contract will count.[10]

---

[1]   Section 210(5).

[2]   This is clear from the wording of s 218(1).

[3]   *Secretary of State for Employment v Globe Elastic Thread Co Ltd* [1979] ICR 706.

[4]   [1987] IRLR 169.

[5]   Formerly Sch 13, paras 17 and 18 of the EPCA 1978.

[6]   *Secretary of State for Employment v Globe Elastic Thread Co Ltd* [1979] ICR 706 at p 711. See also *Collison v British Broadcasting Corporation* [1998] ICR 669. In that case, the EAT held that a compromise agreement, by which the employee had compromised an unfair dismissal claim in 1989, could not have the effect of determining his period of continuous employment.

[7]   See *Carrington v Harwich Dock Co Ltd* [1998] ICR 1112; see also *Secretary of State for Employment v Deary* [1984] ICR 413.

[8]   Section 215(1).

[9]   Section 215(2) and (3).

[10]   *Hyland v JH Barker (North West) Ltd* [1985] ICR 861.

5.   For the dual purpose of eligibility to complain of unfair dismissal
        and of awards of compensation for unfair dismissal, employment
        before the age of 18 counts. So far as redundancy payments are
        concerned, however, the effect of section 211(2) is that no week of
        employment before the age of 18 will count towards the qualifying
        period of two years for the purpose of calculating a redundancy
        payment. This is achieved by providing that an employee's period of
        continuous employment is to be treated as starting on his or her
        18th birthday if that date is later than the actual starting date.
        Section 211(2) only applies to claims for redundancy payments alone;
        it does not apply to unfair dismissal complaints; this includes
        complaints of unfair dismissal where the reason is redundancy.

6.   An employee's continuity of employment will be preserved if he or
        she is reinstated or re-engaged by the employer or a successor or
        associated employer, by virtue of regulation 3 of the Employment
        Protection (Continuity of Employment) Regulations 1996.[1] The
        reinstatement or re-engagement must be in consequence of one of
        the following:[2]

        (i)   the presentation by the employee of a 'relevant complaint of
                dismissal'[3] to a tribunal;
        (ii)   the making by him or her of a claim in accordance with a
                dismissal procedure agreement;
        (iii)   any action taken by a conciliation officer; or
        (iv)   the making of a 'relevant compromise contract'; or[4]
        (v)   the making of an agreement to submit a dispute to arbitration,
                in accordance with the ACAS arbitration scheme.

        For the purposes of the redundancy payments provisions, continuity
        of employment will be broken and the period of previous
        employment will not count if a redundancy payment is paid to the
        employee who is re-employed by the same, or a successor or
        associated, employer.[5] But this rule will not apply if the terms of the

---

[1]   SI 1996 No 3147. These regulations replaced SI 1993 No 2165, which in turn replaced the
      Labour Relations (Continuity of Employment) Regulations 1976, SI 1976 No 660. The 1996
      Regulations came into force on 13 January 1997, and as from that date the 1993
      Regulations were revoked.
[2]   Regulation 2, as amended by the Employment Protection (Continuity of Employment)
      (Amendment) Regulations 2001, SI 2001 No 1188.
[3]   This was defined by s 219(3) of the 1996 Act but that provision was repealed by the
      Employment Rights (Dispute Resolution) Act 1998, s 15 and Sch 1, para 25(1) and (3) and
      Sch 2.
[4]   See para 1.124, n 6. Compromise agreements were discussed earlier in this chapter, at
      para 1.104.
[5]   Section 214(2). Note also s 214(5). These provisions were considered by the Court of
      Appeal in *Lassman v Secretary of State for Trade and Industry* [2000] ICR 1109. In *Senior Heat
      Treatment Ltd v Bell* [1997] IRLR 614, the EAT held that the phrase 'redundancy payment'
      in s 214(2) must mean a statutory redundancy payment, not a voluntary redundancy
      payment or a payment made under an employer's severance scheme.

re-employment include provision for the repayment of the redundancy payment.[1]

1.125   As was mentioned earlier, sections 210–219 set out rules for determining whether a week counts. The following weeks count:

1.   weeks 'during the whole or part of which an employee's relations with his employer are governed by a contract of employment';[2] and
2.   weeks in which the employee is absent from work for certain specified reasons: see below.

In the first case, the wording of the statutory provisions is such that it can be said of an employee away from work because of a holiday or illness that his or her relations with the employer are governed by a contract of employment. The weeks of absence will therefore count under that rule.

(b) The effect of absences

1.126   Employees who are absent may be covered either by section 212(1) or (3). Section 212(1) protects them during absence on holiday, for example, since their relations with their employer during their absence remain governed by a contract of employment. If, during such periods, their relations are not governed by a contract of employment, there must be a question as to whether they are employees at all.

1.127   The question to be discussed here is when section 212(3) applies. The previous statutory provision was Schedule 13, paragraph 9(1) to the EPCA 1978. The heading to that paragraph read 'Periods in which there is no contract of employment'. In previous editions of this book, it has been said that the effect of that heading and the operation of the paragraph were far from clear, not least because it had been applied by the courts in cases when there had been a contract of employment. The present provision seems to make it clear that it is not to apply if the employee's relations with the employer are not governed by a contract of employment – not merely situations in which there is no contract of employment: section 213(3) states that that subsection is to apply to 'any week (not within subsection (1))'.

1.128   A week of absence only counts under section 212(3) if it is caused by the events specified in that paragraph. The events are:

1.   absence because of sickness or injury;
2.   absence on account of a temporary cessation of work; and
3.   absence 'in circumstances such that by arrangement or custom, [the employee] is regarded as continuing in the employment of his employer for all or any purposes'.

Each will be considered in turn.

---

[1]   Regulation 4(1) of the 1996 Regulations.
[2]   Section 212(1).

1.129   It is important to bear in mind that the employee's absence, and the fact that the contract may cease during the absence, will not break continuity, provided that the absence is covered by section 212(3). In certain cases also, the weeks of absence will count. It should also be noted that an employee's continuity of employment will be broken if the absence is not covered by section 212 or any of the other provisions of Part XIV, Chapter I.[1]

(i) Absence because of sickness/injury

1.130   The first situation, which falls within section 212(3)(a), arises where the employee is incapable of work[2] in consequence of sickness or injury, but only if the employee's relations with the employer are not governed by a contract of employment. The employee will be covered by section 212(1) if the contract continues during his or her absence, although there may come a stage when the illness causes the contract to be frustrated.[3] An employee off sick for a long time may at some stage be dismissed, in which case both section 212(1) and (3)(a) would apply. But section 212(3)(a) only applies to absence for up to 26 weeks.[4] After that, continuity is broken. Although the dismissal need not be expressly because of sickness or injury, there must be some causal connection between the two.[5] This view has the support of the Court of Appeal.[6]

(ii) Absence on account of temporary cessation of work

1.131   Any week will count where the employee is absent from work on account of a temporary cessation of work, by virtue of section 212(3)(b). The three main questions which arise here are:

1.   whether there is a cessation of work;
2.   whether the cessation is temporary; and
3.   whether the employee is absent on account of that temporary cessation.[7]

1.132   The House of Lords held, in *Fitzgerald v Hall, Russell & Co Ltd*,[8] that the phrase 'cessation of work' means a cessation of work for the employee to do, because there is no longer any work for him or her to do; it is not necessary that the employer should cease operations in the factory or the

---

[1]   Section 210(4).
[2]   In *Donnelly v Kelvin International Services* [1992] IRLR 496, the EAT said that this phrase does not mean that the employee must be incapable of work of any kind. It refers to the work on which the employee was employed before the period which is in question as a possible interruption of the employment.
[3]   Frustration is discussed in Chapter 3.
[4]   Section 212(4).
[5]   *Scarlett v Godfrey Abbott Group Ltd* [1978] ICR 1106. See also *Green v Wavertree Heating and Plumbing Co Ltd* [1978] ICR 298.
[6]   See *Pearson v Kent County Council* [1993] IRLR 165.
[7]   See *Bentley Engineering Co Ltd v Crown and Miller* [1976] ICR 225.
[8]   [1970] AC 984.

section of it in which the employee works. On the other hand, the provisions of section 212(3)(b) will not apply in situations such as those where an employee is a member of a pool of workers amongst whom the employer distributes work and is not allocated work for some time, the work being given to another member of the pool.[1]

1.133 The reported cases which have considered what is now section 212(3)(b) reveal a diverse approach to the question of what amounts to a cessation of work within the provision and are not easy to reconcile with each other. Many of the cases date from the early days of the legislation and should probably be treated now with caution. It is submitted that the best approach to questions of this sort is to treat an employee's absence from work, whether caused by resignation or dismissal, as a cessation of work, so that the only question which then arises is whether the absence was temporary, looking at the matter with hindsight. That would be to give the words used in section 212(3)(b) a purposive construction, which is warranted by the fact that the legislation has the words 'employment rights' in its title and is presumably, therefore, to be taken as protecting a person's employment.

1.134 The reported cases have not followed this simple approach, however. It has been held, for example, that an employee who leaves voluntarily and then returns, or is dismissed and then re-engaged, may not fall within section 212(3)(b).[2] In *Roach v CSB (Moulds) Ltd*,[3] the EAT decided that there was insufficient continuity of employment in the case of an employee who was dismissed by his employers, went to work for another employer for about 12 days, and then returned to his previous employers at a lower grade for some seven months before being finally dismissed by them. The EAT reached a similar conclusion in *Ryan v Shipboard Maintenance Ltd*,[4] in the case of an employee who was employed on a series of jobs with the same employer and at the end of each was paid off, drawing social security until the next job. On the other hand, it has been held that an employee who takes another job during the period of cessation may still be within section 212(3)(b), but the job must clearly be a stop-gap.[5] Absence caused by a resignation[6] or by a dismissal regarded as permanent (for example, because the dismissal followed a row between employer and employee) has also been held not to count. It is difficult to see why such absences should not be regarded as temporary. It should be noted that an

---

[1]   See *Byrne v Birmingham City District Council* [1987] ICR 519. This was followed by the EAT in *Letheby & Christopher Ltd v Bond* [1988] ICR 480, a case involving a casual worker who ran a bar at race meetings. One of the weeks which fell to be considered was a week in which work was available but was not offered to her. Her absence during that week was held not to be an absence on account of a temporary cessation of work.

[2]   See, for example, *Bunt v Fishlow Products Ltd* (1970) 5 ITR 127. *Cf Ford v Warwickshire County Council* [1983] ICR 273.

[3]   [1991] ICR 349.

[4]   [1980] ICR 88. See also *Hellyer Brothers Ltd v McLeod* [1986] ICR 122.

[5]   *Thompson v Bristol Channel Ship Repairers and Engineers Ltd* (1969) 4 ITR 266 and (1970) 5 ITR 85 (CA).

[6]   See, for example, *Wessex National Ltd v Long* (1978) 13 ITR 413.

employee who works for the same employer in two successive weeks but with a gap between the two periods of work, for example because he or she resigned to go to work for another employer but then left and was re-engaged by the previous employer, will be held to fall within section 212(1).[1]

1.135   The cessation of work must also be temporary, a question which must be determined with hindsight, looking retrospectively at the circumstances of the absence from work. In doing so, the whole period of employment is relevant. Evidence of the intention of the parties at the time is relevant, but absence of such evidence is not conclusive. The test is objective. The question whether a cessation of work is temporary is one of fact and degree in each case. Although there is no limit on the length of the absence, if it is lengthy the question will arise whether it is to be regarded as temporary or permanent.[2]

1.136   Attempts to decide whether any particular absence is or is not 'temporary' have given rise to an extensive body of cases which are not easy to reconcile with each other. The first question is what is meant by the word. In *Ford v Warwickshire County Council*,[3] Lord Diplock said: '... [T]he whole scheme of the Act appears to me to show that it is in the sense of "transient", ie lasting only for a relatively short time, that the word "temporary" is used [in section 212(3)(b)] ...'. Subsequently, the use of the word 'transient' has been deprecated and judges have preferred the phrase 'lasting only for a relatively short time'.[4] What is a short time in one employment is not necessarily a short time in another employment.[5] The whole matter is one of relativity.

1.137   The problems posed by section 212(3)(b) have led to two basic approaches: the 'mathematical' approach and the 'broad' approach. The first approach concentrates on comparing the length of the periods of employment with the length of the intervening gaps. The second approach involves looking at all the circumstances over the whole period of employment (including the intentions of the parties) to see whether the break in question is a temporary cessation. Decisions of the Court of Appeal suggest that the mathematical approach is appropriate where there is a regular seasonal pattern of employment and non-employment and that the broad approach is preferable where the pattern of work is irregular. In this respect, two Court of Appeal decisions may usefully be contrasted with each other.

---

[1]   See *Carrington v Harwich Dock Co Ltd* [1998] ICR 1112 and *Sweeney v J & S Henderson (Concession) Ltd* [1999] IRLR 306, considered above.

[2]   See, for example, *GW Stephens & Son v Fish* [1989] ICR 324. The employee was employed as a full-time coach driver whose main duty was to drive coal miners to and from work. Because of the miners' strike, he stopped driving the miners. This cessation of work was held by the EAT to be temporary.

[3]   [1983] ICR 273 at pp 284–285.

[4]   See, for example, Woolf LJ in *Flack v Kodak Ltd* [1986] ICR 775 at p 781. This was followed by the Court of Appeal in the later case of *Sillars v Charrington Fuels Ltd* [1989] ICR 475.

[5]   *Ibid.*

1.138 In *Flack v Kodak Ltd*,[1] the employees were employed according to seasonal needs on an intermittent basis. The facts of Mrs Flack's employment were examined particularly closely by the Court; they revealed an irregular pattern of employment. Within the final two years of her employment she had bursts of employment and non-employment, following which she worked for 542 days until her dismissal. The Court of Appeal said that in such a case the tribunal should have regard to all the circumstances over the whole period of employment to ascertain whether the breaks in the two-year period before the dismissal were temporary, and should not confine itself to looking only at each such break in relation to the adjoining periods of employment.

1.139 *Sillars v Charrington Fuels Ltd*,[2] on the other hand, involved a regular seasonal pattern of approximately six months in work, followed by approximately six months out of work. The Court of Appeal upheld the employment tribunal's decision, which followed the mathematical approach, that the period out of work relative to the period in work was not short and therefore not 'temporary'. The employee had not, therefore, been in continuous employment.

1.140 Although it is clear that in all cases the process of judging whether a cessation is temporary involves the use of hindsight and consideration of all relevant factors, it is equally clear that the approach to be taken depends upon whether the pattern of employment and unemployment is regular or irregular. The essential difference between the two approaches is that the mathematical approach is objective in its concentration upon comparing the periods during which the employee was in work and out of work. Because the broad approach, on the other hand, enables the tribunal to look at all the factors, including the intention of the parties, it gives far greater flexibility.

1.141 In *Ford v Warwickshire County Council*,[3] the House of Lords held that the provision is applicable to those employed under a series of fixed-term contracts (eg supply or part-time teachers, who have a new contract for every term or each academic year), but the gap between each fixed-term contract and its immediate predecessor must be short in duration relative to the combined duration of the two fixed-term contracts during which work continued. This case was followed by the EAT in *University of Aston v*

---

[1] [1986] ICR 775.
[2] [1989] ICR 475. See also *Berwick Salmon Fisheries Co Ltd v Rutherford* [1991] IRLR 203, which involved seasonal workers with a salmon netting company. Historically, the season ran for 30 weeks, during which the employees worked for the company, followed by 22 weeks not working. In 1986 and 1987, however, economic circumstances caused a shortening of the season, so that the employees worked for 23 weeks and did not work for 29 weeks. During the close season 1987/88, the undertaking was sold and the employees dismissed for redundancy. The EAT held that these periods were not temporary cessations of work and, therefore, that the employees had insufficient continuity of employment.
[3] [1983] ICR 273.

Malik,[1] in which a lecturer employed under a series of consecutive yearly contracts was held to have been continuously employed.

1.142   It should be noted, as was pointed out by the EAT in *Pfaffinger v City of Liverpool Community College,*[2] that the statutory provisions relating to a temporary cessation of work do not have the effect of preventing there being a dismissal or preventing the circumstances of the dismissal from being a redundancy. As it said:[3] 'The computation of periods of employment by reference to [sections 210–219] cannot have the effect of converting a dismissal for redundancy into a nullity'.

(iii) Absence by arrangement or custom

1.143   The third situation is catered for by section 212(3)(c), where the employee is 'absent from work in circumstances such that, by arrangement or custom, he is regarded as continuing in the employment of his employer for all or any purposes'. It is necessary to establish both that there existed an arrangement or custom and that, by virtue of that arrangement or custom, the employee was regarded as continuing in the employment of the employer for all or any purposes; these should be regarded as strict requirements which cannot be made retrospectively.[4] But an agreement to reinstate a dismissed employee and, on reinstatement, to preserve accrued continuity appears to satisfy section 212(3)(c).[5]

1.144   The case-law all dates from a time when the statutory provisions made a distinction between those who worked, or whose contract normally involved employment for, more than 16 hours a week, and those who worked, or whose contract normally involved employment for, less than 16 hours. A number of the cases involved hours which fluctuated. In view of the fact that, for the purposes of continuity of employment, it is now immaterial how many hours a week an employee works, these cases should be treated with considerable caution.

1.145   In *Lloyds Bank Ltd v Secretary of State for Employment,*[6] the EAT held that what is now section 212(3)(c)[7] covered an employee who worked on a 'week on, week off' basis, by using the heading to Schedule 13, paragraph 9 to the 1978 Act ('Periods in which there is no contract of employment'), and construing it as applying to periods not governed by a contract of employment. It went on to say that the weeks when the employee did not work and was not required to work were periods not governed by her contract, and that, accordingly, she was absent by arrangement within

---

[1]   [1984] ICR 492.
[2]   [1997] ICR 142.
[3]   *Ibid* at p 152.
[4]   See *Wishart v National Coal Board* [1974] ICR 460, *Lane v Wolverhampton Die Testing Ltd* (1967) 2 ITR 120 and *Rhodes v Pontins Ltd* (1971) 6 ITR 88. See also *Murphy v A Birrell & Sons Ltd* [1978] IRLR 458 and *Murray v Kelvin Electronics Co* (1967) 2 ITR 622. Reference may also be made to *Southern Electricity Board v Collins* [1970] 1 QB 83.
[5]   *Ingram v Foxon* [1984] ICR 685.
[6]   [1979] ICR 258.
[7]   Formerly Sch 13, para 9(1)(c) to the EPCA 1978.

section 212(3)(c).[1] If this analysis of what is now section 212(3)(c) is correct, it means that an employee will be protected if he or she works a number of hours in one week and none in the next, provided that there is an arrangement or custom.

1.146 In the later case of *Corton House Ltd v Skipper*,[2] the EAT took the view that 'absent from work' has two possible meanings: either simply not working or not at the work-place, or absent from work when under the contract the employee should normally be present. Slynn J favoured the latter interpretation, on the basis of which section 212(3)(c) would not have been satisfied since the employee was not required to be there. Even if the former meaning were applied, as Slynn J felt bound to, in view of the *Lloyds Bank* case, the provision would still have applied, since no special custom or arrangement had been established.

1.147 Arguably, however, the better way of interpreting section 212(3)(c) is that it only applies where an employee has no contract (where the contractual relationship has ceased temporarily or permanently) between two periods during which he or she works full-time under a contract of employment. It should not be used to protect employees whose hours fluctuate, nor should it be used as a safety-net provision to catch hours of work, or periods of employment, which cannot be accommodated within the other paragraphs of Part XIV, Chapter I of the 1996 Act. This view is supported by some of the dicta of the House of Lords in *Ford v Warwickshire County Council*,[3] albeit in the context of section 212(3)(b). If it is correct, the cases discussed above should be regarded as wrongly decided.

1.148 In *Letheby & Christopher Ltd v Bond*,[4] the EAT refused to apply the provisions of section 212(3)(c) to a casual worker who was absent from work for a week when she was on holiday. It said that the tribunal should have asked whether, when the absence took place, the parties regarded the employment as continuing. Since she was employed under single separate contracts, it was not possible to say that her employment was continuing after the cessation of the previous contract. A similar conclusion was reached in the later case of *Booth v United States of America*.[5] The employees worked under a series of fixed-term contracts, which in total exceeded the qualifying period of employment, but between each contract there was a gap of two weeks. At the end of the two-week gap the employees were re-engaged. The EAT upheld the tribunals' decisions that the employees were not protected by section 212(3)(c) as there was no arrangement.

---

[1] [1979] ICR 258 at pp 266–267.
[2] [1981] ICR 307.
[3] [1983] ICR 273 at pp 282 and 288.
[4] [1988] ICR 480.
[5] [1999] IRLR 16.

(c) The effect of industrial disputes

1.149   Special rules operate for weeks during all or part of which an employee takes part in a strike or is absent from work because of a lockout by the employer.[1] The two most important are:

1.   the week will not count but the employee's continuity will not be broken;[2] and
2.   the beginning of the employee's period of continuous employment will be postponed by the amount of time the dispute lasts; ie a dispute lasting two months will cause the starting date of the period of continuous employment to be treated as two months later than it actually was.[3]

It is immaterial whether the strike is unlawful (ie without proper strike notice), unconstitutional (in breach of a procedure agreement) or unofficial (not given official union backing).[4] A period of time after the end of the strike but before an employee returns to work will probably be treated as a 'temporary cessation of work' and covered by section 212(3)(b).[5] Employees laid off because of a strike or lockout at another plant will probably also be covered by section 212(3)(b).

1.150   The employer may not try to contract out of these rules, for example by asking the employee, when taken on again after the strike, to sign a new contract excluding the previous period of employment with the employer. Any such attempt will be made void by section 203. The fact that the employee is dismissed at the beginning of the strike and re-engaged when it has been settled does not avoid the operation of the rules.[6]

3. CONCILIATION

1.151   Conciliation officers designated by the Advisory Conciliation and Arbitration Service are required by section 18(2) of the Employment Tribunals Act 1996 to try to promote a settlement of any complaint presented to an employment tribunal in respect of unfair dismissal. Conciliation officers may be asked to intervene either before or after a complaint of unfair dismissal is presented,[7] and may intervene without being asked to do so if they consider that they could act with a reasonable prospect of success.[8]

---

[1]   'Strike' and 'lockout' are defined in s 235(4) and (5).

[2]   Section 216(1)–(3).

[3]   Section 216(2) (in the case of strikes) or (3) (in the case of lockouts).

[4]   *Bloomfield v Springfield Hosiery Ltd* [1972] ICR 91 and *Clarke Chapman-John Thompson Ltd v Walters* [1972] ICR 83.

[5]   *Clarke Chapman-John Thompson Ltd v Walters* [1972] ICR 83.

[6]   See *Hanson v Fashion Industries (Hartlepool) Ltd* [1981] ICR 35 at p 42.

[7]   Section 18(2) and (3) of the Employment Tribunals Act 1996.

[8]   Section 18(2) of the Employment Tribunals Act 1996.

1.152 When a complaint is presented, the Secretary of the Tribunals must notify the parties of the availability of the conciliation officer's services and must send copies of all documents and notices to him or her.[1] Once the hearing has begun, it may be adjourned to enable conciliation to take place.[2]

1.153 In carrying out their duties under section 18, conciliation officers are particularly required to try to promote the reinstatement or re-engagement of the employee and, where appropriate, to encourage the use of 'other procedures available for the settlement of grievances', ie domestic procedures.[3] If the complainant does not wish to be reinstated or re-engaged, or where such a course is not practicable, but the parties want them to act, they must try to promote agreement as to the amount of compensation.[4]

1.154 The decision in *Moore v Duport Furniture Products Ltd*[5] suggests that the conciliation officer need not do much to satisfy the requirements of what is now section 18 of the Employment Tribunals Act 1996. The House of Lords read into section 18(2)[6] some such words as 'so far as applicable in the circumstances of the particular case' after the expression 'shall act in accordance with [what is now subsection (2)]'.[7] But for such a construction, it is doubtful whether the conciliation officer would have discharged his duty. The House of Lords also held that the phrase 'promote a settlement' in section 18(2) should be given a liberal construction 'capable of covering whatever action by way of such promotion is applicable in the circumstances of the particular case'.[8] It is not necessary to take a positive initiative, nor to go through the motions, if that would not be appropriate.

1.155 There is no statutory obligation to advise or inform an employee of his or her rights under the relevant legislation. In *Slack v Greenham (Plant Hire) Ltd*,[9] the employee was made redundant; with the help of a conciliation officer, the parties reached agreement on the amount of the payment. The employee signed an agreement 'in full and final settlement' of all claims arising from the termination of his employment; it recorded that he understood that he was thereby precluded from presenting a complaint of unfair dismissal. The employee later wanted to present a complaint and claimed that the agreement was a nullity because the conciliation officer should have advised him of his statutory right to claim unfair dismissal. The EAT refused to set aside the agreement and dismissed the employee's complaint.

---

[1] The Employment Tribunals (Constitution and Rules of Procedure) Regulations 2001, SI 2001 No 1171, rr 2 and 23(8).

[2] *Ibid*, r 15(7).

[3] Section 18(6) of the Employment Tribunals Act 1996.

[4] Section 18(4)(b) of the Employment Tribunals Act 1996.

[5] [1982] ICR 84.

[6] Formerly s 134(3) of the EPCA 1978.

[7] *Ibid* at p 97, per Lord Brandon.

[8] *Ibid* at p 98, per Lord Brandon.

[9] [1983] ICR 617.

1.156   The duties imposed upon a conciliation officer by section 18 of the Employment Tribunals Act 1996 do not cease until all questions of liability and remedy have been settled by the employment tribunal. In a case, therefore, where the tribunal has made a finding of liability and adjourned the question of compensation, the parties may invite ACAS to mediate in an attempt to agree the amount of compensation if the tribunal considers that the intervention of ACAS will assist to solve the matter.[1]

1.157   Once the agreement is reached, it will usually be recorded on a COT3 form. The EAT has held that the agreement need not be put into writing and that an oral agreement is valid without the use of a COT3.[2] In cases where an agreement is entered into by an adviser on behalf of an employee and recorded in a COT3, it is unlikely that he or she will be able to have the agreement set aside on the grounds that the agreement was entered into without his or her authority. In *Freeman v Sovereign Chicken Ltd*,[3] the employee advanced this argument in relation to an agreement entered into by her adviser from the Citizens' Advice Bureau, but the EAT rejected it on the grounds that the adviser had ostensible authority to do so and that the scope of the ostensible authority included all actual and potential issues between the parties arising out of the employment relationship which were known to the parties at the time.

1.158   Agreements reached under the auspices of the conciliation officer will not be made void by section 203. Section 203(2)(e) excludes agreements reached both before and after a complaint has been presented to an employment tribunal, but not proceedings under the other legislation.[4] But the agreement must be the consequence of action taken by the conciliation officer which satisfies section 18 of the Employment Tribunals Act 1996. So if the employee wishes to escape the effect of section 203(2)(e), to enable him or her to have the case heard despite the agreement, he or she must argue that the conciliation officer's action in some way fell short of the requirements of section 18, or that the agreement is invalidated in some other way. In *Hennessy v Craigmyle & Co Ltd*,[5] for example, the employee signed an agreement prepared by the conciliation officer, agreeing to forgo his right to bring proceedings in return for a lump sum and certain fringe benefits for a limited period. He later tried to argue that the agreement was voidable on the ground of economic duress. The Court of Appeal held that

---

[1]   See *Courage Take Home Trade Ltd v Keys* [1986] ICR 874 at p 878.

[2]   *Gilbert v Kembridge Fibres Ltd* [1984] ICR 188. See also *Gloystarne & Co Ltd v Martin* [2001] IRLR 15.

[3]   [1991] ICR 853. *Cf Gloystarne & Co Ltd v Martin* [2001] IRLR 15, where the EAT refused to interfere with the employment tribunal's decision that the employee's representative did not have authority to enter into an agreement and that the case should proceed. The employers attempted to raise arguments about the representative's ostensible authority at the appeal but the EAT refused to allow them to do so.

[4]   *Livingstone v Hepworth Refractories Ltd* [1992] ICR 287. The EAT said that the phrase 'proceedings' in what is now s 203(2)(e) does not include proceedings under the Sex Discrimination Act 1975, but presumably this also applies to rights under other legislation such as the Race Relations Act 1976.

[5]   [1986] ICR 461. See also *Slack v Greenham (Plant Hire) Ltd* [1983] ICR 617.

the requirements of section 18(3) were satisfied and rejected the argument of economic duress.

1.159 Section 18(7) of the Employment Tribunals Act 1996 provides that anything communicated to the conciliation officer in connection with the performance of his functions is not admissible in tribunal proceedings, except with the consent of the person who communicated it to him. In *M & W Grazebrook Ltd v Wallens*,[1] it was said that this provision was not 'intended to render evidence inadmissible which could have been given if there had been no communication to the conciliation officer … The test is whether evidence exists in an admissible form apart from evidence based upon such communication to the conciliation officer'.

---

[1]   [1973] ICR 256 at p 258.

Chapter 2

CHANGES OF EMPLOYER

1. TRANSFER OF A TRADE, BUSINESS OR UNDERTAKING

2.01   Until 1982, Schedule 13, paragraph 17(2) to the EPCA 1978 (now section 218(2) of the 1996 Act) was the only provision concerning the continuity of an employee's employment where a business was transferred from one employer to another. Since 1 May 1982, however, the position has been affected by the Transfer of Undertakings (Protection of Employment) Regulations 1981 (as amended), which were introduced in response to EEC Council Directive 187 of 14 February 1977, on the Approximation of the Laws of the Member States relating to the Safeguarding of Employees' Rights in the Event of Transfers of Undertakings, Businesses or Parts of Businesses.[1] The 1977 Directive was subsequently amended by Directive 98/59/EC and both directives have now been consolidated into Council Directive 2001/23/EC. In the text which follows the provisions quoted are those in Directive 2001/23/EC.

2.02   The provisions of the Directive will be considered first, followed by a consideration of the implementing legislation, the Transfer of Undertakings (Protection of Employment) Regulations 1981 (as amended) (TUPE). In any case arising under TUPE, the tribunal or court will need to have regard to the provisions of the Directive and the decisions of the European Court of Justice (ECJ) which bear upon those provisions, bearing in mind that the provisions of TUPE should be construed so as, if possible, to give effect to the Directive.

(a) Directive 2001/23/EC

2.03   The Directive has now been considered in a considerable number of decisions in the ECJ. Until recently, the tendency of the Court was to give a wide construction to the Directive, but, as the consideration of recent cases later in this chapter will suggest, it appears to have moved to a more cautious approach. In *Foreningen af Arbejdsledere i Danmark v Daddy's Dance Hall A/S,*[2] the Court said:

> '... [T]he objective of Directive 77/187 is to ensure as far as possible the safeguarding of employees' rights in the event of a change of proprietor of the undertaking and to allow them to remain in the service of the new proprietor on

---

[1]   77/187/EEC, [1973] OJ L61/26.
[2]   [1988] IRLR 315.

the same condition as those agreed with the vendor. The Directive therefore applies as soon as there is a change, resulting from a conventional sale or a merger, of the natural or legal person responsible for operating the undertaking who, consequently, enters into obligations as an employer towards employees working in the undertaking, and it is of no importance to know whether the ownership of the undertaking has been transferred.'[1]

2.04 Article 1(1)(a) of the Directive[2] states that it is to apply to 'any transfer of an undertaking, business or part of an undertaking or business to another employer as a result of a legal transfer or merger'. Article 1(1) goes on to state:

'(b)   ... there is a transfer within the meaning of this Directive where there is a transfer of an economic entity which retains its identity, meaning an organised grouping of resources which has the objective of pursuing an economic activity, whether or not that activity is central or ancillary.

(c)   This Directive shall apply to public and private undertakings engaged in economic activities whether or not they are operating for gain.' (The Article then goes on to deal with administrative reorganisations; that part of the Article is quoted at para 2.27.)

These new provisions were substituted by Council Directive 98/50/EC and are intended to clarify the legal concept of transfer in the light of the case-law of the ECJ,[3] which is considered more fully below.

2.05 Article 1(2) states that the Directive is to apply 'where and insofar as the undertaking, business or part of the undertaking or business is situated within the territorial scope of the [EC] Treaty'; Article 1(3) excludes its application to 'sea-going vessels'.

2.06 Article 3 provides for the automatic transfer to the transferee of the transferor's rights and obligations arising from a contract of employment or from an employment relationship existing on the date of the transfer.[4] In *Katsikas v Konstantinidis,*[5] the European Court of Justice held that this provision does not preclude an employee employed by the transferor from objecting to the transfer to the transferee of the contract of employment or employment relationship. It said that in such cases it is for the Member States to decide what the fate of the contract of employment or employment relationship with the transferor should be. The United Kingdom's response was to amend the Transfer of Undertakings

---

[1]   [1988] IRLR 315 at p 317. The language used in the slightly earlier case of *Landsorganisationen i Danmark v Ny Molle Kro* [1989] ICR 330 is very similar: see at p 388, para 12.

[2]   Article 1 of the original Directive was replaced by a new text, substituted by Council Directive 98/50/EC, Art 1, para 2. The substituted text is given above.

[3]   See preamble (4) and (5) of Directive 98/50/EC.

[4]   As substituted by Council Directive 98/50/EC, art 1, para 2.

[5]   [1993] IRLR 179. This amounts to a recantation of the Court's previously held view, as set out in *Foreningen af Arbejdsledere i Danmark v Daddy's Dance Hall A/S* [1988] IRLR 315.

Regulations 1981 by introducing a new regulation 5(4A) and (4B) (see paras 2.79 *et seq*).

2.07   Article 4(1) (as substituted) states:

'The transfer of the undertaking, business or part of the undertaking or business shall not in itself constitute grounds for dismissal by the transferor or the transferee. This provision shall not stand in the way of dismissals that may take place for economic, technical or organisational reasons entailing changes in the work force.'

This provision is reflected in regulation 8 of the TUPE 1981 Regulations.

2.08   Article 4(2) (as substituted) goes on to provide that if the contract of employment or the employment relationship is terminated because the transfer involves a substantial change in working conditions to the detriment of the employee, the employer is to be regarded as having been responsible for the termination. This has been given effect to in regulation 5(5) of the 1981 Regulations. The relationship between Article 3(1), as interpreted in the *Katsikas* case (above), and Article 4(2) was considered by the ECJ in *Merckx and Neuhuys v Ford Motors Co Belgium SA*,[1] a case in which the employees objected to the transfer of a car dealership because there was no guarantee by the transferee that their level of remuneration would be maintained. The Court said:[2]

'A change in the level of remuneration awarded to an employee is a substantial change in working conditions within the meaning of that provision, even where the remuneration depends in particular upon the turnover achieved. Where the contract of employment or the employment relationship is terminated because the transfer involves such a change, the employer must be regarded as having been responsible for the termination.'

The distinction is between the employee of his or her own accord deciding not to continue with the employment relationship with the transferee, in which case the *Katsikas* case will apply, and terminating the contract because the transfer involves a substantial change in working conditions, such as a change in the level of remuneration; in the latter case, Article 4(2) will apply. Much will depend upon the facts of any given case.

2.09   In the context of the Directive, the following matters fall to be considered:

1.   the meaning of 'undertaking' and 'business';
2.   what amounts to a 'transfer'; and
3.   enforcement of the Directive.

These matters are considered in the sections that follow.

---

[1]   [1997] ICR 352. See also *Süzen v Zehnacker Gebaudereinigung GmbH Krankenhausservice, Lefarth GmbH (Party joined)* [1997] ICR 662.
[2]   *Ibid* at p 370.

(i) The meaning of 'undertaking' and 'business'

2.10   The question is important since it relates to the coverage of the Directive and the sorts of transfers which are embraced by it. In some of its earlier decisions on this aspect of the Directive, the ECJ said that the Directive applied as soon as there was a change (resulting from a conventional sale or a merger) of the natural and legal person responsible for operating the undertaking, and, as can be seen from the final part of the quotation in the *Daddy's Dance Hall* case (above), was not concerned with whether the ownership of the undertaking had been transferred. It also talked in terms of an undertaking being an 'economic unit'. In *Landsorganisationen i Danmark v Ny Mølle Kro*,[1] the Court made it clear that the transfer must be a transfer of a going concern. In *Allen v Amalgamated Construction Co Ltd*,[2] the Court followed the approach of the two previous cases and said:

> 'It is thus clear that the Directive is intended to cover any legal change in the person of the employer ... and ... it can, therefore, apply to a transfer between two subsidiary companies in the same group, which are distinct legal persons each with specific employment relationships with their employees. The fact that the companies in question not only have the same ownership but also the same management and the same premises and that they are engaged in the same works makes no difference in this regard.'[3]

Thus a transfer between subsidiary companies in the same corporate group is covered by the Directive.

2.11   Decisions of the ECJ in the early 1990s suggested that the Court was prepared to take a broad view of activities which were to be treated as a business or part of a business. In *Dr Sophie Redmond Stichting v Bartol*,[4] the question of the applicability of the Directive arose when the local authority which funded the Redmond Foundation switched its grant to another foundation; the building leased to the Redmond Foundation was transferred to the new foundation, which took over the Redmond Foundation's clients and some of its employees. The question was whether the Directive applied in these circumstances. The ECJ held that it did. It said that 'activities of a special nature' may be regarded as comparable to a business or part of a business and continued:

> 'In order to ascertain whether or not there is such a transfer in a case such as [the present], it is necessary to determine, having regard to all the circumstances surrounding the transaction in question, whether the functions performed are in fact carried out or resumed by the new legal person with the same activities or similar activities, it being understood that activities of a special nature which

---

[1]   [1989] ICR 330. See also *Berg v Besselsen* [1990] ICR 396.
[2]   [2000] ICR 436.
[3]   *Ibid* at p 458.
[4]   [1992] IRLR 366.

pursue independent aims may, if necessary, be treated as a business or part of a business within the meaning of the Directive.'[1]

The decision was applied by the High Court in *Porter v Queen's Medical Centre (Nottingham University Hospital)*,[2] which held that the transfer of the supply of paediatric and neonatal services from two district hospitals to an NHS trust was a legal transfer of an undertaking within Article 1(1) of the Directive.

2.12   In *Rask and Christensen v ISS Kantineservice A/S*,[3] the ECJ took the matter a stage further. The facts of the case were that Phillips A/S decided to contract out the running of a staff canteen to ISS. Phillips agreed to pay ISS a fixed monthly fee to cover costs relating to management, wages, insurance and the provision of work clothing, and to provide premises, equipment, electricity and other services free of charge. ISS undertook to offer employment on the same pay to the staff employed by Phillips at the time the agreement came into force. The two employees complained about changes in their contracts. One of the questions submitted to the ECJ was whether the Directive can apply to a situation where the owner of an undertaking entrusts to the owner of another undertaking, by means of a contract, the responsibility of providing a service for employees, which it had previously operated directly, and which is ancillary to its economic activities. Here too, the ECJ ruled that the Directive applied. The Court said:

'The fact that ... the activity transferred is only an ancillary activity of the transferor undertaking not necessarily related to its objects cannot have the effect of excluding that transaction from the Directive. Similarly, the fact that the agreement between the transferor and the transferee relates to the provision of services provided exclusively for the benefit of the transferor in return for a fee ... does not prevent the directive from applying either ... [T]he decisive criterion for establishing whether there is a transfer ... is whether the business retains its identity, as would be indicated, in particular, by the fact that its operation was either continued or resumed.'[4]

2.13   The Court developed this view further in *Schmidt v Spar- und Leihkasse der Früheren Ämter Bordesholm, Kiel und Cronshagen*,[5] when it decided that the Directive may apply to an ancillary activity where the transfer involves a single employee and does not involve the transfer of any tangible assets.[6]

---

[1]   [1992] IRLR 366 at p 370.

[2]   [1993] IRLR 486. It was conceded that the Directive was directly enforceable against a body such as an NHS trust.

[3]   [1993] IRLR 133.

[4]   *Ibid* at p 136.

[5]   [1995] ICR 237.

[6]   See also *Merckx and Neuhuys v Ford Motors Co Belgium SA* [1997] ICR 352, in which the ECJ reiterated that the transfer of tangible assets is not conclusive of whether the entity in question retains its economic identity.

2.14   This approach to the interpretation of Article 1(1) was confirmed by the ECJ in *Commission of the European Communities v United Kingdom*.[1] It said: '... The Court has already accepted, at least implicitly, in the context of competition law ... or social law ... that a body might be engaged in economic activities and be regarded as an "undertaking" for the purposes of Community law even though it did not operate with a view to profit'.[2] It went on to hold that the United Kingdom had failed to fulfil its obligations under Article 1(1) of the Directive.

These decisions undoubtedly had a significant effect upon the way in which domestic courts and tribunals in the United Kingdom interpreted the 1981 Regulations during the 1990s, and, in turn, had a significant impact on market testing and compulsory competitive tendering.[3]

2.15   Recent decisions of the European Court of Justice have given rise to suggestions that the Court is taking a more cautious approach to interpretation of the Directive. Thus, for example, in *Ledernes Hovedorganisation (Acting on behalf of Rygaard) v Dansk Arbejdsgiverforening (Acting on behalf of Strø Mølle Akustik A/S) (Rygaard's* case),[4] which involved the taking over by a sub-contractor of completion of a building contract, together with the workers and materials assigned to it, the ECJ decided that the Directive did not apply. After stating that the decisive criterion is whether the business in question retains its identity,[5] the Court went on to say:[6]

> 'The authorities cited above[7] presuppose that the transfer relates to a stable economic entity whose activity is not limited to performing one specific works contract ... That is not the case of an undertaking which transfers to another undertaking one of its building works with a view to the completion of that work. Such a transfer could come within the terms of the Directive ... only if it included the transfer of a body of assets enabling the activities or certain activities of the transferor undertaking to be carried on in a stable way ... That is not the case where, as in the case now referred, the transferor undertaking merely makes available to the new contractor certain workers and material for carrying out the works in question.'

2.16   Whilst the decision in *Rygaard's* case arguably suggests a more cautious approach to interpretation of the Directive, it can also be argued that the decision merely shows that there are limits to what is to be considered a business or undertaking and that the view that the taking over of the completion of a contract does not amount to an undertaking is a view consistent with earlier decisions of the ECJ.

---

[1]   [1994] ICR 664.

[2]   *Ibid* at p 717.

[3]   See, for example, *Kenny v South Manchester College* [1993] ICR 934 and *Dines v Initial Healthcare Services* [1995] ICR 11.

[4]   [1996] ICR 333.

[5]   *Ibid* at p 345, paras 15–17.

[6]   *Ibid* at p 346, paras 20–22.

[7]   *Spijkers v Gebroeders Benedik Abattoir* [1968] ECR 1119 and *Schmidt v Spar-und Leihkasse der Früheren Ämter Bordesholm, Kiel und Cronshagen* [1995] ICR 237.

2.17 The decision in *Rygaard's* case may be contrasted with the decision in *Merckx and Neuhuys v Ford Motors Co Belgium SA*,[1] decided some six months later. The case involved the transfer of a car dealership without a transfer of tangible assets from Ford dealers (of which Ford were the main shareholders) to independent dealers. More than three-quarters of the Ford dealer's staff were dismissed but the employees in question were told that they would be transferred to the new dealers; after the transfer the Ford dealers discontinued their activities. The ECJ ruled that Article 1(1) of the Directive applied to the transfer of the dealership, emphasising, in common with the other cases, that the decisive criterion is whether the entity in question retains its economic identity. The Court reiterated its view that the transfer of tangible assets is not conclusive of whether the entity in question retains its economic identity and said:[2] 'The purpose of an exclusive dealership for the sale of motor vehicles of a particular make in a certain sector remains the same even if it is carried on under a different name, from different premises and with different facilities'.

2.18 The difference between the decisions in the two cases resides in the nature of the transactions involved; both decisions may be seen as examples of the difficulty of deciding what amounts to the retention by an entity of its economic identity and tend to suggest that the issue is very much a question of fact in each case. The decision in *Merckx* is certainly consistent with a number of the earlier cases already discussed.

2.19 Separate considerations arise in cases where the employer is an undertaking which is in liquidation. In *Jules Dethier Équipement SA v Dassy*,[3] the ECJ said that the Directive applies to a transfer of an undertaking which subject to an administrative or judicial procedure if the purpose of the procedure is to keep the undertaking in business with a view to its recovery in the future. The Court said that Article 1(1) accordingly applies to the transfer of an undertaking which is being wound up by the court if it continues to trade while it is being wound up so that continuity of the business is assured when the undertaking is transferred. It also said, however, that the Directive does not apply to an undertaking which is in the course of insolvency proceedings or to transfers of undertakings or businesses made in the context of procedures comparable to bankruptcy proceedings.[4] It stressed that the determining factor to be taken into account is the purpose of the procedure in question.

2.20 There is now a specific provision in the Directive[5] dealing with bankruptcy and insolvency proceedings. This is Article 5(1), which provides that, unless Member States provide otherwise, Articles 3 and 4 are not to apply to a transfer of an undertaking or business:

---

[1] [1997] ICR 352. See also *Süzen v Zehnacker Gebäudereinigung GmbH Krankenhausservice, Lefarth GmbH (Party joined)* [1997] ICR 662.
[2] *Ibid* at pp 367–368.
[3] [1998] ICR 541.
[4] See *d'Urso v Ercole Marelli Elettromecanica Generale SpA* [1991] ECR I-4105.
[5] Introduced by Council Directive 98/50/EC, art 1, para 2.

'where the transferor is the subject of bankruptcy proceedings or any analogous insolvency proceedings which have been instituted with a view to liquidation of the assets of the transferor and are under the supervision of a competent public authority (which may be an insolvency practitioner authorised by a competent public authority).'

2.21   This provision effectively states the position set out by the ECJ in *Jules Dethier Équipement* above. Article 5(2)(a), however, enables the Member States to provide that the transferor's debts arising from any contract of employment or employment relationships and payable before the transfer or before the opening of the insolvency proceedings are not to be transferred to the transferee, provided that the proceedings give rise, under the law of the Member State, to protection at least equivalent to that provided for by Council Directive 80/987/EC.[1] It also enables 'the transferee, transferor, or person or persons exercising the transferor's functions', on the one hand, and the representatives of the employees, on the other hand, to agree alterations to the employees' terms and conditions of employment designed to safeguard employment opportunities by ensuring the survival of the undertaking or business.[2] Article 5(2) applies where Articles 3 and 4 apply to a transfer during insolvency proceedings which have been opened in relation to a transferor (whether or not the proceedings have been instituted with a view to the liquidation of the assets of the transferor) and provided that the proceedings are under the supervision of a competent public authority (which may be an insolvency practitioner determined by national law). The provisions of Article 6(1), third paragraph, should also be noted here. Their effect is that where the transferor is the subject of bankruptcy proceedings within Article 5(1), Member States may take the necessary measures to ensure that the transferred employees are properly represented until the new election or designation of representatives of the employees.

2.22   A case which falls to be considered separately is *Henke v Gemeinde Schierke and Verwaltungsgemeinschaft 'Brocken'*,[3] where the issue was whether the Directive applies to a transfer of administrative functions as part of a local government reorganisation. Mrs Henke lost her job as secretary to the mayor of the municipality of Schierke when the municipal administration was dissolved and its functions transferred to a regional authority. She brought proceedings claiming that the termination of her contract was null and void and, in the alternative, that she had been dismissed contrary to the relevant German legislation. The decision of the ECJ was that Article 1(1) of the Directive 'does not apply to the transfer of

---

[1]   As amended by Directive 87/164/EEC.
[2]   Article 5(2)(b). Note also art 5(3) which enables a Member State to apply para 2(b) to any transfers where the transferor is in a situation of serious economic crisis, as defined by national law, provided that the situation is declared by a competent public authority and open to judicial supervision, on condition that such provisions already exist in national law by 17 July 1998.
[3]   [1996] IRLR 701.

administrative functions from a municipality to an administrative collectivity ...'.

2.23 The Court's judgment is extremely brief and terse. At paragraph 13, the Court refers to the first recital in the preamble to the Directive and points out that the Directive 'sets out to protect workers against the potentially unfavourable consequences for them of changes in the structure of undertakings resulting from economic trends at national and Community level, through, inter alia, transfers of undertakings ...'. It goes on to say, in paragraph 14: 'Consequently, the reorganisation of structures of the public administration or the transfer of administrative functions between public administrative authorities does not constitute a 'transfer of an undertaking' within the meaning of the Directive'. The judgment makes no mention of the cases considered above, particularly the *Sophie Redmond Stichting* and *Rask* cases. The ECJ's stress in *Henke* on whether a business has been transferred is incompatible with the language it used in the *Sophie Redmond Stichting* case. It is also surprising, in view of the fact that the Court held the exclusion of non-commercial ventures to be incompatible with the Directive.

2.24 Comparison of the Court's decision with the Opinion of the Advocate-General in the same case merely serves to highlight the inadequacies of the decision and make its conclusions the more surprising. At the end of a carefully reasoned Opinion, which considered the preceding case-law in considerable depth, he proposed that the Court should answer the question whether there was an undertaking in these terms:[1]

> '... A transfer of an undertaking ... is involved where – in the case of a voluntary amalgamation of two or more independent municipalities into an independent collectivity – the municipalities employ persons who are protected as employees under domestic legislation and the operations of the municipalities are actually continued. In this connection, all the facts characterising the transaction in question (the formation of an administrative collectivity) must be taken into consideration, namely the type and extent of the powers transferred, the activities carried out, the area of territorial responsibility, the right to have disposal over records and other administrative materials and whether the workforce is taken over. It is for the national court to make these findings of fact.'

It is arguable that the decision should be given a narrow reading and that its effect is to exclude from the scope of the Directive administrative functions which relate purely to the exercise of public powers and which do not involve any economic activity.[2]

2.25 Two recent cases in the ECJ suggest indeed that the Court is giving a narrow interpretation to *Henke*. In *Mayeur v Association Promotion de*

---

[1] [1996] IRLR 701 at p 708.
[2] See [1996] IRLR 653, where this suggestion is advanced by the Editor of the Reports.

L'Information Messine (APIM),[1] the facts were that the employee was employed as a publicity manager by APIM, a non-profit making organisation which aimed to promote opportunities offered by the City of Metz. In 1997, these activities were taken over by the municipality and APIM was dissolved. Mr Mayeur was dismissed on the grounds that APIM had ceased its activities. The ECJ held that the Directive applies where the activities of a private undertaking are transferred to a public undertaking, even if the private undertaking was a non-profit-making organisation. The ECJ rejected the French Government's argument that APIM was in reality a public service so that what had happened was an administrative reorganisation and outside the scope of the Directive.

2.26   The second case, *Collino and Chiappero v Telecom Italia SpA*,[2] involved the reorganisation of the Italian telephone services and the transfer of employees from a State body to a State-owned company. The ECJ held that the Directive applied and that Article 3(1) requires a transferee to take into account the entire length of service of the employees transferred when calculating rights of a financial nature such as a termination payment. It also pointed out that the persons concerned must be workers subject to national employment law in order to be within the Directive. Thus self-employed contractors or office-holders would be outside the scope of the Directive.

2.27   It should be noted that Article 1(1) of the Directive has been amended[3] so that the relevant part now reads:

'(c) … An administrative reorganisation of public administrative authorities, or the transfer of administrative functions between public administrative authorities, is not a transfer within the meaning of this Directive.'

The amendment serves to confirm the *Henke* decision, above, but does not affect the subsequent cases.

2.28   The final point to note here is that Article 1(1) of the Directive refers to the transfer of 'part of a business'. In *Botzen v Rotterdamische Droogdok Maatschappij BV*,[4] the ECJ ruled on the interpretation of the Directive in the context of the transfer of part of a business and its application to employees assigned to that part. The two questions asked of the Court which are relevant for present purposes were: first, whether the Directive extends to employees whose duties are not performed exclusively with the aid of assets belonging to the transferred part of the undertaking; and secondly, whether the Directive extends to employees employed in a staff department of the undertaking (for example, general management services, personnel matters and the like), where the staff department carries on duties for the benefit of the transferred part of the undertaking but has not itself been transferred. In the case in question, certain departments such

---

[1]   [2000] IRLR 783.
[2]   [2000] IRLR 788.
[3]   By Council Directive 98/90/EC, art 1, para 2.
[4]   [1985] ECR 519.

as marine, general engineering, heavy machinery and turbines were transferred, but not the general administrative and personnel department. The Court ruled that the Directive does not protect employees who, although not employed in the transferred part of the undertaking, carried out duties involved with the use of assets assigned to the part transferred or who, whilst being in an administrative department of the undertaking which has not itself been transferred, carried out certain duties for the benefit of the part transferred.[1] The Court said:

> '[T]he only decisive criterion regarding the transfer of employees' rights and obligations is whether or not a transfer takes place of the department to which they were assigned and which formed the organisational framework within which their employment relationship took effect ... In order to decide whether the rights and obligations under an employment relationship are transferred under [the Directive] ... it is therefore sufficient to establish to which part of the undertaking or business the employee was assigned.'[2]

This case has been applied by the domestic courts to cases arising under the 1981 Regulations (see paras 2.60 *et seq*).

(ii) The meaning of 'transfer'

2.29   The starting-point for a consideration of this question is *Spijkers v Gebroeders Benedik Abattoir*.[3] The ECJ emphasised that the aim of the Directive is to ensure 'the continuity of employment relationships existing within a business, irrespective of a change of owner' and said that the decisive criterion is 'whether the business in question retains its identity'. It went on to say:

> '... [I]t is necessary to consider all the facts characterising the transaction in question, including the type of undertaking or business, whether or not the business's tangible assets, such as buildings and movable property are transferred, the value of its intangible assets at the time of the transfer, whether or not the majority of its employees are taken over by the new employer, whether or not its customers are transferred and the degree of similarity between the activities carried on before and after the transfer and the period, if any, for which those activities were suspended. It should be noted, however, that all those circumstances are merely single factors in the overall assessment which must be made and cannot, therefore, be considered in isolation.'[4]

---

[1]   [1985] ECR 519 at p 528, para 16.
[2]   *Ibid* at p 528, paras 14 and 15.
[3]   [1986] ECR 1119.
[4]   *Ibid* at p 1129.

This approach has been articulated in very similar language in the cases which have followed this decision and the emphasis of the Court has been on whether an undertaking retains its identity.[1]

2.30   In *Landsorganisationen i Danmark v Ny Mølle Kro*,[2] the ECJ said:

'The Directive is ... applicable where, following a legal transfer or merger, there is a change in the legal or natural person who is responsible for carrying on the business and who by virtue of that fact incurs the obligations of the employer vis-à-vis employees of the undertaking, regardless of whether or not ownership of the undertaking is transferred. Employees of an undertaking whose employer changes without any change in ownership are in a situation comparable to that of employees of an undertaking which is sold, and require equivalent protection.'[3]

2.31   This was applied in *Foreningen af Arbejdsledere i Danmark v Daddy's Dance Hall A/S*[4] to the case where the owner of premises revokes a lease granted to one lessee and grants it to a new lessee. The Court said:

'The fact that in such a case the transfer takes place in two phases, in the sense that as a first step the undertaking is transferred back from the original lessee to the owner who then transfers it to the new lessee, does not exclude the applicability of the Directive as long as the economic unit retains its identity. This is the case in particular when, as in the instant case, the business continues to be run without interruption by the new lessee with the same staff that was employed in the undertaking before the transfer.'[5]

2.32   In *P Bork International A/S v Foreningen af Arbejdsledere i Danmark*,[6] the undertaking consisted of a factory which was leased. Notice of termination of the lease was given and the undertaking ceased operating; all the employees were dismissed. About a week later, the new owner bought it from the landlord and took possession, engaging more than half of the staff previously employed there, but taking on no new staff. Shortly after, the new owner bought from the old employer (who was in liquidation) the stock, spare parts, tools, auxiliary materials and furniture. The Court considered the question whether employees dismissed before the undertaking was transferred were protected by the Directive and concluded that they were. It emphasised that 'the undertaking must retain its identity, which is the case where there is an economic entity still in existence, the operation of which is in fact continued or resumed by the

---

[1]   The most recent examples are *Schmidt v Spar- und Leihkasse der Früheren Ämter Bordesholm, Kiel und Cronshagen* [1995] ICR 237, *Ledernes Hovedorganisation (Acting on behalf of Rygaard) v Dansk Arbejdsgiverforening (Acting on behalf of Strø Mølle Akustik A/S)* (Rygaard's case) [1996] ICR 333, *Merckx and Neuhuys v Ford Motors Co Belgium SA* [1997] ICR 352 and *Süzen v Zehnacker Gebäudereinigung GmbH Krankenhausservice, Lefarth GmbH (Party joined)* [1997] IRLR 255. All these cases use the same language in identifying the test to be used.
[2]   [1989] ICR 330. See also *Berg v Besselsen* [1990] ICR 396.
[3]   *Ibid* at p 338.
[4]   [1988] IRLR 315.
[5]   *Ibid* at p 317.
[6]   [1989] IRLR 41.

new employer carrying on the same or a similar business'.[1] It went on to say:

'... [W]orkers employed by the undertaking whose contract of employment or employment relationship has been terminated with effect on a date before that of the transfer, in breach of Article 4(1) of the Directive, must be considered as still employed by the undertaking on the date of the transfer with the consequence, in particular, that the obligations of the employer towards them are fully transferred from the transferor to the transferee, in accordance with Article 3(1) of the Directive. In order to determine whether the only reason for dismissal was the transfer itself, account must be taken of the objective circumstances in which the dismissal occurred and, in particular, ... the fact that it took place on a date close to that of the transfer and that the workers concerned were re-engaged by the transferee.'[2]

2.33   The matter was taken a stage further in *Dr Sophie Redmond Stichting v Bartol*,[3] considered above, when the ECJ ruled that a transfer within Article 1(1) of the Directive may take place where a public body decides to terminate a subsidy paid to one legal person, as a result of which the activities of that legal person are terminated, and to transfer it to another legal person with similar aims. The Court said that the decision by a public body to alter its policy on subsidies is as much a unilateral decision as the decision of an owner to change its lessee.

2.34   In the later case of *Ledernes Hovedorganisation (Acting on behalf of Rygaard) v Dansk Arbejdsgiverforening (Acting on behalf of Strø Mølle Akustik A/S) (Rygaard's case)*,[4] the ECJ ruled that the taking over of the completion of a building contract by a sub-contractor, together with the workers and materials assigned to it, did not fall within the Directive. That case is largely concerned, however, with the question whether there was an undertaking to be transferred, and is considered in more detail above (see para 2.15).

2.35   In recent years, this issue has given rise to a number of significant cases. The first, *Merckx and Neuhuys v Ford Motors Co Belgium SA*,[5] involved the transfer of a car dealership without a transfer of tangible assets from Ford dealers (of which Ford were the main shareholders) to independent dealers. More than three-quarters of the Ford dealers' staff were dismissed but the employees in question were told that they would be transferred to the new dealers; after the transfer the Ford dealers discontinued their activities. The first question, considered at para 2.17, was whether there was an undertaking to be transferred. Having decided that there was, the ECJ noted that Ford transferred the dealership to the new dealers (Novarobel) and 'so transferred the economic risk associated with that

---

[1]   [1989] IRLR 41 at p 43.

[2]   *Ibid* at p 44.

[3]   [1992] IRLR 366. See *also Schmidt v Spar-und Leihkasse der Früheren Ämter Bordesholm, Kiel und Cronshagen* [1995] ICR 237.

[4]   [1996] ICR 333.

[5]   [1997] ICR 352.

business to an undertaking outside its own group of companies, that Novarobel carried on the activity performed by Anfo Motors [the previous dealers in which Ford were majority shareholders], without interruption, in the same sector and subject to similar conditions, that it took on part of its staff and that it was recommended to customers in order to ensure continuity in operation of the dealership'.[1] The employees advanced a number of arguments to the Court, saying that the transfer was outside the Directive:

1.   because there had been no transfer of either tangible or intangible assets and no preservation of the undertaking's structure and organisation;
2.   because the transferor dealer ceased trading and was put into liquidation after the transfer;
3.   because the majority of the staff were dismissed upon the transfer; and
4.   because the notion of a legal transfer within Article 1(1) of the Directive required the existence of a contractual link between the transferor and the transferee.

The Court rejected all these arguments. It said:[2]

'... [T]he Court has given that concept [sc the concept of legal transfer] a sufficiently flexible interpretation in keeping with the objective of the Directive, which is to safeguard employees in the event of a transfer of their undertaking, and has held that the Directive is applicable wherever, in the context of contractual relations, there is a change in the natural or legal person who is responsible for carrying on the business and who incurs the obligations of an employer towards employees of the undertaking ... It is clear ... that, for the Directive to apply, it is not necessary for there to be a direct contractual relationship between the transferor and the transferee. Consequently, where a motor vehicle dealership concluded with one undertaking is terminated and a new dealership is awarded to another undertaking pursuing the same activities, the transfer of undertaking is the result of a legal transfer for the purposes of the Directive ...'

2.36   In *Süzen v Zehnacker Gebäudereinigung GmbH Krankenhausservice, Lefarth GmbH (Party joined)*,[3] the question was whether the termination of a cleaning contract with one contractor and the grant of the contract to another contractor amounts to a transfer within the Directive. As in the *Merckx* case, there was no transfer of tangible or intangible assets. The Court reiterated what it had said in previous cases: that the decisive question is whether the entity in question retains its identity. It said that, although the absence of a contractual link between the transferor and the transferee or (as here) the two undertakings successively granted the cleaning contract might point to the absence of a transfer, it was not

---

[1]   [1997] ICR 352 at p 367.
[2]   *Ibid* at pp 368–369.
[3]   [1997] ICR 662.

conclusive. It added the transfer may take place in two stages, through the intermediary of a third party such as the owner or the person putting up the capital, and stressed that the transfer must relate to a stable economic entity whose activity is not limited to performing one specific works contract (as in *Rygaard's* case).[1] It said:[2]

> 'The term "entity" thus refers to an organised grouping of persons and assets facilitating the exercise of an economic activity which pursues a specific objective ... [T]he mere fact that the service provided by the old and the new awardees of a contract is similar does not therefore support the conclusion that an economic entity has been transferred. An entity cannot be reduced to the activity entrusted to it. Its identity also emerges from other factors, such as its workforce, its management staff, the way in which its work is organised, its operating methods or indeed, where appropriate, the operational resource available to it ... The mere loss of a service contract to a competitor cannot therefore by itself indicate the existence of a transfer ... In those circumstances, the service undertaking previously entrusted with the contract does not, on losing a customer, thereby cease fully to exist, and a business or part of a business belonging to it cannot be considered to have been transferred to the new awardee of the contract.'

2.37 The Court pointed out that the absence of a transfer of assets does not necessarily preclude the existence of a transfer and that, in considering the various criteria which have been identified as relevant to the question whether the business has retained its identity, the degree of importance to be attached to each criterion 'will necessarily vary according to the activity carried on, or indeed the production or operating methods employed in the relevant undertaking'. It said:[3] 'Where in particular an economic entity is able, in certain sectors, to function without any significant tangible or intangible assets, the maintenance of its identity following the transaction affecting it cannot, logically, depend on the transfer of such assets'.

2.38 A similar approach may be detected in *Francisco Hernández Vidal SA v Gomez Perez*[4] and *Sánchez Hidalgo v Asociacion de Servicios ASER*.[5] The first group of cases involved contracting-in, where cleaning work was brought back in-house after being contracted out; the second group involved a change of contractor. In both groups of cases, the ECJ concentrated on whether an 'economic entity' had been transferred. It said in the *Francisco Hernández* case:[6]

> 'Since, in certain labour-intensive sectors, a group of workers engaged in a joint activity on a permanent basis may constitute an economic entity, it must be recognised that such an entity is capable of maintaining its identity after it has been transferred where the new employer does not merely pursue the activity in

---

[1]   [1997] ICR 662 at p 670, paras 10–12.
[2]   *Ibid* at pp 670–671, paras 13, 15 and 16.
[3]   *Ibid* at p 671, para 18.
[4]   [1999] IRLR 132.
[5]   [1999] IRLR 136.
[6]   *Loc cit* at p 135. It used identical words in the *Sánchez Hidalgo* case: see p 139.

question but also takes over a major part, in terms of their numbers and skills, of the employees specially assigned by his predecessor to that task. In those circumstances, the new employer takes over a body of assets enabling him to carry on the activities or certain activities of the transferor undertaking on a regular basis (*Süzen*, cited above, paragraph 21) ... Article 1(1) of Directive 77/187 is to be interpreted as meaning that the Directive applies to a situation in which an undertaking which used to entrust the cleaning of its premises to another undertaking decides to terminate its contract with that other undertaking and in future to carry out that cleaning work itself, provided that the operation is accompanied by the transfer of an economic entity between the two undertakings. The term "economic entity" refers to an organised grouping of persons and assets enabling an economic activity which pursues a specific objective to be exercised. The mere fact that the maintenance work carried out first by the cleaning firm and then by the undertaking owning the premises is similar does not justify the conclusion that a transfer of such an entity has occurred.'

2.39   This approach was followed in the later decision of *Allen v Amalgamated Construction Co Ltd*,[1] which involved the transfer of an employee between subsidiary companies in the same corporate group. Both companies shared the same management and premises and also shared administrative and support functions. The ECJ held that there was a transfer within Article 1 of the Directive. It is worth noting here that the Court approached this case on the basis that it was one involving an activity based essentially on manpower. This was because, although the activity in question (the driving of underground tunnels) required a significant amount of plant and equipment, the mine owner provided those assets and not the contractors. The ECJ pointed out that the fact that ownership of the assets required to run the undertaking does not pass to the new owner does not preclude a transfer.[2]

2.40   The most recent decision of the ECJ in this area is *Oy Liikenne AB v Liskojärvi and Juntunen*.[3] The facts of the case were that the operation of seven bus routes was awarded to Oy Liikenne AB; they had previously been operated by Hakunilan Liikenne Oy. Hakunilan dismissed 45 drivers, of whom 33 were re-engaged by Oy Liikenne, but on less favourable terms and conditions. No vehicles or other assets connected with the operation of the bus routes were transferred, although Oy Liikenne bought uniforms from Hakunilan for some of the drivers who entered its service. The applicants were amongst the 33 drivers who were taken on by Oy Liikenne. They claimed that there had been a transfer of an undertaking and that they were entitled to enjoy the terms and conditions applied by their previous employer. The Court said:[4]

---

[1]   [2000] ICR 436.
[2]   Following *Landsorganisationen i Danmark v Ny Mølle Kro* [1989] ICR 330 and *Foreningen af Arbejdsledere i Danmark v Daddy's Dance Hall A/S* [1988] IRLR 315.
[3]   [2001] IRLR 171.
[4]   *Ibid* at p 175.

'However, bus transport cannot be regarded as an activity based essentially on manpower, as it requires substantial plant and equipment (see, reaching the same conclusion with respect to driveage work in mines, *Allen*, paragraph 30). The fact that the tangible assets used for operating the bus routes were not transferred from the old to the new contractor therefore constitutes a circumstance to be taken into account ... However, in a sector such as scheduled public transport by bus, where the tangible assets contribute significantly to the performance of the activity, the absence of a transfer to a significant extent from the old to the new contractor of such assets, which are necessary for the proper functioning of the entity, must lead to the conclusion that the entity does not retain its identity. Consequently, in a situation such as that in the main proceedings, Directive 77/187 does not apply in the absence of a transfer of significant tangible assets from the old to the new contractor.'

This approach suggests that the decisive criterion in such cases is whether the tangible assets 'contribute significantly' to the activity and does not seem to take into account the possibility that there may be factors pointing towards the conclusion that the entity retains its identity.

2.41   Finally, it should be noted that the ECJ has held that the fact that an undertaking is temporarily closed and does not have any employees at the time of the transfer does not mean that a transfer of an undertaking within the Directive is precluded. It is a factor to be taken into account in deciding whether an economic entity still in existence has been transferred.[1]

(iii) Enforcement of the Directive

2.42   It is not proposed to embark upon a detailed discussion of the direct enforceability of European law by individuals in domestic courts and tribunals, since that is best studied in the appropriate texts. What follows is therefore an outline of this question.

2.43   Provisions of the Treaty Establishing the European Community, for example Article 141 which established the principle of equal pay for equal work, are directly enforceable by individuals in domestic courts and tribunals.[2] That is not a relevant issue in the present context, however. What is relevant is the question whether, and to what extent, the provisions of a Directive are directly enforceable.

2.44   It is possible for employees to make a claim based directly on the Directive, in effect arguing that it has vertical direct effect, first, where the Directive is 'unconditional and sufficiently precise' and, second, where the respondent to the claim is an 'organ' or 'emanation' of the State. A Directive does not have horizontal direct effect against individuals or non-State bodies, such as private-sector employers. The European Court of Justice so decided in *Marshall v Southampton and South West Hampshire Area Health Authority (Teaching)*,[3] accepting as final the Court of Appeal's ruling

---

[1]   See, for example, *P Bork International A/S v Foreningen af Arbejdsledere i Danmark* [1989] IRLR 41 at p 43 and *Landsorganisationen i Danmark v Ny Mølle Kro* [1989] ICR 330 at p 339.

[2]   *Defrenne v SABENA (No 2)* [1976] ICR 547.

[3]   [1986] ICR 335.

that the Health Authority was an emanation of the State. In *Foster v British Gas plc*,[1] the ECJ said:

> '18. … [T]he court has held in a series of cases that unconditional and sufficiently precise provisions of a Directive could be relied on against organisations or bodies which were subject to the authority or control of the state or had special powers beyond those which result from the normal rules applicable to relations between individuals …
>
> 20. … [A] body, whatever its legal form, which has been made responsible, pursuant to a measure adopted by the state and has for that purpose special powers beyond those which result from the normal rules applicable in relations between individuals is included among the bodies against which the provisions of a Directive capable of having direct effect may be relied upon.'

2.45 Applying this opinion, the House of Lords subsequently held that the nationalised British Gas Corporation was an emanation of the State.[2] In reaching this conclusion, the House of Lords said that the principle laid down by the ECJ was that the State must not be allowed to take advantage of its own failure to comply with Community law and there was 'no justification for a narrow or strained construction of the ruling of the European Court of Justice'.

2.46 Subsequently, the Court of Appeal refused to hold that Rolls-Royce plc was an emanation of the State. Applying *Foster*, the Court of Appeal held that Rolls-Royce did not fulfil the requirements of the ECJ's ruling. Even accepting that it provided a 'service' under the control of the State, the company was not 'made responsible, pursuant to a measure adopted by the State for providing a public service' – the 'services' were provided to the State, and not to the public. Nor did the company enjoy any 'special powers' of the type enjoyed by the British Gas Corporation in *Foster*.[3]

2.47 More recently, the privatised utilities have been held to be a State authority,[4] as have the governing bodies of voluntary-aided schools.[5] In this last case, the Court of Appeal said that the formula set out in *Foster v British Gas* is not intended to be an exclusive one and said that the EAT had erred in adopting the tripartite test in *Foster* as if it were a statutory definition of an emanation of the State. Its view was that the test formulated in that case was not appropriate to the case in question, since the *Rolls-Royce* and *Foster* cases were concerned with commercial undertakings in which the Government had a stake. Schiemann LJ, with whom the other members of the Court of Appeal agreed, quoted from the Advocate-General's opinion in *Foster*:[6]

1   [1991] ICR 84 at p 107.
2   See [1991] ICR 463.
3   *Rolls-Royce plc v Doughty* [1992] ICR 538.
4   *Griffin v South West Water Services Ltd* [1995] IRLR 15.
5   *National Union of Teachers v Governing Body of St Mary's Church of England (Aided) Junior School* [1997] ICR 334.
6   *Ibid* at p 349.

'... The point of departure must be ... : a Member State, but also any other public body charged with a particular duty by the Member State from which it derives its authority, should not be allowed to benefit from the failure of the Member State to implement the relevant provision of a Directive in national law.'

He went on to say that a body may be an emanation of the State although it is not under the control of central government.[1]

2.48 In cases where individuals are unable to rely upon the direct effect of a Directive and the domestic legislation does not appear to provide adequate protection, it is still possible that an individual may rely upon what may be called the 'indirect effect' of a Directive. This is exemplified by the House of Lords' decision in *Litster v Forth Dry Dock & Engineering Co Ltd (in receivership)*.[2] There, the House of Lords held that the Transfer of Undertakings Regulations 1981 should be given a purposive construction in a manner which would accord with the decisions of the European Court of Justice on the Directive and, where necessary, words should be implied to achieve that effect. This approach was in pursuance of the principle set out by the ECJ in *Marleasing SA v LA Comercial Internacional de Alimentacion SA*:[3] '[I]n applying national law, whether the provisions in question were adopted before or after the Directive, the national court called upon to interpret it is required to do so, as far as possible, in the light of the wording and the purpose of the Directive in order to achieve the result pursued by the latter'.

2.49 It is also possible that an individual may have a right of reparation against a Member State which fails to fulfil its obligation to implement a Directive, provided that the Directive in question confers rights upon individuals, that it is possible to identify the content of those rights on the basis of the provisions of the Directive and that there is a causal link between the breach of the State's obligation and the loss suffered by the individual.[4] In the United Kingdom, such claims should be brought in the High Court or county court.

(b) The Transfer of Undertakings Regulations 1981

2.50 The effect of the Regulations is that they afford protection to employees where there is a 'relevant transfer' of an 'undertaking'. Particularly significant in the present context is the fact that where there is a relevant transfer, an employee's contract will be automatically transferred to the person to whom the undertaking is transferred. It will be apparent from the preceding section that there has been a steady flow of decisions from the European Court of Justice on the scope of the Directive which caused these Regulations to be made. The importance of these decisions lies in the fact that courts and tribunals in the United Kingdom are required

---

[1] [1997] ICR 334 at p 350.
[2] [1989] ICR 341. For a fuller discussion of this case, see para 2.82.
[3] [1991] 1 CMLR 305.
[4] *Francovich v Italian Republic* [1995] ICR 722.

to interpret the Regulations so that, as far as possible, they conform to the Directive.

2.51   The following matters are considered here:

1.   the meaning of 'undertaking';
2.   the meaning of 'relevant transfer'; and
3.   the effect of a relevant transfer.

The effect of regulation 8 upon dismissals in the context of a relevant transfer will be considered in Chapter 5.

2.52   It should be noted that, as a general rule, a tribunal considering whether there has been a relevant transfer of an undertaking should consider as separate issues, first, whether the entity in question was an undertaking and, secondly, whether there was a relevant transfer. The EAT has made it clear that these two issues should be considered as separate questions and has said that, although it is not invariably an error of law not to raise the two questions as separate questions or to fail to deal with them in that order, a tribunal which fails in this way runs a real risk of error.[1]

(i) The meaning of 'undertaking'

2.53   The definition of 'undertaking' in regulation 1(1)[2] is very brief: '"undertaking" includes any trade or business'. In the light of the interpretation of the ECJ in *Dr Sophie Redmond Stichting v Bartol*[3] and *Rask and Christensen v ISS Kantineservice A/S*,[4] 'undertaking' in the 1981 Regulations is to be given a wide meaning, although recent cases in that Court suggest a move towards a more cautious approach (see para 2.15).

---

[1]   *Cheesman v R Brewer Contracts Ltd* [2001] IRLR 144. See also *Whitewater Leisure Management Ltd v Barnes* [2000] ICR 1049.

[2]   As amended by s 33(2) of the Trade Union Reform and Employment Rights Act 1993.

[3]   [1992] IRLR 366. This case is considered at para 2.11.

[4]   [1993] IRLR 133. The *Sophie Redmond* and *Rask* cases were applied by the High Court in *Kenny v South Manchester College* [1993] IRLR 265, in which employees sought a declaration that their contracts of employment would transfer to the College when it took over the provision of prison education services, which had previously been provided by the local education authority, Cheshire County Council being the employer of the plaintiff employees. The High Court granted the declaration that the prospective transfer from the local education authority to the College was a transfer within the meaning of Art 1 of the Directive. The judge reached this conclusion despite the fact that there was no direct relationship between the authority and the college, no transfer of assets, no transfer of clients and customers, no transfer of employees pursuant to the contract, and the continuing function of providing education would be carried out in a different manner. The judge said that, taking into account all the relevant considerations in accordance with the ECJ decisions, after the transfer the education department at the prison would retain its identity and its operation would continue as a going concern. *Cf Wren v Eastbourne Borough Council* [1993] ICR 955, which involved the transfer of cleansing services from the local authority to a company as a result of compulsory competitive tendering. The EAT remitted the case to the tribunal for it to make a finding as to whether or not there was an undertaking capable of being transferred.

2.54 Cases decided in domestic courts and tribunals over the last few years have shown an increased tendency on the part of the judges to look to ECJ cases when dealing with this issue and to follow the approach suggested by it in cases such as *Spijkers v Gebroeders Benedik Abattoir,*[1] considered above. Bearing in mind that TUPE is intended to transpose the Directive into English law, this is clearly the correct approach. In *Council of the Isles of Scilly v Brintel Helicopters Ltd,*[2] the EAT referred to the fact that the ECJ's decisions tend to speak of an 'economic entity' rather than a business and said:

> 'A "business" implies an activity which is being carried on commercially for profit: that is not a requirement. The use of the word "business" may well lead a tribunal into error, simply because it is associated with the idea that there must be a transfer of a business "as a going concern" with an emphasis on an examination of whether there has been a transfer of outstanding orders and goodwill ... [W]e would respectfully suggest that by using the language of the Court of Justice, [employment] tribunals will find it easier to put aside some of the old case-law, ... which has now been overtaken by more recent cases.'

2.55 Recent decisions in the Court of Appeal and the EAT have drawn heavily on the case-law of the ECJ when considering whether a particular entity amounts to an undertaking. In *Whitewater Leisure Management Ltd v Barnes,*[3] the EAT said that there are two formulations which can be used to identify whether there is an economic entity. The first asks whether there is 'a stable and discrete economic entity'; the alternative version asks whether the entity is 'sufficiently structured and autonomous'. The EAT suggested that the expression 'distinct cost centre' might be helpful. The case itself involved a management contract by which a leisure centre was managed by Whitewater. Whitewater had a number of other operations and the six employees who formed the senior management of the leisure centre were also involved in those other operations. There was also a 'core' team of 14 employees, including a manager and two assistant managers, and a number of other employees, consisting of a mix of part-time, casual and seasonal employees. When the contract expired, Whitewater was unsuccessful in the ensuing tendering process. No tangible or intangible assets were transferred to the successor, nor did the six senior employees transfer. Of the 'core' team, seven transferred and seven (including the manager and assistant managers) did not. The EAT concluded that there was no economic entity capable of transfer. It said:[4]

> 'There is plainly a substantial argument that there was not a stable and discrete entity, or a sufficiently structured and autonomous entity, because of the fact that the Leisure Centre was so intricately bound up with the rest of the operations of Whitewater. The senior management was plainly not discrete, and on the face of it, at least without evidence, which was plainly not adduced,

---

[1]   [1986] ECR 1119.
[2]   [1995] ICR 249 at p 255.
[3]   [2000] ICR 1049.
[4]   *Ibid* at pp 1061–1062.

about the Leisure Centre as a cost centre, the Leisure Centre was, if its senior management is taken into account, not discrete, and if they are left out of account, then not stable, or for that matter autonomous.'

2.56   It is tempting to suggest that had the EAT considered the ECJ decision in *Allen v Amalgamated Construction Co Ltd*.[1] it might have reached a different conclusion. That case, it will be recalled, said that there may be a transfer of an economic entity even where there is no transfer of the plant and equipment necessary to carry out the activity because they are supplied by the person granting the contract.

2.57   The *Whitewater* decision also appears to be inconsistent with the later decision of another division of the EAT, presided over by the President (Lindsay J), in *RCO Support Services and Aintree Hospital Trust v UNISON and others*.[2] There, the EAT held that there may be an undertaking and a transfer of that undertaking despite the fact that neither significant assets nor a majority of the workforce moves over. Lindsay J observed:[3]

> '(iv) ... whilst it is wrong to look merely to see if a given activity continues in order to find whether there is either an undertaking or its transfer, both *Spijkers* (paragraphs 11 and 12) and *Schmidt* (paragraph 17) still stand for the propositions that the decisive criterion as to transfer is whether the business in question retains its identity and as to the importance in relation to that of whether its operation was continued by the new employer with the same or similar activities; (v) *Schmidt* still stands (paragraph 16) as a powerful reminder, when no assets are transferred, that the safeguarding of employees' rights, the very subject-matter of the Directive, cannot depend exclusively on such a factor, a factor which the European Court of Justice had in *Spijkers* held not to be decisive on its own; (vi) *Schmidt* still stands as a reminder of how very little is required to amount to something capable of being an undertaking ... once due regard is paid to the safeguarding of employees' rights, the subject-matter of the Directive ...'

He took a similar approach in *Argyll Training Ltd v Sinclair and Argyll & The Islands Enterprise Ltd*,[4] when deciding that a training contract and the arrangements made for its performance amounted to an undertaking.

2.58   The most recent pronouncement from the President on this vexed question is in *Cheesman v R Brewer Contracts Ltd*.[5] The case again involved the loss of a maintenance contract. The previous contractor, Onyx, took over the contract from a district council; it acquired as part of the contract use of the council's yard, its equipment and its office accommodation. It took on 14 employees who had previously been allocated by the council to the contract. When it lost the contract to Brewer, Onyx dismissed the 14 staff; none of them was taken on by Brewer and no tangible or intangible assets passed from Onyx to Brewer, either directly or indirectly by way of

---

[1]   [2000] ICR 436.
[2]   [2000] ICR 1502.
[3]   *Ibid* at p 1515.
[4]   [2000] IRLR 630.
[5]   [2001] IRLR 144.

the council. The dismissed employees claimed that there had been a transfer of an undertaking to Brewer and brought claims against it. The employment tribunal decided that there had been no transfer of an undertaking. The employees' appeal was allowed by the EAT, which remitted the case to the tribunal to decide whether there had been a transfer of an undertaking. Lindsay J said:[1]

'(i) As to whether there is an undertaking, there needs to be found a stable economic entity whose activity is not limited to performing one specific works contract, an organised grouping of persons and of assets enabling (or facilitating) the exercise of an economic activity which pursues a specific objective – *Sánchez Hidalgo*[2] paragraph 25; *Allen*[3] paragraph 24 and *Vidal*[4] paragraph 6 (which, confusingly, places the reference to "an economic activity" a little differently). It has been held that the reference to "one specific works contract" is to be restricted to a contract for building works – see *Argyll Training*,[5] ... EAT at paragraphs 14–19.

(ii) In order to be such an undertaking it must be sufficiently structured and autonomous but will not necessarily have significant assets, tangible or intangible – *Vidal* paragraph 27; *Sánchez Hidalgo* paragraph 26.

(iii) In certain sectors such as cleaning and surveillance the assets are often reduced to their most basic and the activity is essentially based on manpower – *Sánchez Hidalgo* paragraph 26.

(iv) An organised grouping of wage-earners who are specifically and permanently assigned to a common task may in the absence of other factors of production, amount to an economic entity – *Vidal* paragraph 27; *Sánchez Hidalgo* paragraph 26.

(v) An activity of itself is not an entity; the identity of an entity emerges from other factors such as its workforce, management staff, the way in which its work is organised, its operating methods and, where appropriate, the operational resources available to it – *Vidal* paragraph 30; *Sánchez Hidalgo* paragraph 30; *Allen* paragraph 27.'

2.59   The approach taken in the three cases presided over by Lindsay J lays emphasis on the social objectives of the Directive, the safeguarding of employees' rights. That approach leads to the conclusion that tribunals should be ready to find that an entity is an undertaking and that that undertaking has been transferred.

2.60   The 1981 Regulations apply both to the transfer of an undertaking and the transfer of part of an undertaking. In a case involving the transfer of a part of an undertaking, the same question will arise as with the transfer of an undertaking: whether the part transferred in itself amounts to an

---

[1]   [2001] IRLR 144 at p 147.
[2]   [1999] IRLR 136.
[3]   [2000] ICR 436.
[4]   [1999] IRLR 132.
[5]   [2000] IRLR 630.

economic entity. In *Michael Peters Ltd v Farnfield and Michael Peters Group plc,*[1] the EAT said that the appropriate test to apply when dealing with the transfer of part of an undertaking is the test enunciated by the ECJ in *Botzen v Rotterdamische Droogdok Maatschappij BV,*[2] considered at para 2.28, whether the employee was assigned to the part transferred. The case involved the chief executive of a holding company responsible for overseeing the financial management and operations of 25 subsidiary companies; four of them were sold by receivers but the holding company was not a party to the sale agreement. The employment tribunal held that the four subsidiary companies, together with that part of the holding company's assets belonging to those companies, formed a single economic unit and that part of the holding company was transferred, so that the chief executive was protected on the transfer. The EAT reversed this decision, on the grounds that he could not be said to have been assigned or allocated to the part of the company transferred, ie the four subsidiary companies.

2.61   In *Northern General Hospital National Health Service Trust v Gale,*[3] the Court of Appeal suggested, *obiter*, that the issue is whether the employee in question is 'part of the human stock' of the part transferred. In *Duncan Webb Offset (Maidstone) Ltd v Cooper,*[4] however, the EAT said that that was the same as the *Botzen* test put another way. In that case, the EAT held that three employees who worked for one company ('Maidstone') in a group, but spent some of their time working for other companies in the group, were employed by Maidstone, even though some of their time was spent looking after other parts of the group. The EAT upheld the employment tribunal's decision that when Maidstone was sold, the employees were employed in the undertaking transferred and therefore were protected by regulation 5. The judgment helpfully illustrates the operation of regulation 5 in the context of transfers of part of an undertaking by setting out three factual situations which may arise.[5]

2.62   This approach has been confirmed by the later decision of the EAT in *Buchanan-Smith v Schleicher & Co International Ltd.*[6] The EAT said that for an employee to be employed in part of an undertaking he or she does not have to work exclusively in the part of the undertaking transferred. The question is one of fact to be determined by considering all the relevant circumstances. In that case, the EAT held that an employee who organised and ran the service side of the business, which was sold to a transferee, as well as other parts of the business, was employed in the service side and therefore transferred.

---

[1]   [1995] IRLR 190.
[2]   [1985] ECR 519.
[3]   [1994] ICR 426. See also *Securicor Guarding Ltd v Fraser Security Services Ltd* [1996] IRLR 552.
[4]   [1995] IRLR 633 at p 635. See also *Sunley Turriff Holdings Ltd v Thomson* [1995] IRLR 184.
[5]   See pp 634–635 of the report.
[6]   [1996] ICR 613.

(ii) The meaning of 'relevant transfer'

2.63 A 'relevant transfer' is defined in regulation 3(1) as 'a transfer from one person to another of an undertaking situated immediately before the transfer in the United Kingdom or a part of one which is so situated'. Regulation 3(2) applies the Regulations to transfers by sale or other disposition or by operation of law, but transfers of share capital (eg as in takeovers) and dispositions of physical assets are excluded.[1] The EAT has said that when considering whether there has been a transfer of an undertaking by 'some other disposition' within regulation 3(2) a significant factor is whether the undertaking has retained its identity.[2] So, for example, there may be a transfer of an undertaking where the business of a company which is dissolved is continued after its dissolution with the same assets and employees.

2.64 Regulation 3(4) (as amended)[3] provides that a transfer may be effected by a series of two or more transactions and that it may take place whether or not any property is transferred to the transferee by the transferor.[4] The amendment would appear to give effect to some of the ECJ decisions considered in the preceding section, particularly *Landsorganisationen i Danmark v Ny Mølle Kro*[5] and *Foreningen af Arbejdsledere i Danmark v Daddy's Dance Hall A/S*.[6] Transfers of ships are excluded by regulation 2(2).[7]

2.65 The problem in the context of the meaning of the phrase 'relevant transfer' consists in trying to identify whether there has been a transfer of an undertaking. In the context of the Acquired Rights Directive, this issue has already been looked at. What falls to be considered here is how the courts and tribunals in the United Kingdom have approached the ECJ's decisions.

2.66 The starting-point of any discussion of whether there has been a transfer of an undertaking is the ECJ decisions in *Süzen v Zehnacker Gebäudereinigung GmbH Krankenhausservice, Lefarth GmbH (Party joined)*,[8]

---

[1] In *Brookes v Borough Care Services Ltd* [1998] ICR 1198, the EAT held that reg 3 does not apply where there is a change in the shareholding membership of a company but the company retains its corporate identity. The company in question was a company limited by guarantee.

[2] *Charlton v Charlton Thermosystems (Romsey) Ltd* [1995] ICR 56.

[3] By s 33(3) of the Trade Union Reform and Employment Rights Act 1993.

[4] In *Longden v Ferrari Ltd* [1994] ICR 443, the EAT said that a succession of events causally linked to each other do not constitute a series of transactions by which a transfer of the undertaking is effected.

[5] [1989] ICR 330. See also *Berg v Besselsen* [1990] ICR 396.

[6] [1988] IRLR 315.

[7] In *Addison v Denholm Ship Management (UK) Ltd* [1997] IRLR 389 the EAT held that 'Flotels' used in connection with offshore oil and gas installations are ships.

[8] [1997] ICR 662.

Francisco Hernández Vidal SA v Gomez Perez[1] and *Sánchez Hidalgo v Asociacion de Servicios ASER.*[2] These were considered at paras 2.36–2.38.

2.67   Very soon after the decision in *Süzen*, the Court of Appeal heard the appeal from the High Court in *Betts v Brintel Helicopters Ltd.*[3] The case involved the loss by one company (Brintel) of a contract to provide helicopter services and its transfer to another (KLM). KLM did not take over most of the assets (apart from rights associated with the contract) and engaged none of Brintel's employees. Some of Brintel's employees sought a declaration that there had been a relevant transfer and, therefore, that as from 1 July 1995 (when KLM took over the service) they were employed by KLM. The High Court granted the declaration and said that there had been a relevant transfer. The main issue in the Court of Appeal was whether there was a transfer of an undertaking, in other words whether the undertaking had retained its identity in the hands of the transferee.

2.68   Kennedy LJ reviewed the relevant case-law of the European Court of Justice, which emphasised that the decisive question is whether the business in question retains its identity as an economic entity. He said that the *Süzen* decision represented a change of emphasis and meant that the reasoning of some of the previous decisions might have to be reconsidered. He added that, in the case in question, however, the limited transfer of assets (the right to land on oil rigs and use oil rig facilities) could not lead to the conclusion that the undertaking had retained its identity. He said:

'The real distinction … is between (1) labour-intensive undertakings, of which *Dines*[4] is an example, in which if the staff combine to engage in a particular activity which continues or is resumed with substantially the same staff after the alleged transfer the court may well conclude that the undertaking has been transferred so that it has retained its identity in the hands of the transferee; and (2) other types of undertaking in relation to which the application of the *Spijkers*

---

[1]   [1999] IRLR 132.
[2]   [1999] IRLR 136.
[3]   The High Court's decision is reported at [1996] IRLR 45 and the Court of Appeal's at [1997] ICR 792.
[4]   *Dines v Initial Healthcare Services* [1995] ICR 11. In that case, the facts were that the employees involved were employees of a private company which provided cleaning services at an NHS hospital. As a result of the compulsory competitive tendering process, the contract was awarded to a different company. The employees were dismissed for redundancy but were offered employment at the hospital with the new company, but on less favourable terms and with no continuity of employment. They brought complaints of unfair dismissal under reg 8, on the grounds that they had been dismissed because of a relevant transfer. The EAT refused to interfere with the employment tribunal's decision that, although the provision of cleaning services was a separate economic entity, there had been no transfer of that entity. It took the view that the correct analysis was that one business had ceased and another had begun. The Court of Appeal allowed the employees' appeal, stressing that the correct approach to the interpretation of the Regulations is that they should be interpreted in line with the Directive as interpreted by the ECJ. Following the *Rask* and *Schmidt* cases, it held that, when a company takes over the provision of certain services as a result of competitive tendering, that does not mean that the business or undertaking of the first company did not come to an end. There had therefore been a transfer of an undertaking.

test involves a more wide-ranging inquiry. Consequently I have no difficulty in accepting as appropriate to its facts the approach adopted by this court in *Dines.*'[1]

2.69 This decision may be contrasted with the decision of another division of the Court of Appeal, about a year later, in *ECM (Vehicle Delivery Service) Ltd v Cox.*[2] A contract to distribute cars ('the VAG contract') was lost by one contractor and awarded to ECM. They chose to organise the contracted service in a different way; they dispensed with the previous contractor's base and refused to engage any of the staff employed on the vehicle delivery contract because they had asserted that their employment was protected by TUPE. The Court of Appeal upheld the decision of the tribunal and the EAT that there had been a relevant transfer. The argument of ECM in the Court of Appeal was that there was no transfer of an undertaking, although it accepted that there was an undertaking carried on by the previous contractor. The basis of its argument was that *Süzen* signalled a change of emphasis in the ECJ and that the position on transfers of undertakings following that decision was that, where the only continuing feature is the nature of the activity itself and all that continues is the service itself, it is impossible to find that an undertaking has been transferred. So in the case in question, it was argued, all that continued was the activity of delivering cars under the VAG contract. Mummery LJ, with whom the other Lords Justices agreed, rejected that argument and held that the employment tribunal had applied the correct test, as laid down in *Spijkers* and subsequent cases. He also observed that the tribunal was entitled to have regard, as a relevant circumstance, to the reason why the employees were not taken on by ECM.[3] He suggested that the importance of *Süzen* had been overstated and pointed out that the ECJ had not overruled its previous interpretative rulings. He also observed that the criteria laid down by the ECJ still involve consideration of 'all the facts characterising the transaction in question' as identified in *Spijkers*. He said, however:[4]

'(4) The importance of *Süzen* is that the Court of Justice identified limits to the application of the Directive. On the one hand, it affirmed that: (a) "The decisive criterion for establishing the existence of a transfer within the meaning of the Directive is whether the entity in question retains its identity, as indicated *inter*

---

[1] [1997] ICR 792 at p 806.

[2] [1999] ICR 1162. See also *ADI (UK) Ltd v Willer* [2001] IRLR 542. The EAT held that there was no transfer of an undertaking when a contract to provide security services was awarded to a new contractor but none of the workforce transferred. The EAT said that this was a conclusion which was open to the tribunal. The Court of Appeal allowed the transferor's appeal and remitted the case to a tribunal to consider whether the reason for the transferees not taking on the employees was in order to avoid TUPE. The decision contains a detailed discussion of the ECM case. See also *Lightways (Contractors) Ltd v Associated Holdings Ltd* [2000] IRLR 247, in which the Court of Session said that it was open to the tribunal to take into account a declaration by the transferee before the transfer that TUPE would apply.

[3] *Ibid* at p 1169.

[4] *Ibid* at pp 1168–1169.

alia by the fact that its operation is actually continued ..." (paragraph 10); (b) a
direct contractual link or relationship between the transferor and the transferee
is not conclusive against a transfer (paragraphs 12 and 13); (c) consideration of
all the facts characterising the transaction in question is necessary
(paragraph 14). (5) On the other hand, it set limits by indicating that: (a) "... the
mere fact that the service provided by the old and the new awardees of a
contract is similar does not therefore support the conclusion that an economic
entity has been transferred." Other factors are important – the workforce, the
management staff, its operating methods and its operational resources
(paragraph 15): (b) "The mere loss of a service contract to a competitor cannot
therefore by itself indicate the existence of a transfer within the meaning of the
Directive ... In those circumstances, the service undertaking previously
entrusted with the contract does not, on losing a customer, thereby cease fully to
exist, and a business or part of a business belonging to it cannot be considered
to have been transferred to the new awardee of the contract" (paragraph 16); (c)
The question whether the majority of the employees are taken over by the new
employer to enable him to carry on the activities of the undertaking on a regular
basis is a factual circumstance to be taken into account, as well as the similarity
of the pre- and post-transfer activities and the type of undertaking concerned eg
in labour-intensive sectors (paragraphs 20 and 21).'

He said that the case was unaffected by the limits indicated in *Süzen*.

2.70   Since that decision of the Court of Appeal there have been a
number of decisions of the EAT which are not easy to reconcile with each
other. They represent a difference of approach between other judicial
members of that tribunal and the current President, Lindsay J. The first is
Whitewater Leisure Management Ltd v Barnes,[1] the facts of which were set out
at para 2.55. The EAT, presided over by Burton J, concluded that when
Whitewater lost the contract to manage the leisure centre there was no
transfer of an undertaking, on the basis that no tangible or intangible assets
were transferred and none of the senior managers transferred, with only
half of the 'core' team of 14 employees transferring. As was pointed out
earlier, the decision in this case appears to ignore the ECJ's decision in *Allen
v Amalgamated Construction Co Ltd*,[2] consideration of which might have led
it to a different conclusion. It is also inconsistent with the subsequent
decisions of the divisions of the EAT presided over by Lindsay J, the
President.

2.71   The first of these is *RCO Support Services and Aintree Hospital Trust v
UNISON*.[3] The case involved cleaners and caterers. The cleaners were
employed by Initial Hospital Services Ltd at Walton Hospital, one of two
hospitals run by the Aintree Hospitals NHS Trust. Initial tendered for the
cleaning contract at Fazakerley, the other hospital run by the Trust, but it
was won by RCO. None of the Walton cleaners applied for jobs with RCO
and none was taken on. Subsequently, the employment of cleaners at
Walton ended and a number of them brought unfair dismissal proceedings.
The catering staff were employed at Walton by the Trust itself. Three of the

---

1   [2000] IRLR 456.
2   [2000] ICR 436.
3   [2000] ICR 1502.

support staff were dismissed for redundancy. Applications were invited by RCO, who held the catering contract at Fazakerley. One applicant was not offered a job and another declined the job offered to her. The employment tribunal held that there was a relevant transfer from Initial to RCO in respect of the cleaners and from the Trust to RCO in respect of the caterers. The EAT dismissed the appeals. It said that the absence of movement of significant assets or of a major part of the workforce does not necessarily deny the existence of a relevant transfer and expressed the view that *Süzen* can no longer safely be relied upon. It also favoured the approach taken by the Court of Appeal in *ECM* over that taken by the earlier Court of Appeal in *Betts v Brintel*. Lindsay J emphasised the safeguarding of employees' rights as being the crucial objective. He said:[1]

> '*Schmidt* still stands as a reminder of how very little is required to amount to something capable of being an undertaking ... once due regard is paid to the safeguarding of employees' rights, the subject-matter of the Directive.'

2.72   The second decision follows the same line of thought as the first. It involved the loss of a training contract by one company to another. Mrs Sinclair was employed as a training adviser but lost her job when the training contract was lost by her employers. Despite the decision in *Rygaard's* case, the EAT concluded that there had been a transfer of an undertaking. Again, Lindsay J relied upon the ECJ's decision in *Schmidt* and said that it stands for the proposition that the decisive criterion for establishing whether there is a transfer is whether the business in question retains its identity and that that is indicated by the actual continuation or resumption of the same or similar activities.

2.73   The latest decision from the EAT is also of a division presided over by Lindsay J, in *Cheesman v R Brewer Contracts Ltd*.[2] The case again involved the loss of a maintenance contract. The previous contractor, Onyx, took over the contract from a district council; it acquired as part of the contract use of the council's yard, its equipment and its office accommodation. It took on 14 employees who had previously been allocated by the council to the contract. When it lost the contract to Brewer, Onyx dismissed the 14 staff; none of them was taken on by Brewer and no tangible or intangible assets passed from Onyx to Brewer, either directly or indirectly by way of the council. The dismissed employees claimed that there had been a transfer of an undertaking to Brewer and brought claims against it. After considering the question of what amounts to an undertaking, Lindsay J addressed the question of what constitutes a transfer. He said:[3]

> 'As for whether there has been a transfer:
>
> (i)   As to whether there is any relevant sense a transfer, the decisive criterion for establishing the existence of a transfer is whether the entity in question

---

[1]   [2000] ICR 1502 at p 1515.
[2]   [2001] IRLR 144.
[3]   *Ibid* at pp 147–148.

retains its identity, as indicated, inter alia, by the fact that its operation is actually continued or resumed ...

(ii)   In a labour-intensive sector it is to be recognised that an entity is capable of maintaining its identity after it has been transferred where the new employer does not merely pursue the activity in question but also takes over a major part, in terms of their numbers and skills, of the employees specially assigned by his predecessors to that task. That follows from the fact that in certain labour-intensive sectors a group of workers engaged in the joint activity on a permanent basis may constitute an economic entity ...

(iii) In considering whether the conditions for existence of a transfer are met it is necessary to consider all the factors characterising the transaction in question but each is a single factor and none is to be considered in isolation ...However, whilst no authority so holds, it may, presumably, not be an error of law to consider "the decisive criterion" in (i) above in isolation; that, surely, is an aspect of its being "decisive", although, as one sees from the "inter alia" in (i) above, "the decisive criterion" is not itself said to depend on a single factor.

(iv)   Amongst the matters thus falling for consideration are the type of undertaking, whether or not its tangible assets are transferred, the value of its intangible assets at the time of transfer, whether or not the majority of its employees are taken over by the new company, whether or not its customers are transferred, the degree of similarity between the activities carried on before and after the transfer, and the period, if any, in which they are suspended ...

(v)   In determining whether or not there has been a transfer, account has to be taken, inter alia, of the type of undertaking or business in issue, and the degree of importance to be attached to the several criteria will necessarily vary according to the activity carried on ...

(vi)   Where an economic entity is able to function without any significant tangible or intangible assets, the maintenance of its identity following the transaction being examined cannot logically depend on the transfer of such assets ...

(vii) Even where assets are owned and are required to run the undertaking, the fact that they do not pass does not preclude a transfer ...

(viii) Where maintenance work is carried out by a cleaning firm and then next by the owner of the premises concerned, that mere fact does not justify the conclusion that there has been a transfer ...

(ix)   More broadly, the mere fact that the service provided by the old and new undertaking providing a contracted-out service or the old and new contract-holder are similar does not justify the conclusion that there has been a transfer of an economic entity between predecessor and successor ...

(x)   The absence of any contractual link between transferor and transferee may be evidence that there has been no relevant transfer but it is certainly not conclusive as there is no need for any such direct contractual relationship ...

(xi)   When no employees are transferred, the reasons why that is the case can be relevant as to whether or not there was a transfer ...

(xii) The fact that the work is performed continuously with no interruption or change in the manner or performance is a normal feature of transfers of undertakings but there is no particular importance to be attached to a gap between the end of the work by one subcontractor and the start by the successor ...'

More generally the cases also show:

(i)   The necessary factual appraisal is to be made by the national court ...

(ii)   The Directive applies where, following the transfer, there is a change in the natural person responsible for the carrying on of the business who, by virtue of that fact, incurs the obligation of an employer vis-à-vis the employees of the undertaking, regardless of whether or not ownership of the undertaking is transferred ...

(iii) The aim of the Directive is to ensure continuity of employment relationships within the economic entity irrespective of any change of ownership ... and our domestic law illustrates how readily the courts will adopt a purposive construction to counter avoidance ...'

Lindsay J's remarks are set out at length because of the importance of this decision and the light it sheds on the approach of the EAT to questions of transfer. In view of the emphasis on the social purposes of the Directive, the continuing validity of cases such as *Betts v Brintel* and *Whitewater Leisure Management v Barnes* will need to be reconsidered.

(iii) The effect of a relevant transfer

2.74   The effect of regulation 5(1) is that a relevant transfer does not of itself terminate the employee's contract, so that the transferor will not be liable for a redundancy payment; the contract will be treated as if it had been made between him or her and the transferee (ie the new employer). It applies to the transfer of an undertaking or a part of an undertaking. For a discussion of the cases which consider whether an employee is employed in part of an undertaking, see paras 2.60 *et seq*. It should be noted that regulation 5 will only apply if the employee was employed by the transferor; if not, as was the case in *Askew v Governing Body of Clifton Middle School*,[1] regulation 5 will not apply.

2.75   On the completion of the relevant transfer, regulation 5(2) provides that all the transferor's (ie old employer's) rights, powers, duties and liabilities 'under or in connection with' the employee's contract of employment are transferred and anything done before the transfer is completed by the transferor in relation to the contract is treated as done by

---

[1]   [1999] IRLR 708.

the transferee.[1] The wording of this regulation suggests that, when a relevant transfer takes place, liability passes to the transferee and the transferor drops out of the picture.[2] It should be noted, however, that a transfer under regulation 5 will be effective irrespective of whether the employees knew of the transfer and the identity of the transferee.[3]

2.76   Regulation 5(2) has been held to embrace an employee's accrued right not to be unfairly dismissed,[4] the transferor's right to enforce a restrictive covenant in an employment contract[5] and an employee's complaint of sex discrimination arising from an act of the transferor before the transfer.[6] An employer's contractual obligations arising from a collective agreement incorporated into employees' individual contracts will also transfer under regulation 5.[7] In *Bernardone v Pall Mall Services, Martin v Lancashire County Council*,[8] the Court of Appeal held that regulation 5(2) is wide enough to transfer to the transferee the transferor's tortious liability towards an employee injured at work and thus liability in negligence may pass to the transferee. The Court also held that the transferor's rights under an employer's liability insurance policy transferred to the transferee. In *Unicorn Consultancy Services Ltd v Westbrook*,[9] the EAT held that the payment of sums due to employees under the transferor's profit-related pay scheme was a liability which passed to the transferee on the transfer of the undertaking.

2.77   It should be noted, however, that regulation 5 protects the rights which the employee had against the transferor so that they cannot be varied on a transfer to the transferee. In *Crédit Suisse First Boston (Europe)*

[1]   See *Secretary of State for Employment v Anchor Hotel (Kipford) Ltd* [1985] IRLR 452. *Cf Fenton v Stablegold Ltd (t/a Chiswick Court Hotel)* [1986] IRLR 64. In *Thompson v Walon Car Delivery and BRS Automotive Ltd* [1997] IRLR 343, the EAT refused to find the benefit of a compromise agreement entered into between the transferor and a group of employees as passing to the transferee.

[2]   See *Allan v Stirling District Council* [1995] ICR 1082.

[3]   In *Photostatic Copiers (Southern) Ltd v Okuda and Japan Office Equipment Ltd (in liquidation)* [1995] IRLR 11 the EAT suggested that reg 5 does not take effect unless and until the employee is given notice of the fact of the transfer and the identity of the transferee and said that the employee would be unable to exercise the right to object without such knowledge. In the later case of *Secretary of State for Trade and Industry v Cook* [1997] ICR 288, however, another division of the EAT, presided over by Morrison J, the President, said that the *Okuda* decision should not be followed by employment tribunals.

[4]   See, for example, *BSG Property Services v Tuck* [1996] IRLR 134. See also *Green-wheeler v Onyx (UK) Ltd* (EAT 925/92) IDS Brief 503 and *Euro-Die (UK) Ltd v Skidmore* (EAT 1158/98) (2000) IDS Brief B655/14. In this last case, the transferor's failure to assure an employee that his continuity of employment would be protected following a transfer of the business was held to amount to a breach of the implied term of trust and confidence, so that the employee's resignation amounted to a constructive unfair dismissal, liability for which passed to the transferee.

[5]   *Morris Angel & Son Ltd v Hollande* [1993] ICR 71.

[6]   *DJM International Ltd v Nicholas* [1996] ICR 214. *Cf Tsangacos v Amalgamated Chemicals Ltd* [1997] ICR 154.

[7]   *Whent v T Cartledge Ltd* [1997] IRLR 153.

[8]   [2001] ICR 197.

[9]   [2000] IRLR 80.

Ltd v Lister,[1] the Court of Appeal refused to allow a transferee employer to enforce a restrictive covenant which it had introduced into the employee's contract (with the consent of the employee) when it took over the undertaking. The Court said that, since the transferor employer could not have prevented the employee from working for a competitor after the termination of his employment, the transferee could not do so either. It was irrelevant that the new contract also gave the employee a compensating benefit in return for agreeing to the imposition of the restriction. Clarke LJ quoted with approval the statement of Moore-Bick J (at first instance):[2]

> 'The effect of the decision in the *Daddy's Dance Hall* case is that the agreement is ineffective in so far as it purports to impose on the employee an obligation to which he was not previously subject. To that extent it is disadvantageous to him and it is no answer to say that in the instant case it also gave him a compensating benefit which more than made up for it.'

2.78   In the early days of its dealings with TUPE, the EAT refused to extend the scope of regulation 5 to non-contractual liabilities. In *Angus Jowett Ltd v National Union of Tailors and Garment Workers,*[3] it refused to hold that a transferor employer's liability for a protective award under section 188 of the Trade Union and Labour Relations (Consolidation) Act 1992[4] passed to the transferee. Previous editions of this book criticised the decision on the grounds that it did not accord with the wide construction of the Directive and TUPE which has been common in recent years and that, even if liability for a protective award does not fall within regulation 5(2)(a), it falls within regulation 5(2)(b) as being 'anything done before the transfer is completed ... in respect of' the employee's contract. In *Kerry Foods Ltd v Kreber,*[5] the EAT held that liability for a failure to consult under regulation 10 was a liability arising 'in connection with' an individual worker's contract and so fell within regulation 5(2); it declined to follow the decision in *Angus Jowett*.

2.79   The general position is subject to two provisos. First, regulation 5(5) preserves the employee's right to resign and claim constructive dismissal where a substantial change is made in the working conditions to his or her detriment; but a mere change in the identity of the employer will give the employee no rights unless he or she can show that in all the circumstances the change is significant and is to his or her

---

[1]   [1999] ICR 795. See also *Crédit Suisse First Boston (Europe) Ltd v Padiachy* [1999] ICR 569.
[2]   See [1999] ICR 795 at p 806.
[3]   [1985] ICR 646.
[4]   Formerly s 99 of the Employment Protection Act 1975.
[5]   [2000] ICR 556.

detriment. A wide interpretation of this regulation could embrace non-contractual matters, such as promotion prospects.[1] Secondly, regulation 5(1) and (2) are made expressly subject to regulation 5(4A).[2] The effect of this provision is that regulation 5(1) and (2) will not operate to transfer employees' contracts of employment and the rights, powers, duties and liabilities under or in connection with them, if they inform the transferor or the transferee that they object to becoming employed by the transferee.[3] The effect of an objection will be that the employees' contracts of employment will be terminated by the transfer but they will not be treated as having been dismissed by the transferor.[4] The effect will be the same, therefore, as if they had resigned before the transfer. This is consistent with the decision in the *Katsikas* case, where the ECJ said that, in such cases, it is for the Member States to determine the fate of the contract of employment or employment relationship.[5]

2.80   The relationship between regulation 5(5) and 5(4A) was considered by the Court of Appeal in *Humphreys v University of Oxford*.[6] The facts were that the employee was employed for a number of years by the university, working for its delegacy of local examinations. In 1995, the university indicated that it intended to transfer the business of the delegacy to an examinations board. Before the transfer took place the employee notified the university that he objected to becoming an employee of the board. When the transfer took place he brought an action against the university claiming damages for wrongful dismissal on the grounds that the transfer constituted wrongful dismissal. On an action to strike out the action, the judge rejected the university's argument that under regulation 5 liability had been transferred to the board. The university appealed. At the hearing of the appeal it was conceded for the purposes of the appeal that the transfer would have involved a substantial and detrimental change to the employee's working conditions. The Court of Appeal held that the effect of an objection under regulation 5(4A) was to prevent the operation of regulation 5(1) so that no transfer would take place. In those circumstances, regulation 5(5) preserved the objecting employee's right at common law to terminate his contract in respect of the detrimental change in his working

---

[1]   In *Rossiter v Pendragon plc* [2001] IRLR 256, the EAT held that, when considering whether there has been a constructive dismissal in the context of reg 5(5), the tribunal does not have to find that the employer committed a fundamental breach of contract, as is required under s 95(1)(c) of the ERA 1996. It said that an employee who suffers a substantial change in working conditions to his or her detriment has a right to claim constructive dismissal, even if the employer's actions do not constitute a fundamental breach of contract.

[2]   This provision was inserted by s 33(9) of the Trade Union Reform and Employment Rights Act 1993 with the intention of giving effect to the ECJ's decision in *Katsikas v Konstantinidis* [1993] IRLR 179.

[3]   See reg 5(4A).

[4]   Regulation 5(4B).

[5]   The relationship between the equivalent provisions in the Directive was considered by the ECJ in *Merckx and Neuhuys v Ford Motors Co Belgium SA* [1997] ICR 352, a case in which the employees objected to the transfer of a car dealership because there was no guarantee by the transferee that their level of remuneration would be maintained. It is considered at para 2.08.

[6]   [2000] ICR 405.

conditions and to sue the transferor for wrongful dismissal. The Court rejected the argument advanced on behalf of the university that, if an objection is made by an employee on the ground of detriment, regulation 5(4A) operates to prevent a transfer and regulation 5(4B) operates to deprive the aggrieved employee of the right to sue both the transferor and the transferee for constructive dismissal because regulation 5(5) must be read as subject to it. Potter LJ observed that acceptance of the argument would effectively involve disenfranchising the employee and would be contrary to the overall purpose of the Directive.[1]

2.81   The effect of regulation 5(4A) has been considered in a number of cases. In *Hay v George Hanson (Building Contractors) Ltd*,[2] the EAT said that the question whether the employee has objected to the transfer is a question of fact for the employment tribunal to decide. It also said that an objection for the purposes of the regulation may be defined as 'the withholding of consent' and said that it should not be difficult to distinguish between that and mere expressions of concern or unwillingness. In *Senior Heat Treatment Ltd v Bell*,[3] the facts were that when Lucas Bryce contracted out its heat treatment department it offered a number of options to its employees, including the option of opting out of TUPE by notifying Lucas Bryce of their intention to do so. Employees who took this option would receive a severance package, including a statutory redundancy payment or its equivalent, a further *ex gratia* redundancy payment and a sum equivalent to pay in lieu of notice. The employee chose this option and signed a form saying that he did not wish to transfer. Subsequently, however, he took a job with SHT Ltd, to whom the department was transferred. When he was later dismissed by SHT Ltd, the issue arose as to whether he had sufficient continuity of service with the company. The EAT held that the effect of this action was that, despite his agreement to 'opt out of' the transfer, he had not objected to the transfer within the meaning of regulation 5(4A). This meant that regulation 5 was not disapplied, with the effect that he had sufficient continuity of employment.

2.82   Regulation 5 applies to persons employed 'immediately before' the transfer.[4] The problems which have arisen have concerned the meaning of that phrase. The context in which it arises is one where a transferor agrees to transfer the undertaking to the transferee and, as part of the agreement, agrees to dismiss the workforce before the completion of the transfer. Some two hours before the completion of the transfer, the workforce is dismissed. If the employees concerned are held to be employed immediately before the transfer, their rights against the transferor will be transferred to the transferee by virtue of regulation 5(1). If, on the other hand, they are held not to be employed by the transferor immediately before the transfer, the employees' rights will not be transferred and they will be left to sue the

---

[1]   [2000] ICR 405 at p 419.
[2]   [1996] IRLR 427.
[3]   [1997] IRLR 614.
[4]   Regulation 5(3).

transferor, probably a shell. In *Secretary of State for Employment v Spence*,[1] the Court of Appeal held that regulation 5 was concerned with contracts of employment subsisting at the moment when the undertaking was transferred. As the employees' contracts were not subsisting at the moment of transfer, they had been dismissed before the relevant transfer. This question was subsequently considered by the House of Lords, in *Litster v Forth Dry Dock & Engineering Co Ltd (in receivership)*.[2] The situation was similar to that set out at the beginning of this paragraph. The employees were dismissed with immediate effect by the receivers one hour before the transfer took place. The House of Lords held that the Regulations should be given a purposive construction in a manner which would accord with the decisions of the ECJ on the 1977 Directive and, where necessary, words should be implied to achieve that effect. There should be implied into regulation 5(3) after the words 'immediately before the transfer' the words 'or would have been so employed if he had not been unfairly dismissed in the circumstances described by regulation 8(1)'. In reaching this decision, the House of Lords followed the decision of the European Court of Justice in *P Bork International A/S v Foreningen af Arbejdsledere i Danmark*[3] This approach has been further reinforced by the decision of the ECJ in *Marleasing SA v LA Comercial Internacional de Alimentacion SA*.[4]

2.83   In cases of this kind, the starting-point for considering the position of employees dismissed before the transfer of an undertaking is the reason for the dismissal. The tribunal should start, therefore, by considering regulation 8(1). If the reason for the dismissal is the transfer or is connected with the transfer, the dismissal will be effectively void and the employee will be treated as an employee of the transferee, against whom any action in connection with the dismissal will lie. If the reason for the dismissal is not the transfer and is not connected with the transfer, the law as stated by the Court of Appeal in *Secretary of State for Employment v Spence*[5] will continue to apply. Dismissals in the context of transfers of undertakings and the effect of regulation 8 are considered more fully in Chapter 5.

2.84   The application of these principles in practice can cause problems, as is shown by the differing decisions of the EAT. In *Harrison Bowden Ltd v Bowden*,[6] the EAT applied the decision in *Litster* to the dismissal of an employee by a receiver at a time when a potential buyer was interested in buying the company by which he had been employed, but was not formally committed to buying it. He was later engaged by the transferee but dismissed after a month. The EAT upheld the tribunal's decision that he had sufficient accrued continuity to make a claim. In *Ibex Trading Co Ltd (in administration) v Walton*,[7] on the other hand, the facts were that employees were sent letters of dismissal to take effect on 4 November 1991.

---

[1]   [1986] ICR 651.
[2]   [1989] ICR 341.
[3]   [1989] IRLR 41.
[4]   [1992] 1 CMLR 305.
[5]   [1986] ICR 651.
[6]   [1994] ICR 186.
[7]   [1994] ICR 907. See also *Tsangacos v Amalgamated Chemicals Ltd* [1997] ICR 154.

On 11 November an offer to purchase the business was made and it was sold to the transferee on 13 February 1992. The EAT held that, because of the lapse of time between the dismissals and the sale of the business, they were not employed in the transferred undertaking immediately before the transfer within the meaning of regulation 5(3). It did not follow the decision in *Harrison Bowden*. Subsequently, in *Morris v John Grose Group Ltd*,[1] the EAT said that the views expressed in the *Harrison Bowden* case were to be preferred to those in the *Ibex* case.

2.85 Where there is a series of transactions, regulation 5(3) will not apply where there is a succession of events causally linked to one another. The transfer must be effected by a series of two or more transactions.[2]

2.86 The decision in *Litster* has been followed by the High Court in a case involving a company in administration. In *In re Maxwell Fleet and Facilities Management Ltd (in Administration)*,[3] the facts were that administrators of a company dismissed all the employees on 9 April 1992 and immediately sold the assets and business of the company to a wholly-owned subsidiary company; the agreement provided that the subsidiary would not take any of the employees into its employment. The subsidiary then sold the business as a going concern the same day to an independent third company. Four days later, the transferee offered the employees contracts to carry out similar work to the work they had done for the company in administration. The question was whether liability for the employees' contracts of employment was transferred to the ultimate transferee. The High Court held that regulation 4, which deals with hiving down, should be construed in the same way as regulations 3 and 5 and that, accordingly, the employees were employees 'immediately before the transfer' for the purposes of regulation 5. Liability for their contracts therefore passed to the transferee.

(c) The Employment Rights Act 1996

2.87 Section 218(2) preserves the continuity of employment of an employee of a trade, business or undertaking (whether or not established by or under an Act of Parliament) and counts the period of employment with the transferor as a period of employment with the transferee. The presumption of continuous employment does not apply here, since it only applies to employment by one employer;[4] it cannot be applied to employment with different employers.[5] This means that where a question arises about whether an employee who has had a succession of employers has continuity of employment, the presumption cannot be used to assist in cases of doubt. In *Secretary of State for Employment v Cohen and Beaupress*

---

[1]   [1998] IRLR 499.
[2]   *Longden v Ferrari Ltd* [1994] ICR 443.
[3]   [2000] ICR 717.
[4]   Section 218(1).
[5]   *Secretary of State for Employment v Globe Elastic Thread Co Ltd* [1979] ICR 706.

Ltd,[1] the EAT held that an employment tribunal had erred in applying the presumption of continuity to an employee's employment with three successive employers. It said that the presumption only applies to employment with the one employer, unless the case can be brought within what is now section 218(2)–(6). This means that in a case where there are successive employers, the employment tribunal must make findings as to whether there have been transfers falling within the appropriate provisions.

2.88   An initial question which needs to be addressed concerns the relationship between the 1981 Regulations and the provisions in the Employment Rights Act 1996. This is difficult, since the small number of decisions to consider what is now section 218(2) since the advent of the 1981 Regulations have generally lacked clarity. In *Brook Lane Finance Co Ltd v Bradley*, for example,[2] the EAT dealt with regulation 5 of the Regulations and what is now section 218(2),[3] but without saying which provision it was applying. It did say, however, that the phrase 'at the time of the transfer' in section 218(2)(a) should be construed in the same way as the time of transfer is to be construed in regulation 5. This view was rejected by another division of the EAT in the later case of *Macer v Abafast Ltd*.[4] There, the EAT held that the phrase 'at the time of the transfer' in section 218(2) should not be given the restrictive meaning of 'a moment in time' and that a transfer may therefore be a process taking place over a period of time. In *Clarke & Tokeley Ltd t/a Spellbrook v Oakes*,[5] the Court of Appeal endorsed this approach and applied section 218(2), in a case where the employment tribunal had held that regulation 5 did not apply because the employee had not been employed 'immediately before' the transfer. It held that section 218(2) applied to an employee dismissed a week before being taken into the employment of the transferee on the same day as the transferee concluded the transfer agreement. This meant that the brief period of employment with the transferee could be added to his previous period of employment with the transferor so as to give him the right to complain of unfair dismissal as against the transferee. Thus, it appears that there may be circumstances in which regulation 5 does not apply but where section 218(2) does.

2.89   The question which has recurred frequently in the case-law has been the meaning of transfer of a business. The test generally used has been 'whether the effect of the transaction was to put the transferee in possession of a going concern the activities of which he could carry on without interruption'.[6] This approach means that the provisions will not

---

[1]   [1987] ICR 570.

[2]   [1988] ICR 423.

[3]   Formerly EPCA 1978, Sch 13, para 17(2).

[4]   [1990] ICR 234. See also *Kestongate Ltd v Miller* [1986] ICR 672, *Justfern Ltd v Shaife d'Ingerthorpe* [1994] ICR 286 and *A & G Tuck Ltd v Bartlett and A & G Tuck (Slough) Ltd* [1994] ICR 379.

[5]   [1998] IRLR 577.

[6]   *Kenmir Ltd v Frizzell* [1968] 1 WLR 329 at p 335, approved by the Court of Appeal in *Lloyd v Brassey* [1969] 2 QB 98 and *Woodhouse v Peter Brotherhood Ltd* [1971] ICR 186.

apply where there is a sale of assets only,[1] although special considerations may apply to certain forms of business (for example, farming).[2] Section 218(2) has been held to apply where a part of a business is sold, provided that the transferred part of the business was a recognisable and identifiable part of the whole business.[3] An important consideration will be whether there was an assignment of goodwill, although its absence will not be conclusive if the transferor has effectively deprived himself or herself of the power to compete.[4] The fact that the transferor is insolvent or the business is in a state of substantial decline will not prevent section 218(2) operating if he or she sells the business (or what is left of it) and drops out of the picture.[5]

2.90   The effect of the interpretation of section 218(2) is that an employer who does not know there has been a sale of the business or who is taken on in circumstances which induce the belief that accrued continuity will be preserved, may be left in a weak position.[6] If continuity is broken by the transfer, the employee has six months to pursue a claim for a redundancy payment against the old employer (who may be insolvent) and will have to requalify for the right not to be unfairly dismissed and to receive a redundancy payment.

2.91   The Court of Appeal has refused, however, to treat an employee's continuity of employment as broken where the transferor employer dismissed him on one day and the transferee re-engaged him later that same day (and then dismissed him three days later). The Court said that, by virtue of the definition of 'week' in what is now section 235(1), the employee's period of employment, for continuity purposes, straddled the time of the transfer, and section 218(2) applied.[7] This is consistent with the approach of the courts to regulations 5 and 8 of the 1981 Regulations.

---

[1]   As in *Dallow Industrial Properties Ltd v Else* [1967] 2 QB 449.

[2]   See *Lloyd v Brassey* [1969] 2 QB 98 and *Allman v Rowland* [1977] ICR 201. *Lloyd v Brassey* was applied in *Young v Daniel Thwaites & Co Ltd* [1977] ICR 877 to the surrender of the tenancy of a public house to the landlords (who were brewers) and the replacement of the tenant by a manager.

[3]   *Dallow Industrial Properties Ltd v Else* (above) and *Green v Wavertree Heating and Plumbing Co Ltd* [1978] ICR 928. See also *Secretary of State for Employment v Rooney* [1977] ICR 440. *Cf Melon v Hector Powe Ltd* [1981] ICR 43, which was not in fact a decision upon s 218(2) (formerly EPCA 1978, Sch 13, para 17(2)), but provides an example of the kind of situation which would probably not be treated as a transfer of part of the business.

[4]   *Kenmir Ltd v Frizzell* [1968] 1 WLR 329 at p 335. See also *Ward v Homes Watts* [1983] ICR 231.

[5]   See *Teesside Times Ltd v Drury* [1980] ICR 338 and *Deaway Trading Ltd v Calverley* [1973] ICR 546.

[6]   See, eg, *Woodhouse v Peter Brotherhood Ltd*, above, *Crompton v Truly fair (International) Ltd* [1975] ICR 359 and *Port Talbot Engineering Co Ltd v Passmore* [1975] ICR 234.

[7]   *Teesside Times Ltd v Drury* [1980] ICR 338.

2. OTHER CHANGES OF EMPLOYER

(a) Changes brought about by Act of Parliament

2.92   If one body corporate is substituted for another by virtue of an Act of Parliament, section 218(3) will enable the employee's period of employment with the previous body corporate to count as a period of employment with the substituted body corporate, and the change will not break the continuity of employment.[1]

(b) Changes caused by the death of the employer

2.93   By virtue of section 218(4), an employee taken into the employment of the personal representatives or trustees of a dead employer may count the period of employment before the death as a period of employment with the personal representatives or trustees, and the death will not break the continuity of employment; subsequent changes of the personal representatives or trustees will not affect continuity.[2]

2.94   An employee who is the personal representative of the deceased employer may in that capacity contract with himself or herself as an individual, and thus, *qua* personal representative, employ himself or herself; in such a case, section 218(4) will apply and continuity will not be broken.[3]

(c) Changes of partners

2.95   By virtue of section 218(5), a change of partners in a partnership which employs the employee will not affect the continuity of employment. It has been held in earlier cases that a change from employment by a sole trader to employment by a partnership formed by the former sole trade is not covered;[4] nor is a change from employment by a partnership to employment by one of the former partners after the dissolution of the partnership.[5] Later cases have doubted the correctness of this view.[6] If, however, changes in a partnership mean that only one of the former partners is left, who thus becomes in effect a sole trader, section 218(5) continues to apply.[7]

---

[1]   See *Northern General Hospital NHS Trust v Gale* [1993] ICR 638. The case involved the transfer of the hospital at which the employee worked to trust status. Although he argued that his continuity was preserved by what is now s 218(3), the EAT decided the case on other grounds, s 6 of the National Health Service and Community Care Act 1990. His appeal to the Court of Appeal was dismissed: [1994] ICR 426.

[2]   Section 218(5).

[3]   *Rowley, Holmes & Co v Barber* [1977] ICR 387.

[4]   *Wynne v Hair Control* [1978] ICR 870.

[5]   *Harold Fielding v Mansi* [1974] IRLR 79.

[6]   See *Allen & Son v Coventry* [1980] ICR 9 and *Jeetle v Elster* [1985] ICR 389.

[7]   *Jeetle v Elster* [1985] ICR 389.

2.96 In the situations outlined above, there is no reason why section 218(2) should not apply,[1] provided, of course, that the transferee is put into possession of a going concern. The transfer would also probably be a 'relevant transfer' within the meaning of regulation 3 of the 1981 Regulations. If, however, the business could not be said to be a continuing business, but two separate and distinct ventures, continuity would not be preserved, either by section 218(2) or by the 1981 Regulations.[2]

(d) Employment by associated employers

2.97 An employee taken into the employment of a new employer, associated with the previous employer, may count the period of previous employment as employment with the associated employer, by virtue of section 218(6). The change of employer will not break continuity. It should be noted that, as with section 218(2), the presumption of continuous employment does not apply here, since it only applies to employment by one employer;[3] it cannot be applied to employment with different employers.[4] This means that where a question arises about whether an employee who has had a succession of employers has continuity of employment, the tribunal must look at each change of employer to see whether or not continuity is preserved.[5]

2.98 'Associated employer' is defined in section 231. The definition has two limbs. Under the first limb, two employers are to be treated as associated where 'one is a company of which the other (directly or indirectly) has control'; under the second limb, they will be treated as associated where 'both are companies of which a third person (directly or indirectly) has control'. In both cases, it should be noted that the controlling employer need not be a company and may, therefore, be a sole trader or a partnership. The Court of Appeal has held the definition to be exhaustive, which means that local authorities cannot be associated employers.[6]

2.99 It is not clear from the definition whether the second limb embraces companies which are incorporated in other jurisdictions. In *Hancill v Marcon Engineering Ltd*,[7] the EAT decided that an overseas company may be recognised as a company for the purposes of the

---

[1] The EAT in fact applied s 218(2) in *Allen & Son v Coventry* [1980] ICR 9 and *Jeetle v Elster*, above.

[2] *Allen & Son v Coventry* [1980] ICR 9 at p 12.

[3] Section 218(1).

[4] *Secretary of State for Employment v Globe Elastic Thread Co Ltd* [1979] ICR 706.

[5] See *Secretary of State for Employment v Cohen* [1987] ICR 570, where the EAT held that an employment tribunal had erred in applying the presumption of continuity to an employee's employment with three successive employers. It said that the presumption only applies to employment with the one employer unless the case can be brought within what is now s 218(2)–(6).

[6] *Merton London Borough Council v Gardiner* [1981] ICR 186. See also *Southwood Hostel Management Committee v Taylor* [1979] ICR 813. Note, however, the effect of the Redundancy Payments (Continuity of Employment in Local Government, etc) (Modification) Order 1999 (see para 2.105).

[7] [1990] ICR 103.

definition, provided that the company is one which in its essentials is to be likened to a company limited under the Companies Acts. This means that, if an employee who works abroad for a subsidiary of a multinational incorporated in the country where he or she works and then moves to a subsidiary of the multinational incorporated in this jurisdiction, the two employers will be treated as associated, provided the characteristics of incorporation are similar in the other country. It is worth noting here that an employee in this position would also be able to count the period of employment abroad for most continuity purposes, despite the fact that, when working abroad, he or she might have been excluded from the protection of the legislation.[1] The EAT has also held that a group of companies operating in partnership may fall within the definition.[2]

2.100   The problem which has most frequently arisen in the context of this definition concerns the meaning of 'control'. In *Secretary of State for Employment v Newbold and Joint Liquidators of David Armstrong (Catering Services) Ltd*,[3] the EAT said that control means control by the majority of votes attaching to shares, exercised in general meetings; it is not how or by whom the enterprise is actually run. It is clear, however, that, where a number of companies is involved, one person must have a majority share in all the relevant companies for them to be treated as associated. In *Russell v Elmdon Freight Ltd*,[4] for example, one person held 55% of the shares of the first company and 50% of the shares of the second, and a second person held no shares in the first and 49% of the shares in the second. There was thus no one person who had voting control over both companies. The EAT stressed that, where two companies are involved, there must be one or more persons who have voting control over both companies.

2.101   Problems arise where one person holds a majority of the shares in one company, but holds an equal number of shares in other companies. In *South West Launderettes Ltd v Laidler*,[5] for example, the employer was a company whose majority shareholder shared the entire capital of other companies equally with his wife. The Court of Appeal held that for one company to be an associated employer of another the control of both should be in the hands of the same person, in the sense that he had the power in relation to each to determine the outcome of voting in general meeting. In the present case, although the majority shareholder controlled the employers, he did not also control any of the other companies since the shareholding in them was divided equally between himself and his wife. There was no evidence that he controlled his wife's shares and the Court of Appeal said that there was no presumption of law that he controlled them.

---

[1]   See s 215(1).
[2]   *Pinkney v Sandpiper Drilling Ltd and others* [1989] ICR 389.
[3]   [1981] IRLR 305. See also *Umar v Pliastar Ltd* [1981] ICR 727, *Washington Arts Association Ltd v Forster* [1983] ICR 346, *Charnock v Barrie Muirhead* [1984] ICR 641, *Hair Colour Consultants Ltd v Mena* [1984] ICR 671 and *Poparm Ltd v Weekes* [1984] IRLR 388 (a case on joint control).
[4]   [1989] ICR 629.
[5]   [1986] ICR 455. This case was followed by the EAT in *Strudwick v Iszatt Brothers Ltd* [1988] ICR 796.

In the later case of *Secretary of State for Employment v Chapman*,[1] on the other hand, the employer, Mr Chapman, carried on business as a sole trader. In 1980, he set up a limited company for the purpose of tendering for a maintenance contract, in order to avoid the incidence of VAT. He and his wife were the sole shareholders with one share each. When the maintenance contract ended in 1982, the company ceased trading, and the employer resumed business as a sole trader. The employment tribunal found that Mrs Chapman played no part in the business, that all decisions relating to the company were taken by Mr Chapman and that Mrs Chapman's holding of one share and the company's secretaryship was a matter of formality to comply with the provisions of the Companies Acts. The Court of Appeal held that the tribunal's findings of fact were consistent with Mrs Chapman's holding as a nominee, although the tribunal had not expressly made such a finding. Accordingly, Mr Chapman and the company were associated employers. The Court distinguished the *Laidler* case on the facts as found. It also suggested, *obiter*, that, although voting control is normally the issue to be decided under section 231, exceptionally there may be other circumstances to be taken into account.[2]

2.102 The most recent case to consider this sort of issue is *Tice v Cartwright*.[3] In that case, the employee started employment at a garage owned by a company in which two brothers each held 50% of the shares. He was dismissed and then started work at another garage owned by the same brothers trading as equal partners in a partnership. The employment tribunal found that, as the partnership had indirect control of the company, it was an associated employer of the company. This meant that the employee's period of employment with both the company and the partnership counted towards his continuity of employment. The EAT upheld the tribunal's decision and said that the phrase 'has control' in section 231 is concerned with practical rather than theoretical matters and that an employment tribunal should look at all the circumstances as to the way in which control was in fact exercised to answer the question of who had control.

---

[1]   [1989] ICR 771.

[2]   *Ibid* at pp 776 and 777–778. Note also a similar passage in the judgment of Mustill LJ in the *Laidler* case, above, at p 460. In *Harford v Swiftrim Ltd* [1987] ICR 439, the employment tribunal found that two companies had the same shareholders and that control of both companies depended on a majority of the shareholders acting together. It decided that one could not be said to have control of the other, but the EAT remitted the case to the tribunal for further consideration as to what happened in practice regarding the exercise of voting rights. This decision should now be read in the light of the Court of Appeal's *dicta* in the *Chapman* case.

[3]   [1999] ICR 769.

(e) Transfers between local authority maintained schools and local authorities

2.103   Section 218(7) preserves the continuity of employment of teachers who transfer between employment by a local education authority and employment by the governors of a school maintained by the authority.

(f) Transfers between health service employers[1]

2.104   Section 218(8)–(10)[2] makes special provision for trainee health service employees who move from employment by one health service employer to another such employer.[3] The Redundancy Payments (National Health Service) (Modification) Order 1993[4] applies to persons employed in relevant health services, as specified in the Appendix to Schedule 2 to the Order.

(g) Transfers within local government service

2.105   The effect of the Redundancy Payments (Continuity of Employment in Local Government, etc) (Modification) Order 1999[5] should also be noted. This provides that successive employment in local government service with two or more employers listed in the order will be treated as continuous employment for the purposes of the redundancy payments provisions.

(h) Other relevant provisions

2.106   Section 219[6] enables the Secretary of State to make provision, by Regulations, for the preservation of the continuity of employees who are reinstated or re-engaged by their employer. The relevant Regulations are the Employment Protection (Continuity of Employment) Regulations 1996, which came into force on 13 January 1997.[7] These were considered earlier in Chapter 1, at para 1.124.

---

[1]   Note the Employment Protection (Continuity of Employment of National Health Service Employees) (Modification) Order 1996, SI 1996 No 1023.

[2]   As amended by the Health Act 1999 (Supplementary, Consequential etc Provisions) Order 2000, SI 2000 No 90.

[3]   Section 218(10) specifies what authorities are to be treated as health service employers for the purposes of these provisions.

[4]   SI 1993 No 3167.

[5]   SI 1999 No 2277, as amended by the Redundancy Payments (Continuity of Employment in Local Government, etc) (Modification) (Amendment) Order 2001, SI 2001 No 866.

[6]   As amended by the Employment Rights (Dispute Resolution) Act 1998, s 15 and Sch 1, para 25 and Sch 2.

[7]   SI 1996 No 3147.

Chapter 3

THE MEANING OF DISMISSAL

3.01   It is fundamental to a complaint of unfair dismissal or a claim for a redundancy payment that the employee should have been dismissed. Unless the tribunal is satisfied that there has been a dismissal, the case will fail.

In the case of unfair dismissal complaints, section 95 of the ERA 1996 contains the definition of dismissal; in the case of redundancy payments claims, a similar definition is to be found in section 136, although additional provisions are to be found in sections 138 and 146. In both cases, the statutory provision is exhaustive. The combined effect of the statutory provisions and judicial interpretations of them is that some situations clearly fall within them (for example, an actual dismissal); some situations are deemed to be a dismissal (for example, a resignation prompted by a repudiatory breach on the employer's part or the expiry of a fixed-term contract). Some situations (for example, a frustrating event or a voluntary resignation unprompted by action on the employer's part) are outside the definition.

3.02   It is important when determining whether an action falls within the definition of dismissal to start with the statutory language and then to examine the relevant judicial decisions. This is different from the common-law position involving wrongful dismissal, to which the statutory definition does not apply. It is also important to bear in mind that an event which is treated as a dismissal by the statute may not be a dismissal at common law. For example, the expiry of a fixed-term contract is expressly treated as a dismissal by sections 95(2)(b) and 136(1)(b) of the ERA 1996. At common law, however, it will not amount to a dismissal.

3.03   In this chapter, the events giving rise to a termination of employment will be examined to see which events fall within and which outside the statutory definition. The final part of the chapter will consider the date of termination and the rules which enable it to be determined.

1. THE STATUTORY DEFINITION OF DISMISSAL

3.04   The basic statutory definition of dismissal is as follows:

'... an employee is dismissed by his employer if (and ... only if)—

(a)   the contract under which he is employed is terminated by the employer (whether with or without notice),

(b)   he is employed under a contract for a fixed term and that term expires without being renewed under the same contract, or

(c)   the employee terminates the contract under which he is employed (with or without notice) in circumstances such that he is entitled to terminate it without notice by reason of the employer's conduct.'[1]

3.05   The statutory definition set out above is the basic definition used in both the unfair dismissal and (with a slight difference of wording) the redundancy payments provisions in the Employment Rights Act 1996. The third type of dismissal in the definition is usually called a 'constructive dismissal', but that is not a term to be found in the legislation. In the case of redundancy payments, the constructive dismissal provisions do not include the situation where an employee is entitled to terminate the contract by reason of a lockout by the employer.[2] If there is any dispute in tribunal proceedings as to whether the employee was dismissed or not, the burden is upon the employee to satisfy the tribunal that he or she was dismissed.

In this part of the chapter, the three types of dismissal will be considered in turn, after which consideration will be given to the situations where the employee leaves early and where an offer of alternative employment is made in redundancy cases.

(a) Termination with or without notice

3.06   It is convenient to discuss this topic by considering, first, what amounts to a dismissal in general, and then to examine certain particular situations and the way in which the courts and tribunals have reconciled them with the statutory definition. When considering those situations, it is important to bear in mind that what appears to be a resignation may sometimes be treated as a dismissal. After the particular situations have been considered, the statutory notice requirements will be set out.

3.07   As a general rule, it may be stated that termination occurs when either party informs the other clearly and unequivocally that the contract is to end, or the circumstances are such that it is clear that termination was intended or that it can be inferred that termination was intended. The words used to terminate the contract must be capable of being construed as words of termination. The principles are the same whether the termination consists of a dismissal by the employer or a resignation by the employee.

3.08   A notice of termination must be definite and explicit and must state the date of termination (or enable it to be inferred); a mere warning of impending dismissal or resignation will not be enough.[3] Once a notice of

---

[1]   ERA 1996, s 95(1). The wording of s 136(1) is not exactly the same, but the differences are not of substance.

[2]   Section 136(2).

[3]   *Morton Sundour Fabrics Ltd v Shaw* (1967) 2 ITR 84, discussed more fully below.

termination has been given, it cannot be withdrawn by the party giving it without the agreement of the other party.[1]

(i) What amounts to a dismissal?

3.09   In the case of a dismissal by the employer, phrases such as 'I hereby give you notice of dismissal' are clear. Problems arise, however, where there is a row between the employer and the employee and words are used in the heat of the moment. If the words used by the employer are not ambiguous or could only be interpreted as amounting to words of dismissal, then the conclusion is clear. If, on the other hand, the words used are ambiguous and it is not clear whether they do amount to words of dismissal (eg 'You're finished with me'), it is necessary to look at all the circumstances of the case, particularly the intention with which the words were spoken, and consider how a reasonable employee would, in all the circumstances have understood them.[2] In *Tanner v DT Kean Ltd*,[3] the EAT said:

'No doubt there are some words and acts which as a matter of law could be said only to constitute dismissal or resignation, or of which it could be said that they could not constitute dismissal or resignation. But in many cases they are in the middle territory where it is uncertain whether they do or do not, and there it is necessary to look at all the circumstances of the case, and in particular to see what was the intention with which the words were spoken ... [T]he test which has to be applied in cases of this kind is along these lines. Were the words spoken those of dismissal, that is to say, were they intended to bring the contract of employment to an end? What was the employer's intention? In answering that a relevant, and perhaps the most important, question is how would a reasonable employee, in all the circumstances, have understood what the employer intended by what he said and did?'

There is no reason to suggest that this approach should not also be followed in other cases not involving the statutory rights.

3.10   An example of the kind of problem which can occur is *Martin v Yeoman Aggregates Ltd*.[4] The employee obtained the wrong spare part for a broken-down car. There was an angry exchange between a director and the employee. He refused to collect the correct part and was dismissed by the director. A few minutes later, the director realised that he had acted in anger and that he was in breach of the correct disciplinary procedure. So he told the employee he was suspended without pay for two days. The employee treated what had happened as instant dismissal. The EAT applied the test set out in *Tanner v DT Kean Ltd* (above) and held that there had been no dismissal, saying that it was a matter of common sense, vital to industrial relations, that either an employer or an employee should be

---

[1]   *Riordan v War Office* [1961] 1 WLR 210 and *Harris and Russell Ltd v Slingsby* [1973] ICR 454.

[2]   *BG Gale Ltd v Gilbert* [1978] ICR 1149; *Tanner v DT Kean Ltd* [1978] IRLR 110; *Sothern v Franks Charlesley & Co* [1981] IRLR 278; and *J & J Stern v Simpson* [1983] IRLR 52.

[3]   [1978] IRLR 110.

[4]   [1983] ICR 314. See also *Norrie v Munro's Transport (Aberdeen) Ltd* (EAT 437/88).

given an opportunity of recanting from words spoken in the heat of the moment.

3.11   An employee may be treated as dismissed where the employer unilaterally imposes radically different terms of employment so that, on an objective construction of the employer's conduct, there is a removal or withdrawal of the old contract. This is what happened in *Hogg v Dover College*.[1] The employee, a teacher, became ill and after a period of absence returned to part-time teaching. The headmaster wrote him a letter in which he expressed the view that his ill-health made it impossible for him to continue as a department head and offered him fewer teaching periods at a considerably reduced salary. The employee replied claiming that the letter amounted to a dismissal but that pending his claim of unfair dismissal he would continue to work at the college on the terms offered. The EAT held that the effect of the letter was to terminate the contract and that he had been dismissed. A similar conclusion was reached in the more recent case of *Alcan Extrusions v Yates*,[2] which involved the unilateral imposition of a new shift system on a group of employees. If these decisions are correct, then an employee affected by a unilateral variation could stay on and continue to work for the employer under protest but could also complain of unfair dismissal or, if appropriate, claim a redundancy payment. From a contractual point of view, however, they seem to fly in the face of principle in suggesting that, where the employer commits a repudiatory act such that it can be said that there is a removal or withdrawal of the old contract, that contract ends automatically.[3]

3.12   A further requirement in the case of dismissals with notice is that, to be valid, the notice must specify the date of termination or contain material from which the date is ascertainable. If the employer utters a warning that the employee will be made redundant at some unspecified date in the future or that, if the employee does not resign, he or she will have to be dismissed at some future date, and the employee acts on that warning, finds another job and resigns, that action will be treated as a resignation only; he or she will not be treated as having been dismissed.[4] In *Morton Sundour Fabrics Ltd v Shaw*,[5] for example, the employers told the employee that his employment would cease when the department in which he worked was closed down, but they did not specify when that would occur. The employee made arrangements to find another job, and duly gave notice. He later applied for a redundancy payment, but his claim was rejected. Widgery J said:

---

[1]   [1990] ICR 39.

[2]   [1996] IRLR 327.

[3]   See, eg, Lord Oliver of Aylmerton's observations in *Rigby v Ferodo* [1988] ICR 29 at p 34, quoted in para 9.61.

[4]   *Morton Sundour Fabrics Ltd v Shaw* (1967) 2 ITR 84 and *Haseltine Lake & Co v Dowler* [1981] ICR 222. See also *Pritchard-Rhodes Ltd v Boon* [1979] IRLR 19 and *International Computers Ltd v Kennedy* [1981] IRLR 28.

[5]   (1967) 2 ITR 84. Cf *Wadham Stringer Motor Group t/a Wadham Stringer v Avery* (EAT 405/91) IDS Brief 498.

'As a matter of law an employer cannot dismiss his employee by saying "I intend to dispense with your services at some time in the coming months." In order to terminate the contract of employment the notice must either specify the date or contain material from which that date is positively ascertainable.'

3.13   The irony of cases such as this is that diligent employees who respond to the employer's warning of future dismissal and go out and find another job are likely to exclude themselves from their statutory rights by their diligence, whereas employees who stay on waiting for the axe of dismissal to fall will retain their rights.

3.14   A final point to be noted here is that a dismissal with notice may be converted into a summary dismissal if the employer dismisses the employee on the spot during his or her notice period. Such an action would amount to a wrongful dismissal, but also would have the effect of bringing forward the date of termination for the purposes of the statutory rights.[1]

(ii) Particular situations

3.15   Employee repudiation In the case of an employee whose actions amount to a repudiation of his or her contract of employment, the employer's acceptance of that repudiation will not be treated as a dismissal for the purposes of the employee's common-law rights, but will be treated as a dismissal for the purposes of the statutory definition of dismissal. In contractual terms, the employer's acceptance of the repudiation is the right of the innocent party to a breach or repudiation to treat himself or herself as discharged from further performance of the contract. The acceptance of the repudiation will probably consist of a dismissal of the employee or a refusal to allow him or her to return to work (which is much the same thing), but the common law will not treat that acceptance as a dismissal.

3.16   If an employee's actions amount to a repudiation of his or her contractual obligations, the contract will not be terminated until the repudiation is accepted by the employer; the employer's action will be treated as a dismissal for the purposes of the ERA 1996.[2] In *London Transport Executive v Clarke*,[3] Templeman LJ said:

'If a worker walks out of his job or commits any other breach of contract, repudiatory or otherwise, but at any time claims that he is entitled to resume or to continue his work, then his contract of employment is only determined if the employer expressly or impliedly asserts [sic] and accepts repudiation on behalf of the worker. Acceptance can take the form of formal writing or can take the form of refusing to allow the work to resume or continue his work ... [T]he acceptance by an employer of repudiation by a worker who wishes to continue

---

[1]   *Stapp v The Shaftesbury Society* [1982] IRLR 326. The consequence was that at the date of termination, as brought forward by the summary dismissal, the employee lacked the requisite continuity of employment. The meaning of 'date of termination' is discussed later in this chapter.

[2]   *London Transport Executive v Clarke* [1981] ICR 355, *Rasool v Hepworth Pipe Co Ltd* [1980] ICR 494 and *Pendlebury v Christian Schools North West Ltd* [1985] ICR 174.

[3]   *Loc cit* at p 368.

his employment notwithstanding his repudiatory conduct constitutes the determination of the contract of employment by the employer ...'

3.17   This analysis is sometimes applied to sentences of imprisonment passed on employees. If it is, the employee's conduct is treated as repudiatory and the employer's action in accepting the repudiation, by dismissing him or her or treating the contract as frustrated, as amounting to a dismissal within the statutory definition.[1] Much depends, however, on the facts of each case. In *FC Shepherd & Co Ltd v Jerrom*,[2] for example, the EAT said that a contract of apprenticeship is capable of being frustrated, but held that the employee's contract was not frustrated because it was governed by a nationally negotiated termination procedure which included provision for serious misconduct and which excluded any principle of common law under which the employee's absence at borstal was to be treated as repudiation of his contract. The Court of Appeal reversed the EAT's decision and held that the sentence of borstal training was an event which was neither foreseen nor provided for by the parties at the time of contracting, that it had rendered the performance of the contract radically different from that which the parties had originally contemplated and that, therefore, it frustrated the apprenticeship training agreement: see the next section, where frustration is considered. Cases which have held that the employee's repudiation automatically terminates the contract should now be treated as overruled.[3]

3.18   Frustration   As a general rule, it can be stated that frustration occurs when circumstances beyond the control of either party to a contract make it incapable of being performed in the form which was undertaken by the contracting parties.[4] In that case, the contract will terminate automatically and the frustrating event will not be treated as a dismissal for the purposes of the employee's statutory rights.

3.19   In *Davis Contractors Ltd v Fareham District Council*,[5] Lord Radcliffe set out the basic principle of frustration as follows:

> '... [Frustration occurs whenever the law recognises that without default of either party a contractual obligation has become incapable of being performed because the circumstances in which performance is called for would render it a thing radically different from that which was undertaken by the contract ... [I]t is not hardship or inconvenience or material loss itself which calls the principle of frustration into play. There must be as well such a change in the significance of the obligation that the thing undertaken would, if performed, be a different thing from that contracted for.'

---

[1]   *Norris v Southampton City Council* [1982] ICR 177.
[2]   [1985] ICR 552 (EAT) and [1986] ICR 802 (CA). See also *Chakki v United Yeast Co Ltd* [1982] ICR 140.
[3]   *Cannon v JC Firth Ltd* [1976] IRLR 415, *Smith v Avana Bakeries Ltd* [1979] IRLR 423 and *Kallinos v London Electric Wire* [1980] IRLR 11.
[4]   *Davis Contractors Ltd v Fareham District Council* [1950] AC 696.
[5]   *Ibid* at pp 728–729.

3.20 The doctrine of frustration applies to a contract of employment, the most common examples being illness and imprisonment. The death of either party is also best treated as a frustrating event. The effect of frustration is to terminate the contract automatically without either party having to take steps to bring it to an end. Since the employee will not be treated as having been dismissed, a complaint of unfair dismissal or a claim for a redundancy payment will fail.[1] Section 136(5) of the ERA 1996 only protects an employee's right to a redundancy payment where the frustrating event relates to the employer, not the employee, although, if the event affects both, it will be enough that some of the effect is upon the employer.[2]

3.21 A permanent illness will probably frustrate the contract, as will one which is so prolonged as to prevent the employer from obtaining substantially what was bargained for. Theatrical and similar cases present peculiar problems.[3]

Frustration through illness has come to be reconsidered in the last few years because of its operation in the context of the statutory rights. In *Marshall v Harland & Wolff Ltd*,[4] Sir John Donaldson set out the test as follows:

'Was the employee's incapacity, looked at before the purported dismissal, of such a nature, or did it appear likely to continue for such a period that further performance of his obligations in the future would either be impossible or would be a thing radically different from that undertaken by him and accepted by the employer under the agreed terms of his employment?'

He outlined five factors to be taken into account in answering this question: the terms of the contract, including any provisions as to sick pay; how long the employment was likely to last in the absence of sickness; the nature of the employment; the nature of the illness or injury, how long it had already continued and the prospects of recovery; and the period of past employment.

3.22 In relation to short-term periodic contracts, the EAT has suggested, in *Egg Stores (Stamford Hill) Ltd v Leibovici*,[5] four further factors to be taken into account: the risk to the employer of incurring obligations in respect of redundancy payments or compensation for unfair dismissal to a replacement employee; whether wages have continued to be paid; the acts and statements of the employer in relation to the employment, in particular the dismissal of, or failure to dismiss, the employee; and whether in all the circumstances a reasonable employer could be expected to wait longer. Phillips J said:

---

[1]   *Marshall v Harland & Wolff Ltd* [1972] ICR 101.

[2]   *Fenerty v British Airports Authority* [1976] ICR 361.

[3]   See, eg, *Poussard v Spiers and Pond* (1876) 1 QBD 410, *Bettini v Gye* (1876) 1 QBD 183, *Storey v Fulham Steel Works Co* (1907) 24 TLR 89 and *Condor v Barron Knights* [1966] 1 WLR 87.

[4]   [1972] ICR 101 at p 106. See also *Hebden v Forsey & Son* [1973] ICR 607.

[5]   [1977] ICR 260 at p 265. See also *Hart v AR Marshall & Sons (Bulwell) Ltd* [1977] ICR 539.

'It is possible to divide into two kinds the events relied upon as bringing about the frustration of a short-term periodic contract of employment. There may be an event (eg a crippling accident) so dramatic and shattering that everyone concerned will realise immediately that to all intents and purposes the contract must be regarded as at an end. Or there may be an event, such as illness or accident, the course and outcome of which is uncertain. It may be a long process before one is able to say whether the event is such as to bring about the frustration of the contract. But there will have been frustration of the contract, even though at the time of the event the outcome was uncertain, if the time arrives when, looking back, one can say at some point (even if it is not possible to say precisely when) matters had gone on for so long, and the prospects for the future were so poor, that it was no longer practical to regard the contract as still subsisting.'[1]

3.23   The EAT has returned more recently to the question of frustration of the employment contract by illness. In *Williams v Watsons Luxury Coaches Ltd,*[2] the facts were that after working for her employers for about five and a half years the employee suffered an injury at work. For eight months after the date of the accident she submitted medical certificates stating that she should refrain from work. Fourteen months after the accident she went to the offices of her employers, but there was no real discussion about her future employment. A few months later they disposed of the part of the business where she had been employed, without making any arrangements for her future employment. Nineteen months after the accident, and 11 months after her last medical certificate had expired, she approached her employers with a view to returning to work but was told that her job had disappeared. She claimed unfair dismissal. The employment tribunal decided that her contract had been frustrated and dismissed her application. The EAT reviewed the case-law, particularly *Egg Stores (Stamford Hill) Ltd v Leibovici* (above), and said that, in addition, two further factors should be added: the terms of the contract governing the provisions for sick pay and a consideration of the prospects for the employee's recovery. It made it clear that tribunals should be reluctant to decide that a contract of employment has been frustrated by an employee's illness and that the party alleging frustration should not be allowed to rely upon the frustrating event if that event was caused by the fault of that party. In *Collins v Secretary of State for Trade and Industry,*[3] the EAT held that a contract was frustrated as a result of long-term illness, even though both parties regarded the contract as continuing throughout the illness. When the employers subsequently became insolvent, the Secretary of State rejected his claim for a payment from the National Insurance Fund. The EAT upheld the tribunal's decision that, because of the frustration of his contract, he was not entitled to a payment.

3.24   Despite a suggestion by the EAT in *Harman v Flexible Lamps Ltd.*[4] that frustration is only relevant where the contract of employment is for a

---

[1]   [1977] ICR 260 at p 265.

[2]   [1990] ICR 536. See also *Lawton v Bawden International Ltd* (EAT 421/90).

[3]   (EAT 1460/99) (2001) IDS Brief B687/9.

[4]   [1980] IRLR 418.

long term which cannot be determined by notice, and that, where the contract is terminable by notice, there is no need to consider the question of frustration, the Court of Appeal has reaffirmed, in *Notcutt v Universal Equipment Co (London) Ltd,*[1] that the doctrine of frustration can in appropriate circumstances be applied to a periodic contract terminable by the employer by short notice. In that case, the employee, a skilled workman, started working for the employers in 1957 under a contract which was terminable by one week's notice and which provided that no remuneration would be paid to him when he was absent from work because of sickness. In 1983 he suffered a coronary infarct and was absent from work from then on. By July 1984, when the employers were required to give him 12 weeks' notice under what is now section 86 of the ERA 1996,[2] it had become apparent that he would never be able to work again, so the employers gave him the requisite 12 weeks' notice. The employee claimed sick pay during the period of his notice,[3] but the county court judge dismissed his claim on the grounds that his contract had been frustrated by illness before the notice was given. The Court of Appeal upheld the decision. Dillon LJ said that what was said by the EAT in *Harman v Flexible Lamps Ltd,* above, 'must be taken as no more than a warning that the court must look carefully at any submission that a periodic contract of employment has been discharged by frustration if that submission is put forward to avoid the provisions of the Act'.[4]

It is not clear when the Court regarded the contract as having ended. Dillon LJ seems to suggest that it was when the employee had the coronary; Sheldon J said that the latest moment when the frustration could have occurred was when the medical report was presented.[5]

3.25   It is not entirely clear whether the imposition of a custodial sentence upon an employee frustrates the contract or terminates it by making it impossible for the employee to perform his or her part of the contract, in view of the differences of view of the members of the Court of Appeal in *Hare v Murphy Brothers Ltd.*[6] In the later case of *FC Shepherd & Co Ltd v Jerrom,*[7] the Court of Appeal did not follow its decision in that case, which it regarded as unsatisfactory. It decided that a sentence of borstal training was an event which was not foreseen or provided for by the parties at the time of contracting and that it rendered the performance of the contract radically different from that which the parties had contemplated when they entered into it. There had been no fault or default on the part of the employers and the employee was not entitled to rely on his own default. His criminal conduct, although deliberate, had no effect on

---

[1]   [1986] ICR 414.
[2]   Previously s 49 of the EPCA 1978 (see para 3.37).
[3]   Under what is now ERA 1996, s 89.
[4]   *Ibid* at p 420.
[5]   *Ibid* at p 422.
[6]   [1974] ICR 603. Lord Denning MR was the only member of the Court to conclude that the contract was frustrated.
[7]   [1986] ICR 802. The Court considered, obiter, the question of repudiation: see at pp 815 and 831–832.

the performance of the contract: the imposition of the custodial sentence was the act of the judge. The custodial sentence did frustrate the contract of apprenticeship in this case, since the imposition of the sentence meant that there would be a break in the period of training and at the end of the period of the agreement the employee would not be so well trained as the parties had contemplated he would be. Mustill LJ expressly dealt with the question of self-induced frustration and said that, by asserting that the frustration was self-induced, the employee 'asserts that he himself had repudiated the contract: and this is something which, in my judgment, he should not be allowed to do'.[1]

3.26   This decision appears to settle the question for the moment. Cases which decide that the employee's conduct in such circumstances is repudiatory and that the employer's action in accepting the repudiation amounts to a dismissal should be read in the light of the *Jerrom* case.[2] Further, in view of the fact that no dismissal occurs where there has been a frustration, no question of the fairness or otherwise of the employer's action arises.[3]

3.27   Termination by mutual agreement   At common law, the parties are free to enter into an agreement that the contract should terminate and may insert a term into the contract stipulating for the employee to accept an agreed sum in satisfaction of any claims he or she may have in the event of certain specified events occurring.[4] In the context of the statutory rights, however, the courts have shown reluctance to find that there is a genuine bilateral termination as opposed to an apparent agreement engineered by the employer. Cases in which the employee has been given notice by the employer, but has agreed to bring forward the date of departure at the request of the employer, will not be treated as cases of bilateral termination, but of dismissal.[5] If, however, the date of departure is brought forward by the employer at the employee's request, that may be treated as a case of bilateral termination,[6] although it is probably better to regard it as a case of termination by the employer. The EAT has held that a resignation on agreed terms will not amount to a dismissal, even if preceded by difficulties between the parties.[7] In *Birch v University of Liverpool*,[8] the question was whether an employee who responded to the employer's invitation to apply for early retirement and whose application was approved could claim to have been dismissed for the purposes of a

---

[1]   [1986] ICR 802 at p 820.

[2]   *Norris v Southampton City Council* [1982] ICR 177. *Cf Harrington v Kent County Council* [1980] IRLR 553 and *Chakki v United Yeast Co Ltd* [1982] ICR 140.

[3]   As in *Kingston v British Railways Board* [1982] ICR 392.

[4]   See Chapter 9 for a fuller discussion.

[5]   See *McAlwane v Boughton Estates Ltd* [1973] ICR 470 and *Lees v Arthur Greaves (Lees) Ltd* [1974] ICR 510.

[6]   As in *L Lipton Ltd v Marlborough* [1979] IRLR 178.

[7]   See *Sheffield v Oxford Controls Ltd* [1979] ICR 396, *Staffordshire County Council v Donovan* [1981] IRLR 108 and *Logan Salton v Durham County Council* [1989] IRLR 99. See also *Jones v Mid Glamorgan County Council* [1997] ICR 815.

[8]   [1985] ICR 470. See also *Scott v Coalite Fuels and Chemicals Ltd* [1988] ICR 355.

redundancy payments claim. One of the important factors of the early retirement scheme was that an employee's application was subject to final approval by the employer. The Court of Appeal held that the contract had been terminated by the parties by mutual agreement. The facts that the employee's application was subject to the approval of the employer and that there might have been a redundancy situation did not mean that the final approval, if given, amounted to a dismissal within the statutory definition.

3.28   The expiry of a fixed-term contract may be treated as a termination by agreement if the contract contemplated the termination of the contract in certain specified circumstances and those circumstances occur.[1]

3.29   This is an area which may be affected by section 203 of the ERA 1996, which makes void any agreement which purports to exclude or limit any provision in the Act. This is discussed in Chapter 1, at paras 1.98–1.109, to which reference should be made.

3.30   What amounts to a resignation? The requirements in the case of a resignation by an employee are very similar to those for a dismissal. It is important for employers to know whether an employee has resigned, since if they treat the employee as having resigned when that is not in fact the case, they may be held to have dismissed the employee. If the employee's resignation is prompted by a repudiatory act or breach of contract by the employer, that may be treated as a constructive dismissal by the employer (see para 3.46). A resignation does not require acceptance by the employer and, if the employee wishes to change his or her mind and withdraw the resignation, the withdrawal requires the employer's agreement. Failure to give it does not amount to a constructive dismissal.[2]

3.31   As with dismissal, similar questions have arisen as to what amounts to a resignation, particularly where there has been a row between the employer and the employee and it is not clear from the language used whether the employee was in fact intending to resign. If the employee's words are not ambiguous (eg 'I am resigning') or, when construed, have a clear meaning, he or she will be treated as having resigned, irrespective of whether they were intended to bear that meaning, unless the words of resignation were uttered in the heat of the moment or as a result of pressure exerted by the employer. In *Sovereign House Security Services Ltd v Savage*,[3] May LJ said:

> '... [G]enerally speaking, where unambiguous words of resignation are used by an employee to the employer direct or by an intermediary, and are so understood by the employer, the proper conclusion of fact is that the employee has in truth resigned ... However, in some cases there may be something in the context of the exchange between the employer and the employee or, in the circumstances of the employee himself, to entitle the tribunal of fact to conclude

---

[1]   *Brown v Knowsley Borough Council* [1986] IRLR 102.
[2]   *Denham v United Glass Ltd* (EAT 581/98) (1999) IDS Brief B637/4.
[3]   [1989] IRLR 115 at p 116. See also *Sothern v Franks Charlesly & Co* [1981] IRLR 278.

that notwithstanding the appearances there was no real resignation despite what it might appear at first sight.'

3.32   This area of possible exception suggested by the above dicta was further considered by the EAT in *Kwik-Fit (GB) Ltd v Lineham*.[1] In that case, the EAT said that there may be 'special circumstances' which may make it unreasonable for an employer to assume a resignation. It said:[2]

'Words may be spoken or actions expressed in temper or in the heat of the moment or under extreme pressure ... and indeed the intellectual make-up of an employee may be relevant ... These we refer to as "special circumstances". Where "special circumstances" arise it may be unreasonable for an employer to assume a resignation and to accept it forthwith. A reasonable period of time should be allowed to lapse and if circumstances arise during that period which put the employer on notice that further inquiry is desirable to see whether that resignation was really intended and can properly be assumed, then such inquiry is ignored at the employer's risk ... Thus where words or actions are unambiguous an employer is entitled to accept the repudiation at its face value at once, unless these special circumstances exist, in which case he should allow a reasonable time to elapse during which facts may arise which cast doubt upon that prima facie interpretation of the unambiguous words or action. If he does not investigate these facts, a tribunal may hold him disentitled to assume that the words or action did amount to a resignation ...'

3.33   On the other hand, if the words used are ambiguous, it becomes necessary to look at all the circumstances of the case, and, in particular, the intention with which the words were spoken, and to consider how a reasonable employer would, in all the circumstances, have understood the employee's words.[3] The EAT suggested an approach to these kinds of cases in *Tanner v DT Kean Ltd*[4] (see para 3.09).

3.34   A resignation will be treated as a dismissal if the employee is invited to resign and it is made clear that, unless he or she does so, he or she will be dismissed.[5] In *Martin v Glynwed Distribution Ltd*,[6] Sir John Donaldson MR said of these kinds of cases:

'... Whatever the respective actions of the employer and the employee at the time when the contract of employment is terminated, at the end of the day the question always remains the same, "Who really terminated the contract of employment?" If the answer is the employer, there was a dismissal within [section 95(2)(a)] ... If the answer is the employee, a further question may then

---

[1]   [1992] ICR 183.
[2]   *Ibid* at pp 191–192.
[3]   *Sothern v Franks Charlesly & Co* [1981] IRLR 278 and *J & J Stern v Simpson* [1983] IRLR 52; see also *Tanner v DT Kean* [1978] IRLR 110, *Barclay v City of Glasgow District Council* [1983] IRLR 313 (employee said he wanted his books next day; words held not to be words of termination as he was mentally defective) and *Sovereign House Security Services Ltd v Savage* [1989] IRLR 115.
[4]   [1978] IRLR 110. See also *BG Gale Ltd v Gilbert* [1978] ICR 1149.
[5]   *East Sussex County Council v Walker* (1972) 7 ITR 280. See also *Jones v Mid Glamorgan County Council* [1997] ICR 815.
[6]   [1983] ICR 511 at p 519.

arise, namely, "Did he do so in circumstances such that he was entitled to do so without notice by reason of the employer's conduct?" ...'

In that case, the employee was caught driving the employer's vehicle with excess alcohol. He was threatened with a disciplinary inquiry and was told that it would be in his best interests to resign. He did so. The Court of Appeal held that there was not a dismissal. In *Caledonian Mining Co Ltd v Bassett*,[1] on the other hand, the EAT held that the employers had dismissed employees whom they had inveigled into resigning with the intention of depriving them of their statutory rights. The EAT held that the employees had been dismissed within what is now section 136(1)(a) of the ERA 1996,[2] applying Sir John Donaldson's dictum, above.

3.35   A resignation may also be turned into a dismissal if the employee is forced to leave earlier than the date of expiry of his or her notice of resignation.[3] There will be no dismissal, however, where the employee resigns and the employer invokes a contractual provision entitling him or her to terminate the contract early by making a payment in lieu of notice and, by doing so, brings the contract to an end before the expiry of the employee's notice.[4]

3.36   Finally, it should be noted that if an employer mistakenly construes as a resignation an equivocal expression by the employee of an intention to resign and insists on holding him or her to the resignation, that may amount to a dismissal. However, the employee's behaviour may be relied upon by the employer as supplying the reason for the dismissal which may qualify as 'some other substantial reason' within section 98(1)(b) of the ERA 1996.[5]

(iii) Notice provisions

3.37   At common law, the parties are free to choose whatever notice provision they like, although an employer who sought to impose an excessively long notice period on an employee might be prevented from doing so by the doctrine of restraint of trade. If the contract of employment does not specify a notice period a reasonable period of notice will be implied.[6] In most cases where there are no express notice provisions, the situation is likely to be governed by section 86 of the ERA 1996, which is considered below. There may also be exceptional cases where the contract does not contain a notice requirement but contains an exhaustive enumeration of the grounds upon which the contract may be terminated by either side. This matter is considered in Chapter 9, together with a more

---

[1]   [1987] ICR 425.
[2]   Formerly s 83(2)(a) of the EPCA 1978.
[3]   *British Midland Airways Ltd v Lewis* [1978] ICR 782.
[4]   *Marshall (Cambridge) Ltd v Hamblin* [1994] ICR 362.
[5]   *Ely v YKK Fasteners (UK) Ltd* [1994] ICR 164. The tribunal's decision that the dismissal was fair was upheld by the EAT
[6]   For a recent example, see *Clarke v Fahrenheit 451 (Communications) Ltd* (EAT 591/99) (2000) IDS Brief B666/11.

detailed discussion of the rules governing express and implied notice requirements.

3.38   The statutory right to a minimum period of notice, contained in section 86 of the ERA 1996, does not extend to the following categories:

1.   Crown employees;[1]
2.   House of Commons staff;[2]
3.   House of Lords staff;[3]
4.   employees who are engaged under a contract made in contemplation of the performance of a specific task which is not expected to last for more than three months (unless continuously employed for more than three months);[4] and
5.   merchant seamen.[5]

3.39   Section 86(1) entitles employees continuously employed for one month or more but less than two years to at least one week's notice. After two years' employment, they are entitled to one week's notice for each year of continuous employment, but, if they have been employed for more than 12 years, their statutory entitlement will not exceed 12 weeks. Section 86(2) obliges an employee continuously employed for one month or more to give at least one week's notice. The notice must be definite and explicit and must specify the date of termination or give sufficient facts from which the date of termination can be ascertained.[6] Once a notice has been given, it cannot be withdrawn unilaterally, but only with the agreement of the other party.[7] Although an attempt to provide for a shorter period will be ineffective, section 86(3) provides that either side may waive his or her right to notice or accept a payment in lieu of notice. In *Staffordshire County Council v Secretary of State for Employment*,[8] the Court of Appeal held that this provision is only relevant to an employee's rights in contract, not to the statutory rights on termination of employment. By virtue of section 86(6), the right of either party to treat the contract as terminable without notice because of a serious breach by the other party is not affected by the statutory provisions.

3.40   The statutory periods may also be used for other purposes under the legislation. For example, a failure to give the notice required by section 86 may cause the 'effective date of termination' (in cases of unfair

---

[1]   ERA 1996, s 191(1) and (2).
[2]   ERA 1996, s 195(1) and (2).
[3]   ERA 1996, s 194(1) and (2).
[4]   ERA 1996, s 86(5).
[5]   ERA 1996, s 199(1).
[6]   *Morton Sundour Fabrics Ltd v Shaw* (1967) 2 ITR 84 and *Walker v Cotswold Chine Home School* (1977) 12 ITR 342.
[7]   *Riordan v War Office* [1959] 3 All ER 552 and *Harris and Russell Ltd v Slingsby* [1973] ICR 454.
[8]   [1989] ICR 664. Although the Court of Appeal's remarks are directed to what is now s 86(3) in the context of the employee's statutory right to a redundancy payment, there is no reason why they should not also extend to the right not to be unfairly dismissed.

dismissal) or 'relevant date' (in redundancy payments cases) to be postponed;[1] the statutory notice period is also used as a basis for computing the obligatory period for the purposes of a counter-notice given by an employee dismissed for redundancy,[2] and for the purpose of section 140.[3]

(b) Expiry of fixed-term contract

3.41   Fixed-term contracts may take a number of forms. The contract may specify that it is to continue for a stated period (eg five years from 1 January 2001). In that case, it cannot be terminated before the expiry of that period, unless its terms empower the parties to terminate it earlier or they agree to bring it to an end.[4] A second type of fixed-term contract is one which provides for a definite period of employment but specifies that it may be brought to a premature end by either party giving the other a stated period of notice of termination, for example six months or a year. In *Dixon v British Broadcasting Corporation*,[5] the Court of Appeal held that, in the context of employment protection legislation, such a contract is a contract for a fixed term even though it is terminable by notice on either side before the expiry of the term. Lord Denning MR emphasised that a fixed-term contract must be for a specified period.

3.42   A third type of fixed-term contract is one which provides that it is to continue for a stated period (eg one year) and thereafter until determined by notice. The contract cannot be terminated before the stated period expires, but it is a matter of construction of the words used in the contract whether it can be terminated at the end of the period by a notice given during that period, or whether it can only be determined after the expiry of the definite term by notice given after the end of the term. In *Costigan v Gray Bovier Engines Ltd*,[6] the contract was 'to continue for a period of 12 calendar months and thereafter until determined by three calendar months' notice in writing given by either party at any time to the other'. The court held that, although the contract could not be terminated before the expiration of the 12 months, it could be determined at the end of, or at any time after, the term by notice given either during or after the period of 12 months. In cases where such provisions are to be used, careful consideration will need to be given to the drafting of the clause in question, particularly in view of the one-year qualifying period for the statutory right not to be unfairly dismissed.

3.43   Until 1999, it was possible to insert a clause into a fixed-term contract by which employees might waive their statutory rights.[7] The

---

[1]   ERA 1996, ss 97(2)–(5) and 145(5) and (6). See below for a discussion of these provisions.
[2]   ERA 1996, ss 136(3) and (4) and 142 (see para 3.75).
[3]   See Chapter 6.
[4]   See, for example, *Nelson v James Nelson & Sons Ltd* [1914] 2 KB 770.
[5]   [1979] ICR 281.
[6]   (1925) 41 TLR 372. See also *Morris Oddy & Co Ltd v Hayles* (1971) 219 EG 831.
[7]   By virtue of ERA 1996, s 197.

Employment Relations Act 1999,[1] however, repealed the provisions which permitted clauses waiving employees' unfair dismissal rights, although it is still possible, for the moment, to waive the statutory right to a redundancy payment. For that reason it was important to decide whether or not a particular contract was a fixed-term contract for the purposes of the employment protection legislation. Decisions have drawn a distinction between contracts to perform a particular task or carry out a particular purpose (which are held not to be fixed-term contracts) and contracts for a particular period (which are). The borderline between the two types may often be unclear, as is shown by the case of *Wiltshire County Council v National Association of Teachers in Further and Higher Education and Guy*.[2] The case involved a part-time teacher at a college of further education. She entered into a new contract each year to teach specified subjects on specified occasions for each academic session, which ran from September to around the end of June. The classes were subject to there being sufficient enrolments and did not necessarily continue until the end of the session but could end earlier. She was paid for the hours she taught. She was not offered a new contract at the end of the 1976–1977 session and complained of unfair dismissal. The Court of Appeal held that, since her contract obliged her to work for the period of the academic session if so required, it was a fixed-term contract. Lord Denning MR drew a distinction between a contract for the duration of a voyage or a contract to cut down trees and said:

> 'In neither of those instances is there a contract for a fixed term. It is a contract which is discharged by performance. There is no "dismissal". A contract for a particular purpose, which is fulfilled, is discharged by performance and does not amount to a dismissal.'[3]

Lawton LJ said that 'a "fixed term"… means a term which has a defined beginning and a defined end'.[4]

3.44   Sections 95(1)(b) and 136(1)(b) of the ERA 1996 treat the expiry of a fixed-term contract as a dismissal. A confirmation to an employee of the date of expiry of a fixed term contract is a dismissal falling within section 95(1)(b), not section 95(1)(a). A distinction is to be drawn between telling an employee that his or her contract will end by effluxion of time and exercising a power to bring the contract to an end by notice.[5] If an employee is employed under a succession of fixed-term contracts, there can be a dismissal each time a contract expires. If, after the expiry of one contract, the employer offers the employee a new contract on less favourable terms than previously, there will be no breach of contract, since the employee's previous contract has expired and, at the time of the offer,

---

[1]   Sections 18(1) and 44 and Sch 9, Table 3.
[2]   [1980] ICR 455. See also *Ryan v Shipboard Maintenance Ltd* [1980] ICR 88.
[3]   *Ibid* at p 460.
[4]   *Ibid* at p 462.
[5]   *London Underground Ltd v Fitzgerald* [1997] ICR 271.

he or she has no employment with the employer. That means also that the employee cannot claim to have been constructively dismissed.[1]

3.45 Occasionally, the expiry of a fixed-term contract may be treated as a termination by agreement, as happened in *Brown v Knowsley Borough Council*.[2] The employee was employed as a temporary teacher in a college of further education. She had been employed under a series of fixed-term contracts. In August 1983, she was offered a contract for the academic year from 1 September 1983 which stipulated: 'The appointment will last only as long as sufficient funds are provided either by the Manpower Services Commission (MSC) or by other firms/sponsors to fund it'. On 3 August 1984, the council wrote to her that, as it had not received any contracts from the MSC for courses at the college, her course would not receive funding after the present contract expired and that her employment was to terminate on 31 August in accordance with her contract. The EAT held that, in view of the wording of the letter of appointment, the contract came to an end automatically in the event which happened – when there were insufficient funds provided by the MSC. No action was required of anyone. It is debatable whether this was a genuine contract for a fixed term, but the decision that it was something else would probably have made no difference to the outcome.

The expiry and non-renewal of a fixed-term contract may constitute 'some other substantial reason' for dismissal within section 98(1)(b) of the ERA 1996.[3]

(c) Constructive dismissal

3.46 Constructive dismissal is the term commonly applied to a resignation by the employee in circumstances such that he or she is entitled to terminate the contract without notice because of the employer's conduct, although it is not a term to be found in the legislation. In *Western Excavating (ECC) Ltd v Sharp*,[4] the Court of Appeal affirmed that the question whether an employee is entitled to terminate without notice should be answered according to the rules of the law of contract. Lord Denning MR said:

> 'If the employer is guilty of conduct which is a significant breach going to the root of the contract of employment, or which shows that the employer no longer intends to be bound by one or more of the essential terms of contract, then the employee is entitled to treat himself as discharged from any further performance ... [T]he conduct must ... be sufficiently serious to entitle him to leave at once ...'[5]

Lawton LJ expressed himself differently:

---

[1] *Pfaffinger v City of Liverpool Community College* [1997] ICR 142.
[2] [1986] IRLR 102.
[3] *Fay v North Yorkshire County Council* [1986] ICR 133.
[4] [1978] ICR 221.
[5] *Ibid* at p 226.

'... I do not find it necessary or advisable to express any opinion as to what principles of law operate to bring a contract of employment to an end by reason of an employer's conduct. Sensible persons have no difficulty in recognising such conduct when they hear about it. Persistent and unwanted amorous advances by an employer to a female member of his staff would, for example, clearly be such conduct ...'[1]

3.47   The correct approach, therefore, is to ask whether the employer was in breach of contract, not whether the employer acted unreasonably. There may be circumstances, however, where the employer's conduct is so seriously unreasonable that it provides sufficient evidence that there has been a repudiatory breach of contract.[2]

3.48   The EAT has held that in constructive dismissal cases arising under regulation 5(5) of the Transfer of Undertakings (Protection of Employment) Regulations 1981 (as amended) (TUPE), it is not necessary for there to be a breach of contract before an entitlement to resign and claim constructive dismissal under section 95(1)(c) may arise. It said that, in the case of a transfer of an undertaking, an employee who suffers a substantial change in working conditions to his or her detriment has a right to claim to have been constructively dismissed, even if the employer's actions complained of do not amount to a breach of contract.[3] If this decision is correct, it means that there will be different circumstances in which an employee may claim to have been constructively dismissed, depending upon whether the employee's resignation arose in the context of a transfer governed by TUPE or not. It is questionable whether European law constrained the EAT to reach this conclusion, in the light of the House of Lords' decision in *Wilson v St Helens Borough Council.*[4]

3.49   It is important to note that the evaluation of whether the employer's conduct is repudiatory depends upon whether the conduct, viewed objectively, showed an intention no longer to be bound by the contract. It does not depend upon whether the employer intended the conduct to be repudiatory or could reasonably have believed that it would be accepted as such;[5] nor is the fact that the employer acted on a genuine, though mistaken belief of fact, enough to prevent his conduct amounting to a repudiation.[6] In *Bridgen v Lancashire County Council,*[7] Sir John Donaldson MR said that the mere fact that a party to a contract takes a view of its construction which is ultimately shown to be wrong does not of itself constitute repudiatory conduct: 'It has to be shown that he did not intend to be bound by the contract as properly construed'. These views have

---

1   [1978] ICR 221 at p 229.
2   *Brown v Merchant Ferries Ltd* [1998] IRLR 682.
3   See *Rossiter v Pendragon plc* [2001] IRLR 256.
4   [1998] ICR 1141.
5   *Lewis v Motorwold Garages Ltd* [1986] ICR 157. See also *Post Office v Roberts* [1980] IRLR 347, *Millbrook Furnishing Industries Ltd v McIntosh* [1981] IRLR 309, and *BBC v Beckett* [1983] IRLR 43.
6   *Brown v JBD Engineering Ltd* [1993] IRLR 568.
7   [1987] IRLR 58 at p 60.

received implicit support from the decision of the House of Lords in *Rigby v Ferodo Ltd.*[1]

3.50   A further point to note is that it is not necessary that the person of whose conduct the employee complains should have authority to dismiss, provided that the person concerned acted in the course of employment. In *Hilton International Hotels (UK) Ltd v Protopapa,*[2] the employee complained that the behaviour of her immediate superior amounted to a serious breach of contract; the employers argued that the superior did not have authority to dismiss her and, therefore, that his behaviour could not amount to 'employer's conduct' within the meaning of what is now section 95(1)(c). The EAT rejected this argument and said that, for there to be a constructive dismissal, it has to be by reason of something which the law regards as the conduct of the employer. Whether the conduct of a supervisory employee binds the employer is governed by the general law of contract, according to which the employer is bound by acts done in the course of an employee's employment.

3.51   Analogous to the question raised by the *Protopapa* case, above, is the question whether an employee who resigns as a result of an *ultra vires* action on the part of the employer may claim constructive dismissal. On the other hand, in certain circumstances an *intra vires* act may also constitute a repudiatory act.[3]

3.52   The issue of *ultra vires* actions arose in *Warnes v The Trustees of Cheriton Oddfellows Social Club,*[4] in which the employees (a man and wife steward and stewardess of a club) resigned as a result of a resolution to remove them, passed at the club's annual general meeting. It turned out that the resolution was invalid under the club's rules. The employment tribunal decided that the constructive dismissal claim could not succeed, but its decision was overruled on appeal. The EAT said that an employer is not entitled to rely upon lack of power in one of its officers or organs in acting in a way which, if valid, would constitute a dismissal: 'It is not in general open to an employer to rely upon an abuse of power'.[5] A similar issue arose in *Moores v Bude-Stratton Town Council,*[6] a case in which an employee of a town council resigned after being subjected to abuse and accusations of dishonesty by one of the councillors in front of other council employees. The EAT, by a majority, held that individual councillors are under a duty not to engage in conduct likely to undermine the trust and

---

[1]   [1988] ICR 29; see Chapter 9, where this case is considered.

[2]   [1990] IRLR 316.

[3]   In *BMK Ltd and BMK Holdings Ltd v Logue* [1993] ICR 601, the core argument concerned the effective date of termination, but the EAT proceeded on the assumption that the removal of the employee as a director of the two companies by a valid resolution could amount to a repudiatory act. The matter is therefore unresolved, but it must at least be questionable whether an action which is valid in company law can amount to a repudiatory act. Probably, much depends upon the facts of each case.

[4]   [1993] IRLR 58. For the effect of such an act upon the effective date of termination, see para 3.102.

[5]   *Ibid* at p 59.

[6]   [2001] ICR 271.

confidence required in employment contracts and that the councillor's behaviour amounted to a breach of that duty. Further, it held that the council was vicariously liable for the breach. The President, Lindsay J, dissented, on the grounds that a councillor does not owe such a duty and that, even if he or she did, the council could not be vicariously liable for such a breach.

3.53   In cases of constructive dismissal, the employment tribunal must first consider whether the employer's action is in breach of his or her contractual obligations or is a repudiation of them. That will involve ascertaining the express terms of the contract and considering whether any terms should be implied. But it should be borne in mind that, once the breach or repudiation has been established, it must be serious enough to entitle the employee to leave without notice.[1] This is a mixed question of fact and law.[2] In addition, the tribunal must be satisfied that the employee's resignation was caused by the breach and that the employee did not waive the right to terminate the contract and claim constructive dismissal. These matters are examined after a consideration of the circumstances which amount to a breach.

3.54   In view of the fundamental importance of the payment of wages as an integral part of an employment contract, a failure to pay an employee's wages will amount prima facie to a breach of contract,[3] although there may be circumstances in which a breach of contract will be held not to have occurred or that, although what happened amounted to a breach, the breach was not fundamental. In *RF Hill Lt v Mooney*,[4] Browne-Wilkinson J said:

> 'The obligation on the employer to pay remuneration is one of the fundamental terms of a contract ... [I]f an employer seeks to alter that contractual obligation in a fundamental way, such attempt is a breach going to the very root of the contract and is necessarily repudiation.'[5]

3.55   These issues were considered by the Court of Appeal in *Cantor Fitzgerald International v Callaghan*.[6] What happened there was that the employer refused to honour an agreement relating to the employees' salary packages. The employees resigned in consequence. The issue was whether the failure to honour the agreement was a significant breach going to the root of the contract (although clearly it was a breach). Judge LJ, with whom

---

[1]   *Gillies v Richard Daniels & Co Ltd* [1979] IRLR 457, and *White v London Transport Executive* [1981] IRLR 261.

[2]   *Pedersen v Camden London Borough Council* [1981] ICR 674, *Millbrook Furnishing Industries Ltd v McIntosh* [1981] IRLR 309 and *Woods v WM Car Services (Peterborough) Ltd* [1982] ICR 693 (CA).

[3]   But *Cf Adams v Charles Zub Associates Ltd* [1978] IRLR 551. See also *Reid v Camphill Engravers* [1990] ICR 435.

[4]   [1981] IRLR 258.

[5]   *Ibid* at p 260.

[6]   [1999] ICR 639.

Nourse and Tuckey LJJ agreed, analysed the issues arising from a failure to honour a salary package and said:[1]

> '... [I]t is difficult to exaggerate the crucial importance of pay in any contract of employment ... In my judgment the question whether non-payment of agreed wages, or interference by an employer with an agreed salary package, is or is not fundamental to the continued existence of the contract depends on the critical distinction to be drawn between an employer's failure to pay, or delay in paying, agreed remuneration and his deliberate refusal to do so. Where the failure or delay constitutes a breach of contract, depending on the circumstances, this may represent no more than a temporary fault in the employer's technology, an accounting error or simple mistake, or illness, or accident, or unexpected events ... On the other hand, if the failure or delay in payment were repeated and persistent, perhaps also unexplained, the court might be driven to conclude that the breach or breaches were indeed repudiatory. Where, however, an employer unilaterally reduces his employee's pay, or diminishes the value of his salary package, the entire foundation of the contract of employment is undermined. Therefore, an emphatic denial by the employer of his obligation to pay the agreed salary or wage, or a determined resolution not to comply with his contractual obligations in relation to pay and remuneration, will normally be regarded as repudiatory.'

He concluded that the employer's refusal to pay was deliberate and determined and constituted a repudiatory breach. Issues may also arise relating to the payment of bonuses and whether a refusal to pay a bonus amounts to a breach of contract.[2] For a fuller discussion of such matters, reference should be made to Chapter 9.

3.56   Other examples of a breach of an express term are a refusal of holiday entitlement,[3] the withdrawal of an employee's company car[4] and unilateral alterations in the employee's pay, status or place of work, even on a temporary basis.[5] In *Greenaway Harrison Ltd v Wiles*,[6] the EAT upheld the employment tribunal's decision that an employee's resignation in circumstances where her employers were proposing to vary her hours of work unilaterally and to give her notice of dismissal if she did not agree, amounted to a constructive dismissal. It said that the employer's actions were an anticipatory breach of a fundamental term. In a case involving alterations in the employee's place of work, the tribunal will need to consider whether the employee was subject to an express or implied mobility obligation. This issue is discussed more fully below.

---

[1]   [1999] ICR 639 at pp 648–649.

[2]   See, for example, *Clark v Nomura International plc* [2000] IRLR 766 and *Manor House Healthcare v Hayes and Skinner* (EAT 1196/99) (2000) IDS Brief B674/6.

[3]   *Lytlarch Ltd v Reid* [1991] ICR 216.

[4]   *Triton Oliver (Special Products) Ltd v Bromage* (EAT 709/91) IDS Brief 511.

[5]   See, for example, *Wadham Stringer Commercials (London) Ltd and Wadham Stringer Vehicles Ltd v Brown* [1983] IRLR 46 and *Lytlarch Ltd v Reid* [1991] ICR 216. *Millbrook Furnishing Industries Ltd v McIntosh* [1981] IRLR 309 and *McNeil v Charles Crimin (Electrical Contractors) Ltd* [1984] IRLR 179 both involved temporary alterations.

[6]   [1994] IRLR 380.

3.57   There may be circumstances in which a suspension of the employee on full pay may breach an express term. In *William Hill Organisation Ltd v Tucker*,[1] the employee was the senior dealer in a spread betting business and his contract required him to work such hours necessary to carry out his duties in a proper and professional manner. He gave notice of termination and the employers suspended him on full pay. The question was whether the suspension was a breach of contract. The Court of Appeal held that on its true construction the contract imposed an obligation on the employer to permit the employee, during the period of his notice, to perform the duties of the specific and unique post to which he had been appointed, where the skills necessary to the proper discharge of such duties required their frequent exercise. The employer was in breach of that obligation. Although, as may be seen from the facts, the case was not in fact a constructive dismissal case, nevertheless there may be cases where in effect the employee, as here, is denied the right to work and resigns in consequence. Such cases will depend very much on the nature of the employee's obligations and the fact that, as here also, he or she needs to exercise the skills which are necessary for the effective discharge of the duties under the contract. It should also be noted that the contract in question did not contain an express 'garden leave' clause and the Court refused to imply one.

3.58   The question whether the employer has committed a breach of an express term may also make it necessary for the employment tribunal to consider whether the term alleged to have been breached was incorporated into the employee's contract so as to form part of it. So, for example, in *Bridgen v Lancashire County Council*,[2] the Court of Appeal construed the Burnham Agreement and held that an employee had no entitlement to be regraded and, in *Marley v Forward Trust Group Ltd*,[3] it had to consider the effect of a collective agreement, expressed to be binding in honour only. The agreement contained a provision which gave an employee who accepted redeployment in the event of a redundancy situation arising, six months to assess its suitability without prejudicing his rights to compensation for redundancy. At the end of 1983, the employers decided to close the office where the employee worked. The employee was moved to London, but after two months he told his employers that the new position was unsuitable and that he wished to exercise his 'redundancy option'. The employers took the view that he had been transferred under a mobility clause in his contract and not pursuant to a redundancy situation. The employee's complaint to the employment tribunal and appeal to the EAT were unsuccessful. The Court of Appeal held that the terms of the collective agreement relating to redundancy had been incorporated into the employee's contract and that if a redundancy situation arose the employers could not rely on the mobility clause when redeploying the employee. It

---

[1]   [1999] ICR 291. *Cf SBJ Stephenson v Mandy* [2000] IRLR 233.

[2]   [1987] IRLR 58 (see para 3.49).

[3]   [1986] ICR 891. Reference may also be made to *Henry v London General Transport Services Ltd* [2001] IRLR 132, which considers issues relating to the incorporation of collectively agreed terms.

remitted the case to the employment tribunal to decide whether a redundancy situation did exist when the employee was transferred. More recently, in *Aparau v Iceland Frozen Foods plc*,[1] the facts were that the employers issued new terms and conditions of employment to all their employees, which included a term relating to mobility; the employees were asked to sign and return a duplicate confirming that they had 'read and understood the above conditions of employment and agree to accept the appointment under these terms'. The employee never signed the form but continued to work for a further 12 months before being instructed to move to another branch. She resigned and claimed constructive dismissal. The tribunal rejected her complaint on the ground that she had accepted the new contract by performance. The EAT allowed her appeal and said that her acceptance of the new terms could not be inferred from the fact that she continued to work for a further 12 months. The EAT said also that the tribunal had erred in implying a mobility term into her contract.

3.59   Examples of terms implied into employees' contracts are terms obliging the employer to maintain the relationship of trust between employer and employee, or not to treat the employees arbitrarily, capriciously or inequitably, or not to behave intolerably and not in accordance with good industrial practice.[2] The case of *University of Nottingham v Eyett*[3] suggests, albeit that it arose in the context of pension litigation, that the implied duty of mutual trust and confidence in a contract of employment does not extend so far as to include a positive obligation on the employer. In the case in question, the employer failed to warn an employee who was proposing to exercise important rights in connection with the contract of employment that the way he was proposing to exercise them might not be the most financially advantageous. Hart J said that, although the duty of mutual trust and confidence may in principle impose positive obligations, recognition of a duty to alert an employee to the possibility that he was making a financial mistake would have far-reaching consequences for the employment relationship and would not sit well with other default obligations implied by law in the employment context. On the other hand, the EAT in *BG plc v O'Brien*[4] held that employers acted in breach of the duty of trust and confidence when they offered every permanent employee apart from the complainant the opportunity to benefit from an incentive scheme which included an enhanced redundancy package.

3.60   An example of the application of the duty of trust and confidence is to be found in *TSB Bank plc v Harris*,[5] in which the EAT upheld the tribunal's decision that the employers were in fundamental breach of the

---

[1]   [1996] IRLR 119.

[2]   *Woods v WM Car Services (Peterborough) Ltd* [1981] ICR 666 and [1982] ICR 693 (CA), *Courtaulds Northern Textiles Ltd v Andrew* [1979] IRLR 84, *Wigan Borough Council v Davies* [1979] ICR 411, and *White v London Transport Executive* [1981] IRLR 261. See also *Bliss v South East Thames Regional Health Authority* [1987] ICR 700, considered at para 9.50.

[3]   [1999] ICR 721.

[4]   (EAT 1063/99) (2001) IDS Brief B688/7.

[5]   [2000] IRLR 157.

implied term of trust and confidence by revealing in a reference to a prospective employer complaints against the employee of which she was unaware, thereby blocking her progress in the financial services sector. It rejected the argument that the employers were not in breach of the implied term because they were only doing what was required of them under regulations governing the financial services industry. It said that the obligation of the employers to their regulators is not the measure of their obligation to their employees. In *Euro-Die (UK) Ltd v Skidmore*,[1] the EAT held that an employer's failure to assure an employee that his continuity of employment would be protected following a transfer of the business amounted to a fundamental breach of the term of trust and confidence. The consequence was that the employee was treated as constructively dismissed and the transferee was liable for the unfair dismissal.

3.61   The EAT has treated a failure to deal with a female employee's complaint of alleged sexual harassment as a breach of this type of implied term.[2] It has refused to treat the introduction of a no-smoking policy as a breach of the implied term.[3] It has said, however, that it is an implied term in every contract of employment that an employer will provide for employees a working environment which is reasonably suitable for them for the performance of their contractual duties. It is, therefore, a breach of that implied term to require an employee to work in an environment affected by the smoking habits of fellow-employees.[4] The EAT has also held that it is an implied term in a contract of employment that employers will reasonably and promptly give their employees a reasonable opportunity to obtain redress for any grievances. It therefore held that a failure by employers to provide their employees with a procedure for dealing with their grievances amounted to a breach of the implied term entitling the employees to claim that they had been constructively dismissed.[5] However, the courts are reluctant to imply into an employee's contract terms such as an entitlement to be provided with regular pay increases.[6]

3.62   The question of mobility arose in *Courtaulds Northern Spinning Ltd v Sibson*.[7] The facts were that the employee worked as a lorry driver at the same depot from the start of his employment in 1973. His contract had no express mobility term. All the drivers belonged to the same union, but in 1985 he resigned from the union. To avert strike action, the employer required him to rejoin the union or transfer to another depot. He resigned

---

[1]   (EAT 1158/98) (2000) IDS Brief B655/14. *Cf Sita (GB) Ltd v Burton* [1998] ICR 17.

[2]   See *Bracebridge Engineering Ltd v Darby* [1990] IRLR 3.

[3]   *Dryden v Greater Glasgow Health Board* [1992] IRLR 469.

[4]   *Waltons & Morse v Dorrington* [1997] IRLR 488.

[5]   *WA Goold (Pearmak) Ltd v McConnell* [1995] IRLR 516.

[6]   *Murco Petroleum Ltd v Forge* [1987] ICR 282.

[7]   [1988] ICR 451. See also *Aparau v Iceland Frozen Foods plc* [1996] IRLR 119, where the EAT said that, although there must be some term as to the employee's place of employment in an employment contract, it is not necessary to imply a mobility term. It went on to say that, if that view was wrong, and some term as to mobility fell to be implied, there was no basis for implying a term entitling the employer to transfer the employee against his or her will.

and claimed that he had been constructively dismissed. The Court of Appeal held that, in order to give the contract business efficacy, a term had to be implied in the contract (as being a term which the parties, acting reasonably, would probably have agreed if they had considered the matter) that the employer could, for any reason, direct the employee to work at any place within reasonable daily reach of the employee's home. The employers had therefore acted within their contractual rights and the employee had not been constructively dismissed. The Court rejected the employment tribunal's qualification of the implied term that the employer's request to the employee should be reasonable or 'for genuine operational reasons' as being potentially uncertain and difficult in operation but agreed that the employee could reasonably have demanded that the mobility requirement should be reasonable daily travelling distance.[1]

The Court of Session has held, however, that, where there is an implied right for the employer to transfer an employee from one place of employment to another, the right must be subject to an implied qualification that reasonable notice must be given.[2]

3.63   Similarly, the EAT has applied the implied term not to behave in a manner calculated or likely to destroy or seriously damage the relationship of trust and confidence between employer and employee to the employer's conduct in the exercise of powers conferred by an express term. *United Bank Ltd v Akhtar*[3] concerned the exercise of a mobility clause by employers and its effects upon the employee's right to resign and claim constructive dismissal. The terms of the mobility clause were:

'The bank may from time to time require an employee to be transferred temporarily or permanently to any place of business which the bank may have in the UK for which a relocation allowance or other allowances may be payable at the discretion of the bank.'

The employee was a junior clerk in the Leeds branch of the bank. On 2 June 1987, he learned that he was to be transferred to the Birmingham branch the following Monday, 8 June. He did not receive written confirmation of this until 5 June. In the meantime, he wrote to his manager asking for a postponement of the transfer for three months because of personal difficulties relating to his wife's ill-health and the impending sale of his house. His request was refused. On 8 June he wrote another letter asking for 24 days' leave which was due to him in order to sort out his affairs and start work in Birmingham on 10 July. From 5 June his pay was stopped. He complained that he had been constructively dismissed. The EAT upheld the employment tribunal's decision that he had. It said that the tribunal was entitled to imply into the employee's contract a term that reasonable notice should be given in the exercise of the bank's powers to

---

[1]   [1988] ICR 451 at p 462.

[2]   *Prestwick Circuits Ltd v McAndrew* [1990] IRLR 191.

[3]   [1989] IRLR 507.

require mobility of its employees and that the employers' discretion under the mobility clause was one which they were bound to exercise in such a way as not to make it impossible for him to comply with his contractual obligation to move. It also upheld the tribunal's decision that the employers' conduct in relation to the employee's transfer amounted to a fundamental breach of the implied term that employers must not, without reasonable and proper cause, behave in a manner calculated or likely to destroy or seriously damage the relationship of trust and confidence between employer and employee.

3.64   Whilst there is no reason to suggest that this decision is not perfectly correct in law and on its facts, it is important to bear in mind a decision of this kind should not be seen as a method of avoiding the rule stated in *Western Excavating (ECC) Ltd v Sharp* (see para 3.46) that an employee's entitlement to claim constructive dismissal because of the employer's actions must be determined according to the rules of contract. That rule does not, however, preclude a tribunal from taking a view that an employer's behaviour in the exercise of powers conferred by an express clause amounts to a breach of contract. *United Bank Ltd v Akhtar* was distinguished in the later case of *White v Reflecting Roadstuds Ltd*.[1] In that case, it was argued that the employers' exercise of their rights under a mobility clause was subject to the qualification that they should act reasonably. The EAT rejected this argument and distinguished the *Akhtar* case on the grounds that 'the term implied by Knox J and those sitting with him was that an employer when dealing with a mobility clause ... should not exercise his discretion in such a way as to prevent his employee from being able to carry out his part of the contract'.[2]

It seems clear that the EAT is prepared to imply a fairly narrow term relating to the handling of mobility clauses but that it is aware that to do so too readily would be to go against the authority of *Western Excavating (ECC) Ltd v Sharp*.

3.65   It is important to bear in mind that a series of actions on the part of the employer may cumulatively amount to a breach of the implied contractual obligation of mutual trust and confidence, although each individual action may not. The course of conduct relied upon may include a breach of an express term of the contract committed by the employer but waived by the employee at the time. This was the view of the Court of Appeal in *Lewis v Motorworld Garages Ltd*,[3] a case where the employers demoted the employee in breach of his contract and adversely altered his pay structure. He affirmed the contract, but over a period of eight months the employer persistently criticised him and threatened him with dismissal if he did not improve. He eventually resigned. The employment tribunal decided that the demotion and change in pay structure became spent when the employee affirmed the contract and that the subsequent criticisms and

1   [1991] ICR 733.
2   *Ibid* at p 741.
3   [1986] ICR 157. See also *Abbey National plc v Robinson* (EAT 743/99) (2001) IDS Brief B680/12 and *JV Strong & Co Ltd v Hamill* (EAT/1179/99) (2001) IDS Brief B684/8.

threats did not amount to a repudiation. The Court of Appeal, however, held that the demotion and alteration could be relied upon as part of the course of conduct which cumulatively amounted to a repudiatory breach and that the employment tribunal should have considered the continuing effect of the demotion and change in pay structure.

3.66   If an employee is employed under a succession of fixed-term contracts, and, after the expiry of one contract, the employer offers the employee a new contract on less favourable terms than previously, there will be no breach of contract, since the employee's previous contract has expired and, at the time of the offer, he or she has no employment with the employer. That means that the employee cannot claim to have been constructively dismissed.[1]

3.67   Once the employment tribunal has decided that there has been a breach or repudiation and that it was sufficiently serious to entitle the employee to end the contract immediately, it must then be satisfied that the employee's departure was caused by the breach.[2] In this context questions may arise as to whether the employee need give a reason for leaving and whether that reason need be the real reason for his or her departure. In *Holland v Glendale Industries Ltd*,[3] the employee resigned, saying he was taking early retirement. The real reason in fact was the conduct of the employers towards him. The EAT said that there could not be a constructive dismissal where the employee did not make clear that he was leaving because of the employer's conduct. This view was doubted by the Court of Appeal in the later case of *Weathersfield Ltd v Sargent*.[4] Pill LJ said:[5]

> 'Acceptance of a repudiation of a contract of employment will usually take the form of the employee leaving and saying why he is leaving but it is not necessary in law for the reason to be given at the time of leaving. The fact-finding tribunal is entitled to reach its own conclusion, based on the "acts and conduct of the party" as to the true reason ... [Employment] tribunals will ... be astute to discover the true reason for the employee leaving and reject those claims in which alleged conduct by the employer is no more than a pretext or cover for leaving on other grounds.'

3.68   The tribunal must be satisfied also that he or she has not waived the right to terminate by staying on too long after the conduct in question. Otherwise he or she may be taken to have elected to affirm the contract.[6] In the event of a subsequent resignation, it will not be possible to claim

---

[1]   *Pfaffinger v City of Liverpool Community College* [1997] ICR 142.

[2]   *British Leyland UK Ltd v McQuilken* [1978] IRLR 245 and *Walker v Josiah Wedgwood & Sons Ltd* [1978] ICR 744. See also *Jones v F Sirl & Son (Furnishers) Ltd* [1997] IRLR 493.

[3]   [1998] ICR 493.

[4]   [1999] ICR 425.

[5]   *Ibid* at p 432.

[6]   *Western Excavating (ECC) Ltd v Sharp* [1978] ICR 221 at p 226, *per* Lord Denning MR See also *WE Cox Toner (International) Ltd v Crook* [1981] ICR 823, *Wilton v Cornwall & Isles of Scilly Health Authority* (19 May 1993, CA) IDS Brief 499, and *Abbey National plc v Robinson* (EAT 743/99) (2001) IDS Brief B680/12.

constructive dismissal. In *WE Cox Toner (International) Ltd v Crook*,[1] Browne-Wilkinson J said:[2]

> 'Mere delay by itself (unaccompanied by any express or implied affirmation of the contract) does not constitute affirmation of the contract; but if it is prolonged it may be evidence of an implied affirmation. Affirmation of the contract can be implied. Thus, if the innocent party calls on the guilty party for further performance of the contract, he will normally be taken to have affirmed the contract since his conduct is only consistent with the continued existence of contractual obligation ... However, if the innocent party further performs the contract to a limited extent but at the same time makes it clear that he is reserving his right to accept the repudiation ... such further performance does not prejudice his rights subsequently to accept the repudiation.'

In *Cantor Fitzgerald International v Callaghan*,[3] Judge LJ observed that in such cases the 'ultimate question is one, not of law, but of fact'.

3.69   The employee must also accept a repudiation unequivocally. An example of a failure to do so is *Harrison v Norwest Holst Group Administration Ltd*.[4] The employers wrote to the employee stating that he would lose his directorship in two weeks' time. The employee responded with a letter headed 'Without Prejudice'. The employers later withdrew their threat to deprive him of his directorship, but the employee left anyway. The Court of Appeal treated the original threat as an anticipatory breach but said that the employee's letter was not sufficiently unequivocal to amount to an acceptance of the repudiation. Because the repudiation had not been accepted, the contract continued to run and, during the continued currency of the contract, it was open to the employers to withdraw their threat of breach. A further question which arises in this context is whether an employee is obliged to signify clearly to the employer that he or she is leaving the employment because of the employer's repudiatory conduct, or whether it is sufficient for him or her to leave without indicating the reason but in circumstances where it can be said, looking at the matter objectively, that the departure was caused by the employer's conduct. In the light of *Weathersfield Ltd v Sargent*,[5] considered above, the suggested answer is that the latter approach is to be preferred.

3.70   An employee who does not wish to resign immediately, but who does wish to preserve the right to resign and complain of constructive

---

[1]   [1981] ICR 823.

[2]   *Ibid* at pp 828–829.

[3]   [1999] ICR 639 at p 653. As an example of this, the two cases of *Dixon v London General Transport Services Ltd* (EAT 1265/98) (2000) IDS Brief B666/11 and *Abbey National plc v Robinson* (EAT 743/99) (2001) IDS Brief B680/12 should be contrasted.

[4]   [1985] ICR 668. See also *Lewis v Motorworld Garages Ltd* [1986] ICR 157, *Shook v London Borough of Ealing* [1986] ICR 314 and *Day v Pickles Farms* [1999] IRLR 217. In the last case, the EAT said that there must be 'unequivocal communication' of the acceptance of the repudiation.

[5]   [1999] ICR 425. But see *Logabax Ltd v Titherley* [1977] ICR 369 at p 375 and *Walker v Josiah Wedgwood and Sons Ltd* [1978] ICR 744 at p 751. Reference should also be made to *Chitty on Contracts* (27th edn), para 24-011.

dismissal, should ensure that it is made clear to the employer that he or she is continuing to work under the contract of employment without prejudice to the right to resign later and complain of unfair dismissal.

3.71   In some cases, it may be sensible for the employee to claim constructive dismissal in the alternative, particularly in cases where his or her claim to have been dismissed depends upon ambiguous words spoken by the employer: for a discussion of such dismissals (see paras 3.09–3.10). This is what happened in *Hogg v Dover College*.[1] The employee, a teacher, became ill and after a period of absence returned to part-time teaching. The headmaster wrote him a letter in which he expressed the view that his ill-health made it impossible for him to continue as a department head and offered him fewer teaching periods at a considerably reduced salary. The employee replied claiming that the letter amounted to a dismissal but that pending his claim of unfair dismissal he would continue to work at the college on the terms offered. The EAT held that the effect of the letter was to terminate the contract and that he had been dismissed. Alternatively, the changes in the terms of employment were such that he had been constructively dismissed; his subsequent conduct did not amount to an affirmation of what was a totally different contract.

3.72   Occasionally, a resignation may be treated as an actual dismissal. This was the case in *Caledonian Mining Co Ltd v Bassett*,[2] where the employees were inveigled into resigning by the employers who had the intention of depriving them of their statutory rights.

3.73   Finally, it may be noted that a constructive dismissal is not automatically unfair and that in certain circumstances it may be fair.[3] In *Cawley v South Wales Electricity Board*,[4] however, the EAT said that considerations of fairness under section 98(4) of the ERA 1996 and the considerations affecting constructive dismissal are 'two sides of the same coin'. So if the employer's behaviour is unreasonable enough to amount to a constructive dismissal, it should also be unfair. In cases of constructive dismissal, an employer who maintains that the employee resigned but who wishes to have the chance of arguing, in the event that the employment tribunal decides that there was a constructive dismissal, that the dismissal was fair, should ensure that the notice of appearance (Form IT3) is drafted appropriately.

(d) Employee leaving early

3.74   In respect of unfair dismissal, section 95(2) provides that an employee under notice of dismissal will be treated as dismissed where, within the period of the employer's notice, he or she gives notice to terminate the contract on a date earlier than the employer's notice would

---

[1]   [1990] ICR 39. See also *Millbrook Furnishing Industries Ltd v McIntosh* [1981] IRLR 309 and *McNeill v Charles Crimin (Electrical Contractors) Ltd* [1984] IRLR 179.
[2]   [1987] ICR 425.
[3]   *Savoia v Chiltern Herb Farms Ltd* [1982] IRLR 166.
[4]   [1985] IRLR 89.

expire. If, therefore, the employee, upon being given notice by the employer, walks out without giving any notice at all, he or she will be treated as not having been dismissed.[1] Provided, however, that he or she gives some notice (not necessarily that which is required to be given under the contract or under section 86(2)), the statutory requirement will have been satisfied.[2] On that view, notice amounts to no more than notification. In cases of this kind, the effective date of termination of the employee's contract will be the date on which he or she ceases working in accordance with the counter-notice and not the date when the employer's notice would have expired.[3] This means that the three-month limitation period for presenting a complaint of unfair dismissal will start to run from the date when the counter-notice takes effect.

3.75 Section 136(3) of the ERA 1996 obliges an employee who is given notice of dismissal for redundancy to give a counter-notice in writing during the 'obligatory period of notice', and the counter-notice must terminate the contract earlier than the date of expiry of the employer's notice. An employee who fails to comply with section 136(3) will be treated as not dismissed. The definition of obligatory period in section 136(4) means that, for an employee who is entitled to four weeks' notice and receives four weeks' notice, the obligatory period is the whole of the notice period; if he or she is entitled to four weeks' notice but receives eight weeks' notice, the obligatory period is the last four weeks of that eight-week period. In this context, it should be noted that the relevant date will be the date on which the employee's counter-notice expires.[4]

3.76 The provisions of section 136(3) and (4) are unnecessarily complex and provide a trap for the unwary or ignorant,[5] although the EAT has managed to mitigate their rigour in some cases by finding a mutually agreed variation of the date of expiry of the employer's notice, and thus to protect employees who might otherwise have fallen outside the statutory provisions.[6]

---

[1] *Walker v Cotswold Chine Home School* (1977) 12 ITR 342.
[2] *Ready Case Ltd v Jackson* [1981] IRLR 312. See also *TBA Industrial Products Ltd v Morland* [1982] ICR 686.
[3] *Thompson v GEC Avionics Ltd* [1991] IRLR 488. The employer's notice was given on 15 August 1990 to expire on 9 November. The employee's counter-notice was dated 20 September and she announced that she would be terminating her employment on 21 September. The employment tribunal decided that the effective date of termination was 21 September, and their decision was upheld by the EAT.
[4] Section 145(3).
[5] See, eg, *Pritchard-Rhodes Ltd v Boon* [1979] IRLR 19.
[6] As in *Tunnel Holdings Ltd v Woolf* [1976] ICR 387 and *CPS Recruitment Ltd, trading as Blackwood Associates v Bowen and Secretary of State for Employment* [1982] IRLR 54. *Cf TBA Industrial Products Ltd v Morland* [1982] ICR 686.

(e) Effect of offers of alternative employment in redundancy cases

(i) General rules

3.77   The provisions governing offers of re-engagement and alternative employment are amongst the most complex to be found in Part XI of the ERA 1996 (which deals with employees' right to redundancy payments). They operate in two separate ways: either they affect the question whether or not employees are to be treated as having been dismissed, considered here; or they operate to disentitle them from receiving a redundancy payment which would otherwise be payable; this aspect is considered in Chapter 6. There is the additional complicating factor of the trial period: this comes into operation in both cases where the offer of new employment differs at all from the terms of the previous employment. The trial period provisions are considered separately in the next section. The statutory provisions[1] also apply in certain cases where there is a change of employer; these are considered after the trial period.

3.78   Section 138 deals with the situation where an employee who is under notice of redundancy (or who has been constructively dismissed) is offered alternative employment. The point of its provisions, which follow on from the basic definition of dismissal in section 136 (considered at para 3.04), is to determine in what circumstances the employee is to be treated as having been dismissed. As will be seen from the discussion below, there are circumstances in which an employee will be treated as not having been dismissed. In such circumstances, there will be no entitlement to a redundancy payment, simply because entitlement to a payment depends upon having been dismissed for redundancy and, therefore, if there is no dismissal, there can be no entitlement. However, once the employee is found to have been dismissed, he or she may be disentitled from receiving the payment which would otherwise be payable if there is held to have been an unreasonable refusal of a suitable offer.[2] The disentitling provisions are considered in Chapter 6.

3.79   The trial period provisions in section 138 build on the basic structure of section 136 by setting out the circumstances in which a trial period will come into operation. If an employee unreasonably terminates the employment during the trial period, that act will disentitle him or her from the right to receive a payment.

3.80   Section 138 caters for two alternative possibilities: either that the terms and conditions of the new employment are the same as those of the old, or that they are different. In both cases, there must be an offer of a renewal of the contract or of re-engagement under a new contract; an offer of re-engagement must be made before the ending of the employment under the previous contract. The renewal or re-engagement must take effect immediately on the ending of the previous employment, or within

---

[1]   ERA 1996, s 146(1).
[2]   ERA 1996, ss 141 and 146.

four weeks.[1] If any of the conditions are not complied with, there will be a dismissal. Where the new contract is the same as the old, and all the conditions of section 138(1) are complied with, there will be no dismissal and section 213(2) will preserve continuity of employment. In *SI (Systems and Instruments) Ltd v Grist and Riley,*[2] the EAT said that, on a proper construction of what is now section 138(1) (formerly section 84(1) of the EPCA 1978), a distinction is to be drawn between cases of renewal and re-engagement. In cases of renewal, the offer need not be made before the termination of the contract of employment, but in cases of re-engagement under a new contract, the offer must be made before termination. 'Renewal' includes 'extension'.[3]

(ii) Trial period

3.81   Where the provisions of the new contract differ at all from the provisions of the previous contract, section 138(2) brings a trial period into operation. If the employee leaves or is dismissed during the trial period, he or she will be treated as having been dismissed under the previous contract. An employee whose termination of the contract during the trial period is held to be unreasonable will be disentitled from receiving a redundancy payment: see Chapter 6.

3.82   The coming into operation of the trial period occurs in all cases whether the old contract is renewed or the employee is re-engaged under a new contract and where there is a difference between the terms and conditions of the new contract and the corresponding provisions of the previous contract, unless it is one to which the de minimis rule applies.[4] The trial period generally starts with the ending of the previous contract and ends four weeks from the date on which the employee starts work under the new contract, by virtue of section 138(3). In *Benton v Sanderson Kayser Ltd,*[5] the question arose as to the meaning 'period of four weeks', used by what is now section 138(3)(b). The employee was made redundant from midnight on 21/22 December 1986 and was offered a four-week trial period doing different work, starting immediately following the termination of his employment. On 16 January 1987, he gave notice of his wish to terminate his employment from Monday, 19 January, some eight hours after the expiry of the trial period. The tribunal rejected the employee's argument that, as the employer's premises had been closed for 11 days over the Christmas period, he had not been given the opportunity

---

[1]   For what constitutes a valid offer, see *The Singer Co (UK) Ltd v Ferrier* [1980] IRLR 300. Note the provisions of s 146(2) in relation to contracts which end on a Friday, Saturday or Sunday.

[2]   [1983] ICR 788. The EAT decision in *EBAC Ltd v Wymer* [1995] ICR 466 suggests that what is now s 138(1) is relevant to an unfair dismissal claim. That cannot be regarded as correct, however, since the unfair dismissal provisions of the ERA (Pt X) and the redundancy payments provisions (Pt XI) are self-contained codes. *Cf Jones v Governing Body of Burdett Coutts School* [1997] ICR 390.

[3]   ERA 1996, s 235(1).

[4]   *Rose v Henry Trickett & Sons Ltd* (1971) 6 ITR 211 at p 215.

[5]   [1988] ICR 313 (EAT) and [1989] ICR 136 (CA).

of completing a four-week trial period at work. It held that once the four weeks had expired it had no jurisdiction to hear his claim. The EAT allowed his appeal, and held that 'period of four weeks' had to be related to the words 'trial period' and that 'trial period' could only be understood as meaning a period of trial actually at work. The trial period had not, therefore, expired when the employee terminated his employment. The Court of Appeal rejected that approach and held that 'period of four weeks' means a period of four consecutive weeks calculated according to the calendar, rather than the period of time actually worked.

3.83 The trial period may only be extended, by agreement between the parties, for the purpose of retraining the employee and the agreement must comply with the requirements of section 138(6). An extension for any other reason will have no effect. This means that an employee who decides to leave during the period of the extension will be held to have resigned.[1] An employee who leaves during the trial period or who is dismissed by the employer (for a reason connected with or arising out of the change in the contract) will be treated as having been dismissed on the date on which the previous contract ended and for the reason for which that contract was ended.[2] Similar considerations apply where there is more than one renewal of the original contract or the employee is again re-engaged under a new contract. Section 138 applies also to offers of re-engagement with associated employers.[3] It may be noted that a refusal to offer an employee a trial period may cause the dismissal to be unfair.[4]

3.84 In cases of constructive dismissal, the rules set out above will apply, but with the added complication that a so-called common law trial period will come into existence. This means that if, in breach of the contract, the employee is transferred to another department and takes the job there on trial, he or she has a reasonable period in which to decide whether to take the new job or leave (the 'common law' trial period). If he or she decides to take it, the statutory trial period then comes into operation.[5] The difficulty with this is that, since the employee is granted a reasonable time under the common law trial period to make up his or her mind, it is not easy to know when the statutory trial period has started and whether, when the employee left the employment, the statutory period had ended or not. If it had, there will have been no dismissal and the employee will be held to have resigned.

3.85 If the employee leaves during the trial period, entitlement to a redundancy payment will be lost if the new employment was suitable, and

---

[1]   *Meek v J Allen Rubber Co Ltd and Secretary of State for Employment* [1980] IRLR 21.
[2]   ERA 1996, s 138(4). Note the extended meaning of 'relevant date' in s 145(4) for situations covered by this provision. For a discussion of the date of termination, see below.
[3]   See s 146(1). The meaning of 'associated employer' is discussed in Chapter 1.
[4]   *Elliot v Richard Stump Ltd* [1987] ICR 579.
[5]   *Air Canada v Lee* [1978] ICR 1202 and *Turvey v CW Cheyney & Son Ltd* [1979] ICR 341. See also *East Suffolk Local Health Services NHS Trust v Palmer* [1997] ICR 425.

the termination of the employment during the trial period was unreasonable.[1] For a consideration of what is unreasonable, see Chapter 6.

(iii) Change of employer

3.86 The statutory provisions discussed in the preceding sections apply equally to associated employers of the original employer. This means that an offer of employment made by an associated employer is as good as an offer made by the original employer and the provisions of section 138 apply in the same way to an employee who is offered employment by an associated employer.[2] Provided that the person offering employment is within the definition of 'associated employer', it does not matter that the associated employer has no employees at the time of the offer of employment and is a dormant company reactivated especially for the purpose of offering employment to the redundant employee(s).[3] The effect of these provisions is that an employee who accepts the offer of employment with an associated employer cannot be said to have been dismissed and will not be able to claim a redundancy payment.

3.87 In other cases, the transferee of the business may incur liability. This will depend upon whether there has been a transfer of an undertaking within the Transfer of Undertakings Regulations 1981 or whether section 218(2) of the 1996 Act applies. These issues were considered in Chapter 2, to which reference should be made.

2. THE DATE OF TERMINATION

3.88 One of the most important reasons for identifying the date of termination is that the limitation period for bringing a claim starts to run from that date. An error may mean that the claim is presented late with the consequence that the tribunal has no jurisdiction. A further reason for identifying the date of termination is that that is the date which is relevant for the purposes of calculating unfair dismissal compensation or a redundancy payment.

In this section, the general rules in relation to actual and constructive dismissal cases will be considered first; the rules governing postponements of the date of termination will then be examined.

---

[1] ERA 1996, s 141(4).

[2] ERA 1996, s 146(1).

[3] *Lucas v Henry Johnson (Packers & Shippers) Ltd* [1986] ICR 384. The EAT rejected the argument that the associated company could not be said to be an 'employer' within what is now s 146(1) because it had no employees at the time of the offer of employment. It held that, since the requirements of ss 138(1) and 146(1) were satisfied, the employees taken on by the associated employer could not claim redundancy payments, since they could not be said to have been dismissed by the original employer.

(a) The general rules

(i) In actual dismissal cases

3.89   The date of termination, in cases in which the employee is actually dismissed by the employer or where the expiry of a fixed term contract is treated as a dismissal, is one of the following:

1. if the dismissal is with notice, the date on which the notice expires; or
2. if the dismissal is without notice, the date on which the notice takes effect; or
3. if the dismissal is constituted by the expiry of a fixed-term contract, the date on which the term expires.[1]

The date of termination is called the 'effective date of termination' in the unfair dismissal provisions and the 'relevant date' in the redundancy payments provisions.

3.90   It can often be difficult to decide the difference between a dismissal with notice when the employee is not required to work out the notice and a summary dismissal, particularly if in both cases the employee receives a payment of wages. The speech of Lord Browne-Wilkinson in *Delaney v Staples (t/a De Montfort Recruitment)*[2] contains a discussion of what is meant by payments in lieu of notice, in which he set out four categories of payments in lieu of notice:

1. a termination with notice, where the employer tells the employee not to come to work until the termination date and gives him or her the wages attributable to the notice period in a lump sum;
2. a termination in circumstances where the contract of employment provides expressly that the employment may be terminated either by notice or, on payment of a sum in lieu of notice, summarily;
3. an agreement at the end of the employment between employer and employee that the employment is to terminate immediately on payment of a sum in lieu of notice; and
4. a summary dismissal by the employer, without the agreement of the employee, together with a payment in lieu of notice.

In the first three cases, as Lord Browne-Wilkinson pointed out, there is no breach of contract. In the fourth case, the employer is in breach of contract and 'the summary dismissal is effective to put an end to the employment relationship, whether or not it unilaterally discharges the contract of employment'.[3] These observations are certainly helpful in the present context, although it should be borne in mind that the case in

---

[1]   ERA 1996, ss 97 and 145.
[2]   [1992] ICR 483 at pp 488–489.
[3]   *Ibid* at p 489.

question arose in the context of the Wages Act 1986 (now Part II of the ERA 1996).

3.91   For an employee dismissed with notice who is told that there is no need to work out the notice and given a payment attributable to the notice period in a lump sum (ie effectively on paid or 'garden' leave), the date of termination will be the date when the notice expires.[1] If, on the other hand, he or she is dismissed without notice and with a payment in lieu of notice, the date of termination is either the date when the summary dismissal is communicated,[2] or, if he or she is given notice of an impending dismissal with wages in lieu of notice, the date when the dismissal takes effect.[3] In *McMaster v Manchester Airport plc*,[4] the EAT held that the effective date of termination cannot be earlier than the date on which the employee receives knowledge that he or she is being dismissed. It refused to accept the argument that if the employers could reasonably have expected the employee to be at home to receive the post, he should be deemed to have knowledge of the contents of the letter and said that the doctrine of constructive or presumed knowledge has no place in questions of this kind. In *Newman v Polytechnic of Wales Students Union*,[5] the EAT suggested that, in a case of summary dismissal, the date of termination is the date of communication of the dismissal, irrespective of whether the decision to dismiss was, at the time of communication, invalid as a result of irregularities affecting the meeting at which it was reached.

3.92   The date of termination is the date given in the employer's notice, but it must be clear that the employment is actually being terminated. In *Widdicombe v Longcombe Software Ltd*,[6] for example, letters passed between the parties relating to the employee's continued employment with the employers. The correspondence indicated that there was a continuing situation where the parties were either assuming that the employment was continuing or that it was going to be terminated at some future date. Eventually the employers wrote the employee a letter (dated 26 April 1996) stating that he had relinquished his employment. The EAT treated this letter as a letter of dismissal on the grounds that that was the first letter to contain a clear indication that the employment was being terminated. The employee's complaint was presented within three months of the date of that letter and was therefore treated as presented in time. In cases such as

---

[1]   As in *Dixon v Stenor Ltd* [1973] ICR 157, *Adams v GKN Sankey Ltd* [1980] IRLR 416 and *Chapman v Letheby & Christopher Ltd* [1981] IRLR 440.

[2]   A summary dismissal effected by letter will not take effect until the employee reads the letter or has a reasonable opportunity of reading it: see *Brown v Southall & Knight* [1980] ICR 617 at pp 628–629.

[3]   See *Dedman v British Building and Engineering Appliances Ltd* [1974] ICR 53, *Robert Cort & Son Ltd v Charman* [1981] ICR 816, and *Belling & Lee Ltd v Burford* [1982] ICR 454. In *West v Kneels Ltd* [1987] ICR 146, the employers gave the employee a 'week's notice from now'. The EAT said that it was in accordance with good industrial practice that seven days' notice meant seven clear days.

[4]   [1998] IRLR 112.

[5]   [1995] IRLR 72.

[6]   [1998] ICR 710.

this, it is important for the employer to state the position clearly, since any ambiguity will be resolved against them.

3.93   In cases involving payments in lieu of notice, the tribunal must hear evidence of what actually was said when the employee was dismissed, to enable it to decide whether the dismissal was summary or was with notice but without a requirement to work during the notice period.[1] The P45 form, which an employer should give to the employee when the employment is terminated, generally has nothing to do with the date on which the employment terminates,[2] although the handing of the P45 to the employee may be treated as evidence of a dismissal at the time it is handed over.[3]

3.94   There is nothing in section 97(1) to prevent the parties retrospectively agreeing a date of termination, even though the employee's contract subsists after that date.[4] The parties may also agree that the employee should leave earlier than the date of expiry of the employer's notice. If this takes place at the employee's request, that will not bring forward the date of termination, according to the Court of Appeal in *TBA Industrial Products Ltd v Morland*.[5] The same result would appear to apply if the substitution of the earlier date is at the employer's request, according to the decision of the Court of Appeal in *Staffordshire County Council v Secretary of State for Employment*.[6] In that case, and despite the decision in *TBA Industrial Products Ltd v Morland*, it would seem preferable to treat as the date of termination the earlier date, irrespective of which party initiated the bringing forward of the employee's date of departure. Similar considerations apply in cases where the employee gives a counter-notice to terminate the contract on a date earlier than the date when the employer's notice would expire.[7] In cases of this kind, the effective date of termination of the employee's contract will be the date on which he or she ceases working in accordance with the counter-notice and not the date when the employer's notice would have expired.[8] This means that the three-month

---

[1]   *Leech v Preston Borough Council* [1985] ICR 192.

[2]   *London Borough of Newham v Ward* [1985] IRLR 509.

[3]   *Hassan v Odeon Cinemas Ltd* [1998] ICR 127. The facts of the case were unusual in that the employee was suspended by the employers and subsequently charged with a criminal offence; it was a condition of bail that he was required to live outside London and so he went to Liverpool, but failed to notify his employers of his new address. He did not receive subsequent communications from the employer and on 16 March 1996 returned to London and asked the employers if he could resume work. They handed him a P45 showing a leaving date of 23 September 1995. The EAT held that his employment ended on 16 March when he was handed his P45.

[4]   *Crank v Her Majesty's Stationery Office* [1985] ICR 1, followed in *Lambert v Croydon College* [1999] ICR 409.

[5]   [1982] ICR 686.

[6]   [1989] ICR 664.

[7]   For a discussion of the statutory provisions governing counter-notices, see para 3.75.

[8]   *Thompson v GEC Avionics Ltd* [1991] IRLR 488. The employer's notice was given on 15 August 1990 to expire on 9 November. The employee's counter-notice was dated 20 September and she announced that she would be terminating her employment on 21 September. The employment tribunal decided that the effective date of termination was 21 September, and its decision was upheld by the EAT.

limitation period for presenting a complaint of unfair dismissal will start to run from the date when the counter-notice takes effect.

3.95   A dismissal with notice may be converted into a summary dismissal if the employer dismisses the employee on the spot during his or her notice period (see para 3.14). That will bring forward the date of termination to the date of the summary dismissal.[1]

3.96   Problems may also arise when the employee invokes a domestic appeals procedure, although much will depend upon what the contract actually provides. For example, it may provide that the contract is to continue until the appeal is determined. In that case, there will be no difficulty. As Simon Brown LJ pointed out in *Drage v Governing Body of Greenford High School*,[2] in cases where contractual provision is made for an internal appeal, the critical question is whether during the period between the initial notification of dismissal and the outcome of the appeal the employee is (a) dismissed with the possibility of reinstatement, or (b) suspended with the possibility of the proposed dismissal not being confirmed and the suspension thus being ended. In the former case, the effective date of termination will be the date of the original decision; in the latter it will be the date when the dismissal is confirmed and the employee's appeal is unsuccessful. The facts of the *Drage* case were that the employee, a teacher, was notified of the school's staff committee's decision to dismiss him. He appealed against the decision and remained suspended on full pay until the appeal was heard, when his appeal was dismissed. The question was whether the effective date of termination was the original date of the decision to dismiss or the date on which his appeal was dismissed and the dismissal was confirmed. Simon Brown LJ construed the school's disciplinary procedure and articles of government as referring to a dismissal in the sense of a decision that the teacher should be dismissed with the decision not being implemented until the outcome of the appeal hearing. The date of the dismissal was the date on which the appeal hearing confirmed the original decision to dismiss.

3.97   The other category of case, where there is a dismissal with the possibility of reinstatement, is represented by *J Sainsbury Ltd v Savage*,[3] which Simon Brown LJ in the *Drage* case said was 'clearly rightly decided'.[4] In that case, the contractual scheme provided as follows:

> 'Pending the decision of an appeal to a director against dismissal, the employee will be suspended without pay, but if reinstated, will receive full back pay for the period of suspension.'

Slynn J said:[5]

---

[1]   *Stapp v The Shaftesbury Society* [1982] IRLR 326.
[2]   [2000] ICR 899 at p 909.
[3]   [1981] ICR 1.
[4]   [2000] ICR 899 at p 909D.
[5]   [1979] ICR 96 at p 102.

'In our view, when a notice of immediate dismissal is given, the dismissal takes immediate effect. The provisions of this contract as to the appeal procedure continue to apply. If an appeal is entered, then the dismissed employee is to be treated as being "suspended" without pay during the determination of his appeal, in the sense that if the appeal is successful then he is reinstated and he will receive full back-pay for the period of the suspension. If the appeal is not successful and it is decided that the original decision of instant dismissal was right and is affirmed, then the dismissal takes effect on the original date. In our view, that is the date on which the termination takes effect for the purposes of the Act.'

Beldam LJ said of this statement: 'I find it difficult to improve on the reasoning of the Employment Appeal Tribunal'. The Court of Appeal upheld the decision of the EAT that the effective date of termination in this kind of case is the date of the original dismissal and that, the employee is to be treated, pending the decision on appeal, as suspended without pay; if the appeal is unsuccessful, the date of termination will be the date of the original dismissal.[1] In *West Midlands Co-operative Society Ltd v Tipton*,[2] the House of Lords approved the Court of Appeal's statement of the position.

3.98   In cases where there is no contractual disciplinary procedure but payments of salary are made to the employee in respect of a period after the original dismissal, that may give rise to the conclusion that there was a dismissal with effect from a future date.[3]

3.99   A question associated with the preceding discussion may occasionally arise, although it is unlikely to occur very often: when did the employment terminate? In *Octavius Atkinson & Sons Ltd v Morris*,[4] the facts were that the employee was dismissed summarily on 29 August; he left the site where he was working at about 2 pm and reached home at about 4 pm. At about 4 pm, the employers were asked to supply more men for another job but no attempt was made to contact the employee to offer him the work. He complained of unfair dismissal on the footing that his employment did not terminate until midnight on 29 August and, therefore, that he was still employed when work became available. The employment tribunal and the EAT upheld his complaint, but the Court of Appeal reversed that decision and held that his employment ended when he was summarily dismissed at lunchtime. The employers were not therefore obliged to offer him employment at 4 pm.

---

[1]   See also *Crown Agents for Overseas Governments and Administration v Lawal* [1979] ICR 103. In *Batchelor v British Railways Board* [1987] IRLR 136, a similar conclusion was reached in the case of an employee who was dismissed summarily in breach of British Rail's contractual disciplinary procedure. The Court of Appeal held that the fact that the employers were not entitled to dismiss summarily for the conduct in question did not alter the fact that the date of termination was the date of the summary dismissal.

[2]   [1986] ICR 192.

[3]   *The Board of Governors, The National Heart and Chest Hospitals v Nambiar* [1981] ICR 441. See also *High v British Railways Board* [1978] IRLR 52.

[4]   [1989] ICR 431.

3.100   An employment tribunal is unlikely to extend the limitation period for the presentation of a complaint of unfair dismissal in the case of an employee who fails to present the complaint in time because of a domestic appeals procedure.[1] In such cases, the employee should make sure to present the complaint within three months of the original date of termination and should not wait for a domestic appeals procedure to take its course.

(ii) In constructive dismissal cases

3.101   There is no express provision dealing with the date of termination in constructive dismissal cases. This means that a tribunal will need to apply by analogy the provisions of sections 97 or 145, as appropriate. In *Edwards v Surrey Police*,[2] the EAT said that in a constructive dismissal case the employee must communicate by words or conduct that he or she is terminating the employment. Only then will time start to run for the purposes of the three-month limitation period.

3.102   *BMK Ltd and BMK Holdings Ltd v Logue*[3] involved an employee who, for the purposes of the case, was treated as having been constructively dismissed in consequence of two resolutions of the board of directors removing him as a director of the two companies. He became aware by 17 March 1992 that he had been removed, but was unsure of his position; on that date his solicitors wrote to the controlling shareholder which had been responsible for removing him. On 18 March, he received a letter by fax informing him of his removal. He presented his complaint of unfair dismissal on 17 June. He sought to argue that there was not a termination until he had accepted the repudiation. The EAT held that on the facts of the particular case the relationship of employer and employee had ended by 17 March, and, therefore, his complaint was out of time. It was at pains to stress that it was not laying down a hard and fast rule applicable to all cases.

3.103   The facts of the above case are uncommon, and it is submitted that the decision should be regarded as being confined to its own facts. In many constructive dismissal cases, the employer commits a repudiatory act and the employee continues to work until such time as he or she decides to resign. In such a case, the earliest date for the ending of the employment would be the date of the resignation, but, if it is a resignation with notice, the effective date of termination should be the date when the notice expires. That should be the general rule. In exceptional cases, such as the *Logue* case, the repudiatory act may be treated as putting an immediate end to the relationship, in which case the effective date of termination will be the date when the employment relationship is to be treated as having ended.

---

[1]   See *Bodha (Vishnudut) v Hampshire Area Health Authority* [1982] ICR 200. See also Chapter 12.

[2]   [1999] IRLR 456.

[3]   [1993] ICR 601.

(b) Postponement of the date of termination

3.104   The statutory date of termination may be postponed in the following circumstances:

1.   where the notice given by the employer is shorter than the notice which the employee is entitled to under section 86 of the ERA[1]; and
2.   where the employee terminates the contract with or without notice but the notice required by section 86 to be given to the employee would have expired later, had the employer given such notice.[2]

3.105   In relation to both unfair dismissal and redundancy payments claims, where the notice given by the employer would expire earlier than the notice required to be given by section 86 of the ERA 1996, the later date is treated as the date of termination.[3] For example, if the employee is entitled under section 49 to eight weeks' notice and receives only four, he or she will be treated as having received eight weeks' notice and the date of termination will be when the eight weeks' notice would have expired. This postponement of the date of termination is only for certain purposes, however. The main purposes are:

1.   calculating whether an employee has sufficient continuity of employment under section 108(1) (in the cases of unfair dismissal) or section 155 (in cases of redundancy payments claims);
2.   calculating the years of employment for the purposes of a basic award of compensation; and
3.   calculating the years of employment for the purposes of a redundancy payment: see Chapter 8.

    It should be noted that the date of termination is only extended by the statutory minimum notice entitlement, not by any minimum contractual notice entitlement.[4] It should also be noted that the purposes for which the extensions may take place are limited to those specified in the ERA and to no others.[5] Section 92 of the 1996 Act, which entitles an employee to a written statement of reasons for dismissal, contains a similar provision[6] (see para 4.05).

3.106   It is important to have the statutory provisions in mind in the case of employees who are dismissed with less notice than they are entitled to under section 86. An employee dismissed summarily shortly before the expiry of a complete year of continuous employment may be treated as dismissed on a date falling after the expiry of the complete year of continuous employment, with the result that he or she is treated as having

---

[1]   ERA 1996, ss 97(2) and (3) and 145(5).
[2]   ERA 1996, s 97(4) and (5).
[3]   ERA 1996, ss 97(2) and (3) and 145(5).
[4]   *Fox Maintenance Ltd v Jackson* [1976] ICR 110.
[5]   *Staffordshire County Council v Secretary of State for Employment* [1989] ICR 664 at p 672G.
[6]   See s 92(7).

an extra year of continuous employment; that, in turn, will affect the size of the basic award or redundancy payment.[1]

3.107   The second type of postponement of the date of termination (see above) only operates in relation to unfair dismissal claims where the employee terminates the contract either with or without notice and for the same purposes as those set out above. In that case the date on which the employer's notice under section 86 (had it been given) would have been required to expire is treated as the effective date of termination.

---

[1]   Basic awards of compensation and redundancy payments are calculated according to complete years of employment, not fractions of years: ERA 1996, ss 119(1) and (2) and 162(1)–(3).

Chapter 4

UNFAIR DISMISSAL: THE GENERAL RULES

1. THE REASON FOR DISMISSAL

4.01   Once it has been established that the employee has been dismissed, an unfair dismissal claim will fall to be decided in two stages. The first stage consists of establishing what was the reason for the dismissal. Reasons may be divided into two categories:

1.   what may be called 'potentially fair' reasons; and
2.   reasons which, subject to certain exceptions, make a dismissal automatically unfair (eg dismissals for reasons relating to trade union membership or activities, or relating to leave for family reasons).

4.02   The second category is discussed in the next chapter. At the second stage (discussed later in this chapter), the tribunal must be satisfied that the employer acted reasonably in dismissing for the given reason, unless the reason is one of those which makes the dismissal automatically unfair. The 'potentially fair' reasons are so called because they can potentially justify dismissal, but they do not necessarily justify dismissal, since section 98(4) obliges the tribunal to decide whether the employer acted reasonably or unreasonably in treating the reasons as sufficient for dismissing the employee.

4.03   In a complaint of unfair dismissal involving the potentially fair reasons, section 98(1) places the burden on the employer to show the reason (or, if there was more than one, the principal reason) for the dismissal. He or she must then show that the reason falls within one of the four specific categories set out in section 98(2), namely:

1.   capability or qualifications;
2.   the employee's conduct;
3.   redundancy; or
4.   statutory requirements.

In addition, there is what may be called a residual category, which, in the phraseology of the statute, is 'some other substantial reason of a kind such as to justify the dismissal of an employee holding the position which that employee held'.[1] These are discussed more fully below.

---

[1]   ERA 1996, s 98(1)(b).

4.04   As part of the process of establishing the reason for the dismissal the Employment Rights Act 1996 contains a provision, section 92, under which an employee is entitled to be given a written statement of reasons for the dismissal by the employer. This right is considered first, after which the 'potentially fair' reasons will be considered.

(a) Written statement of reasons under section 92

4.05   Section 92 of the ERA 1996 gives to a dismissed employee[1] the right to be given a written statement giving particulars of the reasons for the dismissal by his or her employer. The following categories of employees are excluded from the right:

1.   employees continuously employed for less than one year,[2] unless dismissed whilst pregnant or after childbirth in circumstances in which their ordinary or additional maternity leave period ends by reason of the dismissal;[3]
2.   share fishermen;[4] and
3.   those employed in police service.[5]

It should be noted that Crown employees are included within the statutory entitlement,[6] as are members of the armed forces,[7] House of Commons staff,[8] and House of Lords staff.[9] These groups are considered more fully in Chapter 1, to which reference should be made.

4.06   The employee's entitlement is to be provided with a written statement giving particulars of the reasons for the dismissal. But the employee must first ask for the written statement, which should be given by the employer within 14 days of the employee's request. In addition, an employee who is dismissed, either while she is pregnant, or after childbirth in circumstances in which her ordinary or additional maternity leave period ends by reason of her dismissal, will be entitled to be provided with a written statement. The entitlement is irrespective of length of

[1]   By virtue of s 92(1), employees who are entitled are those dismissed with or without notice or whose fixed-term contract has expired.
[2]   See s 92(3), (6) and (7). Section 209(1) and (5) gives the Secretary of State the power to vary or exclude the operation of s 92(3) by means of an order under that section. Section 92(3) was amended by the Unfair Dismissal and Statement of Reasons for Dismissal (Variation of Qualifying Period) Order 1999, SI 1999 No 1436, so that with effect from 1 June 1999 the qualifying period of employment was reduced from two years to one year.
[3]   See s 92(4), as amended by the Employment Relations Act 1999, s 9 and Sch 4, Pt III, paras 1, 5 and 12.
[4]   See s 199(2).
[5]   See s 200(1).
[6]   See s 191(1) and (2).
[7]   See s 192(1) and (2). At the time of going to press these provisions had not been brought into effect. Until they are, the provisions in Sch 2, para 16 continue to have effect.
[8]   See s 195(1) and (2).
[9]   See s 194(1) and (2).

employment and does not depend upon the employee first making a request.[1]

4.07   If the employer unreasonably *fails* to provide a written statement in either of the cases set out in the preceding paragraph or provides one containing inadequate or untrue particulars, the employee may present a complaint to the employment tribunal within three months of the date of termination.[2] It should be noted that the emphasised word 'fails' was introduced by the Trade Union Reform and Employment Rights Act 1993. The previous word was 'refuses'. This change clearly extends the possible circumstances in which an employer may be held liable and overrules a previous decision of the EAT[3] that a failure to provide written reasons cannot be equated with a refusal. The case-law relating to the previous version of section 92[4] is set out below, but should be considered in the light of the amendment already mentioned.

If the tribunal finds the complaint well-founded, it may make a declaration as to what it finds to have been the employer's reasons for dismissing the employee; it must also award the employee two weeks' pay.[5]

4.08   Section 93 is a penal section. The EAT has therefore held that it should be rigidly construed and that there should be clear evidence that there has been an unreasonable refusal.[6] A refusal (and, it may be, failure) cannot be said to be unreasonable where it is based upon a conscientious belief that there has been no dismissal.[7] A statement of reasons is not untrue if the employer genuinely believes that the reason given is the reason for the dismissal. It is not necessary for the employment tribunal to embark upon a consideration of whether the reason was good or bad.[8] It is not sufficient compliance with section 93 merely to rely upon the answer put in to the employee's original application; the statute clearly contemplates an independent and separate document.[9]

4.09   The document must be of such a kind that the employee, or anyone to whom he or she may wish to show it, can know from reading the document itself why the employee has been dismissed, and it may refer to other documents provided that the document the employee receives

---

[1]   Section 92(4), as amended by the Employment Relations Act 1999, s 9 and Sch 4, Pt III, paras 1, 5 and 12.

[2]   Section 93.

[3]   In *Ladbroke Entertainments Ltd v Clark* [1987] ICR 585.

[4]   Formerly s 53 of the EPCA 1978.

[5]   Section 93(2).

[6]   *Charles Lang & Sons Ltd v Aubrey* [1978] ICR 168. See also *Lowson v Percy Main & District Social Club and Institute Ltd* [1979] ICR 568 and *Newland v Simons and Willer (Hairdressers) Ltd* [1981] IRLR 359, where the EAT held not to be unreasonable a failure to reply for seven weeks.

[7]   *Brown v Stuart Scott & Co* [1981] ICR 166. See also *Broomsgrove v Eagle Alexander Ltd* [1981] IRLR 127. Cf *Daynecourt Insurance Brokers Ltd v Iles* [1978] IRLR 335.

[8]   *Harvard Securities Ltd v Younghusband* [1990] IRLR 17.

[9]   *Rowan v Machinery Installations (South Wales) Ltd* [1981] IRLR 122.

contains a simple statement of the essential reasons for the dismissal.[1] In *Gilham v Kent County Council (No 1)*,[2] the Court of Appeal said that what is now section 93 is sufficiently complied with if the employer's response to a request refers to other documents containing reasons. It also said that where the employee appoints a legal adviser, the employer need only communicate with the adviser; it is not necessary to communicate with the employee personally.

4.10   In cases under sections 92 and 93, the employment tribunal may only hear complaints relating to statements issued in response to an employee's request;[3] if the employer voluntarily gives a written statement, the employee will not be able to complain about it unless the employer refers to it and effectively adopts it in response to the employee's request.[4]

4.11   Written statements are admissible in evidence in any proceedings.[5] If the employer gives another reason in subsequent litigation, the tribunal would either ignore that other reason and hold the employer to the original statement or treat the change of reason as going to the employer's credibility.

(b) Reasons within the Employment Rights Act 1996

(i) Generally

4.12   As was mentioned at the beginning of this chapter, in a complaint of unfair dismissal involving the potentially fair reasons, section 98(1) places the burden on the employer to show the reason (or, if there was more than one, the principal reason) for the dismissal. He or she must then show that the reason falls within one of the four specific categories set out in section 98(2), namely:

1.   capability or qualifications;
2.   the employee's conduct;
3.   redundancy; or
4.   statutory requirements.

In addition, there is what has been called a residual category, which, in the phraseology of the statute, is 'some other substantial reason of a kind such as to justify the dismissal of an employee holding the position which that employee held'.[6]

4.13   In unfair dismissal cases where the reason is redundancy (which is one of the potentially fair reasons set out above), section 7(6) of the Employment Tribunals Act 1996 suspends the operation of the

---

[1]   *Horsley Smith & Sherry Ltd v Dutton* [1977] ICR 594 at p 597. See also *Marchant v Earley Town Council* [1979] ICR 891.
[2]   [1985] ICR 227.
[3]   See *Catherine Haigh Harlequin Hair Design v Seed* [1990] IRLR 175.
[4]   As happened in *Marchant v Earley Town Council*, above.
[5]   ERA 1996, s 92(5).
[6]   Section 98(1)(b).

presumption of redundancy where, in the same proceedings, the employment tribunal determines a claim for a redundancy payment and a complaint of unfair dismissal. Thus, as in other unfair dismissal cases, the burden is on the employer to show the reason for the dismissal. In pure redundancy cases, that is cases brought under section 135 of the 1996 Act, on the other hand, section 163(2) enacts a presumption that the employer dismissed the employee for redundancy. This means that the burden is on an employer who wishes to dispute liability to prove that the employee was not redundant. Unfair dismissals by reason of redundancy are considered in Chapter 6, together with the other statutory provisions governing dismissals for redundancy.

4.14   The burden of establishing the reason, or principal reason, for the dismissal lies upon the employer. If he or she fails to do so, the dismissal will be deemed unfair.[1] In *Maund v Penwith District Council,*[2] the Court of Appeal gave guidance on applying the burden of proof, particularly where there is a dispute between the parties as to the real reason. Where the employer discharges the burden of proving the reason, but the employee wishes to challenge that reason and show a competing reason, the employee need only show, without actually proving, that there is an issue warranting investigation and capable of establishing the competing reason; once the employee, on evidence, establishes the existence of such an issue, the burden of proving which one of the competing reasons is the principal reason remains on the employer.

4.15   In *Abernethy v Mott, Hay and Anderson,*[3] Cairns LJ said:

'A reason for the dismissal is a set of facts known to the employer, or it may be beliefs held by him, which cause him to dismiss the employee. If at the time of his dismissal the employer gives a reason for it, that is no doubt evidence, at any rate as against him, as to the real reason, but it does not necessarily constitute the real reason. He may knowingly give a reason different from the real reason out of kindness or because he might have difficulty in proving the facts which actually led him to dismiss; or he may describe his reasons wrongly through some mistake of language or of law.'

So an incorrect label will not be fatal to the employer's case. In *Clarke v Trimoco Group Ltd,*[4] the EAT applied the *Abernethy* case to a situation where the reason relied upon in the dismissal letter and the notice of appearance (misconduct) was found by the employment tribunal not to be the real reason for the dismissal, which was different and more serious misconduct. This conclusion was reached on the ground that the real reason why they were dismissed was found to be obvious to the employees concerned. The dismissal was not therefore made unfair by this fact. In *Ely v YKK Fasteners*

---

[1]   See, for example, *Adams v Derby City Council* [1986] IRLR 163.

[2]   [1984] ICR 143.

[3]   [1974] ICR 323 at p 330. The reason given was 'redundancy', but the real reason was the employee's capability. See also *Trust Houses Forte v Aquilar* [1976] IRLR 251, *Stacey v Babcock Power Ltd* [1986] ICR 221 and *Yusuf v Aberplace Ltd* [1984] ICR 850.

[4]   [1993] ICR 237. See also *Burkett v Pendletons (Sweets) Ltd* [1992] ICR 407.

(UK) Ltd,[1] the Court of Appeal said that the *Abernethy* case could be applied by analogy 'to enable resort to be had to a state of facts known to and relied upon by the employer, for the purpose of supplying him with a reason for dismissal, which, as a consequence of his misapprehension of the true nature of the circumstances, he was disabled from treating as such at the time'. That Court upheld the tribunal's decision that the employee's late notification to his employers that he had changed his mind about resigning could amount to 'some other substantial reason' within section 98(1)(b).

4.16   The Court of Appeal has made it clear that, where a dismissal is by notice, the employer's reason for the dismissal should be determined both by reference to the reason for giving the notice of dismissal and by reference to the reason when the dismissal occurs.[2] This means that the tribunal must consider the reasons throughout the notice period. In *Alboni v Ind Coope Retail Ltd,*[3] the tribunal considered evidence relating to what had occurred between the date the employee was given notice of dismissal and the date when the dismissal took effect and concluded that the employers had acted reasonably and that the dismissal was fair. The EAT allowed the employers' appeal and said that the tribunal should not have taken account of what happened after notice of termination had been given. The Court of Appeal allowed the employers' appeal against that decision and restored the decision of the tribunal.

4.17   It may be possible for an employer to have a change of mind in the course of a hearing, provided that the same facts are relied on and the employee is not put at a disadvantage by the change. But in cases involving serious allegations, such as suspected dishonesty, the reason should be stated at the outset; if the employment tribunal allows it to be added, it should make sure that it is put to the employee with sufficient formality and at an early stage in the case, so that he or she has a full opportunity to answer it. In *Hotson v Wisbech Conservative Club,*[4] for example, the employee was dismissed for inefficiency, but in the course of evidence it became clear that she was dismissed for suspected dishonesty. The EAT allowed the employee's appeal against the tribunal's decision that she was fairly dismissed, on the grounds that a great deal more than a change of label was involved and that she was deprived of a proper opportunity of dealing with the much more serious allegation of dishonesty and of being sufficiently prepared to state her answer at the hearing. Particularly in relation to capability and conduct, the employer will discharge the burden of showing the reason if it is possible to establish that he or she held a genuine (even if mistaken) belief, for example, that the employee was guilty of a crime.[5]

---

[1]   [1994] ICR 164.
[2]   See *Parkinson v March Consulting Ltd* [1998] ICR 276 and *White v South London Transport Ltd* [1998] ICR 293.
[3]   [1998] IRLR 131. See also *West Kent College v Richardson* [1999] ICR 511.
[4]   [1984] ICR 859.
[5]   *Monie v Coral Racing Ltd* [1981] ICR 109.

4.18   If, however, the employer relies upon one particular reason and the reason is not established, it is not possible to try to rely upon an entirely different reason either at the tribunal hearing or upon appeal, although it may, of course, be possible to apply for leave to amend the notice of appearance.[1] An error of characterisation of the reason for the dismissal by the tribunal is an error of law, since it is a question of legal analysis to determine under which part of section 98 the reason given by the employer falls.[2] In *Burkett v Pendleton (Sweets) Ltd*,[3] the EAT said that it is an error of law for an employment tribunal to make its decision based on a reason for the dismissal which is different from that pleaded or argued and to fail to give the parties an opportunity to deal with the different ground in presenting their case to the tribunal. It went on to say that, even where the tribunal's finding is merely a different label to that given by the parties to the matters raised in argument, it is desirable where the parties are unrepresented or have lay representatives that the issues should be spelt out during argument rather than merely being left to a question of labelling by the tribunal of the employer's reason for dismissal. The House of Lords' decision in *Smith v Glasgow City District Council*[4] makes it clear that an employment tribunal must be careful in making its finding as to the reason or principal reason for the dismissal.

4.19   The employer may not adduce evidence of what happened after the dismissal or of events which occurred before the dismissal but which did not come to his or her knowledge until afterwards.[5] Although the consequence may be a finding that the employee was unfairly dismissed, the evidence will be relevant to the question of remedies.

4.20   It should be noted that section 107 debars the tribunal from taking into account any industrial pressure exerted on the employer to obtain the dismissal, when determining the reason for the dismissal. This is discussed more fully later: see Chapter 5.

(ii) Capability and qualifications
4.21   'Capability' means 'capability assessed by reference to skill, aptitude, health or any other physical or mental quality', and 'qualifications' means 'any degree, diploma or other academic, technical or professional qualification relevant to the position which the employee held'.[6] In *Shook v Ealing London Borough Council*,[7] the EAT stressed that

---

[1]   *Nelson v BBC (No 1)* [1977] ICR 649. The reason given was redundancy, but the Court of Appeal held that the tribunal was wrong in deciding that he had been dismissed for redundancy, and that the EAT was not entitled to apply the facts found to a possible but unpleaded defence of 'some other substantial reason'. See also *Murphy v Epsom College* [1985] ICR 80.
[2]   *Wilson v Post Office* [2000] IRLR 834.
[3]   [1992] ICR 407.
[4]   [1987] ICR 796. See also *British Railways Board v Jackson* [1994] IRLR 235.
[5]   *W Devis & Sons Ltd v Atkins* [1977] ICR 662. This was applied by the EAT in *Vauxhall Motors Ltd v Ghafoor* [1993] ICR 376.
[6]   Section 98(3).
[7]   [1986] ICR 314.

under section 98(2)(a) the reason for dismissal must relate to the employee's capacity and to the performance of his or her duties under the contract of employment. It is not necessary to show that the employee's incapacity (in this case disabilities caused by back trouble) would have affected the performance of all that he or she might be required to do under the contract.

4.22   A failure to pass aptitude tests may relate to both capability and qualifications.[1] The most common case to arise under this heading is ill-health, which can include mental health.[2] It should be borne in mind that, in cases of serious or long-term illness, the contract of employment may be frustrated (see para 3.18). Questions relating to the discovery of relevant medical reports may arise.[3]

4.23   The other case which commonly arises is lack of capability. The EAT has indicated that it should be viewed relatively narrowly as applying mainly to cases where the employee is incapable of satisfactory work, and that cases where a person has not come up to standard through his or her own carelessness, negligence or idleness, are better dealt with as cases of conduct rather than capability. The difference is between 'sheer incapability due to an inherent incapacity to function' and 'a failure to exercise to the full such talent as is possessed'.[4]

(iii) Conduct

4.24   There is no statutory definition of 'conduct'. Apart from the overlap between conduct and capability, conduct itself has been held to embrace a wide range of actions. Its scope includes gross misconduct, such as theft, violence, negligence and working in competition with the employer, and lesser matters, such as clocking offences or swearing. What may be called 'off-duty' conduct will fall within this head, if it in some way bears upon the relationship between the employer and the employee, particularly where criminal offences are involved.[5] The category may also embrace the situation where the employee conceals previous convictions in order to obtain a job.[6]

It should be noted that, as in the case of capability and qualifications, the reason must relate to the conduct in question.

---

[1]   *Blackman v Post Office* [1974] ICR 151.

[2]   *O'Brien v Prudential Assurance Co Ltd* [1979] IRLR 140. See also *Shook v London Borough of Ealing* [1986] ICR 314.

[3]   See, for example, *Ford Motor Company Ltd v Nawaz* [1987] ICR 434.

[4]   *Sutton & Gates (Luton) Ltd v Boxall* [1978] ICR 67 at p 71. See also *James v Waltham Holy Cross Urban District Council* [1973] ICR 398 and *Cook v Thomas Linnell & Sons Ltd* [1977] ICR 770.

[5]   *Singh v London Country Bus Services Ltd* [1976] IRLR 176, *Nottinghamshire County Council v Bowly* [1978] IRLR 252, *Norfolk County Council v Bernard* [1978] IRLR 220, *Moore v C & A Modes* [1981] IRLR 71 and *P v Nottinghamshire County Council* [1992] ICR 706.

[6]   *Torr v British Railways Board* [1977] ICR 785.

(iv) Redundancy

4.25   This is considered in Chapter 6.

(v) Statutory requirements

4.26   The fourth potentially fair reason, set out in section 98(2)(d), is that 'the employee could not continue to work in the position which he held without contravention (either on his part or that of his employer) of a duty or restriction imposed by or under an enactment'.

An example would be the loss of a driving licence in the case of a person employed as a driver, or a teacher declared unsuitable by the Department of Education.[1] The EAT has held, however, that the fact that the employers genuinely but erroneously believe that they will contravene a statutory requirement cannot be a reason falling within section 98(2)(d), although it might be 'some other substantial reason'.[2] The fact that the continued employment of the employee contravenes a statutory requirement does not exonerate the employer from acting reasonably.[3]

(vi) Some other substantial reason

4.27   The fifth category of reason is what was earlier called a residual category. It is stated in section 98(1)(b) as being 'some other substantial reason of a kind such as to justify the dismissal of an employee holding the position which the employee held'. These words are not to be construed *ejusdem generis* with the other four potentially fair reasons. That means that this is a fairly wide category of reasons.[4] The most common examples relate to the business needs of the employer and have tended to involve a refusal by the employee to agree to a change in contractual terms[5] or a refusal to agree to a reorganisation falling short of redundancy.[6] But this category is wide enough to embrace other reasons, for example the dismissal of one spouse as a result of the dismissal of the other.[7] As a matter of procedure, the EAT has held that an employment tribunal is entitled to find that an employee's dismissal following a reorganisation was for some other substantial reason, despite the fact that the dismissal was by reason of redundancy and the alternative ground was not pleaded nor canvassed in argument at the tribunal hearing: '[W]here the different grounds are really different labels and nothing more then there is no basis for saying that the

---

[1]   As in *Sandhu v Department of Education and Science and London Borough of Hillingdon* [1978] IRLR 208. See also *Sutcliffe & Eaton Ltd v Pinney* [1977] IRLR 349.

[2]   *Bouchaala v Trusthouse Forte Hotels Ltd* [1980] ICR 721.

[3]   *Sandhu v Department of Education and Science and London Borough of Hillingdon*, above.

[4]   *RS Components Ltd v Irwin* [1973] ICR 535.

[5]   *Ibid*. The employee in that case refused to agree to the introduction of a restraint of trade clause into his contract. See also *St John of God (Care Services) Ltd v Brooks* [1992] ICR 715, which involved changes in contractual terms and conditions, particularly pay and benefits.

[6]   *Hollister v National Farmers' Union* [1979] ICR 542.

[7]   See *Kelman v Oran* [1983] IRLR 432 and *Scottish and Newcastle Retail Ltd v Stanton and Durrant* (EAT 1126/96) IDS Brief 596.

late introduction, even without pleading or without argument, is a ground for interference on appeal'.[1]

4.28   Several cases involving this category of reason have reached the Court of Appeal in recent years. In those cases 'some other substantial reason' has been held to include dismissals instigated by a third party,[2] the expiry and non-renewal of a fixed-term contract,[3] the imposition of a sentence of imprisonment,[4] and a mistake as to the employee's intentions (brought about by his late notification to the employers that he had changed his mind about resigning).[5] In *Kent County Council v Gilham (No 2)*,[6] in which the employer's reason for dismissal was the need to achieve economies, the Court of Appeal said the burden on the employer of showing a substantial reason is designed to deter employers from dismissing employees for some trivial or unworthy reason. If, on the face of it, the reason could justify the dismissal, then it passes as a substantial reason. This test must not be confused with the section 98(4) test. The Court of Appeal held that the employer's reason amounted to a substantial reason for the employee's dismissal.

4.29   Section 106 provides that two reasons for dismissal are to be treated as some other substantial reason:

1.   the dismissal of a replacement for a permanent employee suspended on medical grounds; and
2.   the dismissal of a replacement for a pregnant employee absent from work.

For a fuller discussion see Chapter 5.

4.30   The Transfer of Undertakings (Protection of Employment) Regulations 1981 (as amended) also provide[7] that where, either before or after a relevant transfer, the employee is dismissed because of economic, technical or organisational reasons entailing changes in the workforce of either the transferor or transferee, the dismissal will be treated as being for some other substantial reason; the tribunal will then have to consider section 98(4): see Chapter 5. Transfers of undertakings are considered more fully in Chapter 2.

---

[1]   *Hannan v TNT-IPEC (UK) Ltd* [1986] IRLR 165 at p 168.
[2]   *Dobie v Burns International Security Services (UK) Ltd* [1984] ICR 812. See also *Grootcon (UK) Ltd v Keld* [1984] IRLR 302.
[3]   *North Yorkshire County Council v Fay* [1986] ICR 133.
[4]   *Kingston v British Railways Board* [1984] ICR 781.
[5]   *Ely v YKK Fasteners (UK) Ltd* [1994] ICR 164.
[6]   [1985] ICR 233.
[7]   See reg 8(2).

2. THE PROCEDURE USED FOR DISMISSAL

(a) Generally

4.31   Once a potentially fair reason under the ERA 1996 has been established, it is then necessary to consider whether the employer acted fairly in dismissing for that reason. It is important to remember that the effect of section 98(4) is that there is no burden of proof on either the employer or the employee. It is therefore wrong for an employment tribunal to place on the employer the burden of satisfying them that he or she acted reasonably.[1]

4.32   At the outset, it is important to bear in mind that differences in the approach of appellate courts to the question of reasonableness will determine the extent to which the managerial decisions of employers are justiciable by employment tribunals and the judgments of the employment tribunals are subject to control by appellate courts. This is a recurrent theme in the case-law of the EAT and the Court of Appeal.

4.33   The Court of Appeal has stressed that appeals to the EAT and beyond only lie on points of law and has discouraged attempts to dress up questions of fact as questions of law.[2] But it is clear that the question of fairness cannot be considered solely as one of fact, and therefore unappealable. It is best described as a mixed question of fact and law.[3] The tenor of the Court of Appeal decisions is to restrict considerably the circumstances in which appeals may be made to the EAT from employment tribunals' decisions and to discourage the EAT from reversing the tribunal's decisions because it would have reached a different conclusion. In *Neale v Hereford and Worcester County Council*,[4] May LJ in the Court of Appeal said:

> 'Their [*sc* the employment tribunal's] job is to find the facts, and to apply the relevant law and to reach the conclusion to which their findings and their experience lead them. It will not ... be often that when an employment tribunal has done just that, and with the care, clarity and thoroughness which the employment tribunal in the present case displayed, that one can legitimately say that their conclusion "offends reason", or that their conclusion was one to which no reasonable employment tribunal could have come. Deciding these cases is

---

[1]   *Post Office (Counters) Ltd v Heavey* [1990] ICR 1, *Boys and Girls Welfare Society v McDonald* [1996] IRLR 129 and *Hackney LBC v Usher* [1997] ICR 705.

[2]   *Bailey v BP Oil (Kent Refinery) Ltd* [1980] ICR 642, *Thomas & Belts Manufacturing Ltd v Harding* [1980] IRLR 255, *W & J Wass Ltd v Binns* [1982] ICR 486, *Woods v WM Car Services (Peterborough) Ltd* [1982] IRLR 413, *O'Kelly v Trusthouse Forte plc* [1983] ICR 728, *Martin v Glynwed Distribution Ltd* [1983] ICR 511, *Dobie v Burns International Security Services (UK) Ltd* [1984] ICR 812 and *Gilham v Kent County Council (No 2)* [1985] ICR 233 and *Piggott Brothers & Co Ltd v Jackson* [1992] ICR 85. See also *East Berkshire Health Authority v Matadeen* [1992] ICR 723.

[3]   In *Piggott Brothers & Co Ltd v Jackson* [1992] ICR 85 at p 89, Lord Donaldson of Lymington MR said: 'Reasonableness is to be categorised as a mixed issue of fact and law, but the factual element predominates'. See also *British Railways Board v Jackson* [1994] IRLR 235.

[4]   [1986] ICR 471.

the job of employment tribunals and when they have not erred in law neither the appeal tribunal nor this court should disturb their decision unless one can say in effect: "My goodness, that was certainly wrong."'[1]

4.34   In following this in the later case of *Piggott Brothers & Co Ltd v Jackson*,[2] Lord Donaldson of Lymington MR said of the above statement:

> '[This] is an approach which is not without its perils ... The danger of the approach of May LJ is that an appellate court can very easily persuade itself that, as it would certainly not have reached the same conclusion, the tribunal which did so was "certainly wrong" ... It does not matter whether, with whatever degree of certainty, the appellate court considers that it would have reached a different conclusion. What matters is whether the decision under appeal was a permissible option. To answer that question in the negative ..., the appeal tribunal will almost always have to be able to identify a finding of fact which was unsupported by any evidence or a clear self-misdirection in law by the employment tribunal. If it cannot do this, it should re-examine its preliminary conclusion that the decision under appeal was not a permissible option and has to be characterised as "perverse".'

4.35   This approach may be characterised as the 'reasonable decision' approach. It was summarised by Browne-Wilkinson J in *Iceland Frozen Foods Ltd v Jones*,[3] in words quoted with approval by the Court of Appeal in the *Neale* case, above:

> 'The correct approach ... is as follows:
>
> (1)   the starting point should always be the words of section [98(4)] themselves;
> (2)   in applying the section an employment tribunal must consider the reasonableness of the employer's conduct, not simply whether they (the members of the employment tribunal) consider the dismissal to be fair;
> (3)   in judging the reasonableness of the employer's conduct an employment tribunal must not substitute its decision as to what was the right course to adopt for that of the employer;
> (4)   in many, though not all, cases there is a band of reasonable responses to the employee's conduct within which one employer might take one view, another quite reasonably take another;
> (5)   the function of the employment tribunal, as an industrial jury, is to determine whether in the particular circumstances of each case the decision to dismiss the employee fell within the band of reasonable responses which a reasonable employer might have adopted. If the dismissal falls within the band the dismissal is fair: if the dismissal falls outside the band, it is unfair.'

---

[1]   [1986] ICR 471 at p 483.
[2]   [1992] ICR 85 at p 92.
[3]   [1983] ICR 17 at pp 24–25.

4.36   This approach was considered anew by the Court of Appeal in *Foley v Post Office*,[1] as a result of a decision of the EAT in *Haddon v Van den Bergh Foods Ltd*[2] suggesting that the approach was misconceived. Mummery LJ robustly endorsed the *Iceland Frozen Foods* approach saying that the decision itself, which had been approved and applied by the Court of Appeal,[3] 'remains binding on this court, as well as on the employment tribunals and the Employment Appeal Tribunal'. He described the disapproval by the EAT of that approach as 'an unwarranted departure from authority'. Bearing in mind that for some ten months after the EAT's decision in *Haddon* the employment tribunals were confronted with conflicting authorities and did not know what approach to take to this issue, Mummery LJ's remarks might be regarded as restrained. It would not be going too far to characterise the EAT's decision in *Haddon* as irresponsible.

4.37   It has been stressed that the tribunal must not substitute its own view for that of the employer.[4] This has been emphasised by the recent decisions of the EAT (in *Beedell v West Ferry Printers Ltd*) and the Court of Appeal (in *Foley v Post Office*).[5] If, however, the subjective view of the employer were the sole determinant, the tribunal's ability to consider the reasonableness of the action would be almost eliminated; equally, to say that the tribunal could take an entirely objective view would mean that the tribunal would be able to review every case and apply its own views to the facts (and thus to substitute its own views for those of the employer), an approach which the courts have held that the tribunals must not adopt. The favoured approach appears to be a mixture of the two. Thus it is permissible to look at the employer's honest and genuine belief, but the belief must be upon reasonable grounds.[6]

4.38   Another aspect of the tribunal's role concerns the question it should ask, since, if it asks the wrong question, its decision will be liable to be upset on appeal. The appellate courts have stressed that the relevant question is whether it was reasonable of the employer to dismiss the employee and that in many cases there may be a range of courses of action open to the employer, all of which fall within the band of reasonableness; for an employment tribunal to prefer one course of action to another will

---

[1]   [2000] ICR 1283. For a full analysis of the history of the relevant case-law, reference should be made to the EAT's decision in *Beedell v West Ferry Printers Ltd* [2000] ICR 1263, which did not follow the *Haddon* decision.

[2]   [1999] ICR 1150.

[3]   In *Gilham v Kent County Council (No 2)* [1985] ICR 233, *Neale v Hereford and Worcester County Council* [1986] ICR 471, *Campion v Hamworthy Engineering Ltd* [1987] ICR 966 and *Morgan v Electrolux Ltd* [1991] ICR 369.

[4]   Eg by Phillips J in *Grundy (Teddington) Ltd v Willis* [1976] ICR 323 and *NC Watling & Co Ltd v Richardson* [1978] ICR 1049. See also *Securicor Ltd v Smith* [1989] IRLR 356.

[5]   [2000] ICR 1263 and [2000] ICR 1283, respectively.

[6]   See *St Anne's Board Mill Co Ltd v Brien* [1973] ICR 444, *W Devis & Sons Ltd v Atkins* [1977] ICR 662 and *Alidair Ltd v Taylor* [1978] ICR 445 (particularly at pp 450–451, *per* Lord Denning MR).

cause it to apply the test of what it would have done itself and not the test of what a reasonable employer would have done.[1]

4.39   In deciding upon the fairness or otherwise of the dismissal, the tribunal must take into account any relevant provision of the Code of Practice on Disciplinary Practice and Procedures in Employment.[2] Section 207(1) of the Trade Union and Labour Relations (Consolidation) Act 1992[3] stresses that a failure by the employer does not 'of itself' make him or her liable to any legal proceedings; it goes on to say that the Code is admissible in evidence in proceedings in employment tribunals and that 'any provision of the Code which appears to the tribunal ... to be relevant to any question in the proceedings shall be taken into account in determining that question'.[4] In *W Devis & Sons Ltd v Atkins*,[5] Viscount Dilhorne said that non-compliance with the Code does not necessarily make a dismissal unfair, but that a failure to follow a procedure prescribed in the Code may lead to the conclusion that a dismissal was unfair, which, if that procedure had been followed, would have been held to have been fair. This approach was followed by the EAT in *Beedell v West Ferry Printers Ltd*.[6] The decision of the EAT in *Lock v Cardiff Railway Company Ltd*[7] appears to go further by suggesting that a failure by an employment tribunal to take into account the Code of Practice and to examine whether it has been complied with will vitiate the tribunal's decision.

4.40   The effect of the existence of section 98(4) (and its predecessors) and the Code of Practice is that considerable importance has been attached to the notion of procedural fairness, ie the possibility that a dismissal may be made unfair by the use of an unfair procedure (eg lack of warnings or opportunity for the employee to state his or her side of the case), even where the reason is a perfectly good one.

4.41   Two additional points should be noted. First, until the decision of the House of Lords in *Polkey v AE Dayton Services Ltd*[8] it was thought that, if the employment tribunal came to the conclusion that the employer's conduct was unreasonable, but, had a correct procedure been followed in dismissing the employee, the result would still have been the same, the tribunal should go on to find that the dismissal was in fact fair. This approach was based on the cases of *British Labour Pump Co Ltd v Byrne*[9] and

---

[1]   *British Leyland (UK) Ltd v Swift* [1981] IRLR 91 (CA), *NC Watling & Co Ltd v Richardson* [1978] ICR 1049, *Iceland Frozen Food Ltd v Jones* [1983] ICR 17 and *Neale v Hereford and Worcester County Council* [1986] ICR 471. See also *Whitbread & Co plc v Mills* [1988] ICR 776.

[2]   Issued pursuant to ss 199(1) and 200(4) and (5) of the Trade Union and Labour Relations (Consolidation) Act 1992, previously s 6(1) and (8) of the Employment Protection Act 1975. The most recent Code of Practice came into effect on 4 September 2000.

[3]   Formerly, s 6(11) of the Employment Protection Act 1975.

[4]   Section 207(2) of the Trade Union and Labour Relations (Consolidation) Act 1992.

[5]   [1977] ICR 662 at p 679.

[6]   [2000] ICR 1263.

[7]   [1998] ICR 358.

[8]   [1988] ICR 142.

[9]   [1979] ICR 347.

W & J Wass Ltd v Binns,[1] which were overruled by the House of Lords in the *Polkey* case. Lord Mackay of Clashfern LC, who gave the main speech in the House of Lords, adopted the analysis of Browne-Wilkinson J in *Sillifant v Powell Duffryn Timber Ltd.*[2] In that case, the judge stressed that the only test of the fairness of a dismissal is the reasonableness of the employer's decision to dismiss, judged at the time at which the dismissal takes effect. He did suggest, however, that there may be rare cases 'where the offence is so heinous and the facts so manifestly clear that a reasonable employer could, on the facts known to him at the time of dismissal, take the view that whatever explanation the employee advanced it would make no difference …'.[3] Browne-Wilkinson J went on to say that, if the decision to dismiss was unfair in the circumstances, but the observance of fair procedure would have made the dismissal fair, the correct approach would be for there to be a finding of unfair dismissal but a reduction in the employee's compensation.[4] Secondly, the Court of Appeal has said, *obiter*, that it can see no reason why section 98(4) should be construed and applied in any way differently from the way it was before the Human Rights Act 1988 came into force.[5]

(b) Right to be accompanied at disciplinary and grievance hearings

4.42   In view of the fact that much of the text in this part of the chapter is devoted to a consideration of the procedure used by the employer when dismissing the employee, mention should be made of the right given by the Employment Relations Act 1999 to a *worker*[6] to be accompanied at a disciplinary or grievance hearing.[7] Section 10 of the Act applies where a worker is 'required or invited' by the employer to attend a disciplinary or grievance hearing and 'reasonably requests' to be accompanied at the hearing.[8] The employer must allow the worker to be accompanied by a single companion chosen by the worker. The companion must either by a trade union official,[9] an official of a trade union reasonably certified in writing by the union as having experience of, or as having received training in, acting as a worker's companion at disciplinary or grievance hearings, or another of the employer's workers.[10] In this last case, the

---

[1]   [1982] ICR 486.

[2]   [1983] IRLR 91 at p 97.

[3]   *Ibid.*

[4]   *Loc cit* at p 96. This approach was supported in the *Polkey* case at p 157, *per* the Lord Chancellor and at p 163, *per* Lord Bridge of Harwich; Lord Bridge cited *Earl v Slater & Wheeler (Airlyne) Ltd* [1972] ICR 508 as an example of this principle. See also *Mining Supplies (Longwall) Ltd v Baker* [1988] IRLR 417 and Chapter 8.

[5]   *The Post Office v Liddiard* (2001) IDS Brief B690/6, CA.

[6]   'Worker' is defined in ERA 1999, s 13(1)–(3). The definition includes agency workers and home workers (as defined).

[7]   Defined in ERA 1999, s 13(4) and (5).

[8]   ERA 1999, s 10(1).

[9]   Within the meaning of ss 1 and 119 of the Trade Union and Labour Relations (Consolidation) Act 1992.

[10]   ERA 1999, s 10(3).

employer should allow the fellow-worker reasonable time off during working hours to accompany the worker.[1]

4.43   The employer must allow the companion to address the hearing (but not answer questions on the worker's behalf) and to confer with the worker during the hearing.[2] Section 10(4) and (5) provide for the situation where the companion will not be available at the time chosen by the employer for the hearing. In that case, the employer must postpone the hearing to the time proposed by the worker provided that it is reasonable and is within five working days beginning with the first working day after the day proposed by the employer.

4.44   A worker who complains that the right has been infringed may present a complaint to an employment tribunal within three months of the date of the infringement or threatened infringement.[3] If the tribunal finds the complaint well-founded, it must order the employer to pay compensation of up to two weeks' pay.[4] No award should be made if the tribunal makes a supplementary award under section 127A(2) of the ERA 1996.[5]

4.45   The final point to note is that the right not to be unfairly dismissed is extended to workers who exercise or seek to exercise their rights under section 10(2) or (4) *and* to workers who accompany or seek to accompany another worker.[6] Further, the exclusions relating to length of employment and age[7] do not apply. Section 12(6) specifically applies the unfair dismissal provisions to workers.

(c) Capability and qualifications

4.46   Two aspects of this potentially fair reason have given rise to a considerable amount of litigation: unsatisfactory work performance and ill-health. These are considered in turn in this section.

(i) Work performance

4.47   In cases of this kind, the employer must satisfy the employment tribunal that he or she honestly believed on reasonable grounds that the employee was incapable.[8] A full and careful investigation of the facts should be undertaken; if, however, that is done, the employer does not

---

[1]   ERA 1999, s 10(6).

[2]   ERA 1999, s 10(2).

[3]   ERA 1999, s 11(1) and (2). Section 11(2)(b) permits the tribunal to extend the time-limit where it was not 'reasonably practicable' to present the complaint in time. This is the same wording as s 111(2)(b) in the case of complaint of unfair dismissal. See also Chapter 12.

[4]   ERA 1999, s 11(3). Note also s 11(4) and (5).

[5]   These may be made in connection with the employee's failure to use an internal appeal procedure or the employer's failure or refusal to permit use of it (see Chapter 8, para 8.124).

[6]   ERA 1999, s 12(3).

[7]   See ERA 1996, ss 108 and 109.

[8]   *Alidair Ltd v Taylor* [1978] ICR 445.

have to satisfy the tribunal that he or she drew the correct conclusion, only that he or she had sufficient evidence upon which he or she could reach that conclusion.[1] It is necessary for the employer to follow a reasonable procedure, and, in particular, to give the employee a warning and an opportunity to improve, but a failure to do so will not automatically make the dismissal unfair, particularly if it can be shown that the employee is incapable of improving or already knows clearly what is expected,[2] or that the giving of a warning would have made no difference to the result.[3]

4.48   In exceptional cases, it may not be necessary to follow a procedure. But that is only likely to be an option where the employee can be shown to be clearly incapable of improving or to know already what is expected. In *Cook v Thomas Linnell & Sons Ltd*,[4] for example, the employee became manager of the employers' depot concerned with the supply of food to retailers on a cash and carry basis. Before that, he had been manager of a depot dealing with hardware and had had no previous experience of supplying food. The employers were dissatisfied with the standard of his work at the depot, which failed to improve despite warnings and advice. He was offered the managership of a non-food depot elsewhere at the same salary but he refused and was dismissed. The employment tribunal decided that the decision to dismiss was fair; the EAT upheld its decision. It said that the correct question which the employment tribunal ought to consider was whether the employers acted reasonably in treating the employee's lack of capacity as a sufficient reason for dismissing him. It said that when responsible employers genuinely come to the conclusion over a reasonable period of time that a manager is incompetent, that is some evidence of his incapacity to perform the job. But it stressed that there must be supporting evidence. It also said that when dealing with alleged incapability, the complaints must be brought to the employee's attention over a period of time. It added that this is so even where the employee holds a position in which he or she can be expected to monitor his or her own performance.

(ii) Ill-health

4.49   When cases involving ill-health occur, particularly if the employee suffers from long-term or severe illness, the contract may be frustrated, in which case there will be no dismissal. This aspect has already been considered.[5]

---

[1]   *Cook v Thomas Linnell & Sons Ltd* [1977] ICR 770.
[2]   *Hollister v National Farmers' Union* [1979] ICR 542, and *James v Waltham Holy Cross Urban District Council* [1973] ICR 398.
[3]   *AJ Dunning & Sons (Shopfitters) Ltd v Jacomb* [1973] ICR 448. But *cf Polkey v AE Dayton Services Ltd* [1988] ICR 142, in the light of which the principle stated in the text should be re-assessed.
[4]   [1977] ICR 770.
[5]   See Chapter 3.

4.50   The employer must deal with ill employees carefully, particularly if the employee is suffering from mental illness.[1] In cases of prolonged absence, the question is whether the employer can be expected to wait any longer, and, if so, how much longer.[2] Except in exceptional circumstances, the employee should be consulted and the employer should take reasonable steps to find out the true medical position, preferably by means of a sufficiently detailed medical report to enable an informed decision to be made.[3] There is no equivalent duty on an employee to indicate to the employer his or her prospects of recovery.[4] In this context, questions of discovery of medical reports may arise.[5] The EAT has stressed that the decision to dismiss is managerial, not medical, but the employer should consider the possibility of offering alternative work within the employee's capabilities, if it is available.[6] It has been held that, if prior consultation would not have made any difference, the dismissal will not be made unfair by lack of consultation.[7] These cases should probably not be followed now, however, in view of the House of Lords' decision in *Polkey v AE Dayton Services Ltd.*[8]

4.51   In cases of persistent, intermittent absence for minor illness, the employer should conduct a fair review of the employee's attendance record and the reasons for it, and give the employee appropriate warnings and an opportunity to make representations.[9] This type of situation was considered by the EAT in *Lynock v Cereal Packaging Ltd,*[10] in which the employee had a poor attendance record. Despite receiving a final written warning, there was no substantial improvement in his performance and in February 1986, the employers decided to dismiss him. After a successful appeal, the dismissal was rescinded and replaced by two weeks' suspension without pay and a final written warning on an indefinite basis. It was made clear to him that an appreciable and sustained improvement in his attendance was required. He was subsequently off sick for two weeks and two days in July 1986, one day in October 1986, two weeks in April 1987 and one day in June 1987, all for unconnected reasons. That amounted to some improvement but his attendance record was still below average.

---

[1]   As in *O'Brien v Prudential Assurance Co Ltd* [1979] IRLR 140. See also *Gillies v Scottish Equitable Life Assurance Society* (EAT 295/88) and *Halton Borough Council v Hollett* (EAT 559/87).

[2]   *Spencer v Paragon Wallpapers Ltd* [1977] ICR 301 at p 307.

[3]   *East Lindsey District Council v Daubney* [1977] ICR 566, *Williamson v Alcan Ltd* [1978] ICR 104, *A Links & Co v Rose* [1991] IRLR 353 and *Eclipse Blinds Ltd v Wright* [1992] IRLR 133. See also *Seymour v British Airways Board* [1983] ICR 148, which concerned the dismissal of a disabled employee.

[4]   *Mitchell v Arkwood Plastics (Engineering) Ltd* [1993] ICR 471.

[5]   For an example, see *Ford Motor Co Ltd v Nawaz* [1987] ICR 434.

[6]   *Merseyside and North Wales Electricity Board v Taylor* [1975] ICR 185. *Cf Taylorplan Catering (Scotland) Ltd v McInally* [1980] IRLR 53.

[7]   See *Taylorplan Catering (Scotland) Ltd v McInally* [1980] IRLR 53 and *Shook v London Borough of Ealing* [1986] ICR 314. *Cf Townson v The Northgate Group Ltd* [1981] IRLR 382.

[8]   *Loc cit.*

[9]   *International Sports Co Ltd v Thomson* [1980] IRLR 340. See also *London Borough of Tower Hamlets v Bull* (EAT 153/91) IDS Brief 498.

[10]   [1988] ICR 670.

He was dismissed on 1 July 1987 on the grounds that he had failed to reach the required standard of attendance. The employment tribunal held that his dismissal was fair, as did the EAT. The EAT said that where unconnected, intermittent periods of absence are concerned, it is impossible to give a reasonable prognosis or projection of the possibility of what will happen in the future. An employer may make inquiries, but there is no obligation on him or her to do so because the results may produce nothing of assistance to him. The EAT went on to say that in deciding whether to dismiss an employee with a poor record on intermittent sickness absence, a disciplinary approach involving warnings is not appropriate. Factors which may prove important to an employer in reaching the decision to dismiss include the nature of the illness, the likelihood of it recurring or of some other illness arising, the length of the various absences and the periods of good health between them, the need of the employer for the work of the particular employee, the impact of the absences on others who work with the employee, the adoption and carrying out of the policy, the important emphasis on a personal assessment in the ultimate decision and the extent to which the difficulty of the situation and the position of the employer has been made clear to the employee so that he or she realises that the point of no return may be approaching. It emphasised that the approach of the employer should be based on sympathy, understanding and compassion.[1]

4.52 A final point to note concerns claims made both under the Disability Discrimination Act 1995 and the unfair dismissal provisions. The EAT has pointed out that a tribunal should not hold a dismissal which is contrary to the DDA to be automatically unfair.[2] It pointed out that it should be possible to have a disability-related dismissal which is not necessarily unfair, since the criteria applying under the DDA and the unfair dismissal provisions are different.

(d) Conduct

4.53 As with cases of unsatisfactory work performance, the employer must show that his or her view of the facts stemmed from an honest belief based upon reasonable grounds; it is also important to undertake a careful investigation which provides sufficient evidence for the conclusion reached.[3] In *British Home Stores Ltd v Burchell*,[4] the EAT set out the following guidelines for tribunals to apply when dealing with cases of alleged misconduct:

'First ... there must be established by the employer the fact of that belief; that the employer did believe it. Secondly, that the employer had in his mind

---

[1] [1988] ICR 670 at p 675.

[2] In *HJ Heinz Co Ltd v Kenrick* [2000] IRLR 144.

[3] *Trust Houses Forte Leisure Ltd v Aquilar* [1976] IRLR 251 and *Cook v Thomas Linnell & Sons Ltd* [1977] ICR 770. See also *Laughton and Hawley v Bapp Industrial Supplies Ltd* [1986] ICR 634.

[4] [1980] ICR 303. See also *ILEA v Gravetts* [1988] IRLR 497.

reasonable grounds upon which to sustain that belief. And thirdly … that the employer at the stage at which he formed that belief on those grounds, had carried out as much investigation into the matter as was reasonable in all the circumstances of the case.'

This approach was approved by the Court of Appeal in *W Weddel & Co Ltd v Tepper*.[1] The *Burchell* case involved alleged dishonesty, but the test to which it has given its name is generally applied to those cases where the reason for the employee's dismissal is the employer's belief that there has been misconduct of some kind. After some uncertainty about the standing of the *Burchell* test, brought about by the EAT's decision in *Haddon v Van den Bergh Foods Ltd*,[2] the Court of Appeal has re-affirmed that the *Burchell* test 'remains binding on this court, as well as on employment tribunals and the Employment Appeal Tribunal. Any departure from that approach … is inconsistent with binding authority'.[3]

4.54   In *Boys and Girls Welfare Society v McDonald*[4] the EAT stressed that employment tribunals should not fall into the error of placing the burden on employers of satisfying them as to the reasonableness of the dismissal. The *Burchell* case was decided before the enactment of what is now section 98(4) in its present form, which expressly establishes a neutral burden of proof. The EAT also pointed out that, once the tribunal has considered the three-part test of *Burchell*, it must still go on to consider whether the dismissal fell within the range of reasonable responses of a reasonable employer.

4.55   In this section, dismissals for conduct will be considered under the following headings:

1.   conduct of investigations;
2.   decision to dismiss;
3.   procedural fairness;
4.   criminal offences.

4.56   The existence of the statutory right to be accompanied at a disciplinary or grievance hearing should be borne in mind when reading the relevant text. For a discussion of the right, see para 4.42.

4.57   It is particularly important to remember, when looking in detail at aspects of dismissal for conduct, that the overriding consideration for an employment tribunal is to decide whether the employer acted reasonably or unreasonably in dismissing the employee, within the requirements of section 98(4). It is easy to allow decided cases and principles that are thought to be deducible from them to obscure the words used by the statute. It is also easy to forget that the decision in many cases depends on the facts as found by the tribunal. It is tempting to argue that, because a

---

[1]   [1980] ICR 286.
[2]   [1999] ICR 1150.
[3]   *Ibid* at pp 1287–1288.
[4]   [1996] IRLR 129. See also *Conlin v United Distillers* [1994] IRLR 169.

tribunal or another division of the EAT has decided a factual issue in a particular way, a subsequent tribunal should decide a similar factual issue in the same way. It is seldom that the facts of two different cases arising from different contexts are identical. It follows that two different tribunals may reach opposite conclusions on similar sets of facts, without either committing an error of law, simply because it is for each tribunal to decide, on the facts in front of it, whether *that* employer's decision to dismiss *that* employee in *those* circumstances was reasonable or unreasonable. It is essential to concentrate upon the necessarily general words of section 98(4) and the Code of Practice. A tribunal should not allow itself 'to be diverted into the channels created by judicial decisions' but should 'drink at the pure waters of the section'.[1]

(i) Conduct of investigations

4.58   In considering an employer's conduct of an investigation, an employment tribunal will generally follow the three-stage approach set out in the *Burchell* case above, and widely followed. In *Scottish Daily Record & Sunday Mail (1986) Ltd v Laird*,[2] for example, the Court of Session said that the employment tribunal had not erred in holding that the employee's dismissal was unfair because the employers had failed to satisfy the *Burchell* test. The Court pointed out that, although there is no burden on the employer to satisfy the tribunal that it acted reasonably, the employer is still required to produce some evidence to show that the requirements described at each of the three stages of the test were satisfied.[3] Nevertheless, it should not be followed slavishly, particularly where the facts of a particular case do not easily fit within its scope. It is useful in cases where a single employee's misconduct is involved, but may not assist in more complicated cases.

4.59   Thus, for example, in cases where employers conduct an investigation but cannot identify the persons responsible for the acts or omissions in question, they are entitled to dismiss a group of employees, even where it is possible that not all in the group were guilty of the act. But the employment tribunal must be satisfied that the employer conducted a

---

[1]   See Waite J in *Siggs and Chapman (Contractors) Ltd v Knight* [1984] IRLR 83 at p 85. In *Walls Meat Co Ltd v Khan* [1979] ICR 52 at p 57, Lord Denning MR complained that 'if we are not careful, we shall find the [employment] tribunals bent down under the weight of the law books or, what is worse, asleep under them'.

[2]   [1996] IRLR 665. See also *Lovie Ltd v Anderson* [1999] IRLR 164.

[3]   See at p 669.

proper investigation;[1] it need not be a quasi-judicial investigation with cross-examination of witnesses.[2]

4.60   It is important, however, that employers are careful in their handling of the evidence used in the investigation of alleged misconduct. In *Linfood Cash and Carry Ltd v Thomson and Others*,[3] which was approved by the Court of Appeal in *Morgan v Electrolux Ltd*,[4] the employers dismissed three employees for forging credit notes, on the basis of allegations made by an anonymous informant. The employment tribunal which heard their complaints decided that the employers had failed to carry out a reasonable investigation and had no reasonable grounds for their belief in the employees' guilt since the only evidence was the uncorroborated statement of the anonymous informant. The EAT upheld the decision. The importance of the decision lies not so much in the decision itself, but in the guidelines set out by the EAT for employers to follow when informants are involved.[5] Subsequently, however, the High Court has taken the view that, in appropriate circumstances, a dismissed employee is entitled to know the identity of an anonymous informant and to have details of the allegations made.[6] Although this decision was made in the context of actions for breach of contract and conspiracy, it is at least arguable that it should also apply to unfair dismissal claims. If this is correct, the effect will be to deter informants from coming forward. In *Linfood Cash and Carry Ltd*, the EAT also considered the question of the credibility of witnesses and said that the tribunal must not substitute its own view of the credibility of a witness for that of the employer, on the basis of the evidence given to the tribunal. If the tribunal says that the employer could not reasonably have accepted a witness as truthful, that decision must be based upon good grounds. Otherwise, it runs the risk of substituting its own view for that of the employer, and thus committing an error of law. The decision of the EAT in the *Linfood* case, above, has been subsequently applied to the notes taken at a disciplinary hearing. In *Vauxhall Motors Ltd v Ghafoor*,[7] the EAT said that it is permissible for an employment tribunal to find that a failure to keep notes during disciplinary proceedings and to provide them for the employee amounts to a procedural defect.

4.61   The issue in *Louies v Coventry Hood & Seating Co Ltd*[8] was whether the investigation was vitiated by the employer's use of written statements

---

[1]   *Whitbread & Co plc v Thomas* [1988] ICR 135, in which the EAT applied *Monie v Coral Racing Ltd* [1981] ICR 109 (CA). See also *Parr v Whitbread plc, t/a Threshers Wine Merchants* [1990] ICR 427; the EAT suggested (at p 432) an approach for employment tribunals to follow when dealing with such dismissals. See also *Chamberlain Vinyl Products Ltd v Patel* [1996] ICR 113, in which the EAT upheld the employment tribunal's decision that the employer had prematurely concluded the investigation into the employee's misconduct and that no reasonable employer would have dismissed the employee at that stage.

[2]   *Ulsterbus Ltd v Henderson* [1989] IRLR 251.

[3]   [1989] ICR 518.

[4]   [1991] ICR 369.

[5]   [1989] ICR 518 at pp 522–523.

[6]   In *A v Company B Ltd* [1997] IRLR 405.

[7]   [1993] ICR 376.

[8]   [1990] ICR 54. See also *Fuller v Lloyds Bank plc* [1991] IRLR 336.

which were withheld from the employee for no reason. During the disciplinary proceedings the employee was told that the employer had two independent written statements stating that he had been involved in the incident. He appealed, and during the appeal hearing asked to be told what was in the statements. He was not shown the statements and no reason was given for withholding them from him. His appeal was dismissed, and his complaint of unfair dismissal was dismissed by the employment tribunal. The EAT, however, allowed the appeal and said that the dismissal was prima facie unfair if the employee was not permitted to know the contents of statements on which the employer would rely in taking the decision to dismiss. Where there had been an investigation which led to a belief that there had been misconduct on the part of the employee, the subsequent dismissal procedure had to be conducted so that the fairness of the procedure balanced the initial belief of misconduct. Here the tribunal had erred because it had not taken sufficient account of the need for the balance to be maintained. This case was distinguished by the Court of Appeal in the later case of *Hussain v Elonex plc*,[1] on the grounds that in the *Louies* case the substance of the case was contained in statements which the employee had asked to see but which had not been shown to him, with no good reason being shown, and on which substantial reliance had been placed by the employers in reaching the decision to dismiss him; in the *Hussain* case, on the other hand, although the employers failed to disclose to the employee the existence of statements obtained from independent witnesses in relation to the incident which led to his dismissal, nevertheless he was told of the accusations against him and given a full opportunity to respond to them. Mummery LJ pointed out that 'there are no hard and fast rigid rules to be adopted in these cases ... What matters is fairness and reasonableness'.[2]

(ii) Decision to dismiss

4.62   An employer who treats employees differently (for example, by dismissing one and not another) will not be held to have dismissed unfairly provided that the decision was one which a reasonable employer could reach. In *Securicor Ltd v Smith*,[3] the employee's dismissal resulted from an incident in which he and the team leader, a Mr Curry, breached one of the employers' rules governing the handling and transit of cash and put two containers of cash at risk. The incident was investigated and both men were dismissed. At the final appeal, however, the matter was fully investigated and it was decided that Mr Curry was less blameworthy than the employee and it was therefore decided to reject the employee's appeal and confirm his dismissal but to allow Mr Curry's appeal and reinstate him with a final warning. The employment tribunal held that the dismissal was unfair, on the grounds that no reasonable employer in the circumstances of this case

---

[1]   [1999] IRLR 420.

[2]   *Ibid* at p 423.

[3]   [1989] IRLR 356. See also *Cain v Leeds Western Health Authority* [1990] IRLR 168, *Frames Snooker Centre v Boyce* [1992] IRLR 472 and *London Borough of Harrow v Cunningham* [1996] IRLR 256.

could have decided to dismiss the employee's appeal and allow Mr Curry's. The tribunal took the view that there was practically no distinction between the two men's culpability. The EAT dismissed the employers' appeal, but the Court of Appeal allowed their further appeal. The Court said that the question was whether the employers acted reasonably and within the band of reasonable responses in acting upon the findings and conclusions of the appeal panel. In a case such as this, the question when determining the fairness of the dismissal of the employee whose appeal is not allowed is whether the appeal panel's decision was so irrational that no employer could reasonably have accepted it. The Court of Appeal said that although it would have been open to the panel to reach a different conclusion, it did not do so for rational and clear reasons; it could not, therefore, be said that the appeal panel's decision was perverse. The employment tribunal had erred in law by substituting its own view of the facts and the conclusions to be drawn from them.

4.63   Similar considerations arise where the employee in question is dismissed for an offence (eg assaulting another employee) but there is evidence that in the past other employees have not been dismissed for a similar offence. In *Procter v British Gypsum Ltd*,[1] the EAT said that the employer should consider truly comparable cases of which he or she knew or ought reasonably to have known. It stressed, however, that the overriding principle must be that each case should be considered on its own facts and with freedom to consider mitigating aspects. Similarly, in *Paul v East Surrey District Health Authority*,[2] the Court of Appeal stressed that in cases of this kind ultimately the question for the employer is whether in the particular case dismissal is a reasonable response to the misconduct and warned that tribunals should scrutinise arguments based upon disparity of treatment with particular care.

4.64   A similar problem arises in situations where there is a theft, but the employer cannot determine which employee is responsible and dismisses a group of employees (so-called 'blanket dismissal' cases). This is what happened in *Parr v Whitbread & Co plc*.[3] The employee was the manager of an off-licence. He and three assistants were dismissed when a sum of money was stolen in circumstances where each of the dismissed employees had an equal opportunity of committing the theft. The employment tribunal found that the company had carried out a satisfactory investigation to identify those responsible and that it had reasonably believed that one or more of the dismissed employees could have committed the theft. The tribunal held that the employers had acted reasonably. The employee appealed to the EAT which dismissed his appeal. It suggested an approach for dealing with this type of case. Wood J (the President) said:

---

[1]   [1991] IRLR 7. See also *Conlin v United Distillers* [1994] IRLR 169, a decision of the Court of Session.
[2]   [1995] IRLR 305.
[3]   [1990] ICR 427.

'If an employment tribunal is able to find on the evidence before it:

(1)   that an act has been committed which if committed by an individual would justify dismissal;

(2)   that the employer made a reasonable – sufficiently thorough – investigation into the matter with appropriate procedures;

(3)   that as a result of that investigation the employer reasonably believed that more than one person could have committed the act;

(4)   that the employer acted reasonably in identifying the group of employees who could have committed the act and that each member of the group was individually capable of so doing;

(5)   that as between the members of the group the employer could not reasonably identify the individual perpetrator;

then, provided the beliefs were held on solid and reasonable grounds at the date of dismissal, an employer is entitled to dismiss each member of the group.'[1]

The *Burchell* test does not apply where misconduct in fact takes place; in that case the question is not whether the employer had a reasonable belief, but whether the act of dismissal was a reasonable response.

4.65   A final point to note in the context of the present discussion is that, where an employer is relying on an employee's conduct in refusing to obey an instruction as the ground for dismissal, the lawfulness of the instruction, although relevant, will not be decisive when considering the reasonableness of the dismissal.[2] The corollary of that is that it will not be perverse for the tribunal to reach the conclusion in such circumstances that the dismissal was fair.

(iii) Procedural fairness

4.66   There are two House of Lords' decisions which have a particularly important bearing on this area. The first, *Polkey v AE Dayton Ltd*,[3] involves the question whether a dismissal which would be unfair because of a failure to follow a fair procedure can be held to be fair if the employer is able to establish that following a fair procedure would have made no difference to the outcome. In *British Labour Pump Co Ltd v Byrne*,[4] the EAT said that two questions should be asked:

1.   have the employers shown on the balance of probabilities that they would have taken the same course had they held an inquiry, and had they received the information which that inquiry would have produced? and

2.   have the employers shown that in the light of the information which they would have had, had they gone through the proper procedure,

---

[1]   [1990] ICR 427 at p 432. See also *Whitbread & Co plc v Thomas* [1988] ICR 135.

[2]   *Farrant v The Woodroffe School* [1998] ICR 185.

[3]   [1988] ICR 142.

[4]   [1979] ICR 347 at pp 353–354. See also *W & J Wass Ltd v Binns* [1982] ICR 486, *Sillifant v Powell Duffryn Timber Ltd* [1983] IRLR 91 and *Royal Society for the Prevention of Cruelty to Animals v Cruden* [1986] ICR 205.

they would have been behaving reasonably in still deciding to dismiss?

4.67   The House of Lords overruled that decision. It said that the correct question was whether the employer had been reasonable or unreasonable in deciding that the reason for dismissing the employee was a sufficient reason, not whether the employee would nevertheless have been dismissed even if there had been prior consultation or warning. Whether the employer could reasonably have concluded that consultation or warning would be useless so that the failure to consult or warn would not necessarily render the dismissal unfair was a matter for the employment tribunal to consider in the light of the circumstances known to the employer at the time of the decision to dismiss. Lord Mackay of Clashfern LC, who delivered the main speech, adopted the analysis of Browne-Wilkinson J in *Sillifant v Powell Duffryn Timber Ltd.*[1] In that case, the approach suggested by the judge, which was adopted by the Lord Chancellor in the *Polkey* case, was as follows:

> 'The only test of the fairness of a dismissal is the reasonableness of the employer's decision to dismiss judged at the time at which the dismissal takes effect. An employment tribunal is not bound to hold that any procedural failure by the employer renders the dismissal unfair: it is one of the factors to be weighed by the employment tribunal in deciding whether or not the dismissal was reasonable within section [98(4)]. The weight to be attached to such procedural failure should depend upon the circumstances known to the employer at the time of dismissal, not on the actual consequence of such failure. Thus in the case of a failure to give an opportunity to explain, except in the rare case where a reasonable employer could properly take the view on the facts known to him at the time of dismissal that no explanation or mitigation could alter his decision to dismiss, an employment tribunal would be likely to hold that the lack of 'equity' inherent in the failure would render the dismissal unfair. But there may be cases where the offence is so heinous and the facts so manifestly clear that a reasonable employer could, on the facts known to him at the time of dismissal, take the view that whatever explanation the employee advanced it would make no difference ... Where, in the circumstances known at the time of dismissal, it was not reasonable for the employer to dismiss without giving an opportunity to explain but facts subsequently discovered or proved before the employment tribunal show that dismissal was in fact merited, compensation would be reduced to nil ... An employee dismissed for suspected dishonesty who is in fact innocent has no redress: if the employer acted fairly in dismissing him on the facts and in the circumstances known to him at the time of dismissal the employee's innocence is irrelevant. Why should an employer be entitled to a finding that he acted fairly when, on the facts known and in the circumstances existing at the time of dismissal, his actions were unfair but which facts subsequently coming to light show did not cause any injustice? The choice in dealing with section [98(4)] is between looking at the reasonableness of

---

[1]   [1983] IRLR 91 at p 97. *Cf Pritchett v J McJntyre Ltd* [1987] ICR 359, in which the Court of Appeal applied the *British Labour Pump* principles. It is arguable, however, that the same decision could have been reached applying the *Polkey* case.

the employer or justice to the employee. *Devis v Atkins*[1] shows that the correct test is the reasonableness of the employer ...'

4.68 Lord Bridge of Harwich also considered[2] the effect on compensation of taking the procedural steps and quoted a further passage from Browne-Wilkinson J's judgment in the *Sillifant* case:[3]

'There is no need for an "all or nothing" decision. If the employment tribunal thinks there is a doubt whether or not the employee would have been dismissed, this element can be reflected by reducing the normal amount of compensation by a percentage representing the chance that the employee would still have lost his employment.'

This aspect of the decision is explored more fully in Chapter 8.

Although the *Polkey* case was decided in the context of a dismissal for redundancy, it is applicable to other reasons for dismissal, particularly conduct dismissals.

4.69 The second House of Lords' decision which is important in the present context is *West Midlands Co-operative Society Ltd v Tipton*.[4] It concerns appeals. The question was whether the employment tribunal was correct to have regard to the employer's refusal to allow the employee his contractual right of appeal. The employers argued that the tribunal must consider only whether the employer acted reasonably in the original decision to dismiss, and must ignore what happened after that decision. They relied on *W Devis & Sons Ltd v Atkins*.[5] Had the argument succeeded, the employers' failure to allow the employee his contractual right of appeal would have been irrelevant to the fairness or otherwise of the dismissal. The House of Lords rejected the argument and distinguished *W Devis & Sons Ltd v Atkins*. Lord Bridge of Harwich said:

'A dismissal is unfair if the employer unreasonably treats his real reason as a sufficient reason to dismiss the employee, either when he makes his original decision to dismiss or when he maintains that decision at the conclusion of an internal appeal. By the same token, a dismissal may be held to be unfair when the employer has refused to entertain an appeal to which the employee was contractually entitled and thereby denied to the employee the opportunity of showing that, in all the circumstances, the employer's real reason for dismissing could not reasonably be treated as sufficient.'[6]

Lord Bridge did go on to suggest that, in a case of serious dishonesty committed by the employee in the course of employment, the employer could reasonably refuse to entertain a domestic appeal on the ground that

---

[1]   [1977] ICR 662.
[2]   [1988] ICR 142 at p 163.
[3]   [1983] IRLR 91 at p 96.
[4]   [1986] ICR 192. See also *The Post Office v Marney* [1990] IRLR 170.
[5]   [1977] ICR 662.
[6]   *Ibid* at p 204.

it could not affect the outcome. However, that *obiter* dictum should be treated with caution, in the light of the later decision in the *Polkey* case.

4.70   Another question which arises from the role of internal appeals procedures in the dismissal process is whether a fair appeal can rectify an unfair disciplinary hearing and thus render fair a dismissal which might otherwise be unfair. In *Whitbread & Co plc v Mills*,[1] the EAT answered the question in the affirmative. It pointed out that appeal procedures form an important part of the process of ensuring that a dismissal should try to be fair and that both the original and the appellate decision of the employer are necessary elements in the overall process of terminating the employee's contract. It said:

> '... [N]ot every formality of legal or quasi-legal process is required during the disciplinary and appeal procedures. Each set of circumstances must be examined to see whether the act or omission has brought about an unfair hearing. If it has, then whether or not an appeal procedure has rectified the situation must depend upon the degree of unfairness at the original hearing. If there is a rehearing de novo at first instance, the omission may be corrected, but ... if there is to be a correction by the appeal then such an appeal must be of a comprehensive nature, in essence a rehearing and not a mere review.'[2]

4.71   In the instant case, the EAT held that the appeal hearing was in the nature of a review and not a complete hearing and upheld the employment tribunal's decision that the dismissal of the employee was unfair. The Court of Appeal reached a similar conclusion in *Sartor v P & O European Ferries (Felixstowe) Ltd*,[3] although the above case was not referred to in its judgment. The Court did stress, however, that for a procedural defect to be cured by an appeal the appeal must be by way of rehearing.

4.72   Procedural fairness is particularly important in cases of conduct, although the requirements are not absolute. Generally, the employer should go through a procedure appropriate to the nature and size of the organisation and a failure to do so, except in the exceptional cases considered below, will cause the dismissal to be unfair. In *Clarke v Trimoco Motor Group Ltd*,[4] the EAT considered the case of an employee who, as a result of police investigations, was suspended without pay until the outcome of charges brought against him by the police. Two months after his suspension, following an adjournment of the case, his employers wrote to him dismissing him. The employment tribunal held the dismissal to be fair, taking the view that the failure of the employers to call in the employee and give him an opportunity to defend himself against the criminal charges was counterbalanced by the failure of the employee to use the grievance procedure which was failure to him. The EAT held that there was an error of law 'in equating the availability of a grievance procedure

---

[1]   [1988] ICR 776. See also *Post Office v Marney* [1990] IRLR 170, *Clark v Civil Aviation Authority* [1991] IRLR 412 and *Lloyd v Taylor Woodrow Construction* [1999] IRLR 782.
[2]   *Ibid* at p 795.
[3]   [1992] IRLR 271.
[4]   [1993] ICR 237. See also *Lovie Ltd v Anderson* [1999] IRLR 164.

with the affording to an employee of an opportunity of defending himself or herself against a serious charge of dishonesty'. It went on to say:[1]

> '... [A]n employee before being dismissed must, in order to satisfy the requirements of natural justice, be given an opportunity of giving an explanation, save in those rare cases where there is no possibility of the employee giving an explanation of the conduct alleged or where it is plainly admitted so that there may be no cause to ask for an explanation ... The present case is quite plainly not in one of those exceptional categories ...'

4.73 In *Whitbread plc (t/a Whitbread Medway Inns) v Hall*,[2] the Court of Appeal upheld the tribunal's decision that a dismissal was unfair in circumstances where the employee admitted that he had been guilty of misconduct. It said that, although dismissal following the admission was within the range of reasonable responses of a reasonable employer, the disciplinary process was so flawed as to render the dismissal unfair. Hale LJ, with whom the other two members of the Court agreed, said that section 98(4) suggests that there are substantive and procedural elements to the decision to both of which the 'band of reasonable responses' test should be applied.[3] A similar conclusion was reached by the EAT in *John Lewis plc v Coyne*,[4] which involved an employee dismissed for using the company's telephone for making personal calls. It upheld the tribunal's decision that the dismissal was unfair because the employers failed to investigate the seriousness of the offence and dismissed her taking the view that her conduct was dishonest. The EAT pointed out that using an employer's telephone for personal calls is not necessarily dishonest and that much depends upon the circumstances of the particular case.

4.74 A failure to apply a procedure, however, will not cause the dismissal to be unfair, for example if the employee shows himself to be 'determined to go his own way'[5] or has taken up a position which is unlikely to be altered by being given a hearing.[6] But it is important to bear in mind that the decision in the *Polkey* case means that in most cases such questions are not generally relevant. Lord Bridge of Harwich did, however, say:

> 'It is quite a different matter if the tribunal is able to conclude that the employer himself, at the time of the dismissal, acted reasonably in taking the view that, in the exceptional circumstances of the particular case, the procedural steps

---

[1] [1993] ICR 237 at p 248. The EAT followed the decision of the Court of Appeal in *McLaren v National Coal Board* [1988] ICR 370, considered later.

[2] [2001] IRLR 275.

[3] *Ibid* at p 278.

[4] [2001] IRLR 139.

[5] *Retarded Children's Aid Society Ltd v Day* [1978] ICR 437 at p 442.

[6] *James v Waltham Holy Cross Urban District Council* [1973] ICR 398.

normally appropriate would have been futile, could not have altered the decision to dismiss and therefore could be dispensed with."[1]

4.75   The procedure will probably involve the application of the employer's disciplinary rules, which should make clear what amounts to an offence and what the result of a breach of the rules will be, and they should have been brought sufficiently to the employee's notice.[2] If there are no rules, or the rules make no provision for the particular offence, the provisions of the Code of Practice will be relevant.

4.76   In most cases (with the exception of a dismissal for a single act of gross misconduct), the employer should employ a warnings system, eg an oral warning followed by a written warning and then by a final written warning specifying that a further recurrence will lead to dismissal.[3] The employee should also be interviewed and given the opportunity to state his or her case; he or she should also be told of any right to appeal.[4] In this context, it should be noted that a *worker* has a statutory right to be accompanied at a disciplinary or grievance hearing.[5] Further, an employee who fails to use an internal appeal procedure may have his or her compensation reduced and an employer who prevents an employee from using the procedure may be liable to pay a supplementary award of compensation.[6]

4.77   In cases where the employee has a contractual right to have an appeal against dismissal heard and decided by an appeals panel constituted in a particular way, a defect in the composition of such a body will not inevitably make unfair the dismissal of an employee after a flawed hearing. In *Westminster City Council v Cabaj*,[7] the employee was dismissed after his appeal was heard by an internal appeals panel which had not been constituted in accordance with the terms of the disciplinary code incorporated into his employment contract. The EAT decided that the denial of the employee's contractual entitlement was so fundamental a defect that the only possible conclusion must be that the dismissal was unfair. The Court of Appeal agreed that employers ought to follow agreed

---

[1]   [1988] ICR 142 at p 163. For an example see *Ellis v Hammond & Hammond t/a Hammond & Sons* (EAT 1257/95) IDS Brief 582.

[2]   An example of a failure in this respect is *Lock v Cardiff Railway Co Ltd* [1998] IRLR 358, which involved the dismissal of an employee for a one-off act of misjudgment in dealing with a train passenger. The tribunal held that the employer had acted reasonably but the EAT upheld his appeal and said that, since the employee had never been told that he would be dismissed for a one-off act of that sort, no reasonable tribunal properly directing itself could have concluded that dismissal was a fair penalty.

[3]   See the Code of Practice on Disciplinary Practice and Procedures in Employment, para 15. See also *Tower Hamlets Health Authority v Anthony* [1989] ICR 656 and *Bevan Ashford v Malin* [1995] ICR 453. This last case involved a dismissal relying upon a spent warning.

[4]   *Ibid* at paras 14 and 15. See *West Midlands Co-operative Society Ltd v Tipton* [1986] ICR 192.

[5]   See ERA 1999, s 10 and para 4.42.

[6]   See ERA 1996, s 127A, considered at para 8.124.

[7]   [1996] ICR 960. In the light of the Court of Appeal's decision, the decision of the EAT in *Blundell v Christie Hospital National Health Service Trust* [1996] ICR 347, which followed the EAT's decision in the *Cabaj* case, should be treated with caution.

procedures, but said that the issue of fairness fell to be decided in accordance with what is now section 98(4) of the 1996 Act and remitted the case to the employment tribunal. The Court said that there were two issues which the tribunal should consider when determining the fairness of the dismissal: first, whether the council's failure to convene the appeal panel correctly denied the employee the opportunity of demonstrating that the reason for his dismissal was not sufficient; and secondly, the council's reason for dismissing the employee without observing the requirements of the disciplinary code. This decision is significant, in that it suggests a partial retreat from the views of the House of Lords in the *Polkey* case. It also raises an important question as to whether an employer who breaks a significant contractual obligation can be said to have acted reasonably.

4.78 The possibility of finding alternative work for the employee may also be a relevant factor to be taken into account before dismissing an employee, but that will depend upon the size and administrative resources of the undertaking. The investigation into the possibility of alternative work need not be undertaken before the employee is given notice of dismissal, provided that it is undertaken before the notice takes effect.[1] A failure to follow a fair procedure will not automatically make the dismissal unfair.[2] It is important, however, that the procedures are checked from time to time and kept up to date.[3]

(iv) Criminal offences

4.79 One aspect of misconduct which has caused difficulty is the commission by the employee of a criminal offence. The employer must have a genuine belief based upon reasonable grounds, and this requirement has been applied to employees under suspicion of having committed an offence within the employment.[4] The fact that the employee has committed an offence which is contrary to the employer's disciplinary code does not necessarily make the employer's behaviour dishonest and does not generally remove the need for a properly conducted disciplinary inquiry.[5]

4.80 In *McLaren v National Coal Board*,[6] the Court of Appeal made it clear that the standards of fairness which require an employer to give an employee the opportunity of explaining his or her conduct before dismissal are immutable. The case arose from an incident of assault during the miners' strike and the Court of Appeal said that the employment tribunal

---

[1] *P v Nottinghamshire County Council* [1992] ICR 706.

[2] *Hollister v National Farmers' Union* [1979] ICR 542 and *Yate Foundry Ltd v Walters* [1984] ICR 445.

[3] See, eg, *Denco Ltd v Joinson* [1991] ICR 172.

[4] *British Home Stores Ltd v Burchell* [1980] ICR 303, approved by the Court of Appeal in *W Weddel & Co Ltd v Tepper* [1980] ICR 286, although another division of the Court of Appeal, in *Monie v Coral Racing Ltd* [1981] ICR 109, emphasised that each case must depend upon its facts. See also *Royal Society for the Protection of Birds v Croucher* [1984] ICR 604, *Whitbread & Co plc v Thomas* [1988] ICR 135 and *Lovie Ltd v Anderson* [1999] IRLR 164.

[5] *John Lewis plc v Coyne* [2001] IRLR 139.

[6] [1988] ICR 370. See also *Dillett v National Coal Board* [1988] ICR 218.

was wrong to apply a different standard of fairness in the exceptional circumstances of the miners' strike. Sir John Donaldson MR said:

> '[N]o amount of heat in industrial warfare can justify failing to give the employee an opportunity of giving an explanation. What industrial warfare may do is to create a situation in which conduct which would not normally justify dismissal becomes conduct which does justify dismissal, and if there is no possibility of the employee giving any explanation of the conduct which is alleged, or if it is plainly admitted, then there may be no cause to ask him for an explanation ... [T]he standards of fairness never change. They are immutable but are applied in a different situation.'[1]

This was applied by the EAT in *Clarke v Trimoco Motor Group Ltd,*[2] in the case of an employee charged with a criminal offence, who was suspended without pay pending the outcome of the trial but was not given an opportunity to defend himself between the suspension and the dismissal.

4.81   The employer does not have to prove the employee's guilt and, provided his or her belief is genuine and reasonable, the dismissal of the employee will not be made unfair by the latter's subsequent acquittal.[3] This is likely also to be the case where an employee accused of a crime pleads guilty and the employer refuses to accept the explanation that he or she was not guilty but had bowed to pressure to plead guilty to avoid a prison sentence. In such a case, the question is whether on the facts which were known or ought to have been known to the employers, they genuinely believed on reasonable grounds that the employee was guilty. If the procedure by which the employers reached their conclusion was faulty, they will have failed to act reasonably. But, in the absence of any lapse of procedure, it is an error of law for the employment tribunal to seek to reopen the factual issues on the basis of which the employers reached their conclusion.[4] In *P v Nottinghamshire County Council,*[5] which involved a school groundsman dismissed after he had admitted an offence of gross indecency with his daughter, the Court of Appeal said that where an employee has become unsuitable for his or her current work the possibility of alternative employment, depending on the size and administrative resources of the employers' undertaking, may be a relevant factor for them to take into account. Section 98(4) does not, however, require the employers to undertake that investigation before giving the employee notice of dismissal, provided that they do so before the notice takes effect. Finally, the Court of Appeal's decision in *The Post Office v Liddiard*[6] suggests that certain types of dismissal for misconduct unconnected to the workplace (in this case, acts of football hooliganism in France) may be capable of being justified.

---

[1]   [1988] ICR 370 at p 377.
[2]   [1993] ICR 237. See also *Securicor Guarding Ltd v R* [1994] IRLR 633.
[3]   *Da Costa v Optolis Ltd* [1976] IRLR 178.
[4]   *British Gas plc v McCarrick* [1991] IRLR 305 (CA).
[5]   [1992] ICR 706. See also *Secretary of State for Scotland v Campbell* [1992] IRLR 263.
[6]   (2001) IDS Brief B690/6.

(e) Redundancy

4.82   Unfair dismissals where the reason for the dismissal is redundancy are considered in Chapter 6.

(f) Statutory requirements

4.83   The fact that the employer shows that it is not possible to continue to employ the employee in the particular job he or she does, without contravening a statutory requirement, does not mean that there is no need to go through a fair procedure before dismissing the employee.[1]

(g) Some other substantial reason

4.84   The two main areas which have evolved through the cases are reorganisations which fall short of redundancy, and changes in the employee's terms of employment, although this category of reason is wide enough to embrace other matters, for example the dismissal of one spouse as a result of the dismissal of the other.[2] They show the difficulty of drawing the line between fairness and unfairness where there is a clear conflict between the employer's legitimate business interests and the employee's contractual rights, since the employee's contract is static and, prima facie, he or she can insist upon continued performance of it as it stands.

4.85   Reorganisations may produce a redundancy in law, in which case what is said in Chapter 6 will apply. Not infrequently, they tend to lead the EAT to decide the case on the footing that the reason shown by the employer amounted to a redundancy in law, but, if it did not, it was some other substantial reason.[3] But it is important to remember what was said at the beginning of this chapter about the labelling of reasons (see para 4.15).

4.86   The effect of the Court of Appeal's decision in *Hollister v National Farmers' Union*[4] is, in effect, to whittle down the need to comply with what is now section 98(4). There, the Court said that, provided that the employment tribunal has found that there was a substantial reason justifying dismissal, it is not necessary for the employers to consult the employee about the reorganisation of the business. All that needs to be shown is a sound commercial reason for making the reorganisation. In

---

[1]   *Sutcliffe and Eaton Ltd v Pinney* [1977] IRLR 349 and *Sandhu v Department of Education and Science and London Borough of Hillingdon* [1978] IRLR 208.

[2]   See *Kelman v Oram* [1983] IRLR 432 and *Scottish and Newcastle Retail Ltd v Stanton and Durrant* (EAT 1126/96) IDS Brief 596.

[3]   See *Robinson v British Island Airways* [1978] ICR 304 at p 309, *German v London Computer Training Centre Ltd* [1978] ICR 394 at p 399, and *Carry All Motors Ltd v Pennington* [1980] ICR 806 at p 809.

[4]   [1979] ICR 542; see also *Bowater Containers Ltd v McCormack* [1980] IRLR 50, *Genower v Ealing, Hammersmith and Hounslow Area Health Authority* [1980] IRLR 297, *Ladbroke Courage Holidays Ltd v Asten* [1981] IRLR 59, and *Richmond Precision Engineering Ltd v Pearce* [1985] IRLR 179.

Labour Party v Oakley,[1] the Court of Appeal held that the dismissal of an employee because of a reorganisation was unfair. Although the reorganisation was a substantial reason of a kind to justify the dismissal, what made the dismissal unfair was that the employers used the reorganisation as a pretext for her dismissal when they had already decided not to renew her fixed-term contract.

4.87   Often, but not always, allied with reorganisations are unilateral changes in the terms of the employee's contract, which raise difficult issues of law and practice. One of the first cases to be decided on 'some other substantial reason', *RS Components Ltd v Irwin*,[2] concerned the introduction into the employee's contract of a restraint of trade clause. His refusal to accept it made his consequent dismissal fair. In *St John of God (Care Services) Ltd v Brooks*,[3] in which the employees were dismissed for refusing to accept new, and less favourable, terms of employment, the employment tribunal held the dismissals to be unfair on the basis that the crucial question was whether the terms offered were those which a reasonable employer would offer. The EAT allowed the employers' appeal and said that to look only at the offer would necessarily exclude from consideration everything that happened between the time when the offer was made and the dismissal, and would be contrary to the wording of section 98(4), which points to the dismissal. '... [W]hether it was fair or unfair must be judged in the light of the situation when it occurred and not when an earlier step was taken'.[4]

---

[1]   [1988] ICR 403.
[2]   [1973] ICR 535. *Cf Evans v Elemeta Holdings Ltd* [1982] ICR 323.
[3]   [1992] ICR 715. It should be noted that this was a majority decision, with one of the industrial members in the minority. See also *Catamaran Cruisers Ltd v Williams* [1994] IRLR 386 and *Leicester University Students' Union v Mahomed* [1995] IRLR 292.
[4]   *Ibid* at p 722.

Chapter 5

UNFAIR DISMISSAL: SPECIAL CASES

5.01   In the preceding chapter, the general rules of unfair dismissal were considered. These are the rules which generally apply to dismissals for what have been called the 'potentially fair' reasons. In this chapter, what are called 'special cases' are considered. They are so called, because they are cases for which specific statutory provision has been made. In these cases, considerations of reasonableness under section 98(4) are not usually of primary concern, since the question is usually not whether the employer behaved reasonably, but whether it infringed a particular statutory provision. The situations considered here range from dismissals for trade union membership and activities and industrial action, to dismissals in the context of leave for family reasons and in health and safety cases. Dismissals for redundancy are considered in Chapter 6.

5.02   In this chapter, the following matters are considered:

1.   dismissals in connection with trade union membership and activities, or trade union recognition;
2.   dismissals and industrial action, including participation in official industrial action;
3.   dismissal of an employee in connection with leave for family reasons;
4.   dismissal for reasons connected with health and safety;
5.   dismissal of a shop or betting worker for refusing Sunday work;
6.   dismissal in connection with an employee's rights under the Working Time Regulations;
7.   dismissal for reasons relating to an employee's performance of his or her duties as an occupational pension fund trustee;
8.   dismissal for reasons relating to an employee's performance of his or her duties as an employee representative;
9.   dismissal for making a 'protected disclosure';[1]
10.   dismissal for assertion of a statutory right;
11.   dismissal of an employee in connection with the national minimum wage legislation;
12.   dismissal in connection with an employee's rights under the Tax Credits Act 1999;
13.   dismissals of employees arising under paragraph 28 of the Transnational Information and Consultation of Employees Regulations 1999;
14.   dismissals arising under regulation 7 of the Part-time Workers (Prevention of Less Favourable Treatment) Regulations 2000;

---

[1]   Defined in ERA 1996, ss 235(1) and 43A (see para 5.84).

15.   dismissal of a *worker* in connection with the statutory right to be accompanied at a disciplinary or grievance hearing;
16.   dismissals in connection with a transfer of an undertaking; and
17.   dismissals of replacement employees.

In cases 1 and 3 to 14, a selection for redundancy for one of those reasons may also make the dismissal for redundancy unfair.[1] This is considered in Chapter 6, at para 6.42.

1. DISMISSALS IN CONNECTION WITH UNION MEMBERSHIP OR ACTIVITIES AND RECOGNITION OF UNIONS[2]

5.03   In this section two types of dismissal will be considered: dismissals in connection with trade union membership and activities; and (ii) dismissals in connection with trade union recognition. This second type of dismissal arises as a result of the introduction of procedures relating to union recognition by the Employment Relations Act 1999.

(a) Dismissals for trade union membership or activities

5.04   Section 152(1) of the Trade Union and Labour Relations (Consolidation) Act 1992 (TULRCA) provides that a dismissal, or a selection for dismissal for redundancy, will be automatically unfair if the reason for it is one of the following:

1.   membership,[3] or proposed membership, of an 'independent trade union';[4]
2.   participation, or proposed participation, in its 'activities' at an 'appropriate time';[5] and
3.   non-membership of any trade union, or of a particular trade union, or of one of a number of particular trade unions, or refusal or proposed refusal of such membership.[6]

5.05   The reasons set out above are now called 'inadmissible reasons' again, a title which was removed by the Employment Act 1982, but was recalled from abeyance by the Trade Union Reform and Employment

---

[1]   See TULRCA 1992, ss 153 and 238A, and ERA 1996, s 105.
[2]   In this and the following section all references to the 1992 Act or to TULRCA are to the Trade Union and Labour Relations (Consolidation) Act 1992.
[3]   See *Discount Tobacco & Confectionery Ltd v Armitage* [1990] IRLR 15 and [1995] ICR 431, and *Overprint Ltd v Malcolm* (EAT 443/92) IDS Brief 494.
[4]   See below for a definition of this phrase.
[5]   For the meaning of these phrases, see paras 5.13 and 5.15.
[6]   See *Crosville Motor Services Ltd v Ashfield* [1986] IRLR 475.

Rights Act 1993.[1] In the case of a dismissal, or a selection for redundancy, for one of these reasons, employees are protected whether or not they have been continuously employed for one year or have reached retirement age.[2] Further, they may be entitled to higher compensation and interim relief.[3]

5.06 A trade union will be an 'independent trade union', and thus within section 152, if it satisfies the definition set out in section 235(1) of the ERA 1996.[4] Two requirements need to be satisfied:

1. the trade union is not under the domination or control of an employer or a group of employers or of one or more employers' associations; and
2. the trade union 'is not liable to interference by an employer or any such group or association (arising out of the provision of financial or material support or by any other means whatsoever) tending towards such control'.[5]

5.07 If the question arises whether the tribunal has jurisdiction to hear the claim (eg because the employee has been employed for less than one year or has passed retirement age), the burden will be on the employee to satisfy the tribunal that the reason is an inadmissible reason and falls within section 152(1), so it has jurisdiction.[6] In other cases (eg where the employee has been continuously employed for long enough) the burden of establishing a potentially fair reason, and of rebutting any allegations made by the employee that the reason falls within section 152(1), will remain upon the employer.[7]

5.08 Section 152(3) of the 1992 Act treats the following reasons as falling within section 152(1)(c), above:

(a) an employee's refusal, or proposed refusal, to comply with a requirement (whether or not imposed by the contract or in writing) that, in the event of a failure to become or ceasing to remain a

---

[1] See s 49(1) and Sch 7, para 1. With effect from 30 August 1993, para 1(b) introduced a new subs (2) into s 154, which defines an 'inadmissible' reason as one of those specified in s 152(1), which are set out in the text.
[2] TULRCA 1992, s 154(1).
[3] See Chapter 7.
[4] See *Blue Circle Staff Association v Certification Officer* [1977] ICR 224, *Association of HSD (Hatfield) Employees v Certification Officer* [1978] ICR 21 and *Squibb United Kingdom Staff Association v Certification Officer* [1979] ICR 235.
[5] See *Government Communications Staff Federation v Certification Officer* [1993] ICR 163. It was a condition of service of employees of GCHQ that they could not be members of trade unions other than a departmental staff association approved by the Director. The EAT held that the staff federation was 'liable to interference' because it operated under the basic constraint that its continued existence depended on the approval of the Director.
[6] *Smith v Hayle Town Council* [1978] ICR 996. See also *Drew v St Edmundsbury Borough Council* [1980] ICR 513.
[7] *Maund v Penwith District Council* [1984] ICR 143. For a fuller discussion of this case, see Chapter 4.

member of a trade union or one of a number of trade union, he or she must make one or more payments; and
(b)   an objection, or proposed objection, to the operation of a provision under which, in the event mentioned in (a), the employer is entitled to deduct one or more sums from his or her pay.

The Court of Appeal has said that section 152 is not concerned with an employer's reactions to a trade union's activities but with the employer's reactions to an individual employee's activities. If, therefore, a dismissal has nothing to do with anything the employee has personally done or proposed to do, section 152 will not apply.[1]

5.09   The provisions of section 152 apply only to dismissals for the reasons set out above. A distinction, not always easy to draw, needs to be made between such dismissal and dismissal for industrial action. In *Drew v St Edmundsbury Borough Council*,[2] for example, the employee, who was a trade union member, was dismissed after he had been employed for less than the qualifying period of continuous employment (at the material time, 26 weeks) for repeatedly complaining to his employers about health and safety matters. Although he purported to be following a trade union directive to go slow, the directive was not concerned with health and safety matters. The employment tribunal decided that he was not dismissed for taking part in trade union activities, but for taking part in industrial action. He therefore had not been continuously employed for long enough. The EAT upheld its decision.

5.10   It should be noted that, in considering whether the reason for dismissal was a reason relating to trade union membership or activities the tribunal should not take into account whether the employers deliberately or maliciously selected the employee for dismissal. To decide that section 152 does not apply if there is no malice and no deliberate decision to dismiss for trade union activities is to construe the provision too narrowly.[3]

5.11   The first type of dismissal falling within section 152(1) is one where the reason for the dismissal is that the employee 'was ... a member of an independent trade union'. *Discount Tobacco & Confectionery Ltd v Armitage*[4] involved an employee who requested a statement of terms and conditions of employment from her employer some three and a half months into her employment. When she failed to obtain a statement, she went to her trade union official who took up her case with her employer. The matter was not resolved and she was dismissed. The employment tribunal held that the reason for her dismissal was her trade union membership. The EAT upheld its decision. Knox J said:[5]

---

[1]   *Carrington v Therm-a-Stor Ltd* [1983] ICR 208. See also *Discount Tobacco & Confectionery Ltd v Armitage* [1990] IRLR 15.
[2]   [1980] ICR 513. See also *Winnett v Seamarks Brothers Ltd* [1978] ICR 1240.
[3]   *Dundon v GPT Ltd* [1995] IRLR 403.
[4]   [1990] IRLR 15 and [1995] ICR 431.
[5]   [1995] ICR 431 at p 433.

'... [T]he activities of a trade union officer in negotiating and elucidating terms of employment is ... the outward and visible manifestation of trade union membership. It is an incident of union membership which is, if not the primary one, at any rate, a very important one and we see no genuine distinction between membership of a union on the one hand and making use of the essential services of a union, on the other. Were it not so, the scope of section [152(1)(a)] would be reduced almost to vanishing point, since it would only be just the fact that a person was a member of a union, without regard to the consequences of that membership, that would be the subject matter of that statutory provision and, it seems to us, that to construe that paragraph so narrowly would really be to emasculate the provision altogether.'

5.12   This approach was described by the Court of Appeal as 'unquestionably correct' in *Associated British Ports v Palmer*,[1] albeit that the issue in that case was not whether the employees in question had been dismissed for being members of a trade union, but whether action short of dismissal had been taken against them for that reason. In *Speciality Care plc v Pachela*,[2] the EAT followed its previous decision in *Discount Tobacco & Confectionery* and said:[3]

'... [W]here a complaint of dismissal by reason of union membership is made, ... it will be for the tribunal to find as a fact whether or not the reason or principal reason for dismissal related to the applicant's trade union membership not only by reference to whether he or she had simply joined a union, but also by reference to whether the introduction of union representation into the employment relationship had led the employer to dismiss the employee. Tribunals should answer that question robustly, based on their findings as to what really caused the dismissal in the mind of the employer.'

5.13   Section 152(1)(b) uses the phrase 'activities of an independent trade union'. This should not be interpreted restrictively but should be interpreted reasonably; it embraces an employee's participation in trade union activities during the course of his or her previous employment.[4] In *Britool Ltd v Roberts*,[5] the EAT said that actual participation in a strike, whether as a leader or otherwise, will rarely if ever constitute an activity within section 152(1)(b). But, since leading a strike involves not only leading the strike when it is in operation but a preliminary planning and consultation stage, those preliminary activities may be within the provision. In *Lyon v St James's Press*,[6] Phillips J said of these provisions:

[1] [1994] ICR 97. See Dillon LJ at p 102. See also *Harrison v Kent County Council* [1995] ICR 434 (a case in which the employee was refused employment because of trade union membership).
[2] [1996] ICR 633.
[3] *Ibid* at p 643.
[4] *Dixon v West Ella Developments Ltd* [1978] ICR 856 and *Fitzpatrick v British Railways Board* [1992] ICR 221. See also *Brennan and Ging v Ellward (Lanes) Ltd* [1976] IRLR 378 and *Driver v Cleveland Structural Engineering Co Ltd* [1994] ICR 372.
[5] [1993] IRLR 481.
[6] [1976] ICR 413.

'The special protection afforded by [section 152(1)] to trade union activities must not be allowed to operate as a cloak or an excuse for conduct which ordinarily would justify dismissal; equally, the right to take part in the affairs of the trade union must not be obstructed by too easily finding acts done for the purpose to be a justification for dismissal. The marks are easy to describe, but the channel between them is difficult to navigate.'[1]

He went on to add, in relation to acts claimed to come within the protection: '... wholly unreasonable, extraneous or malicious acts done in support of trade union activities might be a ground for a dismissal which might not be unfair'.[2] This approach was followed by the Court of Appeal in *Bass Taverns Ltd v Burgess*,[3] which involved the dismissal of an employee who had made disparaging remarks about the company at an induction course for trainee managers. The Court of Appeal said that the employment tribunal had erred in holding that this was not a reason relating to his trade union activities at an appropriate time. Pill LJ quoted the remarks of Phillips J, above, and went on to say:[4]

'I would add that in dealing with the facts of this case, I am very far from saying that the contents of a speech made at a trade union recruiting meeting, however malicious, untruthful or irrelevant to the task in hand they may be, come within the term "trade union activities" in [section 152].'

5.14   In *Chant v Aquaboats Ltd*,[5] the EAT said that 'activities of an independent trade union' do not include an individual's independent activities as a trade unionist and held that the organising of a petition about safety standards, which was vetted by the local branch of the union before being handed to the employers, was not a trade union activity within the Act. The activities of a union may embrace the discussion of matters which are the concern of a union at a meeting of a group of members of the union, even though the discussion is critical of the union and the meeting is not held in a committee or at a formal meeting of the branch.[6]

5.15   Section 152(2) of the 1992 Act defines 'appropriate time' as a time which is either outside an employee's working hours or 'is a time within his working hours at which, in accordance with arrangements agreed with or consent given by his employer, it is permissible for him to take part' in the activities. 'Working hours' means any time at which an employee is required to be at work in accordance with the contract of employment.[7] In

---

[1]   [1976] ICR 413 at p 418.
[2]   *Ibid* at p 419.
[3]   [1995] IRLR 596.
[4]   *Ibid* at p 599.
[5]   [1978] ICR 643. See also *Lyon v St James's Press* [1976] ICR 413 and *Brennan v Ellward (Lanes) Ltd* [1976] IRLR 378. *Cf SAS Service Partner v MacEachen* (EAT 414/92) IDS Brief 487, where the EAT upheld the tribunal's decision that the real reason for the employee's dismissal was not misconduct but his involvement in trade union activities, even though he did not hold any official union position.
[6]   *British Airways Engine Overhaul Ltd v Francis* [1981] ICR 278.
[7]   TULRCA, s 152(2).

Marley Tile Co Ltd v Shaw,[1] the Court of Appeal said that consent can be express or implied. On the facts of the case, consent could not be inferred and the employee's dismissal was therefore outside the ambit of what is now section 152. The fact that an employee is on the employer's premises and being paid does not mean that the trade union activities are necessarily within working hours.[2]

5.16 By virtue of section 152(4), references in section 152 to being, becoming or ceasing to remain a member of a trade union include references to being, becoming or ceasing to remain a member of a particular branch or section of the union and to being, becoming or ceasing to remain a member of one of a number of particular branches or sections of the union. This also applies to references to taking part in the activities of a trade union.

(b) Dismissals in connection with trade union recognition

5.17 Employees dismissed or selected for redundancy for one of the reasons set out below will be treated as automatically unfairly dismissed.[3] In the case of a dismissal, or a selection for redundancy, for one of these reasons, employees are protected whether or not they have been continuously employed for one year or have reached retirement age.[4] Further, they may be entitled to higher compensation and interim relief.[5]

5.18 The reasons are as follows:

(a) the employee acted with a view to obtaining or preventing recognition of a union or unions by the employer under Schedule A1 to the TULRCA 1992;

(b) the employee indicated that he or she supported or did not support recognition of a union or unions;

(c) the employee acted with a view to securing or preventing the ending under the Schedule of bargaining arrangements;

(d) the employee indicated that he or she supported or did not support the ending of bargaining arrangements;

(e) the employee influenced or sought to influence the way in which votes were to be cast by other workers in a ballot arranged under Schedule A1;

(f) the employee influenced or sought to influence other workers to vote or abstain from voting in such a ballot;

(g) the employee voted in such a ballot;

---

[1] [1980] ICR 72.

[2] *Zucker v Astrid Jewels Ltd* [1978] ICR 1088. The employee discussed union membership with her fellow-employees during the morning and afternoon tea and lunch breaks. The EAT remitted the case to another tribunal to consider whether, on the facts, she was engaging in trade union activities within working hours. Their view was that these were not working hours.

[3] TULRCA 1992, Sch A1, para 161.

[4] TULRCA 1992, Sch A1, para 164.

[5] See s 128, as amended, and Chapter 7.

(h)   the employee proposed to do, failed to do, or proposed to decline to
       do, any of the things referred to above.

5.19   A reason will not fall within the above list if it constitutes an
unreasonable act or omission by the employee.[1]

5.20   The dismissal of an employee selected for redundancy will be
automatically unfair if it is shown that:

(a)   the circumstances constituting the redundancy applied equally to
       one or more other employees in the same undertaking who held
       positions similar to that held by the employee and who have not
       been dismissed by the employer; and
(b)   the reason why the employee was selected was one of the reasons
       listed above.[2]

2. DISMISSALS AND INDUSTRIAL ACTION

5.21   Four types of dismissal fall to be considered here:

1.   dismissals of employees taking part in unofficial industrial action
      under section 237 of the TULRCA;
2.   dismissals in connection with strikes and lockouts;
3.   dismissals for participation in protected industrial action; and
4.   dismissals caused by industrial pressure, under section 107 of the
      ERA 1996.

(a) Unofficial industrial action

5.22   The effect of section 237(1) is to deprive of the right to complain of
unfair dismissal employees who, at the time of dismissal,[3] were taking part
in an unofficial strike or other industrial action. This does not apply,
however, to the dismissal of an employee where it is shown that the reason
(or principal reason) for the dismissal (or, in a 'redundancy case',[4] for
selecting the employee for dismissal) was one of those specified in
sections 99, 100, 101A(d), 103 or 103A of the Employment Rights Act 1996
(dismissals in family, health and safety, working time, employee
representative and protected disclosure cases)[5] (see paras 5.47 *et seq*, 5.57 *et
seq*, 5.73 *et seq*, 5.79 *et seq* and 5.82 *et seq*).

---

[1]   TULRCA 1992, Sch A1, para 161(3).
[2]   TULRCA 1992, Sch A1, para 162.
[3]   Defined in s 237(5); see below.
[4]   Defined in s 105(9) of the ERA 1996 as a case falling within s 105(1)(a) and (b) (see
       para 6.26, in Chapter 6).
[5]   Section 237(1A), introduced by the Trade Union Reform and Employment Rights Act
       1993, s 49(2) and Sch 8, para 76, and amended by the ERA 1996, Sch 1, para 56(15),
       Working Time Regulations 1998, SI 1998 No 1833, reg 32(8) and Employment Relations
       Act 1999, s 9 and Sch 4, Pt III, paras 1 and 2.

5.23   The circumstances in which a strike will be considered to be unofficial are set out in section 237(2). That provision operates in such a way as to place the burden on the employee of showing that the industrial action was not unofficial. The two circumstances in which industrial action is not unofficial are:

1.   where the dismissed employee is a member of a trade union and the action is authorised or endorsed by that union:[1] and
2.   where the employee is not a member of a trade union but amongst those taking part in the industrial action are members of a trade union which has authorised or endorsed the action.[2]

The industrial action is not to be regarded as unofficial if none of those taking part in it are members of a trade union.[3]

5.24   'Time of dismissal' is defined in section 237(5) as meaning either the time when the employee's contract is terminated by notice (when notice is given) or when the termination takes effect (when no notice is given) or when a fixed-term contract expires.

(b) Industrial action

(i) General rules

5.25   Section 238 of the 1992 Act removes from the employment tribunal the jurisdiction to hear a complaint of unfair dismissal where, at the date of dismissal, the employer was conducting or instituting a lockout, or the employee (complainant) was taking part in a strike or other industrial action. But its jurisdiction will be restored if one or more relevant employees of the same employer either have not been dismissed[4] or have been offered re-engagement within three months of their dismissal, but the complainant has not been offered re-engagement.[5] The provisions of section 238 will not cease to be applicable merely because the reason for the dismissal of those taking part in the industrial action is redundancy caused by the action.[6]

---

[1]   By virtue of s 237(3), the provisions of s 20(2) of the 1992 Act apply for the purpose of determining whether industrial action is to be taken to have been authorised or endorsed by a union. This question must be determined by reference to the facts as at the time of dismissal, as defined: see s 237(4). Where an act is repudiated, as mentioned in s 21, the industrial action will not be treated as unofficial before the end of the next working day after the day on which the repudiation takes place: proviso to s 237(4). 'Working day' is defined in s 237(5).

[2]   Note also the provisions of s 237(6).

[3]   Proviso to s 237(2).

[4]   TULRCA, s 238(2)(a).

[5]   TULRCA, s 238(2)(b). See *Tomczynski v JK Miller Ltd* (1976) 11 ITR 127, *Marsden v Fairey Stainless Ltd* [1979] IRLR 103, *Williams v National Theatre Board Ltd* [1982] ICR 715, *Highland Fabricators Ltd v McLaughlin* [1985] ICR 183, and *Bolton Roadways Ltd v Edwards* [1987] IRLR 392. Section 238(4) sets out the meaning of 'offer of re-engagement'.

[6]   *Baxter v Limb Group of Companies* [1994] IRLR 572.

5.26 The provisions concerning re-engagement were considered by the EAT in *Bigham and Keogh v GKN Kwikform Ltd.*[1] The employees were told that they were to be transferred to another site and a number of employees, including the two applicants in this case, were dismissed. Within three months of his dismissal, Bigham applied for a job at a different depot belonging to the same employers, revealing his previous employment and the site where he was employed, but without revealing his dismissal, or giving the date of employment. He was engaged, but was dismissed when his employers discovered the circumstances of his previous dismissal. He and Keogh complained of unfair dismissal, but the tribunal said that they did not have jurisdiction as the employees could not rely on Bigham's re-engagement within three months. The EAT allowed Keogh's appeal, saying that when Bigham applied for a job, the employers must at least have had constructive knowledge of the facts, since the information was available at another depot. Accordingly, Bigham had been offered re-engagement within section 238(2)(b) and the tribunal had jurisdiction to hear Keogh's complaint. The EAT has also held that a general advertising campaign offering employment to those who apply does not in itself amount to an offer of employment to any particular individual; it is merely an offer to treat for re-engagement.[2]

5.27 The provisions of section 238(2) do not apply, however, to the dismissal of an employee where it is shown that the reason (or principal reason) for the dismissal (or, in a 'redundancy case',[3] for selecting the employee for dismissal) was one of those specified in sections 99, 100, 101A(d) or 103 of the Employment Rights Act 1996 (dismissal in family, health and safety, working time and employee representative cases) or section 104 of the Act in its application in relation to time off under section 57A (dependants)[4] (see paras 5.47 *et seq*, 5.57 *et seq*, 5.73 *et seq*, 5.79 *et seq* and 5.95 *et seq*). The provisions of section 238(2) will also not apply in relation to employees who are regarded as unfairly dismissed by virtue of section 238A, which deals with dismissals in connection with participation in official industrial action[5] (see para 5.42).

5.28 The consequences of section 238 are that, if the employer dismisses all the strikers and re-engages none of them, the tribunal has no jurisdiction. Once, however, there is selectivity, either in dismissing or re-engaging, the saving provisions in section 238 will be triggered and the employer will have to beware of various pitfalls they contain.

---

[1]   [1992] ICR 113.

[2]   *Crosville Wales Ltd v Tracey* [1993] IRLR 60.

[3]   Defined in s 105(9) of the ERA 1996 as a case falling within s 105(1)(a) and (b) (see para 6.26 in Chapter 6, where this provision is discussed).

[4]   Section 238(2A), introduced by the Trade Union Reform and Employment Rights Act 1993, s 49(2) and Sch 8, para 77, and amended by the Employment Rights Act 1996, Sch 1, para 56(15), the Working Time Regulations 1998, SI 1998 No 1833, reg 32(8) and the Employment Relations Act 1999, s 9 and Sch 4, Pt III, paras 1 and 3. See *Baxter v LIMB Group of Companies* [1994] IRLR 572.

[5]   TULRCA, s 238(2B), inserted by the Employment Relations Act 1999, s 16 and Sch 5, paras 1 and 2.

5.29   If jurisdiction is given to the tribunal, it will proceed to hear the case in the ordinary way, subject to the amendments made to section 98(4) in cases of non-re-engagement.[1] In such cases also, the limitation period for a complaint is extended to six months from the complainant's date of dismissal.[2] It should also be noted that there may be borderline cases in which the tribunal will have to decide whether the dismissal is for trade union membership or activities (and falls within section 152) or is in connection with industrial action (and falls within section 238).[3] An employee dismissed for trade union membership or activities does not have to have been employed for the qualifying period, whereas an employee dismissed for industrial action does.[4] Industrial action may affect the amount of compensation the employee receives: see Chapter 8.

5.30   The following questions are considered here:

1.   the meaning of 'at the date of dismissal';
2.   the meaning of 'strike', 'lockout' and 'other industrial action'; and
3.   the meaning of 'relevant employees'.

(ii) 'At the date of dismissal'

5.31   Section 238(5) of the TULRCA defines 'date of dismissal' as meaning:

'(a)   where the employee's contract of employment was terminated by notice, the date on which the employer's notice was given, and
(b)   in any other case, the effective date of termination.'

5.32   The EAT considered this definition in *Bolton Roadways Ltd v Edwards*.[5] The question in that case was whether the date of dismissal was the day (24 September 1984) on which the employers handed the striking employees a letter which said: 'if you do not report for duty tomorrow … the company will consider your employment terminated'; or the following day when the employees did not report for work and were dismissed. One of the employees was on strike on 24 September but was ill on 25 September. The employers accepted his explanation and reinstated him. The EAT decided that the date of dismissal was 25 September. Other aspects of this case are considered below in the context of the meaning of 'relevant employees'.

---

[1]   TULRCA, s 239(3), as amended by the ERA 1996, Sch 1, para 56(16)(c). See *Edwards v Cardiff City Council* [1979] IRLR 303.
[2]   TULRCA, s 239(2), as amended by the ERA 1996, Sch 1, para 56(16)(b).
[3]   See, eg, *Winnett v Seamarks Brothers Ltd* [1978] ICR 1240 and *Drew v St Edmundsbury Borough Council* [1980] ICR 513.
[4]   *Drew v St Edmundsbury Borough Council*, above.
[5]   [1987] IRLR 392.

'At the date of dismissal' means 'at the time of dismissal'; so if the strike ends in the morning and the strikers are dismissed in the afternoon, section 238 no longer applies.[1]

(iii) 'Strike', 'lockout' and 'other industrial action'

5.33   Section 235(4) and (5) of the Employment Rights Act 1996 contains definitions of 'strike' and 'lockout', but the Court of Appeal has said that those definitions only apply for the purposes of the provisions specified there; the words in section 238 should be given their ordinary meaning and the definitions in the 1996 Act can only provide guidance in determining what the ordinary meaning is.[2]

5.34   The Court of Appeal has stressed that the question what are the necessary elements of a lockout, strike or other industrial action is not one of law, but of fact.[3] In *Tramp Shipping Corporation v Greenwich Marine Inc,*[4] Lord Denning MR said:

'... [A] strike is a concerted stoppage of work by men done with a view to improving their wages or conditions, or giving vent to a grievance or making a protest about something or other. It is distinct from a stoppage which is brought about by an external event such as a bomb scare or by apprehension of danger.'

In *Coates v Modern Methods & Materials Ltd,*[5] Eveleigh LJ said:

'... [F]or a person to take part in a strike he must be acting jointly or in concert with others who withdraw their labour, and this means that he must withdraw his labour in support of their claim. The fact that a man stays away from work when a strike is on does not lead inevitably to the conclusion that he is taking part in a strike.'

Much of the debate in the cases has in fact concerned the question whether a person was 'taking part' in the strike at the date of dismissal. This is part of the definition of 'relevant employees' and is considered below.

5.35   In *Express & Star Ltd v Bunday,*[6] the Court of Appeal considered the meaning of 'lockout'. After deciding that the definition in what is now section 235(4) of the 1996 Act can only afford guidance as to the meaning of the word, May LJ, with whom Croom-Johnson LJ agreed, quoted the definition in the *Shorter Oxford English Dictionary*: 'An act of locking out a body of operatives; ie a refusal on the part of an employer, or employers acting in concert, to furnish work to their operatives except on conditions

---

[1]   *Heath v JF Longman (Meat Salesmen) Ltd* [1973] ICR 407. See also *Glenrose (Fish Merchants) Ltd v Chapman* (EAT 245/89), a case which arose from a refusal to work overtime.
[2]   *Express & Star Ltd v Bunday* [1988] ICR 379. Cf *Coates v Modern Methods & Materials Ltd* [1982] ICR 763.
[3]   *Express & Star Ltd v Bunday* [1988] ICR 379.
[4]   [1975] ICR 261 at p 266.
[5]   [1982] ICR 763 at pp 778–779.
[6]   [1988] ICR 379. Cf *Fisher v York Trailer Co Ltd* [1979] ICR 834.

to be accepted by the latter collectively'. He stressed, however, that the definition is merely an indication of what does constitute a lockout, but that every case must be decided on its facts. The question whether the employer was in breach of contract in locking out the employees is a relevant consideration in determining whether there has been a lockout, but a breach is not an essential ingredient of a lockout. In the case in question, there was also a question as to whether there had been a lockout or other industrial action. The case involved a dispute over the introduction of new technology. In February 1985, the members of the workforce were instructed by their union not to agree to handle material produced by the new process. The following day the employer closed the premises, except for a management-manned door, and employees were informed that if they refused to handle work, however processed, they would be dismissed. When they refused, they were suspended without pay. The employment tribunal held that they had been taking part in industrial action and that there had been no lockout. The Court of Appeal held that it had not erred in law in reaching that decision.

5.36   Questions have arisen as to whether industrial action for which the employers are to some extent to blame falls within the definition of 'other industrial action' in section 238. Although there are suggestions in *Thompson v Eaton Ltd*[1] that these provisions do not apply to a case where the employer provokes or engineers a strike 'in some gross manner', later decisions have taken the view that an engineered strike falls within the ambit of section 238.[2]

5.37   Other examples of 'other industrial action' have been held to be a refusal to work overtime,[3] taking part in a decision to impose an overtime ban,[4] a refusal to carry out a lawful instruction given by the employer without extra pay,[5] and a threat of withdrawal of labour.[6] In *Rasool v Hepworth Pipe Co Ltd*,[7] the EAT held that attendance at an unauthorised mass meeting for the purpose of ascertaining the views of the workforce with regard to impending wage negotiations fell short of industrial action.

(iv) 'Relevant employees'

5.38   In relation to a lockout, 'relevant employees' means employees who were directly interested in the dispute in contemplation or furtherance of which the lockout occurred;[8] in relation to a strike or other industrial

---

[1]   [1976] ICR 336 at p 342.
[2]   See *Wilkins v Cantrell & Cochrane (GB) Ltd* [1978] IRLR 483 and *Marsden v Fairey Stainless Ltd* [1979] IRLR 103.
[3]   *Power Packing Casemakers Ltd v Faust* [1983] ICR 292. See also *Glenrose (Fish Merchants) Ltd v Chapman* (EAT 245/89).
[4]   *Naylor v Orton & Smith Ltd* [1983] ICR 665. The EAT in fact upheld the employment tribunal's decision that on the facts the relevant employees were not taking part in other industrial action.
[5]   *Lewis and Britton v E Mason & Sons Ltd* [1994] IRLR 4.
[6]   *Ibid.*
[7]   [1980] ICR 494.
[8]   TULRCA, s 238(3)(a); see *Fisher v York Trailer Co Ltd* [1979] ICR 834.

action, it means those employees at the establishment who were taking part in the action at the complainant's date of dismissal.[1] The provisions of section 237, which deal with the dismissal of those taking part in unofficial industrial action (considered above), do not affect the question of who are relevant employees for the purposes of section 238.[2]

5.39   The main question which arises here is what constitutes 'taking part' in a strike or other industrial action. In *McCormick v Horsepower Ltd*,[3] the employee was one of a number of employees who went on strike for more pay. An employee named Brazier, who was employed in a different department which was not involved in the strike, did not wish to cross the picket line and stayed away from work, although he did not tell the employers that he was on strike. After a few weeks he crossed the picket lines and resumed work with the employers. He was later dismissed for redundancy. The Court of Appeal held that in deciding not to cross the picket line he was not acting in concert with the employees who were on strike, nor was he taking part in a sympathetic strike. He was not, therefore taking part in the strike and 'for the purposes of section [238] he was an irrelevancy'.[4] The Court of Appeal has stressed, however, that the words 'taking part in a strike' are ordinary words the meaning of which the employment tribunal is best fitted to decide. It is the employee's actions, and not the reasons or motives behind the actions, that determine whether an employee is taking part in a strike. So, if an employee stops work when other employees come out on strike and neither says nor does anything to indicate disagreement with the strike or indicate a refusal to join the strike, the employee is taking part in a strike.[5] More recently, the EAT has said this:

> '... [T]he question whether an employee is or is not taking part in a strike is to be determined by evidence of what he is in fact doing or omitting to do. If his actions and omissions do not justify the conclusion that he was participating in a strike, then that settles the matter. If his actions and omissions are such as to justify the inferences that he was participating in the strike action, ... the inference [cannot] be invalidated by the circumstance that the employer was unaware of his actions or omissions.'[6]

---

[1]   TULRCA, s 238(3)(b).
[2]   TULRCA, s 238(3).
[3]   [1981] ICR 535.
[4]   *Ibid* at p 540.
[5]   *Coates v Modern Methods & Materials Ltd* [1982] ICR 763. Eveleigh LJ dissented. The relevant employee was certified unfit to attend work for the duration of the strike, and only put in a brief appearance at the beginning. She was held to be a relevant employee. Cf *Hindle Gears Ltd v McGinty* [1985] ICR 111, where on the facts the EAT held to be perverse the tribunal's decision that a sick employee's conduct in talking to strikers when handing in his medical certificates amounted to participation in the strike. See also *McKenzie v Crosville Motor Services Ltd* [1989] ICR 172 and *Rogers v Chloride Systems Ltd* [1992] ICR 198.
[6]   In *Bolton Roadways Ltd v Edwards* [1987] IRLR 392. The employee in question was on strike on the day before the 'date of dismissal', but on the date of dismissal he telephoned the employers and told them he was sick. He was reinstated. The EAT upheld the tribunal's decision that he was taking part in the strike, and was therefore a relevant employee.

5.40 In *McKenzie v Crosville Motor Services Ltd,*[1] the EAT emphasised that an employee who remains away from work must maintain contact with the employer so as to ensure that the employer knows the true reason for his or her absence. Otherwise, the employer is entitled to assume, if the absence occurs when strike action is taking place, that he or she is absent because of participation in the strike action. In the later case of *Manifold Industries Ltd v Sims,*[2] the EAT said that the views expressed in *Bolton Roadways Ltd v Edwards* were to be preferred to those in *McKenzie v Crosville Motor Services Ltd* The EAT emphasised that the question whether or not an employee is taking part in a strike is to be determined by what he or she was in fact doing; the employer's knowledge of the employee's actions is not a relevant consideration.

5.41 A further question which arises here is at what time it has to be shown that there is an employee on strike who has not been dismissed. In *McCormick v Horsepower Ltd* (above), the Court of Appeal suggested, *obiter*, that the relevant time is the start of the employment tribunal hearing. This suggestion has been overruled by the later decision of the Court of Appeal in *P & O European Ferries (Dover) Ltd v Byrne.*[3] The Court held that the relevant time is the end of the hearing at which the tribunal decides whether it has jurisdiction. The Court of Appeal also allowed an appeal against the tribunal's refusal of the employers' application for an order requiring the employee to provide particulars of his allegation that a relevant employee had not been dismissed, including the identity of the employee. This was on the grounds that it was necessary for the employers to know what case they had to meet. The effect of this decision is that an employer who selectively dismisses strikers can prevent the tribunal from acquiring jurisdiction to deal with a dismissed striker's complaint by discovering the identity of any other strikers who were not dismissed and then summarily dismissing them before the end of the tribunal hearing.

The test of who were 'relevant employees' in the context of lockouts is a retrospective one.[4]

(c) Dismissals for participation in official industrial action

5.42 The Employment Relations Act 1999 added a new provision, section 238A, which deals with dismissals for participation in official industrial action. By virtue of section 238A(1), this provision applies to employees who take 'protected industrial action'. This is defined[5] as the commission by the employee of 'an act which, or a series of acts each of which, he is induced to commit which by virtue of section 219 is not

---

[1]   [1990] ICR 172 at pp 177–178.
[2]   [1991] ICR 504. This case was followed by another division of the EAT in *Jenkins v P & O European Ferries (Dover) Ltd* [1991] ICR 652.
[3]   [1989] ICR 779. See also *Manifold Industries Ltd v Sims* [1991] ICR 504.
[4]   *H Campey & Sons Ltd v Bellwood* [1987] ICR 311.
[5]   By s 238A(1). Note s 238A(8) which says that no account is to be taken of the repudiation of any act by a trade union (within s 21) in relation to anything which occurs before the end of the next working day after the day on which the repudiation takes place.

actionable in tort'.[1] An employee who falls within this provision does not have to satisfy the requirements relating to the qualifying period of employment, nor will he or she be excluded if over the normal retiring age.[2]

5.43   An employee will be treated as automatically unfairly dismissed if the reason (or principal reason) for the dismissal is that the employee took 'protected industrial action' and the provisions of section 238A(3), (4) or (5) apply to the dismissal. A dismissal will fall within these provisions if:

(a)   it takes place within eight weeks starting with the day on which the employee started to take protected industrial action;[3] or

(b)   it takes place after the end of the eight-week period and the employee had stopped taking protected industrial action before the end of that period;[4] or

(c)   it takes place after the end of the eight-week period, the employee had not stopped taking protected industrial action before the end of that period, and the employer had not taken such procedural steps as would have been reasonable for the purpose of resolving the dispute to which the protected industrial action relates.[5]

5.44   In the third situation, section 238A(6) sets out the factors to which regard should be had when considering whether the employer has taken reasonable steps; but no regard is to be had to the merits of the dispute.[6] The relevant factors are:

(a)   whether the employer or a union had complied with procedures established by any applicable collective or other agreement;

(b)   whether the employer or a union offered or agreed to start or resume negotiations after the start of the protected industrial action;

(c)   whether the employer or a union reasonably refused, after the start of the protected industrial action, a request that conciliation services should be used;

(d)   whether the employer or a union unreasonably refused, after the start of the protected industrial action, a request that mediation services should be used in relation to procedures to be adopted for the purposes of resolving the dispute.

5.45   Section 239(4)[7] contains provisions relating to complaints that a dismissal was unfair by virtue of section 238A. It provides that the tribunal is not to make a re-employment order under section 113 of the 1996 Act

---

[1]   It is not possible here to discuss the scope and ambit of section 219, but reference should be made to the standard reference works which deal with industrial disputes.

[2]   TULRCA, s 239(1), as amended by the Employment Relations Act 1999, s 16 and Sch 5, paras 1 and 4(1)–(3).

[3]   TULRCA, s 238A(3).

[4]   TULRCA, s 238A(4).

[5]   TULRCA, s 238A(5).

[6]   TULRCA, s 238A(7).

[7]   Inserted by ERA 1999, s 16 and Sch 5, paras 1, 4(1) and (5).

until after the conclusion of the protected industrial action by 'any employee in relation to the relevant dispute'. It also says that regulations under section 7 of the Employment Tribunals Act 1996 may make provision about the adjournment and renewal of applications (including provision requiring adjournment in specified circumstances) and that regulations under section 9 of the Act may require a pre-hearing review to be carried out in specified circumstances. The relevant provision is rule 9 of the Employment Tribunal Rules of Procedure.[1] The new rules of procedure came into effect on 16 July 2001.

(d) Industrial pressure

5.46 Section 107 of the ERA 1996 requires the tribunal to ignore certain kinds of pressure from third parties and to decide upon the reason for the dismissal and its fairness as if there had been no pressure. 'Pressure' is defined in section 107(2) as 'any pressure which, by calling, organising, procuring or financing a strike or other industrial action, or threatening to do so, was exercised on the employer to dismiss the employee'.[2] If the pressure was exercised because the employee was not a trade union member, the employer or the employee may ask the employment tribunal, under section 160 of the TULRCA, to join as a party to the proceedings the person claimed to have exerted the pressure. That person may have to make a total or partial contribution to any compensation awarded against the employer.[3]

3. DISMISSALS AND LEAVE FOR FAMILY REASONS

5.47 The law relating to maternity rights has been substantially overhauled since the last edition of this book. The changes have been brought about by the Employment Relations Act 1999 and the Maternity and Parental Leave Regulations 1999.[4]

5.48 The 1999 Act[5] introduced a new section 99 to the ERA 1996 which is headed 'Leave for family reasons'. A dismissal will be automatically unfair if the reason (or principal reason) is of a kind and it takes place in circumstances prescribed by the Regulations.[6] The reason or set of circumstances prescribed by the Regulations must relate to one of the following situations:

---

[1]   In the Employment Tribunals (Constitution and Rules of Procedure) Regulations 2001, SI 2001 No 1171, Sch 1 (set out at Appendix 2 of this book).

[2]   See *Trend v Chiltern Hunt Ltd* [1977] ICR 612, *Hazells Offset Ltd v Luckett* [1977] IRLR 430, *Ford Motor Co Ltd v Hudson* [1978] ICR 482, and *Colwyn Borough Council v Dutton* [1980] IRLR 420.

[3]   TULRCA, s 160(3). For the calculation of compensation in such cases, see Chapter 8.

[4]   SI 1999 No 3312.

[5]   See s 9 and Sch 4, Pt III, paras 1, 5 and 16.

[6]   Section 99(1). Note s 99(5).

(a)   pregnancy, childbirth, or maternity;
(b)   ordinary, compulsory or additional maternity leave;
(c)   parental leave; or
(d)   time off under section 57A.

It may also relate to redundancy or 'other factors'.[1]

5.49   There is no minimum qualifying period of continuous employment for employees dismissed contrary to this section; nor are they excluded if they are over the normal retirement age.[2]

5.50   The provisions of section 202 of the Employment Rights Act 1996 should be noted here, since, as currently drafted, they contain provisions specific to section 99. Section 202[3] applies where, in the opinion of any Minister of the Crown, the disclosure of any information would be contrary to the interests of national security. In that case, disclosure of the information is not required; further, disclosure is forbidden in any proceedings in any court or tribunal relating to section 99. It should also be noted that section 10(1) of the Employment Tribunals Act 1996[4] provides that an employment tribunal is to dismiss a complaint of unfair dismissal if it is shown that the action complained of was taken for the purpose of safeguarding national security. The new sections 10, 10A and 10B contain no provisions dealing specifically with section 99 as the previous section 10(5) (now replaced) did. These new sections are considered at para 1.90.

5.51   Regulation 20 of the Maternity and Parental Leave Regulations deals with unfair dismissal. An employee is to be regarded as unfairly dismissed if the reason (or principal reason) is connected with:

(a)   the pregnancy of the employee;[5]
(b)   the fact that the employee has given birth to a child;[6]
(c)   'the application of a relevant requirement, or a relevant recommendation, as defined by section 66(2)' of the ERA;

---

[1]   Section 99(3). A reason or set of circumstances satisfies (c) and (d) in the text if it relates to action which an employee takes, agrees to take or refuses to take under or in respect of a collective or workforce agreement which deals with parental leave: see s 99(4).

[2]   See ss 108(3) and 109(2).

[3]   As amended by the Employment Relations Act 1999, s 9 and Sch 4, Pt III, paras 1, 5 and 36.

[4]   As substituted by the Employment Relations Act 1999, s 41 and Sch 8, para 3.

[5]   The previous legislation used a similar phrase. Cases decided under that legislation held that reasons connected with pregnancy included miscarriages and hypertension: see *George v Beecham Group* [1977] IRLR 43 and *Elegbede v The Wellcome Foundation* [1977] IRLR 383. The House of Lords considered the phrase 'any other reason connected with her pregnancy' (the phrase used in the previous legislation) in *Brown v Stockton-on-Tees Borough Council* [1988] ICR 410, a decision followed by the EAT in *Clayton v Vigors* [1990] IRLR 177; see also *Hilton International Hotels (UK) Ltd v Kaissi* [1994] ICR 578. It held that the phrase ought to be read widely. So a pregnant employee who was selected for redundancy because she would require maternity leave was held to have been dismissed for a reason connected with her pregnancy; her dismissal was therefore unfair.

[6]   This only applies where the dismissal ends the employee's ordinary or additional maternity leave period: see reg 20(4).

(d)   the fact that she took, sought to take or availed herself of the benefits of, ordinary maternity leave;[1]
(e)   the fact that she took or sought to take:

(i)   additional maternity leave;[2]
(ii)   parental leave;[3] or
(iii) time off under section 57A;[4]

(f)   the fact that she declined to sign a workforce agreement[5] for the purposes of the Regulations;
(g)   the fact that the employee was a representative of members of the workforce for the purposes of Schedule 1 (which deals with the conclusion of workforce agreements) or a candidate in an election to be such a representative and, as such, performed (or proposed to perform) any functions or activities as a representative or candidate.

5.52   A dismissal for redundancy will be unfair if the employer does not comply with regulation 10. This applies where a redundancy situation develops during the employee's ordinary or additional maternity leave period, and it is not practicable by reason of redundancy for her employer to continue to employ her under her existing contract of employment. In that case, regulation 10(2) entitles her to be offered alternative employment with her employer, or a successor or associated employer, under a new contract of employment, but only if there is a suitable available vacancy. In *Community Task Force v Rimmer*,[6] the EAT held that a suitable 'available' vacancy is not qualified by consideration of what is economic or reasonable. The new contract of employment must comply with regulation 10(3). It must be suitable in relation to her and appropriate for

---

[1]   A woman will be treated as availing herself of the benefits of ordinary maternity leave if, during her ordinary maternity leave period, she avails herself of the benefit of any of the terms and conditions of her employment preserved by s 71 of the ERA during that period: see regs 20(5) and 19(3).

[2]   See ERA, s 73 and regs 5, 6(3) and 7(4). An employee is not entitled to additional maternity leave, unless she is also entitled to ordinary maternity leave and had been continuously employed for a year at the beginning of the eleventh week before the expected week of childbirth: reg 5. The ordinary maternity leave period starts either at the date notified to the employer as the date on which she intends her ordinary maternity leave period to start or the first day of the sixth week before the expected week of childbirth on which she is absent from work wholly or partly because of pregnancy, whichever date is the earlier: reg 6(1); note also reg 6(2). The additional maternity leave period starts the day after the last day of the ordinary maternity leave period and continues until the end of the period of 29 weeks starting with the week of childbirth: regs 6(3) and 7(4). If the employee is dismissed during a maternity leave period, the period ends at the time of the dismissal: reg 7(5).

[3]   The entitlement to parental leave and the extent of the entitlement are set out in regs 13 and 14.

[4]   This section makes provision for time off for dependants in certain circumstances.

[5]   Schedule 1 to the Regulations deals with workforce agreements.

[6]   [1986] ICR 491. The case was decided under the old s 45(3), which used the same phrase, but there is no reason to suppose that the change in the law brought about by the Employment Relations Act 1999 has affected this.

her to do in the circumstances; the terms of the new contract must not be substantially less favourable than if she had continued to be employed under the previous contract. Failure to make an offer of a suitable available vacancy will be treated as an automatic unfair dismissal.[1]

5.53   A dismissal for redundancy will also be automatically unfair if it is shown that:

(a)   the circumstances constituting the redundancy applied equally to one or more employees in the same undertaking who held positions similar to the position held by the employee and were not dismissed by the employer; and

(b)   the reason (or principal reason) for which the employee was selected for a dismissal was one of the reasons set out above.[2]

5.54   There are two exclusions from these provisions. The first applies to small employers in the following circumstances:

(a)   the employer has no more than five employees (including employees of an associated employer)[3] immediately before the end of the employee's additional maternity leave period or, if it is brought to an end by dismissal, immediately before the dismissal; and

(b)   it is not reasonably practicable for the employer (or successor employer) to allow her to return to a job which is both suitable for her and appropriate for her to do in the circumstances or for an associated employer to offer her a job of that kind.[4]

5.55   The second exclusion applies where:

(a)   it is not reasonably practicable for a reason other than redundancy for the employer (or successor employer) to allow her to return to a job which is both suitable for her and appropriate for her to do in the circumstances;

(b)   an associated employer offers her a job of that kind; and

(c)   she accepts or unreasonably refuses the offer.[5]

An employer who wishes to invoke either of the above exclusions will have the burden of showing that they were satisfied.[6]

5.56   There is also a specific exclusion relating to employees dismissed for taking additional maternity leave. Regulation 12(2) excludes from

---

[1]   See reg 20(1)(b).
[2]   Regulation 20(2).
[3]   Defined in reg 2(3). The definition is the same as that in s 231 of ERA 1996.
[4]   Regulation 20(6).
[5]   Regulation 20(7).
[6]   Regulation 20(8).

regulation 20 an employee who has failed to notify her employer of her intention to return in response to a request made in writing.[1]

4. DISMISSALS IN HEALTH AND SAFETY CASES

5.57   Section 100 of the ERA 1996 governs these types of dismissal. For employees covered by this provision there is no minimum qualifying period of continuous employment; nor are they excluded if they are over the normal retirement age.[2]

5.58   A preliminary point to note is whether the person claiming unfair dismissal in these circumstances is an employee of the employer. In *Costain Building & Civil Engineering Ltd v Smith and Chanton Group plc*,[3] the facts were that an engineer was supplied by an agency to Costain. There was an agreement between the agency and Costain for the supply of services by the engineer and the agreement stated that he would be under the strict supervision of Costain. There was no agreement between him and Costain, however, and he did not receive any disciplinary or grievance documentation, he did not expect to receive sick pay or holiday pay, and there was no clause providing for notice of termination. The engineer raised a number of health and safety issues and eventually was appointed a health and safety representative for the site. After he had produced a number of reports critical of Costain's management of the site, Costain informed the agency that they did not want him to continue to work on the site. He claimed that he had been unfairly dismissed by Costain contrary to ERA 1996, section 100(1)(b). The EAT held that he did not become an employee of Costain, and that therefore he could not complain of unfair dismissal. It followed that his appointment as a health and safety representative was ineffective. The EAT pointed out when a health and safety representative is appointed, he or she should already be an employee. It rejected the argument that the appointment of the engineer as a representative had the effect of altering his status.

5.59   It should be noted that selection for redundancy for any of the reasons set out in this section will also be automatically unfair.[4] An employee dismissed for one of the reasons set out below may apply to the employment tribunal for interim relief under section 128. It should be

---

[1] See reg 12(1) and (3). This applies where an employer makes a written request to an employee to notify in writing the date of the child's birth and whether she intends to return to work at the end of her additional maternity leave period. The request must be made no earlier than 21 days before the end of the employee's ordinary leave period; it must be accompanied by a written statement explaining how the employee may determine the date on which her additional maternity leave period will end and warning her of the consequence of a failure to respond in time. The employee must respond within 21 days of receiving the request.

[2] See ss 108(3) and 109(2).

[3] [2000] ICR 215.

[4] See s 105(1) and (3) and Chapter 6, para 6.42.

noted that the statutory limit for a compensatory award of compensation will not apply to these types of unfair dismissal.[1]

5.60   The provisions of section 202 of the Employment Rights Act 1996 should be noted here, since, as currently drafted, they contain provisions specific to section 100. Section 202[2] applies where, in the opinion of any Minister of the Crown, the disclosure of any information would be contrary to the interests of national security. In that case, disclosure of the information is not required; further, disclosure is forbidden in any proceedings in any court or tribunal relating to section 100. It should also be noted that section 10(1) of the Employment Tribunals Act 1996[3] provides that an employment tribunal is to dismiss a complaint of unfair dismissal if it is shown that the action complained of was taken for the purpose of safeguarding national security. The new sections 10, 10A and 10B contain no provisions dealing specifically with section 100 as the previous section 10(5) (now replaced) did. These new sections are considered at para 1.90.

5.61   Section 100(1) provides that the dismissal of an employee will be automatically unfair if the reason (or principal reason) for it is one of the five reasons specified in that subsection. Selection for redundancy for one of these reasons will also be automatically unfair.[4] The burden of proving that a dismissal was for health and safety reasons is on the employee.[5] Where there is more than one possible reason for the dismissal, the tribunal must determine what was the principal reason for the dismissal.[6] The six reasons set out in section 100(1) are as follows:

1.   The employee carried out, or proposed to carry out activities in connection with preventing or reducing risks to health and safety at work, after being designated by the employer to do so.[7]

2.   The employee, as a workers' representative on health and safety matters or member of a safety committee, performed, or proposed to perform, any functions as such a representative or committee member, in accordance with arrangements established under or by virtue of any enactment or by reason of being acknowledged as representative or committee member by the employer.[8]

3.   The employee took part (or proposed to take part) in consultations with the employer pursuant to the Health and Safety (Consultation

---

[1]   See s 124(1A), inserted by the Employment Relations Act 1999, s 37(1), with effect from 25 October 1999.

[2]   As amended by the Employment Relations Act 1999, s 9 and Sch 4, Pt III, paras 1, 5 and 36.

[3]   As substituted by the Employment Relations Act 1999, s 41 and Sch 8, para 3.

[4]   See s 105(1) and (3) and Chapter 6.

[5]   *Tedeschi v Hosiden Besson Ltd* (EAT 959/95). See (2000) IDS Brief B654/5.

[6]   *Ibid.*

[7]   Section 100(1)(a).

[8]   Section 100(1)(b).

with Employees) Regulations 1996 or in the election of safety representatives (whether as a candidate or otherwise).[1]

4. In the case of employees at a place where there was no workers' representative or safety committee or, where there was a representative or a committee, but it was not reasonably practicable for the employees to raise the matter by those means, they brought to the employer's attention by reasonable means circumstances connected with their work which they reasonably believed were harmful or potentially harmful to health and safety.[2]

5. There were circumstances of danger which the employee reasonably believed to be serious and imminent, and which he or she could not reasonably be expected to avert, and he or she left, proposed to leave, or (while the danger persisted) refused to return to, the place of work or any dangerous part of it.[3]

6. There were circumstances of danger which the employee reasonably believed to be serious and imminent and he or she took, or proposed to take, appropriate steps to protect himself or herself or other persons from the danger.[4] Whether the steps were appropriate is to be judged by reference to all the circumstances including, in particular, his or her knowledge and the facilities and advice available to him or her at the time.[5] In the case of a dismissal for this fifth reason, the dismissal will not be automatically unfair if the employer shows that it was (or would have been) so negligent for the employee to take the steps which he or she took, or proposed to take, that a reasonable employer might have dismissed him or her for taking, or proposing to take them.[6]

5.62   The first two cases set out above relate only to the defined activities of safety representatives, employees with designated health and safety functions and members of safety committees. An employee will only be protected by these provisions, however, if he or she is a representative in respect of the area where the health and safety complaint arises. This question arose in *Shillito v Van Leer (UK) Ltd.*[7] The case was decided under what is now section 44(1)(b), the equivalent provision to section 100(1)(b) in the context of an employee's right not to suffer a detriment. In that case, the employee was a safety representative for one area ('line 8'), but took it upon himself to become involved with a health and safety problem which arose in another area ('line 6'). He was disciplined for this. The EAT held that the employment tribunal was entitled to find that his activities as a safety representative were not the reason for his being disciplined because he was not the representative for the area in question, had acted outside the

---

[1]   Section 100(1)(ba), inserted by the Health and Safety (Consultation with Employees) Regulations 1996, SI 1996 No 1513.
[2]   Section 100(1)(c).
[3]   Section 100(1)(d).
[4]   Section 100(1)(e).
[5]   Section 100(2).
[6]   Section 100(3).
[7]   [1997] IRLR 495.

agreed procedures and had acted in bad faith. It also pointed out, however, that it is no defence for the employer to argue that the employee intended to embarrass the employer in front of external authorities, or that he or she performed the functions in an unreasonable way, unacceptable to the employer. Provided that the reason for the dismissal (or, here detriment) is shown to be that the employee was performing the functions of a safety representative, the complaint is made out. The EAT developed this approach in *Goodwin v Cabletel UK Ltd.*[1] It held that it is open to a tribunal to consider whether the manner in which the employee approached the health and safety problem took him or her outside the scope of his or her health and safety activities. It quoted from the judgment of Phillips J in *Lyon v St James's Press,*[2] which was decided in the context of a dismissal for trade union activities:

'... [W]holly unreasonable, extraneous or malicious acts done in support of trade union activities might be a good ground for a dismissal which would not be unfair.'

It went on to add:

'In our judgment a similar approach is appropriate when considering the health and safety activities protected by [section 100]. The protection afforded to the way in which a designated employee carries out his health and safety activities must not be diluted by too easily finding acts done for that purpose to be a justification for dismissal; on the other hand, not every act, however malicious or irrelevant to the task in hand, must necessarily be treated as a protected act in circumstances where dismissal would be justified on legitimate grounds.'[3]

5.63   The fourth case covers any employee, but it should be noted that an employee wishing to raise health and safety issues must go through any safety committee or representative where possible, unless it is not reasonably practicable to do so. Thus, an employee with a grievance must first raise it through the relevant representative; he or she will only be able to rely upon the third reason above if it is possible to satisfy the tribunal that it was not reasonably practicable to use that avenue. Employees who take the issue into their own hands run the risk, therefore, of falling outside section 100(1)(c). In a case covered by this provision, the employee must show that he or she reasonably believed that the circumstances were harmful or potentially harmful to health or safety. In *Kerr v Nathan's Wastesavers Ltd,*[4] which involved an employee who was dismissed for refusing to drive a vehicle which, in his opinion, might become overloaded by the end of the working day, the EAT said that the duty placed on the employee to show reasonable belief should not be too heavy, since the purpose of the legislation is to protect employees who raise matters of health and safety. The EAT nevertheless upheld the tribunal's decision that

---

[1]   [1998] ICR 112.
[2]   [1976] 413 at p 419 (see para 5.13).
[3]   See [1998] ICR 112 at p 117H.
[4]   EAT 91/95.

the case should be dismissed on the grounds that, although the employee's belief was genuine, it was not based on reasonable grounds. Clearly, in cases of this kind, tribunals will need to be careful when deciding upon the reasonableness of the employee's belief.

5.64 *Harvest Press Ltd v McCaffrey*[1] is a decision on the fifth type of health and safety dismissal above, under section 100(1)(d). The employee left his workplace in the middle of a shift because of the abusive behaviour of a fellow-employee which made him fear for his safety. He was dismissed for walking out in the middle of a shift. The EAT upheld the employment tribunal's decision that the dismissal fell within section 100(1)(d) and said that dangers caused by fellow-employees are within the wider scope of that provision. It said that 'danger' is used in the provision without any limitation and is intended to cover any danger, however arising.

5.65 Employees who are tempted to report a health and safety matter to an outside body such as the Health and Safety Executive again run the risk of putting themselves outside section 100. In such a case, the question would be whether the case was covered by section 100(1)(e) and whether the steps taken by the employee were 'appropriate steps to protect himself or other persons from the danger'. Again, the question would arise as to whether the employee should have raised the issue internally with a safety official or the employer before taking more serious action. In *Masiak v City Restaurants (UK) Ltd*,[2] a chef who was dismissed for refusing to cook food which he considered unfit for human consumption complained of unfair dismissal under section 100(1)(e). The tribunal said that the phrase 'other persons' relates only to fellow-employees. The EAT allowed his appeal and said that the statutory provisions are not limited in this way.

5.66 Although section 100 talks in terms of dismissal, there is no reason why the provision should not also apply to constructive dismissals.[3] By analogy with *WA Goold (Pearmak) Ltd v McConnell*,[4] which involved a (successful) claim by an employee that a failure to provide a proper grievance procedure amounted to a breach of an implied term in the contract, it may be argued that an employer's continued or persistent failure to deal with an employee's complaints about health and safety amounts to a breach of a similar sort of implied term.

5. DISMISSALS OF SHOP WORKERS AND BETTING WORKERS WHO REFUSE SUNDAY WORK

5.67 Section 101 embraces 'protected shop workers', 'opted-out shop workers', 'protected betting workers' and 'opted-out betting workers'. An

---

[1] [1999] IRLR 778.
[2] [1999] IRLR 780.
[3] See *Goodwin v Cabletel UK Ltd* [1998] ICR 112.
[4] [1995] IRLR 516.

employee covered by these provisions may complain of unfair dismissal irrespective of age or length of service.[1]

5.68   A shop worker[2] or betting worker[3] is protected if he or she satisfies the conditions set out in section 36(2) or (3). The conditions in section 36(2) are:

1.   he or she must be employed as a shop worker on the day before 26 August 1994 or as a betting worker on the day before 3 January 1995;[4]
2.   on that day, he or she was not employed to work only on Sunday;
3.   he or she has been continuously employed from the day before the commencement date to the 'appropriate date';[5] and
4.   throughout that period, he or she was a shop worker or betting worker.

5.69   The conditions in section 36(3) apply to any shop worker or betting worker whose contract of employment is such that under it he or she is not, and may not be, required to work on Sunday, and could not be required to do so, even if the provisions of Part IV of the Employment Rights Act 1996 (which deal with Sunday working) were disregarded.

5.70   A shop worker or betting worker will be regarded as 'opted-out' if the following conditions[6] are satisfied:

1.   he or she has given an opting-out notice;[7]
2.   he or she has been continuously employed from the date on which the notice was given to the 'appropriate date';[8] and
3.   throughout that period he or she was a shop worker or betting worker.

---

[1]   Sections 108(3) and 109(2).
[2]   'Shop worker' is defined in ERA 1996, s 232(1) as 'an employee who, under his contract of employment, is required to do shop work or may be required to do such work'. 'Shop work' is defined by s 232(2) as 'work in or about a shop in England or Wales on a day on which the shop is open for the serving of customers'. Note also the definitions of 'shop' and 'retail trade or business' in s 232(3) and (6), and s 232(4) and (5).
[3]   'Betting worker' is defined in ERA 1996, s 233(1) as 'an employee who, under his contract of employment, is or may be required to do betting work'. 'Betting work' is defined by s 233(2) as 'work at a track in England and Wales for a bookmaker on a day on which the bookmaker acts as such at the track, being work which consists of or includes dealing with betting transactions' and 'work in a licensed betting office in England and Wales on a day on which the office is open for use for the effecting of betting transactions'. Note also the definitions of 'betting transactions' and 'bookmaker' in s 233(3) and (4).
[4]   Note the provisions of s 36(4), which deal with employees who have ceased to be employed on the day before the commencement date for reasons falling within ERA 1996 s 212(2) or (3) or because the Employment Protection (Continuity of Employment) Regulations 1993 apply.
[5]   Defined by s 101(4) as the effective date of termination.
[6]   Set out in s 41.
[7]   As defined by s 40(1) and (2).
[8]   Defined by s 101(4) as the effective date of termination.

A shop worker or betting worker will cease to be protected or opted-out if he or she gives the employer an opting-in notice and, after giving the notice, has expressly agreed with the employer to work on Sunday or on a particular Sunday.[1]

5.71 A protected shop worker or betting worker will automatically be treated as having been unfairly dismissed if the reason (or principal reason) was that he or she refused, or proposed to refuse, to do shop work on Sunday or on a particular Sunday.[2] This does not apply, however, to an opted-out shop worker or betting worker where the reason for the dismissal was that he or she refused or proposed to refuse to do shop work or betting work on any Sunday or Sundays falling before the end of the 'notice period'.[3] The notice period is defined[4] as 'the period of three months beginning with the day on which the opting-out notice was given'. In other words, the statutory protection given by section 101(1) does not come into effect until three months after the opting-out notice was given.

5.72 A shop worker or betting worker will also be treated as unfairly dismissed if the reason for the dismissal is that he or she gave, or proposed to give, an opting-out notice to the employer.[5]

It should be noted that selection for redundancy or for a reason set out in section 101(1) or (3) is also automatically unfair.[6]

6. DISMISSALS IN CONNECTION WITH AN EMPLOYEE'S RIGHTS UNDER THE WORKING TIME REGULATIONS

5.73 Section 101A of the Employment Rights Act 1996[7] gives the right not to be unfairly dismissed to employees who are dismissed for any of the following reasons:

(a) the employee refused (or proposed to refuse) to comply with a requirement which the employer imposed (or proposed to impose) in contravention of the Working Time Regulations 1998;[8]

(b) the employee refused (or proposed to refuse) to forgo a right conferred by the Regulations;

(c) the fact that he or she refused to sign a workforce agreement[9] for the purposes of the Regulations, or to enter into, or agree to vary or

---

[1]   Sections 41(2) and 36(6).
[2]   Section 101(1).
[3]   Section 101(2).
[4]   See s 41(3).
[5]   Section 101(3).
[6]   Section 105(1) and (4). See Chapter 6.
[7]   Inserted by the Working Time Regulations 1998, SI 1998 No 1833, regs 2(1) and 32(1).
[8]   SI 1998 No 1833.
[9]   As defined in reg 2(1).

extend, any other agreement with the employer provided for in the Regulations;

(d)   the fact that the employee was a representative of members of the workforce for the purposes of Schedule 1 (which deals with the conclusion of workforce agreements) or a candidate in an election to be such a representative and, as such, performed (or proposed to perform) any functions or activities as a representative or candidate.

Selection for redundancy on these grounds is also automatically unfair.[1]

5.74   It is not necessary for employees covered by this provision to serve a minimum qualifying period of employment; nor are employees over the normal retiring age excluded.[2] It should be noted that, although the rights given by the Regulations, are given to 'workers', the unfair dismissal rights which arise in connection with them are conferred upon employees only. This gives rise to the curious consequence that a person may be a worker, but not an employee, and thus able to claim rights under the Regulations, but, if he or she is dismissed for relying on those rights, will not be able to complain of unfair dismissal because of not being an employee.

5.75   The provisions of section 202 of the Employment Rights Act 1996 should be noted here, since, as currently drafted, they contain provisions specific to section 101A(d). Section 202[3] applies where, in the opinion of any Minister of the Crown, the disclosure of any information would be contrary to the interests of national security. In that case, disclosure of the information is not required; further, disclosure is forbidden in any proceedings in any court or tribunal relating to section 101A(d). It should also be noted that section 10(1) of the Employment Tribunals Act 1996 provides that an employment tribunal is to dismiss a complaint of unfair dismissal if it is shown that the action complained of was taken for the purpose of safeguarding national security. The new sections 10, 10A and 10B[4] contain no provisions dealing specifically with section 101A as the previous section 10(5) (now replaced) did. These new sections are considered at para 1.90.

An employee dismissed for a reason falling within (d) above may apply to the employment tribunal for interim relief.[5]

7. DISMISSALS OF TRUSTEES OF OCCUPATIONAL PENSION SCHEMES

5.76   Section 102 of the Employment Rights Act 1996 gives the right not to be unfairly dismissed to employees who are trustees of a relevant occupational pension scheme relating to their employment. If the reason

---

[1]   Section 105(1) and (4A).
[2]   Sections 108(3) and 109(2).
[3]   As amended by the Employment Relations Act 1999, s 9 and Sch 4, Pt III, paras 1, 5 and 36.
[4]   As substituted by the Employment Relations Act 1999, s 41 and Sch 8, para 3.
[5]   ERA 1996, s 128(1), as amended by the Working Time Regulations, regs 2(1) and 32(5).

for the dismissal is that the employee performed, or proposed to perform, any functions as such a trustee, the dismissal will be automatically unfair. Selection for redundancy on these grounds is also automatically unfair.[1]

5.77 The provisions of section 102 apply to an employee who is a director of a company which is a trustee of a relevant occupational pension scheme as they apply to an employee who is a trustee of such a scheme.[2] Section 6 of the Welfare Reform and Pensions Act 1999 has the effect of applying section 102 to employees who are (or directors of companies which are) trustees of a scheme designated by the employer under section 3(2) of that Act.

5.78 It is not necessary for employees covered by this provision to serve a minimum qualifying period of employment; nor are employees over the normal retiring age excluded.[3] An employee dismissed for a reason set out above may apply to the employment tribunal for interim relief.[4]

8. DISMISSALS OF EMPLOYEE REPRESENTATIVES

5.79 Section 103 of the ERA 1996[5] gives the right not to be unfairly dismissed to employee representatives.[6] If the reason for the dismissal is that the employee, as an employee representative, performed, or proposed to perform, any functions or activities as an employee representative, the dismissal will be automatically unfair. This also applies to employees who are candidates for election as an employee representative. Section 103 also extends to employees who are dismissed for taking part in the election of employee representatives.[7] Selection for redundancy on these grounds is also automatically unfair.[8]

5.80 It is not necessary for employees covered by this provision to serve a minimum qualifying period of employment; nor are employees over the normal retiring age excluded.[9] An employee dismissed for a reason set out above may apply to the employment tribunal for interim relief.[10]

---

[1] Section 105(1) and (5).
[2] ERA 1996, s 102(1A), inserted by the Welfare Reform and Pensions Act 1999, s 18 and Sch 2, para 19(1) and (4).
[3] Sections 108(3) and 109(2).
[4] ERA 1996, s 128(1).
[5] As amended by the Collective Redundancies and Transfer of Undertakings (Protection of Employment) (Amendment) Regulations 1999, SI 1999 No 1925, reg 13.
[6] Defined by s 196 of the Trade Union and Labour Relations (Consolidation) Act 1992, which was inserted by the Collective Redundancies and Transfer of Undertakings (Protection of Employment) (Amendment) Regulations 1995, SI 1995 No 2587, reg 6, as amended by the Collective Redundancies and Transfer of Undertakings (Protection of Employment) (Amendment) Regulations 1999, SI 1999 No 1925, regs 2(1) and (2), and 6(1)–(4).
[7] See s 103(2).
[8] Section 105(1) and (6).
[9] Sections 108(3) and 109(2).
[10] ERA, s 128(1).

5.81   The provisions of section 202 of the Employment Rights Act 1996 should be noted here, since, as currently drafted, they contain provisions specific to section 103. Section 202[1] applies where, in the opinion of any Minister of the Crown, the disclosure of any information would be contrary to the interests of national security. In that case, disclosure of the information is not required; further, disclosure is forbidden in any proceedings in any court or tribunal relating to section 103. It should also be noted that section 10(1) of the Employment Tribunals Act 1996[2] provides that an employment tribunal is to dismiss a complaint of unfair dismissal if it is shown that the action complained of was taken for the purpose of safeguarding national security. The new sections 10, 10A and 10B contain no provisions dealing specifically with section 103 as the previous section 10(5) (now replaced) did. These new provisions are considered at para 1.90.

9. DISMISSALS AND PROTECTED DISCLOSURES

5.82   Section 103A[3] provides that a dismissal will be automatically unfair if the reason (or principal reason) is that the employee made a 'protected disclosure'. It is not necessary for employees covered by this provision to serve a minimum qualifying period of employment; nor are employees over the normal retiring age excluded.[4] Selection for redundancy on these grounds is also automatically unfair.[5]

5.83   An employee dismissed for a reason set out above may apply to the employment tribunal for interim relief.[6] It should be noted that the statutory limit for a compensatory award of compensation will not apply to this type of unfair dismissal.[7]

5.84   The phrase 'protected disclosure' means 'a qualifying disclosure (as defined by section 43B) which is made by a worker in accordance with any of sections 43C to 43H' of the Employment Rights Act 1996. As with dismissal in connection with working time, it should be noted that, although the rights given by the relevant provisions of the Act are given to 'workers', the unfair dismissal rights which arise in connection with them are conferred upon employees only. In the text that follows the term 'employee' will be used, since workers who are not employees may not complain of unfair dismissal.

5.85   An employee will be protected by the provisions of the Act if:

---

1   As amended by the Employment Relations Act 1999, s 9 and Sch 4, Pt III, paras 1, 5 and 36.
2   As substituted by the Employment Relations Act 1999, s 41 and Sch 8, para 3.
3   Inserted by the Public Interest Disclosure Act 1998, ss 5 and 18(2).
4   Sections 108(3) and 109(2).
5   Section 105(1) and (6A). See Chapter 6.
6   ERA 1996, s 128(1), as amended by the Public Interest Disclosure Act 1998, s 9.
7   See s 124(1A), inserted by the Employment Relations Act 1999, s 37(1), with effect from 25 October 1999.

(a)   he or she makes a disclosure in relation to one of the specified categories of subject-matter; and

(b)   uses one of the specified manners of procedure to make the disclosure.

There are *six* categories of subject-matter and *six* procedures by means of which a disclosure may be made. Once the circumstances fall within one subject-matter category and one procedure, then the employee is protected.

5.86   A 'qualifying disclosure' is 'any disclosure of information which, in the reasonable belief of the employee making the disclosure, tends to show one or more' of the following:[1]

(a)   that a criminal offence has been committed, is being committed or is likely to be committed;

(b)   that a person has failed, is failing or is likely to fail to comply with any legal obligation to which he or she is subject;

(c)   that a miscarriage of justice has occurred, is occurring or is likely to occur;

(d)   that the health or safety of any individual has been, is being or is likely to be endangered;

(e)   that the environment has been, is being or is likely to be damaged;

(f)   that information tending to show any matter falling within any of the preceding paragraphs has been, is being or is likely to be deliberately concealed.

5.87   The following points should be noted, however:

(1)   the employee's belief must be 'reasonable';[2]

(2)   a disclosure will not qualify for protection if the person making it commits an offence by doing so;[3]

(3)   a disclosure will not qualify if it is one in respect of which legal professional privilege would apply;[4]

(4)   it is irrelevant where the alleged failure takes place, eg that alleged environmental damage has taken place in Brazil.[5]

5.88   The protection only applies to the employee if he or she follows one of the specified procedures to disclose the matter in question. The aim of the legislation is to encourage employees to disclose the information through the appropriate channels first, rather than going directly to an outsider. The Act makes it easier for employees to gain protection by making a disclosure to their employer rather than disclosing information to the press, for example.

---

[1]   See s 43B.
[2]   Section 43B(1).
[3]   Section 43B(3).
[4]   Section 43B(4).
[5]   Section 43B(2).

5.89   There are six procedures which are specified. The first applies where the employee makes a qualifying disclosure in good faith to the employer or another responsible person. Disclosure may only be made to that other person, however, where the employee reasonably believes that the failure relates solely or mainly to the conduct of that person or any other matter for which that other person has legal responsibility.[1] If the disclosure is made to another person in accordance with a procedure whose use by the employee is authorised by the employer, he or she will be treated as making the disclosure to the employer.[2]

5.90   The second procedure applies to a qualifying disclosure made to disclosure to a legal adviser; if it is made in the course of obtaining legal advice.[3] The third procedure applies where the qualifying disclosure is made in good faith to a Minister of the Crown. The procedure applies where the employee's employer is an individual appointed under an enactment by a Minister of the Crown or a member of the Scottish Executive or is a body any of whose members are appointed in this way.[4]

5.91   The fourth procedure applies to a qualifying disclosure made in good faith to a 'prescribed person'.[5] A list of prescribed persons is to be found in the Public Interest Disclosure (Prescribed Persons) Order 1999.[6] The disclosure will be protected if the employee reasonably believes that the relevant failure falls within any description of matters in respect of which the person to whom he or she makes disclosure is prescribed and that the information disclosed, and any allegation contained in it, are substantially true.[7] It is not proposed to set out the complete list here, but it should be noted that the Schedule to the Order contains both a list of prescribed persons and a description of the matters which may be disclosed to them. Thus, for example, the Chief Executive of the Criminal Cases Review Commission is included and the description of matters in respect of which disclosure may be made is 'actual or potential miscarriages of justice'.

5.92   The fifth procedure, set out in section 43G, relates to qualifying disclosures in cases other than those set out above. Such disclosures must comply with the following conditions:

(a)   the employee must make the disclosure in good faith;
(b)   the employee must reasonably believe that the information disclosed, and any allegation contained in it, are substantially true;
(c)   the employee must not make the disclosure for the purposes of personal gain;

---

[1]   Section 43C(1).
[2]   Section 43C(2).
[3]   Section 43D.
[4]   Section 43E, as amended by the Scotland Act 1998 (Consequential Modifications) Order 2000, SI 2000 No 2040, arts 1(1) and 2(1) and Sch, Pt I, para 19.
[5]   Section 43F.
[6]   SI 1999 No 1549.
[7]   Section 43F(1)(b).

(d)   it must be reasonable in all the circumstances of the case for him or her to make the disclosure.

5.93   Section 43G(2) sets out a further list of conditions which must be satisfied and section 43G(3) sets out the factors which should be considered when determining whether it is reasonable for the employee to make the disclosure. The further conditions are as follows:

1.   at the time of making the disclosure the employee must reasonably believe that he or she will be subjected to a detriment by the employer if he or she makes a disclosure to the employer or to a prescribed person in accordance with section 43F;

2.   if there is no prescribed person in relation to the relevant failure, the employee must reasonably believe that it is likely that evidence relating to the relevant failure will be concealed or destroyed if he or she makes a disclosure to the employer;

3.   the employee must have previously made a disclosure of substantially the same information to the employer or in accordance with section 43F.

The factors relating to whether it is reasonable to make the disclosure are:

(a)   the identity of the person to whom the disclosure is made;

(b)   the seriousness of the failure;

(c)   whether the failure is continuing or is likely to occur in the future;

(d)   whether the disclosure is made in breach of a duty of confidentiality owed by the employer to any other person;

(e)   any action which the employer or the person to whom the previous disclosure was made has taken or might reasonably be expected to have taken as a result of the disclosure; and

(f)   whether in making the disclosure to the employer the employee complied with any procedure whose use was authorised by the employer.

The last two factors only come into play, if at all, in cases relating to previous disclosures under section 43G(2)(c).

5.94   The sixth procedure is available where the subject-matter of the disclosure is sufficiently serious to merit the employee bypassing the other procedures. For this to apply, the employee must show:

1.   the disclosure was made in good faith;

2.   he or she reasonably believed that the information disclosed, and any allegation contained in it, were substantially true;

3.   he or she did not make the disclosure for personal gain;

4.   the matter disclosed was of an exceptionally serious nature;

5.   in all the circumstances, it was reasonable for him or her to make the disclosure.[1]

Section 43H(2) provides that, in determining whether it is reasonable for the employee to make the disclosure, regard must be had to the identity of the person to whom the disclosure is made.

10. DISMISSALS FOR ASSERTION OF A STATUTORY RIGHT

5.95   These types of dismissal are governed by section 104 of the Employment Rights Act 1996. It is not necessary for employees covered by this provision to serve a minimum qualifying period of employment; nor are employees over the normal retiring age excluded.[2] Selection for redundancy on these grounds is also automatically unfair.[3]

5.96   The dismissal of an employee will be automatically unfair if the reason (or principal reason) for it was that the employee brought proceedings against the employer[4] to enforce a 'relevant statutory right' or alleged that the employer had infringed a 'relevant statutory right'.[5] In both cases the right must be a right of the dismissed employee, but it is immaterial whether the employee has the right or not and whether it was infringed or not, provided that the claim to the right and its infringement are made in good faith.[6] It is sufficient for this section to apply that the employee made it reasonably clear to the employer what the right claimed to have been infringed was; it is not necessary to specify the right.[7]

5.97   The following statutory rights are 'relevant statutory rights':[8]

1.   any right conferred by the 1996 Act, for which the remedy for its infringement is by way of a complaint or reference to an employment tribunal;
2.   the right conferred by section 86 to a minimum period of notice; and
3.   the right conferred by sections 68, 86, 146, 168, 169 and 170 of the Trade Union and Labour Relations (Consolidation) Act 1992;[9] and

---

[1]   Section 43H(1).
[2]   Sections 108(3) and 109(2).
[3]   Section 105(1) and (7). See Chapter 6.
[4]   References in s 104 to an employer include, where the right in question is given by s 63A (which gives young persons the right to time off for study or training), the principal, as defined by s 63A(3).
[5]   The term 'relevant statutory right' is defined in s 104(4). See also *Philip Hodges & Co v Crush* (EAT 1061/95) and *Mennell v Newell & Wright (Transport Contractors) Ltd* [1997] ICR 1039.
[6]   Section 104(2).
[7]   Section 104(3).
[8]   See s 104(4).
[9]   These deal with deductions of union dues, action short of dismissal on grounds related to trade union membership and activities, and time off for trade union duties and activities.

4.   the rights conferred by the Working Time Regulations.[1]

5.98   In *Mennell v Newell & Wright (Transport Contractors) Ltd,*[2] the EAT said that a dismissal of an employee because of his refusal to sign a new contract permitting his employer to make deductions from his wages could fall within section 104. It said that a threat of dismissal in order to impose a variation of the contract to enable the employer to make deductions from wages may amount to an infringement of the employee's statutory right under Part II of the ERA 1996 not to have deductions made from his or her wages without consent. It is not necessary for the employee to have brought proceedings; it is enough that he or she has alleged in good faith that the employer has infringed a relevant statutory right. When the case reached the Court of Appeal,[3] however, that Court allowed the employers' appeal on the grounds that, on the facts, the reason for the employee's dismissal was his refusal to sign the new contract, not his allegation that a statutory right had been infringed. It is clearly important for tribunals hearing cases under this provision to make a clear finding of fact as to the reason for the dismissal.

11. DISMISSAL OF AN EMPLOYEE IN CONNECTION WITH THE NATIONAL MINIMUM WAGE LEGISLATION

5.99   Section 104A[4] provides that an employee is to be treated as automatically unfairly dismissed if the reason (or principal reason) for the dismissal falls within one of the following categories:

1.   any action was taken by, or on behalf of, the employee with a view to enforcing, or otherwise securing the benefit of, a right of the employee's to which section 104A applies (see below); or
2.   the employer was prosecuted for an offence under section 31 of the National Minimum Wage Act 1998 as a result of action taken by or on behalf of the employee to enforce, or otherwise secure the benefit of, a right of the employee's to which section 104A applies; or
3.   the employee qualifies (or will or might qualify) for the national minimum wage or for a particular rate of national minimum wage.[5]

It is immaterial whether the employee has the right or not and whether it was infringed or not, provided that the claim to the right and its infringement are made in good faith.[6]

5.100   Section 104A applies to the following rights:

[1]   SI 1998 No 1833.
[2]   [1996] IRLR 384.
[3]   See [1997] ICR 1039.
[4]   Inserted by the National Minimum Wage Act 1998, s 25(1).
[5]   Section 104A(1).
[6]   Section 104A(2).

(a)   any right given by (or by virtue of) any provision of the National
         Minimum Wage Act 1998 for which the remedy for its infringement
         is by way of a complaint to an employment tribunal;
(b)   any right given by section 17 of the Act.[1]

5.101   Section 17 gives a right to additional remuneration where the
employee receives less than the national minimum wage.

It is not necessary for employees covered by this provision to serve a
minimum qualifying period of employment; nor are employees over the
normal retiring age excluded.[2] Selection for redundancy on these grounds
is also automatically unfair.[3]

5.102   As with dismissals in connection with working time and protected
disclosures, it should be noted that, although the rights given by the
relevant provisions of the National Minimum Wage Act are given to
'workers', the unfair dismissal rights which arise in connection with them
are conferred upon employees only. In the text the term 'employee' is used,
since workers who are not employees may not complain of unfair
dismissal.

12. DISMISSAL IN CONNECTION WITH AN EMPLOYEE'S RIGHTS UNDER THE TAX CREDITS ACT 1999

5.103   Section 104B[4] provides that an employee is to be treated as
automatically unfairly dismissed if the reason (or principal reason) for the
dismissal falls within one of the following categories:

1.   any action was taken, or was proposed to be taken, by or on behalf
         of, the employee with a view to enforcing, or otherwise securing the
         benefit of, a right given to the employee by regulations under
         section 6(2)(a) or (c) of the Tax Credits Act 1999;[5]
2.   a penalty was imposed on the employer, or proceedings for a
         penalty were brought against it, as a result of action taken by or on
         behalf of the employee to enforce, or otherwise secure the benefit of,
         such a right;
3.   the employee is entitled (or will or might be entitled) to working
         families' tax credit or disabled person's tax credit.[6]

---

[1]   See s 104A(3).
[2]   Sections 108(3) and 109(2).
[3]   Section 105(1) and (7A). See Chapter 6.
[4]   Inserted by the Tax Credits Act 1999, s 7 and Sch 3, para 3(1).
[5]   See the Tax Credits (Payment by Employers) Regulations 1999, SI 1999 No 3219.
[6]   Section 104B(1).

It is immaterial whether the employee has the right or not and whether it was infringed or not, provided that the claim to the right and its infringement are made in good faith.[1]

13. DISMISSALS OF EMPLOYEES IN CONNECTION WITH THE TRANSNATIONAL INFORMATION AND CONSULTATION OF EMPLOYEES REGULATIONS 1999[2]

5.104 Regulation 28 of the Regulations provides that in certain circumstances an employee is to be treated as automatically unfairly dismissed if the dismissal arises in connection with the Regulations. For an employee to be protected he or she must fall within regulation 28(2) or (5) and the reason for the dismissal must fall within regulation 28(3) or (6). It is not necessary for employees covered by this provision to serve a minimum qualifying period of employment; nor are employees over the normal retiring age excluded.[3] Selection for redundancy on these grounds is also automatically unfair.[4]

5.105 An employee will fall within regulation 28 if he or she is one of the following:

(a)   a member of a special negotiating body;[5]
(b)   a member of a European Works Council;[6]
(c)   an information and consultation representative;[7]
(d)   a candidate in an election for the above offices;[8]
(e)   'any employee whether or not he is an employee' [falling within the preceding four categories].[9]

5.106 The following are the reasons which will make a dismissal in the present context automatically unfair:

1.   the employee performed any functions or activities as such a member, representative or candidate;

---

[1]   Section 104B(2).
[2]   SI 1999 No 3323.
[3]   Sections 108(3) and 109(2).
[4]   Section 105(1) and (7D). See Chapter 6.
[5]   Defined in reg 2(1) as 'the body established for the purposes of negotiating with central management an agreement for a European Works Council or an information and consultation procedure'. This last is defined as a procedure agreed under reg 17 or the provisions of the law or practice of another Member State of the European Union.
[6]   Defined in reg 2(1) as a council established under and in accordance with reg 17, or reg 18 and the provisions of the Schedule, or the provisions of the law or practice of another Member State of the European Union.
[7]   Defined in reg 2(1) as a person who represents employees in the context of an information and consultation procedure (as defined in SI 1999 No 3323).
[8]   Regulation 28(2).
[9]   Regulation 28(5).

2.   the employee or a person acting on his or her behalf made a request to exercise an entitlement given to the employee by regulation 25 or 26;

3.   the employee took or proposed to take any proceedings before an employment tribunal to enforce a right or obtain an entitlement given to him or her by the Regulations;[1]

4.   exercised or proposed to exercise any entitlement to apply or complain to the EAT or CAC (or in Northern Ireland, the Industrial Court), given by the Regulations;

5.   asked for, or proposed to ask for information in connection with regulation 7;

6.   acted with a view to securing that a special negotiating body, a European Works Council or an information and consultation procedure did or did not come into existence;

7.   indicated that he or she supported or did not support the coming into existence of a special negotiating body, a European Works Council or an information and consultation procedure;

8.   stood as a candidate to become a member of a special negotiating body or a European Works Council, or an information and consultation representative;

9.   influence or sought to influence the way in which votes were to be cast by other employees in a ballot arranged under the Regulations;

10.   voted in such a ballot;

11.   expressed doubts, whether to a ballot supervisor or otherwise, as to whether such a ballot had been properly conducted; or

12.   proposed to do, failed to do, or proposed to decline to do, any of the things mentioned in items 6–11.

5.107   The first reason set out above does not apply where the reason (or principal reason) for the dismissal is that in the performance (or purported performance) of the employee's functions or activities he or she has disclosed any information or document in breach of the duty imposed by regulation 23, unless he or she reasonably believed the disclosure to be a 'protected disclosure'.[2] The effect of the disapplication of the first reason will be that a dismissal of an employee will not be automatically unfair in the circumstances set out, unless the employee reasonably believed that the disclosure was a protected disclosure. It is not clear, however, whether it would still be open to a tribunal to decide under section 98(4) that the dismissal was unfair or whether the consequence of the disclosure in breach of regulation 23 is that the dismissal is bound to be fair.

---

[1]   If this is the reason for the dismissal, it is immaterial whether the employee has the right or not and whether it was infringed or not, provided that the claim to the right and its infringement are made in good faith: see reg 28(7).

[2]   Regulation 28(4). See s 43A for a definition of 'protected disclosure' (see also para 5.84).

14. DISMISSALS ARISING UNDER THE PART-TIME WORKERS (PREVENTION OF LESS FAVOURABLE TREATMENT) REGULATIONS 2000[1]

5.108   Regulation 7 of the Regulations provides that in certain circumstances an employee is to be treated as automatically unfairly dismissed if the dismissal arises in connection with the Regulations. For an employee to be protected, the reason for the dismissal must fall within regulation 7(3). It is not necessary for employees covered by this provision to serve a minimum qualifying period of employment; nor are employees over the normal retiring age excluded.[2] Selection for redundancy on these grounds is also automatically unfair.[3]

5.109   As with dismissals in connection with working time and protected disclosures, it should be noted that, although the rights given by the relevant provisions of the National Minimum Wage Act are given to 'workers', the unfair dismissal rights which arise in connection with them are conferred upon employees only. In the text the term 'employee' is used, since workers who are not employees may not complain of unfair dismissal.

5.110   The reasons set out in regulation 7(3) are as follows:

1.   the employee has:
    (a)   brought proceedings against the employer under the Regulations;
    (b)   asked for a written statement of reasons under regulation 6;
    (c)   given evidence or information in connection with proceedings brought by any worker;
    (d)   otherwise done anything under the Regulations in relation to the employer or any other person;
    (e)   alleged that the employer has infringed the regulations;
    (f)   refused (or proposed to refuse) to forgo a right given by the Regulations;
2.   the employer believes or suspects that the worker has done or intends to do any of the things mentioned in 1, above.

15. DISMISSALS IN CONNECTION WITH THE STATUTORY RIGHT TO BE ACCOMPANIED AT DISCIPLINARY OR GRIEVANCE HEARINGS

5.111   Section 10 of the Employment Relations Act 1999 introduced a statutory right to be accompanied at a disciplinary or grievance hearing. That right was considered in Chapter 4, at para 4.42. The right is reinforced

---

[1]   SI 2000 No 1551.
[2]   Sections 108(3) and 109(2).
[3]   Section 105(1) and (7E). See Chapter 6.

by provisions which give *workers* the right not be unfairly dismissed. It should be noted that this is the only statutory provision to give unfair dismissal rights to workers.

5.112 Section 12(3) of the 1999 Act provides that a worker is to be regarded as unfairly dismissed if the reason for the dismissal is that:

(a) he or she exercised or sought to exercise the right to be accompanied to a disciplinary or grievance hearing under section 10(2) or to postpone the hearing under section 10(4); or

(b) he or she accompanied or sought to accompany another worker (whether of the same employer or not) after being asked to do so by that other.

It should be noted that it is not necessary for workers covered by this provision to serve a minimum qualifying period of employment; nor are workers over the normal retiring age excluded.[1] The remedy of interim relief is also available.[2]

16. DISMISSALS AND REGULATION 8 OF THE TRANSFER OF UNDERTAKINGS (PROTECTION OF EMPLOYMENT) REGULATIONS 1981

5.113 Dismissals on the transfer of an undertaking are governed by regulation 8 of the 1981 Regulations (TUPE). The general rule is that an employee dismissed either before or after a relevant transfer will be treated as automatically unfairly dismissed, if the transfer or a reason connected with it is the reason or principal reason for the dismissal. The rule applies to employees both of the transferor and the transferee. The general rule does not apply, however, when there is an 'economic, technical or organisational reason entailing changes in the workforce or either the transferor or transferee either before or after a relevant transfer' and that is the reason or principal reason for dismissing the employee.[3] In that case, the reason will be treated as 'some other substantial reason' within section 98(1)(b) of the Employment Rights Act 1996[4] and the fairness of the reason must then be considered by the tribunal under section 98(4).[5] The burden of establishing that the reason falls within regulation 8(2) is on the employer.[6] It is clear from the wording of the regulation and from the decisions of the EAT that the correct approach is to consider, first, whether regulation 8(1) applies so as to make the dismissals automatically unfair; if

---

[1] ERA 1999, s 12(4).
[2] ERA 1999, s 12(5).
[3] Regulation 8(2).
[4] See Chapter 4.
[5] *McGrath v Rank Leisure Ltd* [1985] ICR 527.
[6] See *Litster v Forth Dry Dock & Engineering Co Ltd (in receivership)* [1989] ICR 341 and *Gateway Hotels Ltd v Stewart* [1988] IRLR 287.

it does not, then the tribunal should consider whether regulation 8(2) applies.

5.114 One issue which has now been resolved by the House of Lords concerned the effect of a dismissal which is brought about by the transfer of an undertaking. In *Wilson v St Helens Borough Council* and *Meade v British Fuels Ltd*,[1] two groups of dismissals were involved. The group involved in the *Wilson* case were dismissals for an economic or technical reason and thus within regulation 8(2); the group involved in the *Meade* case were dismissals for a reason connected with the transfer and thus within regulation 8(1). The Court of Appeal held[2] that regulation 8(1) fell to be construed in the light of Article 4(1) of the Acquired Rights Directive and that, so construed, it made a dismissal covered by its terms void and ineffective rather than merely automatically unfair. In the House of Lords, Lord Slynn of Hadley gave the main speech. It centred round the issue whether a dismissal of an employee brought about by a transfer of an undertaking is or is not a nullity. He took the view that the provisions of regulation 8(1) and (2) point to a dismissal being effective and not a nullity and do not create an automatic obligation on the part of the transferee to continue to employ employees who have been dismissed by the transferor. He then went on to consider whether TUPE complies with the Directive. Having considered the relevant case-law of the ECJ,[3] he concluded that the Directive does not create a Community law right to continue in employment which does not exist in national law and that TUPE gives effect to and is consistent with the Directive. The decision restores the law to the position that had been understood to obtain before the decision of the Court of Appeal in 1997. Thus, if an employee is dismissed by the transferor and re-engaged by the transferee, the latter will assume any liability for dismissals incurred by the transferor. The employee will not be able to insist on the observance by the transferee of his or her previous terms or conditions and will be bound by the terms and conditions agreed with the transferee. The dismissal will thus be unfair by virtue of regulation 8(1), but not ineffective.

5.115 It should be noted that regulation 8 only applies for the purposes of the provisions in the ERA 1996 dealing with unfair dismissal. It has no effect on the employee's right to claim a redundancy payment.[4]

5.116 Liability under regulation 8 will only pass to the transferee if the employee was employed in the transferred undertaking immediately before the transfer within the meaning of regulation 5(3), as interpreted by the House of Lords in the *Litster* case. In *Harrison Bowden Ltd v Bowden*,[5] the

---

[1]   [1998] ICR 1141.

[2]   [1998] ICR 387.

[3]   *Wendelboe v LJ Music ApS* [1985] ECR 457, *Foreningen af Arbejdsledere I Danmark v A/S Danmols Inventar* [1985] ECR 2639, *P Bork International A/S v Foreningen af Arbejdsledere I Danmark* [1988] ECR 3057 and *Foreningen af Arbejdsledere I Danmark v Daddy's Dance Hall A/S* [1988] ECR 739.

[4]   *Gorictree Ltd v Jenkinson* [1985] ICR 51.

[5]   [1994] ICR 186.

EAT applied the decision in *Litster* to the dismissal of an employee by a receiver at a time when a potential buyer was interested in buying the company by which he had been employed, but was not formally committed to buying it. He was later engaged by the transferee but dismissed after a month. The EAT upheld the tribunal's decision that he had sufficient accrued continuity to make a claim. In *Ibex Trading Co Ltd (in administration) v Walton,*[1] on the other hand, the facts were that employees were sent letters of dismissal to take effect on 4 November 1991. On 11 November an offer to purchase the business was made and it was sold to the transferee on 13 February 1992. The EAT held that, because of the lapse of time between the dismissals and the sale of the business, they were not employed in the transferred undertaking immediately before the transfer within the meaning of regulation 5(3). It did not follow the decision in *Harrison Bowden*. Subsequently, in *Morris v John Grose Group Ltd,*[2] the EAT said that the views expressed in the *Harrison Bowden* case were to be preferred to those in the *Ibex* case.

5.117   In cases where the transferor gives notice of dismissal but the notice expires after the transfer, any liability for the dismissal will transfer to the transferee, but the reason for the notice of termination will be that of the transferor and the date for determining the reason is the date when notice was given.[3] In cases such as this, therefore, it is very likely that the dismissal will be made unfair by regulation 8(1).

5.118   The relationship between regulation 8(1) and 8(2) was considered by the Court of Appeal in *Warner v Adnet Ltd.*[4] In that case, the argument on behalf of the employee was that the two paragraphs are mutually exclusive and that, if the tribunal concludes that the dismissal was for a reason falling within regulation 8(1), it is precluded from considering the case under regulation 8(2). The Court of Appeal rejected that argument. Mummery LJ, with whom the other members of the Court agreed, said that the Regulations must be read as a whole and that the drafting of regulation 8(2) is such that it expressly contemplates circumstances in which regulation 8(1) will be disapplied and where a view formed by a tribunal under regulation 8(1) is not final or conclusive. He said:[5]

'If the transfer was not the reason, there is no need to inquire further. If it is the reason, regulation 8(2) *may* apply. If it does, regulation 8(1) is disapplied and the dismissal is not *automatically* unfair.'

5.119   This approach was followed by another division of the Court of Appeal in the later case of *Whitehouse v Charles A Blatchford & Sons Ltd.*[6] In that case, the facts were that the employee was employed as a technician at a hospital disablement centre. In 1996, the company employing him lost the

1   [1994] ICR 907. See also *Tsangacos v Amalgamated Chemicals Ltd* [1997] ICR 154.
2   [1998] IRLR 499.
3   *BSG Property Services v Tuck* [1996] IRLR 134.
4   [1998] ICR 1056.
5   *Ibid* at p 1064.
6   [2000] ICR 542.

contract to provide services at the centre to the respondents. The employers took on all the technicians, but, since a condition of obtaining the contract was that the number of technicians working at the centre had to be reduced by one, after making detailed assessments of all the technicians they selected the applicant for dismissal. He complained of unfair dismissal. The tribunal found that the reason was an economic, technical or organisational reason within regulation 8(2) and that, as the selection process had been comprehensively and fairly carried out, the dismissal was not unfair. The Court of Appeal upheld the tribunal's decision. It said that, although the transfer of the undertaking was the occasion for the reduction in the hospital's requirements for the services of technicians, the transfer was not the cause of or the reason for that reduction, and it was open to the tribunal to hold that the transfer was not the reason for the dismissal. Accordingly, regulation 8(1) did not apply. Since also the process of selection had been properly and fairly carried out, he had not been unfairly dismissed. This decision was applied by the EAT in *Kerry Foods Ltd v Kreber,*[1] although the outcome was different inasmuch as the EAT concluded that the reason for the dismissal was the transfer and that the dismissal was, therefore, automatically unfair.

5.120 The words 'economic,'[2] technical or organisational' in regulation 8(2) have been considered in a number of cases. The preferred approach now seems to be that of the EAT in *Wheeler v Patel.*[3] It said that the word 'economic' is to be construed *ejusdem generis* with the other two adjectives and is to be given a limited meaning relating to the conduct of the business. It said that it does not include broad economic reasons for a sale, such as the desire to obtain an enhanced price or a desire to achieve a sale. The EAT has followed this approach in later cases.[4] This approach is consistent with the House of Lords' decision in *Litster v Forth Dry Dock & Engineering Co Ltd (in receivership).*[5]

5.121 A further point is that the reason will not fall within regulation 8(2) unless it also entails changes in the workforce. This aspect of the regulation was considered by the Court of Appeal in *Delabole Slate Ltd v Berriman.*[6] The facts were that a quarryman was employed at a guaranteed weekly wage of £100. The undertaking in which he worked was taken over and his new employers wrote to inform him that they proposed to alter his pay to accord with their existing collective agreement. This would have entailed a substantial reduction in his guaranteed weekly wage. He resigned and

---

[1]   [2000] ICR 556.

[2]   An 'economic' reason includes redundancy: see *Gorictree Ltd v Jenkinson* [1985] ICR 51.

[3]   [1987] ICR 631. They did not follow the previous decision in *Anderson v Dalkeith Engineering Ltd* [1985] ICR 66, where the EAT said that the words are not mutually exclusive but are alternative or cumulative reasons for dismissal and the employment tribunal is not obliged to specify which of the three reasons it is relying on. See also *Trafford v Sharpe & Fisher (Building Supplies) Ltd* [1994] IRLR 325.

[4]   See *Gateway Hotels Ltd v Stewart* [1988] IRLR 287 and *Ibex Trading Co v Walton* [1994] ICR 907.

[5]   [1989] ICR 341.

[6]   [1985] ICR 546.

claimed constructive dismissal. The Court of Appeal held that regulation 8(2) did not protect the employers. It took the view that the employer's reason (to produce standardisation of pay) did not itself involve any change either in the number or the functions of the workforce, and it was not enough that the organisational reason might lead to the dismissal of those employees who did not fall into line. The change in the workforce must be part of the economic, technical or organisational reason and the employer's plan must be to achieve changes in the workforce: 'It must be an objective of the plan, not just a possible consequence of it'.[1] The employee's constructive dismissal was thus automatically unfair because changes in the number of the workforce or the job functions of the transferred employee were not entailed.

5.122   In following the above case, the EAT has subsequently held that the term 'workforce' is an entity separate from the individuals who make up the workforce. It is therefore possible for there to be a change in the workforce if the same people are retained but are given different jobs to do.[2]

17. DISMISSAL OF REPLACEMENT EMPLOYEES

5.123   In view of the fact that the qualifying period for the right not to be unfairly dismissed is one year, the provisions of section 106 are not likely to be needed very often. Section 106 specifically applies to employees engaged to replace employees absent on maternity leave or as a consequence of a medical suspension or suspension on maternity grounds.[3] The replacement must be told in writing that the employment will be ended when the absent employee returns. When he or she is dismissed, the dismissal will be treated as being for some other substantial reason, but the employer will still need to satisfy the requirements of section 98(4), which should not be difficult.

---

[1]   [1985] ICR 546 at p 551.

[2]   *Crawford v Swinton Insurance Brokers Ltd* [1990] ICR 85.

[3]   Section 106(3).

Chapter 6

DISMISSALS FOR REDUNDANCY

6.01   Employees dismissed for redundancy have two main statutory rights:

1.   the right to complain of unfair dismissal under the provisions of Part X of the Employment Rights Act 1996 (sections 94–134); and
2.   the right to claim a redundancy payment under the provisions of Part XI of the 1996 Act (sections 135–181).

In addition, they have the right to time off during their notice period to look for new employment or make arrangements for training for further employment.

6.02   Employees are generally only entitled to the right not to be unfairly dismissed, as has been seen, if they have been continuously employed for one year,[1] although that requirement is sometimes lifted.[2] In the case of the right to claim a redundancy payment, the employee must have been continuously employed for *two* years.[3] In both cases, the employee must have been dismissed. The definition of 'dismiss' is considered in Chapter 3, where it will be noted that, in the case of claims under Part XI, the definition is extended in cases where the employee is offered alternative employment.[4] The definition of 'redundancy', which is the first matter to be considered in this chapter, is common to both the Part X and the Part XI rights. Apart from the definition of redundancy, however, the two Parts are completely self-contained. This means that the provisions of Part XI are not applicable to unfair dismissal claims, nor are those of Part X applicable to redundancy payments claims. It will be an error of law if a tribunal applies the wrong provisions to the wrong type of claim.[5]

---

[1]   ERA 1996, s 108, as amended by the Unfair Dismissal and Statement of Reasons for Dismissal (Variation of Qualifying Period) Order 1999, SI 1999 No 1436.

[2]   See Chapters 1 and 5.

[3]   ERA 1996, s 155.

[4]   In cases where s 136(5) applies and the employee's contract is treated as terminated by reason of the act or event and the contract is not renewed and he or she is not re-engaged under a new contract of employment, the effect of s 139(4) is that the reason for the non-renewal of the contract will be treated as falling within s 139(1); see also s 139(5).

[5]   *Hempell v WH Smith & Sons Ltd* [1986] ICR 365 and *Jones v Governing Body of Burden Coutts School* [1997] ICR 390. *Cf* the EAT decision in *EBAC Ltd v Wymer* [1995] ICR 466, which suggests that what is now s 138(1) is relevant to an unfair dismissal claim. That cannot be regarded as correct, however, and doubt was cast upon its correctness in the *Jones* case. See also *Shawkat v Nottingham City Hospital NHS Trust* [1999] ICR 780.

6.03   In general, an employee dismissed for redundancy will be advised to complain of unfair dismissal or make a dual claim. This is because a complaint under the unfair dismissal provisions enables the employment tribunal to decide whether the employer's decision to dismiss was reasonable in all the circumstances, whereas the redundancy payments provisions merely enable the tribunal to decide whether the statutory presumption of redundancy has or has not been rebutted. Further, the unfair dismissal provisions give an employee the possibility of receiving greater compensation, in the form of the basic award, which is calculated in the same way as a redundancy payment, *plus* a compensatory award, which is not available under the redundancy payments provisions. In the case of a dual claim, the successful employee will either receive a basic award or a redundancy payment, but not both, since section 122(4) contains set-off provisions.

6.04   In this chapter, the following topics will be considered:

1.   the definition of redundancy;
2.   the right to time off;
3.   unfair dismissal claims; and
4.   redundancy payments claims.

1. THE DEFINITION OF REDUNDANCY

6.05   As was mentioned above, the definition of redundancy serves a dual purpose: redundancy is one of the potentially fair reasons in unfair dismissal cases, and an employee who is dismissed by reason of redundancy is also entitled to a redundancy payment, by virtue of section 135(1).

6.06   Redundancy is defined in section 139(1) as follows:

'... [A]n employee who is dismissed shall be taken to be dismissed by reason of redundancy if the dismissal is wholly or mainly attributable to—

    (a)   the fact that his employer has ceased or intends to cease
        (i)   to carry on the business for the purposes of which the employee was employed by him, or
        (ii) to carry on that business in the place where the employee was so employed, or
    (b)   the fact that the requirements of that business
        (i)   for employees to carry out work of a particular kind, or
        (ii) for employees to carry out work of a particular kind in the place where the employee was employed by the employer,

have ceased or diminished or are expected to cease or diminish.'

6.07   Section 139(2) makes clear that the employer's business and that of any associated employer are to be treated as one; subsection (3) states that the activities carried on by a local education authority with respect to schools maintained by it and the activities carried on by the governors of those schools are to be treated as one business for the purposes of subsection (1). Section 139(6) says clearly that 'cease' and 'diminish' mean cease and diminish either permanently or temporarily and for whatever reason.

6.08   In cases involving only a claim for a redundancy payment, section 163(2) enacts a presumption of redundancy. This means that the burden is on the employer who wishes to dispute liability to make the payment to prove that the employee was not redundant. In cases involving a complaint of unfair dismissal and a claim for a redundancy payment, however, the presumption will not operate in relation to the unfair dismissal complaint.[1] In unfair dismissal cases, the burden is on the employer to show what the reason (or principal reason) for the dismissal was. If an employer fails to discharge that burden, the dismissal will be automatically held to be unfair. It is therefore possible for an employer to fail to rebut the presumption of redundancy in the redundancy payment claim and thus become liable for a redundancy payment, and to fail to establish the reason for the dismissal in the unfair dismissal claim and thus be held to have dismissed the employee unfairly.[2]

6.09   A preliminary question which arises is whether the dismissal is by reason of the particular circumstances which constitute a redundancy. In *Hindle v Percival Boats Ltd*,[3] the Court of Appeal held that, provided that the employer honestly believes that the dismissal of the employee is due to some reason other than redundancy (however mistaken the belief may be), the dismissal will not be by reason of redundancy. But it emphasised that employment tribunals must be wary of dishonest employers, or employers who misdirect themselves into thinking that they were influenced by the employee's deficiencies, when the main factor was that the requirements of the business had declined.

6.10   The definition of redundancy in section 139(1) uses the phrase 'in the place where the employee was ... employed'. In previous editions of this book, it was stated that the issue in cases involving the question where an employee was employed was whether the employer had contractual authority, express or implied, to order the employee to move; or, in other words, what degree of contractual mobility the employee was subject to. The effect was that if the employee was required to move to another factory within the radius of the mobility obligation because of the closure of the factory where he or she worked, it would not be possible to claim a redundancy payment, since there had not been a cessation of the business

---

[1]   Section 7(6) of the Employment Tribunals Act 1996.
[2]   *Midland Foot Comfort Centre v Moppett* [1973] ICR 219.
[3]   [1969] 1 WLR 174. See also *Baxter v Limb Group of Companies* [1994] IRLR 572.

in the place where he or she was employed.[1] This has been called the 'contractual test'.

6.11   In *Bass Leisure Ltd v Thomas*,[2] on the other hand, what has been called the 'factual' test was used. There, the EAT said that 'the place' where an employee is employed does not extend to any place where the employee may be contractually required to work; the question is primarily a factual one and the only relevant contractual terms are those which define the place of employment and its extent.

6.12   The question whether the 'contractual' or 'factual' test is to be preferred has been considered by the Court of Appeal, in *High Table Ltd v Horst*.[3] The facts were that three waitresses were employed by employers whose business was that of providing catering services for companies and firms in the City of London and elsewhere. The employees' terms of employment contained the following mobility clause:

> 'Your normal place of work is as stated in your letter of appointment which acts as part of your terms and conditions. However, given the nature of our business, it is sometimes necessary to transfer staff on a temporary or permanent basis to another location. Whenever possible this will be within reasonable daily travelling distance of your existing place of work.'

All the employees worked for all or most of their time with the employers as waitresses with Hill Samuel in the City of London. As a result of redundancies within Hill Samuel, the employers had to reduce their staff. In the EAT the employees argued that there was no redundancy situation because of the mobility clauses in their contracts. This argument was further developed in the Court of Appeal. Peter Gibson LJ, with whom Hobhouse and Evans LJJ agreed, reviewed the relevant case-law[4] and distinguished the cases on the ground that the issue considered there by the Court of Appeal was whether the employees in question were in breach of contract in refusing an instruction to work further afield than they had previously been accustomed to. He was also critical of two decisions of Sir John Donaldson P in the National Industrial Relations Court.[5] He preferred the conclusion of the EAT in the later case of *Bass Leisure Ltd v Thomas* (above) that the place where the employee is employed 'is to be established by a factual inquiry, taking into account the employee's fixed or changing place or places of work and any contractual terms which go to evidence or define the place of employment and its extent, but not those (if any) which

---

[1]   *Stevenson v Teesside Bridge and Engineering Ltd* [1971] 1 All ER 296, *O'Brien v Associated Fire Alarms Ltd* [1968] 1 WLR 1916, *United Kingdom Atomic Energy Authority v Claydon* [1974] ICR 128 and *Sutcliffe v Hawker Siddeley Aviation Ltd* [1973] IRLR 304. An example of what has come to be called the 'contractual' approach is in *Rank Xerox Ltd v Churchill* [1988] IRLR 280.

[2]   [1994] IRLR 104.

[3]   [1997] IRLR 513.

[4]   See para 6.10, n 1.

[5]   *Sutcliffe v Hawker Siddeley Aviation Ltd* [1973] IRLR 304 and *United Atomic Energy Authority v Claydon* [1974] IRLR 6.

make provisions for the employee to be transferred to another'.[1] He went on to say:

> 'The question ... is one to be answered primarily by a consideration of the factual circumstances which obtained until the dismissal. If an employee has worked in only one location under his contract of employment for the purposes of the employer's business, it defies common sense to widen the extent of the place where he was so employed, merely because of the existence of a mobility clause. Of course the refusal by the employee to obey a lawful requirement under the contract of employment for the employee to move may constitute a valid reason for the dismissal, but the issues of dismissal, redundancy and reasonableness in the actions of an employer should be kept distinct ... If the work of the employee ... has involved a change of location, ... then the contract of employment may be helpful to determine the extent of the place where the employee was employed. But it cannot be right to let the contract be the sole determinant, regardless of where the employee actually worked for the employer ...'[2]

6.13   This is an important decision; however it should be remembered that Peter Gibson LJ emphasises that it goes merely to the question whether the employee was redundant and not whether the employer acted reasonably. Equally it will not affect the question whether the employee should lose the entitlement to a redundancy payment because he or she is held to have unreasonably refused a suitable offer of alternative employment.[3]

6.14   Of the two definitions of redundancy given in section 139(1), that relating to cessation of a business has caused little difficulty. It is not necessary to show that the employer is the legal owner of the business in question, only that that person is in control of the business.[4] The other definition, in section 139(1)(b), that there is a cessation or diminution in the requirements of a business for work of a particular kind, is by no means straightforward and has caused considerable difficulties. In a series of cases, the Court of Appeal has held that the fact that there has been a reorganisation of the business does not necessarily mean that there has been a redundancy; it is part of the factual background. The fundamental question is whether the requirement for employees to carry out work of a particular kind has ceased or diminished. So, for example, in *Carry All Motors Ltd v Pennington*,[5] the employee was dismissed from his job as a transport clerk when his employers decided that the work of the transport manager and transport clerk could be carried out by one employee only. The tribunal decided that he had not been dismissed by reason of redundancy because the same work remained. The EAT reversed its decision and held that the question was whether the requirement for

---

[1]   [1994] IRLR 104 at p 112.
[2]   [1997] IRLR 513 at p 518.
[3]   See s 141 and paras 6.56 *et seq*.
[4]   *Thomas v Jones* [1978] ICR 274.
[5]   [1980] ICR 806.

employees to do that work had diminished. Since one employee was doing the work formerly done by two, there was a redundancy.

6.15   A reorganisation does not of itself mean that there is a redundancy situation, particularly if the amount of work remains the same or increases.[1] In *Johnson v Nottinghamshire Police Authority*,[2] Lord Denning MR said:

> '[A]n employer is entitled to reorganise his business so as to improve its efficiency and, in doing so, to propose to his staff a change in the terms and conditions of their employment: and to dispense with their services if they do not agree. Such a change does not automatically give the staff a right to a redundancy payment. It only does so if the change in the terms and conditions is due to a redundancy situation.'

6.16   In *Robinson v British Island Airways*,[3] Phillips J said of these cases:[4]

> '... Cases concerning redundancy arising out of a reorganisation always cause difficulties. Certain passages in ... *Johnson v Nottinghamshire Police Authority* ... and *Lesney Products Ltd v Nolan*[5] ... have been taken as suggesting that if a dismissal has been caused by a reorganisation, the reason for dismissal cannot be redundancy. We do not think that this is the meaning of the passages, or what was intended. In truth, a reorganisation may or may not end in redundancy; it all depends upon the nature and effect of the reorganisation ... The question is whether the definition is satisfied.'

6.17   Subsequent decisions have tended to espouse the idea that, in considering whether there has been a diminution in the requirements of the business for employees to carry out work of a particular kind, the tribunal must look at the terms of the employee's contract. This is called the 'contract test'. An example of this is *Cowen v Haden Ltd*,[6] where an employee was employed as a divisional contracts surveyor and was 'required to undertake, at the direction of the company, any and all duties which reasonably fall within the scope of his capabilities'. The Court of Appeal held that the requirement that the employee should perform the duties within the scope of his capabilities was restricted to the duties of a divisional contracts surveyor; the employers therefore had no right to

---

[1] See *Chapman v Goonvean and Rostowrack China Clay Co Ltd* [1973] ICR 310, *Johnson v Nottinghamshire Police Authority* [1974] ICR 170 and *Lesney Products & Co Ltd v Nolan* [1977] ICR 235. See also *Murphy v Epsom College* [1985] ICR 80 and *MacFisheries Ltd v Findlay* [1985] ICR 160.

[2] *Loc cit* at p 176. See *North Riding Garages Ltd v Butterwick* [1967] 2 QB 56 and *Murphy v Epsom College* [1985] ICR 80.

[3] [1978] ICR 304.

[4] *Ibid* at p 308.

[5] [1977] ICR 235.

[6] [1983] ICR 1. See also *Nelson v BBC (No 1)* [1977] ICR 649, *Nelson v BBC (No 2)* [1979] ICR 110, *Pink v White and White & Co (Earls Barton) Ltd* [1985] IRLR 489 and *Perkins Engine Group Ltd v Overend* (EAT 479/88). See also *Horton v Parrel Electronic Services Ltd* (EAT 755/95) IDS Brief 582, which was decided by the EAT almost four months before the EAT gave its decision in *Burrell*.

require him to transfer from that work to assume the job of a quantity surveyor.

6.18 The authorities in this area were carefully and critically reviewed by the EAT in *Safeway Stores plc v Burrell*,[1] which contains a valuable analysis of the approaches propounded by the courts in recent years. The facts of the case were that the employee's dismissal arose from a reorganisation or 'delayering' of the employers' management structure, with the result that there were less management positions than before, which gave rise to redundancies. The tribunal decided that he had not been dismissed by reason of redundancy, since the work done by the employee still had to be done and, therefore, the requirements of the employers' business for employees to carry out work of a particular kind had not ceased or diminished. The EAT reversed this decision and said that he had been dismissed by reason of redundancy. It said that a three-stage process is involved in determining whether a dismissal for redundancy has taken place:

1. Was the employee dismissed?
2. Had the requirements of the employer's business for employees to carry out work of a particular kind ceased or diminished? If so:
3. Was the dismissal of the employee caused wholly or mainly by the state of affairs identified in stage 2?

6.19 It said that at stage 2, the only question to be asked is whether there is a cessation or diminution in the employer's requirements for employees (not the applicant) to carry out work of a particular kind and that, at this stage, it is irrelevant to consider the terms of the employee's contract. At stage 3, the tribunal is concerned with causation. It said:[2]

'Even if a redundancy situation arises, ... if that does not cause the dismissal, the employee has not been dismissed by reason of redundancy. In *Nelson* the employee was directed to transfer to another job as provided for in his contract. He refused to do so. That was why he was dismissed ... If the requirement for employees to perform the work of a transport clerk and transport manager diminishes, so that one employee can do both jobs, the dismissed employee is dismissed by reason of redundancy ... Conversely, if the requirement for employees to do work of a particular kind remains the same, there can be no dismissal by reason of redundancy notwithstanding any unilateral variation to their contracts of employment.'

6.20 This decision is important and should prompt a re-evaluation of the meaning of a dismissal for redundancy. It is also notable for its emphasis on the words of the statute. The decision was approved by the House of Lords in *Murray v Foyle Meats Ltd*.[3] Lord Irivine of Lairg LC said:[4]

---

[1] [1997] ICR 523. See also *British Broadcasting Corporation v Farnworth* [1998] ICR 1116.
[2] *Ibid* at p 539.
[3] [1999] ICR 827.
[4] *Ibid* at pp 829G and 831C.

'The language of [s 139(1)(b)] … asks two questions of fact. The first is whether one or other of various states of economic affairs exists. In this case, the relevant one is whether the requirements of the business for employees to carry out work of a particular kind have diminished. The second question is whether the dismissal is attributable, wholly or mainly, to that state of affairs. This is a question of causation … The key word in the statute is "attributable" and there is no reason in law why the dismissal of an employee should not be attributable to a diminution in the employer's needs for employees irrespective of the terms of his contract or the function which he performed.'

6.21   In the light of this decision, the decision of the EAT in *Church v West Lancashire NHS Trust*[1] should be treated with caution. The Court of Appeal has looked at this issue again, in *Shawkat v Nottingham City Hospital NHS Trust*.[2] In that case, the employee was employed as a staff grade doctor in thoracic surgery. Following the establishment of a cardio-thoracic unit, he was required to perform both cardiac and thoracic surgery. He refused and was dismissed. The tribunal rejected his claim that his dismissal was for redundancy, but the EAT allowed his appeal and remitted the case to the tribunal, on the footing that it was not clear that a tribunal could only have reached one conclusion. On remission, the tribunal again concluded that there was no diminution in the employers' requirements for employees to carry out work of a particular kind, ie thoracic surgery. It said that there was no reduction in the amount of thoracic surgery or the number of employees required to do that work. It said that the reason why the employee's thoracic sessions was reduced was because they wanted him to do cardiac work in part of his time. It therefore concluded that he was not dismissed by reason of redundancy. The EAT dismissed the employee's appeal, as did the Court of Appeal, which said that the question whether the requirements of section 139 have been satisfied is a question of fact. Here, the tribunal's decision did not disclose an error of law and should not be disturbed.

6.22   It should be borne in mind that a reorganisation which does not fall within the statutory definition of redundancy may amount to 'some other substantial reason', the fifth potentially fair reason.[3]

6.23   Another problem has been caused by economic policy considerations. In *O'Hare v Rotaprint Ltd*,[4] the EAT suggested that if the workforce is expanded to meet a scale of production which fails to materialise, there may not be a cessation or diminution of work because the requirement never materialised. This is arguably inconsistent with the later Court of Appeal decision in *Nottinghamshire County Council v Lee*,[5] in which the Court held that if there is a diminution in the requirement at the time of the dismissal, it makes no difference that when the employee was engaged he or she knew of the diminishing work requirements. In such cases,

[1]   [1998] ICR 423.
[2]   [1999] ICR 780.
[3]   See Chapter 4.
[4]   [1980] ICR 94 at p 97. Cf *Bromby & Hoare Ltd v Evans* [1972] ICR 113.
[5]   [1980] ICR 635. See also *Pfaffinger v City of Liverpool Community College* [1996] ICR 142.

however, the tribunal may hold the dismissal to be for some other substantial reason, an approach followed subsequently by the Court of Appeal in *North Yorkshire County Council v Fay*.[1] In *Association of University Teachers v University of Newcastle-upon-Tyne*,[2] the EAT stressed that the task of the employment tribunal in such cases is to consider whether, on the facts, the dismissal is due to redundancy; it should not consider the reason for the redundancy situation. In that case, an employee was dismissed at the end of his three-year fixed-term contract because funding for the course on which he taught had run out. The employment tribunal's decision was that this did not amount to a redundancy situation, but it was reversed by the EAT, which said that because of the lack of funds the course could no longer be continued and there ceased to be a requirement for the employee's services. This approach is consistent with the EAT's decision in *Safeway Stores plc v Burrell*, above.

2. RIGHT OF EMPLOYEE TO TIME OFF

6.24   Employees given notice of dismissal by reason of redundancy are entitled by section 52(1) to reasonable time off during the notice period to look for new employment or make arrangements for training for further employment. They must have been continuously employed for two years. They need not provide evidence that they have an appointment, although it may be relevant to the reasonableness of the employer's conduct to ask whether the employee has an appointment and to make some enquiries about it.[3] The amount of time off is not statutorily defined, but the employee is not entitled to be paid more than 40% of a week's pay.[4] That does not mean, however, that it would not be reasonable for the employer to allow more time off, although the employee would not be entitled to be paid. Disputes about this entitlement are heard by the employment tribunal.[5]

6.25   It should be noted that only those made redundant are entitled to the right to time off, and not other employees who are dismissed, and that the entitlement to time off does not depend upon the employee's eventual entitlement, or otherwise, to a redundancy payment.[6]

3. UNFAIR DISMISSAL FOR REDUNDANCY

6.26   Two types of complaints of unfair dismissal for redundancy will be considered in this chapter. The first, and most common, type occurs where the employee complains that the way the redundancy dismissal was

---

[1]   [1986] ICR 133. See also *Terry v Sussex County Council* [1976] IRLR 332.
[2]   [1987] ICR 317.
[3]   *Dutton v Hawker Siddeley Aviation Ltd* [1978] ICR 1057.
[4]   Section 53(1) and (5). The pay is calculated at the 'appropriate hourly rate' in accordance with s 53(2) and (3).
[5]   Section 54.
[6]   *Dutton v Hawker Siddeley Aviation Ltd* [1978] ICR 1057.

handled was unfair and therefore contrary to section 98(4) of the Employment Rights Act 1996. The second type of complaint occurs where an employee dismissed for redundancy argues that he or she was selected for redundancy for one of the following reasons:

1.   reasons connected with trade union membership and activities, or trade union recognition;
2.   participation in official industrial action;
3.   reasons in connection with leave for family reasons;
4.   reasons connected with health and safety;
5.   the refusal of a shop or betting worker to do Sunday work;
6.   reasons connected with an employee's rights under the Working Time Regulations;
7.   reasons relating to an employee's performance of his or her duties as an occupational pension fund trustee;
8.   reasons relating to an employee's performance of his or her duties as an employee representative;
9.   reasons relating to the employee making a 'protected disclosure';[1]
10.   the assertion by the employee of a statutory right;
11.   reasons connected with the national minimum wage legislation;
12.   reasons connected with an employee's rights under the Tax Credits Act 1999;
13.   reasons relating to paragraph 28 to the Transnational Information and Consultation of Employees Regulations 1999;
14.   reasons relating to regulation 7 of the Part-time Workers (Prevention of Less Favourable Treatment) Regulations 2000.

6.27   These types of complaint will fall to be considered under section 153 or Schedule A1, paragraph 162 of the Trade Union and Labour Relations (Consolidation) Act 1992, section 105 of the Employment Rights Act 1996 or paragraph 20(1) of the Maternity and Parental Leave Regulations 1999. In such cases, there is no qualifying period of employment, nor does the age exclusion apply.[2]

---

[1]   Defined in ERA, ss 235(1) and 43A (see para 5.84).
[2]   TULRCA 1992, ss 154 (as amended by the Trade Union Reform and Employment Rights Act 1993, ss 49(1) and (2) and 51 and Sch 7, para 1, Sch 8, para 67 and Sch 10) and 239(1) (as amended by the Employment Relations Act 1999, s 16 and Sch 5, paras 1 and 4(1)–(3)); TULRCA 1992, Sch A1, para 164, inserted by s 1 and Sch 1 of the ERA 1999; ss 99(1) and (3), 108(3) and 109(2) of the Employment Rights Act 1996, as amended by the Employment Relations Act 1999, ss 9 and 44 and Sch 4, Pt III, paras 1, 5, 16 and 18 and Sch 9, Table 2, the Working Time Regulations 1998, SI 1998 No 1833, regs 2(1) and 32(4), the Public Interest Disclosure Act 1998, ss 7(1) and 18(2), the National Minimum Wage Act 1998, ss 25(3) and 53 and Sch 3, the Tax Credits Act 1999, ss 7 and 19(4), Sch 3, para 3(3), and Sch 6, the Transnational Information and Consultation of Employees Regulations 1999, SI 1999 No 3323, reg 29(2) and the Part-time Workers (Prevention of Less Favourable Treatment) Regulations 2000, SI 2000 No 1551, reg 10 and Schedule, para 2(2).

(a) Under section 98(4) of the Employment Rights Act 1996

6.28   If the tribunal is satisfied that the reason was redundancy,[1] it is likely that the dismissal will be held to be fair, unless the employer acts with blatant unfairness. Although in recent years the EAT has shown greater preparedness to hold a dismissal for redundancy unfair, by emphasising standards of good industrial relations practice,[2] it has expressed the view that, provided the selection process is fair, an employment tribunal should scrutinise critically a complaint that the dismissal was unfair on some other grounds.[3] Further, if the employee would still have been made redundant had the employer taken reasonable steps to consult with the employee or find him or her other employment, the tribunal may either find that the dismissal was fair or order that (if it was unfair) no compensation, other than the basic award, should be paid.[4] In such a case, in view of the House of Lords' decision in *Polkey v AE Dayton Services Ltd*,[5] the tribunal would normally find the dismissal unfair and award no compensation, although it is open to them to find that the employer could reasonably have concluded that consultation or warning would be useless, so that the failure to consult or warn in the light of the circumstances known to the employer at the time the decision to dismiss was taken was not unreasonable.[6] A tribunal may also conclude that, on the facts as found by it, the dismissal was unfair, but that, had a fair procedure been followed, the employee could have been fairly dismissed within a given period of time. In that case, it may confine the period of loss, for the purposes of assessing compensation, to that period of time.

6.29   A further alternative is that the tribunal may conclude that the dismissal was unfair, but that, had the employer gone through a fair procedure, the employee would have stood a chance of being fairly dismissed at the end of the procedure. If the tribunal reaches such a decision, it may go on to reduce the compensation by the relevant percentage. It is important, however, that the tribunal should consider

---

[1]   See paras 6.05 *et seq.*

[2]   See *Williams v Compair Maxam Ltd* [1982] ICR 156, *Freud v Bentalls Ltd* [1983] ICR 77, *Grundy (Teddington) Ltd v Plummer and Salt* [1983] IRLR 98 and *Stacey v Babcock Power Ltd (Construction Division)* [1986] IRLR 3. Cf *Grundy (Teddington) Ltd v Willis* [1976] ICR 323, *NC Watling & Co Ltd v Richardson* [1978] ICR 1049, and *Holden v Bradville Ltd* [1985] IRLR 483.

[3]   *British United Shoe Machinery Co Ltd v Clarke* [1978] ICR 70 and *Hinckley & Bosworth Borough Council v Ainscough* [1979] ICR 590. See also *Robinson v British Island Airways Ltd* [1978] ICR 304, *Carry All Motors Ltd v Pennington* [1980] ICR 806, and *Cowen v Haden Carrier Ltd* [1982] IRLR 225 (reversed by the Court of Appeal on the meaning of redundancy: see [1983] ICR 1) for examples of the EAT's reluctance to hold a dismissal for redundancy unfair; cf *NC Watling & Co Ltd v Richardson* [1978] ICR 1049, where the selection process was unfair.

[4]   *British United Shoe Machinery Co Ltd v Clarke* [1978] ICR 70, and *Pink v White and White & Co (Earls Barton) Ltd* [1985] IRLR 489. Cf *Howarth Timber (Leeds) Ltd v Biscomb* [1986] IRLR 52.

[5]   [1988] ICR 142. The *Polkey* case was applied by the Court of Appeal in *Walls Meat Co Ltd v Selby* [1989] ICR 601. See also *Dyke v Hereford and Worcester County Council* [1989] ICR 800.

[6]   See, eg, *Duffy v Yeomans & Partners Ltd* [1995] ICR 1.

what would have been the result if the proper procedure had been followed.[1]

6.30   The two main obligations laying upon an employer proposing to dismiss an employee for redundancy are to make reasonable efforts, where practicable, to find him or her suitable alternative employment in the undertaking, or, where appropriate, with an associated employer[2] and to consult with him or her and give reasonable warning of impending redundancy.[3] In *Langston v Cranfield University*,[4] the EAT said that an employment tribunal should consider the two questions of failure to seek alternative employment on the part of the employee and lack of consultation; it should also consider the fairness of the selection. A failure to do so will amount to an error.

6.31   In *R v Gwent County Council ex parte Bryant*,[5] Hodgson J said:

'Fair consultation means:

(a)   consultation when the proposals are still at a formative stage;
(b)   adequate information on which to respond;
(c)   adequate time in which to respond;
(d)   conscientious consideration by an authority of the response to consultation.'

Although this statement was made in a different context, it has been adopted by the Court of Session as appropriate to the consultation requirements for an employer when dismissing for redundancy.[6]

6.32   The important decision of the House of Lords in *Polkey v AE Dayton Services Ltd*[7] is the general starting-point for a consideration of the

---

[1]   *Red Bank Manufacturing Co Ltd v Meadows* [1992] IRLR 209. It should be noted that a different aspect of this case is reported at [1992] ICR 204.

[2]   *Vokes Ltd v Bear* [1974] ICR 1, *Holliday Concreting (Testing) Ltd v Woods* [1979] IRLR 301, *Thomas & Betts Manufacturing Ltd v Harding* [1980] IRLR 255, *Barratt Construction Ltd v Dalrymple* [1984] IRLR 385 and *Wood v Coverage Care Ltd* [1996] IRLR 266 (in which the EAT said that the tribunal had not erred in taking into account the employee's spent convictions when considering her for alternative posts in a residential home which included elderly persons). See also *Sun Valley Poultry Ltd v Mitchell* (EAT 164/96) IDS Brief 582. *Cf MDH Ltd v Sussex* [1986] IRLR 123.

[3]   *Kelly v Upholstery and Cabinet Works (Amesbury) Ltd* [1977] IRLR 91 and *Williams v Compair Maxam Ltd* [1982] ICR 156, which contains a particularly useful discussion of this area. See also *Freud v Bentalls Ltd* [1983] ICR 77, *Grundy (Teddington) Ltd v Plummer and Salt* [1983] IRLR 98, *Gray v Shetland Norse Preserving Co Ltd* [1985] IRLR 53, *Rolls-Royce Motors Ltd v Dewhurst* [1985] IRLR 184, *Holden v Bradville Ltd* [1985] IRLR 483 and *King v Eaton* [1996] IRLR 199. In *Ibex Trading Co Ltd v Walton* [1994] IRLR 564, the EAT upheld the tribunal's decision that the dismissals of employees by the administrator were unfair because of a lack of consultation with them or their union.

[4]   [1998] IRLR 173.

[5]   [1988] *Crown Office Digest* 19. This statement was adopted by the Divisional Court in *R v British Coal Corporation and Secretary of State for Trade and Industry ex parte Price* [1994] IRLR 72.

[6]   See *King v Eaton Ltd* [1996] IRLR 199.

[7]   [1988] ICR 142.

employer's obligations when dismissing for redundancy. It was extensively considered in Chapter 4, but, since it in fact concerned a dismissal for redundancy, it is considered again here. Lord Mackay of Clashfern LC said:[1]

'If the employer could reasonably have concluded in the light of the circumstances known to him at the time of dismissal that consultation or warning would be utterly useless he might well act reasonably even if he did not observe the provisions of the code. Failure to observe the requirement of the code relating to consultation or warning will not necessarily render a dismissal unfair. Whether in any particular case it did so is a matter for the employment tribunal to consider in the light of the circumstances known to the employer at the time he dismissed the employee.'

Lord Bridge of Harwich said:[2]

'... [I]n the case of redundancy, the employer will not normally act reasonably unless he warns and consults any employees affected or their representative, adopts a fair basis on which to select for redundancy and takes such steps as may be reasonable to avoid or minimise redundancy by redeployment within his own organisation ... It is quite a different matter if the tribunal is able to conclude that the employer himself, at the time of dismissal, acted reasonably in taking the view that, in the exceptional circumstances of the particular case, the procedural steps normally appropriate would have been futile, could not have altered the decision to dismiss and therefore could be dispensed with. In such a case the test of reasonableness under section [98(4)] may be satisfied.'

6.33 Subsequently, in *Hooper v British Railways Board*,[3] the Court of Appeal took the view that there is no distinction in substance between the principles formulated by the Lord Chancellor and Lord Bridge. Ralph Gibson LJ said:[4]

'... Lord Bridge did not take the view that he was stating any different test. He was ... emphasising one aspect of the principle stated by Lord Mackay, namely that the reasonableness of the action taken by the employer is to be judged by reference to the facts and factors known to the employer at the time of making the decision.'

6.34 These principles were followed by the Court of Appeal in *Duffy v Yeomans & Partners Ltd*.[5] It said that the test of reasonableness under what is now section 98(4) is objective and it is not necessary for an employer to have applied his or her mind to the question of consultation for a dismissal without consultation to be within the range of reasonable responses under section 98(4). Although normally a dismissal will be unfair where there has

---

1   [1988] ICR 142 at p 153.
2   *Ibid* at pp 162–163.
3   [1988] IRLR 517.
4   *Ibid* at p 528.
5   [1995] ICR 1. The Court of Appeal did not follow the EAT's decision in *Robertson v Magnet Ltd (Retail Division)* [1993] IRLR 512.

been no consultation, the effect of a failure to consult is a matter of fact and degree for the employment tribunal. This view is consistent with the House of Lords' decision in the *Polkey* case and, it is submitted, is correct in taking the view that each case must be decided on its own facts, bearing in mind the general proposition that normally an employer will not act reasonably unless he or she goes through the appropriate procedure. This decision is in accord with the decision in the *Polkey* case.

6.35   The courts have thus continued to emphasise the need for prior consultation and warning, and have been reluctant to find exceptional circumstances which would obviate this requirement. These requirements are not avoided by the fact that the employers are a small company or that immediate decisions needed to be made.[1] In *Ferguson v Prestwick Circuits Ltd,*[2] for example, the employers justified their failure to consult on the grounds that in a previous redundancy exercise three years before they had gone through the recommended consultation process, only to be told by the workforce that they would have preferred simply being told on the day that they were being made redundant. The Scottish division of the EAT said that this was not sufficient reason for departing from the requirements of good industrial relations practice and reiterated what Lord Bridge said in the *Polkey* case; that it is only in exceptional circumstances that there will be no need for consultation. It added:

> 'It would be a convenient matter indeed for employers to state that the workforce did not wish to be consulted before dismissal, and thus to dispense with consultation. The law, however, says otherwise …'[3]

6.36   In *De Grasse v Stockwell Tools Ltd,*[4] the EAT said that while the size of the undertaking may affect the nature or formality of the consultation process, it cannot excuse the lack of any consultation. In *Rolls-Royce Motor Cars Ltd v Price,*[5] which also involved what is now section 105 of the ERA 1996 (see below), the EAT refused to accept the argument that, where consultation with the union on the choice of criteria to be applied in a redundancy situation had been taken as far as was practicable, the employer ceased to be under an obligation to consult with the union or the employees concerned about the application of the criteria to individuals. In

---

[1] See *Heron v Citylink Nottingham* [1993] IRLR 372, which dealt with this last point. The EAT said that a finding that the requirement to consult was obviated by the need for immediate decisions can be supported only if the circumstances made it necessary for the employers to dismiss the employee when they did and at no later date.

[2] [1992] IRLR 266. See also *Rowell v Hubbard Group Services Ltd* [1995] IRLR 195, where the employers sent a letter to all their employees warning them of impending redundancies and setting out the criteria upon which selection would be based. This was followed by a letter of dismissal some two months later, which, after setting out details of compensation, ended by saying that any matters arising from the letter could be discussed with a member of the management. The EAT upheld the tribunal's decision that the dismissal was unfair.

[3] *Ibid* at p 268.

[4] [1992] IRLR 269.

[5] [1993] IRLR 203.

this case, the EAT held that the dismissals were not automatically unfair under section 105, and went on to hold that they were unfair under section 98(4).

6.37 More recently, in *Mugford v Midland Bank plc*,[1] the EAT reviewed the position regarding consultation and said this:[2]

'(1)   Where no consultation about redundancy has taken place with either the trade union or the employee the dismissal will normally be unfair, unless the employment tribunal finds that a reasonable employer would have concluded that consultation would be an utterly futile exercise in the particular circumstances of the case.
(2)   Consultation with the trade union over selection criteria does not of itself release the employer from considering with the employee individually his being identified for redundancy.
(3)   It will be a question of fact and degree for the employment tribunal to consider whether consultation with the individual and/or his union was so inadequate as to render the dismissal unfair. A lack of consultation in any particular respect will not automatically lead to that result. The overall picture must be viewed by the tribunal up to the date of termination to ascertain whether the employer has or has not acted reasonably in dismissing the employee on the grounds of redundancy.'

6.38 In *Warner v Adnet Ltd*,[3] the Court of Appeal upheld the tribunal's decision that a dismissal was fair despite the complete failure by the employers to consult the employee. It said that the tribunal was entitled to find that in view of the appointment of receivers, the dire financial straits of the company and the urgent need to find a purchaser, the normal requirements of consultation did not apply. It added that consultation could not have made a difference to the decision to dismiss. Mummery LJ emphasised[4] that the judgment in that case was not intended to relax the general rule that employment tribunals should scrutinise with the greatest care any case in which an employer dismisses for redundancy without consultation.

6.39 It should be noted that a defect in the employer's consultation process may be cured at the appeal stage, provided that the appeal represents a rehearing and not merely a review of the original decision. In such a case, the dismissal will not be unfair. There is no distinction in principle (as regards a case of procedural deficiency at the dismissal stage being cured by a full rehearing on appeal) between any of the potentially fair reasons under section 98 of the ERA.[5]

6.40 A dismissal for redundancy may be made unfair by events which happen during the period of notice given to the employee, for example by the employer's failure to offer new employment to an employee under

---

[1]   [1997] ICR 399.
[2]   *Ibid* at p 406.
[3]   [1998] IRLR 394.
[4]   *Ibid* at p 398.
[5]   See *Lloyd v Taylor Woodrow Construction* [1999] IRLR 782.

notice of dismissal for redundancy when it became available during the notice period.[1]

6.41   In cases involving selection criteria, the tribunal should beware of rewriting the employer's selection criteria. If it does so, it runs the risk of deciding the case according to what it would have done had it been the employer.[2] So, for example, the tribunal will fall into error if it rewrites the employer's selection criteria so as to include an assessment of the employee's role as a health and safety representative.[3] On the other hand, a decision by the employer to withhold from employees selected for redundancy the details of their individual assessments may cause the dismissal to be unfair.[4] In such cases, it may be appropriate for the employment tribunal to order discovery of documents relating to the selection criteria used by the employer, including documents relating to other employees involved in the process.[5]

(b) Under section 153 of and Schedule A1, paragraph 162 to the TULRCA 1992; section 105 of the ERA 1996; and regulation 20 of the Maternity and Parental Leave Regulations 1999

6.42   The situations covered here are those in which there is a selective dismissal for redundancy and the employee dismissed is complaining that the reason for the selection was an inadmissible reason. It should go without saying, however, that these provisions only apply where the reason for the dismissal is *redundancy*; if the tribunal is satisfied that redundancy was not the reason, then the provisions do not apply.[6]

(i) Under section 153 of the 1992 Act

6.43   A dismissal for redundancy will be in contravention of section 153 and automatically unfair if the following conditions are satisfied:

1.   the circumstances constituting the redundancy applied equally to one or more employees in the same undertaking who held positions similar to that held by the dismissed employee;

---

[1]   *Stacey v Babcock Power Ltd* [1986] ICR 221.
[2]   See the discussion on this matter in Chapter 4, at para 4.35. See also *Byrne v Castrol (UK) Lyf* (EAT 142/96) IDS Brief 590, where an absenteeism criterion was one of the factors applied in a redundancy exercise. The EAT upheld the tribunal's decision that the employer's failure to disregard absences which were not the fault of the employee did not make the dismissal unfair.
[3]   *Smiths Industries Aerospace and Defence Systems v Rawlings* [1996] IRLR 656.
[4]   *John Brown Engineering Ltd v Brown* [1997] IRLR 90. See also *King v Eaton Ltd* [1996] IRLR 199.
[5]   *FDR Ltd v Holloway* [1995] IRLR 400. *Cf* the Court of Appeal's decision in *British Aerospace plc v Green* [1995] IRLR 433.
[6]   See, for example, *Business Post Ltd v Ballard* (EAT 263/90) IDS Brief 490. The employer argued that the reason was redundancy and that the employee did not have sufficient qualifying employment; the employee argued that the reason was that he proposed to join a union and that he did not need any qualifying employment. The EAT agreed with him.

2.   those employees have not been dismissed; and
3.   the employee in question was selected for dismissal for one of the reasons specified in section 152(1), which relate to dismissals for trade union membership and activities.[1]

6.44   Employees dismissed in contravention of section 153 do not need the qualifying period of employment of one year. They are treated like employees who are dismissed in contravention of section 152, for whom there is no minimum qualifying period of employment.[2]

Section 153 is only capable of applying where there are other employees in the undertaking who hold similar positions to that held by the dismissed employee. If there are no other employees holding similar positions, section 153 will not apply.[3]

6.45   In considering whether the reason for the selection of the employee for redundancy was a reason relating to trade union membership or activities, the tribunal should not take into account whether the employers deliberately or maliciously selected the employee. To decide that section 153 does not apply if there is no malice and no deliberate decision to dismiss for trade union activities is to construe the provision too narrowly.[4]

Dismissals for trade union membership and activities are considered in Chapter 5, which should be consulted for a discussion of this group of reasons.

(ii) Under Schedule A1, paragraph 162 to the 1992 Act[5]

6.46   Paragraph 162 is identical in its effect to section 153 of the 1992 Act, except that it applies to employees dismissed for redundancy or selected for redundancy for a reason falling within paragraph 161(2). The reasons are as follows:

1.   the employee acted with a view to obtaining or preventing recognition of a union or unions by the employer under Schedule A1 to the TULRCA 1992;
2.   the employee indicated that he or she supported or did not support recognition of a union or unions;
3.   the employee acted with a view to securing or preventing the ending under the Schedule of bargaining arrangements.
4.   the employee indicated that he or she supported or did not support the ending of bargaining arrangements;

---

[1]   For an example, see *Britool Ltd v Roberts* [1993] IRLR 481.
[2]   TULRCA 1992, s 154, as amended by the Trade Union Reform and Employment Rights Act 1993, s 49(1) and Sch 7, para 1.
[3]   *O'Dea v ISC Chemicals Ltd t/a Rhone-Poulenc Chemicals* [1996] ICR 222.
[4]   *Dundon v GPT Ltd* [1995] IRLR 403.
[5]   Schedule A1 was inserted by s 1 of and Sch 1 to the ERA 1999.

5.   the employee influenced or sought to influence the way in which votes were to be cast by other workers in a ballot arranged under Schedule A1;

6.   the employee influenced or sought to influence other workers to vote or abstain from voting in such a ballot;

7.   the employee voted in such a ballot;

8.   the employee proposed to do, failed to do, or proposed to decline to do, any of the things referred to above.

A reason will not fall within the above list if it constitutes an unreasonable act or omission by the employee.[1]

(iii) Under section 105 of the 1996 Act[2]

6.47   A dismissal for redundancy will be automatically unfair if the following conditions are satisfied:

1.   the circumstances constituting the redundancy applied equally to one or more employees in the same undertaking who held positions similar to that held by the dismissed employee;

2.   those employees have not been dismissed;

3.   the employee in question was selected for one of the following reasons:

(a)   reasons connected with health and safety;

(b)   the refusal of a shop or betting worker to do Sunday work;

(c)   reasons connected with an employee's rights under the Working Time Regulations;

(d)   reasons relating to an employee's performance of his or her duties as an occupational pension fund trustee;

(e)   reasons relating to an employee's performance of his or her duties as an employee representative;

(f)   reasons relating to the employee making a 'protected disclosure';[3]

(g)   the assertion by the employee of a statutory right;

(h)   reasons connected with the national minimum wage legislation;

(i)   reasons connected with an employee's rights under the Tax Credits Act 1999;

(j)   participation in official industrial action;

---

[1]   TULRCA 1992, Sch A1, para 161(3).

[2]   As amended by the Employment Relations Act 1999, ss 9 and 16 and Sch 4, Pt III, paras 1, 5 and 17, Sch 5, paras 1 and 5(1)–(3) and Sch 9, Table 2, the Working Time Regulations 1998, SI 1998 No 1833, regs 2(1) and 32(3), the Public Interest Disclosure Act 1998, ss 6 and 18(2), the National Minimum Wage Act 1998, s 25(2), the Tax Credits Act 1999, ss 7 and Sch 3, para 3(2), and Sch 6, the Transnational Information and Consultation of Employees Regulations 1999, SI 1999 No 3323, reg 29(1) and the Part-time Workers (Prevention of Less Favourable Treatment) Regulations 2000, SI 2000 No 1551, reg 10 and Schedule, para 2(1).

[3]   Defined in ERA, ss 235(1) and 43A (see para 5.84).

(k)   reasons relating to paragraph 28 of the Transnational Information and Consultation of Employees Regulations 1999;

(l)   reasons relating to regulation 7 of the Part-time Workers (Prevention of Less Favourable Treatment) Regulations 2000.

It should be noted that neither the one-year qualifying period nor the age exclusion apply to employees selected for dismissal for redundancy for one of the above reasons.[1]

6.48   If the selection for redundancy infringes section 105, the dismissal will be automatically unfair; if it does not infringe section 105, the employment tribunal should then go on to consider whether the employer has fulfilled the requirements of section 98(4).[2]

6.49   It should also be noted that section 202(2)(g)(ii)[3] permits restrictions on the disclosure of information on grounds of national security in cases arising under section 105(1), where the selection of an employee for a redundancy dismissal is allegedly for any of the reasons falling within section 105(3), (4A) or (6) (health and safety cases, working time cases and cases involving the performance of the employee's functions as an employee representative). Section 202 applies where, in the opinion of any Minister of the Crown, the disclosure of any information would be contrary to the interests of national security. In that case, disclosure of the information is not required; further, disclosure is forbidden in any proceedings in any court or tribunal relating to section 105(1).

Section 10(1) of the Employment Tribunals Act 1996[4] states that the employment tribunal is to dismiss a complaint of unfair dismissal if it is shown that the act complained of was taken for the purpose of safeguarding national security. The new sections 10, 10A and 10B contain no provisions dealing specifically with section 105(2), (3) or (6) as the previous section 10(5) (now replaced) did. These new sections are considered at para 1.90.

6.50   Although section 7(6) of the Employment Tribunals Act 1996 places upon the employer the burden of showing that the reason for the dismissal is redundancy, the burden of showing that section 105 applies lies upon the employee.

(iv)   Under regulation 20 of the Maternity and Parental Leave Regulations 1999

6.51   A dismissal for redundancy will also be automatically unfair if it is shown that:

---

[1]   Sections 108(3)(h) and 109(2)(h).
[2]   *Thomas & Betts Manufacturing Ltd v Harding* [1980] IRLR 255 and *McDowell v Eastern British Road Services Ltd* [1981] IRLR 482.
[3]   As amended by the ERA 1999, s 9 and Sch 4, Pt III, paras 1, 5 and 36.
[4]   As substituted by the Employment Relations Act 1999, s 41 and Sch 8, para 3.

1.   the circumstances constituting the redundancy applied equally to one or more employees in the same undertaking who held positions similar to the position held by the employee and were not dismissed by the employer; and

2.   the reason (or principal reason) for which the employee was selected for a dismissal was one of the reasons set out below.[1]

6.52   The reasons are as follows:

(a)   the pregnancy of the employee;[2]

(b)   the fact that the employee has given birth to a child;[3]

(c)   'the application of a relevant requirement, or a relevant recommendation, as defined by section 66(2)' of the ERA;

(d)   the fact that she took, sought to take or availed herself of the benefits of, ordinary maternity leave;[4]

(e)   the fact that she took or sought to take:

> (i)   additional maternity leave;[5]
>
> (ii)   parental leave;[6] or
>
> (iii)   time off under section 57A;[7]

---

[1]   Regulation 20(2).

[2]   The previous legislation used a similar phrase. Cases decided under that legislation held that reasons connected with pregnancy included miscarriages and hypertension: see *George v Beecham Group* [1977] IRLR 43 and *Elegbede v The Wellcome Foundation* [1977] IRLR 383. The House of Lords considered the phrase 'any other reason connected with her pregnancy' (the phrase used in the previous legislation) in *Brown v Stockton-on-Tees Borough Council* [1988] ICR 410, a decision followed by the EAT in *Clayton v Vigors* [1990] IRLR 177; see also *Hilton International Hotels (UK) Ltd v Kaissi* [1994] ICR 578. It held that the phrase ought to be read widely. So a pregnant employee who was selected for redundancy because she would require maternity leave was held to have been dismissed for a reason connected with her pregnancy; her dismissal was therefore unfair.

[3]   This only applies where the dismissal ends the employee's ordinary or additional maternity leave period: see reg 20(4).

[4]   A woman will be treated as availing herself of the benefits of ordinary maternity leave if, during her ordinary maternity leave period, she avails herself of the benefit of any of the terms and conditions of her employment preserved by s 71 of the ERA during that period: see reg 20(5) and 19(3).

[5]   See ERA, s 73 and regs 5, 6(3) and 7(4). An employee is not entitled to additional maternity leave, unless she is also entitled to ordinary maternity leave and had been continuously employed for a year at the beginning of the eleventh week before the expected week of childbirth: reg 5. The ordinary maternity leave period starts either at the date notified to the employer as the date on which she intends her ordinary maternity leave period to start or the first day of the sixth week before the expected week of childbirth on which she is absent from work wholly or partly because of pregnancy, whichever date is the earlier: reg 6(1); note also reg 6(2). The additional maternity leave period starts the day after the last day of the ordinary maternity leave period and continues until the end of the period of 29 weeks starting with the week of childbirth: regs 6(3) and 7(4). If the employee is dismissed during a maternity leave period, the period ends at the time of the dismissal: reg 7(5).

[6]   The entitlement to parental leave and the extent of the entitlement are set out in regs 13 and 14.

[7]   This section makes provision for time off for dependants in certain circumstances.

(f)   the fact that she declined to sign a workforce agreement[1] for the purposes of the Regulations;

(g)   the fact that the employee was a representative of members of the workforce for the purposes of Schedule 1 (which deals with the conclusion of workforce agreements) or a candidate in an election to be such a representative and, as such, performed (or proposed to perform) any functions or activities as a representative or candidate.

6.53   There are two exclusions from these provisions. The first applies to small employers in the following circumstances:

(a)   the employer has no more than five employees (including employees of an associated employer)[2] immediately before the end of the employee's additional maternity leave period or, if it is brought to an end by dismissal, immediately before the dismissal; and

(b)   it is not reasonably practicable for the employer (or successor employer) to allow her to return to a job which is both suitable for her and appropriate for her to do in the circumstances or for an associated employer to offer her a job of that kind.[3]

6.54   The second exclusion applies where:

(a)   it is not reasonably practicable for a reason other than redundancy for the employer (or successor employer) to allow her to return to a job which is both suitable for her and appropriate for her to do in the circumstances;

(b)   an associated employer offers her a job of that kind; and

(c)   she accepts or unreasonably refuses the offer.[4]

An employer who wishes to invoke either of the above exclusions will have the burden of showing that they were satisfied.[5]

6.55   There is also a specific exclusion relating to employees dismissed for taking additional maternity leave. Regulation 12(2) excludes from regulation 20 an employee who has failed to notify her employer of her intention to return in response to a request made in writing.[6]

---

[1]   Schedule 1 to the regulations deals with workforce agreements.
[2]   Defined in reg 2(3). The definition is the same as that in s 231 of the ERA 1996.
[3]   Regulation 20(6).
[4]   Regulation 20(7).
[5]   Regulation 20(8).
[6]   See reg 12(1) and (3). This applies where an employer makes a written request to an employee to notify in writing the date of the child's birth and whether she intends to return to work at the end of her additional maternity leave period. The request must be made no earlier than 21 days before the end of the employee's ordinary leave period; it must be accompanied by a written statement explaining how the employee may determine the date on which her additional maternity leave period will end and warning her of the consequence of a failure to respond in time. The employee must respond within 21 days of receiving the request.

4. CLAIM FOR REDUNDANCY PAYMENT

(a) Offers of re-engagement or alternative employment

(i) The general rules

6.56   The provisions governing offers of re-engagement and alternative employment operate in two separate ways: either they affect the question whether or not the employee is to be treated as having been dismissed; or they operate to disentitle him or her from receiving a redundancy payment which would otherwise be payable. The first set of provisions is considered in Chapter 3, which considers the meaning of dismissal.

6.57   There is the additional complicating factor of the trial period: this comes into operation in both cases where the offer of new employment differs at all from the terms of the previous employment. The trial period provisions are considered separately in the next section. The statutory provisions also apply where there is a change of employer.[1]

6.58   Section 138 deals with the situation where an employee who is under notice of redundancy (or who has been constructively dismissed) is offered alternative employment. Its provisions have been considered in Chapter 3, to which reference should be made; they follow on from the basic definition of dismissal in section 135. Once the employee is found to have been dismissed, he or she may be disentitled from receiving the payment which would otherwise be payable if there is held to have been an unreasonable refusal of a suitable offer.[2] The effect of the trial period provisions[3] is that, if an employee unreasonably terminates the employment during the trial period, that act will disentitle him or her from the right to receive a payment.

6.59   The provisions of section 141 affect an employee treated as dismissed for redundancy by virtue of section 138. An employee will be disentitled from receiving a redundancy payment where he or she unreasonably refuses an offer of suitable new employment. Section 141(1) applies to an offer made before the ending of the previous employment to renew the contract or re-engage him or her under a new one, the renewal or re-engagement taking effect no more than four weeks after the ending of the previous contract. If the provisions of the new contract are the same as those of the old, the employee will be disentitled, if he or she unreasonably refuses the offer.[4] Where the provisions of the new contract differ, the first question is whether the offer is an offer of 'suitable employment in relation to the employee',[5] since section 141(2) will only disentitle the employee in the case of an unreasonable refusal of a suitable offer. If he or she actually

---

[1]   Sections 141 and 146(1). These provisions are considered after the trial period.
[2]   Section 141. Note s 146(2), which applies where the contract ends on a Friday, Saturday or Sunday.
[3]   Section 141(4). 'Trial period' is defined in s 138(3).
[4]   Section 141(2) and (3)(a).
[5]   See s 141(3)(b).

gives the new contract a try, the statutory trial period will come into operation; if he or she then leaves during it, entitlement will be lost if the new employment was suitable, and the termination of the employment during the trial period was unreasonable.[1] Whether there has been an offer is essentially an issue of fact for the tribunal to decide. A multiplicity of insufficiently specific offers may not be an adequate substitute for an offer of a single suitable alternative employment.[2]

6.60 The two significant questions here concern what is meant by 'suitable' and 'unreasonable'. They must be kept separate and dealt with separately by the tribunal.[3] The suitability of the offer is to be looked at objectively by the employment tribunal and is regarded by the appellate courts as being a matter of fact and degree for it to decide.[4] In *Taylor v Kent County Council*,[5] Lord Parker CJ said that suitability 'means employment which is substantially equivalent to the employment which has ceased', but there are suggestions in later cases that an objectively unsuitable offer may be made suitable (or vice versa) by the employee's attitude towards it.[6]

6.61 In the case of an offer found not to be suitable, it will not be necessary to go on to consider the reasonableness of the employee's refusal. If, however, the offer is found to be suitable, the tribunal must then consider the reasonableness of the refusal by looking at the personal reasons that relate to the employee.[7] This is a subjective matter to be considered from the employee's point of view.[8] This must be judged as at the time the offer is made and not with hindsight,[9] taking account of the personal circumstances of the individual employee, and also his or her reaction in those circumstances; all the relevant factors should be considered as a whole.[10] In looking at the two separate factors of suitability and reasonableness, the employment tribunal is entitled to look at factors which may be common to both questions.[11]

---

[1] Section 141(4).

[2] *Curling v Securicor Ltd* [1992] IRLR 549. In this case, the alleged offer consisted of sending round a list of jobs available and informing the employees concerned that unless they notified the company of their job selection by a specified date so that they could report for duty in an alternative job some 10 days later, they would be deemed to have resigned. The EAT said that to offer employees the choice between accepting alternative employment and applying for redundancy amounted to a dismissal and they upheld the tribunal's decision that no offer of suitable employment had been made to the employees.

[3] *Carron Co v Robertson* (1967) 2 ITR 484 at p 486, and *Hindes v Supersine Ltd* [1979] ICR 517. See also *Taylor v Kent County Council* [1969] QB 560.

[4] *Carron Co v Robertson* (1967) 2 ITR 484 at p 486 and *Taylor v Kent County Council* [1969] QB 560 at pp 565–566.

[5] Above, followed in *Hindes v Supersine Ltd* [1979] ICR 517.

[6] See, eg, *Hindes v Supersine Ltd*, above at p 523 and *Executors of JF Everest v Cox* [1980] ICR 415. See also *Standard Telephones and Cables Ltd v Yates* [1981] IRLR 21.

[7] *Carron Co v Robertson*, above, and *Hindes v Supersine Ltd*, above.

[8] *Cambridge & District Co-operative Society Ltd v Ruse* [1993] IRLR 156.

[9] *Lambert v Warren Bros (Plymstock) Ltd* (EAT 85/88).

[10] *Thomas Wragg & Sons Ltd v Wood* [1976] ICR 313, *Paton Calvert & Co Ltd v Westerside* [1979] IRLR 108, and *Executors of JF Everest v Cox*, above.

[11] *Spencer v Gloucestershire County Council* [1985] IRLR 393.

(ii) Trial period

6.62   Where the provisions of the new contract differ at all from the provisions of the previous contract, a trial period comes into operation.[1] If the employee leaves or is dismissed during the trial period, he or she will be treated as having been dismissed under the previous contract. An employee whose termination of the contract during the trial period is held to be unreasonable will be disentitled from receiving a redundancy payment.

6.63   The coming into operation of the trial period occurs in all cases whether the old contract is renewed or the employee is re-engaged under a new contract and where there is a difference, unless it is one to which the *de minimis* rule applies.[2] The trial period generally starts with the ending of the previous contract and ends four weeks from the date on which the employee starts work under the new contract.[3] In *Benton v Sanderson Kayser Ltd*,[4] the question arose as to the meaning 'period of four weeks' used by what is now section 138(3). The employee was made redundant from midnight on 21/22 December 1986 and was offered a four-week trial period doing different work, starting immediately following the termination of his employment. On 16 January 1987, he gave notice of his wish to terminate his employment from Monday, 19 January, some eight hours after the expiry of the trial period. The tribunal rejected the employee's argument that, as the employer's premises had been closed for 11 days over the Christmas period, he had not been given the opportunity of completing a four-week trial period at work. It held that once the four weeks had expired it had no jurisdiction to hear his claim. The EAT allowed his appeal, and held that 'period of four weeks' had to be related to the words 'trial period' and that 'trial period' could only be understood as meaning a period of trial actually at work. The trial period had not, therefore, expired when the employee terminated his employment. The Court of Appeal rejected that approach and held that 'period of four weeks' means a period of four consecutive weeks calculated according to the calendar, rather than the period of time actually worked.

6.64   The trial period may only be extended, by agreement between the parties, for the purpose of retraining the employee and the agreement must comply with the requirements of section 138(6). An extension for any other reason will have no effect. This means that an employee who decides to leave during the period of the extension will be held to have resigned.[5] An employee who leaves during the trial period or who is dismissed by the employer (for a reason connected with or arising out of the change in the contract) will be treated as having been dismissed on the date on which the previous contract ended and for the reason for which that contract was

---

[1]   This is the combined effect of ss 138(2) and 141(4). The wording of s 141(4) seems to presuppose the coming into effect of the trial period, although it does not actually say so.
[2]   *Rose v Henry Trickett & Sons Ltd* (1971) 6 ITR 211 at p 215.
[3]   Section 138(3).
[4]   [1988] ICR 313 (EAT) and [1989] ICR 136 (CA).
[5]   *Meek v J Allen Rubber Co Ltd and Secretary of State for Employment* [1980] IRLR 21.

ended.[1] Similar considerations apply where there is more than one renewal of the original contract or the employee is again re-engaged under a new contract.[2] Section 141 applies also to offers of re-engagement by associated employers.[3] It may be noted that a refusal to offer an employee a trial period may cause the dismissal to be unfair.[4]

6.65 If the employee leaves during the trial period, entitlement to a redundancy payment will be lost if the new employment was suitable, and the termination of the employment during the trial period was unreasonable.[5] For a consideration of what is unreasonable, see the preceding section.

(iii) Change of employer

6.66 The statutory provisions discussed in the preceding sections apply equally to associated employers of the original employer. This means that an offer of employment made by an associated employer is as good as an offer made by the original employer and the provisions of section 141 apply in the same way to an employee who is offered employment by an associated employer.[6] Provided that the person offering employment is within the definition of 'associated employer', it does not matter that the associated employer has no employees at the time of the offer of employment and is a dormant company reactivated especially for the purpose of offering employment to the redundant employee(s).[7]

6.67 In other cases, the transferee of the business may incur liability. This will depend upon whether there has been a transfer of an undertaking within the Transfer of Undertakings Regulations 1981, or whether section 218(2) of the ERA 1996 applies. These were considered in Chapter 2, to which reference should be made.

(b) Misconduct

6.68 If an employee is dismissed for misconduct, albeit in a redundancy situation, the presumption of redundancy will be rebutted and the dismissal will not have been by reason of redundancy. In such a case, the tribunal should scrutinise the employer's reason carefully, to ensure that it is not a reason trumped up to defeat a legitimate claim. If, on the other

---

[1] Section 138(4). Note the extended meaning of 'relevant date' in s 145(4) for situations covered by this provision. For a discussion of the date of termination, see Chapter 3.

[2] See s 138(5).

[3] Section 146(1). The meaning of 'associated employer' is discussed in Chapter 2.

[4] *Elliot v Richard Stump Ltd* [1987] ICR 579.

[5] Section 141(4).

[6] Section 146(1).

[7] *Lucas v Henry Johnson (Packers & Shippers) Ltd* [1986] ICR 384. The EAT rejected the argument that the associated company could not be said to be an 'employer' within what is now ss 138(1) and 146(1) because it had no employees at the time of the offer of employment. It held that, since the requirements of ss 138(1) and 146(1) were satisfied, the employees taken on by the associated employer could not claim redundancy payments, since they could not be said to have been dismissed by the original employer.

hand, the employer dismisses the employee for redundancy, but discovers misconduct on his or her part, section 140(1) must be complied with. This provision operates so as to disentitle an employee where the employer, 'being entitled to terminate his contract of employment by reason of the employee's conduct', terminates it in one of three ways:

1.   without notice, or
2.   by giving shorter notice than the employee is entitled to, or
3.   by giving the correct notice but also stating in writing that the employer would be entitled to terminate the contract summarily because of the employee's conduct.

6.69   The EAT has expressed the view that what is now section 140(1) applies where there is a single dismissal (ie a dismissal for redundancy and not explicitly for misconduct) as well as a double dismissal (ie a dismissal for redundancy followed by a dismissal for misconduct).[1] So if, for example, the employer gives the employee less notice than he or she is entitled to and subsequently misconduct on the part of the employee comes to light, section 140(1) will relieve the employer of liability; if, on the other hand, the employer gives the correct notice, liability to pay a redundancy payment will not be extinguished unless the employee is dismissed a second time.

6.70   Section 140(1) uses the phrase 'where the employer, *being entitled* to terminate his contract ...'. The effect of the italicised words was considered by the EAT in *Bonner v H Gilbert Ltd*.[2] It held that where the employer raises a defence to a redundancy payments claim based on section 140(1), the question of whether or not he or she is entitled to terminate the employee's contract must be determined according to the 'contractual' approach propounded in *Western Excavating (ECC) Ltd v Sharp*.[3] In other words, the employer must show that the employee was guilty of conduct which was a significant breach of contract or which showed that he or she no longer intended to be bound by one or more of the essential terms of the contract. A reasonable belief that the employee has committed a breach of contract will not be enough.

6.71   Section 140(3) gives the employment tribunal power to award all or part of the redundancy payment, where the employer terminates the contract in accordance with section 140(1) and the second dismissal takes place 'at any relevant time'. This phrase is defined[4] as 'any time within the obligatory period'; 'obligatory period' is defined in section 136(4).[5] In *Simmons v Hoover Ltd*,[6] the EAT expressed the view that what is now section 140(3) applies only where there are two dismissals. If its analysis of

---

[1]   *Simmons v Hoover Ltd* [1977] ICR 61 at p 80.
[2]   [1989] IRLR 475.
[3]   [1978] ICR 221.
[4]   In s 140(5).
[5]   See para 3.75, where its effect is considered.
[6]   *Loc cit.*

section 140(1) and (3) is correct, the result is that some serious anomalies exist, which tend to favour employers who act wrongfully.

6.72 Special considerations apply in the case of strikes. The employee's action in taking part in a strike has been held to be 'employee's conduct' within section 140(1).[1] If the dismissal provokes a strike, section 140(2) operates to negate the effect of section 140(1), so that the employee does not lose the entitlement to a redundancy payment. Section 140(2) will not operate, however, if the strike came first. In that case, section 140(1) will operate. It is a moot point whether section 140(3) will operate, but it is submitted that it does not, since its terms exclude termination by reason of taking part in a strike.

6.73 The report of *Simmons v Hoover Ltd* contains an appendix setting out the various possibilities. In it, the EAT takes an example of a redundant employee (X) who is entitled to three months' notice and postulates seven hypothetical situations.

Situation 1

6.74 X is dismissed on 1 January with two months' notice. The employer knew on 1 January that X had been stealing. In that case, according to the EAT, section 140(1) applies and section 140(3) does not, since there has not been a double dismissal.

Situation 2

6.75 X is dismissed on 1 January with two months' notice and the employers subsequently discover that X had been stealing before the dismissal. The result is the same as in situation 1.

Situation 3

6.76 X is dismissed on 1 January with three months' notice. On 1 February the employers discover that X has been stealing and terminate the contract immediately. The employee is within sections 140(1) and (3) and is entitled to a discretionary payment.

Situation 4

6.77 X is dismissed on 1 January with six months' notice. The employers terminate the contract immediately or on short notice in the following circumstances:

(a) X had been found stealing on 1 February and was dismissed on that day.
(b) The employers discovered that X had been stealing before 1 January and dismissed him on 1 February
(c) X was found stealing on 1 May and was dismissed on that day.

---

[1] *Simmons v Hoover Ltd* [1977] ICR 61.

In cases (a) and (b), X is covered by section 140(1) but not by section 140(3) and therefore receives no payment. This is because the second dismissal does not take place at the 'relevant time' (ie within the obligatory period). In case (c), X is covered by sections 140(1) and (3) and receives a discretionary payment.

Situation 5

6.78   X is dismissed on 1 January with three months' notice and goes on strike immediately afterwards. The employers terminate the contract immediately on 1 February by reason of the strike. X is covered by section 140(1) and (2) and receives a redundancy payment.

Situation 6

6.79   X is dismissed on 1 January with six months' notice and goes on strike immediately afterwards. The employers terminate the contract on 1 February X is covered by section 140(1) but not section 140(2)–(5) and does not receive a redundancy payment. Again, this is because he or she has not taken part in the strike at a 'relevant time'.

Situation 7

6.80   X is dismissed with six months' notice on 1 January. On 1 February he or she is caught stealing. The employers give X one month's notice and the contract terminates on 1 March. X is covered by section 140(1) but not section 140(3), and receives no payment. This is because the second dismissal does not take place at a 'relevant time'.

As can be seen from the above examples, much depends on the coincidence of timing, for example, whether the second dismissal takes place at a 'relevant time', ie the obligatory period. The complexity of this area is unfortunate.

(c) Notification of the Secretary of State

6.81   An employer is obliged to notify the Secretary of State of impending redundancies, at least 90 days before the first dismissal takes effect, where 100 or more employees are to be dismissed over a 90-day period or less, or at least 30 days before the first dismissal where between 20 and 99 employees are to be dismissed over such a period.[1] There is no duty to notify where less than 20 employees are involved. The notice must identify the representatives to be consulted and state when consultation began, and must contain any further information the Secretary of State may

---

[1]   Section 193(1) and (2) of the Trade Union and Labour Relations (Consolidation) Act 1992, as amended by the Collective Redundancies and Transfer of Undertakings (Protection of Employment) (Amendment) Regulations 1995, SI 1995 No 2587, reg 5(2).

require;[1] a copy of the notice must be sent to the representatives, if there are any to be consulted.[2] Failure to give the notice may expose the employer to a fine.[3] Even if there are special circumstances which make it not reasonably practicable for the employer to comply with these requirements, it should still take whatever steps are reasonably practicable towards compliance.[4] Where, however, the decision leading to the proposed dismissals is that of a person controlling the employer (directly or indirectly), a failure on the part of that person to provide information to the employer will not constitute special circumstances making it not reasonably practicable for the employer to comply.[5]

---

[1] TULRCA, s 193(4), as amended by the Collective Redundancies and Transfer of Undertakings (Protection of Employment) (Amendment) Regulations 1995, SI 1995 No 2587, reg 5(3).

[2] TULRCA, s 193(6), as amended by the Collective Redundancies and Transfer of Undertakings (Protection of Employment) (Amendment) Regulations 1995, SI 1995 No 2587, reg 5(4).

[3] TULRCA, s 194(1).

[4] TULRCA, s 193(7), as amended by the Trade Union Reform and Employment Rights Act 1993, s 34(4). See *Secretary of State for Employment v Helitron Ltd* [1980] ICR 523.

[5] This is the effect of the amendment to s 193(7), added by the Trade Union Reform and Employment Rights Act 1993, s 34(4).

Chapter 7

REMEDIES: RE-EMPLOYMENT ORDERS AND INTERIM RELIEF

1. RE-EMPLOYMENT ORDERS

7.01   The main remedies for unfair dismissal were intended to be reinstatement and re-engagement orders, and the whole tenor of the statutory provisions[1] is to suggest that the employment tribunal should apply those remedies first. The statistics show, however, that few re-employment orders are made.[2]

7.02   The first step the tribunal should take, in the case of successful complaints of unfair dismissal, is to explain to the employee what re-employment orders may be made and the circumstances in which they may be made, and to ask whether he or she wishes the tribunal to make an order; if the answer is affirmative, the tribunal *may* then make an order, but is not obliged to do so.[3]

7.03   If the tribunal decides to consider making a re-employment order, it must first consider whether to make a reinstatement order;[4] if it decides not to do so, it must then consider whether to make a re-engagement order.[5] If it decides not to make any order, it must make an award of compensation.[6] A failure by the employment tribunal to comply with section 112(2) by explaining to the successful complainant what orders for re-employment may be made, and to ask whether he or she wishes the

---

[1]   Sections 112–116 of the ERA 1996.

[2]   In the most recent years for which statistics are available (1999–2000 and 2000–2001), re-employment orders were made in 1.2% (38 out of 3,168) and 0.28% (15 out of 5,294) of cases. Apart from 1981, when orders were made in 4.8% of successful cases, the percentage of re-employment orders in recent years has generally been broadly similar: between 3% (1983) and 3.8% (1982). These recent statistics show, however, that the number of cases in which re-employment orders is made has remained consistently small, despite a considerable increase in the number of successful claims, in the context of a substantial increase in the number of complaints presented (for example, from 53,445 in 1992–1993, to 103,935 in 1999–2000).

[3]   Section 112(2) and (3).

[4]   Section 116(1).

[5]   Section 116(2).

[6]   Section 112(4). For compensation, see Chapter 8.

tribunal to make an order will not make its decision on relief a nullity; it is voidable if it results in injustice or unfairness to the complainant.[1]

7.04   It should be noted that where an employee makes a complaint to a tribunal that the dismissal was unfair by virtue of section 238A of the Trade Union and Labour Relations (Consolidation) Act 1992,[2] the tribunal may not make a re-employment order until after the conclusion of the protected industrial action by any employee in relation to the relevant dispute.[3]

(a) Reinstatement orders

7.05   A reinstatement order is an order to the employer to treat the applicant as if he or she had not been dismissed. In deciding whether to make an order, the tribunal must comply with the requirements of section 116(1), and take into account the following factors:

1.   the complainant's wishes;
2.   the practicability for the employer of compliance with the order; and
3.   where the complainant caused or contributed to some extent to the dismissal, whether it would be just to order reinstatement.

7.06   The tribunal must consider all these factors.[4] Although it may be thought that the first factor is paramount, the second and third factors have given rise to such case-law as there is.

The tribunal may have to consider the practicability for the employer of complying with the order at two separate stages: first, when considering whether to make the order; and secondly, if the employer fails to comply with the order, whether it was practicable for the employer to comply with the order.[5] At the first stage, the tribunal has to look forward and 'take into account' whether it is practicable to make the order; at the second stage, the tribunal is looking back.[6] In *Freemans plc v Flynn*,[7] the EAT said that at the first stage, the tribunal is not required to make a finding that it would be practicable for the employer to comply. This proposition is at variance with the later decision of the EAT in *Port of London Authority v Payne*,[8] which in fact concerned a re-engagement order. There, it said that before making an

---

[1]   *Cowley v Manson Timber Ltd* [1995] ICR 367. This decision was applied by the EAT in *Constantine v McGregor Cory Ltd* [2000] ICR 938. The applicant sought reinstatement, but the tribunal omitted to explain to him what re-employment orders might be made and to ask whether he wished the tribunal to make such an order. The EAT said that, although the failure to comply with s 112(2) did not make its decision a nullity, the EAT should be very ready to remit a case for further consideration of remedy in such circumstances.

[2]   This applies to dismissals for taking protected industrial action (see para 5.42).

[3]   TULRCA, s 239(4), added by ERA 1999, s 16 and Sch 5, paras 1, 4(1) and (5).

[4]   *Cf Qualcast (Wolverhampton) Ltd v Ross* [1979] ICR 386, where the tribunal apparently failed to do so.

[5]   This approach has received the approval of the Court of Appeal in *Port of London Authority v Payne* [1994] ICR 555.

[6]   See *Cold Drawn Tubes Ltd v Middleton* [1992] ICR 318 at p 320.

[7]   [1984] ICR 874.

[8]   [1993] ICR 30.

order the tribunal must determine whether it is practicable for the employers to comply with the order and should make a decision on the issue of practicability at this first stage. It refused to follow an earlier decision of the EAT, in *Timex Corporation v Thomson*,[1] in which Browne-Wilkinson J said that the tribunal need only 'have regard' to the practicability of making the order. When the Court of Appeal came to consider this question, it took the view that the EAT's decision on this point did less than justice to the careful assessment which the tribunal made. It said that the determination at the first stage was only provisional, a conclusion in accord with common sense and the authorities.[2] At the first stage, therefore, the tribunal should not be required to make a decision on the practicability of making the reinstatement order; in making its provisional determination, it should be obliged merely to take it into account in the sense of having regard to it. Clearly, however, it will fall into error if it completely fails to take into account the practicability of making the order.

7.07   One consideration is whether the employee is likely to be a satisfactory employee if reinstated, but the employment tribunal should take a broad common sense view of what is practicable.[3] It should use its experience and common sense, looking at what has occurred in the past and what can reasonably be expected for the future and maintaining a fair balance between the parties.[4] 'Practicable' does not, however, mean expedient.[5] In *Clancy v Cannock Chase Technical College*,[6] the President of the EAT, Lindsay J, made it clear that the EAT will be very slow to interfere with the decision of an employment tribunal in relation to the issue of practicability. He said:[7]

'Of all the subjects properly to be left as the exclusive province of an employment tribunal as the "industrial jury", few can be more obviously their territory than the issue of "practicability" within section 116(1)(b) … [or] section 116(3)(b).'

7.08   In *Wood Group Heavy Industrial Turbines Ltd v Crossan*,[8] the EAT said that, where there is a breakdown of trust and confidence between employer and employee, the remedy of reinstatement or re-engagement has very limited scope and will only be practicable in the rarest of cases.

7.09   The second stage of practicability, in cases of non-compliance with a reinstatement order, is considered more fully at para 7.22.

---

[1]   [1981] IRLR 522.

[2]   See [1994] ICR 555 at p 569.

[3]   See *Nothman v London Borough of Barnet* [1980] IRLR 65 at p 66, para 4 (Ormrod LJ), and *Meridian Ltd v Gomersall* [1977] ICR 597 at pp 601–602. *Cf Enessy Co SA t/a The Tulchan Estate v Minoprio* [1978] IRLR 489 at p 490, para 2. See also *Coleman v Magnet Joinery Ltd* [1975] ICR 46.

[4]   *Rao v Civil Aviation Authority* [1992] ICR 503.

[5]   *Qualcast (Wolverhampton) Ltd v Ross* [1979] ICR 386.

[6]   [2001] IRLR 331.

[7]   *Ibid* at p 333.

[8]   [1998] IRLR 680.

7.10   It should be noted that the engagement of a permanent replacement by the employer does not automatically mean that reinstatement is not practicable. When considering the practicability of making an order, the tribunal is not allowed to take that fact into account, unless the employer shows one of the following: either that it was not practicable to arrange for the dismissed employee's work to be done without engaging a permanent replacement, or that the replacement was engaged after a reasonable period had passed without the employer having heard from the dismissed employee that he or she wished to be reinstated, and that when the replacement was engaged it was no longer reasonable for the employer to arrange for the dismissed employee's work to be done except by a permanent replacement.[1]

7.11   In *Boots Co plc v Lees-Collier*,[2] an employee who was dismissed on the grounds of suspected theft of company property was found by the tribunal to have acted absent-mindedly but not dishonestly. The tribunal made an order for reinstatement, but made no express finding as to the practicability of the employer's compliance with such an order or as to whether the employee's conduct had caused or contributed to his dismissal. The tribunal accepted evidence that the employee's superior had lost confidence in his honesty and competence to carry out his duties, but did not consider that factor to be a bar to reinstatement. The employers appealed to the EAT on the grounds that in accepting that evidence the tribunal made a finding inconsistent with a conclusion that reinstatement was practicable and that it had failed to make any finding under section 116(1)(c) (see factor 3, para 7.05). The EAT dismissed the appeal. It said that the tribunal was justified in not considering the question of contributory fault for the express purposes of section 116(1)(c), having concluded that the explanation for the employee's conduct was not dishonesty. Since it had concluded that the employee's conduct had not caused or contributed to the dismissal for the purposes of compensation, there was no room for a finding that he had caused or contributed to his dismissal for the purposes of section 116(1)(c). The tribunal was also not obliged to make a definite finding under section 116(1)(b) that the reinstatement order was practicable, since it was sufficient for them to have examined the relevant evidence relating to practicability.

7.12   The effect of an order of reinstatement is to give the employee his or her old job back. On making the order, the tribunal must make ancillary orders in relation to the following matters:

1.   any amount payable by the employer in respect of any benefit which the employee might reasonably be expected to have had but for the dismissal, including arrears of pay, for the period between the date of termination and the date of reinstatement;
2.   any rights and privileges, including seniority and pension rights, which must be restored to the employee; and

---

[1]   Section 116(5) and (6).
[2]   [1986] ICR 728. See also *British Gas plc v Turton* (EAT 292/89).

3.   the date by which the order must be complied with.[1]

7.13   In calculating the amount of arrears of pay, the tribunal should *deduct* any sums by way of wages in lieu of notice or *ex gratia* payment or remuneration paid in respect of employment with another employer received by the employee. It may also deduct 'such other benefits' as it thinks appropriate in the circumstances.[2] This only affects receipts or benefits between the date of termination of employment and the date of reinstatement.

There is no statutory maximum to the amount which may be ordered to be paid under section 114(2)(a). This means that an order for arrears of pay under section 114(2)(a) cannot be frustrated by an employer's refusal to comply with the reinstatement order.

7.14   A question which arises is whether an award of arrears of pay under section 114(2)(a) is subject to the rules of mitigation. In *City & Hackney Health Authority v Crisp*,[3] the EAT said that the award should not be reduced because of the employee's failure to take steps to mitigate her loss, since an order for reinstatement requires an employer to treat the employee in all respects as if he or she had not been dismissed. If, however, the employee did take steps to mitigate the loss, the earnings by way of mitigation between the date of termination and the date of the reinstatement order are required by section 114(4) to be brought into account.

The continuity of employment of an employee who is reinstated will be preserved.[4]

(b) Re-engagement orders

7.15   If the tribunal decides not to order reinstatement, it should then consider whether to order re-engagement.[5] A re-engagement order is an order that the employee should be engaged by the employer, or by a successor of the employer or an associated employer, in employment comparable to that from which he or she was dismissed, or 'other suitable employment'.[6] In deciding whether to make the order, the tribunal must have regard to the requirements of section 116(3). The three factors it must take into account are similar to those mentioned above in relation to reinstatement orders. In relation to the second factor (practicability), however, the tribunal must consider the practicability of re-engagement

---

[1]   Section 114(2).
[2]   Section 114(4).
[3]   [1990] ICR 95.
[4]   Section 219 of the ERA 1996 and the Employment Protection (Continuity of Employment) Regulations 1996, SI 1996 No 3147, reg 3.
[5]   Section 116(2).
[6]   Section 115(1). In *Rank Xerox (UK) Ltd v Stryczek* [1995] IRLR 568, the EAT said that it is undesirable for the tribunal to order re-engagement in respect of a specific job, as distinct from identifying the nature of the proposed employment.

with a successor of the employer or an associated employer. The engagement of a permanent replacement by the employer does not automatically mean that reinstatement or re-engagement are impracticable. When considering the practicability of making an order, the tribunal should not take into account the engagement of a permanent replacement, unless the employer shows *either* that it was not practicable to arrange for the dismissed employee's work to be done without engaging a permanent replacement, *or* that the replacement was engaged after a reasonable period had passed without the employer having heard from the dismissed employee that he or she wished to be re-engaged and that when the replacement was engaged it was no longer reasonable for the employer to arrange for the dismissed employee's work to be done except by a permanent replacement.[1]

7.16   The fact that the tribunal considers it practicable for the employer to comply does not mean that the issue of practicability is settled once and for all. Practicability falls to be considered at two stages, as with reinstatement orders: at the first stage, it is a consideration which the tribunal must have in mind when considering whether to order re-engagement; at the second stage, the employer may escape the consequences of non-compliance with an order by discharging the burden of showing that it was not practicable to comply with the order, under section 117(4)(a).

The same considerations arise in relation to 'practicability' as with reinstatement orders. The relevant case-law has been fully considered in that context (see para 7.06).

7.17   There is an obvious difference between a re-engagement order and an order to make an offer of re-engagement. The difference is that a re-engagement order writes a new contract for the parties, whereas an order to offer re-engagement merely orders the employer to offer terms. In the latter case, the employee may return to the employment tribunal for its decision as to whether he or she should accept the terms. This matter was considered in *Lilley Construction Ltd v Dunn*[2] by the EAT. It suggested that it is unwise for tribunals to make orders to offer re-engagement, because of the possible sources of confusion. There is also the point that it is doubtful whether tribunals have jurisdiction to make such orders.

7.18   The effect of a re-engagement order will be to give the employee a job similar to the one from which he or she was dismissed. Section 115(2) requires the tribunal when making the order to specify the terms of re-engagement,[3] but, according to the EAT, they should not be significantly more favourable than the employee would have enjoyed had he or she

---

[1]   Section 116(5) and (6).
[2]   [1984] IRLR 483.
[3]   See *Electronic Data Processing Ltd v Wright* [1986] ICR 76. In that case, the tribunal ordered the employee to be re-engaged at a salary less than her previous salary, and ordered the employers to pay compensation under what is now s 115(2)(d) on the basis of her pre-dismissal salary. The EAT upheld the award.

been reinstated in the old job.[1] It is difficult to see why they should be more favourable at all.

7.19 The terms to be specified in the re-engagement order include remuneration, 'any amount payable by the employer in respect of any benefit which the complainant might reasonably be expected to have had but for the dismissal, including arrears of pay, for the period between the date of termination of employment and the date of re-engagement', and 'any rights and privileges, including seniority and pension rights, which must be restored to the employee'. In calculating the amount of arrears of pay, the tribunal should deduct any sums by way of wages in lieu of notice or *ex gratia* payment or remuneration paid in respect of employment with another employer received by the employee. It may also deduct 'such other benefits' as it thinks appropriate in the circumstances.[2] This only affects receipts or benefits between the date of termination of employment and the date of reinstatement.

7.20 As with reinstatement orders, this provision cannot be frustrated by an employer's refusal to comply with the re-engagement order: there is no limit on the arrears of pay which may be ordered under section 115(2)(d). A question which arises here, however, is whether an award of arrears of pay is subject to the rules of mitigation. In *City & Hackney Health Authority v Crisp,*[3] the EAT rejected the employers' argument that the amount in respect of arrears of pay between the date of termination and the date of re-engagement should be reduced because of the employment tribunal's finding that had the employee pursued her claim more vigorously, she would probably have been re-engaged earlier. In effect, the employers were arguing that the employee should be subject to a duty to mitigate his or her loss of earnings. The EAT said that the provisions of what is now section 116(3) were mandatory and were not overridden by the general discretion conferred upon the tribunal by section 113. If, however, the employee did take steps to mitigate the loss, the earnings by way of mitigation between the date of termination and the date of the re-engagement order are required by section 115(3) to be brought into account.

7.21 Except in cases of contributory conduct, the terms of the re-engagement must be as favourable as an order of reinstatement, so far as reasonably practicable.[4] In *Freemans plc v Flynn,*[5] for example, the employment tribunal found that the employee had contributed to his own dismissal to the extent of 20%. Accordingly, the re-engagement order was

1   *Rank Xerox (UK) Ltd v Stryczek* [1995] IRLR 568.
2   Section 115(3).
3   [1990] ICR 95.
4   Section 116(4). See *Nairne v Highlands & Islands Fire Brigade* [1989] IRLR 366, where the Court of Session upheld the EAT's decision that in a case where the employee's degree of contributory fault was assessed at 75% a re-engagement order was not appropriate.
5   [1984] ICR 874. See also *Morganite Crucible Carbon Ltd v Donne* [1988] ICR 18, where the tribunal found that there was a degree of contributory conduct on the employee's part and made a re-engagement order with the requirement that he should forfeit four weeks' pay.

that he should be re-engaged at a salary comparable to 80% of his salary at the effective date of termination of his contract.

(c) Non-compliance

7.22 If the employer does not comply fully with the terms of a reinstatement or re-engagement order, the tribunal must award such an amount of compensation as it thinks fit having regard to the loss sustained by the employee, subject to the maximum permissible.[1] If the employer totally fails to comply, then the tribunal must go on to award compensation in the usual way[2] and it must also make an additional award of compensation.[3] It should be noted that a tribunal may treat an employee who unreasonably prevents a re-employment order from being complied with as having failure to mitigate his or her loss when it makes an award of compensation.[4]

7.23 The EAT considered the difference between partial and total non-compliance in *Artisan Press Ltd v Srawley and Parker*.[5] In that case the employment tribunal made a reinstatement order in respect of employees employed as security staff with minor general duties. The employers re-employed them as cleaners with a few security duties. The employees complained, and the tribunal found that the employers had failed to comply with the order. The employers appealed on the grounds that, since the terms of the reinstatement order had not been fully complied with, the tribunal should have applied section 117(1) and (2). The EAT dismissed their appeal. it said that an employer failed to reinstate the employee, if the employee was re-employed on a less favourable basis than previously, since the requirement of section 114(1) is that the employee should be treated as if he or she had not been dismissed. Since the employers had re-employed the employees as cleaners with minor security duties, they had failed to comply with the reinstatement order. The EAT pointed out that the reason for an award of compensation under section 117(1) and (2) is to compensate an employee where the employer fails to comply fully with the orders made by the tribunal under section 114(2)(a), (b) and (c) relating to ancillary matters.

7.24 In cases of total non-compliance, the employer may escape the consequences of non-compliance by showing that it was not 'practicable' to comply with the re-employment order.[6] In deciding whether it was practicable to re-employ the employee, the tribunal should not take into account the fact that the employer has engaged a permanent replacement,

---

[1] Section 117(1) and (2). The maximum is £51,700. It should be noted that, in certain circumstances, the limit on the amount of compensation may be removed (see para 8.127).
[2] See Chapter 8.
[3] In accordance with s 117(3)(b), as amended by ERA 1999, s 33(2).
[4] ERA 1996, s 117(8).
[5] [1986] ICR 328.
[6] ERA 1996, s 117(4), as amended by ERA 1999, ss 33(1)(a) and 44, and Sch 9, Table 10.

unless the employer shows that it was not practicable for the dismissed employee's work to be done without taking such a step.[1]

7.25 The issue of practicability at this stage is different from the question of practicability as one of the considerations the tribunal must have in mind when deciding whether to order re-employment.[2] The burden is on the employer to show that re-employment was not practicable, but the EAT has stressed that the employment tribunal must not impose too high a duty on the employer to find the employee a job. It is enough for the employer to try to find a suitable job for the employee; if there is none, the duty has been discharged.[3] As the EAT pointed out in *Cold Drawn Tubes Ltd v Middleton*,[4] there is a difference between the two stages at which practicability falls to be considered. At the first stage, when considering whether to make the re-employment order, the tribunal has to look forward and 'take into account' whether it is practicable to make the order; at the second stage, the tribunal is looking back. In doing so, it should take a broad common-sense view. In the case in question, the EAT took the view that the absence of any work for the employee to do made it not practicable for the employee to be reinstated.

7.26 In *Port of London Authority v Payne*,[5] which was commented upon earlier in this chapter, the EAT said that, when considering the issue of practicability at the second stage, the employment tribunal should not substitute its own view for that of the employer. It said that it was imposing too high a duty on the employers to expect them to make room for those ordered to be re-engaged and to make an order which would in effect require the employer to disrupt the workforce, although it also pointed out that a bare assertion by the employer that there were no vacancies would be insufficient to establish that compliance was impracticable. The Court of Appeal said that the standard must not be set too high: the test is practicability, not possibility. It said that a tribunal should pay due regard to the commercial judgment of the employer unless the employer was to be disbelieved, but that an employer could not be expected 'to explore every possible avenue which ingenuity might suggest'.[6]

7.27 In cases of total non-compliance, the tribunal must go on to award compensation in the usual way. In addition, the employee will be entitled to be paid any amount of arrears of pay ordered by the tribunal, under sections 114(2)(a) or 115(2)(d), when making the reinstatement or

---

[1] Section 117(7).
[2] *Freemans plc v Flynn* [1984] ICR 874.
[3] *Ibid.*
[4] [1992] ICR 318 at p 320.
[5] [1993] ICR 30.
[6] [1994] ICR 555 at p 574.

re-engagement order. The tribunal must also make an additional award of between 26 and 52 weeks' pay.[1]

7.28 It is important to note that, in cases in which there is a total failure to comply and the dismissal is unfair because it is contrary to sections 100,[2] 103A,[3] 105(3)[4] or 105(6A)[5] of the ERA 1996, there is no limit to the amount of compensation which the tribunal may award.[6] This is an exception to the general rule that the compensatory award is subject to a limit of £51,700.

2. INTERIM RELIEF

7.29 The remedy of interim relief is available to employees in eight types of unfair dismissal cases, where they allege that they were dismissed for one of the following reasons:[7]

1. a reason connected with health and safety, as specified in section 100(1)(a) and (b) of the ERA 1996;[8]
2. a reason connected with their performance of their functions as an employee representative for the purposes of negotiating a workforce agreement in accordance with Schedule 1 to the Working Time Regulations 1998 or as a candidate in an election for employee representatives, as specified in section 101A(d) of the ERA 1996;
3. a reason connected with the performance of their functions as trustee of an occupational pension scheme, as specified in ERA 1996, section 102(1);
4. a reason connected with the performance of their functions as an employee representative, contrary to ERA 1996, section 103;
5. for making a 'protected disclosure', contrary to ERA 1996, section 103A;
6. a reason connected with trade union recognition as specified in TULRCA, Schedule A1, paragraph 161(2);
7. reasons related to trade union membership or activities, contrary to section 152 of TULRCA 1992; and

---

[1] Section 117(3)(b), as amended by the Employment Rights (Dispute Resolution) Act 1998, s 15 and Sch 1, para 20 and ERA 1999, ss 33(2) and 44, and Sch 9, Tables 10 and 11. See Chapter 8 where additional awards are considered.

[2] Dismissals in health and safety cases (see paras 5.57 *et seq*).

[3] Dismissals for making a 'protected disclosure' (see paras 5.82 *et seq*).

[4] Selection for redundancy for a reason falling within s 100(1).

[5] Selection for redundancy for making a protected disclosure.

[6] ERA, s 124(1A), inserted by ERA 1999, s 37(1).

[7] See ERA, s 128(1), as amended, which makes provision for interim relief to be available in the first six types of unfair dismissal, TULRCA, s 161(1), which provides for the seventh, and ERA 1999, s 12(5), which makes provision for the eighth. See *Barley v Amey Roadstone Corporation Ltd* [1977] ICR 546.

[8] The dismissals covered are dismissals of designated employees, recognised safety representatives or safety committee members for carrying out health and safety duties or activities. See Chapter 5.

8.   reasons relating to the exercise of the right given to a worker to be accompanied at a disciplinary or grievance hearing.

These types of dismissals are considered in more detail in Chapter 5. The employee must apply within seven days of the effective date of termination.[1]

7.30 In trade union cases only, he or she must also, within the seven-day period, present a certificate in writing[2] signed by an authorised official[3] of the union concerned, if the claim is that the case relates to trade union membership or activities (ie if it is within section 152 or 153 of TULRCA 1992). The certificate must state that on the date of the dismissal the employee was (or had proposed to become) a member of the union and that there appear to be reasonable grounds for supposing that the reason for his dismissal was one alleged in the complaint.[4]

7.31 The tribunal must determine the application as soon as practicable after receiving the application and (where appropriate) the certificate, and must give the employer a copy of both and a notice of the date, time and place of the hearing at least seven days before the hearing.[5] The tribunal may only postpone the hearing only in special circumstances.[6]

7.32 At the hearing, if the tribunal considers it likely[7] that on hearing the substantive complaint the tribunal will find that the reason for the dismissal falls within sections 100(1)(a) or (b), 101A(d), 102(1), 103 or 103A of the ERA 1996,[8] section 161 or paragraph 161(2) of Schedule A1 of the TULRCA 1992 or section 12(3) of the Employment Relations Act 1999, it must announce its findings and explain the powers it has and the circumstances in which it will exercise them.[9] It must also ask the employer if he or she is prepared to reinstate the employee or, if not, re-engage him or her.[10] If the employer is prepared to reinstate the employee, the tribunal will make an order to that effect.[11] If the employer is not prepared to reinstate the employee, but to re-engage him or her on specified terms and

---

[1]   Section 128(2) and TULRCA 1992, s 161(2). For the meaning of 'effective date of termination', see Chapter 3.

[2]   A document purporting to be an authorisation of an official by a trade union to act for the purposes of TULRCA 1992, s 161 will be taken to be an authorisation unless the contrary is proved, and a document purporting to be a certificate signed by such an official will be taken to be signed by him or her unless the contrary is proved: TULRCA 1992, s 161(5).

[3]   An 'authorised official' is an official of the union authorised by the union to act for the purposes of TULRCA, s 161: see s 161(4).

[4]   TULRCA 1992, s 161(3). See *Stone v Charrington & Co Ltd* [1977] ICR 248, *Bradley v Edward Ryde & Sons* [1979] ICR 488, and *Sulemany v Habib Bank Ltd* [1983] ICR 60.

[5]   Section 128(3) and (4) and TULRCA 1992, s 162(1) and (2). The procedure will vary slightly if there is a request under s 160 to join a third party; see s 162(3).

[6]   Section 128(5) and TULRCA 1992, s 162(4).

[7]   Interpreted by Slynn J as meaning that the employee must have a 'pretty good' chance of success: see *Taplin v C Shippam Ltd* [1978] ICR 1068.

[8]   See Chapter 5.

[9]   Section 129(1) (as amended) and (2) and TULRCA 1992, s 163(1) and (2).

[10]   Section 129(3) and TULRCA 1992, s 163(2).

[11]   Section 129(5) and TULRCA, s 163(4).

conditions, the tribunal must then ask the employee if he or she is willing to accept re-engagement on those terms; if so, it will make an appropriate order.[1] If the employee is not willing to accept the job on those terms and conditions and the tribunal considers the refusal reasonable, it will make an order for the continuation of the contract of employment; otherwise, it will make no order.[2]

7.33   If the employer does not appear, or refuses to re-employ the employee, the tribunal must make an order for the continuation of the employee's contract.[3] Such an order is an order that the employee's contract is to continue in force until the complainant is determined (or settled), for the purposes of pay, seniority, pension rights and 'any other benefit derived from the employment' and for calculating continuity of employment.[4] The tribunal should also make ancillary orders dealing specifically with pay;[5] it should take into account, however, any payments made by the employer to the employee.[6]

7.34   Between the making of the order and the determination or settlement of the complaint of unfair dismissal, either the employer or the employee may apply to the tribunal for the revocation or variation of the order on the ground of a relevant change of circumstances since the making of the order.[7] The tribunal which hears the application need not be the tribunal which made the original order.[8]

7.35   Section 132 of the ERA 1996 and section 166 of the TULRCA 1992 contain provisions which apply in cases where the employer fails to comply with an interim relief order. If the tribunal made a reinstatement or re-engagement order and the employer fails to comply, the employee may apply to the tribunal. It will make an order for the continuation of the employee's contract and order the employer to pay the employee whatever amount of compensation it considers just and equitable.[9] Section 130 of the EPCA and section 164 of the TULRCA 1992, which govern orders for the continuation of the employee's contract, will then apply.[10] If the employer fails to comply with an order for the continuation of the employee's contract and the non-compliance consists of a failure to pay an amount of pay specified in the order, the tribunal must determine the amount owed by the employer on the date of its determination.[11] In any other case, the tribunal will order the employer to pay whatever amount of compensation

---

[1]   Section 129(6) and (7) of the ERA 1996; TULRCA 1992, s 163(5).
[2]   Section 129(8) and TULRCA, s 163(5).
[3]   Section 129(9) and TULRCA 1992, s 163(6).
[4]   Section 130(1) and TULRCA 1992, s 164(1).
[5]   Under s 130(2)–(4) or TULRCA 1992, s 164(2)–(4).
[6]   Section 130(5) and (6) and TULRCA 1992, s 164(5) and (6).
[7]   Section 131(1) and TULRCA 1992, s 165(1).
[8]   *British Coal Corporation v McGinty* [1987] ICR 912.
[9]   Section 132(1) and TULRCA 1992, s 166(1)(a). Note ERA 1996, s 132(2) and TULRCA 1992, s 166(1)(b), in relation to the calculation of compensation.
[10] Section 132(3) and TULRCA 1992, s 166(2).
[11] Section 132(5) and TULRCA 1992, s 166(4). Note also s 132(5)(b) and the second paragraph of s 166(5) of the respective Acts.

it considers just and equitable in all the circumstances, having regard to any loss suffered by the employee in consequence of the non-compliance.[1]

---

[1] Section 132(6) and TULRCA 1992, s 166(5).

Chapter 8

REMEDIES: COMPENSATION

1. REDUNDANCY PAYMENTS

(a) Calculation of payments

8.01   To calculate a redundancy payment, it is necessary to have the following information:

1.   the employee's age at the relevant date;[1]
2.   the number of years of continuous employment;[2] and
3.   the amount of gross weekly pay.[3]

The calculation is subject to the following limits:

1.   the number of years used in the calculation may not exceed 20;[4] and
2.   the amount of a week's pay may not exceed a figure set by the Secretary of State, the amount being £240.[5]

This figure is now index-linked and is liable to increase or decrease according to whether the retail prices index has increased or decreased between one September and the next.[6] Any change to the limit takes effect from 1 February.

8.02   Redundancy payments are calculated in accordance with section 162 of the ERA 1996 and the total amount arrived at may be subject to a deduction in certain cases, mainly in the case of misconduct or where employees are near retirement age. Social security benefits paid to the employee are not deductible. It should be noted that statutory redundancy payments are exempt from income tax,[7] but they must be aggregated with other termination payments received.[8] Similar considerations apply to *ex*

---

[1]   For the 'relevant date', see Chapter 3.
[2]   Continuity of employment is considered in Chapter 1.
[3]   Calculated in accordance with ERA 1996, ss 220–229 (see paras 8.158 *et seq*). See also *Secretary of State for Employment v John Woodrow & Sons (Builders) Ltd* [1983] IRLR 11 and *Donelan v Kerby Construction Ltd and Secretary of State for Employment* [1983] ICR 237.
[4]   Section 162(3).
[5]   Section 227(1), as amended by the Employment Rights (Increase of Limits) Order 2001, SI 2001 No 21.
[6]   ERA 1999, s 34(1)(e), (2) and (3)(c).
[7]   ICTA 1988, s 579(1). Section 580(1) states that the term 'redundancy payment' has the same meaning as in Part XI of the ERA 1996.
[8]   ICTA 1988, s 580(3). The effect of this is to bring them within s 148 of that Act (see Chapter 10, para 10.84).

gratia payments paid to compensate employees for loss of their statutory or contractual redundancy rights.[1]

8.03   The method of calculation is to take each year of continuous employment, working backwards from the relevant date. For each year of continuous employment, the amount of the redundancy payment is assessed on the basis of the employee's age at the beginning of the year. For each year in which the employee was aged 41 or more (but not more than 64),[2] one and a half weeks' pay is payable; for each year in which he or she was between 22 and 41, one week's pay; for each year over the age of 18 between the time he or she started work and 22, half a week's pay.[3] Thus, an employee employed for 20 years and made redundant at 62 will receive a redundancy payment reckoned on the basis of the years of continuous employment from 62 going back to 42. The maximum redundancy payment that can be awarded at present is thus £7,200.

8.04   Employment before the age of 18 may not be counted.[4] The employee's period of continuous employment will be treated as starting on his or her eighteenth birthday if that date is later than the starting date.

8.05   When the employer pays the redundancy payment, the employee must be given a written statement setting out the calculation of the payment. This does not apply to payments made as a result of a tribunal decision.[5]

8.06   An employee may apply under section 166 to the Secretary of State for a payment direct from the National Insurance Fund.[6] This course of action is available where the employer refuses or fails to pay all or part of a redundancy payment to which the employee claims to be entitled and the employee has taken reasonable steps (other than legal proceedings) to recover the payment;[7] it is also available where the employer is insolvent[8] and the whole or part of the payment remains unpaid.[9] If the Secretary of State makes a payment, he or she will be subrogated to the employee's rights and remedies.[10] Disputes are heard by the employment tribunal.[11]

8.07   Section 14 of the Employment Tribunals Act 1996 empowers the Secretary of State to order sums payable by virtue of employment

---

[1]   See *Mairs v Haughey* [1993] IRLR 551, considered in Chapter 10, at paras 10.79 and 10.84.
[2]   Employees near retirement are liable to have their redundancy payments reduced: see para 8.14.
[3]   Sections 162(2) and 211(2).
[4]   Section 211(2). This provision and the meaning of 'starting date' are considered in Chapter 1.
[5]   Section 165(1).
[6]   Section 13 of the Employment Act 1990 provided for the merger of the Redundancy Fund with the National Insurance Fund.
[7]   Section 166(1)(a).
[8]   As defined by s 166(5)–(7). If the employer ceases trading, but is not 'insolvent' within the definition, s 166(1)(b) will not apply.
[9]   Section 166(1)(b).
[10]   Section 167(3).
[11]   Section 170. For an example of a decision made under this provision, see *Secretary of State for Employment v Reeves* [1993] ICR 508.

tribunals' decisions to carry interest. This provision has been implemented by the Employment Tribunals (Interest) Order 1990,[1] which came into operation on 1 April 1990. Its effect is that a monetary award carries interest if it is unpaid for more than six weeks after the date of the award. The rate of interest from 1 April 1993 is 8% per annum[2] in relation to decisions made on or after 1 April 1993. The Order was considered by the EAT in *Secretary of State for Employment v Reeves*,[3] in which the employees were made redundant and claimed redundancy payments. In the case of one of the employees, the tribunal decided that he had been dismissed for redundancy, but made no payment. In the case of the other two employees, the tribunal made consent orders for specified sums. The employers were insolvent and the employees claimed payments from the National Insurance Fund. The tribunal upheld their claims and also awarded interest calculated by reference to the dates of the original decisions against the employers. The EAT upheld the Secretary of State's appeal, on the grounds that time only started to run from the date of the decision made against the Secretary of State, not against the employers. The case turned on the definitions of 'calculation date' and 'relevant decision' in art 2(1) of the 1990 Order.

It should be noted that redundancy payments are not affected by the Employment Protection (Recoupment of Jobseeker's Allowance and Income Support) Regulations 1996.[4]

Example 1

8.08 Employee aged 27, continuously employed for 10 years, earning £150 a week. Note that employment before the age of 18 does not count.[5]

1 x 5 x £150 =	£750
½ x 4 x £150 =	£300
TOTAL =	<u>£1,050</u>

Example 2

8.09 Employee aged 50, continuously employed for 15 years, earning £290 a week. Since the employee's gross weekly pay exceeds the current statutory maximum, the maximum of £240 must be applied.

---

[1] SI 1990 No 479.
[2] See the Judgment Debts (Rate of Interest) Order 1993, SI 1993 No 564. The previous rate was 15%.
[3] [1993] ICR 508.
[4] SI 1996 No 2349.
[5] Section 211(2).

$1.5 \times 9 \times £240 =$ £3,240.00

$1 \times 6 \times £240 =$ £1,440.00

TOTAL =   <u>£4,680.00</u>

Example 3

8.10   Employee aged 62, continuously employed for 20 years, earning £270 a week.

$1.5 \times 20 \times £240 = $ <u>£7,200.00</u>

(b) Payments liable to discretionary reduction

8.11   The employment tribunal may use its discretion to award all or part of a redundancy payment in the following cases:

1.   in cases involving the giving of a counter-notice by the employee in accordance with the provisions of section 136(3), where the employer has also given a notice under section 142(1) and (2),[1] and
2.   cases involving misconduct by the employee.[2]

There have been very few reported cases concerning payments liable to a discretionary reduction.

Example 4[3]

8.12   Employee aged 40, continuously employed for 10 years, earning £150 a week.

$1 \times 10 \times £150 =$ £1,500

60% of payment awarded for misconduct =   £900

TOTAL =   <u>£900</u>

8.13   The exercise of its discretion by the tribunal in such a case is unlikely to be interfered with by the EAT. The tribunal should consider:

1.   whether it is just and equitable that the employee should receive the whole or part of any redundancy payment to which he or she would have been entitled apart from the supervening dismissal for misconduct, then
2.   decide to award *either* the whole of the payment *or* part of the payment, as it considers just and equitable, then

---

[1]   See para 3.75.
[2]   See Chapter 6.
[3]   See *Lignacite Products Ltd v Krollman* [1979] IRLR 22.

3.   if it decides to award part of the payment, decide how much of the payment to award.[1]

(c) Reductions where employee near retirement

8.14   In the case of employees dismissed after their sixty-fourth birthday, their redundancy payments will be reduced by one-twelfth for each complete month between the sixty-fourth birthday and the relevant date.[2] In such cases, it will be particularly important to ascertain the relevant date; according to the EAT, the provisions in section 145(5) for extending the relevant date do not apply to these cases.[3]

Example 5[4]

8.15   Employee aged 64 years 8 months at relevant date, continuously employed for 20 years, earning £210 a week.

1.5 x 20 x £210 =	£6,300
8/12 x £6,300 =	£4,200
TOTAL =	<u>£2,100</u>

2. COMPENSATION FOR UNFAIR DISMISSAL

8.16   An employment tribunal will award compensation if it makes no order for re-employment, or if it makes such an order but the employer totally fails to comply with it. Compensation may consist of the following elements:

1.   a basic award;
2.   a compensatory award;
3.   an additional award.

Higher additional awards and special awards were abolished by the Employment Relations Act 1999.

8.17   If the employment tribunal makes a finding of unfair dismissal, it must first consider whether to make an order for the re-employment of the applicant. If he or she does not wish such an order to be made or if the tribunal decides against making an order, it will proceed to award compensation. If it does make an order, but the employer totally fails to comply with it, the tribunal will make an additional award[5] and then go on

---

[1]   [1979] IRLR 22 at p 23, paras 4 and 5.

[2]   Section 162(4) and (5).

[3]   *Slater v John Swain & Son Ltd* [1981] ICR 554. See Chapter 3, where the date of termination is considered.

[4]   See *Slater v John Swain & Son Ltd* [1981] ICR 554.

[5]   See paras 8.152 *et seq*, where additional awards are discussed.

to award compensation in the usual way. In most cases, compensation usually consists of a basic award and a compensatory award.

8.18   Section 14 of the Employment Tribunals Act 1996 empowers the Secretary of State to order[1] that sums payable by virtue of employment tribunals' decisions are to carry interest. A monetary award carries interest if it is unpaid for more than six weeks after the date of the award.[2] The rate of interest from 1 April 1993 is 8% per annum[3] in relation to decisions made on or after 1 April 1993.

8.19   Until the implementation of section 34 of the Employment Relations Act 1999, the Secretary of State was required[4] to review the limits on compensation for the time being in force and, in making a review, to consider '(a) the general level of earnings obtaining in Great Britain at the time of the review; (b) the national economic situation as a whole; and (c) such other matters as he thinks relevant'. It was argued in 1994 that, if the limits were to keep pace with the increase in earnings since 1975, they would need to be set at levels of around £470 for a week's pay and £30,400 for the compensatory award and that, to keep pace with the movement in prices, they would need to be set at around £345 for a week's pay and £22,350 for the compensatory award.[5] The changes brought about by the 1999 Act have gone some way to addressing this issue, particularly by raising substantially the limit on the compensatory award, but the current limit on a week's pay is arguably too low. Although it is argued that increasing the limits would cause hardship to employers, it should be borne in mind that a small number of awards of compensation reach the statutory limits, although the percentage of awards above £9,000 has risen steadily in recent years.[6]

8.20   The effect of section 34 of the 1999 Act is to link increases in the limits on compensation to the retail prices index each September. Depending on whether there is an increase or decrease between one September and the next, the limits will be raised or lowered.[7] Section 34(4)

---

[1]   See the Employment Tribunals (Interest) Order 1990, SI 1990 No 479, which came into effect on 1 April 1990.

[2]   See *Secretary of State for Employment v Reeves* [1993] ICR 508, which involved claims for redundancy payments against the employer, followed by a claim from the National Insurance Fund. The tribunal upheld their claims and also awarded interest calculated by reference to the dates of the original decisions against the employers. The EAT upheld the Secretary of State's appeal, on the grounds that time only started to run from the date of the decision made against the Secretary of State, not against the employers. Note the definitions of 'calculation date' and 'relevant decision' in art 2(1) of the 1990 Order.

[3]   See the Judgment Debts (Rate of Interest) Order 1993, SI 1993 No 564. The previous rate was 15%.

[4]   By section 208 of the ERA 1996, repealed by ERA 1999, ss 36(2) and 44 and Sch 9, Table 10.

[5]   See (1994) 1 *Employment Law Briefing* 23, which summarised the submissions of the Employment Lawyers Association to the then Department of Employment on this issue.

[6]   In 2000–2001, awards of compensation over £9,000 constituted about 2% of all awards; the median award was £2,744. In 1.5% of cases, applicants received more than £20,000. Further, 39.9% of awards did not exceed £1,999.

[7]   ERA 1999, s 34(2). Section 34(3) contains provisions for rounding up the figures yielded by the calculation under s 34(2).

raised the limit of the compensatory award to £50,000 and this was further raised with effect from 1 February 2001 to £51,700.[1]

8.21   It is important to note that in two types of unfair dismissal the amount of the compensatory awards is unlimited. These are cases in which the dismissal is unfair because it is contrary to sections 100[2] or 103A,[3] or because the employee was selected for reasons falling within either of those provisions. This is an exception to the general rule that the compensatory award is subject to a limit of £51,700.

(a) Basic awards

(i) Calculation of award

8.22   The basic award is calculated in the same way as a redundancy payment. It is necessary to take the complainant's age, length of continuous employment[4] on the effective date of termination[5] and the amount of gross weekly pay.[6] Starting with the effective date of termination and working backwards, the number of years of continuous employment should be reckoned. For each year of employment between 41 and 64, one and a half weeks' pay should be allowed; for each year between 22 and 41, one week's pay; and for each year between the time the employee started work and 22, half a week's pay.[7] Thus employment before the age of 18 may count, which is not the case with redundancy payments.[8] The week's pay used in the calculation should not include overtime, bonuses and tips.[9] Section 119(3) provides that no more than 20 years of employment may be counted and section 119(4) and (5) contains tapering provisions which reduce the amount of the basic award of an employee over 64.

8.23   In this context, it is important to bear in mind the provisions of section 97,[10] since their operation may affect the effective date of termination of the employment and, in consequence, the length of continuous employment for the purposes of calculating the basic award. So, for example, an employee with nearly eight years' employment, who is given one week's notice, may in fact be treated as having been continuously employed for eight years instead of seven by section 97 operating to extend the effective date of termination into the ninth year of continuous employment.

---

[1]   See the Employment Rights (Increase of Limits) Order 2001, SI 2001 No 21.
[2]   Dismissals in health and safety cases (see paras 5.57 *et seq*).
[3]   Dismissals for making a 'protected disclosure' (see paras 5.82 *et seq*).
[4]   Calculated in accordance with ss 210–219 (see Chapter 1).
[5]   See Chapter 3.
[6]   Calculated in accordance with ss 220–229 (see paras 8.158 *et seq*).
[7]   Section 119(1) and (2).
[8]   See s 211(2) and para 8.04.
[9]   *Brownson v Hire Service Shops Ltd* [1978] ICR 517 and *Palmanor Ltd v Cedron* [1978] ICR 1008.
[10]   See Chapter 3.

8.24   It is not proposed to provide examples here, but reference should be made to examples 1, 2 and 3 earlier in this chapter, although it should be borne in mind, when considering example 1, that employment before 18 would count. The ceiling on the amount of a week's pay is £240.[1] The maximum basic award is thus £7,200. Section 160 of the Trade Union and Labour Relations (Consolidation) Act 1992 makes it possible for a person or trade union responsible for exerting pressure on the employee to be joined as a party to the proceedings and ordered to pay all or part of any compensation awarded.[2]

8.25   The employee is entitled to a minimum basic award:

1.   of two weeks' pay, where the dismissal was by reason of redundancy but he or she is disentitled because of the provisions of section 141, or where he or she is not treated as dismissed because of the operation of section 138;[3] and

2.   of £3,300[4] in cases where the dismissal, or, in redundancy cases, the selection of the employee for dismissal, was for a reason specified in ERA 1996, sections 100(1)(a) or (b), 101A(d), 102(1) or 103,[5] or a reason related to trade union membership or activities, within TULRCA 1992, section 152(1).[6]

8.26   It is unclear how the second of the two provisions above is intended to operate. If, for example, the employee would be entitled to a basic award of £750, is that award increased to £3,300 or £4,050? If he or she would be entitled to £4,500 anyway, should anything more be awarded? There is no clear answer to these questions, but a close reading of the relevant provisions[7] would tend to suggest that if the basic award would be less than £3,300, it is raised to that amount and, if the basic award would exceed £3,300, that higher amount should be awarded.

Reductions from the figure of £3,300 may be made, however, under ERA 1996, section 122: see below.

---

[1]   Section 227(1), as amended by the Employment Rights (Increase of Limits) Order 2001, SI 2001 No 21.
[2]   See para 8.157.
[3]   Section 121; see Chapter 4.
[4]   Section 120(1), as amended by the Employment Rights (Increase of Limits) Order 2001, SI 2001 No 21. The limit may be increased by the Secretary of State by order under ERA 1999, s 34.
[5]   These provisions relate to carrying out duties as a health and safety representative or trustee of an occupational pension scheme, or performing functions or activities as an employee representative; see Chapter 5 where these types of dismissal are considered in more detail.
[6]   Section 120(1) and TULRCA 1992, s 156(1).
[7]   Section 120(1), as amended by the Working Time Regulations 1998, regs 2(1) and 32(5), and TULRCA 1992, s 156(1).

(ii) Reductions in award

8.27   The following reductions in the basic award may be made:

1.   where the employee is near retirement;
2.   where the employee unreasonably refuses an offer of reinstatement;
3.   where the employee's conduct before dismissal makes it just and equitable to make a reduction;
4.   where the employee has already received a redundancy payment;
5.   where the employee has received an award in respect of a dismissal under a designated dismissal procedures agreement; and
6.   where the employee has received an *ex gratia* payment from the employer.

8.28   Reductions may only be made in cases for which there is express statutory provision. So, for example, it will be an error of law for the tribunal to make a reduction in the basic award because of the employee's failure to mitigate, since the statutory provisions relating to mitigation[1] apply only to the compensatory award.[2] By the same reasoning, a basic award is not subject to a *Polkey* reduction.[3]

The order of deductions, together with some further examples, is set out in paras 8.41 *et seq*.

8.29   Reductions where employee is near retirement Section 119(4) and (5) provide for this reduction to be calculated in the same way as in the case of a redundancy payment.

Example 6

8.30   Employee aged 64 years 8 months at effective date of termination, continuously employed for 20 years, earning £210 a week.

1.5 x 20 x £210 =	£6,300
8/12 x £6,300 =	£4,200
TOTAL =	£2,100

8.31   Unreasonable refusal of reinstatement offer   Section 122(1) provides that, if the tribunal finds that the employee has unreasonably refused an offer of reinstatement (but not, it appears, an offer of re-engagement) made by the employer, it may reduce the basic award to whatever extent it considers just and equitable having regard to the

---

[1]   Section 123(4).
[2]   *Lock v Connell Estate Agents* [1994] IRLR 444.
[3]   *Taylor v John Webster, Buildings Civil Engineering* [1999] ICR 561. '*Polkey*' reductions are considered at para 8.53.

finding. Minimum basic awards under ERA 1996, section 120 or TULRCA 1992, section 156[1] are susceptible of reduction under this provision.

8.32   Reduction for conduct   The tribunal has the power, under section 122(2) to reduce the basic award to any extent, where it considers that any conduct of the employee before dismissal (or before notice was given, if that is the case) makes it just and equitable to do so. If the tribunal finds that the employee has contributed to some degree to the dismissal, it must reflect that finding in the award of compensation.[2] The effect of this rule is that *any* conduct before the dismissal is relevant, not merely conduct which caused or contributed to it. So evidence of misconduct before the dismissal, which came to light after the dismissal, would justify a reduction in the basic award.[3] Further, except in redundancy cases, it is perfectly feasible for the employee to receive no basic award at all. In *Optikinetics Ltd v Whooley,*[4] the EAT pointed out that section 122(2) gives the tribunal a wide discretion whether to make any, and if so what, reduction in the basic award on the grounds of the employee's conduct and that it is open to it to conclude that no reduction should be made. On the other hand, section 123(6) (the equivalent provision in relation to compensatory awards) *requires* the tribunal to make a reduction once it has found that there was contributory conduct.

8.33   The equivalent provision in relation to compensatory awards, section 123(6), is somewhat narrower, since it only enables reduction to be made where the conduct *caused or contributed* to the dismissal. There is no reason, therefore, why different percentages of reduction should not be made from the basic award and the compensatory award. In *Charles Robertson (Developments) Ltd v White,*[5] the EAT considered this issue and concluded that a discrepancy in reductions made to the basic and compensatory awards is not wrong in principle but flows from the fact that the discretions in the respective provisions are worded differently and require different factors to be taken into account. In most cases, however, the reductions are likely to be the same.

8.34   The EAT has held that if the employee is dismissed after being charged with a crime and succeeds in a complaint of unfair dismissal before the charge is tried and he or she is convicted, the employer may apply for a review, with a view to arguing that any compensation awarded

---

[1] See para 8.25.

[2] *Morganite Electrical Carbon Ltd v Donne* [1988] ICR 18.

[3] This is what would happen now if a case like *W Devis & Sons Ltd v Atkins* [1977] ICR 662 were to recur. The legislation under which that case was decided has been considerably changed since then, however.

[4] [1999] ICR 984.

[5] [1995] ICR 349. In *Royal Society for the Prevention of Cruelty to Animals v Cruden* [1986] ICR 205, the EAT suggested that there should be different percentages of reduction only in exceptional circumstances. This case was not cited in *Rao v Civil Aviation Authority* [1994] ICR 495, in which there are dicta supporting the notion that there may be different percentages of reduction: see at p 502. See also *Les Ambassadeurs Club v Bainda* [1982] IRLR 5 and *Thompson v Woodland Designs Ltd* [1980] IRLR 423, where the basic award was reduced by 85%, and the compensatory award by 100%, for contributory conduct.

should be reduced.[1] This decision appears to be in conflict with *W Devis & Sons Ltd v Atkins*[2] to the extent that it appears to attach importance to the subsequent conviction.

8.35   In *Courtaulds Northern Spinning Ltd v Moosa*,[3] the EAT suggested that the taking of industrial action should not be characterised as contributory fault meriting a reduction in the amount of compensation. In *Tracey v Crosville Wales Ltd*[4] the Court of Appeal approved the EAT's decision in *Courtaulds Northern Spinning Ltd v Moosa* and said that the tribunal should ignore the conduct represented by the industrial action in which the applicant had participated, but that other blameworthy conduct of the applicant causing or contributing to the dismissal should be taken into account when deciding upon a reduction in compensation. The House of Lords dismissed the employers' appeal against the Court of Appeal's decision and approved the EAT's decision in *Courtaulds Northern Spinning Ltd v Moosa*.[5]

8.36   Reductions under section 122(2) are not permissible, however, if the dismissal was for redundancy, unless it was made unfair because the employee was selected for a reason falling within ERA 1996, sections 100(1)(a) or (b) (dismissals in health and safety cases), 101A(d) (dismissals of employee representatives in working time cases), 102(1) (dismissals of trustees of occupational pension schemes) or 103 (dismissals of employee representatives), or a reason related to trade union membership or activities, within TULRCA 1992, section 152(1); in such cases, only the basic award payable by virtue of ERA 1996, section 120(1) or TULRCA 1992, section 156(1) is susceptible of reduction.[6] In cases where a dismissal is to be regarded as unfair by virtue of TULRCA 1992, sections 152 or 153, certain contributory conduct (in relation to union membership requirements) should be disregarded.[7]

8.37   Deduction in respect of an award under a dismissals procedure agreement   Section 122(3A)[8] provides that, where an employee has received an award under a designated dismissals procedure agreement, the tribunal should reduce the amount of the basic award by whatever amount it considers just and equitable having regard to that award.

8.38   Deduction of redundancy payment   The basic award will be reduced (or further reduced if there have been reductions under the previous headings) by the amount of any redundancy payment awarded by the tribunal, or paid by the employer to the employee, whether in

---

[1]   *Ladup Ltd v Barnes* [1982] ICR 107.
[2]   [1977] ICR 662.
[3]   [1984] ICR 218.
[4]   [1996] ICR 237.
[5]   *Tracey v Crosville Wales Ltd* [1997] ICR 862.
[6]   Section 122(3) and TULRCA 1992, s 156(2).
[7]   TULRCA 1992, s 155.
[8]   Inserted by the Employment Rights (Dispute Resolution) Act 1998, s 15 and Sch 1, para 22.

pursuance of the statutory obligations or otherwise.[1] If the amount of the redundancy payment exceeds the amount of the basic award which would be payable but for section 122(4), the amount of the excess will be deducted from the compensatory award.[2] Section 122(4) only applies, however, to payments made where the dismissal is in fact due to redundancy. So if a payment is expressed to be made to satisfy an employee's entitlement to a redundancy payment but the circumstances are such that there is in fact no redundancy situation, the payment will not fall to be deducted under section 122(4).[3]

8.39   Minimum basic awards,[4] in cases where the dismissal or selection for redundancy is for a reason specified in ERA 1996, sections 100(1)(a) or (b), 101A(d), 102(1) or 103,[5] or a reason related to trade union membership or activities, within TULRCA 1992, section 152(1) are susceptible of reduction under this provision.

8.40   Deduction of *ex gratia* payments   If the employer makes a lump sum payment to a dismissed employee, before a complaint is presented to the employment tribunal, and does not specifically state that it is referable to any possible future liability to pay a basic award, it is a question of construction whether the payment is to be taken to include any liability the employer may have because of the statutory provisions. Although there is a risk that the employer will remain liable to pay a basic award (and also a compensatory award), it seems probable, particularly if the payment is fairly substantial, that it will be held to be compensation for any rights the employee may have under the legislation.[6] In that case, the *ex gratia* payment will be deducted first from the basic award; if there is a surplus, that will then be deducted from the compensatory award.[7]

(iii) Order of deductions

8.41   The final question which requires consideration in relation to basic awards is the order of deductions. A question (which has also arisen in relation to the calculation of compensatory awards) is whether any *ex gratia* payment should be deducted before any contribution in respect of the employee's misconduct or after. There is no direct authority on the question in relation to basic awards, but in relation to compensatory awards the tenor of recent decisions is that the *ex gratia* payment should be

---

[1]   Section 122(4).

[2]   Section 123(7).

[3]   *Boorman v Allmakes Ltd* [1995] ICR 842.

[4]   Made under s 120(1) and TULRCA 1992, s 156(1).

[5]   Section 100 deals with dismissals in health and safety cases, s 101A with dismissals of employee representatives in working time cases, s 102 with dismissals of trustees of occupational pension schemes and s 103 with dismissals of employee representatives (see paras 5.57 *et seq*, 5.73, 5.76, and 5.79).

[6]   *Chelsea Football Club and Athletic Co Ltd v Heath* [1981] ICR 323 at pp 327–328. The employer's *ex gratia* payment was held to discharge liability.

[7]   See *Rushton v Harcos Timber & Building Supplies Ltd* [1993] ICR 230 and *Darr v LRC Products Ltd* [1993] IRLR 257.

deducted first and then the contribution for contributory conduct.[1] It would be sensible to apply the same approach to basic awards.

8.42 Adopting that approach, the order (except if the dismissal was for redundancy) should be:

1. Calculate basic award and deduct *ex gratia* payment;
2. Deduct from net amount in 1:
   (a) contribution for refusal of employer's reinstatement offer; and
   (b) contribution for conduct.

8.43 If the dismissal was for redundancy, step 2 will consist of deducting (a) and (b) and then any redundancy payment paid to the employee. If the redundancy dismissal was automatically unfair by virtue of ERA, sections 100(1)(a) or (b), 101A(d), 102(1) or 103 or TULRCA 1992, section 153, the order will be:

1. Calculate basic award;
2. Add £3,300;[2]
3. Deduct *ex gratia* payment from total of 1 and 2;
4. Then deduct:
   (a) contribution for refusal of employer's reinstatement offer;
   (b) contribution for conduct (but only from the £3,300, or so much of it as represents the basic award);
   (c) redundancy payment.

Example 7

8.44 Employee aged 50, continuously employed for 15 years, earning £230 per week. The employer has paid an *ex gratia* payment of £1,500; the tribunal decides on a reduction of 10% for a refusal of reinstatement and 25% for contributory conduct.

1.5 x 9 x £230 =	£3,105.00
1 x 6 x £230 =	£1,380.00
Sub-total =	£4,485.00
LESS *ex gratia* payment =	£1,500.00
NET AWARD =	£2,985.00
LESS 35% =	£1,044.75
TOTAL =	£1,940.25

---

[1] *Parker & Farr Ltd v Shelvey* [1979] ICR 896. This approach has been approved more recently by the EAT in *Digital Equipment Co Ltd v Clements (No 2)* [1997] ICR 237. Although there was a successful appeal to the Court of Appeal ([1998] ICR 258), the point at issue in the Court of Appeal concerned a contractual redundancy payment. This issue is more fully discussed below, at para 8.120.

[2] See ERA, s 120(1) and TULRCA 1992, s 156(1).

Example 8

8.45 Unfair dismissal for redundancy of employee aged 28, continuously employed for 10 years, earning £145 per week. No *ex gratia* payments, no contribution, but employee receives redundancy payment of £700.

1 x 5 x £145 =	£725.00
½ x 4 x £145 =	£290.00
Sub-total =	£1015.00
LESS redundancy payment =	£700.00
TOTAL =	£315.00

Example 9

8.46 Employee aged 62, continuously employed for 20 years, earning £275 per week. Unfair selection for redundancy contrary to TULRCA 1992, section 153, but employer pays statutory maximum redundancy payment of £7,200. The tribunal decides on a 20% contribution for conduct.

1.5 x 20 x £240 =	£7,200.00
Section 156(1) award =	£3,300.00
Sub-total =	£10,500.00
Deduct 20% of £3,300[1] =	£660.00
Sub-total =	£9,840.00
Deduct redundancy payment =	£7,200.00
TOTAL =	£2,640.00

Note. This example proceeds upon the assumption that, in a TULRCA 1992, section 153 case, £3,300 must be added to the basic award. All that section 156(1) says, however, is that the basic award must be at least £3,300. Since in the above example it is £7,200 anyway, it is at least arguable that section 156(1) would not apply. Similar observations obviously apply when the dismissal is unfair because the employee was selected for redundancy contrary to ERA 1996, sections 100(1)(a) or (b), 101A(d), 102(1) or 103.[2]

---

[1] In accordance with TULRCA, s 156(2), or ERA 1996, s 122(3) in a case of selection for redundancy for a reason falling within ss 100(1)(a) or (b), 101A(d), 102(1) or 103.

[2] The relevant provisions are ss 120(1) and 122(3).

(b) Compensatory awards

(i) Calculation of award

8.47   Section 123(1) states:

'... the amount of the compensatory award shall be such amount as the tribunal considers just and equitable in all the circumstances having regard to the loss sustained by the complainant in consequence of the dismissal in so far as that loss is attributable to action taken by the employer.'

The tribunal should include any expenses reasonably incurred by the complainant and the loss of any benefit which he or she might reasonably expect to have had but for the dismissal.[1] It may only include an amount in respect of loss of entitlement or potential entitlement to a redundancy payment (whether made in pursuance of the 1996 Act or otherwise) if the amount exceeds the amount of the unreduced basic award; in that case it may include the amount of the difference.[2]

8.48   The maximum amount of compensatory award that may be awarded is £51,700.[3] It should be noted, however, that this limit does not apply where an employment tribunal makes an order for reinstatement or re-engagement and, as part of the order, makes an ancillary order for arrears of pay. In such a case, the order for arrears of pay cannot be frustrated by the employer's refusal to comply with the reinstatement or re-engagement order.[4]

8.49   The heads of loss which the compensatory award may cover were set out in *Norton Tool Co Ltd v Tewson*[5] and are:

1.   immediate loss of wages;
2.   manner of dismissal;
3.   future loss of wages; and
4.   loss of protection in respect of unfair dismissal or dismissal by reason of redundancy.

To this, there has been added subsequently a fifth head: loss of pension rights.

8.50   The tribunal must make sure that the various heads of compensation are considered; it is up to the complainant to prove the loss,[6] although 'it is not ... to be expected that precise and detailed proof of every item of loss will be presented'.[7] The common law rules on assessment of

---

[1]   Section 123(2).
[2]   Section 123(3).
[3]   Section 124(1), as amended by ERA 1999, s 34(4) and the Employment Rights (Increase of Limits) Order 2001, SI 2001 No 21.
[4]   Section 124(3). See Chapter 7 for a discussion of re-employment orders.
[5]   [1972] ICR 501.
[6]   *Tidman v Aveling Marshall Ltd* [1977] ICR 506 at p 508.
[7]   *Norton Tool Co Ltd v Tewson* [1972] ICR 501 at pp 504–505.

damages are irrelevant.[1] In *Simrad Ltd v Scott*,[2] the EAT suggested an approach to the calculation of the compensatory award, as follows:

> 'The process is a three-stage one, requiring, initially, factual quantification of losses claimed; secondly, but equally importantly, the extent to which any or all of those losses are attributable to the dismissal or action taken by the employer, which is usually the same thing, the word "attributable" implying that there has to be a direct and natural link between the losses claimed and the conduct of the employer in dismissing, on the basis that the dismissal is the *causa causans* of the particular loss and not that it simply arises by reason of a *causa sine qua non*, ie but for the dismissal the loss would not have arisen. If that is the only connection, the loss is too remote. The third part of the assessment in terms of the reference to the phrase "just and equitable" requires a tribunal to look at the conclusions they draw from the first two questions and determine whether, in all the circumstances, it remains reasonable to make the relevant award. It must again be emphasised, however, that what is to be considered under the third test already has to have passed the second.'

8.51   In general, the purpose of the compensatory award has been regarded as only to compensate the employee for financial loss sustained as a result of the dismissal, not for injury to pride or feelings and the like.[3] This can have the effect that, if the tribunal finds as a fact that the employee has suffered no loss as a result of the employer's action, there should be no compensatory award.[4] An example would be where the employee immediately found another job at the same, or a better, rate of pay; in such a case, however, he or she would still be entitled to receive a basic award, but the tribunal should not make a compensatory award.[5] Another example would be where evidence of misconduct which came to light after the dismissal shows that the employee suffered no injustice.[6] In *Tele-Trading Ltd v Jenkins*,[7] the Court of Appeal said that in such a case what is now section 123(1) applies rather than section 123(6), since conduct which came to light after the dismissal cannot be said to have caused or contributed to it.

8.52   In the light of the House of Lords' decision in *Johnson v Unisys Ltd*,[8] the proposition in the preceding paragraph relating to compensation for non-financial loss may need to be reviewed. In that case, the employee's claim for damages covering the manner of his dismissal was struck out by the House of Lords. In the course of his speech, Lord Hoffmann observed

---

[1]   [1972] ICR 501 at p 504.
[2]   [1997] IRLR 147 at p 149.
[3]   *Norton Tool Co Ltd v Tewson* [1972] ICR 501 at pp 504 and 505.
[4]   *W Devis & Sons Ltd v Atkins* [1977] ICR 662. Cf *Devonshire v Trico-Folberth Ltd* [1989] ICR 747.
[5]   *Isleworth Studios Ltd v Rickard* [1988] ICR 432.
[6]   *W Devis & Sons Ltd v Atkins* [1977] ICR 662.
[7]   [1990] IRLR 430.
[8]   [2001] ICR 480.

that in *Norton Tool Co Ltd v Tewson*[1] the National Industrial Relations Court had said that only financial loss could be compensated. He went on to say:[2]

> 'But I think that is too narrow a construction. The emphasis is upon the tribunal awarding such compensation as it thinks just and equitable. So I see no reason why in an appropriate case it should not include compensation for distress, humiliation, damage to reputation in the community or to family life.'

If this approach is followed in the employment tribunals, the consequence will be the development of a concept of compensation very similar to compensation for injury to feelings in discrimination cases.

8.53   It may also be appropriate for a tribunal to make no award of compensation under section 123(1) in cases where there was a procedural omission by the employer which made the dismissal unfair, but it is clear that, had the employer not acted unfairly, the result would still have been the same (particularly in redundancy cases).[3] The extent to which the compensatory award should be reduced in such circumstances is an issue which has caused much discussion in decided cases since the House of Lords' decision in *Polkey v AE Dayton Services Ltd*.[4] In that case, Lord Bridge of Harwich said:[5]

> 'If it is held that taking the appropriate steps which the employer failed to take before dismissing the employee would not have affected the outcome, this will often lead to the result that the employee, though unfairly dismissed, will recover no compensation or, in the case of redundancy, no compensation in excess of his redundancy payment.'

He went on to quote with approval the dictum of Browne-Wilkinson J in *Sillifant v Powell Duffryn Timber Ltd*:

> 'If the tribunal thinks there is a doubt whether or not the employee would have been dismissed, this element can be reflected by reducing the normal amount of compensation by a percentage representing the chance that the employee would still have lost his employment.'[6]

8.54   In *Mining Supplies (Longwall) Ltd v Baker*,[7] the employment tribunal decided that the dismissal of an employee for redundancy was unfair because of the employers' failure to allow a period for discussions with him. It considered that the discussions would have taken about six weeks,

---

[1]   [1972] ICR 501.

[2]   [2001] ICR 480 at p 500.

[3]   *Earl v Slater & Wheeler (Airlyne) Ltd* [1972] ICR 508, *Clarkson International Tools Ltd v Short* [1973] ICR 70 and *Robertson v Magnet Ltd* [1993] IRLR 512. See also *Tele-Trading Ltd v Jenkins* [1990] IRLR 430 and *Fisher v California Cake & Cookie Ltd* [1997] IRLR 212.

[4]   [1988] ICR 142. See Chapter 4.

[5]   *Ibid* at p 163.

[6]   [1983] IRLR 91 at p 96. See also the decisions of the Court of Appeal in *Rao v Civil Aviation Authority* [1994] ICR 495 and of the Court of Session in *Campbell v Dunoon & Cowal Housing Association* [1993] IRLR 496.

[7]   [1988] IRLR 417.

but that at the end of that period the result would have been the same. It awarded him six weeks' pay as a compensatory award. On appeal the EAT said that the tribunal had not erred in failing to make a nil award of compensation, despite its finding that he would still have been dismissed even if there had been a period of consultation. It held, however, that it was excessive to allow six weeks for consultation with the employee and it reduced the compensatory award. The EAT has said[1] that the assessment of compensation in circumstances where a dismissal is unfair because of a failure to go through a fair procedure involves a two-stage process:[2]

> 'First, the tribunal must ask itself whether if the employer had followed the proper procedures and acted fairly the employee would not have been dismissed ... [I]n many cases the answer will be uncertain, in which situation, in order to give effect to section [123(1)] of the Act of [1996] ... the tribunal must, as the second stage of the process, make a percentage assessment of the likelihood of the employee being retained which must then be reflected in the compensatory award.'

8.55   In *Steel Stockholders (Birmingham) Ltd v Kirkwood*,[3] the EAT in Scotland took the view that the reduction of compensation suggested by Lord Bridge in the *Polkey* case should be confined to cases in which the unfairness of the dismissal arises from a failure to take steps which can properly be categorised as 'procedural' and that his observations do not apply where the grounds for holding a dismissal unfair arise from the substance of the decision: 'In any given case, therefore, it is necessary to consider whether the unfairness can properly be classified as procedural or substantive'.[4] This decision should be treated with considerable caution, however, in view of the criticisms to which it was subjected by the Court of Appeal in *O'Dea v ISC Chemicals Ltd, t/a Rhone-Poulenc Chemicals*.[5]

8.56   Further complications arise where there is a finding of contributory fault on the part of the employee. This matter was considered by the Court of Appeal in *Rao v Civil Aviation Authority*[6] and is discussed later in this chapter.[7]

8.57   In cases such as those which have been discussed above, the burden is in effect on the employer.[8] Theoretically, once an unfair dismissal has been established, the burden of proof in relation to loss lies on the employee. But, particularly where the tribunal is satisfied that the dismissal

---

[1]   See *Red Bank Manufacturing Co Ltd v Meadows* [1992] IRLR 209 and *Wolesley Centers Ltd v Simmons* [1994] ICR 503. It should be noted that the report of the *Meadows* case at [1992] ICR 204 deals with a different aspect of the proceedings. See also *Campbell v Dunoon & Cowal Housing Association Ltd* [1993] IRLR 496, where the reduction was 75%.

[2]   *Wolesley Centers Ltd v Simmons* [1994] ICR 503 at p 508.

[3]   [1993] IRLR 515.

[4]   *Ibid* at p 517.

[5]   [1995] IRLR 599. See in particular the observations of Peter Gibson, LJ at p 604, paras 24 and 25. See also *Boulton & Paul Ltd v Arnold* [1994] IRLR 532.

[6]   [1994] ICR 495.

[7]   At para 8.113.

[8]   *Charles Letts & Co Ltd v Howard* [1976] IRLR 248.

suffers from procedural unfairness, the employee will have a prima facie loss and very little is then required to cause the evidential burden to shift to the employer to show that the dismissal could, or would be likely to, have occurred in any event. If the employer fails to discharge that burden, there should be no reduction in compensation.[1] It follows, therefore, that an employer wishing to argue that there should be a *Polkey* reduction on the grounds that a proper dismissal would have occurred in the near future in any event must adduce the evidence to support that argument. There is no obligation on the tribunal to consider the matter of its own motion and evaluate a reduction in the compensation.[2]

8.58 The degree of unfairness of the employer in dismissing an employee is not a relevant consideration in the assessment of what award is just and equitable in all the circumstances. So it is not permissible for the employment tribunal to take into account a finding of fact that the employers, when dismissing an employee, intended to behave fairly towards their employees.[3] Nor should the tribunal take into account the employee's conduct after the dismissal, when assessing compensation.[4]

8.59 In cases where a dismissal is to be regarded as unfair by virtue of section 152 or 153 of the TULRCA 1992, section 155 of that Act provides that certain contributory conduct (in relation to union membership requirements) should be disregarded.[5] Section 123(5) of the ERA 1996 provides that any industrial pressure threatened against the employer should also be disregarded; the loss sustained by the employee must be computed as if no pressure had been exercised. In such cases, the employer or the employee may join the trade union or person exerting the pressure as a party to the proceedings, and that third party may be ordered to pay all or part of the compensation.[6]

8.60 The effect of *ex gratia* payments paid by the employer should also be noted. If such a payment is made, it should first be set off against the basic award and any surplus should then be carried forward and set off against the compensatory award.[7] This question is considered more fully later in the chapter (see paras 8.121 and 8.132).

---

[1] *Britool Ltd v Roberts* [1993] IRLR 481.
[2] *Boulton & Paul Ltd v Arnold* [1994] IRLR 532.
[3] *Morris v Acco Co Ltd* [1985] ICR 306.
[4] *Soros v Davison* [1994] ICR 590.
[5] The predecessor of this provision (EPCA 1978, s 72A) was considered by the EAT in *Transport and General Workers' Union v Howard* [1992] ICR 106. It said that the provision permits a distinction to be drawn between what was done by the employee and the way in which it was done. Section 155 only requires that the specific circumstances surrounding the exercise of the right not to comply with the requirement to be a member of a trade union should be disregarded when considering a reduction in compensation. If, however, the conduct of the employee before dismissal deserves to be criticised, the tribunal has the power to make an appropriate reduction.
[6] TULRCA 1992, s 160: see para 8.157.
[7] *Chelsea Football Club and Athletic Co Ltd v Heath* [1981] ICR 323 and *Rushton v Harcos Timber & Building Supplies Ltd* [1993] ICR 230.

8.61   The calculation of the compensatory award is considered under the following headings:

1.   loss of earnings to date of hearing;
2.   future loss of earnings;
3.   manner of dismissal;
4.   loss of future protection;
5.   loss of pension rights;
6.   expenses; and
7.   other losses.

8.62   Once the compensatory award has been calculated, it may then be subjected to reductions, which will be applied to it after the initial calculation of the employee's loss under section 123(1)–(3) has been made. Reductions may be made for mitigation, contributory fault, the receipt of statutory or contractual redundancy payments and *ex gratia* payments and the receipt of other payments. These different types of reduction are considered in subsequent sections. Two other points should be noted here:

1.   Once the tribunal has calculated the total amount of the compensatory award, after making necessary reductions, it may then need to adjust the final total to take account of the fact *either* that the employee has not taken advantage of an internal appeals procedure *or* that the employer has prevented the employee from taking advantage of such a procedure;[1]
2.   There are two types of unfair dismissal where there is no limit to the amount of compensation which may be awarded. These are cases in which the dismissal is unfair because it is contrary to sections 100[2] or 103A,[3] or because the employee was selected for reasons falling within either of those provisions. This is an exception to the general rule that the compensatory award is subject to a limit of £51,700.

Both the above points will be considered after the sections on reductions. These are followed by sections which discuss the order of calculation of compensation, the Recoupment Regulations and the way compensation is to be calculated in cases involving dual claims for unfair dismissal and wrongful dismissal. Finally, some worked examples are set out.

8.63   **Loss of earnings to date of hearing** This head of loss is called the 'prescribed element', since it is affected by the Recoupment Regulations

---

[1]   The adjustment will fall to be made by virtue of s 127A, introduced by the Employment Rights (Dispute Resolution) Act 1998, s 13. This is considered more fully below.
[2]   Dismissals in health and safety cases (see paras 5.57 *et seq*).
[3]   Dismissals for making a 'protected disclosure' (see para 5.82).

(see para 8.137). The prescribed element should relate to the period for which the loss of earnings is awarded.[1]

8.64   The general rule is that loss of earnings should be assessed to the date of the tribunal hearing and the employee is required to bring into account earnings from any new employment.[2] If there is a dispute about the level of pay the employee was receiving at the time of dismissal, the tribunal must resolve the dispute.[3] There may be exceptions to the general rule, for example where a long period elapses between the date of dismissal and the date of assessment and the employee obtains new employment. In that case, the loss should be assessed up to the start of the new employment and any loss caused by events after the start of the new employment becomes irrelevant.[4] In dealing with cases of this kind, it is important that tribunals should not allow themselves to be bound by the formulae established by case-law, but should remember the overriding words of section 123(1) and award the amount they consider just and equitable.

8.65   In *Fentiman v Fluid Engineering Products Ltd*,[5] the EAT refused to apply the general rule in a case where a dismissed employee obtained new employment at a significantly higher rate of pay between the date of the dismissal and the date of the employment tribunal hearing and where there was a considerable gap between the date of dismissal and the promulgation of the tribunal's decision. The tribunal assessed the loss of earnings from the date of his dismissal to the date of promulgation of its decision, and deducted the earnings from his new employment. That produced a net loss of £2,373. The EAT said that in a case such as this the tribunal should decide whether the new employment is permanent; if so, it should calculate the loss as between the date of dismissal and the date the new employment was obtained. It said that the general rule is unrealistic if applied to all cases and is based on an arbitrary selection of the date of assessment being the date of the tribunal hearing. It took the view that the operation of the general rule meant that the employers who dismissed the employee unfairly would be called upon to pay compensation only for a fraction of the loss sustained by the employee during the period of unemployment. In its view, it was 'just and equitable' in these circumstances that the employee should be compensated for the full loss he sustained until he obtained new employment.[6] It therefore substituted the maximum compensatory award, since in fact the loss exceeded that.

8.66   The approach taken in *Fentiman* was followed by the EAT in *Whelan v Richardson*.[7] That was also a case where the employee obtained

---

[1]   *Homan v A1 Bacon Co* [1996] ICR 721.
[2]   *Ging v Ellward Lancs Ltd* (1978) 13 ITR 265; see also the text on mitigation at paras 8.100 *et seq.*
[3]   *Kinzley v Minories Finance Ltd* [1988] ICR 113.
[4]   *Courtaulds Northern Spinning Ltd v Moosa* [1984] ICR 218. See also *Gilham v Kent County Council (No 3)* [1986] ICR 52.
[5]   [1991] ICR 570.
[6]   *Ibid* at pp 575–576.
[7]   [1998] ICR 318.

employment at a higher level of salary before the date of the tribunal hearing. The EAT upheld the tribunal's approach of basing its calculation of the compensatory award on the loss between the date of the employee's dismissal and the date she obtained permanent employment at a higher rate than her pre-dismissal earnings, but making a deduction in respect of earnings during a period of temporary employment. His Honour Judge Peter Clark said:[1]

'... [W]e think it might be helpful to reduce our conclusions to a series of propositions, making it clear that we are not seeking to fetter the exercise of discretion by [employment] tribunals on the facts of any individual case, nor is the list which follows in any way exhaustive.

(1)   The assessment of loss must be judged on the basis of the facts as they appear at the date of the assessment hearing ("the assessment date").
(2)   Where the applicant has been unemployed between dismissal and the assessment date then, subject to his duty to mitigate and the operation of the recoupment rules, he will recover his net loss of earnings based on the pre-dismissal rate. Further, the [employment] tribunal will consider for how long the loss is likely to continue so as to assess future loss.
(3)   The same principle applies where the applicant has secured permanent alternative employment at a lower level of earnings than he received before his unfair dismissal. He will be compensated on the basis of full loss until the date on which he obtained the new employment, and thereafter for partial loss, being the difference between the pre-dismissal earnings and those in the new employment. All figures will be based on net earnings.
(4)   Where the applicant takes alternative employment on the basis that it will be for a limited duration, he will not then be precluded from claiming a loss down to the assessment date, or the date on which he secures further permanent employment, whichever is the sooner, giving credit for earnings received from the temporary employment.
(5)   As soon as the applicant obtains permanent alternative employment paying the same or more than his pre-dismissal earnings his loss attributable to the action taken by the respondent employer ceases. It cannot be revived if he then loses that employment either through his own action or that of his new employer neither can the respondent employer rely on the employee's increased earnings to reduce the loss sustained prior to his taking the new employment. The chain of causation has been broken.'

8.67   In *Dench v Flynn & Partners*,[2] Beldam LJ, with whom Mummery LJ and Sir Christopher Staughton agreed, said:

'I consider that statement needs qualification. No doubt in many cases a loss consequent upon unfair dismissal will cease when an applicant gets employment of a permanent nature at an equivalent or higher level of salary or wage than the employee enjoyed when dismissed. But to regard such an event as always and in all cases putting an end to the attribution of the loss to the termination of employment cannot lead in some cases to an award which is just and equitable. Although causation is primarily a question of fact, the principle

---

[1]   [1998] ICR 318 at pp 325–326.
[2]   [1998] IRLR 653.

to be applied in deciding whether the connection between a cause, such as unfair dismissal, and its consequences is sufficient to found a legal claim to loss or damage is a question of law. The question for the industrial tribunal was whether the unfair dismissal could be regarded as a continuing cause of loss when she was subsequently dismissed by her new employer with no right to compensation after a month or two in her new employment. To treat the consequences of unfair dismissal as ceasing automatically when other employment supervenes is to treat as the effective cause that which is simply closest in time.'[1]

8.68 The point about these cases is that it is of overriding importance that the tribunal should decide upon a compensatory award which is just and equitable in all the circumstances and should be careful of slavishly following other cases, where the facts may have been different. The point about the discretion given by section 123(1) is that, although it should be exercised in a principled way, it gives a tribunal power to make an appropriate order according to the facts of the case in front of it.

8.69 A further problem arises in cases where the employee is dismissed, obtains a job at a lower rate of pay, and is then dismissed from that second job. The question in such cases is whether the compensation against the first employer should be awarded in respect of a time after the dismissal by the second employer. According to the Court of Appeal,[2] the tribunal should award compensation in respect of the difference between the wages paid in the first job and the second job, had the employee continued in it. It should not award compensation in respect of the loss of wages from the first job only, since the dismissal from the second job breaks the chain of causation. If there was a reduction for contributory fault in respect of the first dismissal, that should continue to affect the compensation awarded, but there should be no reduction for contributory fault in respect of the second (see para 8.104, for a discussion of contributory fault).

8.70 Loss under this head is based on the employee's net take-home pay (after deduction of tax and social security contributions),[3] but it may include regular overtime (net) and bonus earnings and tips.[4] If the employee was dismissed without wages or wages in lieu of notice, the net wages for the notice period to which he or she was entitled will be included here.

8.71 The figure thus arrived at is subject to deductions. Wages paid in lieu of notice are deductible, but not wages earned by the employee during the period covered by the wages in lieu of notice.[5] No deduction will be made in respect of any jobseeker's allowance or income support received,

---

[1] [1998] IRLR 653 at p 655.

[2] In *Mabey Plant Hire Ltd v Richens* (6 May 1993, CA) IDS Brief 495.

[3] *Norton Tool Co Ltd v Tewson* [1972] ICR 501 at p 506.

[4] *Brownson v Hire Service Shops Ltd* [1978] ICR 517 and *Palmanor Ltd v Cedron* [1978] ICR 1008.

[5] *Addison v Babcock FATA Ltd* [1987] ICR 805 and *TBA Industrial Products Ltd v Locke* [1984] ICR 228. If, as is usual, the wages in lieu of notice are paid gross, the gross amount should be deducted: *ibid* at p 235.

since this will be subject to recoupment;[1] nor should there be a deduction in respect of an educational grant received by the employee in connection with a course embarked upon following the dismissal.[2] On the other hand, statutory sick pay and invalidity benefit should be deducted.[3]

8.72   The loss of benefits in kind (eg low interest mortgage, use of company car, medical insurance) should not be dealt with under this head, since the Recoupment Regulations only affect loss of earnings. Such losses should be dealt with under the heading of other losses: see below. It may be proper to include an amount in respect of loss of holiday leave and loss of a tax rebate; the tribunal should generally disregard the incidence of tax in respect of the tax on loss of earnings.[4]

8.73   The effect of *ex gratia* payments paid by the employer should also be noted. If such a payment is made, it should first be set off against the basic award and any surplus should then be carried forward and set off against the compensatory award.[5] *Ex gratia* payments are considered more fully at para 8.121.

8.74   Future loss of earnings This should be calculated on the basis of the difference between the employee's net take-home pay in the former job and that in the new job, if he or she has obtained one.[6]

8.75   Although the calculation of future loss is speculative, particularly where the employee has not obtained another job at the time of the tribunal hearing, the tribunal must have some evidence of the probable future loss and its scale before making an award.[7] Awards for future loss in respect of a period of six or nine months are not unlikely. In *Morganite Electric Carbon Ltd v Donne*,[8] the EAT said that the award for future loss is not restricted to 26–52 weeks' pay and that the range must be determined by the evidence in any particular case. This is subject to the statutory maximum. Where, however, the unfair dismissal arises from the closure of the employer's business, the future loss element cannot extend beyond the date of complete closure of the business.[9]

---

[1]   Under the Employment Protection (Recoupment of Jobseeker's Allowance and Income Support) Regulations 1996, SI 1996 No 2349.

[2]   *Justfern Ltd v D'Ingerthorpe* [1994] ICR 286 at p 294.

[3]   *Puglia v C James & Sons* [1996] ICR 301. The EAT did not follow the earlier decision of another division in *Hilton International Hotels (UK) Ltd v Faraji* [1994] ICR 259. *Cf Rubenstein and Roskin t/a McGuffies Dispensing Chemists v McGloughlin* [1997] ICR 318, in which it was decided that it was just and equitable to deduct half of the invalidity benefit received by the employee.

[4]   *Tradewinds Airways Ltd v Fletcher* [1981] IRLR 272, *Lucas v Lawrence Scott Electromotors Ltd* [1983] ICR 309 and *MBS Ltd v Calo* [1983] ICR 459.

[5]   *Chelsea Football Club and Athletic Co Ltd v Heath* [1981] ICR 323 and *Rushton v Harcos Timber & Building Supplies Ltd* [1993] ICR 230.

[6]   *Norton Tool Co Ltd v Tewson* [1972] ICR 501.

[7]   *Adda International Ltd v Curcio* [1976] ICR 407.

[8]   [1988] ICR 18. The EAT upheld an award covering a period of 82 weeks.

[9]   *James W Cook (Wivenhoe) Ltd v Tipper* [1990] ICR 716.

8.76 Where the employee has obtained another job, a comparison between the two jobs must obviously be made. If the new job is at the same or a higher salary, the amount of compensation under this head is likely to be nominal. If, on the other hand, there is a shortfall, the tribunal will first need to compare the employee's salary prospects for the future in each job and see as best it can how long it will be before he or she reaches with the new employers the equivalent salary to that which he or she would have reached but for the dismissal.[1] It should then select an appropriate multiplier. The multiplier should reflect the tribunal's estimate of the future loss but should also take into account various discounting factors, such as the possibility that the employee might have resigned in the future. The fact that the receipt of earnings will be accelerated by the payment to the employee of a lump sum of compensation will also be a discount factor. In *Cartiers Superfoods Ltd v Laws*,[2] the tribunal satisfied itself that the employee was right to take a lower-paid job. It found that in the new job there was a shortfall of £18 a week. It then applied a multiplier of three years to that figure and to a figure attributable to probable increases in wages and achieved a total of £3,744. The EAT refused to interfere with that assessment.

8.77 If the employee has not obtained another job, the exercise becomes more speculative. The tribunal will again have to find an appropriate multiplier, based on its local knowledge and experience of the labour market, but it should make clear its reasons for the period chosen.[3] In arriving at a multiplier, the tribunal must also consider the circumstances of the employee's age and state of health or injuries suffered by him or her, which may make finding another job more difficult.[4] The tribunal must decide upon an appropriate cut-off point for the award for future loss. In *Holroyd v Gravure Cylinders Ltd*,[5] the dismissed employee embarked on a 12-month postgraduate university course. He tried to argue that the tribunal should have allowed for loss of earnings during the period of study and for some unspecified time after that. The EAT rejected that argument, on the grounds that the employee effectively took himself out of the labour market by deciding to embark on the course. Any future loss at the end of the course was so remote as to be incapable of calculation. A similar conclusion was reached in the later case of *Simrad Ltd v Scott*,[6] a case in which the employee decided to retrain as a nurse and embarked on a three-year course of study. The EAT distinguished the *Simrad* case in *Khanum v IBC Vehicles Ltd*,[7] which also involved the question of compensation being

---

[1]   *Tradewinds Airways Ltd v Fletcher* [1981] IRLR 272 at p 274, para 8. See also *Mabey Plant Hire Ltd v Richens* (6 May 1993, CA) IDS Brief 495.

[2]   [1978] IRLR 315.

[3]   *Qualcast (Wolverhampton) Ltd v Ross* [1979] ICR 386.

[4]   *Fougère v Phoenix Motor Co Ltd* [1976] ICR 495 and *Brittains (Arborfield) Ltd v Van Uden* [1977] ICR 211. See also *Devine v Designer Flowers Wholesale Florist Sundries Ltd* [1993] IRLR 517, which considered the *Fougère* case.

[5]   [1984] IRLR 259. See also *Forth Estuary Engineering Ltd v Litster* [1986] IRLR 59 and *Gilham v Kent County Council (No 3)* [1986] ICR 52.

[6]   [1997] IRLR 147.

[7]   (EAT 685/98) (2000) IDS Brief B654/5.

awarded to cover a period after the complainant's enrolment on a degree course. It said that the *Simrad* case does not create a rule of law that embarking upon a course of further education necessarily breaks the chain of causation and that the issue for the tribunal is whether the decision to attend university is a direct result of the dismissal. Here, it said it was.

8.78   Compensation may be awarded for a time beyond the normal retiring age, if the tribunal finds that the employee would probably have stayed on beyond that time.[1] If the employee in fact succeeds in finding another job fairly soon after the tribunal hearing, the employer may be able to apply to the tribunal for a review to consider reducing the amount of compensation.[2]

8.79   Manner of dismissal   This has not generally been a head of compensation hitherto, unless there is cogent evidence that the manner of the dismissal caused financial loss, for example by making it more difficult to find future employment.[3] In the light of the comments of Lord Hoffmann in *Johnson v Unisys Ltd*,[4] however, it may be that this head of compensation will acquire a new lease of life.

8.80   Loss of future protection   An employee who succeeds in finding another job will not acquire the right not to be unfairly dismissed and the right to receive a redundancy payment for two years. This head of loss is effectively compensated for by the basic award, and so a nominal amount is usually awarded.[5] In *SH Muffett Ltd v Head*,[6] the EAT said that £100 was the correct sum under this head. That case was decided some years ago, however, and the figure of £100 should presumably be revised. In the later case of *Harvey v Institute of the Motor Industry*,[7] however, the EAT said that 'there is no rule of law which requires such a head of compensation to be awarded and no need for an employment tribunal to spell out why sums were not being awarded'. In *Puglia v C James & Sons*,[8] the EAT refused to interfere with the tribunal's decision to make no award under this head in the light of its finding that he would have been fairly dismissed at a later date.

---

[1] *Barrel Plating & Phosphating Co Ltd v Danks* [1976] ICR 503.
[2] The Employment Tribunal (Constitution and Rules of Procedure) Regulations 2001, SI 2001 No 1171, Sch 1, rule 13; see also *Yorkshire Engineering & Welding Co Ltd v Burnham* [1974] ICR 77 and *Help The Aged Housing Association (Scotland) Ltd v Vidler* [1977] IRLR 104.
[3] *Vaughan v Weighpack Ltd* [1974] ICR 261 at pp 265–266.
[4] [2001] ICR 480 at p 500 (see para 8.52).
[5] *Cf*, however, *Daley v AE Dorsett (Almar Dolls) Ltd* [1982] ICR 1, where an amount to reflect loss of notice entitlement was awarded.
[6] [1987] ICR 1.
[7] [1995] IRLR 416 at p 420.
[8] [1996] ICR 301.

8.81   Loss of an advantageous position in relation to redundancy (eg where the employee's contract gives an entitlement to a larger redundancy payment, if he or she is made redundant, than he or she would receive under the statutory entitlement) is a matter to be taken into account.[1]

8.82   Loss of pension rights   This head has provided considerable difficulty, and it is potentially capable of substantially increasing the amount of compensation. In 1980, the Government Actuary's Department produced a paper (*A suggested method for assessing loss of pension rights under an occupational pension scheme following a finding of unfair dismissal by an employment tribunal*). Although it was intended to provide a simple system for calculating this head of loss, it was not easy to operate, not least because tribunals often found themselves with insufficient information to enable them to do the calculations. Nevertheless, the EAT indicated that it was preferable to follow the guidance set out by the Government Actuary's Department, rather than the opinions of experts called by either side, although all such matters are matters of opinion, which the tribunal must itself consider and evaluate.[2] The EAT also discouraged the use of elaborate statistical or other evidence on the assessment of pension rights, and stressed that it was essentially a rough and ready matter.[3]

8.83   By the end of the 1980s, it was clear that the 1980 guidelines required revision. A committee of chairmen of employment tribunals considered this question, and, in consultation with the Government Actuary's Department, produced a new set of guidelines.[4] It is intended that these will be reviewed and updated in line with changes in the field of pensions and pensions law. In *Clancy v Cannock Chase Technical College*,[5] Lindsay J said that careful consideration should be given to whether the guidelines can still be relied upon to give the help they have given in the past and whether a fresh edition ought to be prepared.

8.84   It is important to bear in mind in relation to use of the guidelines, however, as the authors observe, that 'any party is free to canvass any method of assessment which he considers appropriate'.[6] Even so, it is likely that the methods set out will be the most commonly used, since they are fairly simple to use and utilise information which the tribunal is likely to have before it by the end of the hearing. In *Bingham v Hobourn Engineering Ltd*,[7] the EAT said that there is no duty on an employment tribunal to follow the guidelines and, therefore, no error of law in not giving precise effect to the scheme it recommends. In each case, it is a question of

---

[1]   *Lee v IPC Business Press Ltd* [1984] ICR 306.
[2]   *Tradewinds Airways Ltd v Fletcher* [1981] IRLR 272.
[3]   In *Manpower Ltd v Hearne* [1983] ICR 567.
[4]   *Industrial Tribunals: Compensation for Loss of Pension Rights* (HMSO, 1990). A second edition was published in 1991. Extracts from the guidelines are reproduced in Appendix 1 of this book.
[5]   [2001] IRLR 331 at p 336.
[6]   At p 31, para 11.2.
[7]   [1992] IRLR 298.

evaluating the factors on either side to see what adjustment should be made or whether the guidelines are a safe guide at all.

8.85   The one figure which is likely to trouble tribunals is the percentage of reduction for the likelihood of withdrawal (ie that the employee would have left before retirement for reasons other than death or disability). This is a matter for the tribunal to assess after hearing all the evidence. In *TBA Industrial Products Ltd v Locke*,[1] the tribunal applied a withdrawal factor of 70% because of its view that there was 'a very high degree of probability that the employee would have left the employment in any event due either to a continuation of his unsatisfactory work performance or to overall redundancy'. It also applied a 70% reduction in the total compensation awarded for contributory conduct. The employee appealed on the grounds that he had been penalised twice. The EAT upheld the tribunal's approach, saying that the employee's unsatisfactory work performance had to be taken into account for two quite separate purposes.

8.86   Under the guidelines, loss of pension rights falls to be assessed under three heads:

1.   loss of pension rights from the date of dismissal to the date of hearing;
2.   loss of future pension rights; and
3.   loss of enhancement of accrued pension rights.

Appendix 2 of the guidelines contains a set of tables, in the form of flow charts, for calculating each head of loss. A copy of Appendix 2 is set out in Appendix 1 of this book.

8.87   The first head is calculated by taking the employee's gross weekly pensionable pay and the employer's normal contribution as a percentage of the payroll. If the tribunal does not know it or cannot find it out from the employers, it should assume 10% for contributory schemes and 15% for non-contributory schemes. The weekly continuing pension loss thus ascertained should then be multiplied by the number of weeks between the effective date of termination and the date of the hearing: see Appendix 2, table 1 (set out in Appendix 1 of this book, at para A1.04). This figure is not part of the prescribed element.

8.88   The second head is calculated by ascertaining the employee's weekly continuing pension loss in the same way as under the first head. From the figure there should be deducted the new employer's weekly contribution in the new pension scheme (if the employee has found a new job); if there is no scheme, 3% of the weekly wages should be deducted. The figure thus arrived at should be multiplied by the number of weeks allowed for future loss of earnings whether total or partial. See Appendix 2, table 2 (set out in Appendix 1 of this book, at para A1.05).

---

[1]   [1984] ICR 228.

8.89 In *Clancy v Cannock Chase Technical College*,[1] the EAT said that the tribunal erred in calculating compensation in respect of loss of pension rights solely on the basis of the employer's contributions. It said that a system of computation based on the value of the employer's contributions is not appropriate in assessing loss of pension rights under a scheme which yields not only an income benefit but also a lump sum arising as of right rather than by commutation. It commented that the 1991 Guidelines provide no yardstick for the computation of loss in such a case. The resulting figure in the EAT's view could not be just and equitable, since it produced a figure which could not begin to replace the reduction the lump sum and annual pension which the employee would suffer as a result of the dismissal.

8.90 The third head, loss of enhancement of accrued pension rights, is arrived at by taking the deferred pension the employee will receive based on salary at leaving and his or her anticipated age of retirement. The appropriate multiplier should then be applied as set out in the table in Appendix 4 (set out in Appendix 1 of this book, at para A1.07). This amount should then be reduced by a percentage reflecting the tribunal's view of the likelihood of withdrawal (see Appendix 2, table 3 (set out in Appendix 1 of this book, at para A1.06)). There are various situations in which an employee will receive no award under this head. They are also catered for in the flow chart in Appendix 2, table 3 (set out in Appendix 1 of this book, at para A1.06). Examples are employees in public sector schemes, employees in the private sector who are near retirement age, and employees in whose case the tribunal has found that their employment would have terminated in any event within a period of up to a year.

The worked examples at the end of this section contain an example dealing with loss of pension rights.

8.91 **Expenses** Section 123(2)(a) enables any expenses reasonably incurred to be included. These may include the cost of setting up one's own business,[2] but not the cost of presenting a complaint of unfair dismissal.[3] The costs of travel to interviews and of subscribing to appropriate trade journals or papers with job advertisements would be properly included under this head. It is arguable that the tribunal should take into account interest on an overdraft incurred as a result of the dismissal. Assuming that the employee can satisfy the tribunal that the overdraft interest was incurred as a result of the dismissal, section 123(2)(a) is wide enough to cover such an expense.

8.92 **Other losses** As was mentioned earlier, compensation has hitherto only been awarded in respect of financial loss, so that, for example, injury to pride or feelings, or loss of job satisfaction, will not be compensated. This

---

[1]   [2001] IRLR 331.
[2]   *Gardiner-Hill v Roland Berger Technics Ltd* [1982] IRLR 498.
[3]   *Nohar v Granitstone Ltd* (1974) 9 ITR 155.

approach to compensation will now need to be reassessed in the light of Lord Hoffmann's comments in *Johnson v Unisys Ltd*.[1]

8.93   The EAT has also said that the calculation of the compensatory award should exclude loss of allowances, since allowances are either a component of the employee's remuneration and chargeable to tax accordingly, or are paid to reimburse expenses actually incurred. In the latter case, the employee will suffer no loss if the new job has fewer allowances than the old job.[2] Loss caused to the employee by the employer's delay in giving a promised written reference, or failure to do so, should not be included in the calculation of the award.[3]

8.94   A specific head of loss mentioned in section 123(3) is 'loss of any entitlement or potential entitlement to, or expectation of, a payment on account of dismissal by reason of redundancy, whether in pursuance of Part XI or otherwise'. But the loss is to include only the amount by which the redundancy payment would have exceeded the basic award, apart from any reductions under section 122. This is likely to arise where the employee is contractually entitled to a payment on redundancy which is in excess of his or her statutory entitlement. So if, for example, the contractual entitlement is to a payment of double the statutory amount, so that the employee is entitled to £1,500 by way of statutory payment and £3,000 by way of contractual entitlement, the £3,000 will be brought in at this stage. If it has already been paid, then it will be deducted by virtue of section 123(7) (see para 8.119). In this context, the decision of the EAT in *Boorman v Allmakes Ltd*[4] should be noted. Although it is a decision on the equivalent provision relating to basic awards, section 122(4), it is arguable that its reasoning applies in this context also. If that is correct, section 123(7) will only apply to payments made where the dismissal is in fact due to redundancy. (See also para 8.119.) It should be noted that a payment made under section 123(7) falls to be deducted after all other deductions have been made, thus giving the employer full benefit for the payment.[5] The order of deductions is considered more fully at para 8.132.

8.95   Compensation in respect of the loss of fringe benefits will also be dealt with under this head, rather than under the head of loss of earnings to the date of hearing. This is because the Recoupment Regulations only affect actual earnings. A common head of loss, which would fall to be dealt with here, is the loss of a company car. There is little guidance on how to calculate this loss, and the calculation will depend upon whether the employee has the use of the car as well as for the purposes of the job. One way to assess the loss is to take the scale charge for the car and for the petrol provided by the employer for private mileage by reference to which the employee is assessed to tax. For the purposes of taxation, this scale charge is increased if there is a low element of business mileage and

---

[1]   [2001] ICR 480 at p 500.
[2]   *Tradewinds Airways Ltd v Fletcher* [1981] IRLR 272.
[3]   *Gallear v JF Watson & Son Ltd* [1979] IRLR 306.
[4]   [1995] ICR 842.
[5]   *Digital Equipment Co Ltd v Clements (No 2)* [1998] ICR 258.

decreased if there is a high element of business mileage. For the current rate of scale charges, reference should be made to the up-to-date tax tables.

8.96   An alternative method of calculating the loss would be to use the schedule of running costs published by the Automobile Association. This tends to give a higher figure, particularly where the car involved is an expensive model with a large engine capacity.

8.97   There is no direct authority which offers any guidance on which of these two methods of calculating the loss is to be preferred. In *Shove v Downs Surgical plc*[1] (a wrongful dismissal case), Sheen J took the view that the scale charges used to calculate an employee's liability to tax do not afford a useful guide to calculating this head of loss as part of the damages to be awarded; he seems to have preferred the AA guidelines.[2]

8.98   Other fringe benefits which may be included under this head are loss of medical insurance, loss of preferential treatment (for example, low interest or interest-free loans) and loss of rights under a share option scheme.[3] This last type of loss was considered by the Court of Session in *Leonard v Strathclyde Buses Ltd*.[4] During their employment, the employees participated in a share option scheme. On dismissal, they were required to sell back the shares at the then current value of £1.50 per share. Some months after the dismissals, their former employer was acquired by another bus operator; at the time of the takeover, the value of each share was £5.10, with a terminal bonus of 75p per share. The employment tribunal took the change in share value into account in assessing the employees' compensatory award, taking the view that the increase in share value was a benefit which they would have had if their employment had not ended when it did. The Court of Session upheld that approach.

8.99   The effect of *ex gratia* payments paid by the employer should also be noted. If such a payment is made, it should first be set off against the basic award and any surplus should then be carried forward and set off against the compensatory award.[5] If it is an *ex gratia* payment rather than a statutory or contractual redundancy payment, it will be dealt with in calculating the employee's loss and will be brought into the calculation as part of the first stage of calculating the loss from the date of dismissal to date of hearing. It will thus precede any deductions to be made for contributory fault. If, on the other hand, it is a genuine statutory or contractual redundancy payment, it will be deducted *last*, after any deductions for contributory fault and the like. These are considered more fully at para 8.120.

---

[1]   [1984] ICR 532.
[2]   *Ibid* at pp 541–542.
[3]   See, eg, *Casey v Texas Homecare Ltd* (EAT 632/87).
[4]   [1998] IRLR 693.
[5]   *Chelsea Football Club and Athletic Co Ltd v Heath* [1981] ICR 323 and *Rushton v Harcos Timber & Building Supplies Ltd* [1993] ICR 230.

(ii) Mitigation

8.100   Section 123(4) requires the employment tribunal to apply the common law rules relating to mitigation of damages. That provision does not prevent a tribunal taking into account as a failure on the part of an employee to mitigate his or her conduct in unreasonably preventing a re-employment order[1] from being complied with by the employer.[2]

8.101   The tribunal must address its mind to the question of mitigation; a failure to do so will be good grounds for an appeal.[3] It should be noted, however, that it is for the employer to establish that the employee ought reasonably to have taken steps to mitigate his or her loss.[4] The employee's conduct before the dismissal should not be taken into account in determining the question of mitigation.[5] The rules require a dismissed employee to take reasonable steps to minimise his or her loss by looking for another job. If he or she fails to accept a reasonable offer, or to take any reasonable steps, an appropriate amount representing what he or she could have earned will be deducted from the award of compensation.[6] In *Gardiner-Hill v Roland Berger Technics Ltd*,[7] the EAT said that the tribunal in such cases should follow a three-stage process: (1) identify what steps should have been taken by the employee to mitigate his or her loss; (2) find the date upon which such steps would have produced an alternative income; (3) thereafter reduce the amount of compensation by the amount of income which would have been earned. The tribunal should not calculate the compensatory award and reduce the whole award by a percentage.[8] If the employee has obtained another job, the earnings from that job[9] will go towards reducing the amount of compensation; this general rule is subject, however, to exceptions (see paras 8.64 and 8.65).

8.102   The rule to be applied in making deductions for mitigation is that, if the employee is dismissed without notice, net wages will be awarded for the notice period without making a deduction for earnings or potential earnings during the notice period.[10] But credit must be given for payment of salary or wages in lieu of notice received from the employers.[11] This

---

[1]   Under s 114 or 115.

[2]   Section 117(8).

[3]   *Morganite Electrical Carbon Ltd v Donne* [1988] ICR 18.

[4]   *Sturdy Finance Ltd v Bardsley* [1979] IRLR 65 and *Fyfe v Scientific Furnishings Ltd* [1989] ICR 648.

[5]   *Prestwick Circuits Ltd v McAndrew* [1990] IRLR 191.

[6]   *Savage v Saxena* [1998] ICR 357, following *Gardiner-Hill v Roland Berger Technics Ltd* [1982] IRLR 498.

[7]   [1982] IRLR 498.

[8]   *Peara v Enderlin Ltd* [1979] ICR 804. See also *Gardiner-Hill v Roland Berger Technics Ltd* [1982] IRLR 498.

[9]   This includes earnings from part-time employment: see *Justfern Ltd v D'Ingerthorpe* [1994] ICR 286.

[10]   *Norton Tool Co Ltd v Tewson* [1972] ICR 501, *Everwear Candlewick Ltd v Isaac* [1974] ICR 525 and *TBA Industrial Products Ltd v Locke* [1984] ICR 229. *Cf Tradewinds Airways Ltd v Fletcher* [1981] IRLR 272.

[11]   *TBA Industrial Products Ltd v Locke, loc cit.*

position was confirmed by the Court of Appeal in *Addison v Babcock FATA Ltd.*[1]

8.103 It is clear that the employee may be awarded no compensation in respect of loss of earnings, if he or she unreasonably refuses the employer's offer to consider him or her for vacancies which arise after the dismissal[2] or unreasonably refuses an offer of reinstatement (in which case the tribunal may make no compensation award at all).[3] If, however, the employee's refusal of alternative employment precedes the dismissal, the employment tribunal should treat that as contributory conduct rather than a failure to mitigate.[4] In an appropriate case, for example where the employee is in his or her fifties, has occupied a senior position, and tries to utilise the experience gained in the employment by setting up his or her own business, it may be reasonable to try to do that rather than seek alternative employment, and it will not be right to treat that failure as a failure to mitigate.[5] In such cases, it is important to make sure that adequate evidence is put before the tribunal. If the evidence shows that the employee's earnings as a self-employed person will be lower than his or her previous earnings, that fall must be reflected in the amount of compensation awarded.[6] A failure by a dismissed employee to utilise an employer's internal appeal procedure cannot as a matter of law amount to a failure to mitigate his or her loss,[7] although it may cause an adjustment to be made to the compensatory award under section 127A (see para 8.124).

(iii) Contributory fault

8.104 Section 123(6) says:

'Where the tribunal finds that the dismissal was to any extent caused or contributed to by any action of the complainant it shall reduce the amount of the compensatory award by such proportion as it considers just and equitable having regard to that finding.'

The wording of this provision is narrower than the equivalent provision relating to the basic award, section 122(2). If the tribunal finds that the employee has contributed to some extent to the dismissal, it must reflect that finding in the award of compensation.[8] In *Optikinetics Ltd v Whooley,*[9] the EAT pointed out that section 122(2) gives the tribunal a wide discretion

---

[1] [1987] ICR 805.

[2] *Gallear v JF Watson & Son Ltd* [1979] IRLR 306.

[3] *Sweetlove v Redbridge & Waltham Forest Area Health Authority* [1979] IRLR 195. See also *Johnson v Hobart Manufacturing Co Ltd* (EAT 210/89).

[4] *Trimble v Supertravel Ltd* [1982] IRLR 451. See also *Martin v Yeoman Aggregates Ltd* [1983] ICR 314.

[5] *Gardiner-Hill v Roland Berger Technics Ltd* [1982] IRLR 498.

[6] *Lee v IPC Business Press Ltd* [1984] ICR 306.

[7] *Lock v Connell Estate Agents* [1994] ICR 983. The EAT did not follow its previous decision in *Hoover Ltd v Forde* [1980] ICR 239, but instead followed the later decision of the Scottish division of the EAT in *William Muir (Bond 9) Ltd v Lamb* [1985] IRLR 95.

[8] *Morganite Electrical Carbon Ltd v Donne* [1988] ICR 18.

[9] [1999] ICR 984.

whether to make any, and if so what, reduction in the basic award on the grounds of the employee's conduct and that it is open to it to conclude that no reduction should be made. On the other hand, section 123(6) *requires* the tribunal to make a reduction once it has found that there was contributory conduct. It is not open to the tribunal, once it has found the employee guilty of contributory conduct, not to reduce the compensatory award at all; nor is it open to it to override its finding of causative conduct on the part of the employee by reference to the conduct of the employer. Thus, it is not possible for the tribunal to reflect its view of the employer's conduct by making no deduction for contributory conduct, where the employee is in fact guilty of such conduct.

A finding of contributory fault may also affect the tribunal's decision as to whether to make a re-employment order: see Chapter 7.

8.105 The contributory conduct relied upon by the employer must be conduct of which the employer was aware at the time of the dismissal, as a result of which the employer dismissed the employee. If the employer was not aware of the misconduct, then section 123(6) is not applicable and section 123(1) will apply.[1] Similarly, conduct which occurs after the dismissal is not relevant to the issue of whether the employee's conduct caused or contributed to the dismissal.[2]

8.106 In cases where a dismissal is to be regarded as unfair by virtue of section 152 or 153 of the Trade Union and Labour Relations (Consolidation) Act 1992, section 155 of that Act provides that certain contributory conduct (in relation to union membership requirements) should be disregarded.[3]

8.107 To make a reduction, the tribunal must make three findings:

1. that there was conduct on the part of the employee which was culpable or blameworthy, in the sense that it was 'perverse or foolish, or ... bloody-minded ... or unreasonable in all the circumstances';
2. that the dismissal was caused or contributed to to some extent by that conduct; and
3. that it was just and equitable, having regard to the first and second findings, to reduce the assessment of the employee's loss to a specified extent.[4]

8.108 Of the second, the EAT has said this:

'... [W]hen one looks at what the Act requires, which is a finding that the dismissal was to any extent caused or contributed by any action of the complainant it is ... clear that no such direct and exclusive causal connection as

---

[1] *Tele-Trading Ltd v Jenkins* [1990] IRLR 430 (see also para 8.51).
[2] *Soros v Davison* [1994] ICR 590.
[3] See *Transport and General Workers' Union v Howard* [1992] ICR 106, considered at para 8.59.
[4] *Nelson v BBC (No 2)* [1979] ICR 110 at pp 121–122 (Brandon LJ).

a sole or principal or operative cause, is to be discerned in the statutory requirements. It is much looser than that ...'[1]

8.109   It appears also to be possible to make a reduction in cases of dismissal for lack of capacity.[2] It will not amount to unreasonable conduct if the employee's action is lawful and proper, such as a refusal to obey an unlawful order.[3]

8.110   The assessment of contributory fault is a separate stage in the procedure of fixing compensation, which should be clearly indicated by the tribunal.[4] The Scottish division of the EAT has said that, in cases of constructive dismissal, it would be exceptional for the employee to be held to have contributed to the dismissal.[5] But, as the Northern Ireland Court of Appeal has made clear, the statutory provisions allow a reduction for contributory fault in every kind of unfair dismissal, whether express or constructive, and their language does not suggest than an exception should or may be made in cases of unfair constructive dismissal. As that Court pointed out, the three concepts of constructive dismissal, unfair dismissal and contributory fault are distinct and each requires a separate consideration and decision at a different stage in an unfair dismissal claim.[6] This was followed in *Polentarutti v Autokraft Ltd*[7] by the EAT, which also observed that in constructive dismissals cases it is not necessary to show exceptional circumstances before a finding of contributory conduct can be made.

8.111   The tribunal should approach the question of contributory fault in a broad common-sense manner and the EAT is not entitled to interfere with its conclusion unless the tribunal is wrong in law or its conclusion is one which no reasonable tribunal could have reached on the evidence; the apportionment of responsibility for the dismissal is a matter of impression, opinion and discretion.[8] There must be a causal connection between the actions of the employee and the dismissal, but the connection need not be direct and exclusive. In *Hutchinson v Enfield Rolling Mills Ltd,*[9] for example, the employee was dismissed for attending a union demonstration in Brighton, after presenting a sick note to his employers for that day. The EAT said, *obiter*, that that fact made a causative contribution to the dismissal, but indicated that the tribunal had been wrong to take other facts into consideration, such as that he had been a troublemaker throughout his employment and that his political views were affecting his work. The Court of Appeal has made it clear that in assessing contributory fault, the

---

[1]   In *Polentarutti v Autokraft Ltd* [1991] ICR 757 at p 769.
[2]   *Finnie v Top Hat Frozen Foods* [1985] ICR 433.
[3]   *Morrish v Henlys (Folkestone) Ltd* [1973] ICR 482.
[4]   *Nudds v W & JB Eastwood Ltd* [1978] ICR 171.
[5]   *Holroyd v Gravure Cylinders Ltd* [1984] IRLR 259.
[6]   *Morrison v Amalgamated Transport & General Workers' Union* [1989] IRLR 361.
[7]   [1991] ICR 757.
[8]   *Maris v Rotherham CBC* [1974] ICR 435, *Hollier v Plysu Ltd* [1983] IRLR 260 (CA) and *Warrilow v Robert Walker Ltd* [1984] IRLR 304.
[9]   [1981] IRLR 318, particularly at p 320, para 11.

statutory provisions require the tribunal to confine its inquiry to the conduct of the employee and decide whether that conduct requires the amount of compensation to be reduced.[1] This means that, for example, in the case of an employee involved in a fight who is dismissed, whereas the other person involved is not, it is not permissible to reduce the contributory element to take into account the way the other employee is treated. This decision must cast doubt on whether it is permissible to reduce the contribution if the employers are to some extent at fault.[2] In assessing contributory fault, acts of the employee's agent (eg advice given by solicitors) may be taken into account.[3]

8.112   The EAT has suggested that if facts come to light after the tribunal's decision (such as a subsequent criminal conviction), the employer may apply to the tribunal for a review of its decision on contribution and the tribunal may reduce the award of compensation.[4] This decision appears to be in conflict with the House of Lords' decision in *W Devis & Sons Ltd v Atkins*.[5] In such cases, where misconduct is discovered by the employer after the dismissal, that should be reflected in the initial assessment of the compensatory award (which may be reduced to nil in consequence) and is not a matter of contributory fault. Conduct which occurs after the dismissal is not relevant to the issue of whether the employee's conduct caused or contributed to the dismissal.[6]

8.113   A further question which needs to be addressed in the light of the fact that tribunals are required to consider reducing compensation in circumstances covered by *Polkey v AE Dayton Services Ltd*[7] is the effect of contributory fault on a *Polkey* reduction. This question was considered by the Court of Appeal in *Rao v Civil Aviation Authority*.[8] The question arises in cases where the tribunal takes the view that there is a degree of uncertainty as to whether the employee would have been fairly dismissed if the proper procedure had followed. In that case, the tribunal should calculate the loss of earnings and make appropriate deductions for mitigation. This order – reduction for contribution followed by *Polkey* reduction – is the order set out by the employment tribunal and supported by the EAT.[9] The Court of Appeal, however, whilst agreeing with the general approach, reversed the order, so that the *Polkey* reduction is made first and the deduction for conduct is made after that.[10] These differences of approach do not appear to affect the amount of compensation, which will be the same whichever

---

[1]   In *Parker Foundry Ltd v Slack* [1992] ICR 302. See also *Allders International Ltd v Parkins* [1981] IRLR 68.

[2]   As was held in *Gibson v British Transport Docks Board* [1982] IRLR 228, in which *Allders International Ltd v Parkins* appears not to have been cited.

[3]   *Allen v Hammett* [1982] ICR 227.

[4]   In *Ladup Ltd v Barnes* [1982] ICR 107.

[5]   [1977] ICR 662.

[6]   *Soros v Davison* [1994] ICR 590.

[7]   [1988] ICR 142 (see paras 8.53 *et seq*, where the relevant cases are considered).

[8]   [1994] ICR 495.

[9]   See [1992] ICR 503.

[10]   [1994] ICR 495 at p 501F.

order is used. It is important to note that a *Polkey* reduction is separate from a reduction for contributory fault under section 123(6).[1]

8.114   Finally, the effect of the taking of industrial action to be considered in relation to contributory fault. In *Courtaulds Northern Spinning Ltd v Moosa*,[2] the EAT said that the taking of industrial action should not be characterised as contributory fault. In *TNT Express (UK) Ltd v Downes*,[3] however, it decided that the previous decision should not be followed, and employment tribunals were entitled to examine the facts and circumstances surrounding the dismissal, including the circumstances surrounding the industrial action. In *Tracey v Crosville Wales Ltd*,[4] however, the Court of Appeal approved the EAT's decision in *Courtaulds Northern Spinning Ltd v Moosa* and said that the tribunal should ignore the conduct represented by the industrial action in which the applicant had participated, but that other blameworthy conduct of the applicant causing or contributing to the dismissal should be taken into account when deciding upon a reduction in compensation. The House of Lords dismissed the employers' appeal against the Court of Appeal's decision and approved the EAT's decision in *Courtaulds Northern Spinning Ltd v Moosa*.[5]

8.115   The actual amount of the reduction for contributory fault is a question of fact for the tribunal, but it may be up to 100%.[6] Although section 123(5) does not allow compensation to reflect the loss suffered by the employee as a consequence of industrial pressure, his or her conduct in provoking that pressure may be relevant in assessing contributory fault.[7]

8.116   As has been seen, the amount of contribution is to be assessed in a broad common sense manner by the employment tribunal, and much will depend upon its findings. This makes it difficult to cite cases, except as illustrations. Examples of a 25% reduction are dismissal after being in a fight with another employee[8] and dismissal for a relatively minor and unintentional mistake (the placing of bodies in the wrong coffins).[9] Examples of a 50% reduction are dismissal for a refusal to co-operate and perform the required duties[10] and a (constructive) dismissal contributed to by the employee's over-sensitiveness, which caused her to over-react.[11] An example of a 75% reduction is the dismissal of a union shop steward for a

---

[1]   *Campbell v Dunoon & Cowal Housing Association* [1993] IRLR 496.
[2]   [1984] ICR 218.
[3]   [1994] ICR 1.
[4]   [1996] ICR 237.
[5]   *Tracey v Crosville Wales Ltd* [1997] ICR 862.
[6]   See, eg, *Smith v Lodge Bros (Funerals) Ltd* (EAT 92/88) and *Chaplin v HJ Rawlinson Ltd* [1991] ICR 553.
[7]   *Sulemanji v Toughened Glass Ltd* [1979] ICR 799 (the employee stopped paying his union subscriptions); see also *Colwyn BC v Dutton* [1980] IRLR 420.
[8]   *Taylor v Parsons Peebles NEI Bruce Peebles Ltd* [1981] IRLR 119. Cf *Munif v Cole and Kirby Ltd* [1973] ICR 486, where the reduction was 75% because of a threat of direct physical violence to a manager.
[9]   *Coalter v Walter Craven Ltd* [1980] IRLR 262.
[10]   *UBAF Bank Ltd v Davis* [1978] IRLR 422.
[11]   *Associated Tyre Specialists (Eastern) Ltd v Waterhouse* [1977] ICR 218. Cf *Holroyd v Gravure Cylinders* [1984] IRLR 259.

serious contravention of an agreement between the management and the workforce concerning the length of a lunch break just before Christmas.[1] An example of a 90% reduction is *Gibson v British Transport Docks Board*,[2] where the employees were held to be substantially to blame, because they set out to intimidate, in the course of picketing, fellow-employees whose conduct they disapproved of and stood by when physical violence developed; the contribution was reduced from 100% by the EAT because it held the employers 10% to blame. Examples of a 100% contribution are *Thompson v Woodland Designs Ltd*,[3] where the employee left work without telling anyone he was going and induced in the minds of his employers the view that he had been at a meeting called to consider strike action, and *Allders International Ltd v Parkins*,[4] where the 100% contribution was based on the employment tribunal's finding that, had the correct procedure been followed, the employee could have been fairly dismissed. Notwithstanding this authority, it must remain debatable whether an unfair dismissal in which the employee is held to be 100% to blame should be held to have been unfair.

8.117   In certain cases, the employment tribunal may have to consider carefully whether to categorise the employee's conduct as amounting to a failure to mitigate or as contributory conduct. In *Trimble v Supertravel Ltd*,[5] for example, the employee was dismissed after she refused to transfer from one job to another. The employment tribunal held that this amounted to a failure to mitigate, but the EAT suggested that this was an error, since mitigation follows a breach of contract and does not precede it, and that the conduct might be better characterised as contributory conduct.

8.118   The amount of the contribution should be deducted from the total amount of the compensatory award, ignoring the statutory maximum (£51,700). The maximum only operates if the reduced figure exceeds £51,700.[6] (See also the section on the order of calculation, below.)

(iv) Other deductions

8.119   Section 123(7) provides that, if the amount by which any redundancy payment paid by the employer to the employee (whether paid in pursuance of the employer's statutory obligation or otherwise) exceeds the basic award which would be payable but for section 124(4), that amount will be deducted from the compensatory award. This provision is the obverse of section 123(3), which provides for the tribunal to take into account an employee's entitlement to a redundancy payment in excess of

---

[1]   *Wells v Derwent Plastics Ltd* [1978] ICR 425.

[2]   [1982] IRLR 228.

[3]   [1980] IRLR 423.

[4]   [1981] IRLR 68. The view that the employer's conduct was not relevant was not followed in the later case of *Gibson v British Transport Docks Board, loc cit* in which the instant case was not cited.

[5]   [1982] IRLR 451.

[6]   Section 124(1). See *Walter Braund (London) Ltd v Murray* [1991] ICR 327.

the statutory amount. The entitlement is to be taken into account in calculating the compensatory award, but must be deducted if actually paid. The sort of payments likely to be affected here are payments to which employees are contractually entitled on redundancy under schemes set up by their employers. Such payments are likely to be calculated by reference to the employee's statutory entitlement, but to exceed it. Thus an employee entitled to a statutory payment of £1,500 may also be entitled to receive £3,000 from an employer's scheme, if, for example, the scheme provides for payments to be made of double the statutory amount.

8.120 It is important to note that there is a difference between statutory or contractual redundancy payments, on the one hand, and *ex gratia* payments, on the other hand. A statutory or contractual redundancy payment is one made *by reason of the employee's redundancy*, whereas, as its name implies, an *ex gratia* payment is one made by the employer to offset contingent liability. Although it might be thought that there is little difference between the two types of payment, there is considerable significance when it comes to their position in the order of deductions. An *ex gratia* payment should be taken into account at the point of initial assessment of the employee's loss and before making a *Polkey* deduction or a deduction for contributory fault. On the other hand, a statutory or contractual redundancy payment should be deducted last, after all the other deductions – including *Polkey* deductions and deductions for contributory fault. This is made clear by the Court of Appeal's decision in *Digital Equipment Co Ltd v Clements (No 2)*,[1] where the Court of Appeal expressed its view that the reason for this must have been that Parliament intended that an employer who pays compensation for redundancy on a more generous scale than the statutory scale is to be entitled to full credit for the additional payment against the amount of loss which makes up the compensatory award.[2]

8.121 If an *ex gratia* payment is made, it should first be set off against the basic award and any surplus should then be carried forward and set off against the compensatory award.[3] If there is any surplus after that, and an additional award falls to be made, the surplus should be set off against any additional award.[4] The *ex gratia* payment or any other amount of money paid by the employer must expressly or impliedly be referable to the award

[1] [1998] ICR 258.
[2] Beldam LJ at p 267C.
[3] *Chelsea Football Club and Athletic Co Ltd v Heath* [1981] ICR 323 and *Rushton v Harcos Timber & Building Supplies Ltd* [1993] ICR 230. *Cf Roadchef Ltd v Hastings* [1988] IRLR 142, where the tribunal did not offset an *ex gratia* payment since it considered that an employer acting reasonably would have made the same payment after a period of prior warning. The EAT held that the tribunal was entitled to make that finding: there was nothing to indicate that the employers would not have paid the same moneys after a period of warning.
[4] *Darr v LRC Products Ltd* [1993] IRLR 257.

of compensation.[1] If the dismissal is for redundancy and the employer pays a redundancy payment and an *ex gratia* payment, the redundancy payment will be set off against the basic award and the *ex gratia* payment against the compensatory and, if appropriate, additional award.[2] If the amount of the redundancy payment exceeds the basic award, the surplus will be set off against the compensatory award, but the *ex gratia* payment will already have been used to assess the employee's loss.

8.122   A deduction should only be made in respect of sickness benefit received by the employee if, had the employment continued, the benefit would have been deducted from his or her wages or he or she would have been disentitled from receiving any sickness benefit.[3] Statutory sick pay and invalidity benefit should be deducted.[4]

8.123   If the employee receives a tax rebate of any size, that may be deductible, as may any damages for wrongful dismissal already awarded. No deductions are made in respect of jobseeker's allowance or income support received by the employee, but part of the compensatory award is subject to the Employment Protection (Recoupment of Jobseeker's Allowance and Income Support) Regulations 1996 (see below).

(v) Internal appeal procedures

8.124   The provisions of section 127A[5] enable a tribunal to reduce or increase the compensatory award, but by no more than two weeks' pay either way. The tribunal may *reduce* the award where the employee has failed to take advantage of an internal appeals procedure. For this to apply, the tribunal must find that:

(a)   the employer provided an internal appeals procedure;
(b)   the employee was given, at the time of dismissal or within a reasonable period afterwards, written notice of its existence and including written details of it; and
(c)   the employee did not appeal against the dismissal under the procedure (unless the employer prevented him or her from doing so).[6]

---

[1]   *Chelsea Football Club & Athletic Co Ltd v Heath* [1981] ICR 323 at p 327. In *Simrad Ltd v Scott* [1997] IRLR 147, the EAT said that the employment tribunal had erred in treating as an *ex gratia* payment a loan whose repayment was waived by the employers when they dismissed the employee.

[2]   *Rushton v Harcos Timber & Building Supplies Ltd* [1993] ICR 230.

[3]   *Sun & Sand Ltd v Fitzjohn* [1979] ICR 268.

[4]   *Puglia v C James & Sons* [1996] ICR 301. The EAT did not follow the earlier decision of another division in *Hilton International Hotels (UK) Ltd v Faraji* [1994] ICR 259. *Cf Rubenstein and Roskin t/a McGuffies Dispensing Chemists v McGloughlin* [1996] IRLR 557, in which it was decided that it was just and equitable to deduct half of the invalidity benefit received by the employee.

[5]   Introduced by the Employment Rights (Dispute Resolution) Act 1998, s 13.

[6]   Section 127A(1).

If the tribunal makes these findings, it may reduce the compensatory award by an amount it considers just and equitable, subject to a maximum of two weeks' pay.[1]

Conversely, if the tribunal finds that the employer provided an internal appeals procedure but prevented the employee from appealing against the dismissal under the procedure, it may make a supplementary award of an amount it considers just and equitable, again subject to a maximum of two weeks' pay.[2]

In both cases, when determining the amount of the reduction or supplementary award, the tribunal must 'have regard' to all the circumstances of the case, 'including in particular the chances that an appeal under the procedure ... would have been successful'.

8.126   It is not immediately clear whether the supplementary award falls within the statutory limit or not. Section 124 speaks of compensation awarded under section 123 and says that such compensation is not to exceed the limit. That being so, it is submitted that a supplementary award should be added or subtracted at the very end, after the statutory limit has been applied. Needless to say, the circumstances in which such an issue might arise must be rare indeed.

(vi) Removal of statutory limit on the amount of compensation

8.127   There are two types of unfair dismissal where there is no limit to the amount of compensation which may be awarded. These are cases in which the dismissal is unfair because it is contrary to section 100[3] or 103A,[4] or because the employee was selected for reasons falling within either of those provisions.[5] This is an exception to the general rule that the compensatory award is subject to a limit of £51,700.

8.128   It should be noted that these two types of dismissal are the first types of unfair dismissal in respect of which compensation may be unlimited. Hitherto, compensation for all types of unfair dismissal has been limited, although in certain types of situation provision has been made for the compensation to be increased, for example, by a special award.[6] This change is important and it gives rise to issues relating to how compensatory awards of compensation for the types of unfair dismissal covered by sections 100 and 103A should be calculated and whether an award of compensation may include aggravated damages. The analogy that comes to mind is that of compensation in discrimination cases, where the principles of calculation of compensation are analogous to those used when calculating damages for personal injury. It is suggested, therefore,

---

[1]   Section 127A(1) and (4).
[2]   Section 127A(2) and (4).
[3]   Dismissals in health and safety cases (see paras 5.57 *et seq*).
[4]   Dismissals for making a 'protected disclosure' (see para 5.82).
[5]   Section 124(1A), introduced by ERA 1999, s 37(1).
[6]   The provisions relating to special awards were repealed by the ERA 1999.

that a tribunal confronted with this type of unfair dismissal will need to have regard, in appropriate circumstances, to the Ogden Tables.[1] In such cases, an appropriate multiplier will be applied to a 'multiplicand', which is one year's total loss. The multiplier should be selected from the Ogden Tables, but will need to be discounted to reflect the contingencies of life, eg the geographical region in which the applicant worked, the type of employment (manual or sedentary) in which he or she would have remained, and the state of the economy.

8.129   When using the Ogden Tables, the following steps should be taken:

1.   Choose the appropriate table (from Tables 13–16) depending on the pension age and sex of the applicant.
2.   Choose the appropriate rate of return, at present 2.5%, following the House of Lords' decision in *Wells v Wells*.[2]
3.   Find the figure under the column in the table chosen given against the age at the date of the hearing.
4.   Adjust the figure to take account of the contingencies of life using Section B of the Tables.
5.   Multiply the annual loss by the adjusted multiplier.

8.130   Use of the Ogden Tables will not always be appropriate, and it is suggested that they are most likely to be appropriate where the dismissal of the employee involves a claim for future loss extending over a fairly lengthy period, if not to retirement.

8.131   In addition, in cases where the payment made exceeds £30,000, it will be necessary to take into account the tax position and the effect of the relevant tax legislation. This is considered more fully below and in Chapter 10.

(vii) The order of calculation

8.132   Section 124(5) provides that the statutory maximum for a compensatory award (£51,700) should be ignored until the very end of the calculation. There has been disagreement in recent cases as to the correct order for calculating a compensatory award. The issue has concerned the stage of the calculation at which termination payments made by the employer, the *Polkey* reduction and a deduction for contributory fault should be applied. Clearly, the order in which these matters are dealt with will affect the size of the award. In *Digital Equipment Co Ltd v*

---

1   The Government Actuary's Department *Actuarial Tables for use in Personal Injury and Fatal Accident cases* (3rd edn).
2   [1999] AC 345. This was confirmed in *Warren v Northern General Hospital Trust (No 2)* [2000] 1 WLR 1404, but a reduced rate of 2% was allowed by Latham J in *Barry v Ablerex Construction (Midlands) Ltd* [2000] PIQR Q263. The rate was reduced from 3% with effect from 28 June 2001.

Clements (No 2),[1] the President of the EAT, Morison J, set out the principles to be followed when dealing with payments made by the employer and deductions for contributory fault and/or *Polkey* reductions. The case went to the Court of Appeal.[2] Although that Court allowed the appeal, the only point at issue on the appeal concerned a contractual redundancy payment and the point at which it ought to have been deducted. In other respects, the Court of Appeal does not appear to have overturned the EAT's decision; rather, it seems to have made an addition to it.

8.133   As a result of these two decisions, it is submitted that the position is as set out by the EAT, but subject to the addition made by the Court of Appeal. The first task of the employment tribunal in calculating the compensatory award is to ascertain the 'loss' sustained by the employee in consequence of the dismissal. The loss is the balance struck after losses and gains have been reckoned, and will include any *ex gratia* payment. To that loss there should be applied a percentage reduction, if appropriate, to reflect the possibility that he or she might have been dismissed in any event, and any deduction for contributory fault. Thus, any *ex gratia* payment should be deducted before any contribution for contributory fault[3] and before the statutory maximum is applied.[4] If the payment made by the employer was a statutory or contractual redundancy payment, that payment should be deducted last, thus giving the employer the full benefit of the payment. Clearly, an employer who makes such a payment will pay a smaller compensatory award than one who pays an *ex gratia* payment and it might, therefore, be tempting for employers to attempt to disguise an *ex gratia* payment as a statutory or contractual redundancy payment. The point, however, is that such a payment would only fall within the relevant statutory provisions[5] if it was made where the dismissal was *by reason of redundancy*, since the statutory provisions only apply to dismissals for redundancy. If the dismissal was not, for this reason it would not be possible to dress up an *ex gratia* payment to attract the benefit of being added last in the order of deductions.

8.134   The order is, therefore, as follows:

1.   Take the loss of earnings to the date of hearing (after allowing for failure to mitigate); then

2.   (a)   deduct the amount of the *ex gratia* payment not deducted from the basic award;

    (b)   deduct the amount of any wages paid in lieu of notice; and

---

[1]   [1997] ICR 237. The EAT followed its previous decisions in *UBAF Bank Ltd v Davis* [1978] IRLR 422 and *Parker & Farr Ltd v Shelvey* [1979] ICR 896. It did not follow its previous decisions in *Clement-Clarke International Ltd v Manley* [1979] ICR 74, *Derwent Coachworks v Kirby* [1995] ICR 48 and *Cox v Camden London Borough Council* [1996] ICR 815.

[2]   [1998] ICR 258.

[3]   *Parker & Farr Ltd v Shelvey* [1979] ICR 896, followed in *Digital Equipment Co Ltd v Clements (No 2)* [1997] ICR 237.

[4]   *McCarthy v BICC plc* [1985] IRLR 94.

[5]   Sections 122(4) and 123(7).

(c)   deduct any earnings received to the date of the hearing (but excluding wages earned from alternative employment during the period covered by the wages in lieu);
3.   the sub-total arrived at is the employee's 'loss';
4.   deduct from that figure any amount for contributory fault;
5.   the total thus far is the 'prescribed element';
6.   add up the other heads of compensation as follows:
        (a)   estimated future loss of wages;
        (b)   loss of other benefits (before and after hearing);
        (c)   loss of statutory industrial rights;
        (d)   loss of redundancy rights in excess of statutory entitlement;
        (e)   loss of pension rights;
        (f)   expenses incurred; then
7.   from the sub-total arrived at after step 6, deduct amount for contributory fault;
8.   aggregate sub-totals arrived at in steps 5 and 7; then
9.   if appropriate, make a *Polkey* reduction, but only from the compensatory award;
10.   deduct any excess of redundancy payment (whether statutory or contractual) over the basic award paid by the employer;
11.   if the total exceeds £51,700, reduce to £51,700;
12.   if a supplementary award is made under section 127A, add that award; if a reduction falls to be made, make that adjustment.

8.135   It is important when reducing the total to £51,700 to reduce all the elements in the compensatory award *pro rata.*[1] Otherwise, the prescribed element would bear the wrong proportion to the rest of the compensatory award, and there would be either too little or too much recoupment.

8.136   In a case where the compensatory award exceeds £30,000, the amount of the excess over £30,000 should be grossed up and £30,000 then added to it. In other words, if the compensatory award is £45,000, £15,000 should be grossed up and then added to £30,000. If the total arrived at exceeds £51,700, the award should be reduced to that amount. It would be an error, it is submitted, to make an award in excess of £51,700, even if the figure arrived at results from doing a grossing-up calculation.

(viii) Recoupment of job seeker's allowance and income support

8.137   The compensatory award is not subject to deductions in respect of any jobseeker's allowance and/or income support received by the employee. However, to prevent the employee recovering twice over for days on which jobseeker's allowance has been paid, the Employment Protection (Recoupment of Jobseeker's Allowance and Income Support) Regulations 1996[2] have been brought into effect. Regulation 4(8) provides

---

[1]   See the Recoupment Regulations, reg 4(2). See also *Mason v Wimpey Waste Management Ltd and Secretary of State for Employment* [1982] IRLR 454 and *Tipton v West Midlands Co-operative Society Ltd (No 2)* (EAT 859/86).

[2]   SI 1996 No 2349.

that the Regulations do not apply if the employee has not received or claimed jobseeker's allowance, and, accordingly, the tribunal will need to satisfy itself on this score. In setting out the award of compensation (called the 'monetary award'), regulation 4(3) or (4) obliges the tribunal to indicate the amount of the 'prescribed element' (whether it announces its decision after the hearing or sends it to the parties later). The prescribed element is the amount awarded for loss of wages for the period up to the date of the hearing (if the decision is announced then) or the date on which the decision is sent to the parties, if the decision is reserved;[1] it is net of all deductions (eg for contributory fault) and does not take into account any jobseeker's allowance or income support received by the employee.[2] Losses of benefits other than earnings incurred during the period covered by the prescribed element should not be included, since they are not losses of earnings. Regulation 4(4) obliges the tribunal to explain the effect of the Regulations when it announces its decision.

8.138 Regulation 7 provides that the amount of any jobseeker's allowance or income support paid to the employee is liable to be recouped by the Department of Employment from the prescribed element. When paying the compensation to the employee, the employer must be told to retain the prescribed element until the Department of Employment has served a recoupment notice or given written notification that it does not intend to serve a recoupment notice.[3] The recoupment notice (or the notification that there will be no recoupment) must be served within 21 days after the conclusion of the hearing or within nine days of the decision being sent to the parties, whichever is the later (in the case of a decision announced at the hearing), or within 21 days of the decision being sent to the parties (if judgment was reserved), or, in both cases, as soon as reasonably practicable afterwards.[4] If after recoupment any of the prescribed element remains, regulation 8(8) provides that the employer must pay the balance to the employee. There is no appeal against the amount specified in the recoupment notice.

8.139 Recoupment will not operate where there is a private settlement or a settlement reached after conciliation.

(ix) Compensation in cases of unfair dismissal and wrongful dismissal

8.140 As a result of the Employment Tribunals Extension of Jurisdiction (England and Wales) Order 1994[5] employment tribunals now have jurisdiction in breach of contract cases. The maximum amount of compensation they may award in such cases is £25,000. The question which arises is how compensation should be calculated in cases where the employee launches a successful dual claim in the tribunal for unfair dismissal and wrongful dismissal.

---

[1] Regulations 3(1)(a) and 2(1) and Col 3 of the Schedule.
[2] Regulation 4(1) and (2).
[3] Regulation 7(1) and (2).
[4] See reg 8(5) and (6).
[5] Discussed in Chapter 9, at paras 9.65 *et seq.*

8.141   As will be seen from Chapter 10, where the common law principles of damages are discussed, the measure of damages is limited to the loss sustained by the employee until the time when the employment could have been lawfully terminated by the employer. Thus, an employee who is entitled to three months' notice is only entitled at common law to the loss of wages and other benefits to which he or she was contractually entitled during the notice period.

8.142   In a case where a dual claim is involved, the principle of double recovery means that, in calculating compensation for unfair dismissal, the tribunal should not compensate an employee twice for the same loss. As may be seen from paras 8.63 *et seq*, one of the main heads of loss which may be covered by a compensatory award is the immediate loss of wages, that is the loss of wages from the date of termination to the date of hearing of the claim. In calculating that head of loss, the tribunal would breach the principle of double recovery if it were to award damages under the 1994 Order in respect of the loss of earnings for three months from the date of termination, and compensation for unfair dismissal in respect of the same period. To the extent that the damages and compensation are in respect of the same period, they should be set off against each other. Further, it should be noted that damages under the 1994 Order could not include any element of future loss, unless the employee's notice period was so long that it extended beyond the date of the hearing. Even so, however, the measure of damages would still be the loss sustained by the employee as a result of the employer's failure to give the notice required by the contract.

8.143   On the other hand, the principle of double recovery would not be breached if the tribunal awarded damages under the 1994 Order for the period of the employee's notice starting with the date of termination and then calculated compensation for unfair dismissal so as to start from the end of the notice period. If it were to take such a step, there would be a risk, from the employer's point of view, that the level of compensation would be higher. This is particularly likely to arise in the case of an employee who has had a fairly high rate of pay, but not sufficiently high to warrant suing in the High Court or county court. Bearing in mind that the maximum compensation that may be awarded under the 1994 Order and the 1996 Act is £76,700 (ie £25,000 + £51,700), a tribunal could use up the £25,000 limit first by awarding damages for the employee's notice period. A compensatory award of unfair dismissal in respect of the remaining period up to the date of the hearing might then use up the limit of £11,300. That would be reduced if some of the compensatory award were set off against the damages.

This issue is potentially important, but it has not yet been considered in a decided case and awaits the attention of the tribunals and the EAT.

(x) Examples

8.144 The following examples illustrate the calculation of the various heads of the compensatory award, including deductions, and the operation of the Recoupment Regulations.

Example 10

8.145 Employee continuously employed for five years, earning £150 per week, aged 27. Summarily dismissed, obtains new job at same wages after four weeks. No contributory fault; no loss of pension rights. Hearing takes place 20 weeks after dismissal.

1. **Basic award** =	£750
2. **Compensatory award**	
(a) Net average wages of, say, £115 per week for 20 weeks =	£2,300
LESS earnings =	£1,725
PRESCRIBED ELEMENT =	£575
(b) Other losses	
Loss of future protection =	£100
Expenses incurred =	£25
TOTAL of (b) =	£125
Total 1 =	£750
Total 2(a) =	£575
Total 2(b) =	£125
GRAND TOTAL =	£1,450

Notes

1. The Recoupment Regulations will not apply if the employee has not received or claimed jobseeker's allowance.

2. The deduction of £1,725 for earnings is calculated from the end of the notice period to which he was entitled (five weeks) to the date of the hearing, ie 15 weeks.

Example 11

8.146 Employee aged 55, continuously employed for 10 years, earning £15,000 per annum, plus company car. Dismissed with two months' wages in lieu of notice of £2,500 (ie 2 x £1,250), and obtains new job at salary of £16,000 per annum after six months. Contributory fault of 25%. No loss of pension rights. The date of the tribunal hearing is seven months after the date of dismissal.

1. Basic award =	£3,600.00
LESS 25% =	£900.00
TOTAL =	<u>£2,700.00</u>
2. Compensatory award	
(a) Net wages of, say, £850 per calendar month for seven months =	£5,950.00
LESS payment in lieu of notice =	£2,500.00
LESS earnings in new employment, of, say, £950 per month, for one month =	£950.00
Sub-total =	<u>£2,500.00</u>
LESS 25% =	£625.00
PRESCRIBED ELEMENT =	<u>£1,875.00</u>
(b) (i) Loss of use of car for period unemployed =	£1,350.00
(ii) Loss of statutory rights =	£150.00
(iii) Expenses =	£75.00
Sub-total =	<u>£1,575.00</u>
LESS 25% =	£393.75
TOTAL of (b) =	<u>£1,181.25</u>
Total 1 =	£2,700.00
Total 2(a) =	£1,875.00
Total 2(b) =	£1,181.25
GRAND TOTAL =	<u>£5,756.25</u>

Notes

1. The basic award is calculated on the basis of the maximum permissible week's pay of £240, although the actual week's pay exceeds that.

2. The actual net wages would depend upon the employee's circumstances (eg mortgage, plus personal allowances).

Example 12

8.147   Employee aged 46, continuously employed for 15 years, earning £17,500 per annum. Dismissed with *ex gratia* payment of £4,375 (ie three months' gross salary). Obtains new job at salary of £18,000 after two months. Contributory fault of 10%. Tribunal hearing is four months after date of dismissal.

1. Basic award

(1.5 x 5 x £240) =	£1,800.00
+ 1 x 10 x £240 =	£2,400.00
Sub-total =	£4,200.00
LESS ex *gratia* payment =	£4,375.00
Sub-total =	NIL

(NB Surplus of £175 to be deducted from compensatory award.)

2. Compensatory award

(a) Net wages of, say, £1,050 per month for the four months to the date of the hearing =	£4,200.00
LESS two months' net earnings from new employment @, say, £1,100 pcm =	£2,200.00
LESS balance of *ex gratia* payment =	£175.00
Sub-total =	£1,825.00
LESS 10% =	£182.50
PRESCRIBED ELEMENT=	£1,642.50
(b) Loss of statutory rights =	£100.00
Expenses =	£40.00
Sub-total =	£140.00
LESS 10% =	£14.00
TOTAL of (b) =	£126.00
Total 1 =	NIL
Total 2(a) =	£1,642.50
Total 2(b) =	£126.00
GRAND TOTAL =	£1,768.50

Notes

1. Had he not received the *ex gratia* payment, he would have received compensation as follows:

Basic award (£4,200.00 less 10%) = £3,780.00

Compensatory Award

1. Prescribed element

(Lost earnings less receipts less 10%) = £1,800.00

2. Other losses (less 10%) =   £126.00

TOTAL =   £5,706.00

2. In the example, the employee received an *ex gratia* payment, whose effect is as above. If the payment were three month's salary in lieu of notice, the result would be that that amount would be deducted from the amount representing the loss to the date of hearing, but only one month's salary from the new employment would be taken into account, in accordance with the Court of Appeal's decision in *Addison v Babcock FATA Ltd.*[1]

Example 13

8.148   Employee aged 40, continuously employed for 10 years, earning £17,500 per annum (£336.50 pw gross, say £250 net). Member of final salary pension scheme by which pension on retirement at 65 would have been n/60ths of final salary, n being the years of service. Employers normally pay 9% of payroll into scheme; he contributed 4% of salary. Hearing takes place 36 weeks after dismissal; employee is due to start a new job the following week, earning £16,000 per annum (£307.70 pw gross, say £230 net). The new job has no pension scheme except SERPS. Tribunal assesses that in one year he should have regained a comparable position in salary and fringe benefits and decides to apply a withdrawal factor of 25% to his loss of enhancement of accrued pension rights and to take into account the chance that he would have left his employment before he reached 65 even if he had not been dismissed.

1. Basic award

(10 x 1 x 240) =   £2,400.00

2. Compensatory award

(a) Loss to date of hearing

(36 weeks @, say, £250 pw)

PRESCRIBED ELEMENT=   £9,000.00

(b) Future loss of earnings at £20 pw for 52 weeks
(£250 – 230 = £20) =   £1,040.00

(c) Loss of pension rights

    (i)   To hearing date

    (ie 9% x 336.50 = 30.30 x 36) =   £1,090.80

    (ii) Future loss

    (ie 30.30 – 9.20 = 21.10 x 52) =   £1,097.20

---

[1]   [1987] ICR 805.

(iii) Loss of enhancement

(10/60ths of £17,500 = £2,196.67 x 1.5 = £4,375, less 25% (£1,093.75)) =	£3,281.25
Total 1 =	£2,400.00
Total 2(a) =	£9,000.00
Total 2(b) =	£1,040.00
Total 2(c) =	£5,469.25
TOTAL COMPENSATORY AWARD =	£15,509.25
TOTAL MONETARY AWARD =	<u>£17,909.25</u>

Notes

1. The multiplier of 1.5 used to calculate the loss of enhancement is taken from Appendix 4 of the 1991 edition of the *Industrial Tribunals: Compensation for Loss of Pension Rights* (set out in Appendix 1 of this book, at para A1.07).

2. The figure for future loss of pension rights is calculated by taking the former employer's contribution of 9% of the gross weekly wage (9% x £336.50 = £30.30) and deducting from it the contribution from the new employer into SERPS (3% x £307.70 = £9.20). Thus the future loss is £30.30 – £9.20 = £21.10, assessed over a year.

Example 14[1]

8.149 Employee aged 49 dismissed summarily after five years' continuous employment as Assistant General Manager of hotel after investigation by hotel into allegations that depletions in the wine cellar were due to the employee's dishonesty. Tribunal finds that the investigation was inadequate and that the dismissal was unfair. It also decides, however: (i) that the employee was 10% to blame for his dismissal; and (ii) that, had the employers carried out a fair and reasonable investigation, there was a 25% chance of the employee being dismissed fairly. It is satisfied that he has taken adequate steps to mitigate his loss, although he has still not found another job by the date of the hearing, which takes place 15 months (65 weeks) after the dismissal. Tribunal takes view that employee should be able to find another job at same rate of pay within three months of date of hearing. Gross pay: £25,500 (£2,125 pcm); net pay: £1,425 pcm No fringe benefits; no loss of pension rights. Has claimed jobseeker's allowance. He claims expenses of £125, a figure accepted by the tribunal.

---

[1]   This example is based on *Rao v Civil Aviation Authority* [1994] ICR 495.

1. Basic Award

(5 x 1.5 x 240) =	£1,800.00
LESS 10% =	£180.00
TOTAL =	<u>£1,620.00</u>

2. Compensatory Award

(a) Loss to date of hearing (15 months)

(15 x £1,425) =	£21,375.00
LESS 10% =	£2,137.00
SUB-TOTAL (PRESCRIBED ELEMENT) =	<u>£19,237.50</u>

(b) Estimated future loss

(3 x £1,425) =	£4,275.00
(c) Loss of statutory industrial rights =	£100.00
(d) Expenses =	£125.00
TOTAL 2(b)–(d) =	<u>£4,500.00</u>
LESS 10% =	£450.00
TOTAL =	<u>£4,050.00</u>
Total 2(a) =	£19,237.50
2(b)–(d) =	£4,050.00
TOTAL COMPENSATORY AWARD=	<u>£23,287.50</u>

LESS *Polkey* reduction of 25%

2(a) =	£4,809.38
2(b)–(d) =	£1,012.50
SUB-TOTAL =	£5,821.88
TOTAL =	<u>£17,465.62</u>
TOTAL MONETARY AWARD =	<u>£19,085.62</u>

Note

Application of the *Polkey* reduction of 25% means that the prescribed element (2(a) above) is reduced to £14,428.12 (ie £19,237.50 less £4,809.38) and the other heads of loss (2(b)–(d) above) are reduced to £3,037.50 (ie £4,050.00 less £1,012.50).

Example 15

8.150   Employee dismissed at the beginning of May 2000 from her job as a deputy manager of the haberdashery department in a large department store. Dismissal with the notice to which she was entitled; reason given by employers was her inability to perform the job to a satisfactory standard. Hearing takes place 15 weeks after the dismissal. Tribunal decides that her dismissal was unfair and that, because of her age, she is unlikely ever to find another job at the level of her previous employment. It indicates that it intends to make an award of compensation in respect of future loss up to the age (60) when she would have retired. She has just taken a part-time job as a shelf-filler with a local superstore. Her age at dismissal was 56 (she turned 57 just before ET hearing); 15 years of continuous employment; gross pay of £30,000 pa (net pay: £1,650 pcm); no fringe benefits or loss of pension rights; earnings from part-time employment of £625 pcm; period up to retirement at 60: 3 years.

1. Basic award

(1.5 x 15 x 240) =   £5,400.00

2. Compensatory award

(a) Loss to date of hearing (15 weeks)

15 x (£1,650 x 12 ÷ 52 =) £380 =   £5,700.00

PRESCRIBED ELEMENT=   £5,700.00

(b) Estimated future loss

3 x 12 x £1,650 =   £59,400.00

LESS earnings: 3 x 12 x £625 =   £22,500.00

Sub-total =   £36,900.00

TOTAL COMPENSATORY AWARD =   £42,600.00

(c) Taxation of the award

Gross up £12,600.00 (ie amount over £30,000) by 100 ÷ 77=   £16,363.64

Add £30,000 =   £46,363.64

TOTAL COMPENSATORY AWARD =   £46,363.64

TOTAL MONETARY AWARD =   £51,763.64

Notes

1. It has been assumed that the employee is a basic rate taxpayer.

2. The grossing up fraction (100 ÷ 77) is arrived at as follows: assume that £100 gross will yield £77 net of tax. To gross up the *net* amount (£77) to the original figure, the £77 must be multiplied by 100 and divided by 77. Thus 77 x 100 ÷ 77 = 100.

3. Had the employee been a higher rate tax payer, the net amount would have been grossed up by 100 ÷ 60.

Example 16

8.151   Employee employed as a scaffolder by a construction company in the North West. Employed for 10 years; is dismissed for making a 'protected disclosure' within section 103A of the ERA. The tribunal decides that the dismissal was unfair, as being contrary to section 103A, but, because of his age, considers that he will be unlikely to find another job as a scaffolder and that he would have had nine full years of employment. He is due to start in part-time employment the week after the hearing. Age at date of hearing: 50; gross annual pay (including overtime): £25,000; net annual pay: £18,285; net weekly pay: £350 pw (£1,525 pcm); number of weeks from date of dismissal to date of hearing: 25; no fringe benefits or loss of pension rights; annual earnings from part-time employment: £13,000 gross (£10,245 net); retirement age: 60.

1. Basic award

1.5 x 9 x 240 =	£3,240 +
1 x 1 x 240 =	£240
TOTAL =	<u>£3,480</u>

2. Compensatory award

(a) Loss to date of hearing

25 x £350 =	<u>£8,750</u>

(b) Future loss

   (i) Multiplicand

£18,285 – £10,245 =	£8,040

   (ii) Multiplier = 8.65 (assuming rate of return of 2.5%)

   Adjusted by:

   1. 0.94 (for contingencies other than mortality)

   2. –0.04 (adjustment for occupation) = .90

   3. –0.04 (adjustment for region) = .86

   THUS 8.65 x 0.86 = 7.44

(iii) Total future loss = 7.44 x £8,040.00 =	<u>£59,817.60</u>

(c) Taxation of the award

£38,567.60 grossed up by 100 ÷ 77 =	£50,087.79
Add back £30,000 =	£80,087.79
TOTAL COMPENSATORY AWARD =	<u>£80,087.79</u>
TOTAL MONETARY AWARD =	<u>£83,567.79</u>

Notes

1. The multiplier of 8.65 and the adjustments are derived from the Ogden Tables, as discussed in the text.

2. The example assumes that the employee is a basic rate taxpayer; if not, the grossing up fraction will be 100 ÷ 60.

3. It is not clear whether there should be a reduction for accelerated receipt, bearing in mind that the adjustments made under the Ogden Tables are supposed to take account of the contingencies of life.

4. It is unclear whether the tribunal may award aggravated damages if it takes the view that the manner in which the employee was dismissed warrants such an award.

(c) Additional awards

8.152   These will be made where the following conditions are fulfilled:

1.   the employer totally fails[1] to comply with a re-employment order;
2.   the employer fails to satisfy the tribunal that it was not practicable to comply with the order.[2]

If the failure is partial, the tribunal may award whatever amount it considers fit with regard to the employee's loss caused by the non-compliance, under section 117(1) and (2) of the ERA 1996. This is subject to a statutory limit of £51,700, but the statutory limit does not apply to ancillary orders for arrears of pay in cases where the tribunal has made a reinstatement or re-engagement order.[3] The effect of section 124(4) in such cases is that the limit under section 124(1) may be exceeded to the extent only of the loss of arrears of pay and the like less the additional award.[4]

In the case of a total failure to comply, the additional award will be between 26 and 52 weeks' pay.[5] The maximum is £12,480 (ie 52 x £240).[6] The employer will be liable to pay the award unless the tribunal is satisfied that it was not practicable to comply with the re-employment order.[7] It should be noted that what is 'practicable' in the context of non-compliance is different from what is 'practicable' when the tribunal is considering

---

[1]   For an analysis of the difference between total and partial non-compliance, see *Artisan Press Ltd v Srawley and Parker* [1986] ICR 328, and Chapter 7, where the case is considered.
[2]   Section 117(3) and (4), as amended by the Employment Rights (Dispute Resolution) Act 1998, s 15 and Sch 1, para 20 and ERA 1999, s 33(2).
[3]   Section 124(3).
[4]   See *Selfridges Ltd v Malik* [1998] ICR 268.
[5]   Section 117(3)(b), as amended by ERA 1999, s 33(2).
[6]   Note that by virtue of s 227(1) additional awards are subject to the statutory ceiling on the amount of a week's pay.
[7]   Section 117(3)(b) and (4)(a), as amended by ERA 1999, ss 33(1)(a) and (2) and 44 and Sch 9, Table 10. See *Timex Corporation v Thomson* [1981] IRLR 522 and *Artisan Press v Srawley and Parker* [1986] ICR 328 (a case which considers what amounts to partial and total non-compliance).

whether to make a re-employment order. This matter is considered fully in Chapter 7.

8.153   In *Mabirizi v National Hospital for Nervous Diseases*,[1] the EAT said that the additional award is not intended to be a precisely calculated substitute for financial loss, but a general solatium to be arrived at by fixing the appropriate point on the scale specified. The tribunal must exercise its discretion in deciding where in the range of 13 to 26[2] weeks the award should fall. In deciding where to pitch the award, it must address its mind to the fact that it is exercising a discretionary power and must consider what factors ought properly to affect the exercise of that discretion. Some sort of proper assessment and balancing must take place.[3] In considering the amount of the award, the tribunal is entitled to have regard to the employer's conduct and to make an award which registers disapproval of that conduct.[4]

8.154   The following points should also be noted:

1.   In addition to awarding an additional award of compensation, the tribunal will also award compensation in the usual way. It should be noted, however, that in cases where the employee has unreasonably prevented a re-employment order from being complied with by the employer, the tribunal must take that conduct into account when making a compensatory award of compensation and treat it as a failure to mitigate.[5]

2.   Additional awards are not subject to deductions for contributory conduct or, indeed, to any other form of deduction.

3.   There is no reason why an employer should not make an *ex gratia* payment to an employee which is expressed to be in satisfaction of, or as a contribution towards, any additional award which may be made by a tribunal in due course.[6]

Example 17

8.155   Facts taken from example 10. Total of basic and compensatory award £1,450. Total non-compliance with re-employment order; employers fail to satisfy tribunal that it was not practicable to comply.

---

[1]   [1990] ICR 281.

[2]   This case was decided in the context of different provisions which contained a lower range of weeks.

[3]   *Morganite Electrical Carbon Ltd v Donne* [1988] ICR 18 at pp 28–29.

[4]   *Motherwell Railway Club v McQueen* [1989] ICR 418. The EAT refused to interfere with an award of 20 weeks' pay. This was arrived at because the tribunal took the view that the blatancy of the employers' refusal to reinstate made a substantial award appropriate; they also took account of the fact, however, that the employee had been certified unfit for work (a fact which the employers did not know when the order was made), which made a maximum award inappropriate.

[5]   Section 117(8).

[6]   *Darr v LRC Products Ltd* [1993] IRLR 257.

1. Total of basic and compensatory award =   £1,450.00

2. Additional award (say, 30 weeks' pay) =   £4,500.00

GRAND TOTAL =   £5,950.00

(d) Contributions to compensation

8.156   Sections 107 and 123(5) of the ERA 1996 oblige an employment tribunal to ignore industrial pressure when determining the reason for the employee's dismissal and to determine the amount of the compensatory award, ignoring the effect of any actual or threatened industrial pressure. However, the employee's conduct in provoking the pressure (eg by ceasing to pay union subscriptions) may be relevant in reducing the amount of compensation.[1]

8.157   In cases of this kind, where the pressure was exercised because the employee was not a member of any trade union or a particular trade union (or one of a number of particular trade unions), however, section 160 of the Trade Union and Labour Relations (Consolidation) Act 1992 enables the employer or employee to ask the tribunal to join as a party to the proceedings anyone claimed to have exercised the pressure. The tribunal must grant the request if it is made before the hearing, but has a discretion as to whether to do so once the hearing has begun; once compensation has been awarded or a re-employment order made, no request for joinder may be made. If the tribunal considers the claim made by the employer or employee against the third party well-founded, section 160(3) enables it to order the party to make a total or partial contribution to the compensation, as it considers just and equitable in the circumstances.

3. CALCULATION OF A WEEK'S PAY

8.158   It is necessary to calculate the week's pay of an employee to enable the amount of a redundancy payment and of a basic and additional award of compensation to be calculated. It is a gross figure, rather than a net figure as in the calculation of a compensatory award. A week's pay is calculated in accordance with sections 220–229 of the ERA 1996 and depends upon whether the employment in question has normal working hours or not.

(a) Employment with normal working hours

8.159   The first step is to determine whether there are 'normal working hours' or not. To do so, it is necessary to look at the employee's contract; if that specifies a minimum number, that will usually be conclusive. Alternatively, the working hours may be specified in the written statement under section 1 of the ERA 1996.

---

[1]   See *Morris v Gestetner Ltd* [1973] ICR 587 and *Sulemanji v Toughened Glass Ltd* [1979] ICR 799.

8.160   Section 234 of the ERA 1996 provides that normal working hours are the number of hours to be worked before overtime becomes payable. So if the contract states that overtime is payable after a certain number of hours per week have been worked, the hours of overtime will not count. What is now section 234 has been held to apply to cases where the hours are not 'fixed' by the employee's contract but by some other source, eg an Agricultural Wages Order.[1] Overtime will only count if the employer is obliged to provide overtime and the employee is obliged to work it. The fact that the employee regularly works overtime is not sufficient.[2]

8.161   If there are normal working hours, sections 221–223 apply. Section 221(2) applies to time workers, ie those whose remuneration for employment in normal working hours does not vary with the amount of work done. A week's pay for such workers is the amount payable under the contract in force on the calculation date.[3] For the purposes of the calculations which fall to be made, the amount of the gross pay should be taken, not the net amount.[4]

8.162   The amount payable has been held to exclude amounts covered by an agreement (made after the employment ends) to give a back-dated increase.[5] On the other hand, if the employee is entitled to a statutory minimum wage (for example, by virtue of the Wages Councils legislation), the week's pay should be calculated according to the amount the employee is entitled to receive, rather than the amount that he or she actually receives.[6] In *WA Armstrong & Sons Ltd v Borrill*,[7] the facts were that the employee, an agricultural worker, was entitled to a rate of pay payable under the Agricultural Wages Order 1997 (Number 1) 'less board and lodging paid to [his] mother'. The question was whether the amount of a week's pay for the purpose of calculating his redundancy payment should be the payment to the employee plus the money paid to his mother for his board and lodging, or whether it should have been the payment to him alone. The EAT upheld the tribunal's decision that the amount paid to his mother was part of the minimum wages payable under the Order, which could not therefore be reduced.

8.163   Section 221(3) of the ERA 1996 applies to piece workers, ie those who have normal working hours, but whose pay varies according to the amount of work done, eg on the basis of payment per piece or of a commission related to output. Here a week's pay is the amount of remuneration[8] for the number of normal working hours in a week

---

[1]   *Fox v C Wright (Farmers) Ltd* [1978] ICR 98.
[2]   *Tarmac Roadstone Holdings Ltd v Peacock* [1973] ICR 273. See also *Lotus Cars Ltd v Sutcliffe and Stratton* [1982] IRLR 381.
[3]   The 'calculation date' is defined in s 226 and is considered below.
[4]   *Secretary of State for Employment v John Woodrow & Sons (Builders) Ltd* [1983] ICR 582. See also *Donelan v Kerby Constructions Ltd and Secretary of State for Employment* [1983] ICR 237, concerning the payment of a site bonus.
[5]   *Leyland Vehicles Ltd v Reston* [1981] ICR 403.
[6]   *Cooner v PS Doal & Sons* [1988] ICR 495.
[7]   [2000] ICR 367.
[8]   This includes 'any commission or similar payment which varies in amount': see s 221(4).

calculated at the average hourly rate of remuneration payable in respect of a 12-week period ending with the 'calculation date' (if that day is the last day of the week), or, in any other case, with the last complete week before the calculation. Section 221(3) (formerly Schedule 14, paragraph 3(3) to the EPCA 1978) has been held by the EAT to apply to waiters remunerated according to a system by which a fixed charge of 15% was placed in a fund and distributed to all waiters (and some kitchen staff) in proportions calculated by reference to the relative importance of the various employees in the service hierarchy.[1]

8.164 Section 222 applies to shift and rota workers, ie those required to work during their normal working hours 'on days of the week or at times of the day which differ from week to week or over a longer period so that the remuneration payable for ... any week varies according to the incidence of the said days or times'. Here the amount of a week's pay is the amount of remuneration for the average number of weekly normal working hours at the average hourly rate of remuneration.[2] The average number of weekly hours is the total number of the employee's normal working hours during a 12-week period, divided by 12.[3] The average hourly rate of remuneration is the average hourly rate for the hours actually worked in a 12-week period.[4] The provisions of section 228 apply where the employee has not been employed long enough for a calculation to be made under the above rules. In such a case, the tribunal must determine an amount 'which fairly represents a week's pay'.[5]

8.165 In arriving at the average hourly rate of remuneration, section 223(1) allows to be brought in only those hours when the employee was working and only the remuneration payable for, or apportionable to, those hours of work.[6]

8.166 The term 'remuneration' has been extended to include commission, production bonuses and unconsolidated supplements.[7] If commission is payable on a periodic basis (eg quarterly or yearly), it may be apportioned *pro rata* to ascertain the amount of a week; pay is the amount of a week's pay in a 12-week period.[8] Benefits in kind (eg free accommodation) and payments which reimburse expenditure incurred or to be incurred by the employee are excluded (though any element of profit or surplus would be included).[9]

---

[1] *Keywest Club Ltd t/a Veeraswamy's Restaurant v Choudhury* [1988] IRLR 51.
[2] Section 222(2).
[3] Section 222(3)(a).
[4] Section 222(3)(b).
[5] Section 228(1). See also s 228(2) and (3).
[6] Note, however, s 223(3), which provides that a premium for working overtime should be ignored. See *British Coal Corporation v Cheesbrough and Secretary of State for Employment* [1990] ICR 317.
[7] *Weevsmay Ltd v Kings* [1977] ICR 244, *Ogden v Ardphalt Asphalt Ltd* [1977] ICR 604, and *AB Marcusfield Ltd v Melhuish* [1977] IRLR 484.
[8] Section 229(2) and *J & S Bickley Ltd v Washer* [1977] ICR 425.
[9] *S & U Stores Ltd v Wilkes* [1974] ICR 645. See also *Palmanor Ltd v Cedron* [1973] ICR 1008.

(b) Employment with no normal working hours

8.167		Section 224 of the ERA 1996 applies to cases where there are no working hours and provides for the amount of a week's pay to be the amount of the employee's average weekly remuneration in a 12-week period ending with the calculation date (if that is the last day of a week) or, in any other case, ending with the last complete week before the calculation date. No account is to be taken of a week in which no remuneration was payable.[1]

(c) The 'calculation date'

8.168		Section 226[2] sets out the calculation dates for each of the statutory rights. Generally, the calculation date is the 'effective date of termination' (in unfair dismissal cases) or the 'relevant date' (in redundancy cases).[3] If the employer gives shorter notice than that required to be given by section 49, however, the calculation date will be the (later) date on which the proper notice would have expired.

8.169		This definition of calculation date means that, if the amounts to be used in a calculation of compensation change between the effective date of termination or relevant date and the date of the employment tribunal hearing, the amount to be used is the amount in force at the effective date of termination or relevant date. So in the case of an employee whose effective date of termination is 15 January and the limit of a week's pay is raised with effect from 1 February, the limit in force at the date of termination will be used, not the limit in force when the case is heard.

---

[1]		See *Secretary of State for Employment v Crane* [1988] IRLR 238.
[2]		See *Port of London Authority v Payne* [1994] IRLR 9 at p 17.
[3]		See Chapter 3.

Part II:

THE COMMON LAW RIGHTS

Chapter 9

WRONGFUL DISMISSAL

1. WAS THE EMPLOYEE DISMISSED?

(a) Termination by act of either party

9.01   A contract which is not expressed to be for a fixed term or the completion of a specific task will be a contract of indefinite duration; it will go on indefinitely until terminated by either party by notice. It is usual for a contract of employment, particularly one that is in writing, to contain an express notice provision. Indeed, that is one of the items that should be included in a written statement of particulars of employment.[1] In the absence of express agreement, the contract will be impliedly terminable by reasonable notice on either side. In practice, the implication of a period of notice required to be given by the employer has been largely overtaken by the provisions of section 86 of the Employment Rights Act 1996: see Chapter 3.

(i) Dismissal by employer

9.02   In general, the first requirement for any claim arising from dismissal is that the employee was in fact dismissed. In certain circumstances, a resignation may be treated as a dismissal by the employer, but the resignation must have been prompted by an action on the employer's part which amounts to a breach of an important term of the contract or a repudiation: see below.

9.03   Most contracts are terminable by notice, express or implied, unless they are contracts for a fixed term or for the performance of a specific task. It may happen, however, that the contract does not contain a notice requirement, but contains an exhaustive enumeration of the grounds upon which the contract may be terminated by either side. This was the case in *McLelland v Northern Ireland Health Services Board*,[2] in which the employee was appointed to a post expressed to be 'permanent and pensionable'. The conditions of service contained a clause providing for dismissal for 'gross misconduct' or if the employee proved 'inefficient and unfit to merit continued employment'. There were also provisions for dismissal on failure to take or to honour the oath of allegiance and termination by reason of permanent ill-health or infirmity. There was no provision for termination in other circumstances. The Board purported to terminate Mrs McClelland's contract with six months' notice on the ground of

---

[1]   ERA 1996, s 1.
[2]   [1957] 1 WLR 594, [1957] 2 All ER 129.

redundancy. The House of Lords (by a majority) held that on the true construction of the terms and conditions of service, the express powers of the Board to dismiss an employee were comprehensive and exhaustive and no further power could be implied. Accordingly, her employment had not been validly terminated. The majority based their construction on the construction of the contract before them and particularly the clause whose terms have been summarised above. It is doubtful whether the case would now be followed, unless the circumstances were virtually identical.

9.04   Dismissal with notice   The parties are free to choose whatever notice provision they like, although an employer who sought to impose an excessively long notice period on an employee might be prevented from doing so by the doctrine of restraint of trade.

9.05   Questions of construction may arise in relation to a notice provision, particularly where an initial fixed term is specified followed by a provision allowing either party to terminate on giving a stated period of notice, for example 'for 12 months certain, after which time either party should be at liberty to terminate the agreement, by giving the other three months' notice'.[1] It is important that such clauses should be clearly drafted.

9.06   A dismissal which does not comply with the notice to which an employee is expressly or impliedly entitled will be in breach of contract and thus wrongful. This is an important consideration, since an employer who is tempted to dismiss in contravention of a notice provision may not be able to enforce any restrictive covenants in the contract governing the employee's freedom to work for other employers after the dismissal (see para 14.21).

9.07   A contract of employment which contains no notice provision is impliedly terminable by reasonable notice. To determine what amount of notice is reasonable, the circumstances of the particular contract must be looked at, for example the type of employment, the position of the employee within the employer's operation, the length of service and the intervals at which remuneration is paid. Decided cases do not propound any principles; they are merely examples of what may be held to be reasonable in different circumstances. Many skilled employees are likely to be entitled to at least six months' notice. Those who are senior and in highly paid positions, of whom considerable skill, expertise and effort is demanded, are probably entitled to between six months' and one year's notice. It is unlikely that any employee would be entitled to more than one year's notice. Of course, an express term may provide for longer notice. In

---

[1]   *Langton v Carleton* (1873) LR 9 Ex 57: the court held that the employment could be terminated by either party at the end of 12 months, without giving any notice. *Cf Jacks v Palmers Shipbuilding & Iron Co* (1928) 98 LJKB 366: agreement provided that it was to last for 12 months, with six months' notice thereafter to terminate. It was held that notice could not be given until the 12 months had expired but could be given at any time after the expiration of the 12 months. See also *Costigan v Gray Bovier Engines Ltd* (1925) 41 TLR 372.

most cases, it is unlikely that the amount of implied notice entitlement will exceed the amount of statutory notice to which the employee is entitled.

9.08 There have been very few reported cases in recent years which have considered the question of an implied entitlement to reasonable notice. The most recent is *Clark v Fahrenheit 451 (Communications) Ltd.*[1] The case involved an employee who became a director of the company in June 1998. She produced a draft contract which specified no period of notice for directors. When the working relationship between her and her fellow-directors broke down she suggested that they accept one month's paid notice as part of a termination package, but she herself was subsequently dismissed with one month's notice. She complained to a tribunal that she should have been given six months' notice. The tribunal decided that one month's notice was reasonable in all the circumstances. The EAT said that the issue of reasonable notice is a mixed question of fact and law and that determining a reasonable period of notice depends on all the circumstances of the case. It said that the tribunal was entitled to interpret her intention to dismiss fellow-directors on one month's notice as evidence that she considered one month's notice reasonable. It also said that the tribunal had not erred in taking into account her short length of service. The tribunal had failed, however to take into account her status and seniority in the company and had erred in using the company's financial status as an indicator of what is reasonable. In the circumstances, the EAT said that it could not uphold the tribunal's decision and substituted a finding that the correct period of notice was three months. This decision is set out at some length since it gives some guidance on how to approach these sorts of cases when they occur.

The issues which arise in this context are very similar to those which arise in the context of the statutory rights. Reference should, therefore, be made to Chapter 3 for a discussion of what amounts to a dismissal.

9.09 Dismissal without notice This form of dismissal is often called summary dismissal; it is a creature of the common law relating to the contract of employment. The dismissal of an employee without notice will be wrongful, unless the employer can prove that the summary dismissal was justified because of a serious breach of contract on the part of the employee. The effect of a breach or repudiation upon the contract is considered later in this chapter as are the circumstances in which a dismissal will be wrongful (see paras 9.51 and 9.28).

(ii) Resignation by employee

9.10 It is sometimes thought that a resignation by an employee requires an acceptance by the employer. In circumstances where the employee terminates the employment by giving the notice required by his or her contract, this is erroneous, since the employee is terminating the contract

---

[1] (EAT 591/99) (2000) IDS Brief B666/11.

according to its terms.[1] It should also be noted, as was mentioned in Chapter 3, that the withdrawal of a resignation requires the employer's agreement. Failure by the employer to agree to the withdrawal of a resignation cannot amount either to an actual dismissal or a constructive dismissal.[2]

9.11　In a case where the employee's resignation breaches the contract, for example because he or she gives shorter notice than is stipulated in the contract, the employer's consent is unlikely to be material. It is more likely that the employer will wish to sue the employee, either for the loss occasioned by the employee's breach or to enforce restraints contained in the contract. An example of the latter situation is *Thomas Marshall (Exports) Ltd v Guinle*,[3] which is considered at para 9.16.

9.12　Where an employee resigns and the employer invokes a contractual provision entitling him or her to terminate the contract early by making a payment in lieu of notice, and, by doing so, brings the contract to an end before the expiry of the employee's notice, there will be no dismissal.[4]

9.13　Resignation because of breach or repudiation　An employee is entitled to terminate the contract summarily if the employer breaches an important term (express or implied) or behaves in a way which amounts to a repudiation of the contract. In that case, the employee has the choice of waiving the breach or repudiation and continuing with the contract or of treating the contract as at an end and resigning. In the case of a resignation, he or she may sue the employer for breach of contract at common law. Breaches by the employer are considered at the end of the chapter.

9.14　The employee must accept the employer's breach or repudiation unequivocally. A failure to do so may lead to the consequence that the employer withdraws the repudiation before it has been unequivocally accepted. If the employee then purports to accept the repudiation after it has been withdrawn and resigns, he or she will not succeed in an action for breach of contract. An example of this is *Harrison v Norwest Holst Group Administration Ltd.*[5] The employers wrote to the employee stating that he would lose his directorship in two weeks' time. The employee responded with a letter headed 'Without Prejudice'. The employers later withdrew their threat to deprive him of his directorship, but the employee left anyway. The Court of Appeal treated the original threat as an anticipatory breach but said that the employee's letter was not sufficiently unequivocal to amount to an acceptance of the repudiation. Because the repudiation had not been accepted, the contract continued to run and, during the continued

---

[1]　See *Denham v United Glass Ltd* (EAT 581/98) (1999) IDS Brief B637/4.
[2]　*Ibid.*
[3]　[1978] ICR 905. See Ewing's remarks on this case: [1993] CLJ 405 at pp 411–412.
[4]　*Marshall (Cambridge) Ltd v Hamblin* [1994] ICR 362.
[5]　[1985] ICR 668. See also *Lewis v Motorworld Garages Ltd* [1986] ICR 157 and *Shook v London Borough of Ealing* [1986] IRLR 46.

currency of the contract, it was open to the employers to withdraw their threat of breach.

9.15   Resignation in breach of contract There are many cases where an employee resigns in breach of contract but it is not worth the employer's while to sue for the breach. There are also cases, however, where the employee is skilled and has been privy to confidential information. Here the failure to give the proper notice required by the contract may be significant. Employees of this type may be subject to long notice periods of a year or more and may also have what are called 'garden leave' clauses in their contracts.[1] If such an employee leaves without giving correct notice, the employer may wish to enforce the contractual notice period so as to prevent him or her utilising skills or confidential information whilst they are still fresh.[2] The question whether it is possible to do so then becomes of acute importance, since an employer is likely to have more extensive powers of restraint against someone who is still an employee than against an ex-employee.

9.16   *Thomas Marshall (Exports) Ltd v Guinle*[3] is an example of a situation in which an employer has successfully claimed that the employee's resignation in breach of contract should be treated as ineffective, at least for the purpose of enforcing restraints applicable during the continuance of his employment. In that case, the employee purported to resign when his fixed-term contract still had four and a half years to run. The contract had clauses in it dealing with competition and the use of confidential information. Megarry V-C held that the employee's wrongful termination of the contract required acceptance by the employer and did not automatically terminate it. He accepted that the court was powerless to compel the employee to continue to work in accordance with his contract, but said that his repudiation did not release him from his obligations. These were more extensive than they would have been had the repudiation been treated as effective to terminate the contract and had the employee been in the position of an ex-employee. The injunctions sought against the employee in this case were to restrain solicitation of the employer's customers and to restrain the disclosure or use of confidential information.

9.17   *Evening Standard Co Ltd v Henderson*[4] is the starting-point for a consideration of the development of 'garden leave' clauses. The employee was employed as the production manager of the *Standard*. His contract required one year's notice of termination and provided that, while it lasted, he was not to engage in work outside the company without special permission. He was offered a similar position with a competitor newspaper and gave his employers two months' notice of termination. The employers

---

[1]   For an example of such a clause, see *Provident Financial Group plc v Hayward* [1989] ICR 160. Although in that case an injunction was not granted, there is nothing in the judgments of the Court of Appeal to suggest that a clause of this type is not enforceable.
[2]   As happened in *GFI Group Inc v Eaglestone* [1994] IRLR 119: see below.
[3]   [1978] ICR 905. See Ewing's remarks on this case: [1993] CLJ 405 at pp 411–412.
[4]   [1987] ICR 588. See also *Provident Financial Group plc v Hayward* [1989] ICR 160.

sought an injunction to restrain him from undertaking employment with or providing assistance to any competitor of theirs in breach of his contract of employment. The Court of Appeal said that there was no serious issue as to liability, since the employee's contract would continue until the expiration of the one-year notice period, unless his employers accepted his repudiation. If, during that time, he were to work for the competitor, he would be in breach of contract. The Court went on to hold that the balance of convenience favoured the granting of an injunction. The factors which weighed with them in reaching this decision are considered in Chapter 11.

9.18   In *GFI Group Inc v Eaglestone*,[1] on the other hand, Holland J refused to hold an employee to his 20-week notice period, when he joined a competitor during the notice period. Instead, the judge granted an injunction to restrain him from joining the competitor for 13 out of the 20 weeks. The rationale for the decision was that two of the employee's colleagues, who were only on four weeks' notice, had already joined the competitor after the expiry of their notice. This approach was implicitly endorsed by the Court of Appeal in *Crédit Suisse Asset Management Ltd v Armstrong*.[2] The Court held that, although the court may exercise its discretion in deciding the permissible length of paid leave during a notice period, there is no relationship between a garden leave clause and a restrictive covenant; if the covenant is valid, the employer is entitled to have it enforced, subject to the usual grounds upon which the grant of an injunction may be refused. The Court also pointed out, *obiter*, however, that the existence of a garden leave clause may be a factor to be taken into account in determining the validity of a restrictive covenant.[3]

9.19   In *Hutchings v Coinseed Ltd*,[4] the Court of Appeal said that the mere fact that an employee takes another job during the notice period does not necessarily amount to a repudiatory breach entitling the employer to elect to bring the contract to an end. Whether there is a repudiatory breach depends upon whether taking the new job is wholly inconsistent with the employee's obligations to the employer at that time. In the case in question, there was no express provision in the contract prohibiting the employee from taking another job and the Court refused to imply an obligation, given that she had been released from further work by the employers under a garden leave clause. Although her contract contained a confidentiality clause, there was no allegation that she was in breach of that clause. In *Symbian Ltd v Christensen*,[5] on the other hand, the employee's contract contained an express provision which precluded him from engaging in any employment during the term of the contract. The Court of Appeal refused to interfere with the decision of the Vice-Chancellor to grant an injunction restraining the employee from being employed by a competitor firm, albeit in a non-competitive capacity, during the six-month

---

[1]   [1994] IRLR 119; see below.
[2]   [1996] ICR 882.
[3]   *Ibid* at p 894.
[4]   [1998] IRLR 190.
[5]   [2001] IRLR 77.

period when he was on garden leave during notice. As can be seen from these two contrasting cases, much depends upon the individual provisions in an employee's contract.

9.20 The Court of Appeal has made it clear, in *William Hill Organisation Ltd v Tucker*,[1] that an employer who wishes to have the power to send the employee home on garden leave must do so by inserting an express stipulation to that effect in the contract. In the case in question, in the absence of an express stipulation, the Court refused to imply a stipulation and said that on its true construction the employee's contract imposed an obligation on the employer to allow the employee during his notice period to perform the duties of the specific and unique post to which he had been appointed, where the skills necessary to the proper discharge of those duties required their frequent exercise. It also said that the court should be careful not to grant interlocutory relief to enforce a garden leave clause to any greater extent than would be covered by a justifiable covenant in restraint of trade.[2]

(b) Effect of agreed damages clause

9.21 At common law, the parties are free to enter into an agreement that the contract should terminate. In such circumstances, it is likely that they would do so on terms providing for the employee to be compensated for the premature termination of the contract. It is also open to them to agree in advance that, if certain specified events occur (eg a fixed-term contract being brought to a premature end by the employer), the employer will pay to the employee an agreed sum in satisfaction of any claims that he or she may have. Such a clause is called an agreed damages clause.

9.22 If the courts regard the clause as a liquidated damages clause, the amount recoverable will be as stipulated in the clause without the employee having the necessity of proving the actual loss suffered. If, however, the stipulated sum is not a genuine pre-estimate of the loss but is in the nature of a penalty intended to secure performance of the contract, then it is not recoverable and the plaintiff must prove what damages he or she can. The essential question for the court to decide is whether the stipulated sum is a genuine pre-estimate of the loss which is likely to flow from the breach. The principles to be used in dealing with this question are set out in the speech of Lord Dunedin in the leading case of *Dunlop Pneumatic Tyre Co Ltd v New Garage and Motor Co Ltd*.[3] He summed up the law in the following propositions:[4]

> '(1) Though the parties to a contract who use the words "penalty" or "liquidated damages" may prima facie be supposed to mean what they say, yet the expression is not conclusive. The court must find out whether the payment stipulated is in truth a penalty or liquidated damages ...

---

[1] [1999] ICR 291.
[2] *Ibid* at pp 301–302.
[3] [1915] AC 79.
[4] *Ibid* at pp 86–88.

(2)   The essence of a penalty is a payment of money stipulated as *in terrorem* of the offending party; the essence of liquidated damages is a genuine pre-estimate of damage.

(3)   The question whether a sum stipulated is a penalty or liquidated damages is a question of construction to be decided upon the terms and inherent circumstances of each particular contract, judged of at the time of the making of the contract, not as at the time of the breach.

(4)   To assist this task of construction various tests have been suggested which, if applicable to the case under consideration, may prove helpful or even conclusive. Such are:

(a)   It will be held to be a penalty if the sum stipulated for is extravagant and unconscionable in amount in comparison with the greatest loss which could conceivably be proved to have followed from the breach.

(b)   It will be held to be a penalty if the breach consists only in not paying a sum of money, and the sum stipulated is a sum greater than the sum which ought to have been paid ...

(c)   there is a presumption (but no more) that it is penalty when "a single lump sum" is made payable by way of compensation, on the occurrence of one or more or all of several events, some of which may occasion serious and others but trifling damage.

On the other hand:

(d)   It is no obstacle to the sum stipulated being a genuine pre-estimate of damage, that the consequences of the breach are such as to make precise pre-estimation almost an impossibility. On the contrary, that is just the situation when it is probable that pre-estimated damage was the true bargain between the parties.'

9.23   In *Law v Local Board of Redditch*,[1] Lopes LJ put the matter rather more briefly when he said:[2]

'The distinction between penalties and liquidated damages depends on the intention of the parties to be gathered from the whole of the contract. If the intention is to secure performance of the contract by the imposition of a fine or penalty, then the sum specified is a penalty; but if, on the other hand, the intention is to assess the damages for breach of the contract, it is liquidated damages.'

9.24   A more recent example of the application of this principle is to be found in *Neil v Strathclyde Regional Council*,[3] which involved a clause by which the employee agreed to refund to her employers a proportion of their outlays in respect of a period of leave of absence during which she took a training course, if she left their service within two years of completion of the course. She tried to argue that the provision was a penalty and therefore unenforceable, but the Sheriff Principal upheld the employers' claim against her, applying the principles set out above. In

---

[1]   [1892] 1 QB 127.

[2]   *Ibid* at p 132.

[3]   [1984] IRLR 14.

Giraud UK Ltd v Smith,[1] EAT upheld the tribunal's decision that a clause which provided that 'failure to give the proper notice and work it out will result in a reduction from your final payment equivalent to the number of days short' was an unlawful penalty clause rather than a liquidated damages clause. The clause did not represent a genuine pre-estimate of loss.

9.25   If the clause is treated as a liquidated damages clause, the sum stipulated will be recoverable. The employee may not disregard the sum and prove that he or she has suffered greater damages, nor may the employer prove that the employee has suffered less.[2] The employee may be able to recover additional damages in respect of a default which it was not within the parties' contemplation that the agreed damages should cover. If a dispute arises between the parties, it will fall to be dealt with by a county court or the High Court. An example is *Gothard v Mirror Group Newspapers,*[3] where an employee was offered certain financial arrangements as an incentive to take early retirement. These included a payment in lieu of notice. The issue which arose was whether the payment in lieu of notice should be calculated on the basis of gross pay or net pay. The Court of Appeal decided that, in the circumstances, the county court judge was entitled to conclude that the natural meaning of the employer's offer was that the payment in lieu of notice should be calculated on the basis of gross pay. Much, of course, depends upon the circumstances of each individual case, but here the determinant factor was that the employer's offer to the employees, which was described by him as 'fair and generous', was of 'tax-free payments for unexpired notice and redundancy payments'.

9.26   Finally, it should be noted that a termination of employment which is within the scope of an agreed damages clause will not be a wrongful dismissal. In *Rex Stewart Jeffries Parker Ginsberg Ltd v Parker,*[4] for example, the employee's contract contained a provision that the employment could be 'determined by the giving in writing of six calendar months' notice on either side or the payment of six months' salary in lieu thereof'. He was informed that he was to be made redundant in a week's time and that he would be paid six months' salary in lieu of notice in accordance with the agreement. When he set up in competition to his former employers, they sought to enforce a non-solicitation clause against him. He argued that his dismissal was in breach of contract and that the clause was unenforceable. The Court of Appeal held that his contract entitled him to be dismissed with six months' notice or six months' salary in lieu of notice and, therefore, that his dismissal was not in breach of contract. A similar conclusion was reached by the Court of Appeal in *Abrahams v Performing Right Society Ltd.*[5] The employee was employed under a contract entitling

---

[1]   [2000] IRLR 763.
[2]   *Diestal v Stevenson* [1906] 2 KB 345 and *Cellulose Acetate Silk Co Ltd v Widnes Foundry (1925) Ltd* [1933] AC 20.
[3]   [1988] ICR 729.
[4]   [1988] IRLR 483.
[5]   [1995] ICR 1028.

him to two years' notice of termination, or salary in lieu of notice. The employers summarily terminated his employment. The Court of Appeal held that in doing so they were acting lawfully and were effectively electing to pay money in lieu of notice under the contract. The Court went on to hold that, in those circumstances, the employee was not obliged to mitigate his loss.[1] See also para 9.44, where the sorts of clauses considered in the two preceding cases are considered in more detail, together with more recent case-law.

(c) Termination by operation of law

9.27   Certain events may occur whose effect is such that, although the employment relationship comes to an end, the employee may not be not treated as dismissed. They are the insolvency of the employer and a supervening external event which amounts to frustration of the contract.

The first event is considered in Chapter 13; frustration is considered in Chapter 3.

2. WAS THE DISMISSAL WRONGFUL?

9.28   At common law, summary termination of the contract of employment by either party gives the innocent party the right to sue for breach of contract. The defendant may have a defence if the court is satisfied that the plaintiff was guilty of conduct which amounted to a serious breach of contract or to a repudiation of the contract.

9.29   This principle is an extension of the general rule of contract, that if a party to a contract breaches an important term of the contract or evinces an intention no longer to be bound by one or more of its essential terms, the innocent party has a choice: he or she may either waive the breach or repudiation and choose to treat the contract as continuing or may accept the breach or repudiation and treat himself or herself as discharged from the performance of any further obligations under the contract, which is thus at an end. As a general rule, the breach or repudiation, whether by employer or employee, requires to be accepted by the other party before the contract comes to an end. This issue has been the subject of considerable discussion and debate, particularly in relation to the summary dismissal of an employee by an employer, and is considered more fully below (see para 9.51).

9.30   It was stated at the beginning of this chapter that a contract of employment is terminable by notice, express or implied, unless the contract is for a fixed term or for the completion of a specific task or contains an exhaustive enumeration of the grounds upon which it may be terminated. If, therefore either party terminates the contract summarily, ie without notice, the other party has the right at common law to sue for breach of contract. If the defendant's summary termination of the contract was a

---

[1]   See paras 10.47 *et seq*, where the duty to mitigate is considered.

response to an action on the part of the plaintiff, a defence may be available. But he or she must be able to show that the plaintiff's behaviour amounted to a breach of a serious term of the contract or a repudiation of the contract which entitled him or her to terminate the contract summarily. The plaintiff's breach need not have been known at the time of the summary dismissal.[1]

9.31 If the summary dismissal by the employer is not justified, the employee will be treated as having been wrongfully dismissed; if the employer's conduct causes the employee to resign and that conduct is held to be repudiatory or in breach of contract, the employee's contract will be treated as having been breached. An action for wrongful dismissal or breach of contract is heard in the County Court or High Court; the employment tribunals also now have jurisdiction in such cases where damages are claimed.

(a) Breach by employee

9.32 A dismissal will be wrongful, if the employer dismisses the employee without giving him or her the notice he or she is entitled to, or, in the case of a fixed-term contract with no notice provision, allowing him or her to see out the fixed term. In this kind of case, the employer's defence will rest upon breaches of contract alleged to have been committed by the employee.

9.33 There must be a breach by the employee of the express or implied terms of the contract, and the breach must amount to a repudiation or be sufficiently fundamental.[2] In *Wilson v Racher*, Edmund-Davies LJ said: 'Reported decisions provide useful, but only general guides, each case turning upon its own facts ... [A] contract of service imposes upon the parties a duty of mutual respect'.[3]

9.34 This means that opposite conclusions may be reached on similar facts[4] and that, whilst in one context one single, relatively minor, breach may be sufficient to justify summary dismissal,[5] the same will not be true of other, different contexts. The most common instances of breaches of

---

[1]   *Boston Deep Sea Fishing & Ice Co v Ansell* (1888) 39 ChD 339 and *Cyril Leonard & Co v Simo Securities Trust Ltd* [1972] 1 WLR 80.
[2]   See, eg, *Laws v London Chronicle (Indicator Newspapers) Ltd* [1959] 1 WLR 698 at p 700, *per* Lord Evershed MR.
[3]   [1974] ICR 428 at p 430.
[4]   As in *Pepper v Webb* [1969] 1 WLR 514 and *Wilson v Racher* [1974] ICR 428.
[5]   See, eg, *Sinclair v Neighbour* [1967] 2 QB 279.

contract giving rise to summary dismissals are misconduct,[1] disobedience to lawful orders[2] and negligence.[3] Although every case turns upon its own facts, a single act is less likely to justify summary dismissal than a series of actions; the quality of the breach is what counts, not the consequences flowing from it. The more serious the breach, the more likely it is that it will be held to justify summary dismissal. Although much of the law in this area was developed in the late nineteenth and earlier twentieth centuries, it remains important and forms the basis of the modern law relating to confidential information. It has given rise to a number of important cases. *Sybron Corporation v Rochem Ltd,*[4] for example, concerned the question whether an employee was under a duty to disclose breaches of duty to his employers. The Court of Appeal said that he was, on the ground that, although an employee has no general duty to disclose his own misconduct, and there is no general requirement to disclose misconduct of fellow-employees, the terms and nature of the employment may be such that there is a contractual duty to disclose the misconduct of other employees, even if that disclosure would inevitably lead to disclosure of the employee's own misconduct. The Court found such a duty. On the other hand, in *University of Nottingham v Fishel,*[5] the court held that the employee was not obliged to disclose to his employers that he was doing outside work in breach of his contract, nor was he obliged to apply for consent, although his contract required him to do so. He was, however, in breach of contract in doing what he did.

9.35   A slightly different issue arose in *Horcal Ltd v Gatland.*[6] A director of a company agreed to perform work for a client, but decided to keep the proceeds for himself. This happened during negotiations to resolve differences with the principal shareholder. The negotiations led to an agreement that Mr Gatland should receive a golden handshake and resign at a future specified date. After making the agreement, he accepted payments from the client for the work he had performed but failed to account for them to Horcal. Horcal tried to recover the golden handshake on the grounds that Mr Gatland was in breach of his duty. The Court of

---

1   See, eg, *Clouston & Co v Corry* [1906] AC 122, *Sinclair v Neighbour* [1967] 2 QB 279, and *Wilson v Racher* [1974] ICR 428. In *Laughton and Hawley v Bapp Industrial Supplies Ltd* [1986] IRLR 245, the EAT held that an employee's expressed intention of setting up in competition with the employer was not in itself a breach of the implied duty of loyalty to the employer and did not amount to misconduct. Misconduct is sometimes given the epithet 'gross'. In *Wilson v Brett* (1843) 11 M & W 113 at pp 115–116, Rolfe B said that he 'could see no difference between negligence and gross negligence ... that it was the same thing, with the addition of a vituperative epithet'.
2   See, eg, *Laws v London Chronicle (Indicator Newspapers) Ltd* [1959] 1 WLR 698 and *Pepper v Webb* [1969] 1 WLR 514.
3   See, eg, *Baster v London & County Printing Works* [1899] 1 QB 901, *Power v British India Steam Navigation Co Ltd* (1930) 46 TLR 294, and *Jupiter General Insurance Co Ltd v Shroff* [1937] 3 All ER 67. Negligence sometimes has the epithet 'gross' added to it but in *Dietman v Brent London Borough Council* [1987] ICR 737 at p 748, Hodgson J characterised this usage as unhelpful.
4   [1983] ICR 801.
5   [2000] ICR 1462.
6   [1984] IRLR 288.

Appeal held that there was no breach of the agreement at the time the agreement was made; the golden handshake could not, therefore, be recovered. This made it unnecessary to consider whether, had there been a breach of duty, Mr Gatland should have disclosed it. The possibilities of *Sybron* thus remain undeveloped.

9.36 A more recent example of the problem of deciding what amounts to misconduct (or, indeed, gross misconduct) is *Dietman v London Borough of Brent*.[1] Mrs Dietman was a senior social worker whose performance was criticised by an inquiry into a case of child abuse. When the council received the report, the council's chief executive decided to dismiss her instantly; his decision was confirmed by the appropriate sub-committee. Mrs Dietman was given no opportunity of attending any of the relevant meetings or putting forward her case. The council's disciplinary procedure provided that, in the case of more serious offences, the employees should be invited to a formal disciplinary meeting but that certain types of gross misconduct 'may lead to a recommendation to the council for instant dismissal ...'. Clause 7 of the contract of employment was as follows: 'Any breach of disciplinary rules will render you liable to disciplinary action, which will normally include immediate suspension followed by dismissal, or instant dismissal, for offences of gross misconduct[2] unless there are mitigating circumstances ...'.

She lodged an appeal under the council's disciplinary procedure, which was rejected. She sued the council for wrongful dismissal, claiming damages, a declaration that the dismissal was 'invalid, void and of no effect' and an injunction restraining the council from purporting to dismiss her. Hodgson J held that she had been wrongfully dismissed and awarded her damages. He found that the failure to achieve the standard required did not amount to gross misconduct and that the council was not entitled to dismiss her summarily without giving her a hearing under the disciplinary procedure. The Court of Appeal dismissed the council's appeal and held that it was not entitled to dismiss her summarily without giving her a hearing under the disciplinary procedure. The correct construction of clause 7 of her contract was that, if the alleged breach of a disciplinary rule amounted to gross misconduct, this would normally mean immediate suspension, pending the outcome of the disciplinary hearing; the hearing might result in a recommendation of either instant dismissal without notice or ordinary dismissal on proper notice. The Court rejected the employers' argument that the relevant words meant that for offences of gross misconduct, instant dismissal, not preceded by suspension, and without the need for the delay caused by a formal disciplinary hearing, was permissible. The Court of Appeal also upheld the judge's decision that Mrs Dietman's admitted gross negligence did not constitute 'gross misconduct'

---

[1] [1988] IRLR 299 (CA).

[2] 'Gross misconduct' was defined as 'misconduct of such a nature that the authority is justified in no longer tolerating the continued presence at the place of work of the employee who commits an offence of gross misconduct'.

as defined by the contract, but added that it was not prepared to say that gross negligence can never amount to gross misconduct.

9.37   It was said earlier that cases involving an employee's behaviour, whether it is categorised as misconduct, negligence or disobedience, all turn on their own facts. The *Dietman* case is one such case, but is considered at length here as an example of the problems of construction which can arise. This point was stressed by Balcombe LJ in the Court of Appeal: 'This appeal has raised purely technical issues on the construction of the plaintiff's contract of employment with the council'.[1] It should be noted that if an employee under notice of dismissal is dismissed summarily during the notice period, the dismissal will be changed into a summary dismissal.[2]

9.38   At common law the employer is not obliged to give a reason for the dismissal, provided that grounds for dismissal exist.[3] It will be a complete defence in an action for wrongful dismissal if the employer can establish that, unknown to him or her at the time of dismissal, there existed a reason which, had it been known, would have justified the summary dismissal.[4]

9.39   The fact that a dismissal is wrongful does not mean that it necessarily follows that it is unfair. The reason for this is that the principles which determine whether a dismissal is wrongful are common law principles of contract. To determine whether a dismissal is unfair, on the other hand, it is necessary to consider whether the employer has breached section 98(4) of the ERA 1996. The two causes of action are totally different and are governed by different principles.

(b) Breach by employer

9.40   A breach by the employer may take two forms. First, there may be a breach of an express term of the contract, for example by a failure to observe a notice provision or to allow the employee to fulfil a fixed-term contract. In such a case, the employer may be able to justify the action on the grounds of the employee's breach: see above. Otherwise, the question is principally one of how much the employee should receive by way of damages, since the remedies of injunction and specific performance are unlikely to be available.[5] The employer may wish to pay a golden handshake to buy off future litigation (and its attendant, and possibly unwelcome, publicity) and will, therefore, need to know on what principles a court would calculate the compensation (in the form of damages) to be paid to the employee. A golden handshake is, in other words, a payment by the employer intended to reflect the estimate of liability to the employee

---

[1]   [1988] IRLR 299 at p 304.

[2]   *Stapp v The Shaftesbury Society* [1982] IRLR 326.

[3]   *Ridgeway v Hungerford Market Co* (1835) 3 Ad & Ee 171.

[4]   *Boston Deep Sea Fishing and Ice Co Ltd v Ansell* (1888) 39 ChD 339, approved in *Cyril Leonard & Co Ltd v Simo Securities Trust Ltd* [1972] 1 WLR 80.

[5]   See Chapter 11.

in a successful wrongful dismissal case. The principles involved are set out in Chapter 10.

9.41 The first question which arises here is whether there has been a breach at all. In *Brigden v American Express Bank Ltd*,[1] the employee's contract contained a clause providing that he might be dismissed by notice and/or payment in lieu of notice without implementation of the company's disciplinary procedure. He was dismissed with a payment in lieu of notice but sought to claim that the clause in question was void as being unreasonable, contrary to section 3 of the Unfair Contract Terms Act 1977. Morland J accepted that a contract of employment falls within section 3 of the Act but said that the clause was not void as it was not a contract term excluding or restricting the liability of the employers in respect of breach of contract; nor did it entitle the employers to render a contracted performance substantially different from that which was reasonably expected of them or to render no performance in respect of any part of their contractual obligation, as required by section 3(2)(a) or (b). The judge said that the clause set out the employee's entitlement and the limit of his rights.

9.42 A dismissal which does not comply with the notice to which an employee is expressly or impliedly entitled will be in breach of contract and thus wrongful. This is an important consideration, since an employer who is tempted to dismiss in contravention of a notice provision may not be able to enforce any restrictive covenants in the contract governing the employee's freedom to work for other employers after the dismissal.[2] The employee raised this argument in *Rex Stewart Jeffries Parker Ginsberg Ltd v Parker*.[3] His contract contained a provision that the employment could be 'determined by the giving in writing of six calendar months' notice on either side or the payment of six months' salary in lieu thereof'. He was informed that he was to be made redundant in a week's time and that he would be paid six months' salary in lieu of notice in accordance with the agreement. When he set up in competition to his former employers, they sought to enforce a non-solicitation clause against him. He argued that his dismissal was in breach of contract and that the clause was unenforceable. The Court of Appeal held that his contract entitled him to be dismissed with six months' notice or six months' salary in lieu of notice and, therefore, that his dismissal was not in breach of contract. Accordingly, it upheld the non-solicitation clause. A similar conclusion was reached by the Court of Appeal in *Abrahams v Performing Rights Society Ltd*.[4] The employee was employed under a contract entitling him to two years' notice of termination, or salary in lieu of notice. The employers summarily terminated his employment. The Court of Appeal held that in doing so

---

[1]   [2000] IRLR 94.
[2]   *General Billposting Co Ltd v Atkinson* [1909] AC 118. The decision of the Court of Appeal in *Rock Refrigeration Ltd v Jones and Seward Refrigeration Ltd* [1996] IRLR 675 suggests, however, a desire to move away from the rigour of this principle.
[3]   [1988] IRLR 483.
[4]   [1995] ICR 1028.

they were acting lawfully and were effectively electing to pay money in lieu of notice under the contract.[1]

9.43   This type of case depends on the express provisions of the employee's contract and was distinguished by the Court of Appeal in *Abrahams* from the case where the employer gives the employee wages in lieu of notice, which the employee accepts. In the latter case, the analysis is that there has been a summary and wrongful dismissal and the wages in lieu represent the measure of damages to which the employee would ordinarily be entitled.[2]

9.44   The problems posed by what are called PILON[3] clauses have led to a number of cases, which usually involve careful construction of the relevant clause.[4] The differences between the approach of the High Court and the Court of Appeal in *Gregory v Wallace*[5] show how difficult this can sometimes be. In that case, the employee was employed by Mountleigh Management Services Ltd (MMS) as group financial controller of Mountleigh Finance plc ('the company'). His contract contained a series of clauses. Clause 1(a) made provision for termination of his appointment, either by MMS or the company giving two years' written notice or by him giving one year's notice in writing. Clause 1 went on as follows:

'(b) If MMS or the company gives such notice to terminate, the executive shall not be required to attend the office regularly during the notice period and the executive may accept other full-time employment during such notice period.
(c)   Upon the giving by MMS or the company of such notice to terminate, MMS or the company shall be entitled to terminate this agreement henceforth. In such event, MMS shall, at the election of the executive, either: (i) pay to the executive, in monthly instalments in arrears over the two-year period of the notice, the executive's gross basic salary at the rate in force at the date of termination of the employment; or (ii) pay to the executive the aggregate of all such monthly instalments, discounted to reflect the present value as at the date of termination.'

9.45   In 1992, an administration order was made against MMS and the administrators subsequently gave him oral notice that his employment was being terminated. He obtained new employment some six weeks later. He

---

[1]   The main issue in this case was whether the employee was obliged to mitigate his loss. This is considered in Chapter 10, at para 10.38.
[2]   This analysis is implicitly supported by the speech of Lord Browne-Wilkinson in *Delaney v Staples (t/a De Montfort Recruitment)* [1992] ICR 483, particularly at pp 488–489, although that case concerned the definition of 'wages' in the Wages Act 1986 (consolidated into Part II of the ERA 1996). See, eg, *Dixon v Stenor Ltd* [1973] ICR 157, as an example of the type of dismissal where the employer gives the employee wages in lieu. See also *Marsh v National Autistic Society* [1993] ICR 453.
[3]   Ie pay in lieu of notice.
[4]   See *Skilton v T & K Home Improvements Ltd* [2000] ICR 1162, in which the Court of Appeal said that a clause which said that the employee 'may be dismissed' with immediate effect for failing to meet sales targets did not terminate or exclude the employee's right under another clause in the contract to three months' notice or payment of salary in lieu of three month's notice.
[5]   [1998] IRLR 387.

began proceedings against the administrators claiming that he was entitled to two years' salary, discounted in accordance with clause 1(c)(ii) of his agreement, as a debt without deduction of the income which he received from his new employment during the two-year period. The administrators argued that clause 1(c) never came into operation as the required two years' notice of termination had not been given; he was dismissed summarily when he was told orally of his immediate dismissal. The judge at first instance concluded that he was entitled to the sums referred to in clause 1(c) as a debt without deduction of earnings from other employment. The Court of Appeal dismissed the administrators' appeal and upheld the judge's decision on different grounds. It said that the judge had erred in holding that the employee was entitled to two years' discounted salary as a debt and said that, since the termination was oral, it was not effected under the terms of the contract, but was a deliberate breach of contract giving rise to a claim for damages. Further, damages were to be assessed on the basis that the contract would be duly performed in the way that was most beneficial to the employer paying the damages. In the present case, had the contract been duly performed, the employee would have been given two years' notice, leaving the employers with the choice of either letting the employee serve out the notice period or terminating the contract forthwith and making the appropriate payments. In those circumstances, it could not be said that those payments represented liquidated damages payable on repudiation of the contract. The employee was entitled to unliquidated damages, against which he was not obliged to give credit for his earnings from other employment during the notice period. The reason for that was that, if he had been given notice in accordance with his contract, under its terms he could have obtained other full-time employment during the notice period and also received payment due from the company. Accordingly, since he was entitled to be put in the position he would have been in had his contract been performed, he was entitled to damages undiminished by earnings in his new employment because that was the sum he lost as a result of the employer's breach.

9.46 In *Cerberus Software Ltd v Rowley*,[1] the employee was employed under a contract determinable by either party giving six months' notice but which provided that the employers might make a payment in lieu of notice to the employee. The relevant part of the clause stated: 'It is agreed that the employer may make a payment in lieu of notice to the employee'. On 26 June 1996, he was summarily dismissed and, on 1 August, he started a new job. The employment tribunal upheld his complaint of wrongful dismissal and awarded him six months' pay without requiring him to give credit for earnings in his new job, on the ground that, since the contract expressly provided that employment might be terminated on payment of a sum in lieu of notice, the summary dismissal was a lawful act and the claim was for a sum due under the contract rather than for damages. The EAT dismissed the employers' appeal, holding that, whether or not the

---

[1]   [2001] ICR 376.

employers breached the contract by summary dismissal itself, they were in breach by not paying money in lieu of notice, that the money in lieu was claimable either as money due under the contract or as damages for breach of contract, and that in neither event were the employers entitled to receive the benefit of the employee's mitigation because they had promised to pay the whole sum. The Court of Appeal, by a majority,[1] allowed the employers' appeal. It said that inclusion of the sentence quoted above ('It is agreed …') meant that the employer was given the right to elect whether or not to make a payment in lieu of notice and language whereby the employer was given the choice to pay or not to pay was inconsistent with the provision of a contractual right to the employee to insist that he should be paid six months' salary in lieu of notice. Since in the circumstances the employers were in breach of their obligation to give six months' notice, the employee's remedy was not recovery of the sum payable under the contract as a debt, but damages for wrongful dismissal reduced by any amount earned by way of mitigation of his loss. The majority distinguished *Abrahams v Performing Right Society Ltd* (above) on the grounds that the relevant clause in that case was differently worded and the clause in question gave the employers an election as to whether or not to make a payment in lieu of notice. Sedley LJ would have dismissed the appeal. He said that the contract gave Cerberus only the choice of giving notice or paying in lieu; on that view the payment would have been a debt due under the contract and not subject to mitigation, thus following the *Abrahams* case.

9.47   A final point to note is that a contractual provision in a share option scheme which provides for an option to lapse if the contract is terminated will only operate if the contract is terminated lawfully, unless there is clear language to the contrary in the scheme.[2]

9.48   This lengthy consideration of the most recent cases on the subject of payments in lieu of notice shows that a great deal depends upon the drafting of the clause in question, as is shown by a comparison of those cases. It must be remembered, however, that an employer which chooses to go down the path of a summary and wrongful dismissal, as Cerberus did, will be unable to insist upon the enforcement of post-termination restrictive covenants.

9.49   A second type of breach by the employer may be a breach of an implied term. In that case, the term[3] and its breach must be established. It must then be established that the breach was sufficiently serious to be repudiatory. Finally, the employee must have accepted the repudiation. For

---

[1]   Sedley LJ dissenting.

[2]   *Levett v Biotrace International plc* [1999] ICR 818.

[3]   In *McLory v Post Office* [1992] ICR 758, for example, the Court refused to imply a term that the employees were entitled to be provided with work and the opportunity to earn overtime during a period of suspension for conduct or alleged misconduct, since there was an express term governing suspension; in *Morley v Heritage plc* [1993] IRLR 400, the Court of Appeal refused to imply a term that the employee, who was a chief financial director, was entitled to accrued holiday pay on termination of his employment.

a fuller discussion of implied terms, see Chapter 3, where constructive dismissal is considered.

9.50 The case-law shows the problems that can arise. An example is *Bliss v South East Thames Regional Health Authority*,[1] where the employers acted in a way which the Court of Appeal held to be a repudiation of the employee's contract, by requiring him to submit to a medical examination and suspending him when he refused. It held that the employers' action was in breach of contract by requiring the employee, without reasonable cause, to submit to the medical examination and, when he refused, by suspending him. That was a breach of the implied term that they would not without reasonable cause conduct themselves in a manner likely to damage or destroy the relationship of trust and confidence between employer and employee. The breach was so serious as to go to the root of the contract and to entitle the employee to treat the contract as at an end. The breach was a continuing breach until the employers lifted the suspension. After the employers withdrew the requirement and lifted the suspension, they offered to give him time to make up his mind about his future intentions and to pay him while he did so. They then tried to argue that his acceptance of his salary affirmed the contract so as to preclude him from accepting their repudiation, as he purported to do. The Court of Appeal held that he had not affirmed the contract by his conduct in accepting the salary payments and he was entitled to accept the repudiation. The Court took the view that the cardinal factor was that the employer was prepared to give the employee time to make up his mind and to pay while he was doing so.

(c) Effect of breach or repudiation on the contract

9.51 The question of the effect of a breach or repudiation on the contract of employment has given rise to considerable judicial and academic discussion.[2] It has not always been clear whether a distinction should be drawn between a summary dismissal or termination, on the one hand, and breach or repudiation, on the other.

9.52 It is arguable that a distinction should be made between conduct which actually terminates the contract and therefore amounts to a wrongful dismissal, and conduct which amounts to a failure to observe a basic term of the employment relationship (eg a reduction by the employer of the employee's wages). In the former case, the conduct arguably

---

[1]   [1987] ICR 700. See also *Dietman v London Borough of Brent* [1987] ICR 737 (QBD) and [1988] ICR 842 (CA), where the employee's acceptance of the offer of employment was held to amount to acceptance of the employer's repudiation so as to preclude her from injunctive relief. This point was made at first instance, but did not arise in the Court of Appeal.

[2]   See, eg, Elias (1978) 7 ILJ 16, McMullen [1982] CLJ 110, Kerr (1984) 47 MLR 30, Carty (1989) 52 MLR 449, Macdonald (1991) 22 *Cambrian Law Review* 26, McColgan (1992) 21 ILJ 58 and Ewing [1993] CLJ 405. See also *Deakin and Morris, Labour Law* (2nd edn, 1998), pp 414–418.

terminates the contract without more.[1] In the latter case, the question is whether the conduct in question automatically terminates the contract or whether it gives the innocent party the choice of affirming the contract or accepting the breach as a repudiation and treating the contract as at an end.

9.53   A repudiation, or repudiatory breach, generally requires acceptance by the innocent party before there is a termination, but it has been argued that contracts of employment are an exception. The argument is often put on the basis that a contract of employment cannot be ordered by the courts to be performed, by means of an order of specific performance.[2]

9.54   In *Decro-Wall International SA v Practitioners in Marketing Ltd*, Salmon LJ said:[3]

> 'I doubt whether a wrongful dismissal brings a contract of service to an end in law, although no doubt in practice it does. Under such a contract a servant has a right to remuneration ... in return for services. If the master, in breach of contract, refuses to employ the servant, ... the contract will not be specifically enforced ... [T]he only result is that the servant, albeit he has been prevented from rendering services by the master's breach, cannot recover remuneration under the contract because he has not earned it ... His only money claim is for damages for being wrongfully prevented from earning his remuneration.'

9.55   The reasoning of the judges in this case was criticised by Sir John Donaldson, President of the National Industrial Relations Court, in *Sanders v Ernest A Neale Ltd*, as follows:[4]

> 'In essence it proceeds by the following stages. (i) A servant cannot sue for wages if he has not rendered services. (ii) This leaves him with a claim for damages as his only remedy. (iii) Any claim for damages is subject to a duty to mitigate the loss and the only way to perform this duty is to accept the repudiation as terminating the contract of employment and seeking other employment. If there is any fault in this line of reasoning, it lies in point (i). Why should not the servant sue for wages if it is the act of the employer which has prevented his performing the condition precedent of rendering services? And if he can sue in debt for his wages, no duty to mitigate would arise and there would be no practical necessity to accept a wrongful dismissal as terminating the contract of employment ...'

9.56   Despite these reservations, however, in the later case of *Gunton v Richmond-upon-Thames London Borough Council*,[5] Buckley LJ developed

---

[1]   This question was left open by the House of Lords in *Rigby v Ferodo Ltd* [1988] ICR 29, see below. Lord Oliver of Aylmerton said that the question did not arise on the facts of the case.

[2]   See, eg, Shaw LJ in *Gunton v Richmond-upon-Thames London Borough Council* [1981] Ch 448 at p 459.

[3]   [1971] 1 WLR 361 at p 369.

[4]   [1974] ICR 565 at pp 570–571.

[5]   [1980] ICR 755.

further the view of wrongful dismissal expressed in the reasoning in the *Decro-Wall* case. He said:[1]

'... [C]ases of wrongful dismissal in breach of a contract of personal service have certain special features. In the first place, as the term "wrongful dismissal" implies, they always occur after the employment has begun and so involve an immediate breach by the master of his obligation to continue to employ the servant. Secondly, a wrongful dismissal is almost invariably repudiatory in character ... Thirdly, the servant cannot sue in debt under the contract for remuneration in respect of any period after the wrongful dismissal, because the right to receive remuneration and the obligation to render services are mutually interdependent. Fourthly, the servant must come under an immediate duty to mitigate his damages and so must almost invariably be bound to seek other employment in fulfilment of that obligation ... It follows ... that at least as soon as the servant finds, and enters into, other employment he must put it out of his power to perform any continuing obligations on his part to serve his original employer. At this stage, if not earlier, the servant must ... be taken to have accepted his wrongful dismissal as a repudiatory breach leading to a determination of the contract of service.'

In the same case, Brightman LJ said:[2]

'It is clear beyond argument that a wrongfully dismissed employee cannot sue for his salary or wages as such, but only for damages. It is also ... equally clear that such an employee cannot assert that he still retains his employment under the contract. If a servant is dismissed and excluded from his employment, it is absurd to suppose that he still occupies the status of a servant.'

9.57   These principles were followed subsequently by the High Court in *Marsh v National Autistic Society*,[3] in which the principal of a school established by the Society was dismissed in breach of contract by them. The employee argued that, in the absence of any notice terminating his employment in accordance with his contract, the dismissal amounted to a repudiatory breach of contract, which was only capable of bringing his contract to an end if he accepted it, which he did not, and that the contract therefore remained in force until he either accepted the repudiation or was given proper notice by the Society. He sought an interlocutory injunction to restrain the Society from dismissing him or purporting to dismiss him otherwise than in accordance with the provisions of his contract of employment and an order that he should continue to be paid his remuneration. Both were refused by the judge. Ferris J reviewed the authorities quoted above, and went on to say:[4]

'[T]hey [sc the authorities] show ... that where ... a contract of employment has been wrongfully terminated by the employer the ordinary contractual principles relating to acceptance of repudiatory breach apply and to some extent at least

---

[1]   [1980] ICR 755 at p 771.
[2]   *Ibid* at p 778.
[3]   [1993] ICR 453.
[4]   *Ibid* at p 459.

the authorities show that the contract continues to subsist ... The very same authorities show, however, ... that, although it is the employer who in those circumstances is in breach of contract by having committed a repudiatory breach, the employee is not thereafter entitled to remuneration as a matter of debt.'

9.58   In the later case of *Boyo v Lambeth London Borough Council*,[1] the Court of Appeal reviewed the authorities dealing with this issue, particularly the *Gunton* case and *Saunders v Ernest A Neale Ltd*.[2] It felt constrained to follow *Gunton*, but it is clear, particularly from the judgments of Ralph Gibson and Staughton LJJ, that the majority would have preferred to decide the case unconstrained by the decision in that case. Ralph Gibson LJ's view[3] was that a wrongful dismissal requires a real acceptance by the employee and that the court should not easily infer acceptance, as suggested by Buckley LJ in the *Gunton* case. He said:[4]

'... [I]f there is a requirement of law for acceptance by the servant of the repudiation by the master, I am unable to see why it is not a requirement for real acceptance, that is to say a conscious acceptance intending to bring the contract to an end or the doing of some act which is inconsistent with continuation of the contract. If that is right, I do not understand how the courts would apply the notion of "easily infer[ring] that the innocent party has accepted the ... repudiation".[5] Further, I do not understand why the taking of employment should automatically constitute acceptance. If I tell my employer ... that I do not accept his repudiation; and that I shall get another job but remain willing and able to do my work when sent for by him, why should I be treated as having accepted what I have not accepted?'

He went on to say[6] that if it were open to the Court to depart from the conclusion in the *Gunton* case, he would prefer the views expressed by Sir John Donaldson in *Saunders v Ernest A Neale Ltd*, but added that the Court was not free to depart from that decision.

9.59   Staughton LJ's view was that a direct repudiation, whether by employer or employee, determines a contract of employment and that, in that respect, such contracts are in a class of their own; he also said that, 'although there is powerful authority to the contrary, I do not accept that an employee has no right to salary if he has done no work'.[7] He concluded his judgment by saying that the law in this area 'is distinctly lacking in rhyme and reason'.

9.60   More recently, this matter was considered by Sedley LJ in his dissenting judgment in *Cerberus Software Ltd v Rowley*.[8] His view was that

---

[1]   [1994] ICR 727.
[2]   [1974] ICR 565.
[3]   See [1994] ICR 727.
[4]   *Ibid* at p 743.
[5]   *Per* Buckley LJ in the *Gunton* case at p 772E.
[6]   *Ibid* at pp 743–744.
[7]   *Ibid* at p 747.
[8]   [2001] ICR 376. See pp 387–388.

the case in question offered strong support to the elective theory but that it also has attendant problems. In any case, his views must regarded as *obiter*.

For the moment, therefore, the principle is that a wrongful dismissal requires acceptance by the employee, but that acceptance will be easily inferred. Clearly, however, this area is ripe for re-examination by the House of Lords.

9.61   The alternative type of case is that in which the employer does not dismiss the employee but engages in actions which seek to change 'the nature of the work required to be done or the times of employment'.[1] An example of such a case is the House of Lords' decision in *Rigby v Ferodo Ltd*.[2] The employee was employed as a lathe operator at a wage of £192 per week and his contract was terminable by 12 weeks' notice. In 1982, because of a severe financial crisis, the employers tried unsuccessfully to agree a wage reduction with the unions representing their employees. The employers then imposed the wage reductions unilaterally. The employee continued to work at the reduced rate, but instituted proceedings for damages to recover the difference between the wages to which he was entitled under his contract and the wages actually paid to him by his employers. It was agreed that the employers' action amounted to a fundamental and repudiatory breach. The first point dealt with by the House of Lords was the employers' argument that the breach constituted the giving of the necessary 12 weeks' notice required under the contract to terminate the employment. The House of Lords rejected this, on the footing that it was an impossible contention on the facts of the case, since the employers were concerned to keep their workforce and never purported to give such a notice. The main argument was that contracts of employment are an exception to the general rule that an unaccepted repudiation leaves the contractual obligations of the parties unaffected and that the wrongful repudiation of the fundamental obligations of either party not only brings to an end the relationship of employer and employee, but also terminates the contract immediately without the necessity of any acceptance by the party not in default. It followed, therefore, according to this argument, that the unilateral reduction in the employee's wages amounted to a termination of the contract and his sole remedy was damages limited to the shortfall from his original contractual wage over a 12-week period. Lord Oliver of Aylmerton, who gave the main speech in the House of Lords, rejected this argument and said that there was no reason why a contract of employment should be on any different footing from any other contract. He did appear, however, to make a distinction between a repudiatory breach and a wrongful dismissal. Although he was at pains to point out that the case was not one of wrongful dismissal and said that it would not be appropriate to decide that question, which, on the facts, did not arise, he did say this:

---

[1]   See Shaw LJ in the *Gunton* case [1981] Ch 448 at p 459.
[2]   [1988] ICR 29. See also *Dietman v London Borough of Brent* [1988] IRLR 299.

'Whatever may be the position under a contract of service where the repudiation takes the form either of a walk-out by the employee or of a refusal by the employer any longer to regard the employee as his servant, I know of no principle of law that any breach which the innocent party is entitled to treat as repudiatory of the other party's obligations brings the contract to an end automatically.'[1]

9.62   In view of these statements of the law, it is possible to say that an employee who is a victim of a repudiatory act is effectively confined to a claim for damages (if the repudiation takes the form of a wrongful dismissal) or unpaid, or under-paid, wages (if the repudiation takes the form of a unilateral reduction in wages, as in *Rigby v Ferodo Ltd*). In other cases, such as a unilateral change in non-financial terms of the employee's contract), the choice is between waiving the breach and thus affirming the contract, or accepting the repudiation and resigning. In all these cases, it is highly unlikely that the court will grant injunctive relief.

9.63   On the other hand, if the act of termination or repudiatory act is the employee's, there are circumstances in which, despite the impossibility of forcing the employee to work in accordance with the contract, nevertheless the court is prepared to treat the contract as subsisting for the purposes of restraining him or her from committing breaches of the contract. The breaches in question are often breaches of a clause in the contract governing competition or the use of confidential information and the like. An example is *Thomas Marshall (Exports) Ltd v Guinle*,[3] considered at para 9.16. This case may be contrasted with *Evening Standard Co Ltd v Henderson*,[4] which was also considered earlier in this chapter. The employee was obliged to give one year's notice of termination, but purported to give two months' notice. There was a clause in his contract to the effect that, during its duration, he was not to engage in work outside the company without special permission. His purpose in giving shorter notice than he was obliged to was to enable him to accept a position on a rival newspaper which would be in competition with his employer's newspaper. In this case, the injunctions sought were to restrain him from undertaking or continuing employment with any competitor of the employers and from disclosing confidential information relating to them for the duration of the contractual notice period. The employers gave an undertaking to the trial judge to continue to pay the employee's salary until his contract lawfully expired but without requiring him to continue working for them, although in fact they were also willing to allow him to continue working for them. In those circumstances, the Court of Appeal granted the injunctions sought, on the footing that the employee would not be forced to work for the employers or be reduced to a condition of starvation or idleness.

9.64   Although there are perceptible differences between the two cases, the important point about both, at least for present purposes, is that the

---

[1]   [1988] ICR 29 at p 34.
[2]   See Ewing's observations on this issue: [1993] CLJ 405 at pp 415–423.
[3]   [1978] ICR 905. See Ewing's remarks on this case: [1993] CLJ 405 at pp 411–412.
[4]   [1987] ICR 588.

courts held that there are circumstances in which, and purposes for which, an employer may be allowed to refuse to accept a repudiation. In the *Evening Standard* case, however, Lawton LJ stressed that the hearing of an interlocutory appeal is not the time to examine these issues in depth.[1] They therefore await fuller analysis and examination on some future occasion.

3. THE EMPLOYMENT TRIBUNAL JURISDICTION

9.65 Section 3 of the Employment Tribunals Act 1996 gives the Lord Chancellor[2] the power to confer jurisdiction on employment tribunals in respect of damages for breach of a contract of employment.[3] The power is exercisable by order, and the relevant order is the Employment Tribunals Extension of Jurisdiction (England and Wales) Order 1994.[4]

9.66 Section 3 of the Employment Tribunals Act 1996 embraces the following claims:

1. claims for damages for breach of a contract of employment[5] or any other contract connected with employment;
2. claims for sums due under such contracts; and
3. claims for the recovery of sums in pursuance of any enactment relating to the terms or performance of such a contract.

In all three cases, the claim must be such that a court has jurisdiction to hear and determine an action in respect of the claim under existing law;[6] further, the tribunal jurisdiction is exercisable concurrently with such a court.[7] The enabling order may specify which claims are to be within the tribunal's jurisdiction and may also include exceptions.[8] Personal injuries claims are excluded.[9] The definition of 'personal injuries' includes 'disease and any impairment of a person's physical or mental condition'.[10]

9.67 The Employment Tribunals Act 1996 provides that the order may include provisions governing the manner in which proceedings are to be brought and the time within which they are to be brought and may modify any other enactment.[11] It may also make different provision in relation to

---

[1] [1987] ICR 588 at pp 594–595.

[2] In Scotland, the Lord Advocate.

[3] This does not include a claim for damages, or for a sum due, for personal injuries: see s 3(3) of the ETA 1996.

[4] SI 1994 No 1623. The Order applicable to Scotland is SI 1994 No 1624. The Orders came into effect on 12 July 1994.

[5] A breach of contract includes a breach of a term implied by contract, statute or otherwise, a term of a contract as modified by or under an enactment or otherwise, and a term incorporated in the contract: see s 3(6) of the Employment Tribunals Act 1996.

[6] Section 3(2).

[7] Section 3(4).

[8] Section 3(1) of the Employment Tribunals Act 1996.

[9] Section 3(3).

[10] Section 3(5).

[11] Section 8(3).

proceedings in respect of different descriptions of claims.[1] It does not, therefore, follow that the same limitation period for claims under section 3 will apply as for other claims, although, in fact, a limitation period of three months has been specified.

9.68   The final point to note here is that section 8(1) gives the tribunal power to order the respondent in the proceedings to pay whatever amount it finds to be due to the applicant. The order may set a maximum limit to the amount that may be awarded.

9.69   The Extension of Jurisdiction Order applies to claims covered by section 3 of the Employment Tribunals Act 1996 which arise or are outstanding on the termination of the employee's employment.[2] The following categories of claims are excluded:

1.   claims for breach of a contractual term requiring the employer to provide living accommodation or in connection with the provision of it;
2.   claims for breach of a term relating to intellectual property or imposing an obligation of confidence; and
3.   claims for breach of a restrictive covenant.[3]

It is arguable that a claim involving pensions rights may be possible, on the footing that such a claim is for breach of a contract 'connected with employment' within section 3(2)(a). There is no minimum qualifying period of employment to qualify for the right to claim, but a claim may not be brought during employment. The Court of Appeal has confirmed that an employment tribunal does not have jurisdiction to entertain a claim for damages for breach of contract presented before the effective date of termination.[4] Premature claims are thus not possible.

9.70   A claim must be presented within three months beginning with the effective date of termination or, where there is no effective date of termination, three months 'beginning with the last day upon which the employee worked in the employment which has terminated'. The test for extending the time for presenting the claim is the same as for unfair dismissal complaints, that it was not reasonably practicable to present the complaint in time.[5]

9.71   The employer may make a claim against the employee only where the employee has presented a complaint already and the claim is not excluded by article 5.[6] The employer's claim may not be presented if the

---

[1]   Section 8(4).
[2]   Article 3. This provision has been held to apply to an employee's claim for breach of contract where she contracted to work for the employers but the contract was terminated before she started work under it: see *Sarker v South Tees Acute Hospitals NHS Trust* [1997] IRLR 328.
[3]   Article 5, which also defines 'intellectual property'.
[4]   *Capek v Lincolnshire County Council* [2000] ICR 878.
[5]   Article 7.
[6]   Articles 4 and 8(a).

employee's claim has been withdrawn and must be presented within six weeks beginning with the day on which the employer received[1] a copy of the employee's originating application.[2] Extensions of time are dealt with in the same way as for employees' claims.[3] Article 4 specifies the types of claims that an employer may bring. It appears to be wide enough to embrace, for example, claims for damage to the employer's property or business through negligence, claims for damages against an employee who leaves early, and claims for recovery of training costs or relocation costs. The EAT has held that an employer's counter-claim may proceed even if the employee's claim fails, for example because it is presented out of time. Provided that it fulfils the criteria set out in article 4 of the Extension of Jurisdiction Order and is presented within the time-limit imposed by article 8, the counter-claim may still be heard and dealt with by the tribunal.[4]

9.72 The maximum compensation the tribunal may award is £25,000.[5] Questions may arise as to how compensation should be calculated where there is a successful claim under the Order and a successful complaint of unfair dismissal. This matter is considered in Chapter 8, at para 8.140.

---

[1] The Order does not say from whom.

[2] Article 8(c).

[3] For an example, see *Schultz v Esso Petroleum* [1999] ICR 1202.

[4] *Patel v RCMS Ltd* [1999] IRLR 161.

[5] Article 10.

Chapter 10

REMEDIES FOR WRONGFUL TERMINATION

1. DAMAGES

10.01 The general rule governing the measure of damages to which the employee is entitled is that the award will be limited to the amount of wages or salary he or she would have earned but for the premature termination of the contract by the employer. Compensation may also include the loss of any benefit to which he or she is contractually entitled and of which he or she is deprived in consequence of the breach. The period by reference to which the losses are assessed is that period until the date when the employer could lawfully terminate the contract. If the contract is for an indefinite period, the employee will receive the wages he or she would have earned during the notice period to which he or she was entitled. In the case of an employee employed under a fixed-term contract with no notice provision, the measure of damages will be the wages he or she would have received during the unexpired part of the contract. The general rule in calculating damages is that an employee is entitled to recover damages which will put him or her in the position he or she would have been in had the employers fulfilled their contractual obligations in the way most beneficial or least burdensome to themselves.[1]

10.02 The employee must 'mitigate' (ie minimise) the loss and an award of damages will be reduced by the amount he or she could reasonably be expected to earn in other employment, or the amount he or she actually earned during the notice period. All reasonable steps must be taken to mitigate the loss, which means that the employee must look for, and accept, any reasonable offer of alternative employment. He or she is also entitled to the amount of wages earned but not paid at the date of dismissal.[2]

10.03 In calculating the measure of damages to which a wrongfully dismissed employee is entitled, the court will need to take into account the relevant tax rules. These are considered at the end of this section.

10.04 An employee who breaches the contract is also liable for damages.[3] Until recently, claims for damages by employers against employees were relatively rare. It is possible, however, that the coming into force of the Employment Tribunals Extension of Jurisdiction Order,[4] which conferred wrongful dismissal jurisdiction upon the employment tribunals, may lead

---

[1] *Lavarack v Woods of Colchester Ltd* [1967] 1 QB 278.

[2] *Hochster v De La Tour* (1853) 2 E & B 678, *Frost v Knight* (1872) LR 7 Exch 111 and *Brace v Calder* [1895] 2 QB 253.

[3] See, eg, *National Coal Board v Galley* [1958] 1 WLR 16.

[4] SI 1994 No 1623 (see Chapter 9, paras 9.65 *et seq*, where it is considered).

to a greater number of claims by employers. The Regulations contain provisions enabling an employer to make a counterclaim against a former employee and are considered later in this chapter (see para 10.76).

(a) Recoverable losses

10.05   Two important considerations should be borne in mind when assessing the recoverable losses:

1.   the benefit lost must have been one to which the employee was contractually entitled; and
2.   the period for which the contract might have lasted must be ascertained.

So far as the second consideration is concerned, the general rule is that the employer may be assumed to have terminated the contract in the way most beneficial to itself. This means that, in the context of an employment contract, the period for which damages will be awarded will be the period for which the contract might have been expected to last had it been terminated according to its terms.

10.06   It is possible, however, that this period may be extended in cases where the employee is claiming 'stigma' damages arising from a breach of contract by the employer likely to affect his or her future employment prospects. This type of claim has been made possible by the House of Lords' decision in *Malik v Bank of Credit and Commerce International SA (in compulsory liquidation)* and is considered at paras 10.40 *et seq*.

10.07   The period for which damages may be awarded may also be extended in cases involving a contractual disciplinary procedure. In *Boyo v Lambeth London Borough Council*,[1] an employee whose contract incorporated a disciplinary procedure was dismissed without notice. The county court judge said that damages should be assessed on the basis of one month's notice and an estimated five months for the disciplinary proceedings. The Court of Appeal expressed reservations about this,[2] but regarded itself as bound by the previous Court of Appeal decision in *Gunton v Richmond-upon-Thames London Borough Council*.[3] In the later case of *Focsa Services (UK) Ltd v Birkett*,[4] a case arising from the employment tribunals' new jurisdiction in wrongful dismissal cases, the EAT reiterated the general rule that an employee's entitlement is to receive damages to reflect the pay he or she would have received during the notice period and no more. The EAT distinguished the *Boyo* and *Gunton* cases on the grounds that in the instant case there was no evidence to suggest that use of the employer's disciplinary procedure would have extended beyond the contractual notice which was given. Clearly, therefore, if the time over which damages are to

---

[1]   [1994] ICR 727.
[2]   See at pp 743H, 745H and 747G–748A.
[3]   [1980] ICR 755.
[4]   [1996] IRLR 325.

be awarded is to be extended beyond the contractual notice period, evidence will need to be adduced as to the time likely to have been taken by the operation of the disciplinary procedure. In *Janciuk v Winerite Ltd*,[1] the EAT said that the measure of loss for an employer's breach of contract in dismissing an employee without first having followed a contractual disciplinary procedure is based upon an assessment of the time for which, had the procedure been followed, the employee's employment would have continued, not upon an analysis of the chances that if the procedure had been followed the employee might never have been dismissed. This issue is considered further at para 10.34, where consideration is given to the question whether an employee may be compensated for the loss of statutory rights brought about by a breach of contract, including a failure to observe a contractual disciplinary procedure.

(i) Remuneration

10.08 The term 'remuneration' covers not only the payment of basic salary, but also additions to, and increases in, that basic salary. So commission, bonuses, tips and the like may be included.

10.09 **Basic salary** The reported cases show that there are at least three possible ways of calculating the loss of basic salary. One way is to work out the cost of buying an annuity which would provide the amount of the claimant's salary until the lawful termination date of the contract. This was done in *Bold v Brough, Nicholson & Hall Ltd*,[2] in the case of an employee paid £4,000 a year, plus a commission agreed at £500. His 10-year fixed-term contract was terminated wrongfully after it had run for just over three years. He claimed £26,312 on the basis of the cost of annuities to provide £4,000 and £500 a year until the date of the expiry of his contract. The judge upheld this claim, although he actually awarded £21,000 because of various amounts he deducted from the £26,312.

10.10 A second method is to take the gross amount of salary until the date of lawful termination, as was done in *Lavarack v Woods of Colchester Ltd*.[3] The third method is to take the net salary over the relevant period and, after the other sums have been done, gross up the total due to the claimant so as to leave him or her with that sum after taking account of any tax liability, as was done in *Shove v Downs Surgical plc*.[4] The plaintiff earned £36,000 a year and was entitled to not less than 30 calendar months' notice in writing. The judge considered schedules of calculations estimating the plaintiff's net income for that period. He said of these:

> 'I do not think that calculations such as these can be made with precision, or, if they can, that the results should be treated as more than a guide to the loss suffered by the plaintiff. These calculations assume that the rate of income tax

---

[1]   [1998] IRLR 63.
[2]   [1964] 1 WLR 201.
[3]   [1967] 1 QB 278.
[4]   [1984] ICR 532.

will remain the same during the whole period in question. No one can say now with certainty whether the amount of tax payable by a man earning £36,000 per annum will be higher or lower in the tax year 1984/85.'[1]

He concluded that the plaintiff would probably have received £53,000 net. He added various other heads of loss to that figure and then made various deductions, and decided that the plaintiff was entitled to net compensation of £60,728. To leave the plaintiff with that sum after payment of the tax payable on such compensation, he decided that damages of £83,477 should be awarded. In both cases, the social security contributions the employee would have had to pay will fall to be deducted.[2]

10.11	Whatever approach is adopted, the incidence of taxation will affect the amount of money received by the employee. In the light of the current rules on the taxation of golden handshakes, which are considered later in this chapter, the best approach is that of Sheen J in the _Shove_ case.

**10.12	Additions to basic salary** Additions to, or increases in, basic salary may be included in the calculation of damages only if the employee was contractually entitled to them. Since the employer generally does not have an obligation to increase the employee's salary, a claim for an increase of salary would be irrecoverable.[3] But an employee whose contract has an inflation-proofing clause may claim whatever increase the working of the clause would have given.[4] In cases where an employee's contract contains a provision stating that the employer's policy is normally to review salaries annually, the employee's entitlement to an increase will depend upon the construction of the agreement. In _Clark v BET plc_,[5] for example, the relevant clause is stated as follows:

'The executive's salary shall be reviewed annually and be increased by such amount if any as the board shall in its absolute discretion decide. In making their decision the board shall consider a comparative group of companies similar to that used in section 4 of the report "Review of executive Remuneration" dated 14 December 1993 produced by William M. Mercer Ltd.'

Timothy Walker J took the view that this clause was to be construed as obliging the employers to provide an annual upward adjustment in salary but leaving the amount (if any) of the increase to the absolute discretion of the board. He considered the relevant evidence, which was to the effect that the employee and other comparable employees had achieved annual increases of at least 10% over the previous five years and that the employers were a profitable company which could reasonably expect increases in profitability in the future. He therefore assessed damages

[1]	[1984] ICR 532 at p 538.
[2]	_Cooper v Firth Brown Ltd_ [1963] 1 WLR 418.
[3]	_Lavarack v Woods of Colchester Ltd_ [1967] 1 QB 278.
[4]	_Re Crowther and Nicholson Ltd_ (1981) _The Times_, June 10.
[5]	[1997] IRLR 348.

under this head on the basis that the employee would have been awarded an annual 10% increase.

10.13 The contract may also contain a clause giving the employee entitlement to performance- or profit-related pay. The amount the employee will be entitled to by way of damages will depend upon the particular scheme adopted by the employer, but there is no reason in principle why damages should not be awarded in respect of this type of loss. Damages for the loss of rights given by a share option scheme are considered at para 10.32.

10.14 Commission will not be a recoverable head of damage unless the employer's failure to provide the employee with an opportunity to earn commission constituted a breach of contract. It may be hard to decide whether there has been a breach, particularly if the wrongful dismissal is caused by the employer closing down the business. In *Rhodes v Forwood*[1], the House of Lords refused to imply a term into a contract between a principal and an agent that the business should continue to be carried on for the duration of the contract, largely because there was a clause in the agreement which expressly provided for the events which would enable the agreement to be terminated. In *Turner v Goldsmith*,[2] on the other hand, the Court of Appeal held that the defendant was liable, despite the fact that his factory had been burnt down. *Rhodes v Forwood* was distinguished on the ground that since there was no express contract to employ the agent, such a contract could not be implied. But a failure to give an opportunity to earn commission may not constitute a breach. In *Re RS Newman Ltd, Raphael's Claim*[3] the employee was entitled to a commission of 5% 'on the amount realised from and paid upon all sales effected of the goods of the company'. Astbury J said: 'It is only a contract to pay on such turnover as the company, so long as it continues to exist as a company, shall in fact make ...'.[4]

10.15 Even if the employee is entitled to damages for loss of future commission, the damages will not necessarily be calculated on the assumption that the employer's business would have continued to flourish. In *Reigate v Union Manufacturing Company (Ramsbottom) Ltd*,[5] two of the judges pointed out that the assessment of damages might reflect predictions of the probable state of the defendant's business and business conditions generally. In *Roberts v Elwell Engineers Ltd*,[6] the plaintiff was entitled to commission on all orders received from customers introduced by him. The Court of Appeal held that the commission had to be taken into account beyond the date at which the contract could have been lawfully terminated by the employers (three months), but pointed out that allowance would have to be made for the vicissitudes of trade, the

---

[1] (1876) 1 App Cas 256.
[2] [1891] 1 QB 544.
[3] [1916] 2 Ch 309.
[4] *Ibid* at p 320.
[5] [1918] 1 KB 592.
[6] [1972] 2 QB 586.

possibility of the customers ceasing to deal with the employers, and the likelihood of the employers receiving repeat orders from customers introduced by the employee.[1] Generally speaking, a reasonable yardstick for assessing lost commission would be the average amount of the employee's commission earnings before the dismissal.[2]

10.16   Another possible addition to salary is a bonus, but, since bonuses are usually given at the discretion of the employer, the loss of a possible bonus is not likely to be a recoverable head of damage. In *Lavarack v Woods of Colchester Ltd*,[3] the employers ended a bonus scheme after the employee's wrongful dismissal. This head of his claim failed, although Diplock LJ suggested that had the employers continued the scheme he might have been entitled to be compensated for the loss of bonus.[4] Lord Denning MR dissented, on the grounds that the employee was entitled to what he might reasonably have expected to have received but for the wrongful dismissal. In *Clark v BET plc*,[5] which was discussed above in the context of an employee's contractual entitlement to a salary increase, a second issue was whether the employee in question was entitled to a bonus. The relevant clause stated as follows: 'The executive will participate in a bonus arrangement providing a maximum of 60% of basic salary in any year'. The judge construed this as conferring a right on the employee to participate in a bonus scheme providing within its terms for a maximum of 60% bonus of salary. He distinguished *Lavarack v Woods* and said that the evidence established that, making realistic assumptions, the employee would have continued to achieve significant bonuses; he assessed the level of bonus at 50% of salary for three years.

10.17   In *Clark v Nomura International plc*,[6] the employee's contract provided for a 'discretionary bonus scheme which is not guaranteed in any way and is dependent on individual performance and after the first 12 months your remaining in our employment on the date of payment'. The plaintiff was a senior proprietary equities trader who in the relevant period was responsible for profits for his employers of around £6.5 million. He was dismissed with three months' notice but, although he was still in employment at the date of payment of the bonus, he did not receive it. He made a claim for damages alleging that the employers' failure to pay him any bonus amounted to a breach of contract. The judge upheld his claim. According to Burton J, an employer exercising a discretion which, on the face of the contract of employment, is unfettered or absolute, will be in breach of contract if no reasonable employer would have exercised the discretion in that way. On that basis, he awarded damages to the employee in respect of the bonus he would have received had the employer complied with its contractual obligations.

---

[1]   [1972] 2 QB 586 at p 596.
[2]   See *Devonald v Rosser & Sons* [1906] 2 KB 728.
[3]   [1967] 1 QB 278.
[4]   *Ibid* at p 297.
[5]   [1997] IRLR 348.
[6]   [2000] IRLR 766.

10.18   The employee may also be entitled to compensation for loss of tips, if there was a term in the contract (express or implied) entitling him or her to receive them.[1]

10.19   A claim for holiday pay is likely to be a claim for money due under the employee's contract and not as part of the damages for breach of contract, since the claim will be in respect of accrued holiday pay.[2] The amount of holiday pay the employee will be entitled to claim will depend on the terms of the contract and how much holiday he or she has had in the period of holiday entitlement ('holiday year') before the termination of the employment.[3] If the amount due cannot be ascertained under the contract, the proper claim will be for damages.

(ii) Benefits in kind

10.20   Company car   The head of loss of a company car was considered in some detail by the judge in *Shove v Downs Surgical plc*.[4] The employee's service contract provided for him to have a Daimler car; the company agreed to 'bear the entire cost of servicing, repairing, maintaining, taxing and insuring the said motor car and any replacement and shall in addition reimburse to the [employee] all sums expended by him on petrol and oil consumed in the performance of [his] duties'.

10.21   The company tried to argue that he had no contractual entitlement to use the car for his own private purposes and that he was not entitled to charge the company for petrol consumed when using the car for his own purposes. Sheen J rejected the first argument on the ground that, as a matter of construction, the clause in question entitled the employee to use the car in the performance of his duties and for private use. The second argument did not fall to be considered because of a concession made by the company's counsel. The employee's evidence was that he drove about 17,000 miles in the last year of his employment. The judge assessed his private use of the car at 5,000 miles each year and assessed compensation on that basis. He rejected the argument that he should assess the plaintiff's loss by reference to the notional taxable emolument specified by the Taxes Act 1988 (as it now is) for the benefit, which would have been £2,680. He

---

[1]   *Manubens v Leon* [1919] 1 KB 208.

[2]   See, eg *Shove v Downs Surgical plc* [1984] ICR 532, where the claim was agreed at £553.84. There is no reason why the employer should not include a contractual provision requiring an employee to take some or all of any outstanding holiday entitlement during the notice period.

[3]   In *Morley v Heritage plc* [1993] IRLR 400, the Court of Appeal upheld a county court judge's decision that, in the absence of an express provision, there was no implied term in the employee's contract that if his employment terminated without his having taken all his holiday entitlement, his employers would pay him in lieu. The contract contained an express term, but the employee sought to amplify it by the implication of a further term relating to a payment in respect of remaining holiday entitlement on termination of his employment. This decision reinforces the point that, if there is an express term covering a particular matter, there is limited scope for the implication of any further term relating to that matter.

[4]   [1984] ICR 532.

also dismissed the argument that he should calculate the employee's loss by reference to the cost of providing the type of car which the employee might reasonably be expected to acquire in his present circumstances, on the ground that the contract expressly provided for the employee to be provided with a Daimler, the benefit of which he would have enjoyed for the two and a half years of his notice entitlement. He appears to have accepted evidence provided by the Automobile Association as to the cost of running cars of various sizes, but he stressed that it was impossible to make an exact calculation of the loss. He awarded damages under this head of £10,000.

10.22   If the AA figures are used when assessing damages under this head, in preference to the car and fuel benefit scales for directors and higher paid employees used for tax purposes, then clearly the measure of damages will be considerably greater than otherwise they would be. It is not clear on what basis loss of a company car should be calculated for the purposes of a compensatory award for unfair dismissal, but there seems no reason not to use the AA figures there too.

It is important, however, to bear in mind that the starting-point for calculations is the employee's contract of employment.

10.23   Accommodation The term 'accommodation' covers a number of different possible arrangements, but the most likely arrangement is the provision of rent-free or low-rent accommodation under the terms of a licence. Other costs may also be borne by the employer, such as rates, heating, electricity, use of telephone, and provision of domestic services.

It is accepted that a claim in respect of rent-free accommodation is permissible, and the court will assess the loss on the basis of the market value of the premises if they are freehold, as to which evidence should be available.[1]

10.24   Pension schemes This head of loss is potentially complex, because of the actuarial problem of deciding upon the amount of damages to be awarded to compensate for the loss of a future entitlement. Much depends upon the provisions of a particular pension scheme, and the assistance of an actuary will be essential. As with the other heads of loss, the benefit lost must be one to which the employee was contractually entitled. In *Silvey v Pendragon plc*[2] the Court of Appeal held that damages may be awarded in respect of pension benefits to which the employee would have become entitled had he been given the correct period of notice and not been

---

[1]   See *Re English Joint Stock Bank, Yelland's Case* (1867) LR 4 Eq 350, *British Guiana Credit Corporation v Da Silva* [1965] 1 WLR 248 and *Ivory v Palmer* [1975] ICR 340. See also *Norris v Checksfield* [1991] 1 WLR 1241, which concerned the enforcement of a contractual provision that the employee's licence to occupy accommodation would end immediately on termination of his employment. The Court of Appeal upheld the county court judge's decision that the provision created a service licence and that no notice to quit was required to be served on the employee.

[2]   (2001) IDS Brief B689/7, CA.

summarily dismissed. It said that the loss of pension rights was not too remote to be recoverable and rejected the employers' argument that the particulars of the pension scheme meant that the loss in question was not foreseeable.

10.25 The rules of the scheme will probably provide the options available to a member of the scheme who leaves for any reason except retirement or death. In *Acklam v Sentinel Insurance Company Ltd*,[1] the rules provided that a member 'leaving the service of the company for any reason except retirement on pension or death' had to exercise one of three options: to take a pension beginning at normal pension date for the amount secured by his own contributions; or to continue his contributions and secure a pension starting at normal pension date; or to take a refund of all his contributions. Salmon J rejected the argument that the provision did not apply to members who had been wrongfully dismissed. In fact, the employee chose to take a refund of all his contributions. The judge held that he was not thereby precluded from recovering damages for the loss of the pension rights which he suffered because of the wrongful dismissal.

10.26 The employee's entitlement may be considerably affected if the employer has the right to terminate any participant's assurance under the pension scheme at any time. In *Beach v Reed Corrugated Cases Ltd*,[2] the employers had such a right. When the employee was dismissed, they discontinued his assurance and paid him his entitlement under the terms of the scheme, a life annuity purchasable by the sum of £10,647. Had he continued to be employed by them until his sixty-fifth birthday (as his contract entitled him) or died before that date, he (or his estate) would have been entitled to £27,379. He tried to argue that the entitlement under the scheme should be confined to cases where the employment was rightfully terminated, and that, by wrongful termination of his contract, his employers deprived him of the opportunity of receiving the larger sum. He therefore claimed £13,462, which represented actuarially the present value of the difference between the sum actually received and £27,379. The judge rejected this argument, saying:

> '... [O]nce it is conceded that the plaintiff's deprivation of a chance of obtaining enhanced benefits under the scheme does not sound in damages because the defendants have fulfilled their obligations under the scheme, I find it quite impossible to see how the plaintiff can be entitled to swell the amount of damages to which he is entitled owing to the defendants' wrongful repudiation of his service agreement by including in his claim an item in respect of which no damages is recoverable.'[3]

10.27 The later case of *Bold v Brough Nicholson & Hall Ltd*[4] distinguished the *Beach* case on the grounds that there the employers had a discretion to discontinue contributions in respect of a particular employee, whereas in

---

[1]   [1959] 2 WLR 683.
[2]   [1956] 1 WLR 807.
[3]   *Ibid* at p 817.
[4]   [1964] 1 WLR 201.

the *Bold* case they could only discontinue the scheme as a whole. Here the employee's fixed-term contract was wrongfully terminated just under seven years before its expiry. His sixty-fifth birthday would have fallen about three and three-quarter years after its expiry. He claimed loss of pension rights on three possible bases:

1. that if he had remained in the defendant's employment until his sixty-fifth birthday or if they had become liable to maintain the premiums due under the scheme, he would have become entitled to a pension of £729 10s a year, the then value of which was actuarially agreed at £5,743;
2. in the alternative, that if he had remained in their employment until the expiry of the fixed-term contract, he would have become entitled to a reduced pension (of £678, present value £5,388) afforded by the joint contributions to that date made by him and the employers;
3. alternatively, that had he continued in the employment of the defendants until the expiry of the fixed term and had his contract then been terminated, he would have become entitled to a pension reflecting his own contributions (in accordance with a rule in the scheme allowing for the provision of a reduced pension payable from pension age in the event of membership terminating at any time before the attainment of pension age), the agreed figure being £729.

10.28   The judge rejected the first basis, since, on the facts, the company had no legal obligation to make such payments as might be necessary to provide him with a pension at 65 of an amount equal to what he would have received at that age. He decided in favour of the third basis, because the defendants had the right to terminate the employee's contract with six months' notice expiring on the date of expiry of the fixed-term contract. This method of termination could have fallen within two rules of the scheme, one covering discharge of a member from his employment (rule 8(e)), the other covering the departure of the member with the consent of the employer (rule 13). The judge held that a termination of the plaintiff's services by six months' notice expiring at the end of the contract was a discharge, not a departure with consent.

10.29   The judge also applied the rule that damages against a contract breaker must be assessed on the footing that he or she will perform the contract in the manner most beneficial to himself or herself.[1] This meant in the present context that the court must assume that the employers would terminate the employee's contract by appropriate notice rather than agree upon his early retirement.

10.30   The judge also rejected the argument that damages under this head should be assessed upon the basis that the employers had the right to discontinue the whole scheme. He stressed that in assessing damages he

---

[1]   See *Cockburn v Alexander* (1846) 6 CB 791 and *Robinson v Robinson* (1851) 1 De GM & G 247.

had to compensate the employee for what he had lost, bearing in mind all the probabilities, and rejected the likelihood of them terminating the scheme solely to defeat a claim by the employee.[1]

10.31   Other benefits in kind Such losses may include loss of medical insurance,[2] loss of preferential treatment (eg low-interest or interest-free loans) and loss of luncheon vouchers.[3]

10.32   A more recent head of loss is the loss of a right pursuant to a share option scheme. In this type of case, much will depend upon the wording of the relevant clause. In *Micklefield v SAC Technology Ltd*,[4] for example, the clause said: 'If an option holder ceases to be employed … for whatever reason whatsoever, then the option granted to him shall … lapse and not be exercisable'. Another clause further stipulated:

> 'If any option holder ceases to be an executive for any reason he shall not be entitled, and by applying for an option an executive shall be deemed irrevocably to have waived any entitlement, by way of compensation for loss of office or otherwise howsoever to any sum or other benefit to compensate him for the loss of any rights under the scheme'.

The judge held that, on the construction of the relevant clauses, the employee was not entitled to damages for the loss of his option to purchase shares. He said that the second clause quoted above was an exemption clause which exempted the employers from part of the liability for their wrongful act. He also held that the clear terms of the clause had the effect of excluding the principle that a person cannot be permitted to take advantage of his or her own wrong. It should be noted, however, that the judge accepted that employment contracts outside Scotland[5] are covered by the Unfair Contract Terms Act 1977, despite the absence of express statutory provision.[6]

10.33   In *Chapman v Aberdeen Construction Group plc*,[7] a case which arose in Scotland, there was a similar rule in the option scheme which excluded the employee's right to damages or compensation in the event of his dismissal. The Court of Session applied section 23 of the Unfair Contract Terms Act 1977 (which only applies in Scotland) and held that its effect was to render the exclusion clause void. The majority rejected the employer's argument that the share option scheme did not create a contract, saying that once an option had been granted to an employee under the scheme a contractual

---

[1]   [1964] 1 WLR 201 at pp 211–212.

[2]   In *Shove v Downs Surgical plc* [1984] ICR 532, the judge found that the employee was entitled to have paid a subscription to BUPA of £350 per annum for himself and his wife, and awarded £700 under this head. See also *Clark v BET plc* [1997] IRLR 348 at p 352.

[3]   *McGrath v De Soissons* (1962) 112 LJ 60.

[4]   [1990] IRLR 218.

[5]   In Scotland, they are expressly included, by virtue of s 15(2)(b) of the Act.

[6]   This view has also been taken by the Court of Appeal: see *Johnstone v Bloomsbury Health Authority* [1991] ICR 269. See also *Brigden v American Express Bank Ltd* [2000] IRLR 94.

[7]   [1991] IRLR 505.

relationship arose between him or her and the employers. It said that the purpose of section 23 is to prevent rights in a primary contract being cut down or extinguished by a provision in a secondary contract.

(iii) Loss of statutory rights

10.34   In *Robert Cort & Son Ltd v Charman*,[1] the EAT suggested that damages for wrongful dismissal may include the loss of the right to compensation for unfair dismissal which the employee would have had if the correct notice had been given. So an employee would be entitled to damages under this head if he was entitled to three months' notice, but was dismissed summarily after 23 months. This suggestion was approved by the Court of Appeal in *Stapp v The Shaftesbury Society*.[2]

10.35   The issue has surfaced more recently in the context of cases involving contractual disciplinary procedures. In such cases, the argument is that the employer, by failing to observe a contractual disciplinary procedure and thus terminating the employee's contract earlier than would have been the case had the procedure been followed, should compensate the employee not only in respect of the wages he or she would have earned during the time taken by observance of the procedure, but also in respect of the loss of unfair dismissal rights which has occurred as a result of the employer's failure. Such an argument is clearly only possible when the employee is close to reaching the end of the qualifying period of employment for the right not to be unfairly dismissed and can thus argue that the period of time it would have taken to conclude a disciplinary procedure would have taken the employee over the threshold of the qualifying period.

10.36   The Court of Session decision in *Morran v Glasgow Council of Tenants Associations*[3] concerned an employee who started employment on 8 October 1991 and was dismissed summarily on 16 September 1993; he was thus unable to satisfy the then requirement of two years' qualifying employment. Under his contract he was entitled to four weeks' notice, but that entitlement was subject to the right of the employer to make a payment in lieu of notice. He received neither notice nor pay in lieu. The Court of Session rejected his claim for compensation in respect of the loss of the right to complain of unfair dismissal. It pointed out the principle that in an action for damages for breach of contract, an employee is entitled to recover damages which will put him or her in the position he or she would have been in if the employers had fulfilled their contractual obligation in the way which would have been least burdensome to them. It said that where the contract gives the employer the option of terminating the contract with due notice or making a payment in lieu of notice, the less burdensome way for them to fulfil their obligation is to dismiss the employee and make a payment in lieu of notice.

---

[1]   [1981] ICR 816.
[2]   [1982] IRLR 326.
[3]   [1998] IRLR 67.

10.37 This case was distinguished by the EAT in the later case of *Raspin v United News Shops Ltd.*[1] The facts were that the employee started work for the employers on 16 May 1994; she was summarily dismissed on 27 May 1996 in breach of the contractual disciplinary procedure to which she was entitled. The tribunal concluded that following a proper procedure would have taken an additional three weeks and awarded her damages in respect of that period. She appealed to the EAT arguing that since, on the tribunal's finding, the earliest she would have been dismissed had a proper procedure been followed was 16 May 1996 and she would then have been qualified to complain of unfair dismissal, there should be a further award of damages to reflect the fact that her dismissal in breach of contract had deprived her of the opportunity to bring an unfair dismissal claim. The EAT allowed her appeal. It said that the employment tribunal had found, and was entitled to do so, that but for the breach of the contractually binding disciplinary procedure, the applicant's employment would not have been terminated before 16 May 1996. Regardless of how the employers might then have terminated her employment, whether lawfully or unlawfully, or fairly or unfairly, that was the earliest date on which it could have happened and there would then have been jurisdiction to entertain a claim for unfair dismissal. It therefore remitted the case to the tribunal for assessment of damages under this head. This would involve the evaluation of a lost opportunity, which would entail assessing what the losses would have been as well as the chances that an unfair dismissal claim would have been successful.

(b) Irrecoverable losses

10.38 The House of Lords case of *Addis v Gramophone Company Ltd.*[2] is the leading authority for the principle that damages may not be awarded to compensate for the manner of dismissal, the injured feelings of the employee, or the loss he or she may sustain from the fact that the dismissal of itself makes it more difficult to obtain new employment. It has been affirmed in *Shove v Downs Surgical plc,*[3] *Bliss v South East Thames Regional Health Authority,*[4] *O'Laoire v Jackel International Ltd (No 2)*[5] and *French v Barclays Bank plc.*[6] The House of Lords has now reviewed it in its decision in *Malik v Bank of Credit and Commerce International SA (in compulsory liquidation)*[7] (see para 10.40).

10.39 In *Cox v Phillips Industries Ltd,*[8] damages were awarded to an employee to compensate him for depression, anxiety, frustration and illness caused by a demotion. Lawson J accepted that the *Addis* principle

---

[1] [1999] IRLR 9.
[2] [1909] AC 488.
[3] [1984] ICR 532.
[4] [1987] ICR 700.
[5] [1991] ICR 718.
[6] [1998] IRLR 646.
[7] [1997] ICR 606. The Court of Appeal's decision is reported at [1995] IRLR 375.
[8] [1976] ICR 138.

prevented the employee from claiming any further damages for wrongful dismissal, since he had already been paid the appropriate compensation.[1] But he went on to decide that the employers had entered into an express contractual obligation with the employee to offer him a better position with greater responsibility and an increased salary and that it was within the contemplation of the parties that, if the contractual obligation was breached, the effect would be to expose the employee to the degree of distress he underwent. So these damages were for breach of a separate contractual obligation and not wrongful dismissal. This case should be regarded as turning on its own particular facts. Indeed, in *Bliss v South East Thames Regional Health Authority,* Dillon LJ, with whom the other members of the Court of Appeal agreed, described the views of Lawson J as 'wrong' and said that the approach taken by him was not open to the court until the House of Lords reconsidered its decision in the *Addis* case.[2]

10.40   *Addis v Gramophone Company Ltd*[3] has been taken as authority for the proposition that loss caused by injury to one's reputation is irrecoverable. Lord Loreburn LC said that damages 'cannot include compensation ... for the loss the employee may sustain from the fact that his having been dismissed of itself makes it more difficult for him to obtain fresh employment'.[4] In *Malik v Bank of Credit and Commerce International SA (in compulsory liquidation),*[5] the Court of Appeal struck out a claim for damages by an employee who claimed that his existing reputation had been damages by the employer's breach of an implied term that it would not, without reasonable and proper cause, conduct itself in a manner likely to destroy or seriously damage the relationship of trust and confidence between employer and employee. The claim arose from the liquidation of the bank and the fraudulent practices which later came to light. The House of Lords decided unanimously,[6] however, that in certain cases what have come to be called 'stigma damages' may be awarded and allowed the employees' appeal against the Court of Appeal's decision. Lord Nicholls of Birkenhead stressed that the issue in *Malik* was whether damages are recoverable in respect of the financial loss suffered by the employee because of the dismissal and said that he was not concerned with whether damages for injured feelings are recoverable. He said of Lord Loreburn's comments in *Addis*:

'In my view, these observations cannot be read as precluding the recovery of damages where the manner of dismissal involved a breach of the trust and confidence term and this caused financial loss. *Addis v Gramophone Co Ltd* was decided in the days before this implied term was adumbrated. Now that this term exists and is normally implied in every contract of employment, damages for its breach should be assessed in accordance with ordinary contractual

---

[1]   [1976] ICR 138 at p 146.
[2]   [1987] ICR 700 at pp 717–718.
[3]   [1909] AC 488.
[4]   *Ibid* at p 491. See also *Withers v General Theatre Corporation* [1933] 2 KB 536.
[5]   [1995] IRLR 375.
[6]   See [1997] ICR 606.

principles. This is as much true if the breach occurs before or in connection with the dismissal or at any other time.'[1]

He also pointed out that, so far as the recoverability of continuing financial losses are concerned, there is no basis for distinguishing wrongful dismissal following a breach of the trust and confidence term, constructive dismissal following a breach of the trust and confidence term, and a breach of the trust and confidence term which, as in the present case, only becomes known after the contract has ended.[2] Both Lord Nicholls and Lord Steyn emphasised that it is consistent with general contractual principle that an employee should be compensated for a financial loss arising from a breach of contract. So stated, the principle excludes claims based on events other than a breach of contract. This means that compensation for loss of reputation may be awarded, provided that it is caused by a breach of contract. If the loss is caused by a breach of the implied term of trust and confidence, it is consistent with principle that damages should be awarded.

10.41   Whilst it is tempting to regard this decision as having far-reaching implications, it is important to note that both Lord Nicholls and Lord Steyn pointed to the difficulties in practice of mounting successful claims based on a breach of the implied term. Lord Nicholls observed that it was likely that it would rarely happen that the employer was conducting a 'dishonest and corrupt' business and made it clear that an employee's association with an unsuccessful business, even if run incompetently, would not found a claim.[3] Lord Steyn said:

'... [T]he implied obligation applies only where there is no "reasonable and proper cause" for the employers' conduct, and then only if the conduct is calculated to destroy or seriously damage the relationship of trust and confidence. That circumscribes the potential reach and scope of the implied obligation ... The limiting principles of causation, remoteness and mitigation present formidable practical obstacles to such claims succeeding.'[4]

10.42   The issues canvassed in the *Addis* and *Malik* decisions have been further considered by the House of Lords in *Johnson v Unisys Ltd*.[5] The employee was summarily dismissed in 1994; he won an unfair dismissal claim against his employers and was awarded the maximum compensatory award available, subject to a deduction for contributory fault. He later started a wrongful dismissal action, claiming that, because of the manner of his dismissal, he suffered a psychiatric illness which made it impossible for him to find work. He claimed damages in respect of that loss. The House of Lords upheld the decision of the county court judge to strike out the claim on the ground that it disclosed no cause of action. The main speeches were given by Lord Hoffmann and Lord Millett, with whom Lord Bingham of

---

[1]   [1997] ICR 606 at p 615.
[2]   *Ibid* at pp 613–614.
[3]   *Ibid* at pp 617–618.
[4]   *Ibid* at pp 628–629.
[5]   [2001] IRLR 279.

Cornhill (expressly) and Lord Nicholls of Birkenhead (impliedly) agreed.
There were two grounds for its decision: (1) the implied duty of trust and
confidence does not apply to a dismissal or to the way in which
employment is terminated, because an implied term cannot contradict an
express term giving a right to dismiss on due notice and because the
implied duty of trust and confidence is concerned with preserving the
employment relationship;[1] and (2) the statutory scheme of unfair dismissal
gives employment tribunals a broad jurisdiction to award compensation in
respect of the manner in which an employee is dismissed and that a
common law right embracing the same matter cannot co-exist with the
statutory right.[2] Lord Hoffmann said:[3]

> '... [T]his statutory system for dealing with unfair dismissals was set up by
> Parliament to deal with the recognised deficiencies of the law as it stood at the
> time of *Malloch v Aberdeen Corporation*.[4] The remedy adopted by Parliament was
> not to build upon the common law by creating a statutory implied term that the
> power of dismissal should be exercised fairly or in good faith, leaving the courts
> to give a remedy on general principles of contractual damages. Instead, it set up
> an entirely new system outside the ordinary courts, with tribunals staffed by a
> majority of lay members, applying new statutory concepts and offering
> statutory remedies. Many of the new rules, such as the exclusion of certain
> classes of employees and the limit on the amount of the compensatory award,
> were not based upon any principle which it would have been open to the courts
> to apply. They were based upon policy and represented an attempt to balance
> fairness to employees against the general economic interests of the community
> ... For the judiciary to construct a general common law remedy for unfair
> circumstances attending dismissal would be to go contrary to the evident
> intention of Parliament that there should be such a remedy but that it should be
> limited in application and extent.'

10.43   In *Gogay v Hertfordshire County Council*,[5] the Court of Appeal
distinguished both the *Malik* case and *Johnson v Unisys*. The case involved a
claim for damages in respect of a depressive illness allegedly brought
about by the employers' breach of the implied duty of trust and confidence.
The Court upheld the claim and awarded damages in respect of the
psychiatric illness, distinguishing *Addis* on the grounds that the employee
suffered psychiatric illness rather than hurt feelings, and *Addis* and *Johnson
v Unisys* on the grounds that in the instant case what was involved was a
suspension rather than a dismissal from employment.

10.44   In the *Malik* case, both Lord Nicholls and Lord Steyn also
commented upon the conflict between *Marbé v George Edwardes (Daly's
Theatre) Ltd*.[6] and *Withers v General Theatre Corporation*[7] and said that *Withers*

---

[1]   See Lord Hoffmann at pp 286 (para 38) – 287 (para 47) and Lord Millett at p 291, para 78.
[2]   See Lord Hoffmann at pp 288 (para 54) – 289 (para 58) and Lord Millett at p 291, paras 79
      and 80.
[3]   *Ibid* at pp 288–289.
[4]   [1971] 1 WLR 1581.
[5]   [2000] IRLR 703.
[6]   [1928] 1 KB 269.
[7]   [1933] 2 KB 536.

was wrong in saying that damages may never be recovered in respect of damage to an existing reputation caused by a breach of contract.[1] It is consistent with the stated principles, however, that, if the enhancement of the plaintiff's reputation by publicity was contemplated specifically by the contract, then it may be regarded as a head of damage contemplated by the parties when entering into the contract for which damages may be claimed. This head of damage has been established in relation to actors[2] and extended to authors.[3]

10.45 Although the Court of Appeal has refused to give damages to a company director for the loss of the publicity or prestige he would have gained by being in the defendant's employment,[4] the contemporary importance of the media means that there are classes of employees (eg broadcasters, journalists, etc) whose career depends upon their receiving publicity through the media. In such cases, it is arguable that enhancement of their reputation is contemplated by their contract, but no reported cases have considered this question. In this context, however, it is worth recalling the words of Goddard J in *Tolnay v Criterion Film Productions Ltd:*[5] 'All persons who have to make a living by attracting the public to their works, be they ... painters or ... literary men ... or ... pianists, must live by getting known to the public'. Those words are as true now as when they were uttered.

10.46 Another question which arises here concerns the amount of damages that should be awarded. The decided cases are mostly from the late nineteenth or early twentieth century and the amount of damages was left to the jury after directions from the judge. In a number of these cases, the appellate court felt that the amount was more than it would have awarded itself, but declined to interfere with the award.[6] This means that there is relatively little guidance as to the principles which should apply when calculating damages under this head.

It should be noted that wrongfully dismissed apprentices may recover for loss of future prospects and the opportunity of completing their apprenticeship, since the object of apprenticeship is to enable the apprentice to be trained for future employment.[7]

---

[1]   [1997] ICR 606 at pp 617, 627 (Lord Nicholls) and 470, para 67 (Lord Steyn).
[2]   *Marbé v George Edwardes (Daly's Theatre) Ltd* [1928] 1 KB 269. See also *Banning v Lyric Theatre Ltd* (1894) 71 LT 396, *Clayton and Waller Ltd v Oliver* [1930] AC 209 and *Withers v General Theatre Corporation* [1933] 2 KB 536.
[3]   *Tolnay v Criterion Film Productions Ltd* [1936] 2 All ER 1625.
[4]   *Re Golomb* (1931) 144 LT 583.
[5]   [1936] 2 All ER 1625 at p 1626.
[6]   See, eg, *Clayton and Waller Ltd v Oliver* [1930] AC 209, where the House of Lords described the jury's award as 'extravagant'.
[7]   *Dunk v George Waller & Sons Ltd* [1970] 2 QB 163.

(c) Mitigation

10.47   In *Beckham v Drake*,[1] Erle J said:

'The measure of damages ... is obtained by considering what is the usual rate of wages for the employment here contracted for, and what time would be lost before a similar employment could be obtained. The law considers that employment in any ordinary branch of industry can be obtained by a person competent for the place, and that ... it is the duty of the servant to use diligence to find another employment.'

This remains a useful general statement of this area of the law.

10.48   The duty to mitigate means that the wrongfully dismissed employee must take reasonable steps to minimise the loss he or she has suffered as a result of the wrongful dismissal; it is not permissible just to do nothing and wait until the time when the contract could have been lawfully terminated and then sue for the remuneration which would have been earned during that period.[2] It should be noted that the duty to mitigate does not arise in circumstances where the employee's contract contains a provision entitling him or her to a period of notice or to salary in lieu of notice. This was the conclusion reached by the Court of Appeal in *Abrahams v Performing Right Society Ltd*.[3] The employee was employed under a contract entitling him to two years' notice of termination, or salary in lieu of notice. The employers summarily terminated his employment. The Court of Appeal held that in doing so they were acting lawfully and were effectively electing to pay money in lieu of notice under the contract. The Court went on to hold that, in those circumstances, the employee was not obliged to mitigate his loss. Hutchison LJ, with whom Aldous LJ agreed, said that, since the contractual provision gave rise to a claim for a sum due under the contract, there was no duty to mitigate. He went on to say that, if that view was wrong and the payment in lieu was to be regarded as liquidated damages, the employee still had no duty to mitigate. After quoting from *McGregor on Damages* and *Chitty on Contracts*, he said:[4] 'It seems to me that, as a matter of principle, where there is a liquidated damage clause which is valid ... there is no room for arguments on mitigation of damages, a concept relevant only in cases where damages are at large'.

10.49   In *Gregory v Wallace*,[5] the Court of Appeal considered *Abrahams v Performing Right Society Ltd* but concluded that, on the basis of the drafting of the clause in issue in that case, the employee was entitled to unliquidated damages but was not subject to a duty to bring into account earnings from other employment during the notice period. The reason for

---

[1]   (1849) 2 HLC 579 at pp 607–608.
[2]   *British Westinghouse Electric Co Ltd v Underground Electric Ry* [1912] AC 673 at p 689, and *Denmark Productions Ltd v Boscobel Productions Ltd* [1969] 1 QB 699.
[3]   [1995] ICR 1028.
[4]   *Ibid* at p 1041.
[5]   [1998] IRLR 387.

that was that, if he had been given notice in accordance with his contract, under its terms he could have obtained other full-time employment during the notice period and also received payment due from the company. Accordingly, since he was entitled to be put in the position he would have been in had his contract been performed, he was entitled to damages undiminished by earnings in his new employment because that was the sum he lost as a result of the employer's breach. The facts of this case and the decision are considered in more detail at para 9.44.

10.50   In *Cerberus Software Ltd v Rowley*,[1] also considered in more detail at para 9.46, the employee was employed under a contract determinable by either party giving six months' notice but which provided that the employers might make a payment in lieu of notice to the employee. The relevant part of the clause stated: 'It is agreed that the employer may make a payment in lieu of notice to the employee'. On 26 June 1996, he was summarily dismissed and on 1 August, he started a new job. The employment tribunal upheld his complaint of wrongful dismissal and awarded him six months' pay without requiring him to give credit for earnings in his new job, on the ground that, since the contract expressly provided that employment might be terminated on payment of a sum in lieu of notice, the summary dismissal was a lawful act and the claim was for a sum due under the contract rather than for damages. The Court of Appeal, by a majority,[2] allowed the employers' appeal and said that inclusion of the sentence quoted above ('It is agreed ...') meant that the employer was given the right to elect whether or not to make a payment in lieu of notice, and language whereby the employer was given the choice to pay or not to pay was inconsistent with the provision of a contractual right to the employee to insist that he should be paid six months' salary in lieu of notice. Since in the circumstances the employers were in breach of their obligation to give six months' notice, the employee's remedy was not recovery of the sum payable under the contract as a debt, but damages for wrongful dismissal reduced by any amount earned by way of mitigation of his loss. The majority distinguished *Abrahams v Performing Right Society Ltd* (above) on the grounds that the relevant clause in that case was differently worded and the clause in question gave the employers an election as to whether or not to make a payment in lieu of notice.

10.51   The rules relating to mitigation cover two possibilities: first, that the employee finds alternative employment, and secondly, that he or she does not. If he or she finds other employment, the amount earned during the relevant period (ie the period between the wrongful dismissal and the time when the contract could lawfully have ended) will be deducted from the prima facie damages; if the wages are the same as, or higher than, the wages earned in the previous employment, he or she will only be entitled to nominal damages.[3] If, on the other hand, he or she fails to take other employment when it would have been reasonable to do so, a deduction

---

[1]   [2001] ICR 376.
[2]   Sedley LJ dissenting.
[3]   *Reid v Explosives Co* (1887) 19 QBD 264.

will be made in respect of the wages he or she would have earned from such employment, and only nominal damages may be awarded.[1]

(i) The duty to mitigate

10.52   The burden is on the employer to show that the employee ought, as a reasonable person, to have taken steps to mitigate the loss,[2] and the defendant is entitled to particulars of other employment obtained by the plaintiff after the dismissal.[3]

10.53   The first point to note is that the duty does not arise until there has been a breach of contract. In *Shindler v Northern Raincoat Co Ltd*,[4] the employers, during the course of the employee's employment under a 10-year contract, wrongfully repudiated the contract by telling the employee that his service with them would terminate at a specified date. He was later removed from office at an extraordinary general meeting of the company. The judge held that the repudiation gave him the right to choose whether to affirm the contract or accept the repudiation and treat himself as discharged. Because he elected to affirm, there was no breach until the meeting at which he was removed. Between the date of the repudiation and the date of the meeting, the employers could have changed their minds and decided to continue employing him.

10.54   The obligation upon the employee to take reasonable steps to find alternative employment means that he or she is not bound to accept employment of a different kind, or a lower position in the same kind of employment, even if the rate of remuneration offered is the same.[5] An employee will not necessarily be expected to accept an offer of employment in a different part of the country, or in a different type of work, even if of equal status to that from which he or she was dismissed. In *Yetton v Eastwoods Froy Ltd*,[6] Blain J said:

> '... [F]actually, even if not as a strict matter of law, personal factors are clearly more likely to be of weight or are likely to be of greater weight in cases of personal services than in ... cases of sale of goods contracts where money may be the only important factor. Certainly personal factors do not have to be ignored in the making up of a dismissed servant's mind when he comes to make a decision reasonable or unreasonable.'

10.55   At some stage, however, the plaintiff may be expected to drop his or her sights. In *Yetton v Eastwoods Froy Ltd*, it was held not to be unreasonable for the plaintiff to try for something like his previous salary in the early stages of his applications for new jobs (the first six months or so

---

1   *Brace v Calder* [1895] 2 QB 253.
2   *Edwards v SOGAT* [1971] Ch 354. There is a brief discussion of issues relating to mitigation in *Clark v BET plc* [1997] IRLR 348 at pp 352–353, paras 42–53.
3   *Monk v Redwing Aircraft Ltd* [1941] 1 KB 182.
4   [1960] 1 WLR 1038.
5   See *Yetton v Eastwoods Froy Ltd* [1967] 1 WLR 104, *Edwards v SOGAT* [1971] Ch 354 and *Basnett v J & A Jackson Ltd* [1976] ICR 63.
6   [1967] 1 WLR 104 at p 118.

after his dismissal). After that, he did drop his sights. The judge suggested that he might have dropped his sights sooner, but did not treat this as a failure to mitigate. He awarded damages on the assumption that the plaintiff would find employment 18 months after his dismissal, at which time the five-year fixed-term contract which was broken would have had 19 months to run. The judge brought into account a notional salary of £3,000 a year (£250 a month over the 19-month period); the plaintiff's gross earnings had previously been around £10,000 a year.

10.56   A reasonable offer of alternative employment may come from the employer; but to decide whether the employee's refusal is reasonable or not it will be necessary to look at the circumstances of the dismissal.[1]

(ii) The effect of mitigation

10.57   As a general rule, any amount the plaintiff has earned in new employment since the breach is deducted. If he or she has taken on employment on the same terms as, or better terms than, the previous employment, he or she will not be entitled to any damages.[2] Since, however, in most cases, the employee is unlikely to obtain a new job immediately after the dismissal but may have to wait a month or more, even one month's loss of earnings may be a significant amount if he or she has been earning a fairly high salary.

10.58   The amounts deducted are the amounts earned in the new employment. That includes the same amounts that may be taken into account in assessing the plaintiff's loss. So commission, benefits in kind and the like will have to be brought into account. In *Roberts v Elwell Engineers Ltd*,[3] a commission agent was entitled to commission on all orders received from customers introduced by him, even after the termination of his employment. The Court of Appeal upheld that as a head of damage, but said that allowance would have to be made for, amongst other things, the possibility of the agent's customers ceasing to deal with the defendants, since they were open to being canvassed by the agent on behalf of a new company. In *Clark v BET plc*,[4] the judge took the view that a wrongfully dismissed senior executive would be likely to find some non-executive directorship during his notice period. He accepted evidence as to the maximum number which can be held and the likely level of remuneration and made an appropriate deduction from the calculation of damages.

10.59   In certain cases, the court may take into account matters other than the wages earned from the new employment, subject to the qualification that they must not be too remote. In *Lavarack v Woods of Colchester Ltd*,[5] the

---

[1]   *Brace v Calder* [1895] 2 QB 253. Cf *Jackson v Hayes* [1938] 4 All ER 587 and *Shindler v Northern Raincoat Co Ltd* [1960] 1 WLR 1038. See also *Yetton v Eastwoods Froy Ltd*, above and *Eley v Bedford* [1972] 1 QB 155.

[2]   *Reid v Explosives Co Ltd* (1887) 19 QBD 264 and *Re RS Newman Ltd, Raphael's Claim* [1916] 2 Ch 309.

[3]   [1972] 2 QB 586.

[4]   [1997] IRLR 348 at p 353, para 52.

[5]   [1967] 1 QB 278.

dismissed employee made an investment in another company and took employment in it at a depressed salary; he also made a substantial investment in a third company. The Court of Appeal held that he should give credit for the salary he earned from the company and for the estimated improvement in the value of his shareholding during the relevant period. He did not have to give credit for the benefit from his investment in the third company, albeit that he could not have invested in it at all had he continued to be employed by the employer.

(iii) Failure to mitigate

10.60   Failure to mitigate may arise from two separate causes: an inability to mitigate, for example, because of adverse market conditions for the kind of skill possessed by the employee, or a refusal to mitigate, ie a refusal to accept reasonable alternative offers of employment. In the latter case, the court must decide on the reasonableness of the employee's actions so far[1] or decide how much longer it is reasonable to expect him or her to continue to refuse alternative employment. In *Yetton v Eastwoods Froy Ltd*,[2] the judge held that the plaintiff's failure to obtain new employment up to the date of trial was reasonable; he also took the view that he would be likely to find a new job at a reduced salary of £3,000 a year two months after the trial. Averaging that salary out over the remaining 19 months of the five-year contract at £250 per month, the judge arrived at a sum of £4,250, which, by agreement, was reduced to £3,750 after adjustment for tax. In reaching this conclusion, the judge acknowledged that he was doing the best he could in a necessarily arbitrary way; but projections into the future are bound to be arbitrary.

10.61   Cases of inability to mitigate pose more difficult problems. The court will have to consider the reasonableness of the plaintiff's response to offers of alternative employment (if any), but in the nature of things it is likely that his or her actions will be held to have been reasonable. In *Edwards v SOGAT* (in fact, a case involving wrongful expulsion from a trade union),[3] the judge calculated the plaintiff's loss by taking the difference between the wage he would have been earning had he not been dismissed and the wage from the only job he could have obtained within the industry and applied a multiplier of 10, which represented an estimate of the plaintiff's probable earning life subject to a discount. The Court of Appeal disagreed with that approach (based on the way the courts deal with personal injury cases), on the grounds that in personal injury cases the permanent incapacity cannot be overcome, whereas in this kind of case the difficulty can be overcome by learning another skill or being reinstated by

---

[1]   See, eg, *Brace v Calder* [1895] 2 QB 253, where on the dissolution of a partnership the continuing partners offered to keep on the employee but he refused; he was only awarded nominal damages.

[2]   [1967] 1 WLR 104. See also *Shove v Downs Surgical plc* [1984] ICR 532 at p 542, where the judge held that the plaintiff would be able to mitigate his loss to the extent of £5,000 over the relevant period.

[3]   [1971] Ch 354.

the union. It said that the matter should be viewed broadly. The case was complicated by the fact that during the Court of Appeal hearing the union agreed to take the plaintiff back into full membership. That fact altered the prognostications of the future and undoubtedly played a considerable part in the Court's decision. It is clear from the three judgments, however, that the three judges adopted different approaches to the question.[1]

(d) Other deductions

(i) Earnings from new employment

10.62 Any earnings from new employment will be brought into account and deducted from the award of damages to the employee, whether or not he or she would have been under a duty to mitigate by taking such employment. The reasonable expenses of travelling and advertising incurred in finding the new job are, however, deductible from those earnings.[2] Earnings up to the date at which the contract could have been terminated will be brought into account, as will anticipated (or hypothetical) future earnings.[3]

(ii) Social security benefits and contributions

10.63 Any unemployment (or equivalent) benefit received by the employee will have to be brought into account.[4] In *Westwood v Secretary of State for Employment*,[5] the House of Lords considered the way in which the amount of the deduction should be calculated. Lord Bridge said:[6]

> 'First, as a matter of causation, it is clear that the loss of earnings and the receipt of benefit both flow from the same cause: indeed the whole purpose of the compulsory scheme which makes unemployment benefit available to all those who lose their employment is to provide the unemployed man with a substitute for earnings. Secondly, if the benefits are not deducted, the dismissed employee during the period of notice to which he was entitled recovers double compensation.'

He went on to observe that the consequence of the employee's dismissal without the 12 weeks' notice to which he was entitled was that he received unemployment benefit and earnings-related supplement 12 weeks earlier than if he had received the notice to which he was entitled; since he remained unemployed, that meant that his entitlement to those two benefits was exhausted 12 weeks earlier than it otherwise would have been. He said that the correct approach was to set against the lost earnings

---

[1] [1971] Ch 354 at p 378, *per* Lord Denning MR at p 385, *per* Sachs LJ and at p 387, *per* Megaw LJ.

[2] *Westwood v Secretary of State for Employment* [1985] ICR 209.

[3] *Yetton v Eastwoods Froy Ltd* [1967] 1 WLR 104.

[4] *Parsons v BNM Laboratories Ltd* [1964] 1 QB 95 and *Nabi v British Leyland (UK) Ltd* [1980] 1 WLR 529.

[5] [1985] ICR 209.

[6] *Ibid* at p 220.

caused by the dismissal without notice the lesser sum received as supplementary benefit after the premature expiry of the unemployment benefit and earnings-related supplement periods caused by the wrongful dismissal, not the actual benefits received during the 12-week notice period. So the supplementary benefit received during the first 12 weeks after the unemployment benefit period expired was deducted. Mr Westwood was thus £212.67 better off than he would have been had the other approach been adopted.

10.64   It is not clear to what extent other benefits and contributions are to be accounted for, since many of the cases on deductibility are personal injury cases and it is debatable whether the same conclusion should be reached by analogy in the case of damages for wrongful dismissal. It is likely, however, that the analogy would be followed. On this footing, supplementary benefit (now income support) probably would be deductible, at any rate where the effect of not deducting it would be doubly to compensate the employee.[1] Mobility and attendance allowances are probably also deductible.[2] It has also been held that family income supplements (now family credit) actually received would be deductible, but not payments which would be received in respect of loss of future earnings, because of the difficulty of valuing the future benefits.[3] Again in the context of personal injuries, it has been held that statutory sick pay should be taken into account when assessing loss of earnings,[4] as it has in the context of calculating the compensatory award of compensation for unfair dismissal.[5] In the context of compensation for unfair dismissal, the EAT has held that invalidity benefit should be taken into account.[6]

10.65   Deductions will be made for the employee's social security contributions which the employer would have been obliged to deduct from his earnings. In *Shove v Downs Surgical plc*,[7] Sheen J took a net figure for loss of earnings over the remainder of the contractual period, accepting that the gross figure should be reduced to take account of the employee's tax liability, pension contributions and National Insurance contributions.

---

[1]   *Plummer v PW Wilkins & Son Ltd* [1981] 1 All ER 91. See also *Lincoln v Hayman* [1982] 1 WLR 488.

[2]   *Hodgson v Trapp* [1988] 3 WLR 1281. The House of Lords reached its decision on the footing that there was no rational ground or principle of public policy to justify the plaintiff achieving double recovery and that the attendance and mobility allowances paid to her were to be regarded as available to meet the cost of care generally and thus mitigating the damages recoverable in respect of the cost of the care. It overruled *Bowker v Rose* (1978) 122 SJ 147; see also *Basnett v J & A Jackson Ltd* [1976] ICR 63.

[3]   *Gaskill v Preston* [1981] 3 All ER 427.

[4]   *Palfrey v Greater London Council* [1985] ICR 437.

[5]   In *Puglia v C James & Sons* [1996] ICR 301.

[6]   *Ibid.* In *Rubenstein and Roskin t/a McGuffies Dispensing Chemists v McGloughlin* [1997] ICR 318, the EAT held that it was just and equitable to deduct half of the invalidity benefit received by the employee. *Quaere*, whether it is appropriate to follow that approach when dealing with damages.

[7]   [1984] ICR 532. See also *Cooper v Firth Brown Ltd* [1963] 1 WLR 418.

(iii) Redundancy payments

10.66   In *Wilson v National Coal Board*,[1] the House of Lords held that it is not normally reasonable to deduct a redundancy payment, since it represents compensation for the loss of an established job and not for loss of future earnings. It may be deductible, however, if the dismissal for redundancy is the result of the incident in respect of which the employee is awarded damages.[2] A redundancy payment will fall to be deducted if the employee would not have received it but for a failure by the employer to give proper notice.[3] This constitutes an exception to the general principle enunciated by the House of Lords in the *Wilson* case.

(iv) Compensation for unfair dismissal

10.67   The basic award of compensation for unfair dismissal will probably not be deducted, since it is similar to a redundancy payment.[4]

10.68   So far as the compensatory award is concerned, the best view is that those elements of the compensatory award which are capable of being allocated to any of the heads of damages for wrongful dismissal should be deducted from the award of damages, but only to the extent that they are capable of being so allocated. This question was considered in *O'Laoire v Jackel International Ltd (No 2)*.[5] The case involved a wrongful dismissal claim and a successful unfair dismissal complaint. The outcome of the latter was that the employment tribunal made a reinstatement order with which the employers refused to comply and went on to award the maximum amount of compensation (then £8,000), which was all it had power to do, as the Court of Appeal held in an earlier decision involving the same parties.[6] In the present case, the Court of Appeal held that in assessing damages for wrongful dismissal the trial judge should not have deducted the maximum compensatory award made by the employment tribunal. The Court did not rule out the principle of double recovery, but said that, if the rule is to be invoked, it must be shown that the employee will be obtaining compensation under two heads for the same loss.[7] In the case in question, this could not be done, because the tribunal had calculated the compensation due to the employee as being around £100,000 but had then had to apply the statutory maximum (which was then £8,000, but is now £51,700). Sir Nicolas Browne-Wilkinson V-C, who gave the judgment of the Court, said:[8]

---

[1]   (1980) 130 NLJ 146. The decision of the Court of Appeal in *Hansa Northey v Bromsgrove and Redditch Health Authority* (unreported, 12 July 1994) in which the *Wilson* case appears to have been cited, is to contrary effect, but is best regarded as turning on its own facts.

[2]   See *Rees v British Steel Corporation* (1981) 131 NLJ 803; see also *Colledge v Bass Mitchells & Butlers Ltd* [1988] ICR 125, *Basnett v J & A Jackson Ltd* [1976] ICR 63 and *Cf Stocks v Magna Merchants Ltd* [1973] ICR 530.

[3]   *Baldwin v British Coal Corporation* [1995] IRLR 139.

[4]   *Shove v Downs Surgical plc* [1984] ICR 532 at pp 542–543.

[5]   [1991] ICR 718. *Cf Berry v Aynsley Trust Ltd* (1977) 127 NLJ 1052.

[6]   See [1990] ICR 197. For this aspect of the litigation, see Chapter 7.

[7]   [1991] ICR 718 at p 731.

[8]   *Ibid* at pp 731–732.

'How ... can the [employers] demonstrate that the £8,000 actually awarded by the employment tribunal is not attributable to loss of earnings after the first six months' notice period or to some other head of damages included in the total figure of £100,700? ... In the ordinary case, where it is clear that the actual loss will greatly exceed the statutory maximum, the employers normally pay ... the maximum award without the employment tribunal having to make any computation of the total loss suffered by the complainant.'

10.69 Since in any case in which it awards compensation a tribunal should make an actual calculation of the total loss suffered by the employee before applying the statutory maximum, and should set out its calculations, it should be possible to see from the computation what, if any, heads of the compensation are also capable of being allocated as damages. It is submitted, however, that the *O'Laoire* case is not authority for the proposition that no element of the compensatory award is to be set off against an award of damages.

(v) Other benefits

10.70 In *Parry v Cleaver*,[1] which contains an extensive analysis of the principles applicable in cases involving collateral benefits, the House of Lords refused to deduct a disability pension payable as of right to an injured policeman. It is probable that such payments from charitable and pension schemes will not be deductible, irrespective of whether the payment is discretionary or obligatory or the fund contributory or not.[2] The House of Lords also held that monies received under an insurance policy and pension money received by the employee are not deductible.[3] Lord Reid said:

'As regards monies coming to the [employee] under a contract of insurance, I think that the real and substantial reason for disregarding them is that the [employee] has bought them and that it would be unjust and unreasonable to hold that the monies which he prudently spent on premiums and the benefit from it should enure to the benefit of the tortfeasor.'[4]

10.71 In *Smoker v London Fire and Civil Defence Authority, Wood v British Coal Corporation*,[5] the House of Lords decided that pensions payable to employees as a result of injuries were not deductible from the damages payable by their employers. It said that the principle applicable was that the employees' pension benefits were the fruits, through insurance, of monies set aside in the past in respect of their past work and could not be appropriated by their employers; double recovery was not involved. The same conclusion was reached in *Hopkins v Norcros plc*,[6] a case in which a

---

[1]　[1970] AC 1. See also *Dews v National Coal Board* [1987] ICR 602.

[2]　*Ibid* at p 14, *per* Lord Reid.

[3]　*Ibid* at pp 14 and 16, *per* Lord Reid at pp 37–38, *per* Lord Pearce and at p 42, *per* Lord Wilberforce.

[4]　*Ibid* at p 14.

[5]　[1991] ICR 449. See also *Longden v British Coal Corporation* [1995] ICR 957.

[6]　[1993] ICR 338.

wrongfully dismissed employee received payments under an occupational pension scheme for the period between his summary dismissal and his sixtieth birthday. The judge said that there was no distinction between damages for lost earnings arising out of a claim for wrongful dismissal and damages arising out of a claim for lost earnings as a result of injury. He said that the approach should be the same irrespective of whether the claim is in contract or tort. His decision was upheld by the Court of Appeal.[1]

10.72   The House of Lords considered this matter again in *Longden v British Coal Corporation*.[2] The case involved an employee who received injuries which resulted in his early retirement at the age of 37. He was entitled to an incapacity pension consisting of a lump sum and a pension. Had he remained in employment until the age of 60 he would have been entitled to substantially higher payments. He claimed damages for personal injuries including a claim for loss of pension after retirement age, consisting of the lump sum he would have received on retirement and the difference between the annual pension he would have received and the pension he was currently receiving and would continue to receive after the normal retirement age. The House of Lords held that the incapacity pension payable to him between his early retirement on medical grounds following an accident at work and normal retiring age did not have to be set off against his damages for the difference between the retirement pension he would have received and the incapacity pension he would receive after normal retiring age. It said that the effect of *Parry v Cleaver* and *Smoker v London Fire and Civil Defence Authority* was that incapacity and disability pensions fall outside the general rule that prima facie all receipts due to the accident which gives rise to damages for personal injuries must be set against losses claimed to have arisen because of the accident. It also said that the only reason why incapacity and disability pension payments received after the normal retirement age must be brought into account in computing the claim for loss of pension after that age, is that the claim at this stage is for loss of pension, which cannot properly be calculated without taking into account receipts of the same character arising in the same period. It would therefore be contrary to principle to set off incapacity and disability payments received prior to normal retiring age against loss of retirement pension. It said that it would also be unfair to deduct pre-retirement payments in order to arrive at net pension loss after retiring age. A plaintiff cannot reasonably be expected to set aside sums previously received as incapacity pension in order to make good his loss of pension after his normal retirement age. On the other hand, there can be no injustice in setting off the sums received by way of incapacity pension against the sums lost by way of retirement pension arising in the same period. Finally, it said that an appropriate portion of the lump sum payment which the employee received when he was retired prematurely on grounds of ill health would be set off against his claim for loss of retirement pension. Payment of a lump sum on retirement is a

---

[1]   [1994] ICR 11.
[2]   [1998] ICR 26.

commutation in part of the annual pension to which the plaintiff is entitled and has the effect of reducing the amount of the annual pension, not only during the period up to normal retirement age, but for the whole period that the pension remains payable. Accordingly, in the same way as the annual incapacity pension for the period to which the claim for loss of retirement pension relates must be brought into account, it is right to bring into account that part of the lump sum which represents the commutation of a part of the annual payments which otherwise he would have received as income during the same period.

10.73   On the other hand, the House of Lords has held[1] that payments under a health insurance scheme to an employee injured in an accident in the course of his employment are deductible from damages for personal injuries. Under his contract, the employee was entitled to 13 weeks' sick pay, and thereafter to payments equal to half his pre-accident earnings under the employers' health insurance scheme. This scheme entitled the employers to be reimbursed by the insurers for payments made under the scheme. Lord Bridge of Harwich said of the payments:[2]

> 'Looking at the payments made under the scheme by the defendants in the first weeks after the expiry of the period of 13 weeks of continuous incapacity, they seem to me to be indistinguishable in character from the sick pay which the employee receives during the first 13 weeks. They are payable under a term of the employee's contract by the defendants to the employee qua employee as a partial substitute for earnings and are the very antithesis of a pension, which is payable only after employment ceases. The fact that the defendants happen to have insured their liability to meet these contractual commitments as they arise cannot affect the issue in any way.'

Rebates of income tax will be taken into account.[3]

(vi) Reduction for accelerated receipt

10.74   The total amount of damages to which the plaintiff is entitled (ie the total recoverable loss minus deductions) will suffer a further reduction to reflect the fact that the payment of damages to the employee is an accelerated single receipt of entitlements covering the whole unexpired fixed term or notice period, and the fact that the so-called vicissitudes of life might shorten the period of salary entitlement. These vicissitudes include the possibility of death or of the employee deciding to resign from the job before the unexpired portion of the fixed term or the notice period.

10.75   One approach to this question is to find out the current value of an annuity which would yield annually, throughout the unexpired portion of

---

[1]   In *Hussain v New Taplow Paper Mills Ltd* [1988] ICR 259. The Court of Appeal distinguished this case in *Berriello v Felixstowe Dock & Railway Co* [1989] ICR 467, on the footing that the employee would not be compensated twice for the same loss, since the amounts he received from the relevant fund would be recoverable if he was awarded damages in respect of losses for which the payments were made.

[2]   [1988] ICR 259 at p 267.

[3]   *Hartley v Sandholme Iron Co Ltd* [1974] 3 All ER 475.

the fixed term or the employee's notice period, such remuneration as the employee would have received, subject to the duty to mitigate.[1] The alternative is to reduce the total of damages arrived at by a percentage for accelerated receipt. In *Shove v Downs Surgical plc*,[2] the percentage was 7%, a figure agreed by counsel. It has been suggested[3] that a 10% reduction is rather high, and that a deduction in the range of 2% to 6% is appropriate.

(vii) Damages counter-claimed by the employer

10.76   It should be borne in mind that in an action for wrongful dismissal the employer may make a counterclaim for damages against the employee, irrespective of whether the proceedings are heard in the employment tribunal or the county court or High Court. As with an employee's claim against the employer, the employer's counterclaim must prove a breach of contract by the employee. In *Pearce v Roy T Ward (Consultants) Ltd*,[4] the employers counter-claimed for relocation expenses which had been paid to him to facilitate his move to the company and for loans made to him to assist him with his accommodation expenses. The relocation expenses were expressed to be repayable if his contract did not last the full 12 months of its declared duration. The employee was summarily and wrongfully dismissed before the expiration of the contract. The EAT held that the letter offering him the relocation expenses had been incorporated into his employment contract and that the wrongful repudiation by the employers released the employee from further performance of the contractual agreement in relation to the relocation expenses. It said that the loans were clearly separate and distinct from the main contract and concluded that he was still bound to repay the loans as agreed.

(e) Taxation of termination payments

10.77   Taxation is an important factor in the calculation of damages which can be awarded for loss of office. This section considers the taxation principles relevant to such awards and their application.

10.78   A number of different situations may give rise to the payment of a lump sum on the termination of an employment. If the contract of employment requires or provides for such a payment,[5] the whole of the lump sum will be taxable under the provisions of section 19 of the Income and Corporation Taxes Act 1988, in spite of the fact that the employment

---

[1]   *Bold v Brough, Nicholson & Hall Ltd* [1964] 1 WLR 201.

[2]   [1984] ICR 532. *Cf Lavarack v Woods of Colchester Ltd* [1967] 1 QB 278, where the percentage was 1%.

[3]   By Owen and Shier in 'The Actuary in Damages Cases – Expert Witness or Court Astrologer?' at p 19.

[4]   (EAT 180/96) IDS Brief 585.

[5]   As in *Rex Stewart Jeffries Parker Ginsberg Ltd v Parker* [1988] IRLR 483. The contract provided for determination of the contract by six months' notice on either side or the payment of six months' salary in lieu of notice. The issue was whether the employers were in breach of contract when they made a payment as contemplated by the contract. See Chapter 3.

has ceased. Other types of termination payments such as compensation and *ex gratia* payments will be within the scope of section 148 of and Schedule 11 to the Income and Corporation Taxes Act 1988.[1] As will be seen, the provisions of Schedule 11 grant a measure of relief to non-contractual payments made on the termination of an employment.

10.79 Sums received by virtue of the terms of a contract of employment are treated as emoluments for services past, present or future, and are taxed in full under Schedule E. It is therefore rarely beneficial to include compensation clauses in service agreements. In *Dale v de Soissons*,[2] a director's three-year service agreement provided that he would receive compensation of £10,000 or £6,000 if his employment was terminated at the end of the first or second year respectively. The contract ceased at the end of the first year. The £10,000 received by the director was liable to tax under section 181 of the Income and Corporation Taxes Act 1970 (now ICTA 1988, section 19), since it was paid by reason of a contractual obligation. In *Richardson v Delaney*[3] the High Court held that a lump sum payment made to an employee as part of a negotiated agreement to terminate his employment was not compensation for breach of contract by the employer. This meant that the payment was treated as an emolument from employment and the whole sum was chargeable to tax under section 19. *Mairs v Haughey*[4] involved a payment made to employees of a company in public ownership which was due to be privatised. The employees were covered by a non-statutory enhanced redundancy scheme. As an inducement to the employees to enter the employment of the new company on new terms and conditions of employment (including the loss of the enhanced redundancy scheme), they were offered an *ex gratia* payment which consisted of two elements: element A was 30% of the amount of the enhanced redundancy payment to which they would have been entitled had they been made redundant at the time of the privatisation; element B was £700 or £100 per complete year of service with the company, whichever was the greater. The employee received an *ex gratia* payment of £5,806, comprising £4,506 under element A and £1,300 under element B. He was assessed to tax under section 19 on the entire amount and appealed. A Special Commissioner held that the sum should be apportioned between element A and element B and that element A should be treated as compensation for the loss of the contingent rights under the enhanced redundancy scheme and element B as consideration for the acceptance of the new terms and conditions. He therefore held that element A was not taxable but that element B was taxable as an inducement to enter into employment with the privatised company. The Crown appealed to the Northern Ireland Court of Appeal and the House of Lords, both of which dismissed their appeal. Most of Lord Woolf's speech (with which the other

---

[1] As substituted by the Finance Act 1998, s 58(1)–(4) and Sch 9, Pt I. Section 188 was repealed by ss 58(4) and 165 and Sch 27, Pt III(9) of the same Act.

[2] 32 TC 118, [1950] 2 All ER 460.

[3] (2001) IDS Brief B691/6, ChD. See also *EMI Group Electronics Ltd v Coldicott* [1999] IRLR 630.

[4] [1993] 3 All ER 801, [1993] IRLR 551.

Lords of Appeal agreed) was devoted to a discussion of why element A was not taxable. This is considered more fully below.

10.80 *Ex gratia* payments or 'golden handshakes' will not generally be within the scope of the normal charging provisions of section 19 of ICTA 1988, and thus will be liable to tax under the specific provisions contained in section 148. Section 148(1) (as substituted) states:

'Payments and other benefits not otherwise chargeable to tax which are received in connection with—

> (a)   the termination of a person's employment, or
> (b)   any change in the duties of or emoluments from a person's employment,

are chargeable to tax under this section if and to the extent that their amount exceeds £30,000.'

10.81 'Benefit' is defined in section 148(2) as including 'anything which, if performed for performance of the duties of the employment (a) would be an emolument of the employment or (b) would be chargeable to tax as an emolument of the employment'. Section 148(5) provides that the section is to apply 'whether the payment or benefit is provided by the employer or former employer or by another person' and 'whether or not the payment or other benefit is provided in pursuance of a legal obligation'. Schedule 11, paragraph 2(1) provides as follows:

'section 148 applies to all payments and other benefits received directly or indirectly in consideration or in consequence of, or otherwise in connection with, the termination or change—

> (a)   by the employee or former employee,
> (b)   by the spouse or any relative or dependant of the employee or former employee, or
> (c)   by the personal representatives of the former employee.'

10.82 The effect of these provisions is that payments made by persons other than the employer, for example a payment made by another company within the same group as the employer company, are within section 148. Furthermore, payments made to relatives, or dependants or otherwise at the direction of the person whose employment has been terminated, are treated as if they had been paid directly to the ex-employee. The provisions also embrace payments in kind, with the effect that, if an ex-employee is given a company car in compensation for the termination of his or her employment, the section 148 charge will include the market value of the car at that date.

10.83 Payments and other benefits are chargeable to tax under section 148 when they are received and not, as previously, upon termination of the employment.[1] The lump sum payment will therefore augment the recipient's total taxable income for the year of assessment in which the payment or benefit is received. Schedule 11 to ICTA 1988 (as substituted) sets out the most important of the reliefs and exemptions currently available; paragraph 7 makes provision for what is now expressed as a threshold. The £30,000 threshold applies to the aggregate amount of payments and other benefits provided in respect of the same person either in respect of the same employment or different employments with the same employer or associated employers.[2] There appears to be no limitation to one exemption of £30,000 in each tax year. Thus, an employee who receives termination payments from two different employers in the same tax year would appear to be entitled to the £30,000 exemption in respect of each payment. Where payments and other benefits are received in different tax years, the £30,000 threshold is set against the amount of payments and other benefits received in earlier years before those of later years.[3]

10.84   Section 579(1) provides that statutory redundancy payments are exempt from income tax under the normal Schedule E provisions. However, section 580(3) specifically brings such payments within the scope of section 148. These payments must therefore be aggregated with other termination payments received.[4] In *Mairs v Haughey*,[5] whose facts were set out above, the House of Lords considered an *ex gratia* payment (called element A) paid to an employee to compensate him for the loss of a contingent right to a payment under an enhanced redundancy scheme. Lord Woolf, with whose speech the other Lords of Appeal agreed, said:

> 'A redundancy payment has ... a real element of compensating or relieving an employee for the consequences of his not being able to continue to earn a living in his former employment ... It is distinct from the damages to which he would be entitled if his employment were terminated unlawfully. It is also unlike a deferred payment of wages in that the entitlement to a redundancy payment is never more than a contingent entitlement ... Instead of being an emolument from employment, it is a payment to compensate the employee for not being able to receive emoluments from his employment ... The other significant characteristic of a redundancy payment is that it is payable after the employment has come to an end. Prima facie a payment made after the termination of employment is not an emolument from that employment. It can be, however, an emolument from the employment if for example it is a lump sum payment in the nature of deferred remuneration ... [T]he payment made to satisfy a contingent right to a payment derives its character from the nature of

---

[1]   Section 148(3) of ICTA 1988, as substituted.

[2]   Under ICTA 1988 Sch 11, para 8(1), as substituted, employers are treated as associated employers if one of them is under the control of the other or one of them is under the control of a third person who controls the other employer or who is under the control of the other employer. 'Control' for this purpose is defined by s 840 of ICTA 1988, by virtue of Sch 11, para 8(2).

[3]   ICTA 1988 Sch 11, para 7(3).

[4]   As to what is regarded as a genuine redundancy payment see the Inland Revenue Statement of Practice, SP 1/81.

[5]   [1993] 3 All ER 801, [1993] IRLR 551.

the payment which it replaces. A redundancy payment would not be an emolument from the employment and a lump sum paid in lieu of the right to receive the redundancy payment is also not chargeable as an emolument under Sch. E.'[1]

The House of Lords therefore upheld the Special Commissioner's decision that the *ex gratia* payment made to compensate the employee for his loss of a contingent right under the employer's enhanced redundancy scheme was not taxable.

Example 1

10.85   Employee employed under a contract of employment which does not provide for the payment of a 'golden handshake' on termination. On 1 August 2001 he is dismissed and compensation of £50,000 is paid to him. His other taxable income for 2001/02 is sufficient to make him a higher-rate taxpayer. Tax chargeable on the compensation payment will be 40% of the excess of £50,000 over £30,000, ie 40% of £20,000, which is £8,000.[2]

Example 2

10.86   A Ltd is a wholly owned subsidiary of B Ltd D is a director of A Ltd and B Ltd. She resigns from B Ltd on January 1, 2001 and from A Ltd on 1 May 2001. She receives termination payments of £20,000 from B Ltd and £15,000 from A Ltd The £20,000 received in 2000/2001 will be exempt from income tax under Schedule 11, paragraph 7(2). £10,000 of the payment from A Ltd (treated under section 148(4) as received in 2001/2002) will be exempt under Schedule 11, paragraph 7(2) and the balance will be chargeable in full under section 148 of ICTA 1988.

10.87   As has been discussed earlier in this chapter, it is an established principle that, where an individual sustains a loss by reason of a breach of contract, he or she will be entitled to an amount of damages which will (in so far as money is able to) place him or her in the same situation as if the contract had been performed.

10.88   Damages for wrongful dismissal will be liable to tax under section 148, but will qualify for the relief given under Schedule 11, paragraph 7. Thus an ex-employee who receives damages of, say, £28,000 will suffer no income tax on that payment. On the other hand, if he or she had remained in employment income tax would have been payable on the whole of the emoluments and he or she would have received a net sum after tax.

10.89   In order to ensure that dismissed employees in receipt of damages are no better off than if they had remained in employment, the courts have followed the rule in *British Transport Commission v Gourley*.[3] This case involved the assessment of damages payable to an eminent civil engineer

---

[1]   [1993] 3 All ER 801 at pp 811–814.
[2]   ICTA 1988, s 188(4).
[3]   [1955] 3 All ER 796.

(taxable under Schedule D) who was severely injured in a passenger train derailment in 1951. He was awarded the sum of £47,720 which was made up as follows:

(a) Pain and suffering	£9,000
(b) Out of pocket expenses	£1,000
(c) Actual loss of earnings	£15,220
(d) Estimated future loss of earnings	£22,500
TOTAL	£47,720

Both sides were agreed that the amount awarded would not be liable to tax. The point at issue was whether the judge should have taken into account taxation in awarding items (c) and (d), since only the net amount would have been received by Gourley if his injuries had not prevented the continuation of his professional activities. The House of Lords decided that the amounts awarded in respect of actual loss of earnings (ie items (c) and (d)) should be awarded net of income tax. Item (c) was therefore reduced to £4,945 and item (d) was reduced to £1,750. Thus the total award for damages became £16,695.

10.90   Although the *Gourley* decision involved damages for personal injuries, Lord Goddard considered that the principle of awarding an amount of damages net of income tax could equally be applied in actions for wrongful dismissal. His view was shared by Lords Radcliffe and Somerville and was adopted in *Beach v Reed Corrugated Cases Ltd*[1] and by the majority of the Court of Appeal in *Parsons v BNM Laboratories Ltd*.[2]

10.91   It will be apparent that *Gourley* will only apply in the following circumstances:

1.   the damages awarded for the loss of earnings are not taxable; and
2.   the emoluments lost as a result of the breach of contract would have been taxable had they been received normally by the employee, rather than by way of compensation.

Clearly, if the damages are within the normal charging provisions of Schedule E there will be no need for a *Gourley* adjustment. Awards of damages for wrongful dismissal may therefore be split into:

1.   awards which do not exceed £30,000; and
2.   awards greater than £30,000.

10.92   Claims for awards of damages amounting to less than £30,000 will not be liable to income tax and therefore will be subject to the *Gourley* rule. Interestingly, it was argued in *Parsons v BNM Laboratories Ltd* that the first

[1]   [1956] 2 All ER 652.
[2]   [1963] 2 All ER 285.

£25,000 (the exempt figure at that time) was within the charge to income tax by virtue of section 148 of ICTA 1988, and thus tax should not be deducted from the award, although it was not actually chargeable to tax because of the exemption in what is now Schedule 11, paragraph 7 to ICTA 1988, as substituted. This approach was rejected by Harman LJ, a view endorsed by Pearson LJ.

10.93   When the claim for damages exceeds the £30,000 exempt limit, two methods of arriving at the net amount to be awarded have been used. In *Bold v Brough, Nicholson & Hall Ltd,*[1] a managing director was dismissed approximately six and a half years before his service contract expired. In awarding him damages, the court decided that the *Gourley* rule should be applied to the exempt portion of the amount due, which at that time was £5,000. This amount was spread over the remaining years of the service contract and reduced by a notional amount of income tax payable for each year. The balance of the damages in excess of £5,000 were not within the *Gourley* principle and, thus, were paid gross. This balance would, however, have been subject to tax under section 148.

10.94   An alternative, and rather more sophisticated, method of dealing with awards of damages greater than the exempt limit was adopted in the case of *Stewart v Glentaggart Ltd.*[2] In this Scottish case, Lord Hunter estimated the tax which would have been payable on the amount of earnings involved, and deducted this to leave a net sum. He then grossed up the net sum by adding the tax which would be payable under section 148. In this way the net amount received by the ex-employee was calculated to equal exactly, as far as possible, the actual loss suffered because of the wrongful dismissal. Lord Hunter saw this method as taking the *Gourley* rule to its logical conclusion. It has been criticised, eg in *Parsons v BNM Laboratories Ltd,* as being too complicated, but it was applied in the case of *Shove v Downs Surgical plc.*[3] In this case, the court was provided with full information regarding the salary and benefits which would have been received by the plaintiff if the 30 months' notice required by the service agreement had been given. The total emoluments receivable after deduction of income tax was £70,300. This was reduced by £5,000 for mitigation of the loss and the balance was discounted by a further 7% to take account of early payment. The result of these calculations was the conclusion that the plaintiff had suffered a net loss of £60,729. Part of such a compensation payment would be liable to tax under section 148 and in order to ensure that the ex-employee was left with the sum of £60,729 in his hands the court awarded him damages of £83,447.

10.95   In a case in which the calculation of damages is made in accordance with the *Shove* case, the steps in the calculation are therefore as follows:

---

[1]   [1963] 3 All ER 849.
[2]   (1963) 42 ATC 318.
[3]   [1984] ICR 532.

1.   take value of gross salary and benefits;
2.   calculate taxable value of salary and benefits;
3.   calculate tax and national insurance contributions payable after deduction of allowances;
4.   deduct tax and NIC from gross salary and benefits;
5.   figure arrived at is net annual loss, which should be multiplied by damages period (ie period until contract could lawfully be terminated). Thus multiplier is 1.5 if damages period is 18 months;
6.   make deduction for mitigation;
7.   make reduction for accelerated receipt;
8.   deduct £30,000;
9.   gross up taxable slice;
10.   add £30,000.

10.96   Clearly, if the courts are being asked to make adjustments under the *Gourley* rule and to take account of section 148 tax liabilities, it is necessary and important to provide the relevant tax information. In this way an award may be made which reflects as accurately as possible the actual loss suffered by the ex-employee.

2. OTHER AVAILABLE REMEDIES

(a) Declarations

10.97   The effect of a declaration is that it states what the rights of the parties are, without containing any coercive order. In practice, however, a declaration is obeyed, despite the absence of a sanction. Most commonly, a party seeking a declaration will also seek discretionary relief, for example a prohibitory injunction.

10.98   An employee who is wrongfully dismissed will generally not be able to obtain a declaration[1] except, perhaps, in 'special circumstances'.[2] A likely example of special circumstances is the situation where the parties retain mutual confidence or where the party claiming to have lost confidence is found by the court to have done so on irrational grounds.[3] In *Saeed v Inner London Education Authority*,[4] an employee who had been acquitted of a criminal charge and against whom disciplinary proceedings were subsequently started by the employers applied to the court for a declaration that the disciplinary proceedings were null and void and seeking an injunction restraining the employers from continuing the proceedings or starting new proceedings on the same or similar grounds. The facts on which the criminal charge and the disciplinary proceedings were based were identical and the employee argued that he was being put in double jeopardy. Popplewell J refused the declaration and held that the

---

[1]   *Taylor v National Union of Seamen* [1967] 1 WLR 532 at pp 551–553.
[2]   See *Hill v CA Parsons & Co Ltd* [1972] Ch 305 at pp 314 and 319.
[3]   See para 10.90.
[4]   [1985] ICR 637.

rule of double jeopardy has no application as between criminal and civil proceedings or as between criminal proceedings and disciplinary proceedings, where the disciplinary tribunal applies the civil and not the criminal standard of proof.

10.99 Civil Procedure Rules 1998,[1] rule 24.2 now provides as follows:

'The court may give summary judgment against a claimant or defendant on the whole of a claim or on a particular issue if—

> (a)   it considers that—
>> (i)   that claimant has no real prospect of succeeding on the claim or issue; or
>> (ii)   that defendant has no real prospect of successfully defending the claim or issue; and
>
> (b)   there is no other compelling reason why the case or issue should be disposed of at a trial.'

Paragraph 1.3 of the accompanying *Practice Direction* makes plain that:

'An application for summary judgment under rule 24.2 may be based on:

> (1)   a point of law (including a question of a document),
> (2)   the evidence which can reasonably be expected to be available at trial or the lack of it, or
> (3)   a combination of these.'

10.100 The predecessor to CPR rule 24.2[2] was used by Chadwick J in *Jones v Gwent County Council*,[3] when he granted a declaration that a purported dismissal was not valid and effective because it failed to comply with the employee's contract of employment. He rejected the employers' argument that the matter could not be decided without the court forming a view as to the relationship of trust and confidence between the parties and said that whether the letter of dismissal was a valid notice of dismissal did not depend upon any questions of trust or confidence. He also granted a permanent injunction restraining the employers from dismissing the employee pursuant to their dismissal letter.

10.101 It might be thought that the main significance of the remedy is that it may be available to an employee who enjoys a special status,[4] eg the status of office-holder or a special statutory status, so that such employees may have the right to be dismissed only after the rules of natural justice or the requirements of a statutory or contractual procedure have been complied with. But the case of *Jones v Gwent County Council*, above, tends to suggest that it may have a wider significance, at least in cases where the court is prepared to take the view that the employer should go through a contractual disciplinary procedure before dismissing an employee.

---

[1]   SI 1998 No 3132.
[2]   Order 14A, r 1 of the Rules of the Supreme Court 1965.
[3]   [1992] IRLR 521.
[4]   See Chapter 11.

(b) Specific performance

10.102 In practice, an order for specific performance and an injunction restraining a breach of contract may have the same effect – that of maintaining the relationship of employer and employee. But, in cases where one of the parties wishes to stop the other from taking or threatening to take an action which would be to his or her detriment, the most common relief sought is an injunction restraining the action or threatened action.[1] In cases of this kind, discussion of the principles governing orders of specific performance tend to feature, since it is a principle common to both types of remedy that 'the courts are bound to be jealous lest they turn contracts of service into contracts of slavery'.[2]

10.103 In *Ridge v Baldwin*,[3] Lord Reid said: 'There cannot be specific performance of a contract of service …'. It is clear, however, that the courts are prepared to consider granting an order of specific performance where mutual confidence continues to subsist between employer and employee.[4] Not every contract for personal services constitutes a contract of employment, but it is well established that contracts which are personal in nature or involve personal services will not be specifically enforced.[5] The rule is not absolute and the court will not always refuse an order as soon as any element of personal service appears.[6] The remedy is discretionary and will only be awarded where damages are inadequate and the court can ensure performance.

10.104 There is the additional factor – which does not arise in the case of injunctions – that, so far as contracts of employment are concerned (as distinct from contracts for personal services), section 236 of the Trade Union and Labour Relations (Consolidation) Act 1992 forbids specific enforcement.

(c) Injunctions

10.105 The general rule was stated by Fry LJ in *De Francesco v Barnum:*[7]

> 'I should be very unwilling to extend decisions the effect of which is to compel persons who are not desirous of maintaining continuous personal relations with one another to continue those personal relations … [T]he courts are bound to be

---

[1] See, eg, *Powell v Brent London Borough Council* [1988] ICR 176.

[2] *De Francesco v Barnum* (1890) 45 Ch 430 at p 438, *per* Fry LJ.

[3] [1964] AC 40 at p 65.

[4] *Powell v Brent London Borough Council* [1988] ICR 176.

[5] *Lumley v Wagner* (1852) 1 De GM & G 604. See also *Thomas Marshall (Exports) Ltd v Guinle* [1978] ICR 905 and *De Francesco v Barnum* (1890) 45 Ch 430.

[6] *Beswick v Beswick* [1968] AC 58 at p 97 and *CH Giles & Co Ltd v Morris* [1972] 1 All ER 960 at p 970.

[7] (1890) 45 Ch 430 at p 438. See also *Lumley v Wagner* (1852) 1 De GM & G 604, *Whitwood Chemical Co v Hardman* [1891] 2 Ch 416, *Rely-a-Bell Burglar and Fire Alarm Co v Eisler* [1926] Ch 609, *Warner Bros v Nelson* [1937] 1 KB 208 and *Page One Records Ltd v Britton* [1968] 1 WLR 157. For a more recent example of the application of these principles, see *Warren v Mendy* [1989] ICR 525.

jealous lest they turn contracts of service into contracts of slavery; and ... I should lean against the extension of the doctrine of specific performance and injunction in such a manner.'

There is an exception to this general rule, where the employer and the employee still have complete confidence in each other.[1] The grant of an injunction is discretionary and subject to the proviso that damages is an inadequate remedy. It should also be noted that an injunction will be refused, where it is sought on the grounds of the employer's repudiatory act but the employee has accepted the repudiation.[2]

10.106 Recent case-law makes clear that the courts are prepared to grant injunctions, particularly interlocutory injunctions, where mutual confidence continues to subsist between the parties. This is likely to be so in the case where the employer is a large organisation such as a local authority. There are also suggestions, however, that where the employer claims to have lost confidence in the employee (or no doubt vice versa), the court must be satisfied that the loss of confidence is on reasonable grounds, and not some irrational ground.[3]

10.107 An example of a case where the court has held that confidence has not been lost and has granted interlocutory relief is *Powell v Brent London Borough Council*.[4] The employee was employed as a Senior Benefit Officer in the Housing Department. In November 1986, she applied for the post of Principal Benefits Officer. The candidates were interviewed on 27 November and she was later told that she had been selected for the post and should report to her new place of work next day. On that day, it was agreed that she should start the new job on 1 December. The same day, one of the unsuccessful candidates, who suspected a breach of the council's code on equality of opportunity, made a written request for an explanation why he had not been selected for the job. The matter was referred to the council's Director of Law and Administration, as a result of which the council decided to readvertise the post. The plaintiff was told of this and invited to reapply. She was later told that her appointment had not been confirmed and told to return to her job as Senior Benefits Officer. She claimed that she should be allowed to continue as Principal Benefits Officer and started proceedings in which she sought an injunction restraining the council from treating her as other than Principal Benefits Officer and from

---

[1]   *Hill v CA Parsons & Co Ltd* [1972] Ch 305 and *Powell v Brent London Borough Council* [1988] ICR 176.

[2]   *Dietman v Brent London Borough Council* [1988] ICR 842. The employee was summarily dismissed in breach of the council's disciplinary procedure and started proceedings claiming, inter alia, an injunction restraining the council from acting upon the decision purporting to dismiss her and from treating the decision as anything other than invalid, void and of no effect. The judge refused an injunction, on the grounds that, although injunctive relief could have been granted to prevent the plaintiff's wrongful dismissal from taking effect, such relief was no longer available once she had accepted their repudiation. This part of the judge's decision was not appealed to the Court of Appeal.

[3]   See, eg, *Ali v Southwark London Borough Council* [1988] ICR 567 at pp 582–583 and *Powell v London Borough of Brent* [1988] ICR 176 at 195.

[4]   [1988] ICR 176.

treating the post as vacant or taking any steps to fill it. The Court of Appeal granted an interlocutory injunction, on the grounds that on the evidence available to it (but not to the first instance judge) it was satisfied that there was sufficient mutual confidence to justify the grant of an injunction. Ralph Gibson LJ said:

> 'Sufficiency of confidence must be judged by reference to the circumstances of the case, including the nature of the work, the people with whom the work must be done and the likely effect upon the employer and the employer's operations if the employer is required by injunction to suffer the [employee] to continue in the work.'[1]

Sir Roger Ormrod hinted that the question is whether the situation would be unworkable if the injunction were granted.[2]

10.108 A similar decision was reached in *Hughes v Southwark London Borough Council*,[3] where the employees complained that the council was unreasonably requiring them to do work which was not part of their contractual duty and sought an interlocutory injunction to prevent it from requiring compliance with the instruction. Here too, the court found that there was mutual confidence between the parties.

10.109 On the other hand, in *Alexander v Standard Telephones & Cables plc*,[4] in which the employees sought injunctions to restrain the employers from dismissing them for redundancy without going through a selection procedure in accordance with a collective agreement, Aldous J refused the applications. He said that, since the employers wished to retain those members of the workforce who were most suitable for the available jobs and did not have confidence that the employees seeking the injunctions were as able to carry out those jobs as others who would have to be dismissed if the plaintiffs were retained, to grant the injunction would be contrary to the principle by which courts refuse to grant injunctions to retrain a breach of contract of personal service which would either compel an employer to provide work for an employee or an employee to work for an employer once the relationship of mutual trust and confidence had broken down. He distinguished the *Powell* case on the grounds that the 'sufficiency of confidence' referred to in that case was lacking in the instant case.

1 [1988] ICR 176 at p 194.
2 *Ibid* at p 201.
3 [1988] IRLR 55. See also *Wadcock v London Borough of Brent* [1990] IRLR 223.
4 [1990] ICR 291. *Cf Anderson v Pringle of Scotland Ltd* [1998] IRLR 64, in which the Court of Session (Outer House) held that the employee was entitled to require his employers to operate the last in, first out method of selection for redundancy agreed with the union. The Court granted an interdict (the term used in Scotland for an injunction) restraining the employers from selecting employees for redundancy on any other basis that that agreed. See also *Wishart v National Association of Citizens Advice Bureaux Ltd* [1990] ICR 794. In the latter case, the employee was offered a job 'subject to the receipt of satisfactory written references' but the offer was withdrawn. The Court of Appeal discharged injunctions granted by the High Court and again distinguished the *Powell* case.

10.110 Other cases in which questions of injunctive relief tend to arise are those where a disciplinary procedure is involved. For example, in *Irani v Southampton and South-West Hampshire Health Authority*,[1] the court intervened to grant an interlocutory injunction, on the grounds that the employee was seeking the protection of a procedure for resolving disputes laid down by the Whitley Councils, in circumstances where there was no criticism of his conduct or professional competence and damages would not be an adequate remedy for the loss of his employment. A similar conclusion was reached in *Robb v Hammersmith and Fulham London Borough Council*,[2] in which the judge took the view that the employers' loss of confidence in the employee did not make the continuation of the contract unworkable, given that he had been, and would remain, suspended from duty during the disciplinary procedure and that a resumption of the procedure was necessary to allow him to seek to defend the conduct for which they were trying to dismiss him.

10.111 In *Ali v Southwark London Borough Council*,[3] on the other hand, Millett J refused to grant an interlocutory injunction restraining the council from proceeding with a disciplinary hearing. The effective purpose behind the application for the injunction was to compel the council to conduct the procedure in the manner sought by the plaintiff. The judge, however, refused to intervene in the council's conduct of the hearing. In doing so, he followed the Court of Appeal's decision in *Longley v National Union of Journalists*[4] that the court should not interfere to prevent a domestic tribunal from hearing and adjudicating a matter unless the court is satisfied that no reasonable tribunal acting bona fide could reach that decision. Here the judge refused to say that, relying on the evidence which it proposed to rely upon, the tribunal acting bona fide could not possibly uphold the disciplinary charge against the plaintiff. He added that, even if his decision on this point was wrong, he would also refuse to grant an injunction to the plaintiff on the grounds that mutual confidence between the parties had ceased, in that the council, on reasonable grounds, had lost confidence in the employee.[5]

10.112 The cases considered above are cases in which interlocutory relief has been sought and, sometimes, granted. In *Jones v Gwent County Council*,[6] on the other hand, the judge granted a permanent injunction against the employers to restrain them from dismissing the employee pursuant to a letter of dismissal which he had found to be invalid and ineffective because it failed to comply with her contract of employment. He also granted a declaration that the purported letter of dismissal was not a valid and effective dismissal. This aspect of the case is considered at para 10.100.

---

[1]   [1985] ICR 590. In this case, the procedure was incorporated into employees' contracts of employment by virtue of statutory provisions.

[2]   [1991] ICR 514. See also *Peace v City of Edinburgh Council* [1999] IRLR 417.

[3]   [1988] ICR 567.

[4]   [1987] IRLR 109.

[5]   [1988] ICR 567 at pp 582–583.

[6]   [1992] IRLR 521.

10.113 The cases are all cases involving employees seeking injunctions against their employers. Needless to say, employers often wish to obtain injunctions against employees, most commonly to stop them working for a competitor by leaving during their notice period or breaking a restrictive covenant in their contract. Cases involving employees who resign in breach of contract are considered in Chapter 9; restrictive covenant cases are considered in Chapter 14.

10.114 Most of the cases concern applications for what are now called interim injunctions,[1] ie orders restraining the breach of an employment contract until the full trial of the claimant's action. Whilst on such applications the courts consider the substantive principles governing the claimant's entitlement to injunctive relief, and the evidence adduced by the parties in support of their respective cases,[2] this is only for the purpose of establishing whether the claimant has an arguable case for a permanent injunction at the trial.

10.115 The principles formerly applied to claims for an interlocutory injunction have survived the introduction of the Civil Procedure Rules 1998 and apply to any application for an interim injunction. The relevant principles therefore remain those stated by the House of Lords in *American Cyanamid Co v Ethicon Ltd*,[3] which held that, with limited exceptions, the grant or refusal of interlocutory injunctions should be determined according to the 'balance of convenience', and not the substantive merits of the parties' cases as revealed by the evidence. Lord Diplock described the position as follows:[4]

> '… [U]nless the material available to the court at the hearing of the application for an interlocutory injunction fails to disclose that the plaintiff has any real prospect of succeeding in his claim for a permanent injunction at the trial, the court should go on to consider whether the balance of convenience lies in favour of granting or refusing the interlocutory relief that is sought.'

10.116 The primary consideration in determining where the balance of convenience lies is the degree to which an award of damages would adequately compensate the claimant and the defendant for any loss caused by an interim decision to refuse or grant an injunction respectively which proves on a full consideration of the merits at the trial to be incorrect. For example, in the *Powell* case,[5] the Court of Appeal's decision to grant an interim injunction rested on the Court's finding that the defendant would suffer no loss of 'real significance' as a result of being required to keep the plaintiff in post pending trial, whereas the plaintiff would not be

---

[1] Referred to hitherto as 'interlocutory injunctions'.

[2] Evidence for an interim remedy may be contained in the parties' Statements of Case (if verified by a Statement of Truth), or in a witness statement; the former requirement for evidence by affidavit is confined to applications for Freezing Injunctions or Search Orders (para 3 of the *Practice Direction* accompanying CPR Part 25).

[3] [1975] AC 396.

[4] *Ibid* at p 408.

[5] [1988] ICR 176 at p 196.

compensatable for the frustration and unhappiness of being returned to her old work, nor for the denial of the satisfaction and challenge of doing the work which she had been selected to do. Where both the claimant and the defendant stand to suffer uncompensatable losses from the grant or refusal of an injunction, the question of where the balance of convenience lies will involve consideration of other factors. These will vary from case to case, but may include, for example, the relative extent to which the parties' losses will be uncompensatable by an award of damages, or considering whether the effect of the injunction will be to restrain the defendant from embarking upon the activity complained of or interrupting an established pattern of activity which may cause greater inconvenience. In addition, the court may take into account any evidence which is not in dispute, but: '[t]he court is not justified in embarking upon anything resembling a trial of the action upon conflicting affidavits in order to evaluate the strength of either party's case'.[1] If the balance of convenience is evenly balanced, the court should take such steps as are necessary (by either granting or refusing the interim injunction) to ensure the preservation of the status quo pending the trial of the action.[2]

10.117 In some circumstances a full consideration of the merits of the claimant's claim is justified at the interlocutory stage. A number of exceptions to the *American Cyanamid* principles have developed, but in the employment context an important exception emerged in *NWL Ltd v Woods*.[3] There, the House of Lords held that where the interlocutory decision will effectively dispose of the dispute between the parties, because, for example, they are both likely in practice to accept the decision as final, the correct approach is to consider the evidence in full at the interlocutory application and decide the question of the plaintiff's entitlement to an injunction on the merits. Cases falling within this exception are rare, and typically involve applications for injunctions to restrain industrial action where the mutual need to preserve the employment relationship will often inhibit the parties from proceeding with the action to trial.[4] Other cases, such as applications by employees to restrain breaches of contract by the employer, are difficult to bring within the exception, and the *American Cyanamid* principles will be applied. For example, in *Hughes v London Borough of Southwark*,[5] Taylor J refused to regard the plaintiffs' application as falling within the *NWL Ltd v Woods* exception and applied the *American Cyanamid* test, holding that it was not a case in which the interlocutory decision would be decisive of the action. This was because, although the parties may have settled the action by the time of the trial, the question as to the validity of the employers' instruction to carry out different work would not become of 'merely historic or academic interest' with the passage of time, since there was likely to be a continuing problem over the work involved so that a question of the validity of further similar instructions was likely to arise. Further, a

---

[1]   [1975] AC 396 at p 409.
[2]   *Ibid* at p 408. See also *Hughes v London Borough of Southwark* [1988] IRLR 55 at p 58.
[3]   [1979] ICR 867.
[4]   See also Trade Union and Labour Relations Act 1974, s 17(2).
[5]   [1988] IRLR 55.

claim for damages brought by one plaintiff would not disappear by the effluxion of time and would remain to be determined at the trial. Similarly, in *Marsh v National Autistic Society*,[1] the judge refused an injunction to restrain a dismissal in breach of contract on the ground that, since the claim was a claim for damages only, there could not be the slightest doubt that damages was an adequate remedy.

(d) Restitution

10.118   *Avon County Council v Howlett*[2] draws attention to the possibility of restitutionary claims being made against employees. In that case, an employee was injured and the council claimed that, from the date of his injury to the date of retirement (just under three years), it had overpaid him in respect of his salary and sickness benefit, as a result of a mistake of fact. The employee had spent the money. Sheldon J held that the council was entitled to restitution of some of the money but that they were estopped from reclaiming the rest, amounting to £546.61, which the employee had lost or expended in reliance upon the employers' representations. Although, on the facts of the case as pleaded, the Court of Appeal held that the employers were estopped from claiming the whole of the overpaid amount, the chances of similar claims succeeding should not be overlooked.

---

[1]   [1993] ICR 453.
[2]   [1981] IRLR 447 (QBD) and [1983] IRLR 171 (CA).

Chapter 11

DISMISSALS GOVERNED BY PUBLIC LAW

11.01   The law relevant to this topic derives from the development of principles of administrative law in a series of judicial decisions over the last 30 years or so. The consequences, so far as they are relevant to the termination of the employment relationship, are that employees with a special legal status may have another basis for challenging their dismissal, in addition to their common law and statutory rights. The width of the category is unclear, but if an employee falls within it he or she may be able to argue that the dismissal was *ultra vires*, in breach of a prescribed procedure, or in breach of the principles of natural justice. The rules to be discussed derive solely from case-law.

11.02   If a person is a pure employee, it will not be possible to invoke public law remedies.[1] But an employee dismissed from an office, 'where the body employing [him or her] is under some statutory or other restriction as to the kind of contract which it can make with its servants, or the grounds on which it can dismiss them', will not be disentitled.[2] Similar considerations apply where the relationship involves a 'specific statutory status' or is of a 'sufficient public character' with a sufficient 'element of public employment or service'.[3] An office-holder (who may or may not be an employee) is entitled to the protection of the rules of natural justice.[4] An employee who falls within one of these categories is required to bring proceedings by way of judicial review.[5]

11.03   Dicta in the more recent cases have tended to suggest that there are cases when the courts may be prepared to permit an extension of these principles, but they remain chary of doing so with any degree of frequency. Essentially, of course, an extension of the principles means that there are more circumstances in which employees have access to public law remedies.

11.04   In *Stevenson v United Road Transport Union*,[6] the Court of Appeal upheld the grant of a declaration that the dismissal of a trade union official was in breach of the requirements of natural justice and void. The case can be fitted into the category of cases where some further element is involved,

---

[1]   *Vine v National Dock Labour Board* [1957] AC 488 at pp 500 and 507, *per* Viscount Kilmuir LC and Lord Keith respectively.
[2]   *Ridge v Baldwin* [1964] AC 40 at p 65, *per* Lord Reid.
[3]   *Malloch v Aberdeen Corporation* [1971] 1 WLR 1578 at p 1582, *per* Lord Reid and at p 1596, *per* Lord Wilberforce.
[4]   *Ridge v Baldwin* [1964] AC 40.
[5]   See *McLaren v The Home Office* [1990] ICR 824.
[6]   [1977] ICR 893.

but there are dicta which suggest that the Court did not regard the principle as being confined to any particular category.[1]

11.05   In *R v British Broadcasting Corporation ex parte Lavelle*,[2] an employee whose contract gave her the right to an elaborate domestic disciplinary appeals procedure sought judicial review of the decision to dismiss her. The application was refused on the grounds that the prerogative orders have never been used to enforce private rights and are inappropriate for enforcing the performance of an employer's obligations to an employee. The judge suggested, however, that in appropriate circumstances the court will intervene to grant injunctions or declarations to protect the contractual rights of employees dismissed in breach of a procedure specified in their contract.[3]

11.06   If, then, the contract of the protected employee makes provision for a procedure to be followed, the employer will not be able to dismiss validly until the procedure is carried out;[4] if the procedure involves a hearing or investigation, the rules of natural justice must be observed. Where the appointment and dismissal of the employee are regulated by statute, the statutory requirements must be complied with, and, if the employee has the right to a hearing (either expressly or by implication), the hearing must comply with the rules of natural justice.

11.07   The category of office-holders is far from clear, although it can be said to involve the exercise of some public function (eg a police constable). Although it might be thought that large numbers of employees are potentially capable of being given enhanced protection, it is doubtful whether this is so. In the reported cases, the employees so protected appear to be regarded as exceptional, but the difficulty is to decide who falls within the category. In *R v East Berkshire Health Authority ex parte Walsh*,[5] a nurse employed by the Authority alleged that he was unlawfully dismissed for misconduct in breach of the Authority's disciplinary procedures. He sought an order for *certiorari*. The Court of Appeal held that there was nothing in the case to take it out of the sphere of the ordinary employer/employee relationship; there was no special element, as indicated by Lord Wilberforce in *Malloch v Aberdeen Corporation*.[6] The Court also said that employment by a public authority does not itself inject any

---

[1]   [1977] ICR 893 at pp 902–903.

[2]   [1983] ICR 99.

[3]   *Ibid* at pp 111–112. For an example of a case in which an interlocutory injunction was granted see *Irani v Southampton and South-West Hampshire Health Authority* [1985] ICR 590; see also Chapter 10, where injunctions and declarations are discussed.

[4]   This was one of the grounds for the decision in *Gunton v Richmond-upon-Thames London Borough Council* [1980] ICR 755 at pp 765 and 777, *per* Buckley and Brightman LJJ respectively.

[5]   [1984] ICR 743. See also *R v Chief Rabbi ex parte Wachman* [1992] 1 WLR 1036 and *R v Derbyshire County Council ex parte Noble* [1990] ICR 808: a deputy police surgeon whose appointment was terminated failed in his application for judicial review of the decision. The Court of Appeal upheld the Divisional Court's decision that there was not a sufficient public element in his claim.

[6]   [1971] 1 WLR 1578.

element of public law. Similarly, in *R v Lord Chancellor's Department ex parte Nangle*,[1] the Divisional Court reached the conclusion that the correct construction of the documents by which the applicant was appointed led to the conclusion that a contract of employment had been created and that his claim was a matter of private law not susceptible to judicial review.

11.08   In *R v Secretary of State for the Home Department ex parte Benwell*,[2] on the other hand, judicial review and *certiorari* were granted to a prison officer who, as such, held the office of constable and who was dismissed. As a holder of the office of constable, he was expressly excluded by the legislation as it was then drafted from the right not to be unfairly dismissed. Since that decision, however, the legislation has been amended so that prison officers are now excluded from the right not to be unfairly dismissed.[3] *Ex parte Walsh*[4] was applied by the Divisional Court in *R v Civil Service Appeal Board ex parte Bruce*.[5] The civil servant appealed against a decision to dismiss him to the CSAB, and, when the Board rejected his appeal, sought judicial review of the decision. The Divisional Court said that in appropriate cases the decisions of the CSAB could be susceptible of judicial review, but that leave to proceed by way of judicial review should only be granted in exceptional circumstances since there was an adequate remedy by way of complaint to an industrial tribunal (to which in fact the civil servant had complained). The Court therefore refused relief. The Court of Appeal upheld this decision.[6] On the other hand, in *R v Civil Service Appeal Board ex parte Cunningham*,[7] the Court of Appeal upheld the grant of a declaration that the CSAB acted unlawfully in refusing to give reasons for an award of compensation following his dismissal. The difference between the two cases arguably lies in the fact that in *Cunningham*, the Court was dealing with an employee who, being a prison officer and within what is now section 200(2) of the 1996 Act,[8] was excluded by section 200(1) from the right not to be unfairly dismissed. (His case was therefore similar to that of *Benwell* above.) The Court of Appeal reiterated what it had said in *Bruce*, that the CSAB is a body whose decisions are susceptible of judicial review but here, because the decision of the CSAB was regarded as similar to that of an employment tribunal, to which the employee did not have access, the Court said that fairness and natural justice required a tribunal such as the CSAB to give reasons for its decision sufficient to enable the parties to know the issues to which it had addressed its mind, the means by which it had arrived at its decision and that it had

---

1   [1991] ICR 743.
2   [1984] ICR 723.
3   See s 200(2)(b) and s 126 of the Criminal Justice and Public Order Act 1994.
4   [1984] ICR 743.
5   [1988] ICR 649.
6   [1989] ICR 171.
7   [1992] ICR 816.
8   Formerly s 146(3) of the 1978 Act, as amended by s 126 of the Criminal Justice and Public Order Act 1994, which states that a prison officer is not to be regarded as in police service for the purposes of the 1996 Act.

acted lawfully. Lord Donaldson of Lymington, MR quoted the words of Lord Lane CJ in *R v Immigration Appeal Tribunal ex parte Khan (Mahmud)*:[1]

> 'Where one gets a decision of a tribunal which either fails to set out the issue which the tribunal is determining either directly or by inference or fails either directly or by inference to set out the basis upon which they have reached their determination upon that issue, then that is a matter which will be very closely regarded by this court, and in normal circumstances will result in the decision of the tribunal being quashed ... A party appearing before a tribunal is entitled to know, either expressly stated by the tribunal or inferentially stated, what it is to which the tribunal is addressing its mind.'

The Master of the Rolls said that the Board should have given outline reasons sufficient to show to what it was directing its mind and to show indirectly whether its decision was lawful: 'Any other conclusion would reduce the Board to the status of a free-wheeling palm tree'. Both McCowan and Leggatt LJJ agreed that all the Board needed to do was to take a 'a few simple sentences' to give 'a concise statement of the means by which they arrived at the figure awarded'.[2]

11.09 A similar conclusion was reached in *R v Secretary of State for Education ex parte Prior*,[3] a case involving the dismissal of a teacher in a grant-maintained school. The teacher was dismissed and complained that the dismissal procedure was flawed because the chairman of the school staff committee which dismissed him had not been properly appointed. He asked the Secretary of State to intervene, but he declined to do so on the grounds that it was not appropriate because the teacher had not alleged any bias and since any defaults were primarily of a technical nature. Brooke J quashed the decision, on the grounds that the Secretary of State could not reasonably have downplayed the seriousness of the teacher's complaint. He was entitled to act as a forum for determining disputes between a school and its employees, unless, for example, he judged that the dispute raised issues of wider application or there were other reasons why he ought to exercise his powers of intervention.[4]

11.10 In *R v The Chief Constable of the Thames Valley Police ex parte Cotton*,[5] the Court of Appeal refused judicial review to a constable who was dismissed for obesity by the Deputy Chief Constable. Mr Cotton alleged that the Deputy Chief Constable's decision was vitiated by procedural impropriety because he had failed to show him and ask him to comment on the adverse report he had received from the Assistant Chief Constable, and upon which he had relied. Simon Brown J dismissed the application. He took the view that the applicant must 'establish that there is a real, as opposed to a purely minimal, possibility that the outcome would have been different' and said that, even if Mr Cotton had been shown the

---

[1] [1983] QB 790 at pp 794–795.
[2] [1992] ICR 816 at pp 831 and 835.
[3] [1994] ICR 877.
[4] Under s 99 of the Education Act 1944, as amended.
[5] [1990] IRLR 344.

Assistant Chief Constable's report, there would have been 'no substantial chance of any further observation or action on the applicant's part in any way altering the final decision in his case'. The Court of Appeal dismissed the appeal. Slade LJ said:

> 'Save in cases where an applicant has a statutory or contractual right to demand that a particular procedure be followed in dealing with his case, his right (if any) to complain of the procedure stems from his right to have his case fairly dealt with in accordance with natural justice. Save in such cases, it will not ... be right for the court to hold that the failure of the respondent to take certain steps during the course of the procedure has involved "procedural impropriety" unless it is satisfied that such failure was, in all the circumstances the subsisting, unfair to the applicant ... [T]he occurrence or otherwise of a relevant procedural impropriety does not ... fall to be determined in any given case merely by reference to abstract rules. An applicant seeking judicial review on these grounds must ... show that on the particular facts he has not been given "fair play" ... An applicant who cannot show that here has been any breach of natural justice in substance cannot ... expect to be granted a bare declaration that "procedural impropriety" has occurred.'[1]

All three Lords Justices stressed that there can be no such thing as a technical breach of natural justice and that, in cases such as this, the court is concerned with matters of substance rather than of form.

11.11   As was mentioned above, the category of those to whom public law remedies are available is far from clear. In *McLaren v The Home Office*,[2] however, Woolf LJ laid down the following principles which should be borne in mind in determining whether an employee of a public body (including an office-holder) is required to bring proceedings by way of judicial review:[3]

1. In relation to his personal claims against an employer, an employee of a public body is normally in exactly the same situation as other employees and can bring proceedings for damages, a declaration or an injunction in the ordinary way, although an employee of the Crown may have limited rights against the Crown.

2. An employee of a public body can seek judicial review and obtain a remedy which would not be available to an employee in the private sector, where there exists some disciplinary or other body established under the prerogative or by statute to which the employer or the employee is entitled or required to refer disputes affecting their relationship.

3. In addition, an employee of the Crown or other public body who is adversely affected by a decision of general application of the employer and contends that the decision is flawed can be entitled to challenge that decision by way of judicial review.

---

[1]   [1990] IRLR 344 at pp 350–351.
[2]   [1990] ICR 824.
[3]   *Ibid* at pp 836–837.

4.   There can be situations where, although there are disciplinary procedures which are applicable, they are of a purely domestic nature and therefore, albeit that their decisions might affect the public, the process of judicial review will not be available.

In the instant case, the employee argued that the Home Office had broken his contract, and brought a private law action. The Home Office argued that no cause of action in private law was involved and sought to have his claim struck out. The Court of Appeal held that the matter was one of private law and allowed the employee's appeal against the decision of Hoffmann J to allow the Home Office's application to strike out.

11.12   In *Roy v Kensington and Chelsea and Westminster Family Practitioner Committee*,[1] which contains an extensive review of the authorities, the House of Lords considered whether it was appropriate to strike out the claim of a person who began a private law action by writ, on the grounds that he should have proceeded by way of judicial review. It refused to do so, taking the view that a litigant asserting his or her entitlement to a private law right cannot be prevented from seeking to establish the right by action begun by writ or originating summons by the circumstance that the existence and extent of the private right asserted may incidentally involve the examination of a public law issue. It said that the rule in *O'Reilly v Mackman*[2] that an aggrieved person must proceed by judicial review in cases in which public law acts or decisions are challenged, is subject to exceptions where private law rights are involved, based on the nature of the claim and the undesirability of erecting procedural barriers.

11.13   From a consideration of these cases it is clear that the courts, particularly the Court of Appeal, are reluctant to allow ready access to public law remedies and take the view that the principal recourse should be to private law remedies.

---

[1]   [1992] IRLR 233.
[2]   [1983] AC 237.

Part III:

PROCEDURAL CONSIDERATIONS

Chapter 12

LIMITATION PERIODS

1. WRONGFUL DISMISSAL

12.01 Since 12 July 1994, employees have had the right to bring wrongful dismissal claims in employment tribunals as well as the High Court and county court.[1]

12.02 The limitation period for claims in the High Court or county courts will start to run when the cause of action, ie the breach of contract, accrues.[2] Section 28 of the Limitation Act 1980 extends the period of limitation in the case of certain persons under a disability (eg minors and persons of unsound mind). The statutory period of limitation will not start to run in certain cases of fraud until the plaintiff has discovered the fraud, or could with reasonable diligence have discovered it; similar considerations arise in relation to mistake.[3]

12.03 Claims in the employment tribunal must be presented within three months of the effective date of termination of the contract or, where there is no effective date of termination, three months 'beginning with the last day upon which the employee worked in the employment which has terminated'.[4] The tribunal may extend the time for presenting the complaint, where it is satisfied that it was not 'reasonably practicable' for the complaint to be presented in time.[5] This power is couched in the same language as in cases of unfair dismissal under section 111(2) of the Employment Rights Act 1996, which is considered in the next section. It should be noted that premature applications are not possible and that a claim may only be presented once the contract has ended.[6]

2. UNFAIR DISMISSAL

12.04 Section 111(2) of the 1996 Act provides that an employment tribunal may not consider a complaint of unfair dismissal unless it is presented to the tribunal within three months[7] of the 'effective date of termination' or such further period as the tribunal considers reasonable in a

---

[1] See s 3 of the Employment Tribunals Act 1996 and the Employment Tribunals Extension of Jurisdiction (England and Wales) Order 1994, SI 1994 No 1623. These types of wrongful dismissal claim are considered at the end of Chapter 9.

[2] Limitation Act 1980, s 2.

[3] Limitation Act 1980, s 32.

[4] Article 7 of the Order.

[5] For an example, see *Schultz v Esso Petroleum Co Ltd* [1999] ICR 1202.

[6] *Capek v Lincolnshire County Council* [2000] ICR 878.

[7] 'Month' means calendar month: Interpretation Act 1978, s 5 and Sch 1.

case where it is satisfied that it was not reasonably practicable for the complaint to be presented within three months. This period will be extended to six months in cases involving dismissals in connection with a strike or lockout under sections 238 or 238A of the Trade Union and Labour Relations (Consolidation) Act 1992 where the tribunal is given jurisdiction.[1]

12.05   This provision goes to the tribunal's jurisdiction. So if the complaint is presented out of time, the tribunal must consider as a preliminary issue whether to allow the complaint to proceed; the respondents (employers) cannot agree to raise no objection to the claim being presented out of time. The burden is on the applicant to satisfy the tribunal that it was not reasonably practicable to present the complaint in time.[2]

12.06   It should be noted that section 111(4) enables a complaint to be presented during the currency of the notice of termination or of an employee's notice of termination in a constructive dismissal case,[3] but not where the dismissal consists of the expiry of a fixed term of contract without its renewal.[4] This provision applies to an employee who is dismissed with notice and during the notice period presents a complaint, but is subsequently summarily dismissed.[5]

12.07   When dealing with a question involving the time-limit, the employment tribunal has essentially four questions to consider:

1.   When was the complaint presented?
2.   When did the limitation period expire?
3.   Was it reasonably practicable for the complaint to be presented within three months of the effective date of termination?
4.   If not within what period was it reasonable for the complaint to have been presented?

The employment tribunal must first decide when the effective date of termination was: see Chapter 3. That may not always be easy, as the relevant text demonstrates.

The four questions set out above are considered individually below.

(a) Date of presentation of complaint

12.08   Once the effective date of termination has been established, the first question is when the date of presentation was. A complaint is 'presented' when it arrives at the Central Office of Employment Tribunals

---

[1]   TULRCA 1992, s 239(2), as amended by the ERA 1999, s 16 and Sch 5, paras 1 and 4(1) and (4).
[2]   *Porter v Bandridge Ltd* [1978] ICR 943.
[3]   *Presley v Llanelli Borough Council* [1979] ICR 419.
[4]   *Throsby v Imperial College of Science and Technology* [1978] ICR 357 at p 367.
[5]   *Patel v Nagesan* [1995] ICR 988.

(COET) or an office of the tribunals.[1] It can be pushed through the letter-box (if the relevant office has one), but it should be marked with the date and time at which that happens. If the tribunal office does not have a letter-box, for example because it is in multiple occupation, the time-limit may be extended to the next working day.[2] If the office of the tribunal does not have a letter-box and the date of presentation is a Sunday or bank holiday, the day will be treated as a *dies non* and the time for presentation will be extended to the next day. In *Ford v Stakis Hotels & Inns Ltd*,[3] the employee resigned on 28 February and his solicitor delivered the originating application to the regional office of the employment tribunals on 28 May, a day after the expiry of the limitation period. The regional office to which it was delivered had no letter-box and the date of expiry of the limitation period (27 May) was a bank holiday. The EAT held that, in those circumstances, 27 May was a *dies non*, and the time for presenting the complaint was extended to the next day. The complaint was therefore presented in time.

12.09   Special arrangements exist between the COET and the Post Office,[4] and an application may be treated as arriving earlier. In *Lang v Devon General Ltd*,[5] for example, the effective date of termination was 17 September 1985. The application was sent on Friday, 14 December to the Central Office. Because of the arrangement between the Central Office and the Post Office, the application was delivered on Monday, 17 December. The EAT held that, as a result of the special arrangement, the application could be said to have been presented on Saturday, 15 December, within the limitation period.

12.10   Fax facilities now exist at the Central Office and Regional Offices. If that method of transmission of an application is used, care should be taken to ensure that the date of transmission is clearly marked.

(b) Date of expiry of three-month period

12.11   The complaint must be presented within three months of that date. That means, for example, that an employee whose effective date of termination is 16 September must present the complaint by midnight on 15 December. The question which arises, however, concerns the position when the effective date of termination is the last day of a month and there is no corresponding date in the month three months later. An example of this would be an employee whose effective date of termination was 30 November. The corresponding date three months later is the end of February. The question is whether the limitation period expires on

---

[1]   *PO v Moore* [1981] ICR 623. See also *Hammond v Haigh Castle & Co Ltd* [1973] ICR 148, *Bengey v North Devon District Council* [1977] ICR 15, *House v Emerson Electric Industrial Controls* [1980] ICR 795, and *Hetton Victory Club Ltd v Swainston* [1983] ICR 341.

[2]   *Hetton Victory Club Ltd v Swainston* [1983] ICR 341.

[3]   [1987] ICR 943.

[4]   That post which arrives on a Saturday will be held until the following Monday.

[5]   [1987] ICR 4. See also *Goodman v Worthing District Health Authority* (EAT 941/93) IDS Brief 588.

28 February. (It should be noted that that date will also be the expiry date for a dismissal whose effective date of termination was 1 December.) A further complication arises where the effective date of termination is the end of a short month, for example February, but the relevant month three months later is longer. So, for example, an employee is dismissed and the effective date of termination is 28 February. Does the limitation period expire on 27 June or 30 June? In this last case, the argument is that, since the effective date of termination is the end of a month, so the expiry of the limitation period should be the end of the month three months later.

12.12   These issues were considered by the EAT in *University of Cambridge v Murray,*[1] which in fact involved an employee who was dismissed on 30 April and whose complaint was presented on 30 July 1991. The employee's representative argued that if the effective date of termination had been 1 May, she would have had until 31 July and that, therefore, since she was dismissed one day before 1 May, she ought to have until one day before 31 July, ie 30 July, to present her complaint. The EAT said that the three-month limitation period must be computed by reference to the day before the corresponding date in the third month after the date of termination; if there is no such day, for example because the dismissal takes place on 30 November and the following year is not a leap year, the date of expiry is 28 February. In the instant case, therefore, its conclusion was that the limitation period expired on 29 July. It rejected the employee's argument on the grounds that it was an argument that one should count backwards rather than forwards, which was contrary to the authorities and that, if one continued to count backwards, the process would distort the whole month. In *Pruden v Cunard Ellerman Ltd,*[2] another division of the EAT, presided over by the President, reached the same conclusion, but by a simpler route. It said that the tribunal should determine the effective date of termination, take the day before and then go forward three months. When February is involved, because the effective date of termination is 30 November or 1 December, the limitation period expires on the last day of February.

12.13   Once it has been determined that the complaint was presented out of time, the next question is whether it was reasonably practicable for the complaint to have been presented within the limitation period.

(c) Practicability of presentation within limitation period

12.14   The approach of the Court of Appeal in *Dedman v British Building & Engineering Appliances Ltd,*[3] is still followed, although that case was decided under provisions whose relevant wording was 'practicable', and in the context of a 28-day limitation period. This approach has been affirmed in subsequent Court of Appeal decisions, and it has been stressed that employment tribunals should be fairly strict in enforcing the time-limits

---

[1]   [1993] ICR 460.
[2]   [1993] IRLR 317.
[3]   [1974] ICR 53.

and that questions of reasonable practicability are questions of fact.[1] In *Palmer v Southend-on-Sea Borough Council*,[2] May LJ said that 'reasonably practicable' means more than what is reasonably capable physically of being done and that to construe the words as 'reasonable' would be to take a view too favourable to the employee. He also emphasised that, since the issue is pre-eminently one of fact, the EAT and the Court of Appeal should be slow to interfere with the employment tribunal's decision.

12.15 The decided cases can be grouped into various categories, which are considered separately below. It should be noted, however, that a theme which is common to all of them is that there is a noticeable, and regrettable, tendency to erect the dicta of the Court of Appeal into principles to be followed in the various categories and to move away from the words of the statute, which are fairly simple and straightforward. It is submitted that the views of the judges in the Court of Appeal have been misunderstood and that it has been forgotten that the Court of Appeal in cases of this kind is dealing with cases which it acknowledges to be cases where the issue is pre-eminently a question of fact for the employment tribunal. The words of Stephenson LJ should be borne in mind: 'When judges elaborate, or qualify, the plain words of a statute by gloss upon gloss, the meaning of the words may be changed, the intention of Parliament not carried out but defeated, and injustice done instead of justice'.[3]

(i) Ignorance

12.16 This category embraces, first, ignorance of the right to claim and of the time-limit, and secondly, ignorance of relevant facts which were outside the claimant's knowledge during the three-month period.

12.17 So far as the first type is concerned the approach of the Court of Appeal is fairly strict: if the employee ought to have known, but did not know of the right to claim, then it was reasonably practicable to present the complaint in time.[4] In *Walls Meat Co Ltd v Khan*, Brandon LJ said:[5]

> 'The performance of an act, in this case the presentation of a complaint, is not reasonably practicable if there is some impediment which reasonably prevents, or interferes with, or inhibits, such performance. The impediments may be physical, for instance the illness of the complainant, or a postal strike; or the impediment may be mental, namely the state of mind of the complainant in the form of ignorance of, or mistaken belief in regard to, essential matters. Such states of mind can, however, only be regarded as impediments, making it not reasonably practicable to present a complaint within the period of three months, if the ignorance on the one hand, or the mistaken belief on the other, is itself reasonable. Either state of mind will … not be reasonable if it arises from the fault of the complainant in not making such inquiries as he should reasonably

---

[1]   *Walls Meat Co Ltd v Khan* [1979] ICR 52.
[2]   [1984] ICR 372 at p 384.
[3]   In *Riley v Tesco Stores Ltd* [1980] ICR 323 at p 334. See also the view of Lord Bingham, quoted below at para 12.25.
[4]   *Porter v Bandridge Ltd* [1978] ICR 943 and *Walls Meat Co Ltd v Khan* [1979] ICR 52.
[5]   [1979] ICR 52 at pp 60–61.

have made, or from the fault of his solicitors or other professional advisers in not giving him such information as they should reasonably in all the circumstances have given.'

12.18   Although such ignorance might be excusable in the circumstances of the case, the publicity given to the right not to be unfairly dismissed must make it unlikely that ignorance will be excused. Ignorance will not be excused if it arises from the fault of the complainant in not making such inquiries as he or she should reasonably in all the circumstances have made.[1]

12.19   Considerations similar to those set out above arise in relation to ignorance of the time-limit, although there have been suggestions that such ignorance may make it harder to prove that it was not reasonably practicable to present the complaint within the time-limit.[2] A reasonable mistake is capable of affording just cause.[3]

12.20   Ignorance of the second type was considered by the Court of Appeal in *Machine Tool Industry Research Association v Simpson*.[4] In that case, the Court of Appeal said that it is not reasonably practicable for an employee to bring a complaint of unfair dismissal until he or she has knowledge of a fundamental fact that rendered the dismissal unfair. The Court accepted the argument that, in cases of this kind, the subjective state of mind of the employee must be approached in three stages. First, it must have been reasonable for the employee not to be aware of the factual basis on which he or she could bring an application during the limitation period. Secondly, the applicant must establish that the knowledge which he or she gains has, in the circumstances, been reasonably gained and that the knowledge is crucial to his or her change of belief, from one in which he or she does not believe that there are grounds for making an application, to a belief which he or she reasonably or genuinely holds that there is a ground for making an application. Thirdly, the acquisition of this knowledge must be crucial to the decision to bring the claim in any event. Purchas LJ said:[5]

---

[1]   *Wall's Meat Co Ltd v Khan* [1979] ICR 52. See also *Riley v Tesco Stores Ltd* [1980] ICR 323, *Avon County Council v Haywood-Hicks* [1978] ICR 646, *Churchill v A Yeates & Sons Ltd* [1983] ICR 380 and *Trevelyans (Birmingham) Ltd v Norton* [1991] ICR 488.
[2]   See, eg, *Riley v Tesco Stores Ltd* [1980] ICR 323 at p 328, *per* Stephenson LJ.
[3]   As in *Wall's Meat Co Ltd v Khan* [1979] ICR 52.
[4]   [1988] ICR 558. This case was applied by the EAT in *Grampian Health Board v Taylor* (EAT 37/91) IDS Brief 453 to a case where an employee dismissed for ill-health thought that she was entitled to a pension but was later told that she did not qualify. She brought the complaint within a month of being informed that she did not qualify but some five and a half months after being dismissed. The EAT upheld the tribunal's decision that it was not reasonably practicable for her to bring her complaint within the time-limit. See also *Post Office v Sanhotra* [2000] ICR 866, which involved an allegation by the employee that the employers made a fraudulent misrepresentation when they promised him a reference if he resigned. The EAT said that until he discovered that he had not been given a good reference he had no reason to think that the representation made by it was fraudulent.
[5]   *Ibid* at p 564.

'I see little difficulty in the view that fundamentally the exercise to be performed is a study of the subjective state of mind of the employee when, at a late stage, he or she decides that after all there is a case to bring before the employment tribunal. There is no indication in the wording of the section that it is necessary for an applicant to be relieved of the strict time limit to establish, as facts, those facts which have caused a genuine frame of mind, and reasonably so caused it, to form a decision to present a complaint to the tribunal out of time.'

12.21   Where the employee has all the facts which he or she needs to know to enable a complaint to be presented, it is reasonably practicable to present the complaint in time. An offer of re-employment does not make it reasonably impracticable to present the complaint in time, nor does the offer and its subsequent withdrawal alter any such fact.[1]

12.22   In *Marley (UK) Ltd v Anderson*,[2] the issue was whether the employment tribunal is bound to regard the moment at which the employee first develops a belief in a right to claim unfair dismissal (on any ground) as fixing the point at which it becomes 'reasonably practicable' for him or her to present a complaint. In the instant case, the facts which the employee subsequently discovered were facts relating to the reason alleged by the employer (a redundancy situation) to be the reason for his dismissal. The Court of Appeal said that the tribunal should not regard the moment at which the employee first develops the belief as fixing the point at which it becomes reasonably practicable to present the complaint. Waite LJ, with whom the other members of the Court agreed, accepted the argument of counsel for the employee that it would be unjust and unfair to allow employers, who have through inadvertence or ignorance failed to disclose to an employee circumstances or documents solely within their own purview, to plead lapse of time before disclosure as a reason for denying a right of complaint on that ground to the employee.[3] Of the employers' argument to the contrary, he said:[4]

'If employers wish to protect themselves from late claims presented by dismissed employees on the basis of newly discovered information, the remedy will in most cases lie in their own hands. They will see to it that the fullest information is made available to the employee at the time of dismissal ...'

12.23   The report of the decision contains a useful review of the case-law in this area. Towards the end of his judgment, Waite LJ referred to the 'ever-present danger, which the tribunals are frequently, and for good reason, exhorted to avoid, of the members becoming deflected from their task of applying statutory rules of principle to differing factual situations by citation of judicial pronouncements culled from other cases'.[5] This echoes similar sentiments by other judges noted elsewhere in this chapter.

---

[1]   See *London Underground Ltd v Noel* [2000] ICR 109, considered in more detail at para 12.29.
[2]   [1996] ICR 728.
[3]   *Ibid* at p 738B–738D.
[4]   *Ibid* at p 738.
[5]   *Ibid* at p 739.

(ii) Reliance upon advisers and others

12.24   The second category of cases concerns employees who rely upon advisers. It is immaterial whether or not they are skilled or whether or not they are engaged. In *Riley v Tesco Stores Ltd,*[1] which concerned wrong advice given by a Citizens Advice Bureau, Stephenson LJ said:

> 'What matters is that the employee cannot of necessity prove reasonable impracticability by saying "I took advice": and a third party, skilled or unskilled, only comes to be considered a possible excuse for the employee's delay if he gives advice or is authorised to act in time and fails to act or advise acting in time.'

It should be noted that the Lord Justice is not saying that the effect of taking advice from a third party is that the employee is necessarily prevented from establishing reasonable practicability. But a failure by an adviser to give correct advice will generally prevent the employee from claiming that it was not reasonably practicable to apply in time.[2] In *Rybak v Jean Sorelle Ltd,*[3] the EAT upheld the tribunal's decision that it was not reasonably practicable for the employee to have presented her complaint in time as a result of being misled by a member of the employment tribunal staff.

12.25   In *London International College Ltd v Sen,*[4] the Court of Appeal considered anew the cases involving the taking of advice. The case concerned an employee who took legal advice from a solicitor but then sought further advice by contacting the employment tribunal office, from which he received erroneous advice. As a result, his complaint was presented out of time. The tribunal found that the effective cause of his failure was the advice of the employment tribunal and concluded that it was not reasonably practicable for him to present his complaint in time. In the course of giving the judgment of the Court of Appeal upholding the decision of the tribunal, Sir Thomas Bingham MR accepted that the authorities suggest that an employee who consults an adviser can no longer say that it was not reasonably practicable to comply with the time-limit even if the advice was wrong. But he went on to question the rationale of the principle and also to question whether the previous cases were purporting to lay down a rule of law 'to govern what is essentially a question of fact'. He concluded his judgment with an expression of unease that 'the overlay of authority does seem ... to have distracted attention

---

[1]   [1980] ICR 323 at p 330. This has been extended to delay in presenting a claim because of reliance on the advice of the Free Representation Unit: see *Croydon Health Authority v Jaufurally* [1986] ICR 4. Cf *Papparis v Charles Fulton & Co Ltd* [1981] IRLR 104. See also *Harrington v Kent County Council* [1980] IRLR 353.

[2]   So too a confusion between the employee and the adviser as to who is to initiate the claim; see *Dowty Aerospace Gloucester Ltd v Ballinger* (EAT 45/93) IDS Brief 494. The adviser in this case was a trade union official.

[3]   [1991] ICR 127.

[4]   [1993] IRLR 333.

from what started out ... as a simple and readily comprehensible statutory test'.[1]

(iii) Criminal proceedings

12.26   The third category embraces employees who are prosecuted for alleged crimes. A failure by the employee to present a claim of unfair dismissal because of outstanding criminal charges is not an acceptable reason for saying that it was not reasonably practicable to present the complaint in time.[2]

(iv) Delay for good reason

12.27   The fourth category concerns employees who delay presenting a complaint of unfair dismissal for what appear to them at the time good reasons. An example is delay because of the operation of domestic appeals procedures. Here, the question is whether the fact of a pending appeal makes it not reasonably practicable to present a complaint. In *Palmer v Southend-on-Sea Borough Council*,[3] the Court of Appeal refused to interfere with the decision of the employment tribunal that it was reasonably practicable for employees in such circumstances to have presented their complaints within three months. The Court emphasised that the answer to whether it is reasonably practicable to present the complaint within the time-limit is an issue of fact for the employment tribunal to determine in the circumstances of the case. It also said that 'reasonably practicable' should not be construed so widely as to mean simply 'reasonable', nor so narrowly as to mean 'reasonably capable physically of being done' and that its meaning lay between those two limits.

12.28   The approach of the Court of Appeal in the *Palmer* case was followed by the Court of Appeal in the later case of *Schultz v Esso Petroleum Co Ltd*.[4] The case involved the late presentation of a complaint by an employee who suffered from depression and who was too ill to give instructions to his solicitors during the last six weeks of the limitation period, although he was well enough to have done so during the first part of the period. The tribunal decided that it was reasonably practicable to have presented the complaint within the three-month period, since he was well enough during the first part of the period to have instructed his solicitors to present the complaint. The Court of Appeal said that that was too restrictive a construction of section 111(2)(b). Potter LJ, with whom the other members of the Court agreed, said that the tribunal must consider the surrounding circumstances and the aim to be achieved, including whether the employee was hoping to avoid litigation by pursuing other remedies. He also said that where illness is relied upon, although its effects have to be

---

[1]   [1993] IRLR 333 at p 335, para 16 and p 336, para 23.
[2]   *Wall's Meat Co Ltd v Khan* [1979] ICR 52 and *Porter v Bandridge Ltd* [1978] ICR 943. See also *Norgett v Luton Industrial Co-operative Society Ltd* [1976] ICR 442 and *Trevelyans (Birmingham) Ltd v Norton* [1991] ICR 488.
[3]   [1984] ICR 372.
[4]   [1999] ICR 1202.

assessed in relation to the overall period of limitation, the weight to be attached to a period of disabling illness varies according to whether it occurs in the earlier weeks or the more critical weeks leading up to the expiry of the limitation period. He said that it may make all the difference between practicability and *reasonable* practicability.[1]

12.29   An example of a delay for which there is no good reason is *London Underground v Noel*.[2] The facts were that the employee was dismissed on 10 April 1997 but, following an appeal, offered re-employment in a new job at a lower rank with reduced pay. Before taking up the new employment, she was required to undergo a medical examination, as a result of which the offer of re-employment was withdrawn, on 28 July. She presented a complaint of unfair dismissal on 7 August. The tribunal decided that it had jurisdiction to hear the complaint, but the Court of Appeal allowed the employers' appeal. It said that where the employee has all the necessary facts to found a complaint within the limitation period it is 'reasonably practicable' to present the complaint in time. It also said that an offer of re-employment made during the period does not make it reasonably impracticable to present the complaint and the existence of an offer does not alter the right to present a complaint. As she knew all the relevant facts to enable her to make a complaint before the expiry of the limitation period and the offer of re-employment and its subsequent withdrawal did not alter any such fact, it was reasonably practicable to present the complaint in time.

12.30   Another example is delay because the employee believes that dismissal may be averted. In *James W Cook & Co (Wivenhoe) Ltd (in liquidation) v Tipper*,[3] employees were given notice of dismissal for redundancy after the company went into voluntary liquidation. They delayed making applications to the employment tribunal because they were led to believe that work would pick up and that they would be offered their jobs back. In fact, there was no intention to keep the shipyard where they worked going, but they did not realise that their dismissals were final and irreversible until the yard closed down. The Court of Appeal held that their belief that work would pick up again was a relevant factor in deciding that it was not reasonably practicable for them to present their complaints within the time-limit and refused to interfere with the tribunal's decision on this point. The Court of Appeal reiterated that the question whether or not it was reasonably practicable to present the complaint within the time-limit is essentially a question of fact for the tribunal and that appellate courts should be slow to interfere with such findings.

---

[1]   [1999] ICR 1202 at p 1210.

[2]   [2000] ICR 109.

[3]   [1990] IRLR 386. See also *Birmingham Optical Group v Johnson* [1995] ICR 459.

(v) Postal delays

12.31 The postal system has added its own problems to this area of the law, by such matters as delay and loss of applications.[1] A common feature of such cases is that the application is posted by first class post the day before the expiry of the limitation period, but, instead of arriving the next day, arrives the day after. It is, of course, risky to leave the posting of an application so late and the EAT has regularly warned against it.[2] In cases of this kind, the tribunal should go into the circumstances in which the application was posted and, if solicitors were involved, whether it could reasonably have expected the application to be delivered the next day: 'It is not a question of what can be guaranteed of the postal services; it is a question of what a reasonable solicitor would have expected, or might reasonably have expected, at the time, date and place in question'.[3] In such cases it is open to the employment tribunal to examine the procedures in a solicitors' office to see whether it considers they are reasonable in the circumstances.[4] In *St Basil's Centre v McCrossan,*[5] the EAT said that to encourage uniformity it would be reasonable for tribunals to look to the guidance given in the Rules of the Supreme Court and work on the basis that first class mail is delivered on the second working day after posting. That general approach should be subject, however, to evidence to the contrary in a particular situation.

12.32 If the application is delayed and arrives outside the time-limit, it has not been 'presented' within the time-limit. In such a case, however, the tribunal should consider all the relevant evidence and decide whether in the circumstances it was reasonably practicable for the complaint to have been presented in time. Thus, in a case where the application was completed and signed on 10 May, but was not posted until 13 May and did not arrive until 15 May, the EAT upheld the tribunal's decision that, since the application was ready to be sent on 10 May, it was reasonably practicable to have presented it within the limitation period.[6]

12.33 The problem is much the same with applications which are lost in the post. A lost application cannot be said to be presented, but it is arguable that the assumption that the application had arrived would make it not reasonably practicable to present a second application in time. The EAT's

---

[1] See *Beanstalk Shelving Ltd v Horn* [1981] ICR 273, *Burton v Field Sons & Co Ltd* [1977] ICR 106 and *House v Emerson Electric Industrial Controls* [1980] ICR 795.

[2] See, eg, *Beanstalk Shelving Ltd v Horn* [1980] ICR 273 at p 277, and *Birmingham Midshires Building Society v Horton* [1991] ICR 648 at p 651.

[3] *Burton v Field Sons & Co Ltd* [1977] ICR 106 at 111, quoted in *St Basil's Centre Ltd v McCrossan* [1992] ICR 140 at 142. In *Birmingham Midshires Building Society v Horton* [1991] ICR 648, the EAT refused to interfere with the tribunal's decision to accept the evidence of the applicant's solicitor that he believed that 99% of first class post arrived the day after it was posted and to allow the complaint to proceed out of time.

[4] *Birmingham Midshires Building Society v Horton* [1991] ICR 648 at p 652.

[5] [1992] ICR 140.

[6] *Bellaby v Stanton plc* (EAT 450/89) IDS Brief 438.

decision *in Capital Foods Retail Ltd v Corrigan,*[1] however, makes it clear that a solicitor with conduct of an unfair dismissal case must have in place a system for ensuring that the time-limits are complied with. In that case, the application was posted some five weeks before the expiry of the limitation period but nothing happened until almost three months after the expiry when the applicant asked her solicitors what was going on and they discovered that there was no acknowledgement that the complaint had been received by the Central Office; nor was the application returned as undelivered by the Post Office. The solicitors immediately sent a copy of the original application with a copy of their original covering letter. The employment tribunal took the view that there is a presumption that what is posted will be delivered and that in the circumstances it was not reasonably practicable to present the complaint in time. The EAT allowed the employers' appeal. It said that the unexplained failure of an application to reach the tribunal is not sufficient to satisfy section 111(2) unless all reasonable steps were taken to confirm that the application had been duly received. It said:

> 'It seems to us to be a matter of ordinary and prudent practice to employ some system of checking that replies which might reasonably be expected within a certain period have in fact been received, and that the conduct of business is taking a normal course.'[2]

To a certain extent this case turns on its own facts, but it provides an important reminder for advisers that they should check on the progress of cases. On the other hand, bearing in mind that all these cases are a question of fact and degree, it is possible to envisage cases where the application is presented nearer to the expiry of the limitation period, but the non-arrival of the application is discovered shortly afterwards. In such a case, the tribunal might well take a different view.

(d) Presentation outside limitation period

12.34   It is important to bear in mind that the decision that it was not reasonably practicable for a complaint to be presented within the time-limit is not the end of the matter. The tribunal must go on to decide upon the period within which it was reasonable to present the complaint. In *James W Cook & Co (Wivenhoe) Ltd v Tipper,*[3] for example, which involved employees who delayed making applications because they were led to believe that work would pick up, the Court of Appeal took the view that it would not be right to fix a date earlier than two weeks after the expiry of the limitation period as the date when the employees should have realised that hope has gone; it then allowed a further two weeks after that as a reasonable period within which to make an application. Two employees,

---

[1]   [1993] IRLR 430. See also *Camden & Islington Community Services NHS Trust v Kennedy* [1996] IRLR 381. In this last case, the EAT described the test in *Corrigan* as 'stringent'.

[2]   *Ibid* at p 431.

[3]   [1990] ICR 716.

whose complaints were presented outside that period, had their complaints dismissed for want of jurisdiction. In *Schultz v Esso Petroleum Co Ltd*,[1] the Court of Appeal reversed the tribunal's decision that a complaint presented almost six months out of time was time-barred. This is a surprisingly long time outside the time-limit, but the explanation for the Court of Appeal's decision probably lies in the unusual facts of the case (see para 12.28).

12.35   The conclusion to be drawn from the above cases is that, in general, a tribunal should be careful about extending the time for presenting a complaint much beyond a month, except in exceptional circumstances. Clearly, too, the longer the period that elapses after the expiry of the limitation period, the less likely becomes an extension of time.

12.36   In cases of this kind, the employment tribunal should give proper consideration to all the relevant circumstances in which the delay occurred, rather than concentrate upon the length of the delay itself. There are no laid down time-limits as to what should and should not be regarded as a reasonable period.[2]

3. REDUNDANCY PAYMENTS

(a) Under the ERA 1996

12.37   In contrast to the problems outlined in the preceding section, the limitation period for claims for redundancy payments appears to have caused relatively little litigation. It is set out in section 164 and is a jurisdictional provision.[3]

12.38   By virtue of section 164(1), an employee will be deprived of the right to a redundancy payment, unless before the end of a six-month period beginning with the relevant date[4] one of the following events occurs:

1.   the payment has been agreed and paid; or
2.   the employee has made a claim[5] for the payment by notice in writing given to the employer; or
3.   a question as to the right to a payment, or the amount of the payment, has been referred[6] to an employment tribunal; or

---

[1]   [1999] ICR 1202.
[2]   *Marley (UK) Ltd v Anderson* [1996] ICR 728.
[3]   *Secretary of State for Employment v Atkins Auto Laundries Ltd* [1972] ICR 76.
[4]   See Chapter 3.
[5]   In *Price v Smithfield & Zwanenberg Group Ltd* [1978] ICR 93, the EAT said that the test of whether there was sufficient written notice of a claim was whether the notice or writing relied upon was of such a character that the recipient would reasonably understand in all the circumstances of the case that it was the employee's intention to seek a redundancy payment.
[6]   In *Nash v Ryan International Ltd* [1977] ICR 560, the EAT held that it will be sufficient if the employee's application is posted, even though it is not received. This case was distinguished in *Secretary of State for Employment v Bank and Others* [1983] ICR 48, in which the EAT held that an application was referred when it was received by the tribunal office, not on the date it was sent by the employee.

4.   he or she has presented a complaint of unfair dismissal to the tribunal.[1]

12.39   It seems that, if the employee makes a claim to the employer (step 2, above) within the six-month period, there is no time-limit within which the employee should to follow that up by making a claim to the tribunal.[2] Section 164(1) merely states that the employee must take one of the steps specified within six months. In *Crawford v Secretary of State for Employment*,[3] the EAT made it clear that an employee will lose the right to claim a redundancy payment if he or she fails to comply with the requirements of section 164, irrespective of the reasons for the delay in claiming. This is particularly important where it is unclear whether or not there has been a transfer of an undertaking, as in the *Crawford* case. Mummery J said that in such cases an employee of an insolvent company should make a claim as soon as possible and not await the outcome of proceedings to determine whether there has been a relevant transfer or not.[4]

12.40   If none of the steps set out above is taken within the six-month limit, the tribunal has power, by virtue of section 164(2), to award a payment if it considers it just and equitable to do so, having regard to the reason shown by the employee for failing to take the relevant steps and all the other relevant circumstances. But he or she must make the claim, in one of the three ways described in (2)–(4) above, during the six-month period immediately following the initial six-month period. A claim which is made outside 12 months after the relevant date will be time-barred.

It should be noted that the employee's claim will be invalid if it is made before his employment comes to an end.[5]

(b) Under contractual arrangements

12.41   Crown employees are excluded from the statutory right to receive a redundancy payment,[6] since special schemes exist for them which are more beneficial than the statutory scheme. An example of such a scheme is the Whitley Council Agreement, which provides for redundancy payments. Such schemes may include a provision for referring disputes to an employment tribunal, as does the Whitley Council Agreement. In that case, they have the right to refer questions of entitlement to an employment

---

[1]   In *Duffin v Secretary of State for Employment* [1983] ICR 766, the EAT held that a complaint of unfair dismissal presented within six months entitles the employee to a redundancy payment even though the complaint would have been out of time for the purposes of the tribunal's unfair dismissal jurisdiction.

[2]   *Price v Smithfield & Zwanenberg Group Ltd* [1978] ICR 93. See also *Bentley Engineering Co Ltd v Miller* [1976] ICR 225.

[3]   [1995] IRLR 523.

[4]   *Ibid* at p 526.

[5]   *Watts v Rubery Owen Conveyancer Ltd* [1977] ICR 429. Cf s 111(4), which allows complaints of unfair dismissal to be presented during the notice period.

[6]   By s 159.

tribunal under section 177, which does not provide a limitation period for the bringing of claims. References under section 177 are, therefore, governed by the ordinary limitation rules and must be brought within six years.[1]

---

[1] *Greenwich Health Authority v Skinner* [1989] ICR 220 and *Stevens v Bexley Health Authority* [1989] ICR 224.

Chapter 13

INSOLVENCY OF THE EMPLOYER

1. INSOLVENCY REGIMES

13.01   The consequences of termination of employment in the context of an insolvency depend to some extent on the type of insolvency in question.

13.02   An insolvent employer (broadly, one which cannot pay its debts as they fall due) will usually become subject to the control of a qualified insolvency practitioner[1] under one of the insolvency regimes provided for by the Insolvency Act 1986 (IA 1986). In cases where the employer is completely bereft of assets, there may be no one willing to incur the expense of imposing a formal insolvency regime.

Insolvent individuals and insolvent companies are dealt with under distinct procedures. The main regimes are as follows:

1.   bankruptcy;
2.   liquidation;
3.   administrative receivership; and
4.   administration.

Each will be dealt with in turn.

(a) Bankruptcy

13.03   Bankruptcy[2] is the collective regime under which the assets of an insolvent individual are distributed by the trustee in bankruptcy. A partnership may be subjected to compulsory liquidation by the court as an unregistered company.[3]

(b) Liquidation

13.04   The liquidation or winding-up of an insolvent company[4] involves ceasing its business (except to the extent necessary for beneficial winding-up), selling its assets and paying its debts so far as its funds allow. A liquidation may be either compulsory (ordered and supervised by the court) or voluntary (instigated by the shareholders and supervised by the creditors). At the end of the liquidation process, the company will cease to exist.

---

[1]   See Insolvency Act 1986, Pt XIII.
[2]   See IA 1986, Pt IX.
[3]   See IA 1986, Pt V and the Insolvent Partnerships Order 1994.
[4]   See IA 1986, Pt IV.

(c) Administrative receivership

13.05   A receiver[1] is sent into a company by a creditor to take possession of and realise assets which are subject to a charge in favour of the creditor. A receiver who takes possession of substantially the whole of the assets (which will be the case where the company has given a floating charge over its entire undertaking) will be an administrative receiver;[2] receiverships other than administrative receiverships will not be dealt with in this chapter.[3] In theory, once the creditor has been paid off, the receiver will be able to return the company to the management of its directors as a going concern but, in fact, a receivership is usually accompanied or followed by a liquidation. A liquidator appointed whilst a receiver is in office will monitor the progress of the receivership and distribute any remaining assets once the receivership ends. The business, or part of it, may survive in the hands of a new owner.

(d) Administration

13.06   Administration[4] is a procedure intended to rescue insolvent companies. The court can appoint an administrator with power to run the business; such an appointment will bring about a moratorium protecting the company from legal action. An administrator will draw up a rescue plan which, if approved by the creditors, he or she will then implement.

2. TERMINATION OF EMPLOYMENT AND INSOLVENCY

(a) Pre-existing claims

13.07   When an employer becomes insolvent, there may be claims outstanding which arise out of previous dismissals. The imposition of an insolvency regime may affect the procedural ability of the employees to

---

[1]   See IA 1986, Pt III.

[2]   See IA 1986, s 29.

[3]   In fact, much of what is said in this chapter about administrative receivers applies equally to other receivers appointed out of court. Administrative receivers are declared by IA 1986, s 44 to be the agents of the company until it goes into liquidation, but most other receivers will be agents of the company under the charge document appointing them. Section 40 of the IA (payment of preferential debts) applies to all receivers. Both types of receiver incur personal liability on new contracts which they enter into (ordinary receivers under s 3 of the IA 1986 and administrative receivers under s 44); since the IA 1994 has amended s 44 (discussed in detail later in the chapter) but left s 37 alone, the liability of administrative receivers on adopted contracts of employment appears to be more restricted than that of ordinary receivers. Other main differences between the two types of out of court receiver are that a wide variety of powers is conferred on administrative receivers by the IA 1986, whereas those of ordinary receivers depend on the charge document, and that administrative receivers are under some obligations to inform ordinary creditors of the progress of the receivership.

[4]   See IA 1986, Pt II.

bring legal action or to enforce judgment against the employer.[1] By definition, the insolvent employer will have insufficient funds to meet all claims in full. The funds available to meet claims submitted by employees are considered below.[2]

(b) Dismissal at onset of insolvency

13.08   The onset of insolvency may be accompanied by the closure of the business and the dismissal of most or all of the employees. Dismissed employees may have claims arising out of the dismissals;[3] there will be a redundancy situation and, in the absence of the correct notice period, wrongful dismissals.

13.09   Dismissals, although for the potentially fair reason of redundancy, may be held to be unfair on the basis of procedure.[4] If the business ceased at the time of dismissal, it may not be worth bringing an unfair dismissal claim since an employment tribunal may hold that the employee had suffered no loss from the unfairness. This said, for a long-serving employee, the entitlement to the basic award for unfair dismissal may amount to several thousand pounds and claims may also exist for a compensatory award in respect of loss of statutory rights and the right to long notice. If some of the employees are retained, there may be a claim for unfair dismissal based on a procedurally flawed selection; subsequent dismissal of the remaining employees would place a limit on the period of loss incurred by those dismissed earlier.

13.10   In addition to claims arising from the dismissal, it is possible that the employees will have remuneration owing to them.[5]

(c) Dismissals in the course of insolvency

13.11   The insolvency practitioner may carry on the employer's business in order to effect a more beneficial sale of the assets or in an attempt to effect a rescue; he or she may, consequently, retain the services of some or all the employees. The effect of insolvency regimes on contracts of employment and change of terms by an insolvency practitioner are considered below. The question of who will be responsible for meeting any claims arising out of a subsequent dismissal of the employees is also considered below.[6] Where dismissals are connected with a sale of all or part

---

[1]   See paras 13.12 *et seq.*
[2]   See paras 13.24 *et seq.*
[3]   For the procedural ability to bring claims, see paras 13.12 *et seq.*
[4]   In *Fox Brothers (Clothes) Ltd v Bryant* [1979] ICR 64, the EAT doubted whether there could be an unfair dismissal where there was a properly conducted entry into liquidation, but this seems questionable. However, in *Pambakian v Brentford Nylons Ltd* [1978] ICR 665, the EAT held that receivers and managers should be aware of the requirements of good industrial relations practice in connection with consulting employees prior to closing down or selling off the whole or part of the employer's business.
[5]   The funds available to meet successful claims are considered at paras 13.24 *et seq.*
[6]   See paras 13.52 *et seq.*

of the business of the insolvent employer, the implications of the Transfer of Undertakings (Protection of Employment) Regulations 1981 clearly become very important and a number of the landmark decisions on the Regulations arose in the context of an insolvency. The Regulations are considered elsewhere in this book and are not further addressed in this chapter.

3. RESTRICTIONS ON PROCEEDING AGAINST AN INSOLVENT EMPLOYER[1]

(a) Bankruptcy

13.12   Once a bankruptcy petition has been presented, the court may stay any proceedings or execution against the person or property of the debtor.[2] Once a bankruptcy order has been made, the consent of the court will be necessary to commence proceedings or enforce a judgment in respect of a debt provable in the bankruptcy.[3] The benefit of any execution can only be retained if it was completed before the bankruptcy order was made.[4]

13.13   Instead of bringing legal proceedings, those who have claims against the bankrupt at the commencement of the bankruptcy must submit their claim to the trustee in bankruptcy ('prove their debt');[5] appeal lies to the court against rejection by the trustee in bankruptcy of their claim.

(b) Compulsory liquidation

13.14   After presentation of a petition for a winding-up order, a stay of proceedings against the company may be sought.[6] If a winding-up order is subsequently made, any disposition of the company's property after the presentation of the petition will be void, unless the court orders otherwise.[7] Any execution which has not been completed before the commencement of the winding-up will be set aside unless the court orders otherwise.[8] Once the winding-up order has been made, no action or proceeding can be commenced against the company or its property without leave of the court.[9] Claims (which can be unliquidated) must be submitted to the liquidator and appeal lies to the court if the proof of debt is rejected.[10]

---

[1]   An employee may be able to circumvent these difficulties by claiming from the National Insurance Fund, see para 13.24.
[2]   Section 285 of the IA 1986.
[3]   *Ibid.*
[4]   Section 346 of the IA 1986.
[5]   Section 322 of the IA 1986 and Chapter 8, Pt 6 of the Insolvency Rules 1986, SI 1986 No 1925.
[6]   Section 126 of the IA 1986.
[7]   Section 127 of the IA 1986.
[8]   Section 183 of the IA 1986. For time of commencement of a winding-up, see s 129 of the IA 1986.
[9]   Section 130(2) of the IA 1986.
[10]   Chapter 9, Pt 4 of the Insolvency Rules 1986, SI 1986 No 1925.

(c) Voluntary liquidation

13.15 There is no automatic stay of proceedings in a voluntary liquidation, but application may be made to the court for an order imposing a stay.[1]

(d) Administrative receivership

13.16 There is no moratorium on legal action against a company in administrative receivership, but the assets in the possession of the receiver will not be available to meet the claims of ordinary creditors until after the secured creditor who has appointed the receiver has been paid off. The employees will be able to enforce their claims in the ordinary way against assets returned to the company at the end of the receivership, or submit their claim to the liquidator in any subsequent liquidation.

(e) Administration

13.17 Once a petition for an administration order has been presented, no proceedings or execution against the company or its property may be commenced or continued except with the consent of the administrator or the leave of the court.[2] There has been some debate as to whether proceedings in an employment tribunal fall within this moratorium, but in *Kenneth Carr v British International Helicopters Ltd*,[3] the Scottish EAT held that complaints and applications to employment tribunals are within the description 'other proceedings' and that it is not possible to construe the Insolvency Act 1986 so as to exclude claims under the employment protection legislation from the scope of the moratorium. Lord Coulsfield, delivering the judgment of the EAT, observed that it was likely that it would only be in rare cases that it will be appropriate for consent to be refused to the bringing of proceedings for unfair dismissal or in respect of redundancy. Consent would also be required for subsequent enforcement of any award.

4. THE EMPLOYEE AS CREDITOR

13.18 An employee is in a better position than the ordinary creditors of the employer in two respects. First, some of the debts owed to an employee carry preferential status and, secondly, some debts to employees (including some which also carry preferential status) are guaranteed by the State.

---

[1]   Section 112 of the IA 1986 gives the liquidator, creditors or the company the power to ask the court to exercise any of the powers it might exercise in a court winding-up.
[2]   Section 10 of the IA 1986 imposes the moratorium during the period between the presentation of the petition and the court's decision; s 11 of the IA 1986 imposes the moratorium during the period for which the administration order is in force.
[3]   [1994] ICR 18. The EAT held in that case that an application presented without the necessary consent should be adjourned to allow the applicant an opportunity to apply for the necessary consent; the application did not have to be treated as a nullity.

(a) Preferential status

13.19	The basic principle governing the distribution of assets of an insolvent is that of *pari passu* or equal distribution of those assets over which there is no prior secured claim. An exception is created by statute in respect of those debts classified as preferential;[1] these rank ahead of the other unsecured creditors and ahead of any floating charge over the assets of a corporate insolvent. An administrative receiver has to pay preferential creditors in priority to the debts secured by the charge under which he has been appointed.[2]

13.20	The provisions relating to preferential status are relevant where an employee is owed money in respect of remuneration at the onset of the insolvency.[3] In respect of all other debts, including wrongful dismissal damages and awards of compensation made by an employment tribunal, the employee will rank as an ordinary creditor in the insolvency.

13.21	Preferential status was originally conferred only on certain debts owing to employees, but has been extended to include a number of debts owing to government agencies. The *pari passu* principle obtains amongst the preferential creditors; any shortfall will abate rateably between them. In so far as there are insufficient assets to meet the preferential claims in full, any floating chargee and the ordinary unsecured creditors (including employees in respect of non-preferential debts) will receive nothing.

13.22	Preferential status is conferred on remuneration owing to employees for the four months prior to the onset of the insolvency, up to a maximum of £800, together with accrued holiday pay.[4] Remuneration is defined to include guarantee payments, medical suspension payments, payments for time off and remuneration under a protective award.

13.23	In so far as employees are owed more than £800 remuneration, they will rank *pari passu* with the ordinary unsecured creditors. There will be no preferential claim to an amount earned more than four months before the onset of the insolvency or which becomes due after the commencement of the insolvency (subsequent termination payments and protective awards, for example, are excluded).

---

[1]	Sections 386 and 387 and Sch 6 of the IA 1986. Section 175 of the IA 1986 relates to liquidations; s 328(1) of the IA 1986 relates to bankruptcy.

[2]	Section 40 of the IA 1986 (there is some debate as to whether the preferential creditors will have priority over a floating charge which has priority over the charge under which the receiver was appointed: see conflicting first instance decisions in *Griffiths v Yorkshire Bank* [1994] 1 WLR 1427 and *Re H & K (Medway) Ltd* [1997] 2 All ER 321). The receiver may recoup the payments from assets available to the ordinary creditors.

[3]	'The relevant date', defined in s 387 of the IA 1986. Where an administration is followed by a liquidation, the relevant date is the commencement of the administration.

[4]	IA 1986, Sch 6.

(b) Guaranteed payments

13.24 Certain payments owing to the employees of an insolvent employer are guaranteed by the state and will be met out of the National Insurance Fund ('the Fund').[1] If payment is made to an employee, the Department for Trade and Industry becomes subrogated to his or her rights against the employer, including any priority in respect of preferential debts; any sums recovered from the employer are paid back into the Fund. In some circumstances, the ability to claim from the Fund will circumvent procedural difficulties facing an employee in taking action against an insolvent employer.

(i) Redundancy payments

13.25 Redundancy payments are guaranteed,[2] both where the employer is formally insolvent and where the employee has taken all reasonable steps (other than legal proceedings to enforce an employment tribunal decision) to recover the payment, and the employer has refused or failed to pay (this will cover the situation where the employer has so few assets that it is not worth putting it into formal insolvency).

(ii) Maternity pay

13.26 Any statutory maternity pay is guaranteed in the same way as redundancy pay.[3]

(iii) Other guaranteed payments

13.27 Other payments guaranteed on a formal insolvency are set out in section 184 of the Employment Rights Act 1996. Before a payment will be made out of the Fund, the Department for Trade and Industry must be satisfied that:

1.   the debt claimed is within the specified categories;
2.   the employer is insolvent, as defined in section 183;[4]
3.   the employment of the employee has been terminated; and
4.   the debt was due on the appropriate date.[5]

---

[1]   The requirement for a State guaranteed fund is created by EC Directive 80/987 ('the Employment Insolvency Directive').

[2]   Section 166 of the ERA 1996.

[3]   Regulation 7 of the Statutory Maternity Pay Regulations 1986.

[4]   In *Secretary of State for Employment v Stone* [1994] ICR 761 it was held that appointment of a receiver pursuant to a fixed charge over book debts did not fall within the then equivalent of s 183 and therefore the employer was not insolvent.

[5]   *Secretary of State for Employment v Wilson* [1996] IRLR 330 is authority for the view that, if the employee owes money to the employer, that sum will reduce or eliminate the debt owed by the employer in accordance with the normal insolvency set-off provisions under r 4.90 of the Insolvency Rules 1986.

13.28 '**The appropriate date**'[1] In relation to arrears of pay and holiday pay, this is the date on which employer became insolvent.[2] In relation to protective awards under section 189 of the Trade Union and Labour Relations (Consolidation) Act 1992 and basic awards of compensation for unfair dismissal, the appropriate date is the latest of the date on which the employer became insolvent, the date of the termination of the employee's employment, and the date on which the award was made. In relation to any other guaranteed payment, it is the later of the date on which the employer became insolvent and the date of termination of the employee's employment.

13.29   Categories of payment[3] Categories of payment in respect of which a claim may be made are, broadly:

1.   remuneration due during the eight weeks prior to the commencement of the insolvency;
2.   section 86 (but not any greater contractual) notice moneys;
3.   holiday pay; and
4.   unfair dismissal basic award (but not the compensatory element).

Periodic payments guaranteed by the Fund are subject to a statutory maximum currently set at £240 per week[4] per item (this maximum is the gross figure and is subject to deduction for tax and National Insurance).

13.30   The House of Lords in *Westwood v Secretary of State for Employment*[5] decided that a claim from the Fund for payment in lieu of what is now section 86 notice was of the same nature as a breach of contract claim, and that sums received in mitigation of the loss must therefore be deducted from the amount paid. In *Westwood*, the Department of Employment argued that unemployment benefit received by Mr Westwood should be deducted from the 12 weeks' notice money to which he was entitled. The precise issue in *Westwood* has been dealt with by a subsequent alteration to the social security regulations, providing that the maximum period of unemployment benefit will be in addition to days in respect of which the employee receives a notice payment from the Fund.[6] The general principle of obligation to mitigate is also shown by *Secretary of State for Employment v*

---

[1]   Section 185 of the ERA 1996.
[2]   As defined in s 183 of the ERA 1996.
[3]   See s 184 of the ERA 1996.
[4]   In *Potter v Secretary of State for Employment* [1997] IRLR 2, the Court of Appeal left open the question of whether the statutory ceiling is in accordance with the social objective of the Insolvency Directive. This case related to protective awards and the Court of Appeal decided that such awards do not fall within the Insolvency Directive. The issue is likely to arise again in the future in relation to claims of arrears of remuneration clearly falling within the Directive and reference may well be made to the ECJ under Art 234 of the Treaty of Rome for guidance on the issue.
[5]   [1984] IRLR 209.
[6]   See *Secretary of State for Employment v Wilson* [1996] IRLR 334, which reiterated the application of the normal principle of mitigation and explained how the interrelationship of guaranteed payment and unemployment benefit is usually dealt with in practice.

Cooper[1] in which the EAT held that the payment made from the Fund should be reduced by an amount equivalent to the basic rate of income tax.

13.31   Need for a formal insolvency Unlike redundancy and maternity pay, sums can only be paid from the Fund under section 182 where the employer is insolvent as defined in section 183; that is, broadly, where the employer is subject to a formal insolvency regime. *Pollard v Teako*[2] is an example of the situation where a company has so few assets that it is not worth liquidating. In such a case, the only way in which employees can become entitled to claim under section 182 is by putting the company into formal insolvency themselves.

13.32   A rather unusual case in which this actually happened was *Re Eloc Electro-Optieck and Communicatie BV*.[3] This concerned a Dutch company which had ceased trading and had no assets within the jurisdiction of the court. Two employees, both foreign nationals, were owed several thousand pounds each for unpaid salary and unfair dismissal. Nourse J said that normally there would be no point in, and the court would refuse to make, a winding-up order against a foreign company with no assets within the jurisdiction. Here, however, there was the prospect of some benefit to the creditors, albeit from the Fund, not from the company itself. He made a compulsory winding-up order, subject to an undertaking to indemnify the Official Receiver.

13.33   Further, *Secretary of State for Trade and Industry v Walden*[4] has again recently confirmed that the factual existence of insolvency is not enough to trigger a payment from the Fund; one of the specific events in section 183 of the Employment Rights Act 1996 must be established in order for the Fund to be required to make a payment.

13.34   Right to appeal An employee may complain to an employment tribunal that the Fund has either paid nothing to the employee or has paid too little.[5] Such application must be presented within three months of the decision of the Department of Trade and Industry; there is no right to complain of an unreasonable delay in the Department of Trade and Industry reaching a decision. If the complaint is proved the employment tribunal will make a declaration as to the amount due, but it does not actually order payment.

(c) Inter-relationship of preferential debts and guaranteed payments

13.35   Where employees are owed amounts which both carry preferential status and are guaranteed, they will generally recover more of what is

---

[1]   [1987] ICR 766.
[2]   [1967] 2 ITR 357.
[3]   [1981] 2 All ER 1111.
[4]   [2000] IRLR 168.
[5]   Section 188 of the ERA 1996.

owed (since the monetary limit on guaranteed payments is higher) more quickly under section 182 than from claiming as a preferential creditor in the insolvency proceedings. There are items which will be paid out of the Fund which do not carry preferential status (section 86 notice moneys, basic award, redundancy payments and protective award made after the onset of insolvency).

13.36   The only circumstances in which an employee will be forced to claim in the insolvency, relying on his or her preferential status, will be in respect of sums due for periods outside the Fund limits or where the employee is still employed by the insolvent employer.

13.37   For other sums not forthcoming from the Fund (unfair dismissal compensation, for example), the employee will have a non-preferential claim in common with the unsecured creditors.

(d) Directors and controlling shareholders

13.38   Until relatively recently, no distinction was made between ordinary employees and those who are also controlling shareholders of an insolvent company. However, a group of cases[1] has resulted in a six-point set of guidelines being required to be examined in each case to determine whether, in fact, a controlling shareholder is also an employee. The matters that employment tribunals must consider are:

(a)   whether there was a genuine contract between the shareholder and the director;
(b)   whether the contract gave rise to an employer/employee relationship;
(c)   whether there were other such shareholders;
(d)   whether the constitution of the company allows the shareholder rights such that the shareholder is, in effect, answerable only to himself/herself and can thereby block the shareholder's own dismissal;
(e)   what voting rights the shareholder had in connection with matters in which he was personally interested;
(f)   the conduct of the parties pursuant to the contract.

13.39   If a director (including a shadow director) is found guilty of wrongful trading under section 214 of the Insolvency Act 1986 (that is, in very broad terms, failing to take steps to avoid loss to creditors once he or she should realise that the business is going to collapse), any debts owing to him or her by the company may be subordinated to all the other debts of the company.[2]

---

[1]   *Buchan and Ivey v Secretary of State for Employment* [1997] IRLR 80, *Fleming v Secretary of State for Trade and Industry* [1997] IRLR 682, *Secretary of State for Trade and Industry v Bottrill* [1999] IRLR 326 and *Sellars Arenascene Limited v Connolly* [2001] IRLR 222.
[2]   Section 215 of the IA 1986.

5. EFFECT OF INSOLVENCY REGIMES ON CONTRACTS OF EMPLOYMENT

(a) Bankruptcy

13.40   The general rule is that the trustee in bankruptcy takes over the benefit of contracts made with the bankrupt. Contracts of a personal nature may remain with the bankrupt; inability to pay wages under a contract of employment would, however, repudiate the contract. A person who has made a contract with someone subsequently made bankrupt may apply to the court for an order discharging the obligations under the contract.[1]

13.41   Where the trustee in bankruptcy takes over or re-engages the employee, it would appear that (since the business vests in the trustee) the two periods of employment are continuous under section 218(2) of the Employment Rights Act 1996 and that the Transfer of Undertakings (Protection of Employment) Regulations 1981 would also apply.[2]

13.42   The Insolvency Rules 1986 provide that the remuneration of employees will be payable out of the insolvent's estate in priority to the trustee's own fees.[3]

(b) Liquidation

13.43   A compulsory winding-up is usually said to operate as an automatic dismissal (by repudiation of contract) of the employees. There seems in principle, to be no reason why this should be so if the business does not cease at the same time. It is not apparent from the case-law[4] that any obligation universal to every employer is necessarily rendered incapable of performance as a result of a winding-up order where the company continues to trade and retain employees through the agency of the liquidator. Even if this traditional view is correct,[5] the re-engagement of those employees who continue to work is by the liquidator as agent for the

---

[1]   Section 345 of the IA 1986.

[2]   *Bellhaven v Berekis*, 17 March 1993 EAT, Scotland (unreported). The relevant law (Bankruptcy (Scotland) Act 1985) is to the same effect as English law.

[3]   See r 6.224 of the Insolvency Rules 1986; either (b) an expense incurred in the carrying on of the business of the bankrupt, or (n) remuneration of those employed to perform services for the estate.

[4]   *Chapman's Case* (1866) LR 1 Eq 346 has been taken as authority for this proposition but the issue was when the notice of termination (whose existence was assumed in that case) was given, and not whether a winding-up order necessarily involves termination of employment. *Re English Joint Stock Bank ex parte Hording* (1867) 3 Eq 341 seems a more sensible approach in this regard. In *Macdowell's Case* (1866) 32 Ch D 366, Chitty J held that, following *Chapman's Case*, a winding-up order operated as a dismissal, but that there could be a waiver or new contract between liquidator and employee. He provided no explanation of why the order should have this effect, other than that *Chapman* had been universally accepted as based on this proposition.

[5]   The Privy Council case of *Commercial Finance Company Ltd (in liquidation) v Indira Ramsingh-Mahabir* [1994] 1 WLR 1297 was decided on the basis that the traditional view is correct.

company, and if there is no gap between contracts for the purposes of section 218(2) of the Employment Rights Act (that is, in most cases, provided the liquidator confirms continued employment by the end of the week following the making of the winding-up order), continuity should be maintained.[1]

13.44　A resolution for voluntary winding-up has no effect on the contracts of employment, at least where the business does not entirely cease.[2]

13.45　In the case of a voluntary winding-up, all expenses properly incurred by a liquidator in winding up the affairs of a company are payable out of company assets in priority to any obligations incurred before the liquidation began.[3] In the case of a court winding-up, however, the court may make an order as to the payment of the expenses in such order of priority as it thinks fit.[4] Persons who are employed by the liquidator in connection with the liquidation are entitled to be subrogated to the liquidator's claim to be indemnified, and may recover from the company's assets if the liquidator does not pay them.

(c) Administrative receivership

13.46　The appointment of an administrative receiver does not, of itself, terminate the contracts of employment, since the receiver is the agent of the company. This was finally settled in *Griffiths v Secretary of State for Social Services*,[5] in which it was said that there were three situations in which there might be exceptions to this rule. First, the appointment of a receiver accompanied by the sale of the business would terminate the contracts (this now has to be considered in the light of the Transfer of Undertakings (Protection of Employment) Regulations 1981). Secondly, contracts will be terminated where the receiver enters into new agreements with employees. Thirdly, a contract of employment may be terminated where it is inconsistent with the existence of a receiver; in some circumstances, the role of a managing director may be inconsistent with that of a receiver (an argument which had been raised in *Griffiths*, although, on the facts, that particular managing director had not been dismissed).

13.47　The position is more complicated if a company in receivership goes into liquidation. Section 44 of the Insolvency Act 1986 enacts the common law position established by the House of Lords in *Gaskell v Gosling*,[6] that the receiver can be the company's agent only unless and until the company

---

[1]　*Golding & Howard v Fire, Auto & Marine Insurance* (1968) 3 ITR 372 appears wrongly decided.
[2]　*Fowler v Commercial Timber Company* [1930] 2 KB 1.
[3]　Section 115 of the IA 1986. Rule 4.218 of the Insolvency Rules 1986 provides for the order of payment.
[4]　Section 156 of the IA 1986. In the absence of such an order, the order of priority set out in r 4.218 of the Insolvency Rules 1986 will apply.
[5]　[1974] 1 QB 468.
[6]　[1897] AC 575.

goes into liquidation. It would seem that, if the receiver continues to trade after the company goes into liquidation, he or she must be trading and employing those working in the undertaking as principal. This was the position in *Deaway Trading Ltd v Calverley*;[1] the issue arose because the receiver had transferred the business to a new owner who subsequently dismissed the employees. The employees claimed that their employment had been continuous with that for the original owner under the then equivalent of section 218(2) of the Employment Rights Act 1996. Deaway claimed there was no continuity because the employees had been employed by the receiver, not the owner, at the time of sale. The National Industrial Relations Court ignored the technicalities and said that the receiver, although technically the employer, was not employer in his personal capacity but as receiver of the original owner and, looking at the realities of the case, the employees had been transferred with the business in such a way as to preserve their continuity. A similar argument could arise in relation to the operation of the Transfer of Undertakings (Protection of Employment) Regulations 1981 where a business is sold by a receiver when the company is in liquidation; the courts would probably adopt a similarly bold approach. Indeed, it could perhaps be argued that the effect of the termination of the receiver's agency is to effect a transfer of the undertaking (and, therefore, of the contracts of the employees) to the receiver; receivers would argue strenuously against such an interpretation.[2]

13.48   The effect of section 44 of the Insolvency Act 1986, as amended by the Insolvency Act 1994, is that administrative receivers will be personally liable for any new contracts which they make and will be liable for wages, salaries[3] and pension contributions arising during the receivership of those whose contracts of employment they have adopted. The question of the circumstances in which contracts are adopted is addressed below in the section of this chapter dealing with dismissal by a receiver (see para 13.59), since it is in this context that the issue has arisen. The receiver will not be taken to have adopted the contract of any employee dismissed within 14 days of the start of the receivership. An administrative receiver will be entitled to an indemnity out of the company's assets in respect of this personal liability but if the assets prove insufficient the loss will fall on the receiver.[4] Insofar as section 44 deals with the receiver's liability for the continuing remuneration of the employees, it adds nothing to what would be the position anyway since, in order to keep the employees, the receiver has always had to make funds available for paying them. Receivers will only retain the services of employees where they are confident that such funds will be available without putting themselves or their debenture holders at risk.

[1]   [1973] 3 All ER 776.
[2]   See para 13.63, for other problems connected with the ending of the receiver's agency which have no satisfactory legislative answer.
[3]   Defined by s 44(2C) of the IA 1986 to include wages or salary payable in respect of periods of absence for holiday, sickness or other good cause and sums payable in lieu of holiday.
[4]   Receivers may be able to pass the loss on to their appointors under the terms of the agreement between them.

(d) Administration

13.49   The appointment of an administrator has no effect upon the contracts of the employees since section 14(5) of the Insolvency Act 1986 deems him to act as the company's agent.

13.50   Unlike a receiver, an administrator incurs no personal liability to the employees. Section 19 of the Insolvency Act 1986, as amended by the Insolvency Act 1994, does confer priority on certain sums which become due to employees in the course of an administration. Sums payable under new contracts entered into by an administrator and wages, salaries[1] and pension contributions arising during the administration of those whose contracts of employment have been adopted[2] by the administrator are to be paid out of the company's assets in priority to the administrator's own fees and expenses. Administrators will, therefore, be unwilling to retain the services of employees unless confident that there will be sufficient assets remaining to meet the costs of the administration after paying the employees. The claims of creditors with security which, as created, was floating and of unsecured creditors are postponed to payments of the costs of administration.

6. CHANGE OF TERMS BY THE INSOLVENCY PRACTITIONER

13.51   An insolvency practitioner, when retaining employees, may seek unilaterally to vary the terms of the employees' contracts of employment, particularly those relating to the employer's obligations on termination. However, such a course of action is likely to give rise to potential claims of constructive dismissal. Where the employees continue to work for a considerable period after being notified of the changes, they may be deemed to have waived the right to complain of the breach.

7. DISMISSAL BY AN INSOLVENCY PRACTITIONER

13.52   An employee dismissed by an insolvency practitioner due to a requirement identified by the insolvency practitioner to streamline the employer's business is likely to be redundant. However, such employees may have wrongful dismissal claims if dismissed without being given the correct notice and they may also have unfair dismissal claims in the event that proper procedures are not followed in relation to their dismissals.[3] Where the dismissal is connected with the sale of the business, it may be

---

[1]   Defined by s 19(9) of the IA 1986 in identical terms to s 44(2C) of the IA 1986. See para 13.48, n 3.

[2]   See discussion of adoption at para 13.48.

[3]   See para 13.09. There have been findings of unfair dismissal against administrators (see, eg *Powdrill v Watson* [1994] 2 All ER 513). One of the difficulties in establishing the legal principles in this area, however, is that it is rarely worthwhile for an insolvency practitioner to expend funds defending a claim.

necessary to consider the implications of the Transfer of Undertakings (Protection of Employment) Regulations 1981.

13.53   It is necessary to consider whether the fact that the employee has been retained during the insolvency alters the employee's chances of having his or her claims met. As already seen, redundancy payments, basic awards and section 86 notice moneys are guaranteed by the State in the case of an insolvent employer. There is technically a problem with this where the dismissal is by a receiver where the company is in liquidation, since the receiver's agency has been terminated and he or she is employing as a principal. Similarly, the trustee in bankruptcy is not the agent of the bankrupt and is not insolvent and, therefore, the requirement for the employer to be insolvent does not seem to be met. Neither of these points appears to be taken by the Department for Trade and Industry. Dismissals by liquidators, administrators and receivers of companies not in liquidation will be dismissals as agents for the insolvent employer and, therefore, by an insolvent employer.

13.54   The questions arise as to the priority in the distribution of the insolvent's assets of the claims of the employees (including those to which the National Insurance Fund is subrogated) which arise on dismissal by an insolvency practitioner and as to whether the insolvency practitioner incurs any personal liability.

(a) Trustee in bankruptcy

13.55   The expenses of the bankruptcy have first claim on the available assets of the insolvent.[1] Expenses incurred carrying on the business of the bankrupt are high in the order of priority, ahead of the trustee in bankruptcy's own fees.[2] It is arguable that termination payments fall within the category of expenses of running the business; trustees in bankruptcy would argue that they do not.

(b) Liquidator

13.56   Remuneration of those properly employed during the liquidation will be an expense of the liquidation;[3] whether it can be argued that termination payments fall within the same category is not clear, but insolvency practitioners would argue that they do not.

(c) Administrative receiver

13.57   The position at common law would be that a receiver, as agent of the company, would not be personally liable for the termination of the contracts of the company's employees by the company. A receiver incurs no personal liability by repudiating a contract in the name of the company

---

[1]   Section 328 of the IA 1986.

[2]   Rule 6.224 of the Insolvency Rules 1986.

[3]   See paras 13.09 *et seq* for order of priority of payment.

or by refusing to allow the company to perform its part of a contract and would, therefore, bear no liability for termination payments to employees whom he or she had made the company dismiss. The employees would be left with a probably worthless claim against the company and, where relevant, a claim on the National Insurance Fund.

13.58 Since 1947 receivers have been statutorily personally liable on new contracts entered into by them, except to the extent that such contracts have excluded liability and have been entitled in respect of such liability to an indemnity out of the assets of the company. An example of a receiver incurring personal liability was *Re Mack Trucks (Britain) Ltd*,[1] in which the receiver expressly terminated the old contracts (apparently under the impression that this was in any event the effect of going into receivership) and entered into new contracts of employment on the same terms in November 1964. The company ceased trading in July 1965 and it was held that the receiver could be sued for the wrongful dismissals since he was personally liable on the new contracts.

13.59 The case of *Nicoll v Cutts*,[2] which was decided whilst the Insolvency Act 1986 was in the course of being drafted, led to the hasty insertion into that Act of provisions under which the personal liability of receivers was extended to contracts which they had 'adopted'. The plaintiff in *Nicoll* was the managing director of a company which went into receivership whilst he was in hospital; the receivers did not pay him but did not actually dismiss him until some weeks later. The Court of Appeal held that he had no claim against the receivers for unpaid salary since they had not entered into a contract with him. Contracts continued by receivers could not be equated with contracts entered into by them.

13.60 Section 44(2) of the Insolvency Act 1986, as originally enacted, provided that an administrative receiver would be personally liable on any contract of employment adopted by him (with the right to an indemnity against the assets of the company). The Insolvency Act 1994 has amended section 44 to restrict the personal liability of administrative receivers on contracts adopted after 15 March 1994 to wages, salary and pension contributions,[3] so that in respect of contracts adopted after that date receivers will be at no risk of personal liability for payments arising out of the termination of the contracts.[4]

13.61 The insolvency legislation provides no definition of the circumstances in which a receiver adopts a contract of employment; section 44(2) simply provides that the administrative receiver is not to be

---

[1] [1967] All ER 977.

[2] [1985] BCLC 322.

[3] As defined in s 44(2C) of the IA 1986 as amended.

[4] The legislation has no retrospective effect (despite the pleas of insolvency practitioners that it should have) and the House of Lords has held (in *Re Leyland DAF* [1995] 2 All ER 65) that in respect of contracts adopted before 15 March 1994 receivers will be liable for payments in lieu of notice, including pension contributions in respect of the notice period, and to holiday pay referable to the months of employment following the receiver's appointment.

taken to have adopted a contract of employment by reason of anything done or omitted to be done within 14 days after his appointment. In *Powdrill v Watson*,[1] Lord Browne-Wilkinson said that adoption connotes some conduct by the receiver which amounts to an election to treat the continued contract of employment with the company as giving rise to a separate liability in the receivership.

13.62   There has been considerable debate as to whether it is possible to refuse to adopt a contract of employment whilst retaining the services of the employees. After the enactment of the original version of section 44, receivers developed the practice of sending a letter to employees, informing them that they would continue to be employed by the company and that the receiver would continue to make funds available to the company to cover their remuneration, but that the company alone remained their employer and that the receiver was not adopting or accepting any personal liability in respect of the contracts. Harman J in *Re Specialised Mouldings* upheld the efficacy of this practice in protecting receivers from liability.[2] The House of Lords, however, held in *Powdrill v Watson*[3] that letters of this type do not work; it is not possible to 'cherry-pick' and adopt part only of a contract. The contract of any employee whose services are retained after the 14-day period should automatically be taken to be impliedly adopted. The effect of the amendment to section 44 is to remove the impetus on administrative receivers to argue that they have not adopted contracts since their liability is restricted to that which they would anyway accept.

13.63   The question seems never to have arisen as to whether the liability of the receiver for dismissals differs if the company has gone into liquidation. Once that has happened, the receiver will be employing as principal since his agency for the company has come to an end; it might be expected that he should be treated as any other employer. No conclusive answer is provided by the insolvency legislation on this issue. Section 44 starts by providing that 'the administrative receiver of a company is deemed to be the company's agent unless and until the company goes into liquidation' and it would be possible to read the subsequent parts of the section dealing with the imposition of liability on the receiver as applying solely to the period of that agency. Insofar as section 44 provides for liability on new contracts, the position on termination would be the same whether the receiver is agent or principal (if the latter, the receiver's right to an indemnity will have ceased). Receivers seeking to avoid personal liability for the termination of the contracts of employment of those whose contracts they had continued at the start of the receivership would have to argue that those contracts retained the status of 'adopted' (and, therefore, did not impose liability for termination on the receiver) despite the ending of the receiver's agency. It might be thought that the notion of 'adoption' of contracts is inappropriate where the receiver has replaced the company as

---

[1]   [1995] 2 All ER 65.
[2]   3 February 1987, ChD (unreported).
[3]   [1995] 2 All ER 65.

principal on the contract. Receivers might argue that those drafting the Insolvency Act 1986 clearly thought that liability for adopted contracts could be imposed on receivers who were acting as principals, since that is what section 37 appears to provide in the case of ordinary receivers. Section 37 provides that they are to be 'to the same extent as if appointed by order of the court ... personally liable on any contract entered into by him ... and on any contract of employment adopted by him'; a receiver appointed by order of the court will be a principal. Equally, however, one might argue that section 37 is incompetently drafted and does not achieve its aim since it would not be possible for a receiver appointed by the court to adopt contracts. All that can be said with any certainty is that some rather more thoroughly considered legislation dealing with this area would not come amiss.

(d) Administrator

13.64   Administrators, as has been seen, do not incur personal liability towards employees. The question which arises in this context is that of the order of priority in the distribution of the company's assets of an employee's claim arising out of the termination of employment. As explained above, section 19 of the Insolvency Act 1986 (as amended by the Insolvency Act 1994) provides for priority of payment of certain sums. In respect of contracts adopted[1] after 15 March 1994,[2] an employee will be unable to argue that termination payments carry any priority and, unless the sum claimed is payable out of the National Insurance Fund, he or she will be left with an unsecured claim against the company in common with the ordinary creditors which it may be impossible to pursue until after the end of the administration.

---

[1]   See discussion of meaning of 'adopted' in para 13.50.

[2]   For contracts adopted before 15 March 1994, priority will be given to amounts due in respect of payments in lieu of notice, including pension contributions in respect of the notice period, and to holiday pay referable to the months of employment following the administrator's appointment: *Powdrill v Watson* [1995] 2 All ER 65.

Part IV:

PROBLEMS AFTER TERMINATION

Chapter 14

COMPETITION BY EX-EMPLOYEES

14.01 Although it is not possible for employers to prevent their ex-employees absolutely from competing with them, they are entitled to protect their legitimate trade interests to a certain extent. There are two ways in which this may be done. First, they may seek to rely upon what is usually called the implied duty of loyalty and fidelity, by arguing that the ex-employees' contracts contained an implied term obliging them to respect confidential information relating to the employers' trade secrets and trade connections acquired during the course of their employment. Alternatively, they may rely upon an express restrictive covenant, but only if the employees' contracts contained one and the dismissal was not in breach of contract.

14.02 It is perfectly clear that in an appropriate case an ex-employee who commits a breach of the implied duty of loyalty and fidelity may be restrained from committing or continuing to commit the breach. As the cases show, however, the implied duty is of fairly limited ambit. Employers who are concerned about protecting their trade secrets and trade connections are therefore well advised to ensure that their employees' contracts contain express restraints which can then be sought to be enforced after termination.

14.03 It should also be borne in mind that the contractual doctrine of repudiation[1] may operate so as to affect the situation. In *Thomas Marshall (Exports) Ltd v Guinle*,[2] for example, the employee was subject to various express restraints, which, to differing extents, affected him both during and after his employment. He purported to resign when his service contract still had four and a half years to run. Sir Robert Megarry V-C held that this repudiatory act did not automatically terminate the contract[3] and that, although the court could not force him to work, it could restrain him from committing other breaches of his obligations during the continuance of his contract. The Vice-Chancellor then went on to restrain him from dealing with the company's customers and suppliers and from using confidential information belonging to the company, on the basis of the employee's breach of the implied duty of loyalty and fidelity. The clause expressly restraining him during his employment covered only the *disclosure*, not the *use* of confidential information, but the implied term was held to cover both. The *Guinle* case is, therefore, a good example of the interaction of the implied duty and express restraints; it also suggests that the courts are more prepared to use the implied duty against employees during their

---

[1] For a discussion of this, see Chapter 9.
[2] [1978] ICR 905.
[3] *Ibid* at pp 917 and 920–921.

employment and express restraints against them once their employment has ended. In an appropriate case, however, the implied duty may be invoked against an ex-employee. If it is, it should be noted that it will not be subject to any limitation of time; on the other hand, it is essential that an express restraint be limited in time since it will otherwise be held to be unreasonable.

Both types of protection are considered in the following sections. Enforcement is considered at the end of the chapter.

1. THE IMPLIED DUTY OF LOYALTY AND FIDELITY

14.04   As the *Guinle* case shows, the implied duty of loyalty and fidelity may be invoked against an employee during the course of the employment.[1] That aspect of the case is not, however, relevant to the present discussion, which concerns ex-employees.

14.05   An examination of the case-law suggests two important points: first, that the implied term will probably be invoked only where the breach is actually committed before the employment ceased;[2] and secondly, that the courts are more likely to restrain the use of tangible, rather than intangible, information.

14.06   It is clear that the ex-employee will be restrained from using a list of the ex-employer's customers copied out before leaving the employment[3] and from deliberately soliciting the employer's customers, before leaving, to transfer their custom after his or her departure.[4] But if there is no written list, the court will be reluctant to restrain the ex-employee who solicits those customers whose names he or she can remember,[5] unless there is evidence to suggest that he or she has deliberately committed an entire list to memory.[6] In this last situation, the case may be difficult to prove, as happened in *Baker v Gibbons*.[7]

14.07   A distinction must be made between an individual employee's general knowledge or individual skill, which he or she may legitimately put to use in the future, and a trade secret which the employer is entitled to protect. In *Printers and Finishers Ltd v Holloway*,[8] Cross J said:

---

[1]   See also *Hivac v Park Royal Scientific Instruments Ltd* [1946] Ch 169.

[2]   As in *Robb v Green* [1895] 2 QB 315, *Worsley and Co Ltd v Cooper* [1939] 1 All ER 290 and *Wessex Dairies Ltd v Smith* [1935] 2 KB 80.

[3]   As in *Robb v Green* [1895] 2 QB 315.

[4]   *Wessex Dairies Ltd v Smith* [1935] 2 KB 80. See also *Adamson v B & L Cleaners Ltd* [1995] IRLR 193, which arose in the context of unfair dismissal. The employers' dismissal of the employee for competing with them for the future business of one of their customers was held to be fair.

[5]   *Hart v Colley* (1890) 59 LJ Ch 355.

[6]   This proposition is inferable from the dicta of Sir John Pennycuick, V-C in *Baker v Gibbons* [1972] 2 All ER 759.

[7]   [1972] 2 All ER 759.

[8]   [1964] 3 All ER 731.

'The mere fact that the confidential information is not embodied in a document but is carried away by the employee in his head is not of itself a reason against the granting of an injunction to prevent its use or disclosure by him. If the information in question can fairly be regarded as a separate part of the employee's stock of knowledge which a man of ordinary honesty and intelligence would recognise to be the property of his old employer and not his own to do as he likes with, then the court, if it thinks that there is a danger of the information being used to the detriment of the old employer, will do what it can to prevent that result by granting an injunction. Thus an ex-employee will be restrained from using or disclosing a chemical formula or a list of customers which he has committed to memory.'[1]

14.08 A further requirement in cases of this kind is that the employee must not be allowed to acquire an unfair advantage. This rule particularly applies where he or she deliberately obtains, memorises or copies lists of customers in breach of the implied duty. An example of this type of situation is *Robb v Green*,[2] in which an employee was restrained from using after his employment had ended a list of his employers' customers which he had copied out before his departure. More recently, in *Roger Bullivant Ltd v Ellis*,[3] the Court of Appeal said that 'it is of the highest importance that the principle of *Robb v Green* ... which ... is one of no more than fair and honourable dealing, should be steadfastly maintained'. When he left his employment, the employee took with him a card index showing the names and addresses of his employer's customers. The Court of Appeal said that in such circumstances it was appropriate to grant an injunction, but that the injunction should be limited to the period during which the unfair advantage might be expected to continue. This was limited to 12 months, as there was an express restraint limited to this period. Nourse LJ conceded that the employee might have contacted some of the customers without using the card index, but said that he was far from convinced that he would have been able to contact all those he did without using it. He said:[4]

'Having made deliberate and unlawful use of the [employer's] property, [the employee] cannot complain if he finds that the eye of the law is unable to distinguish between those whom, had he so chosen, he could have lawfully contacted and those whom he could not.'

14.09 Although the confidential information need not be of a complicated nature,[5] the question is whether, in any particular case, the information is confidential. This is far from easy to establish. In *Thomas Marshall (Exports) Ltd v Guinle*,[6] Sir Robert Megarry, V-C suggested, *obiter*, a test containing four elements:

---

1   [1964] 3 All ER 731 at pp 735–736.
2   [1895] 2 QB 315.
3   [1987] ICR 464.
4   *Ibid* at p 475.
5   As in *Cranleigh Precision Engineering Ltd v Bryant* [1965] 1 WLR 1293.
6   [1978] ICR 905 at p 926.

'First ... the information must be information the release of which the owner believes would be injurious to him or of advantage to his rivals or others. Second ... the owner must believe that the information is confidential or secret, i.e. that it is not already in the public domain ... Third, the owner's belief under the previous two heads must be reasonable. Fourth ... the information must be judged in the light of the usage and practices of the particular industry or trade concerned. It may be that information which does not satisfy all these requirements may be entitled to protection as confidential information or trade secrets; but I think that any information which does satisfy them must be of a type which is entitled to protection.'

14.10   The Court of Appeal considered this issue fully in *Faccenda Chicken Ltd v Fowler*.[1] It upheld the existence of an implied duty in relation to the use and disclosure of information, but in effect confined it to trade secrets or their equivalents, ie information which has a sufficiently high degree of confidentiality to warrant protection after the employment has ended by means of an implied term. It is, therefore, necessary to distinguish between information which amounts to a trade secret or its equivalent and information which is confidential and which an employee is free to use for his or her own advantage. At first instance, Goulding J identified three classes of information which an employee might acquire in the course of employment. He said:[2]

'First there is information which, because of its trivial character or its easy accessibility from public sources of information, cannot be regarded by reasonable persons or by the law as confidential at all. The servant is at liberty to impart it during his service or afterwards to anyone he pleases, even his master's competitor ... Secondly, there is information which the servant must treat as confidential (either because he is expressly told it is confidential, or because from its character it obviously is so) but which once learned necessarily remains in the servant's head and becomes part of his own skill and knowledge applied in the course of his master's business. So long as the employment continues, he cannot otherwise use or disclose such information without infidelity and therefore breach of contract. But when he is no longer in the same service, the law allows him to use his full skill and knowledge for his own benefit in competition with his former master; and ... there seems to be no established distinction between the use of such information where its possessor trades as a principal, and where he enters the employment of a new master, even though the latter case involves disclosure and not mere personal use of the information. If an employer wants to protect information of this kind, he can do so by an express stipulation restraining the servant from competing with him (within reasonable limits of time and space) after the termination of his employment. . . Thirdly, however, there are, to my mind, specific trade secrets so confidential that, even though they may necessarily have been learned by

---

[1]   [1986] ICR 297. See also *Balston Ltd v Headline Filters Ltd* [1987] FSR 330. In *Berkeley Administration Inc v McClelland* [1990] FSR 505, the information sought to be protected was information derived from financial projections in an appendix to the employers' own business plan. The court said that the information was not sufficiently confidential to be protectable after the termination of the employee's employment and applied the *Faccenda* case.

[2]   [1984] ICR 589 at pp 598–600.

heart and even though the servant may have left the service, they cannot lawfully be used for anyone's benefit but the master's.'

Neill LJ, giving the judgment of the Court of Appeal, said that the court must consider all the circumstances of a case, taking into account the following factors:[1]

'(a) The nature of the employment. Thus employment in a capacity where "confidential" material is habitually handled may impose a high obligation of confidentiality because the employee can be expected to realise its sensitive nature to a greater extent than if he were employed in a capacity where such material reaches him only occasionally or incidentally.

(b) The nature of the information itself ... [T]he information will only be protected if it can be properly classed as a trade secret or as material which, while not properly to be regarded as a trade secret, is in all the circumstances of such a highly confidential nature as to require the same protection as a trade secret ...

(c) Whether the employer impressed upon the employee the confidentiality of the information ... [T]hough an employer cannot prevent the use or disclosure merely by telling the employee that certain information is confidential, the attitude of the employer towards the information provides evidence which may assist in determining whether or not the information can properly be regarded as a trade secret ...

(d) Whether the relevant information can be easily isolated from other information which the employee is free to use or disclose ... [W]e would not regard the separability of the information in question as being conclusive, but the fact that the alleged "confidential" information is part of a package and that the remainder of the package is not confidential is likely to throw light on whether the information in question is really a trade secret.'

14.11   In the *Faccenda* case, the information in issue was sales information which the employers were very anxious to keep confidential; there were no express restrictive covenants in the employees' contracts. The Court of Appeal concluded that the information fell into Goulding J's second category and not the third category but did not rule out the possibility that information relating to an employer's commercial interests could be protected in certain circumstances. On the facts in the instant case, the employers had not done enough, however, to be able to protect their business information. A similar conclusion was reached in *Wallace Bogan & Co v Cove*,[2] where the Court of Appeal refused to imply a term into the contracts of solicitors whose effect would be to restrain them from canvassing or doing business with clients of their former employees. The Court's view was that the way for employers to protect themselves in a case of this kind was for them to extract a restrictive covenant from the employees concerned. A similar conclusion was reached by the Court of Appeal in *Brooks v Olyslager OMS (UK) Ltd*,[3] which involved the disclosure by a former employer of information relating to his former employers'

---

[1] [1986] ICR 297 at pp 310–311.
[2] [1997] IRLR 453.
[3] [1998] IRLR 590. See also *AT Poeton (Gloucester Plating) Ltd v Horton* [2000] ICR 1208.

financial position. The Court said that the information did not amount to trade secrets falling within the third category.

14.12   In *Lancashire Fires Ltd v SA Lyons & Co Ltd,*[1] on the other hand, the Court of Appeal said that for information to amount to a trade secret falling within Goulding J's third category (see above), it is not necessary for the employer to point out to the employee the precise limits of what is sought to be protected as confidential. In the instant case, the employee acquired information about the processes involved in producing artificial coals and logs for use in gas fires. Carnwath J at first instance said that the information did not fall within the third category, but the Court of Appeal reversed his decision on that point. It rejected the argument that the employee did not owe a duty of confidence to the employers after leaving their employment because the employers had not precisely defined and pointed out to him those aspects of the production process which they sought to protect as a trade secret.

14.13   The final point to note here is that the public interest may require the disclosure of confidential information to those who have a 'proper interest' to receive it. In *Gartside v Outram,*[2] Wood VC said: 'There is no confidence as to the disclosure of iniquity'. In *Initial Services Ltd v Putterill,*[3] the Court of Appeal held that an exception to the implied duty arises where the information relates to iniquity or misconduct on the part of the employer which is of such a nature that it ought in the public interest to be disclosed to someone who has a proper interest in receiving it. This was followed in *Re a Company's Application,*[4] in which an injunction was granted to restrain the disclosure of confidential information but was expressed not to cover disclosure to the appropriate regulatory body (FIMBRA) which had the power to investigate whether the employers were complying with the regulatory scheme, or information concerning fiscal matters to the Inland Revenue.

14.14   The remedies most likely to be sought by the employer are an injunction against the ex-employee to restrain him or her from continuing to disclose or use the trade secrets or confidential information, and damages for breaches of contract already committed. The employer may also seek injunctions and/or damages against third parties to whom the trade secrets or confidential information have been passed. Injunctions are considered at the end of this chapter.

---

[1]   [1997] IRLR 113.
[2]   (1856) 3 Jur NS 39, (1856) 26 LJ (Ch) 113.
[3]   [1968] 1 QB 396. See also *Beloff v Pressdram Ltd* [1973] 1 All ER 241 at p 260.
[4]   [1989] ICR 449.

2. EXPRESS RESTRICTIVE COVENANTS

(a) General rules

14.15   The current state of the law in relation to the implied term of loyalty and fidelity makes it clear that it is preferable for employers who wish to protect their business interests to do so by means of express restrictive covenants. But, to be enforceable, such covenants must protect the employer's legitimate business interests, either trade secrets or goodwill and trade connections. It is not possible to prevent competition as such.

14.16   It is well settled that the doctrine of restraint of trade applies to restrictive covenants in contracts of employment.[1] This means that such covenants are prima facie void, but will be enforceable if they are reasonable:

> '... reasonable, that is, in reference to the interests of the parties concerned and reasonable in reference to the interests of the public, so framed and so guarded as to afford adequate protection to the party in whose favour [they are] imposed, while at the same time ... in no way injurious to the public.'[2]

The burden is on the person, in the present context the employer, seeking to enforce the restraint to satisfy the court that it is reasonable.[3] But the restraint must be no more than is reasonably necessary to afford the protection sought.[4]

14.17   There must be a clear proprietary interest requiring protection; the covenants most likely to be enforced are those which are reasonably necessary to protect the employer's trade secrets and trade connections. It is possible that employees and suppliers may also be legitimate interests, but they would need to be clearly defined. An employee who accepts employment in which he or she would be likely to damage these interests may be restrained. If, therefore, an employee would be likely to use the employer's trade secrets in new employment, he or she may be restrained. He or she may also be restrained from soliciting the ex-employer's customers or from setting up his or her own business or accepting a position with one of the ex-employer's competitors, if that is likely to damage the employer's trade connections by a misuse of his or her acquaintance with the employer's customers or clients. In *Spafax Ltd v Harrison*,[5] Stephenson LJ said:

> 'An employer is entitled to take and enforce promises from an employee which the employer can prove are reasonably necessary to protect him, the employer,

---

[1]   *Esso Petroleum Ltd v Harpers' Garage (Stourport) Ltd* [1968] AC 269.
[2]   *Nordenfelt v Maxim Nordenfelt Guns and Ammunition Co* [1894] AC 535 at p 565, *per* Lord Macnaghten.
[3]   *Herbert Morris Ltd v Saxelby* [1916] 1 AC 688.
[4]   *Gledhow Autoparts Ltd v Delaney* [1965] 1 WLR 1366.
[5]   [1980] IRLR 442 at p 446, para 25.

his trade connection, trade interests and goodwill, not from competition by the employee if he leaves his employment or from his then using the skill and knowledge with which his employment had equipped him to compete, but from his then using his personal knowledge of his employer's customers or his personal influence over them, or his knowledge of his employer's trade secrets, or advantages acquired from his employer to his employer's disadvantage.'

14.18   The factors to be taken into account include:

1.   the area of restraint;
2.   the period of restraint;
3.   the nature of the interest sought to be protected; and
4.   the subject-matter of the restraint.

14.19   Although it is clear that the reasonableness of the restraint must be judged at the time when the contract is made,[1] the approach of the courts in construing restrictive covenants tends to fluctuate. In *Littlewoods Organisation Ltd v Harris*,[2] the Court of Appeal construed a clause which, on its face, prevented an ex-employee from working for a rival organisation or any of its subsidiaries throughout the world, so as to prevent him from working for the rival in the United Kingdom. Lord Denning MR said:[3] '... I think that limiting words ought to be read into the clause so as to limit it to the part of the business for which the [employers] are reasonably entitled to protection'. On the other hand, in the later case of *JA Mont (UK) Ltd v Mills*,[4] the Court of Appeal had to consider the enforceability of the following restrictive covenant entered into by the employee on termination of his employment: 'This [termination] payment is made on condition that you do not join another company in the tissue industry within one year of leaving our employment'. Within a year, he became joint managing director of trade competitors of his former employers, who sought an injunction whose effect was to restrain him from working for the competitor. In discharging the injunction granted by the judge at first instance, Simon Brown LJ, who gave the judgment of the Court of Appeal said that 'there was no attempt whatever to formulate the covenant so as to focus upon the particular restraint necessary to guard against the [employee's] possible misuse of confidential information, the only legitimate target for imposing any restraint upon his future employment.' He went on to say:[5]

'There is, moreover, this further consideration. If the Court here were to construe this covenant as the [employers] desire, what possible reason would

1   *Home Counties Dairies Ltd v Skilton* [1970] 1 WLR 526. See also *GW Plowman & Son Ltd v Ash* [1964] 1 WLR 568, *Business Seating (Renovations) Ltd v Broad* [1989] ICR 729 and *Credit Suisse Asset Management Ltd v Armstrong* [1996] ICR 882 at p 892B, *per* Neill LJ.
2   [1977] 1 WLR 1472.
3   *Ibid* at p 1483.
4   [1993] IRLR 172. See also *Hollis & Co v Stocks* [2000] IRLR 712 and *Wincanton Ltd v Cranny and SDM European Transport Ltd* [2000] IRLR 716.
5   *Ibid* at p 176. See also Lord Moulton in *Mason v Provident Clothing and Supply Company Ltd* [1913] AC 724 at p 745.

employers ever have to impose restraints in appropriately limited terms? It would always be said that the covenants were "just and honest", and designed solely to protect the employers' legitimate interests in the confidentiality of their trade secrets rather than to prevent competition as such ... Thus would be perpetuated the long-recognised vice of ex-employees being left subject to apparently excessive restraints and yet quite unable, short of expensive litigation and at peril of substantial damages claims, to determine precisely what their rights may be.'

14.20 Subsequently, however, in *Hanover Insurance Brokers v Shapiro*[1] a different division of the Court of Appeal took an approach which had more in common with that of the Court in *Littlewoods Organisation Ltd v Harris*, above. In view of this divergence of approach, the sensible course of action for an employer is to assume that a court will take a strict approach and ensure that restrictive covenants in employees' contracts are drafted only as widely as is absolutely necessary for the protection of the employers' legitimate business interests.

14.21 As a general rule, an employer who breaches the contract of employment, for example by wrongfully dismissing the employee, will not be allowed to enforce any restrictive covenants contained in the contract. This was established by the House of Lords in *General Billposting Ltd v Atkinson*,[2] and reiterated by the majority of the Court of Appeal in *Rock Refrigeration Ltd v Jones and Seward Refrigeration Ltd*.[3] In the latter case, Phillips LJ, although concurring in the result, said that the rule in *General Billposting* 'accords neither with current legal principle nor with the requirements of business efficacy'.[4] An issue which has been to the fore in recent litigation has concerned the enforceability of a restrictive covenant expressed to be enforceable in the event of the termination of the employee's contract 'howsoever caused'. In *Briggs v Oates*[5] Scott J said, *obiter*:

'A contract under which an employee could be immediately and wrongfully dismissed but would nevertheless remain subject to an anti-competition restraint seems to me to be grossly unreasonable. I would not be prepared to enforce the restraint in such a contract.'

The two main reasons for his decision were that: (i) the premature and wrongful termination of the employee's contract meant that there was an absence of mutuality by which the employee was deprived of the full consideration in exchange for which he accepted the post-termination restraint; and (ii) the wrongful repudiation of the contract by the employers put an end to the entire contract, including the restraint clause. Scott J's approach was followed in *Living Design (Home Improvements) Ltd v*

---

[1]   [1994] IRLR 82.
[2]   [1909] AC 118. See also *Rex Stewart Jeffries Parker Ginsberg Ltd v Parker* [1988] IRLR 483.
[3]   [1996] IRLR 675.
[4]   *Ibid* at p 683, para 63. His critique of the *General Billposting* case is in paras 64–67.
[5]   [1990] ICR 473 at p 484.

Davidson[1] by Lord Coulsfield, who said that such a restrictive covenant was 'manifestly wholly unreasonable' and said that Scott J's observations were clearly correct, albeit that they were *obiter*.[2] Subsequently, a number of cases have revolved around this issue.

14.22   In *PR Consultants Scotland Ltd v Mann*,[3] Lord Caplan in the Court of Session (Outer House) treated the matter as an issue of construction and said that a provision which refers to termination 'howsoever caused' is not apt to cover unlawful termination. In *D v M*,[4] Laws J took Scott J's comments in *Briggs v Oates* (above) a stage further. The relevant clause referred to the termination of the contract 'for any reason whatsoever at any time hereafter'. Laws J concluded that that phrase in the restrictive covenant of itself made the clause unreasonable and unenforceable. *PR Consultants Scotland Ltd v Mann* was not cited to him.

14.23   This whole area was reviewed by the Court of Appeal in *Rock Refrigeration Ltd v Jones and Seward Refrigeration Ltd*.[5] Simon Brown LJ said that the argument that covenants containing such clauses should be dealt with by a process of construction proceeded on a 'fundamentally false footing'. He said:[6]

'… [T]he most basic premise upon which the whole restraint of trade doctrine is founded is that, but for the doctrine's application, the covenant in question would otherwise operate to restrain the employee unduly. In other words the doctrine applies only where there exists an otherwise enforceable covenant … The whole point about the *General Billposting* principle is that, in cases of repudiatory breach by the employer, the employee is on that account released from his obligations under the contract and restrictive covenants, otherwise valid against him, accordingly cannot be enforced … [L]ogically it matters not whether covenants include or exclude such phrases as "whether lawful or not". If they do, then to that extent they are merely writ in water, unenforceable under the *General Billposting* principle.'

He went on to hold that *D v M* was wrongly decided. Morritt LJ agreed with him. Phillips LJ agreed with the conclusion that the covenants involved were enforceable but went on to raise questions about the *General Billposting* rule.[7] Whatever the benefits of abrogating the rule, in terms of 'current legal principle' or 'business efficacy', the argument appears to ignore the principle that contract-breakers should not be allowed to take advantage of their own wrong.

14.24   Five other points should be noted here:

[1]   [1994] IRLR 69.
[2]   *Ibid* at p 71, para 4.
[3]   [1996] IRLR 188.
[4]   [1996] IRLR 192.
[5]   [1996] IRLR 675.
[6]   *Ibid* at pp 678–679.
[7]   *Ibid* at pp 683–684.

1. It is for the judge to decide, on the basis of the appropriate evidence, whether in the particular facts of the case a restraint is reasonable or not. This means that a decision in one case that a particular restraint is reasonable (for example, two years in the case of a milk roundsman) does not mean that in all subsequent cases involving the same type of employment a judge is bound by that decision.[1]

2. If there is a change of employer, in circumstances such that the Transfer of Undertakings (Protection of Employment) Regulations 1981[2] apply, the transferee employer may be able to enforce a restrictive covenant entered into between the transferor employer and the employee.[3] But a transferee employer will not be able to enforce a restrictive covenant introduced into the transferring employees' contracts as a result of the transfer.[4]

3. In appropriate cases, 'severance' may be possible. This is considered below.

4. Restrictive covenants and garden leave clauses are often found together in employment contracts. The question which has arisen is whether employees who have already had a period of garden leave should also have a restrictive covenant enforced against them. In *Credit Suisse Asset Management Ltd v Armstrong*,[5] the Court of Appeal said that there is no relationship between a garden leave clause and a restrictive covenant and that, if the covenant is valid, the employer is entitled to have it enforced. It concluded, therefore, that there is no basis for allowing a period of garden leave to be set off against the period for which the restrictive covenant is expressed to last. Neill LJ, with whom the other members of the Court agreed, did leave open the possibility, however, that 'in an exceptional case where a long period of garden leave had already elapsed, perhaps substantially in excess of a year, without any curtailment by the court, the court would decline to grant any further protection based on a restrictive covenant'.[6]

5. The fact that a restrictive covenant is not restricted to the United Kingdom will not necessarily make it unreasonable.[7]

---

[1] See *Dairy Crest Ltd v Piggott* [1989] ICR 92. The Court of Appeal said that the judge was wrong in considering that he was bound by principle to hold that in the case of a milk roundsman a two-year restraint was not unreasonable.

[2] See Chapter 2.

[3] See *Morris Angel & Son Ltd v Hollande* [1993] ICR 71.

[4] *Credit Suisse First Boston (Europe) Ltd v Lister* [1999] ICR 794.

[5] [1996] ICR 882.

[6] *Ibid* at p 894. Although the courts have been prepared to enforce shorter periods of garden leave than those contemplated by the original contract, that does not apply to restrictive covenants, which must stand or fall by the duration originally stipulated.

[7] *Scully UK Ltd v Lee* [1998] IRLR 259.

(b) Particular types of covenant

(i) Non-solicitation covenants

14.25 These covenants are intended to prevent ex-employees from soliciting the business of clients or customers of their former employer in competition with their former employer for a period of time after the employment ends. In covenants of this kind, it must be shown that the employee's contact with the customers is sufficiently direct or influential as to give rise to the real possibility of misuse of the employee's knowledge of the customers.

14.26 A covenant not to solicit customers may be enforced so as to prevent the solicitation of those who were customers not only at the date of termination of the employment but at any other time during the period of employment (even if they had ceased to be customers before its termination);[1] it will not be reasonable to restrain solicitation of persons who might become the employer's customers after termination, for example by a clause restraining an employee from soliciting anyone in the relevant trade in the area in which he or she used to operate for the employer.[2] In *The Marley Tile Co Ltd v Johnson*,[3] the court refused to restrain the solicitation of those who were customers of the employer within the 12 months preceding the termination of the employee's employment, on the grounds that the number of customers involved (said to be some 2,500) was so large that he could not possibly have known of or come into contact with more than a small percentage of them. In *Office Angels Ltd v Rainer-Thomas*,[4] the covenant in question prohibited the employees from setting up or being employed in or otherwise engaged in the trade or business of an employment agency within 1,000 metres of the branch where they had previously worked for a period of six months after the termination of their employment. The employees involved worked in one of the employers' four branches in the City of London, at Bow Lane. After leaving the employers, they set up in an employment agency operating from premises within 1,000 metres of Bow Lane. The Court of Appeal refused to enforce the restrictive covenant. It noted that the effect of the restriction was to preclude the employees from opening an office anywhere within an area of about 1.2 square miles, including most of the City of London. It said that an area restriction was not appropriate because it would do little to protect the employers' connection with their clients. Client orders were placed over the telephone and it was of no concern to them where the office was located. It took the view that this was not an appropriate form of covenant for the protection of the employers' connection with its clients and was wider than was necessary, although it acknowledged that they were entitled to protect their goodwill.

---

[1]   *GW Plowman & Son Ltd v Ash* [1964] 1 WLR 568 and *Home Counties Dairies Ltd v Skilton* [1970] 1 WLR 526.

[2]   *Gledhow Autoparts Ltd v Delaney* [1965] 1 WLR 1366. See also *Jack Allen (Sales & Service) Ltd v Smith* [1999] IRLR 19.

[3]   [1982] IRLR 75.

[4]   [1991] IRLR 214. See also *Hollis & Co v Stocks* [2000] IRLR 712.

14.27 A second type of non-solicitation covenant which is much less common is a covenant restricting the solicitation or employment of former colleagues.[1] This type of covenant, which is sometimes called a 'non-poaching' covenant, was considered by the Court of Appeal in *Hanover Insurance Brokers v Shapiro*,[2] but at no great length. It refused to enforce the particular covenant. Although such covenants are not inherently unenforceable, it is clear that the courts are wary of enforcing them.[3] To stand any chance of being enforced, they will have to be narrowly drawn and applicable only to employees who were colleagues of the ex-employees at the same time; probably, too, they will need to be applicable only to particular types of employees.[4] An example of this approach is to be found in *Dawnay, Day & Co Ltd v de Braconier d'Alphen*.[5] The Court of Appeal upheld the decision of the High Court that the maintenance of a stable workforce is a legitimate interest for protection by means of a restrictive covenant and that a clause preventing the poaching of directors or senior managers for one year was enforceable. On the other hand, in *TSC Europe (UK) Ltd v Massey*,[6] the judge refused to uphold a non-solicitation covenant involving employees of a company on the two grounds that: (a) the covenant prohibited solicitation of any employee without reference to his or her importance in the business or technical knowledge or experience; and (b) that it applied to any employee who joined the company during the prohibited period including those whose employment began after the employee sought to be restrained had ceased to be an employee.

(ii) Non-competition covenants

14.28 These types of covenants are used to protect employers where the employee has a close relationship with clients[7] or has knowledge of the employer's trade secrets or confidential information.[8] In both cases, the restraint must be restricted to activities connected with the goodwill or trade secrets the employer is trying to protect; duration and area limitations are particularly important.[9] An example is *Littlewoods Organisation Ltd v Harris*,[10] which was considered at para 14.19. Another

---

[1] See *Kores Manufacturing Co Ltd v Kolok* [1959] 1 Ch 108.

[2] [1994] IRLR 82.

[3] See Dillon LJ's remarks at p 84, para 15, where he stresses that employees have the right to work for whatever employer they want to work for if the employer is willing to employ them. Two cases in which non-poaching clauses have been upheld are *Ingham v ABC Contract Services Ltd* (unreported) and *Alliance Paper Group plc v Prestwich* [1996] IRLR 25.

[4] This is supported by Dillon LJ's remarks at p 84, para 15.

[5] [1998] ICR 1068.

[6] [1999] IRLR 22.

[7] As in *Marion White Ltd v Francis* [1972] 3 All ER 857.

[8] See *Commercial Plastics Ltd v Vincent* [1964] 3 All ER 546.

[9] See *Spencer v Marchington* [1988] IRLR 392, *Greer v Sketchley Ltd* [1979] IRLR 445 and *Dairy Crest Ltd v Piggott* [1989] ICR 92. In this last case, the Court of Appeal stressed that it is for the judge to decide whether in the particular case a restraint is reasonable or not. They said that the judge was wrong in considering that he was bound by principle to hold that in the case of a milk roundsman a two-year restraint was not unreasonable.

[10] [1977] 1 WLR 1472. See also *Lansing Linde Ltd v Kerr* [1991] ICR 428 and *Turner v Commonwealth & British Minerals Ltd* [2000] IRLR 114.

example of a covenant involving an attempt by an employer to protect trade secrets is to be found in the case of *FSS Travel and Leisure Systems Ltd v Johnson*,[1] in which the relevant clause read as follows:

> 'For a period of one year after termination of your employment hereunder (howsoever caused) you shall not:
>
> > (i) either alone or jointly as a manager or agent for any person directly or indirectly carry on or be engaged or concerned in any business in the United Kingdom which competes with the business of the FSS Group in which you shall have been personally concerned at the date of such termination.'

14.29   At first instance the judge held that the company had trade secrets which it was entitled to protect, but that the duration of the restraint was not reasonable. The Court of Appeal dismissed the appeal, although it held that the judge had erred in holding that the employers had trade secrets which they were entitled to protect. It said that the critical question in deciding whether an employer has trade secrets which are legitimately protectable by means of a restrictive covenant is whether there are trade secrets which can fairly be regarded as the employer's property, as distinct from the skill, experience, know-how and general knowledge which can fairly be regarded as the property of the employee to use without restraint for his or her own benefit or in the services of a competitor. In each case, it is a question of examining closely the detailed evidence relating to the employer's claim for secrecy and deciding, as a matter of fact, on which side of the boundary line it falls. In the present case, the evidence adduced by the employers was not sufficiently specific, precise or cogent to identify and establish a separate body of objective knowledge qualifying for protection as a trade secret by means of a restrictive covenant. Subsequently, in *SBJ Stephenson Ltd v Mandy*,[2] Bell J reiterated that the true distinction to be made is between 'objective knowledge' which is the property of the employer and 'subjective knowledge' which is the employee's own property, following Lord Shaw's dictum in *Herbert Morris Ltd v Saxelby*.[3]

14.30   In *Scully UK Ltd v Lee*,[4] the Court of Appeal refused to uphold a non-competition clause on the ground that it was not limited to a business which was in competition with the employers. It said that it was wider than was necessary to protect the employers' legitimate interest in their customer connection and confidential information.

(iii) Non-dealing covenants

14.31   Such covenants prevent employees from having any dealings with customers of their former employer. They are clearly wider than

---

[1]   [1998] IRLR 382.
[2]   [2000] ICR 233.
[3]   See [1916] 1 AC 688 at p 714.
[4]   [1998] IRLR 259. See also *Jack Allen (Sales & Service) Ltd v Smith* [1999] IRLR 19.

non-solicitation covenants since they apply irrespective of whether the initiative for doing business comes from the customer or the former employee. Non-solicitation clauses will only prevent employees taking the initiative, but will not prevent them dealing with a customer who has approached them. The enforcement of such clauses obviously affects the rights of third parties to deal with whomever they choose.

14.32 In *John Michael Design plc v Cooke*,[1] the relevant clause stated that the employee would not 'canvass, solicit or accept from any client who is or was in the four years prior to the termination of this employment a client' of the employers. The Court of Appeal granted an injunction restraining the employee from dealing with a client of the employers who made it clear that they were not in any event going to do business with the employers. Nicholls LJ said:[2] 'The mere fact that a particular customer no longer wishes to remain a customer of the [employer] but wishes in future to deal with the [ex-employee] is not *per se* a sound reason for excluding the customer from the scope of the injunction'.

14.33 The same considerations apply to the enforceability of non-dealing covenants as to non-solicitation covenants – duration, area, interest to be protected, and the like. In particular, it is desirable to limit this type of covenant to those clients or customers with whom the employee actually had dealings and not extend it to all clients of the employer.[3]

(c) Severance

14.34 Apart from the possibility, considered earlier in this chapter, that a potentially wide restrictive covenant may be saved by a construction which renders it reasonable,[4] there is also the possibility that the court may 'sever' the covenant. When severance is applied, the effect is to remove the offending parts of the covenant, whose retention would make the covenant too wide, leaving the remainder to be enforced. Severance will be easier when the contract contains a series of restrictive covenants, for example, a non-competition covenant, a non-dealing covenant, and a non-solicitation covenant. If one of the covenants is unreasonably wide, it can be removed without damage to the others. If, however, there is only one restraint and it is unreasonably wide, the court will only sever it if the severed parts are independent of each other and can be severed without this affecting the meaning of the part remaining.[5] This is sometimes called the 'blue pencil' test. The courts will not write a new covenant, nor will they alter the nature of the agreement. In *Mason v Provident Clothing Co Ltd*,[6] Lord Moulton said:

'It would be in my opinion be *pessimi exempli* if when an employer had exacted a covenant deliberately framed in unreasonably wide terms, the courts were to

---

[1] [1987] ICR 445. See also *International Consulting Services (UK) Ltd v Hart* [2000] IRLR 227.
[2] *Ibid* at p 449.
[3] See *The Marley Tile Co Ltd v Johnson* [1982] IRLR 75.
[4] As in *Littlewoods Organisation Ltd v Harris* [1977] 1 WLR 1472.
[5] See *Attwood v Lamont* [1920] 3 KB 571.
[6] [1913] AC 724 at p 745.

come to his assistance and, by applying their ingenuity and knowledge of the law, carve out of this void covenant the maximum of what he might validly have achieved ... I do not doubt that the court may, and in some case will, enforce a part of a covenant in restraint of trade, even though taken as a whole the covenant exceeds what is reasonable. But, in my opinion, that ought only to be done in cases where the part so enforceable is clearly severable, and even so only in cases where the excess is of trivial importance, or merely technical, and not a part of the main purport and substance of the clause.'

14.35   There is no doubt that in an appropriate case the court will apply severance to restrictive covenants in a contract of employment.[1] Thus, a covenant seeking to restrict solicitation of 'customers of the Group' is not severable; on the other hand, a covenant applicable to 'customers of the [employer] Company and other companies in the Group' would be severable. Deletion of the phrase 'or other companies of the Group' may enable the rest of the clause to be enforced. The only possibility with the non-severable phrase would be to argue that it should be construed narrowly, but that is a risky undertaking.

14.36   The process of severance will be assisted by a clause expressly permitting deletions insofar as any covenant is too wide. In *Hinton & Higgs (UK) Ltd v Murphy*,[2] the employees' contract contained the following clause:

'The restrictions contained in clause 14 [the restrictive covenant clause] are considered reasonable by the parties, but in the event that any such restriction shall be found to be void [but] would be valid if some part thereof were deleted or the period of application reduced such restrictions shall apply with such modifications as may be necessary to make them valid or effective.'

Lord Dervaird, in the Outer House of the Court of Session, said that he regarded the first part of the clause as an 'illegitimate attempt to oust the jurisdiction of the Court'. He went on:

'The second part, however, contemplates that the parties will abide by a result which may be effected by the deletion of some unreasonable part of the contract, rendering the contract as a whole reasonable. It has often been said that the courts will not make contracts for the parties. Here, however, ... the parties have agreed in advance they will accept as continuing to bind them such part of the arrangements ... as the Court finds by deletion only to be alterations which permit the restriction to be regarded as reasonable ... I do not see why the Court should refuse to perform that role ... .'[3]

14.37   One of the issues in *Rex Stewart Jeffries Parker Ginsberg Ltd v Parker*[4] was whether a non-solicitation clause in the employee's contract could be enforced. The clause was worded as follows:

---

[1]   See *T Lucas & Co Ltd v Mitchell* [1974] Ch 129. In *Marshall v NM Financial Management Ltd* [1997] IRLR 449 a non-competition clause in a sales agent's contract was severed by the court.
[2]   [1989] IRLR 519.
[3]   *Ibid* at p 520.
[4]   [1988] IRLR 483.

'... [Y]ou will not for a period of 18 months ... solicit the custom or business of any person, concern, firm or company who to your knowledge is or has been during the period of your employment a customer of the company or associated companies so as to harm the good will of the company or so as to compete with the company.'

14.38   The Court of Appeal held that the clause in effect prohibited the employee from soliciting those who were customers up to the moment of termination of his employment; it also prohibited him from soliciting anyone who might have become a customer thereafter and it sought to prevent him from soliciting customers of the employer's associated companies. These were separate prohibitions and were severable so as to leave standing the central prohibition preventing the employee soliciting those who were customers up to the time of the termination of his employment.

14.39   The judge took a similar view in *Business Seating (Renovations) Ltd v Broad*,[1] in which the relevant clause read:

'For a period of one year after the termination of the agreement for any cause whatsoever the employee shall not canvass, solicit or endeavour to take away from the company or any associated employer the business of any customers or clients of the company or any associated employer who have been customers or clients of the company or any associated employer during the period of one year immediately preceding the termination of the employment.'

He said that there were in effect two separate covenants, each taken for the protection of the respective businesses of each company. He said there was no difficulty grammatically in severing the two covenants, and that severance left unaffected the covenant relating to the customers of the employer. He therefore granted an injunction confined to the business of the employer and excluding any reference to an associated employer.

3. ENFORCEMENT

14.40   In the context of the enforcement of an employer's rights against competition by an ex-employee, the remedy of most value will be an injunction. This remedy has been discussed already in Chapter 11. Here, the question to be discussed concerns the basis upon which interim injunctions are granted by the courts.

14.41   Generally, the sort of injunction granted in cases of this kind is a prohibitory injunction – an order restraining the doing or continuance of some wrongful act such as the breach of a reasonable restrictive covenant. An interim injunction is an injunction granted before the trial of the action with the object of maintaining the status quo until the trial of the action. The grant of an interim injunction does not necessarily mean that a perpetual injunction will be granted at the trial. The importance to an

---

[1]   [1989] ICR 729.

employer of seeking an interim injunction is that, if the court is satisfied that the injunction should be granted, it will not be necessary to wait until the trial of the action. This is particularly important in a case involving the disclosure of confidential information, for example, since the trial of the action might take some time to come on and the employer's position might be substantially prejudiced by the disclosure of such information; an interim injunction in such a case will protect the employer's position. In general, a person seeking an interim injunction will be required to offer the court an undertaking that he or she will meet any award of damages made at trial in the event that the employer fails to make out its claim and it is considered that the interim injunction has caused the employee loss.

14.42   The procedure for obtaining any interim remedy (including an interim injunction) is laid down by Part 25 of the Civil Procedure Rules 1998. The old procedural distinction between the Queen's Bench and Chancery Divisions of the High Court is swept away with application for interim relief being made in both by application notice[1] and supported by evidence in the form of statements of case and/or witness statements.[2] It used to be the case that an application for an interim injunction would be heard in private in the Queen's Bench Division, but in public in the Chancery Division. This was an important factor in selecting the appropriate division in any case where maintaining confidentiality was in any way in issue. However, the right of everyone to a trial in public[3] has resulted in the general rule[4] that hearings are to be in public. Rule 39.2(3) of the Civil Procedure Rules 1998 lays down the circumstances in which a hearing, or part of it, may be in private and it is for the judge hearing the application to consider any representations made before determining whether to sit in public or private. Of particular relevance to employers seeking interim relief will be the provisions enabling the court to sit in private if the hearing involves confidential information and publicity would damage that confidentiality,[5] or if the application is made without notice and it would be unjust to any respondent for there to be a public hearing[6] or, finally, if the court considers it necessary, in the interests of justice.[7] It is not necessary for proceedings to have been started in order to apply for an interim injunction,[8] although an applicant for pre-issue relief will be expected to undertake to issue proceedings promptly. Application for an interim injunction may be made without notice to the respondent if it appears to the court that there are good reasons for not giving notice,[9] such reasons having been stated in the evidence in support of the application.[10] In any application made without notice, the applicant is under a duty to give full and frank disclosure of all matters, including those harmful to his or her

---

[1]   CPR Part 23.
[2]   CPR r 25.3(2).
[3]   Article 6 of the ECHR states that 'everyone is entitled to a fair and public hearing ...'.
[4]   CPR r 39.2.
[5]   CPR r 39.2(3)(c).
[6]   CPR r 39.2(3)(e).
[7]   CPR r 39.2(3)(g).
[8]   CPR r 25.2.
[9]   CPR r 25.3(1).
[10]   CPR r 25.3(3).

own case and a failure to comply with the duty may result in the discharge of the injunction even if, after full enquiry, the court determines that the order made was just and convenient and would probably have been made even if there had been full disclosure.[1] In many cases of the kind covered by this chapter, the parties tend to treat the decision in the interim proceedings as effectively determining the likely result of the trial.

14.43   The principles governing the grant of interim injunctions were set out in *American Cyanamid Co v Ethicon Ltd*,[2] which was considered in Chapter 10. In general, this means that the court is relieved of the task of considering the evidence and making a provisional assessment of the likely prospect of success in the action. However, in certain types of case, a different approach may be followed, one of these types being cases involving the enforcement of a restrictive covenant. In these cases, where the relevant facts are clear, the covenant is prima facie valid and there has been an infringement of it, the court should consider the grant or refusal of relief by deciding whether or not the employer will succeed at the trial.[3] In *Lawrence David Ltd v Ashton*,[4] however, the Court of Appeal allowed an appeal against the first instance judge's refusal of an interim injunction, on the grounds that he had failed to apply the *American Cyanamid* principles in refusing the application. Balcombe LJ, who gave the main judgment in the Court of Appeal, stressed[5] that the *American Cyanamid* principles should be applied in restrictive covenant cases and rejected the view that they were not applicable.[6]

14.44   In *Lawrence David Ltd v Ashton*, Balcombe LJ did indicate, however, that the exception to the *American Cyanamid* principles will apply where the action cannot be tried before the period of the restraint has expired or the period of restraint has run a large part of its course. In that case, the grant of the interim injunction will effectively dispose of the action, and the judge 'may properly go on to consider the prospects of the employers' succeeding in the action'.[7] This was followed by another division of the Court of Appeal in *Lansing Linde Ltd v Kerr*,[8] which formed the view that it would not be possible to hold a trial before the expiry of the majority of the restraint period and went on to consider the likelihood of success.

---

[1]   *R v Kensington Income Tax Commissioners ex parte de Polignac* [1917] 1 KB 486, recently restated by Jacob J in *OMV Supply & Training AG v Clarke* (14 January 1999, unreported).
[2]   [1975] AC 396.
[3]   See *Office Overload Ltd v Gunn* [1977] FSR 39.
[4]   [1989] ICR 123.
[5]   *Ibid* at p 132. The Lord Justice also referred to *Dairy Crest Ltd v Piggott* [1989] ICR 92, in which he was also a member of the Court of Appeal. In *John Michael Design plc v Cooke* [1987] ICR 445, O'Connor LJ seems to have used the approach criticised by Balcombe LJ, whereas Nicholls LJ applied the *American Cyanamid* principles.
[6]   See also *Dairy Crest Ltd v Piggott* [1989] ICR 92, in which Balcombe LJ applied the various stages of Lord Diplock's speech in *American Cyanamid* and concluded that an interim injunction should be granted: see at pp 96–97.
[7]   [1989] ICR 123 at p 135.
[8]   [1991] ICR 428. This case was applied by another division of the Court of Appeal in the later case of *Credit Suisse Asset Management Ltd v Armstrong* [1996] ICR 882.

Chapter 15

REFERENCES

15.01   An employer is not obliged to provide a reference for an employee but, if he or she does so, the reference must be accurate. An inaccurate reference may make the employer liable to a subsequent employer or a former employee.

15.02   An employer may be liable in deceit for fraudulent misstatement if he or she knowingly makes a false statement in a reference intending a subsequent employer to rely upon it and that employer does rely upon it and suffers damage as a result.[1] The motives of the employer giving the reference are irrelevant. The House of Lords' decision in *Hedley Byrne & Co Ltd v Heller & Partners Ltd*[2] also suggests the possibility of a claim for negligent misstatement, since the House of Lords accepted the possibility of a claim being brought for pure economic loss where a special relationship exists between the parties. Such a relationship exists in all relationships where the person seeking the information trusts the other, who claims to have some specialist knowledge of the subject. Lord Morris of Borth-y-Gest, for example, said:

> '... [I]f in a sphere in which a person is so placed that others could reasonably rely upon his judgment ..., a person takes it upon himself to give information or advice to, or allows his information or advice to be passed on to, another person who, as he knows or should know, will place reliance upon it, then a duty of care will arise.'[3]

15.03   These principles would appear to cover the situation where an employer provides a reference to a subsequent employer, but there is no direct authority on the point.[4] The decision of the House of Lords in *Spring v Guardian Assurance plc*,[5] which held that the giver of a reference owes a duty to the subject of it, tends to support this view.

15.04   An employee has three possible causes of action against a former employer: defamation, injurious or malicious falsehood and negligent misstatement. So far as defamation is concerned, the reference is protected by qualified privilege, since the employer and the potential employer have a common interest in it.[6] The defence of qualified privilege is lost if it can be shown that the person giving the reference was motivated by malice or

---

[1]   *Foster v Charles* (1830) 7 Bing 105.
[2]   [1964] AC 465.
[3]   *Ibid* at pp 502–503.
[4]   The case of *Lawton v BOC Transhield Ltd* [1987] ICR 7 is indirect authority for this.
[5]   [1994] ICR 596.
[6]   See *Jackson v Hopperton* (1864) 16 CB (NS) 829.

spite. In *Horrocks v Lowe*,[1] Lord Diplock gave the following guidance on what amounts to malice:

> '[W]hat is required on the part of the defamer to entitle him to the protection of the privilege is positive belief in the truth of what he published or ... "honest" belief. If he publishes untrue defamatory matter recklessly, without considering or caring whether it is true or not, he is ... treated as if he knew it to be false. But indifference to the truth of what he publishes is not to be equated with carelessness, impulsiveness or irrationality in arriving at a positive belief that it is true ... Even a positive belief in the truth of what is published on a privileged occasion ... may not be sufficient to negative express malice if it can be proved that the [defamer] misused the occasion for some purpose other than that for which the privilege is accorded in law.'

15.05 In addition, it will not be possible for the employee to sue in defamation if he or she is taken to have consented to the publication of the allegations. In *Friend v Civil Aviation Authority*,[2] the Court of Appeal held that an employee who accepts a disciplinary code as part of the contract of employment consents to the republication of an accusation or complaint as part of that process and cannot, therefore, bring an action for defamation on the republication.

15.06 An injurious or malicious falsehood occurs where false statements are made to a third party (the potential employer), who is deceived into doing something which causes loss to the plaintiff (employee), who must show that the referee acted maliciously intending the false statement to cause damage.[3] The test of what constitutes malice is the same as in the torts of libel and slander.[4] The statement need not amount to an attack on the employee's reputation, as in defamation.

15.07 Until the Court of Appeal's decision in *Spring v Guardian Assurance plc*,[5] the courts seemed to be moving in the direction of accepting that a referee owed a duty of care to the employee to whom the reference related. This was accepted by the judge in *Lawton v BOC Transhield Ltd*,[6] although the employee lost the case on the grounds that the reference in question did not amount to a negligent misstatement. Tudor Evans J held that it was obvious to the employers that the request for a reference concerned the employee's future employment, that he had given their name to support his application for employment and that he relied on them to give an accurate reference. There was a sufficient proximity between him and them in circumstances where they clearly foresaw loss to him in giving the reference and they therefore owed him a duty to take reasonable care to ensure that the opinions expressed in the reference were based on accurate

---

[1] [1975] AC 135 at p 150.
[2] [1998] IRLR 253.
[3] See *Ratcliffe v Evans* [1892] 2 QB 524 and *Horrocks v Lowe* [1975] AC 135.
[4] *Spring v Guardian Assurance plc* [1993] ICR 412 at p 430.
[5] [1993] ICR 412.
[6] [1987] ICR 7.

facts. Tudor Evans J said:[1] 'opinions must ... [be] based on facts and I can see no difficulty in requiring that reasonable care be taken to ensure that opinion [is] based on accurate facts'.

15.08 This case was followed by the High Court in *Spring v Guardian Assurance plc*,[2] which involved a reference given by former employers in accordance with the requirements of the LAUTRO rules that persons cannot be employed in the insurance industry without a reference, which has to be obtained from their former employers. The employee had been involved in a large investment deal in which he recommended a totally inappropriate investment. This did not take place, but the employers formed the view that he had been motivated by the desire to generate a high commission for himself rather than to give the best advice. He was dismissed when the employers learned that he was proposing to leave and go to work for a competitor. He later applied to become a representative of Scottish Amicable, but they decided to have no dealings with him on the basis of the reference written by his former employers. This reference said that the employee had kept the best leads for himself with little regard for the sales team he was supposed to manage and that he was a man of little or no integrity and could not be regarded as honest. It also referred to the case of misselling and other cases where there had been bad advice. The employee sued for negligent misstatement, malicious falsehood and breach of an implied term in his contract that any reference would by compiled with reasonable care. The last two claims failed. The judge upheld the first claim on the footing that the compiler of the reference had a duty to exercise reasonable care in the compiling of an employment reference and knew that the consequence of a negligent misstatement was that the employee's entire career might be blighted. He found that, in relation to the misselling case and the observations on the employee's honesty and integrity, those who provided information to the compiler of the reference made negligent misstatements. The employers were therefore liable in damages. On appeal, the Court of Appeal allowed the employers' appeal against liability for negligence and disallowed the employee's appeal against the judge's decision that the employers were not liable for malicious falsehood or breach of an implied term. In allowing the employers' appeal, it overruled *Lawton v BOC Transhield Ltd*[3] and held that the giver of a reference owes no duty of care in negligence to the subject of the reference.

15.09 The House of Lords, however, allowed the employee's appeal and held that the former employers did owe their ex-employee a duty of care in respect of their preparation of the reference.[4] It said that all the elements necessary for the application of the principle in *Hedley Byrne & Co Ltd v Heller & Partners Ltd*[5] were present; it also said that the balance of public

---

[1]   [1987] ICR 7 at p 19.
[2]   [1992] IRLR 173.
[3]   [1987] ICR 7.
[4]   [1994] ICR 596.
[5]   [1964] AC 465.

interest favoured allowing a remedy in negligence. Lord Woolf said that the case clearly showed that the need to establish malice in defamation made defamation a 'wholly inadequate remedy'. Three of the Law Lords went on to say that there are certain types of contract in which a term may be implied that the employer will provide a reference based upon careful inquiry. Lord Lowry dissented on this last point and Lord Keith of Kinkel gave a dissenting judgment.

15.10   Subsequently, in *Bartholomew v London Borough of Hackney*,[1] the Court of Appeal said that the duty of care owed by an ex-employer to an ex-employee in accordance with the *Spring* case does not mean that a reference must in every case be full and comprehensive. It said that, although the reference in the instant case might have been improved upon in some respects, it was not as whole unfair, inaccurate and false. The reference in dispute referred to the fact that, at the time of the employee's voluntary severance, he was suspended from work because of a charge of gross misconduct and that the disciplinary action had lapsed automatically with the end of his employment; it gave no details as to the nature of the misconduct, the fact that he strongly denied the charge and the terms of the voluntary severance. The Court of Appeal said that the employers were not in breach of the duty of care which they owed him.

15.11   Subsequently, in *Kidd v Axa Equity & Law Life Assurance Society plc*,[2] Burton J said that the duty owed by the giver of a reference to the subject of that duty is a duty to take reasonable care not to give misleading information about him or her, whether as a result of the unfairly selective provision of information, or by the inclusion of facts and opinions in such a manner as to give rise to a false or mistaken inference in the mind of a reasonable recipient. He said that the giver of a reference does not owe an additional duty to the subject to take reasonable care to give a full and comprehensive reference, or to include in a reference all material facts, and said that the nature and extent of such a duty would be difficult to formulate and define. He added that to impose an obligation on employers to give employees a full, frank and comprehensive reference was not necessary in the public interest nor in the interests of employees, since such a reference would have to include the bad as well as the good.

15.12   It is possible that an employer may breach the implied duty of mutual trust and confidence in the way it provides a reference. In that case, an employee who resigns as a consequence may be able to claim to have been constructively dismissed.[3]

15.13   Finally, it should be noted that the Rehabilitation of Offenders Act 1974 protects from liability a referee who fails to acknowledge or disclose a conviction which is 'spent'.

---

[1]   [1999] IRLR 246. See also *Cox v Sun Alliance Life Ltd* (2001) IDS Brief B689/5, in which the Court of Appeal upheld the judge's decision that the employer's reference was negligent on the basis of the facts as found.

[2]   [2000] IRLR 301.

[3]   *TSB Bank Ltd v Harris* [2000] IRLR 157.

APPENDICES

Appendix 1

COMPENSATION FOR LOSS OF PENSION RIGHTS

[This material comprises extracts taken from Appendices 1, 2 and 4 of *Industrial Tribunals: Compensation for Loss of Pension Rights* (2nd edn, 1991), is Crown copyright, and is reproduced with the permission of the Controller of Her Majesty's Stationery Office.]

PART A: SUMMARY

A1.01

1. Loss of pension rights from date of dismissal to the hearing

Unless there are arguments to the contrary we consider that the following formula should apply:—

(a) Ascertain the employer's contribution as a percentage of the applicant's pay. It may be necessary to adjust this figure if exceptional circumstances pertain; if for example the pension fund is over-funded and the employer is having a pension contribution holiday. If the pension is a non-contributory one which is not funded e.g. a civil service pension, then it may be necessary to impute a notional employer's contribution.

(b) If the figure for the employer's contribution is not readily forthcoming then assume that the employer's contribution is 10 per cent (15 per cent in the case of non-contributory schemes.)

(c) Treat the employer's contribution as a weekly loss, in the same manner as a weekly loss of earnings.

A1.02

2. Loss of future pension rights

Use the same rate of contributions as for 1 and the same multiplier as for assessment of future loss of earnings.

A1.03

3. Loss of enhancement of accrued pension rights

Assume no loss of enhancement of accrued pension benefit unless the contrary is proved in:—

(a) Schemes in which pension benefit are referable to contributions made and not final salary (*i.e.* company money purchase schemes, personalised plans etc.).
(b) Public sector schemes – funded and non-funded.
(c) Private sector final salary schemes where the applicant has less than five years until retirement.

Loss of accrued benefit in final salary schemes (where condition 5c(i) and c(ii) do not apply):

1. Ascertain the deferred pension he will receive (ignoring any anticipated increases or additional benefits).
2. Ascertain the applicant's present age and his anticipated age of retirement.
3. Apply the appropriate multiplier as set out in Appendix 4 [Part E, below].
4. Reduce the resulting figure by a reasonable percentage for the likelihood of withdrawal (*i.e.* that he would have left before retirement for reasons other than death or disability).

PART B: FLOW CHART FOR CALCULATION OF LOSS OF PENSION RIGHTS FROM DATE OF DISMISSAL TO THE HEARING

A1.04

1. Ascertain the employee's gross weekly pensionable pay	£
2. Ascertain the employer's normal contribution as a percentage of the pay-roll	
3. If the figure for the employer's contribution is not readily forthcoming then assume that the employer's contribution is 10% (15% for non-contributory schemes)	
Weekly continuing pension loss	£
4. Multiply by number of weeks between effective date of termination and date of hearing	X
AWARD	£

N.B. This is not part of the prescribed element

PART C: FLOW CHART FOR CALCULATION OF LOSS OF FUTURE PENSION RIGHTS

A1.05

1. Ascertain the employee's gross weekly pensionable pay	£
2. Ascertain the employer's normal contribution as a percentage of the pay-roll	
3. If the figure for the employer's contribution is not readily forthcoming then assume that the employer's contribution is 10% (15% for non-contributory schemes)	
Weekly continuing pension loss	£
4. Multiply by number of weeks allowed for future loss of earnings whether total or partial	X
AWARD	£

PART D: FLOW CHART FOR CALCULATION OF LOSS OF ENHANCEMENT OF ACCRUED PENSION RIGHTS

A1.06

1. Is it a final salary or a money purchase scheme?

Final | Salary   Money | Purchase

2. Is it a private sector or public sector scheme?

Private | Sector   Public | Sector
(fully index | linked)

3. Has the applicant less than 5 years until retirement?

No   Yes

4. (i) Ascertain the deferred pension he will receive (ignoring any anticipated increase in benefit) — £

(ii) Apply the appropriate multiplier as set out in the Table at Appendix 4 [see para A1.07 of this book] — X

sub total

(iii) Reduce the resulting figure by a reasonable percentage for the likelihood of withdrawal (*i.e.* that he would have left before retirement for reasons other than death or disability)

less %

AWARD — £   NO AWARD

PART E: TABLES OF MULTIPLIERS TO BE APPLIED TO THE DEFERRED ANNUAL PENSION TO ASSESS COMPENSATION FOR LOSS OF ENHANCEMENT OF ACCRUED PENSION RIGHTS

A1.07

Age last birthday at dismissal	Normal retirement age 60	Normal retirement age 65
Under 35	1.9	1.5
35–44	1.8	1.5
45–49	1.7	1.4
50	1.6	1.4
51	1.5	1.4
52	1.4	1.3
53	1.3	1.3
54	1.1	1.3
55	1.0	1.2
56	0.86	1.2
57	0.6	1.1
58	0.3	1.0
59	0.1	0.9
60	NIL	0.8
61		0.6
62		0.4
63		0.3
64		0.2

Appendix 2

RULES OF PROCEDURE

[This material is taken from Schedule 1 to the Employment Tribunals (Constitution and Rules of Procedure) Regulations 2001, SI 2001 No 1171, which came into force on 16 July 2001.]

1. Originating application

(1) Where proceedings are brought by an applicant, they shall be instituted by the applicant presenting to the Secretary an originating application, which shall be in writing and shall set out—

(a)   the name and address of the applicant and, if different, an address within the United Kingdom to which he requires notices and documents relating to the proceedings to be sent;

(b)   the names and addresses of the person or persons against whom relief is sought; and

(c)   the grounds, with particulars thereof, on which relief is sought.

(2) Two or more originating applications may be presented in a single document by applicants who claim relief in respect of or arising out of the same set of facts.

(3) Where the Secretary is of the opinion that the originating application does not seek or on the facts stated therein cannot entitle the applicant to a relief which a tribunal has power to give, he may give notice to that effect to the applicant stating the reasons for his opinion and informing him that the application will not be registered unless he states in writing that he wishes to proceed with it.

(4) An application in respect of which such a notice has been given shall not be treated as having been received for the purpose of rule 2 unless the applicant intimates in writing to the Secretary that he wishes to proceed with it; and upon receipt of such an intimation the Secretary shall proceed in accordance with that rule.

(5) In the case of an originating application in respect of a complaint under section 6(4A) of the 1986 Act relating to a term of a collective agreement, the following persons, whether or not identified in the originating application, shall be regarded as the persons against whom relief is sought and shall be treated as respondents for the purposes of these rules, that is to say—

(a)   the applicant's employer (or prospective employer), and
(b)   every organisation of employers and organisation of workers, and every association of or representative of such organisations, which, if the term were to be varied voluntarily, would be likely, in the opinion of the tribunal, to negotiate the variation;

provided that such an organisation or association shall not be treated as a respondent if the tribunal, having made such enquiries of the applicant and such other enquiries as it thinks fit, is of the opinion that it is not reasonably practicable to identify the organisation or association.

(6)   Where proceedings are referred to a tribunal by a court, these rules shall be applied to them, except where the rules are inappropriate, as if the proceedings had been instituted by the presentation of an originating application.

(7)   Paragraph (1)(b) does not apply to an originating application in respect of an application under section 3C of the Employment Agencies Act 1973 for the variation or revocation of a prohibition order, but on any application the Secretary of State shall be treated as the respondent for the purpose of these rules.

2. Action upon receipt of originating application

(1)   Upon receiving an originating application the Secretary shall—

(a)   send a copy of it to the respondent;
(b)   give every party notice in writing of the case number of the application (which shall constitute the title of the proceedings) and of the address to which notices and other communications to the Secretary shall be sent; and
(c)   send to the respondent a notice in writing which includes information, as appropriate to the case, about the means and time for entering an appearance, the consequences of failure to do so, and the right to receive a copy of the decision.

(2)   The Secretary shall enter such of the details of an originating application as are referred to in paragraph (4) in the Register either within 28 days of receiving it or, if that is not practicable, as soon as reasonably practicable thereafter.

(3)   The Secretary shall also, in all cases, notify the parties that, in every case where an enactment provides for conciliation, the services of a conciliation officer are available to them.

(4)   The details of an originating application to be entered in the Register are—

(a)   the case number;
(b)   the date the Secretary received the application;
(c)   the name and address of the applicant;
(d)   the name and address of the respondent;
(e)   the Regional Office of the Employment Tribunals dealing with the application; and
(f)   the type of claim brought in general terms without reference to its particulars.

(5)   In any case appearing to the Secretary to involve allegations of the commission of a sexual offence, where any person referred to in paragraph 4(c) or 4(d) appears to the Secretary to be a person affected by or making the allegations he shall omit from the Register the details in paragraph 4(c) or 4(d), as the case may be, relating to that person.

3. Appearance by respondent

(1)   A respondent shall, within 21 days of receiving the copy of the originating application, enter an appearance to the proceedings by presenting to the Secretary a written notice of appearance—

(a)   setting out his full name and address and, if different, an address within the United Kingdom to which he requires notices and documents relating to the proceedings to be sent;
(b)   stating whether or not he intends to resist the application; and
(c)   if he does intend to resist it, setting out sufficient particulars to show on what grounds.

Upon receipt of a notice of appearance the Secretary shall send a copy of it to each other party.

(2)   Two or more notices of appearance relating to originating applications in which the relief claimed is in respect of or arises out of the same set of facts may be presented in a single document, provided that in respect of each of the originating applications to which the notices so presented relate—

(a)   the respondent intends to resist the applications and the grounds for doing so are the same in each case; or
(b)   the respondent does not intend to resist the applications.

(3)   A respondent who has not entered an appearance shall not be entitled to take any part in the proceedings except—

(a)   to apply under rule 17 for an extension of the time appointed by this rule for entering an appearance;
(b)   to make an application under rule 4(1) for a direction requiring the

> applicant to provide further particulars of the grounds on which he relies and of any facts and contentions relevant thereto;
>
> (c)   to make an application under rule 13(4) in respect of rule 13(1)(b);
> (d)   to be called as a witness by another person;
> (e)   to be sent a copy of a document or corrected entry in pursuance of rule 12(5), 12(9) or 12(10);

and in the rules which follow, the word 'party' only includes such a respondent in relation to his entitlement to take such a part in the proceedings, and in relation to any such part which he takes.

4. Case management

(1)   A tribunal may at any time, on the application of a party or of its own motion, give such directions on any matter arising in connection with the proceedings as appear to the tribunal to be appropriate.

(2)   An application under paragraph (1)—

(a)   may be made by presenting to the Secretary a notice of application, which shall state the title of the proceedings and set out the grounds of the application, or
(b)   may be made at the hearing of the originating application.

(3)   Directions under paragraph (1) may include any requirement relating to evidence (including the provision and exchange of witness statements), the provision of further particulars, and the provision of written answers to questions put to a party by the tribunal.

(4)   A tribunal may appoint the time at or within which and the place at which any act required in pursuance of this rule is to be done and may direct that a copy of any document furnished pursuant to any requirement imposed under this rule be sent to the tribunal.

(5)   A tribunal may, on the application of a party or of its own motion,—

(a)   require the attendance of any person in Great Britain, including a party, either to give evidence or to produce documents or both and may appoint the time and place at which the person is to attend and, if so required, to produce any document; or
(b)   require one party to grant to another such disclosure or inspection (including the taking of copies) of documents as might be granted by a court under rule 31 of the Civil Procedure Rules 1998.

(6)   Every document containing a requirement imposed under paragraph (5) shall state that, under section 7(4) of the 1996 Act, any person who without reasonable excuse fails to comply with the requirement shall be liable on summary conviction to a fine, and the document shall also state the amount of the current maximum fine.

(7) Where a requirement has been imposed under paragraph (1) or (5)—

(a)   on a party in his absence; or
(b)   on a person other than a party,

that party or person may apply to the tribunal by notice to the Secretary to vary or set aside the requirement. Such notice shall be given before the time at which or, as the case may be, the expiration of the time within which the requirement is to be complied with, and the Secretary shall give notice of the application to each party, or where applicable, each party other than the party making the application.

(8)   If a requirement under paragraph (1) or (5) is not complied with, the tribunal—

(a)   may make an order in respect of costs under rule 14(1)(a), or
(b)   before or at the hearing, may strike out the whole or part of the originating application, or, as the case may be, the notice of appearance, and, where appropriate, direct that a respondent be debarred from defending altogether;

but a tribunal shall not exercise its powers under this paragraph unless it has sent notice to the party who has not complied with the requirement giving him an opportunity to show cause why the tribunal should not do so, or the party has been given an opportunity to show cause orally why the powers conferred by this paragraph should not be exercised.

5. Time and place of hearing

(1)   The President or a Regional Chairman shall fix the date, time and place of the hearing of the originating application and the Secretary shall send to each party a notice of hearing together with information and guidance as to attendance at the hearing, witnesses and the bringing of documents, representation by another person and the making of written representations.

(2)   The Secretary shall send the notice of hearing to every party not less than 14 days before the date fixed for the hearing except—

(a)   where the Secretary has agreed a shorter time with the parties; or
(b)   on an application for interim relief made under section 161 of the 1992 Act or section 128 of the Employment Rights Act 1996.

6. Entitlement to bring or contest proceedings

(1)   A tribunal may at any time before the hearing of an originating application, on the application of a party made by notice to the Secretary or of its own motion, hear and determine any issue relating to the entitlement

of any party to bring or contest the proceedings to which the originating application relates.

(2)   A tribunal shall not determine such an issue unless the Secretary has sent notice to each of the parties giving them an opportunity to submit representations in writing and to advance oral argument before the tribunal.

7. Pre-hearing review

(1)   A tribunal may at any time before the hearing of an originating application, on the application of a party made by notice to the Secretary or of its own motion, conduct a pre-hearing review, consisting of a consideration of—

(a)   the contents of the originating application and notice of appearance;
(b)   any representations in writing; and
(c)   any oral argument advanced by or on behalf of a party.

(2)   If a party applies for a pre-hearing review and the tribunal determines that there shall be no review, the Secretary shall send notice of the determination to that party.

(3)   A pre-hearing review shall not take place unless the Secretary has sent notice to the parties giving them an opportunity to submit representations in writing and to advance oral argument at the review if they so wish.

(4)   If upon a pre-hearing review the tribunal considers that the contentions put forward by any party in relation to a matter required to be determined by a tribunal have no reasonable prospect of success, the tribunal may make an order against that party requiring the party to pay a deposit of an amount not exceeding £500 as a condition of being permitted to continue to take part in the proceedings relating to that matter.

(5)   No order shall be made under this rule unless the tribunal has taken reasonable steps to ascertain the ability of the party against whom it is proposed to make the order to comply with such an order, and has taken account of any information so ascertained in determining the amount of the deposit.

(6)   An order made under this rule, and the tribunal's reasons for considering that the contentions in question have no reasonable prospect of success, shall be recorded in summary form in a document signed by the chairman. A copy of that document shall be sent to each of the parties and shall be accompanied by a note explaining that if the party against whom the order is made persists in participating in proceedings relating to the matter to which the order relates, he may have an award of costs made against him and could lose his deposit.

(7) If a party against whom an order has been made does not pay the amount specified in the order to the Secretary either—

(a)   within the period of 21 days of the day on which the document recording the making of the order is sent to him, or
(b)   within such further period, not exceeding 14 days, as the tribunal may allow in the light of representations made by that party within the said period of 21 days,

the tribunal shall strike out the originating application or notice of appearance of that party or, as the case may be, the part of it to which the order relates.

(8) The deposit paid by a party under an order made under this rule shall be refunded to him in full except where rule 14(8) applies.

(9) No member of a tribunal which has conducted a pre-hearing review shall be a member of the tribunal at the hearing of the originating application.

8. National security

(1) A Minister of the Crown (whether or not he is a party to the proceedings) may, if he considers it expedient in the interests of national security, direct a tribunal by notice to the Secretary to—

(a)   sit in private for all or part of particular Crown employment proceedings;
(b)   exclude the applicant from all or part of particular Crown employment proceedings;
(c)   exclude the applicant's representatives from all or part of particular Crown employment proceedings;
(d)   take steps to conceal the identity of a particular witness in particular Crown employment proceedings.

(2) A tribunal may, if it considers it expedient in the interests of national security, by order—

(a)   do anything of a kind which a tribunal can be required to do by direction under paragraph (1);
(b)   direct any person to whom any document (including any decision or record of the proceedings) has been provided for the purposes of the proceedings not to disclose any such document or the content thereof to—

(i)   any excluded person,
(ii)   in any case in which a direction has been given under paragraph (1)(a) or an order has been made under

paragraph (2)(a) read with paragraph (1)(a), to any person excluded from all or part of the proceedings by virtue of such direction or order, or

(iii)   in any case in which a Minister of the Crown has informed the Secretary in accordance with paragraph (3) that he wishes to address the tribunal with a view to the tribunal making an order under paragraph (2)(a) read with paragraph (1)(b) or (c), to any person who may be excluded from all or part of the proceedings by virtue of such an order, if an order is made, at any time before the tribunal decides whether or not to make such an order;

(c)   take steps to keep secret all or part of the reasons for its decision.

The tribunal shall keep under review any order it makes under this paragraph.

(3)   In any proceedings in which a Minister of the Crown considers that it would be appropriate for a tribunal to make an order as referred to in paragraph (2), he shall (whether or not he is a party to the proceedings) be entitled to appear before and to address the tribunal thereon. The Minister shall inform the Secretary by notice that he wishes to address the tribunal and the Secretary shall copy the notice to the parties.

(4)   When exercising its functions, a tribunal shall ensure that information is not disclosed contrary to the interests of national security.

9. Dismissals in connection with industrial action

(1)   In relation to a complaint under section 111 of the Employment Rights Act 1996 (unfair dismissal: complaint to employment tribunal) that a dismissal is unfair by virtue of section 238A of the 1992 Act (participation in official industrial action) a tribunal may adjourn the proceedings where specified civil proceedings have been brought until such time as interlocutory proceedings arising out of the specified civil proceedings have been concluded.

(2)   In this rule—

'specified civil proceedings' means legal proceedings brought by any person against another person in which it is to be determined whether an act of that other person, which induced the applicant to commit an act, or each of a series of acts, is by virtue of section 219 of the 1992 Act not actionable in tort or in delict; and

the interlocutory proceedings shall not be regarded as having concluded until all rights of appeal have been exhausted or the time for instituting any appeal in the course of the interlocutory proceedings has expired.

10. The hearing

(1)   Any hearing of an originating application shall be heard by a tribunal composed in accordance with section 4(1) and (2) of the 1996 Act.

(2)   Any hearing of or in connection with an originating application shall take place in public.

(3)   Notwithstanding paragraph (2), a tribunal may sit in private for the purpose of hearing evidence from any person which in the opinion of the tribunal is likely to consist of—

(a)   information which he could not disclose without contravening a prohibition imposed by or by virtue of any enactment, or

(b)   information which has been communicated to him in confidence, or which he has otherwise obtained in consequence of the confidence reposed in him by another person, or

(c)   information the disclosure of which would, for reasons other than its effect on negotiations with respect to any of the matters mentioned in section 178(2) of the 1992 Act, cause substantial injury to any undertaking of his or any undertaking in which he works.

(4)   A member of the Council on Tribunals shall be entitled to attend any hearing taking place in private in his capacity as a member.

(5)   If a party wishes to submit representations in writing for consideration by a tribunal at the hearing of the originating application he shall present his representations to the Secretary not less than 7 days before the hearing and shall at the same time send a copy to each other party.

(6)   The tribunal may, if it considers it appropriate, consider representations in writing which have been submitted to the Secretary less than 7 days before the hearing.

(7)   The Secretary of State if he so elects shall be entitled to appear as if he were a party and be heard at any hearing of or in connection with an originating application in proceedings which may involve a payment out of the National Insurance Fund, and in that event he shall be treated for the purposes of these rules as if he were a party.

11. Procedure at hearing

(1)   The tribunal shall, so far as it appears to it appropriate, seek to avoid formality in its proceedings and shall not be bound by any enactment or rule of law relating to the admissibility of evidence in proceedings before the courts of law. The tribunal shall make such enquiries of persons appearing before it and witnesses as it considers appropriate and shall otherwise conduct the hearing in such manner as it considers most

appropriate for the clarification of the issues before it and generally to the just handling of the proceedings.

(2)   Subject to paragraph (1), at the hearing of the originating application a party shall be entitled to give evidence, to call witnesses, to question any witnesses and to address the tribunal.

(3)   If a party fails to attend or to be represented at the time and place fixed for the hearing, the tribunal may, if that party is an applicant, dismiss or, in any case, dispose of the application in the absence of that party or may adjourn the hearing to a later date; provided that before dismissing or disposing of any application in the absence of a party the tribunal shall consider his originating application or notice of appearance, any representations in writing presented by him in pursuance of rule 10(5) and any written answer furnished to the tribunal pursuant to rule 4(3).

(4)   A tribunal may require any witness to give evidence on oath or affirmation and for that purpose there may be administered an oath or affirmation in due form.

12. Decision of tribunal

(1)   Where a tribunal is composed of three members its decision may be taken by a majority; and if a tribunal is composed of two members only, the chairman shall have a second or casting vote.

(2)   The decision of a tribunal, which may be given orally at the end of a hearing or reserved, shall be recorded in a document signed by the chairman.

(3)   The tribunal shall give reasons for its decision in a document signed by the chairman. That document shall contain a statement as to whether the reasons are given in summary or extended form and where the tribunal—

(a)   makes an award of compensation, or
(b)   comes to any other determination by virtue of which one party is required to pay a sum to another (excluding an award of costs or allowances),

the document shall also contain a statement of the amount of compensation awarded, or of the sum required to be paid, followed either by a table showing how the amount or sum has been calculated or by a description of the manner in which it has been calculated.

(4)   The reasons for the decision of the tribunal shall be given in summary form except where—

(a)   the proceedings involved the determination of an issue arising under or relating to the 1970 Act, the 1975 Act, the 1986 Act, the 1976 Act or the 1995 Act;

(b)   a request that the reasons be given in extended form is made orally at the hearing by a party;

(c)   such a request is made in writing by a party after the hearing either—

      (i)   before any document recording the reasons in summary form is sent to the parties, or

      (ii)   within 21 days of the date on which that document was sent to the parties; or

(d)   the tribunal considers that reasons given in summary form would not sufficiently explain the grounds for its decision;

and in those circumstances the reasons shall be given in extended form.

(5)   The clerk shall transmit the documents referred to in paragraphs (2) and (3) to the Secretary who shall enter them in the Register and shall send a copy of the entry to each of the parties and, where the proceedings were referred to the tribunal by a court, to that court.

(6)   The document referred to in paragraph (3) shall be omitted from the Register in any case in which evidence has been heard in private and the tribunal so directs. In such a case the Secretary shall send that document to each of the parties; and where there are proceedings before a superior court relating to the decision in question, he shall send the document to that court, together with a copy of the entry in the Register of the document referred to in paragraph (2).

(7)   In any case appearing to involve allegations of a sexual offence, the document referred to in paragraph (3) shall be entered on the Register with such deletions or amendments as have been made in accordance with rule 15(6).

(8)   Clerical mistakes in the documents referred to in paragraphs (2) and (3), or errors arising in those documents from an accidental slip or omission, may at any time be corrected by the chairman by certificate.

(9)   If a document is corrected by certificate under paragraph (8), or if a decision is—

(a)   revoked or varied under rule 13, or

(b)   altered in any way by order of a superior court,

the Secretary shall alter any entry in the Register which is affected to conform with the certificate or order and send a copy of any entry so altered to each of the parties and, where the proceedings were referred to the tribunal by a court, to that court.

(10) Where a document omitted from the Register pursuant to paragraph (6) is corrected by certificate under paragraph (8), the Secretary shall send a copy of the corrected document to the parties; and where there are proceedings before any superior court relating to the decision in question, he shall send a copy to that court together with a copy of the entry in the Register of the document referred to in paragraph (2), if it has been altered under paragraph (9).

(11) Where this rule requires a document to be signed by the chairman of a tribunal composed of three or two persons, but by reason of death or incapacity the chairman is unable to sign it, the document shall be signed by the other members or member of the tribunal, who shall certify that the chairman is unable to sign.

13. Review of tribunal's decision

(1) Subject to the provisions of this rule, a tribunal shall have power, on the application of a party or of its own motion, to review any decision on the grounds that—

(a) the decision was wrongly made as a result of an error on the part of the tribunal staff;
(b) a party did not receive notice of the proceedings leading to the decision;
(c) the decision was made in the absence of a party;
(d) new evidence has become available since the conclusion of the hearing to which the decision relates, provided that its existence could not have been reasonably known of or foreseen at the time of the hearing; or
(e) the interests of justice require such a review.

(2) A tribunal may not review a decision of its own motion unless it is the tribunal which issued the decision.

(3) A tribunal may only review a decision of its own motion if—

(a) it has sent notice to each of the parties explaining in summary form the ground upon which and reasons why it is proposed to review the decision and giving them an opportunity to show cause why there should be no review; and
(b) such notice has been sent on or after the date of the hearing, but within 14 days of the date on which the decision was sent to the parties.

(4) An application for the purposes of paragraph (1) may be made at the hearing. If no application is made at the hearing, an application may be

made to the Secretary on or after the date of the hearing, but within 14 days of the date on which the decision was sent to the parties. Such application must be in writing and must state the grounds in full.

(5) An application for the purposes of paragraph (1) may be refused by the President or by the chairman of the tribunal which decided the case or by a Regional Chairman if in his opinion it has no reasonable prospect of success.

(6) If such an application is not refused under paragraph (5) it shall be heard by the tribunal which decided the case, or—

(a)   where it is not practicable for it to be heard by that tribunal, or
(b)   where the decision was made by a chairman acting alone under rule 15(8),

by a tribunal appointed by either the President or a Regional Chairman.

(7) On reviewing its decision a tribunal may confirm the decision, or vary or revoke the decision; and if it revokes the decision, the tribunal shall order a re-hearing before either the same or a differently constituted tribunal.

14. Costs

(1) Where, in the opinion of the tribunal, a party has in bringing the proceedings, or a party or a party's representative has in conducting the proceedings, acted vexatiously, abusively, disruptively or otherwise unreasonably, or the bringing or conducting of the proceedings by a party has been misconceived, the tribunal shall consider making, and if it so decides, may make—

(a)   an order containing an award against that party in respect of the costs incurred by another party;
(b)   an order that that party shall pay to the Secretary of State the whole, or any part, of any allowances (other than allowances paid to members of tribunals) paid by the Secretary of State under section 5(2) or (3) of the 1996 Act to any person for the purposes of, or in connection with, his attendance at the tribunal.

(2) Paragraph (1) applies to a respondent who has not entered an appearance in relation to the conduct of any part in the proceedings which he has taken.

(3) An order containing an award against a party ('the first party') in respect of the costs incurred by another party ('the second party') shall be—

(a)   where the tribunal thinks fit, an order that the first party pay to the second party a specified sum not exceeding £10,000;

(b)   where those parties agree on a sum to be paid by the first party to the second party in respect of those costs, an order that the first party pay to the second party a specified sum, being the sum so agreed; or

(c)   in any other case, an order that the first party pay to the second party the whole or a specified part of the costs incurred by the second party as assessed by way of detailed assessment (if not otherwise agreed).

(4)   Where the tribunal has on the application of a party postponed the day or time fixed for or adjourned the hearing, the tribunal may make orders, of the kinds mentioned in paragraphs (1)(a) and (1)(b), against or, as the case may require, in favour of that party as respects any costs incurred or any allowances paid as a result of the postponement or adjournment.

(5)   A tribunal shall make orders against a respondent of the kinds mentioned in paragraphs (1)(a) and (1)(b) as respects any costs or any allowances paid as a result of the postponement or adjournment of a hearing where, on a complaint of unfair dismissal, the applicant has expressed a wish to be reinstated or re-engaged which has been communicated to the respondent not less than 7 days before the hearing of the complaint and the postponement or adjournment has been caused by the respondent's failure, without a special reason, to adduce reasonable evidence as to the availability of the job from which the applicant was dismissed, or of comparable or suitable employment.

(6)   Any costs required by an order under this rule to be assessed by way of detailed assessment may be so assessed in the County Court in accordance with the Civil Procedure Rules 1998.

(7)   Where—

(a)   a party has been ordered under rule 7 to pay a deposit as a condition of being permitted to continue to participate in proceedings relating to a matter;

(b)   in respect of that matter, the tribunal has found against that party in its decision, and

(c)   there has been no award of costs made against that party arising out of the proceedings on the matter,

the tribunal shall consider whether to award costs against that party on the ground that he conducted the proceedings relating to the matter unreasonably in persisting in having the matter determined by a tribunal; but the tribunal shall not make an award of costs on that ground unless it has considered the document recording the order under rule 7 and is of the opinion that the reasons which caused the tribunal to find against the party in its decision were substantially the same as the reasons recorded in that document for considering that the contentions of the party had no reasonable prospect of success.

(8)   Where an award of costs is made against a party who has had an order under rule 7 made against him (whether the award arises out of the proceedings relating to the matter in respect of which the order was made or out of proceedings relating to any other matter considered with that matter), his deposit shall be paid in part or full settlement of the award—

(a)   where an award is made in favour of one party, to that party, and

(b)   where awards are made in favour of more than one party, to all of them or any one or more of them as the tribunal thinks fit, and if to all or more than one, in such proportions as the tribunal considers appropriate,

and if the amount of the deposit exceeds the amount of the award of costs, the balance shall be refunded to the party who paid it.

15. Miscellaneous powers

(1)   Subject to the provisions of these rules, a tribunal may regulate its own procedure.

(2)   A tribunal may—

(a)   if the applicant at any time gives notice of the withdrawal of his originating application, dismiss the proceedings;

(b)   if both or all the parties agree in writing upon the terms of a decision to be made by the tribunal, decide accordingly;

(c)   subject to paragraph (3), at any stage of the proceedings, order to be struck out or amended any originating application or notice of appearance, or anything in such application or notice of appearance, on the grounds that it is scandalous, misconceived or vexatious;

(d)   subject to paragraph (3), at any stage of the proceedings, order to be struck out any originating application or notice of appearance on the grounds that the manner in which the proceedings have been conducted by or on behalf of the applicant or, as the case may be, respondent has been scandalous, unreasonable or vexatious; and

(e)   subject to paragraph (3), on the application of the respondent, or of its own motion, order an originating application to be struck out for want of prosecution.

(3)   Before making an order under sub-paragraph (c), (d) or (e) of paragraph (2) the tribunal shall send notice to the party against whom it is proposed that the order should be made giving him an opportunity to show cause why the order should not be made; but this paragraph shall not be taken to require the tribunal to send such notice to that party if the party

has been given an opportunity to show cause orally why the order should not be made.

(4) Where a notice required by paragraph (3) is sent in relation to an order to strike out an originating application for want of prosecution, service of the notice shall be treated as having been effected if it has been sent by post or delivered in accordance with rule 23(4) and the tribunal may strike out the originating application (notwithstanding that there has been no direction for substituted service in accordance with rule 23(7)) if the party does not avail himself of the opportunity given by the notice.

(5) A tribunal may, before determining an application under rule 4 or rule 19, require the party making the application to give notice of it to every other party. The notice shall give particulars of the application and indicate the address to which and the time within which any objection to the application shall be made, being an address and time specified for the purposes of the application by the tribunal.

(6) In any case appearing to involve allegations of the commission of a sexual offence, the tribunal or the Secretary shall omit from the Register, or delete from the Register or any decision, document or record of the proceedings, which is available to the public, any identifying matter which is likely to lead members of the public to identify any person affected by or making such an allegation.

(7) A chairman may postpone the day or time fixed for, or adjourn, any hearing (particularly where an enactment provides for conciliation in relation to the case, for the purpose of giving an opportunity for the case to be settled by way of conciliation and withdrawn) and vary any such postponement or adjournment.

(8) Any act required or authorised by these rules to be done by a tribunal may be done by a chairman except—

(a)   the hearing of an originating application under rule 10;
(b)   an act required or authorised to be so done by rule 11 or 12 which

       the rule implies is to be done by the tribunal which is hearing or heard the originating application;
(c)   the review of a decision under rule 13(1), and the confirmation, variation or revocation of a decision, and ordering of a re-hearing, under rule 13(7).

(9) Any act required or authorised by rule 17 and paragraph (7) to be done by a chairman may be done by a tribunal or on the direction of a chairman.

(10) Any function of the Secretary may be performed by a Regional Secretary or by a person acting with the authority of the Secretary or of a Regional Secretary.

16. Restricted reporting orders

(1) In any case which involves allegations of sexual misconduct the tribunal may at any time before promulgation of its decision in respect of an originating application, either on the application of a party made by notice to the Secretary or of its own motion, make a restricted reporting order.

(2) In proceedings on a complaint under section 8 of the 1995 Act in which evidence of a personal nature is likely to be heard by the tribunal, it may at any time before promulgation of its decision in respect of an originating application, either on the application of the complainant made by notice to the Secretary or of its own motion, make a restricted reporting order.

(3) Where the tribunal makes a restricted reporting order under paragraph (2) and that complaint is being dealt with together with any other proceedings, the tribunal may direct that the order applies also in relation to those other proceedings or such part of them as the tribunal may direct.

(4) The tribunal shall not make a restricted reporting order unless it has given each party an opportunity to advance oral argument at a hearing, if they so wish.

(5) Where a tribunal makes a restricted reporting order—

(a)   it shall specify in the order the persons who may not be identified;
(b)   the order shall remain in force until the promulgation of the decision of the tribunal on the originating application to which it relates unless revoked earlier; and
(c)   the Regional Secretary shall ensure that a notice of that fact is displayed on the notice board of the tribunal with any list of the proceedings taking place before the employment tribunal, and on the door of the room in which the proceedings affected by the order are taking place.

(6) A tribunal may revoke a restricted reporting order at any time if it thinks fit.

(7) For the purposes of this rule 'promulgation' occurs on the date recorded as being the date on which the document recording the determination of the originating application was sent to the parties.

17. Extension of time

(1)   A chairman may, on the application of a party or of his own motion, extend the time for doing any act appointed by or under these rules (including this rule) and may do so whether or not the time so appointed has expired.

(2)   An application under paragraph (1) shall be made by presenting to the Secretary a notice of application, which shall state the title of the proceedings and shall set out the grounds of the application.

(3)   The Secretary shall give notice to each of the parties of any extension of time granted under this rule.

18. Devolution issues

(1)   In any proceedings in which a devolution issue arises, the Secretary shall as soon as reasonably practicable by notice inform the relevant authority thereof (unless the person to whom notice would be given is a party to the proceedings) and shall at the same time—

(a)   send a copy of the notice to the parties to the proceedings; and
(b)   send the relevant authority a copy of the originating application and the notice of appearance.

(2)   A person to whom notice is given in pursuance of paragraph (1) may within 14 days of receipt thereof by notice to the Secretary take part as a party in the proceedings, so far as they relate to the devolution issue. The Secretary shall send a copy of the notice to the other parties to the proceedings.

19. Joinder and representative respondents

(1)   A tribunal may at any time, on the application of any person made by notice to the Secretary or of its own motion, direct any person against whom any relief is sought to be joined as a party, and give such consequential directions as it considers necessary.

(2)   A tribunal may likewise, on such application or of its own motion, order that any respondent named in the originating application or subsequently added, who appears to the tribunal not to have been, or to have ceased to be, directly interested in the subject of the originating application, be dismissed from the proceedings.

(3)   Where there are a number of persons having the same interest in an originating application, one or more of them may be cited as the person or persons against whom relief is sought, or may be authorised by the tribunal, before or at the hearing, to defend on behalf of all the persons so interested.

20. Combined proceedings

(1)   Where, in relation to two or more originating applications pending before the employment tribunals, it appears to an employment tribunal, on the application of a party made by notice to the Secretary or of its own motion, that—

(a)   a common question of law or fact arises in some or all the originating applications, or
(b)   the relief claimed in some or all of those originating applications is in respect of or arises out of the same set of facts, or
(c)   for any other reason it is desirable to make an order under this rule,

the tribunal may order that some (as specified in the order) or all of the originating applications in respect of which it so appears to the tribunal shall be considered together, and may give such consequential directions as may be necessary.

(2)   The tribunal shall only make an order under this rule if—

(a)   each of the parties concerned has been given an opportunity at a hearing to show cause why such an order should not be made; or
(b)   it has sent notice to all the parties concerned giving them an opportunity to show such cause.

(3)   The tribunal may, on the application of a party made by notice to the Secretary or of its own motion, vary or set aside an order made under this rule but shall not do so unless it has given each party an opportunity to make either oral or written representations before the order is varied or set aside.

21. Transfer of proceedings

(1)   On the application of a party made by notice to the Secretary or of his own motion, the President or a Regional Chairman may at any time, with the consent of the President of the Employment Tribunals (Scotland), direct any proceedings to be transferred to the Office of the Employment Tribunals (Scotland) if it appears to him that the proceedings could be, and would more conveniently be, determined in an employment tribunal (Scotland) established in pursuance of the Employment Tribunals (Constitution and Rules of Procedure) (Scotland) Regulations 2001; but no such direction shall be made unless notice has been sent to all parties concerned giving them an opportunity to show cause why a direction should not be made.

(2)   Where proceedings have been transferred to the Office of the Employment Tribunals (England and Wales) under rule 21(1) of the Employment Tribunals Rules of Procedure (Scotland) 2001 they shall be

treated as if in all respects they had been commenced by an originating application pursuant to rule 1.

22. References to the European Court of Justice

Where a tribunal makes an order referring a question to the European Court of Justice for a preliminary ruling under Article 234 of the Treaty establishing the European Community, the Secretary shall send a copy of the order to the Registrar of that Court but shall not do so until the time for appealing against the order has expired or, if an appeal is made within that time, until the appeal has been determined or otherwise disposed of.

23. Notices, etc

(1)   Any notice given under these rules shall be in writing.

(2)   All notices and documents required by these rules to be presented to the Secretary, other than an originating application, may be presented at the Office of the Tribunals or such other office as may be notified by the Secretary to the parties.

(3)   An originating application may be presented at the Office of the Tribunals or at any Regional Office of the Employment Tribunals.

(4)   All notices and documents required or authorised by these rules to be sent or given to any person hereinafter mentioned may be sent by post (subject to paragraph (6)) or delivered to or at—

(a)   in the case of a notice or document directed to the Secretary of State in proceedings to which he is not a party (or in respect of which he is treated as a party for the purpose of these rules by virtue of rule 10(7)), the offices of the Department of Trade and Industry (Employment Relations Directorate 2) at 1 Victoria Street, London, SW1H 0ET, or such other office as may be notified by the Secretary of State;

(b)   in the case of a notice or document directed to the Attorney General pursuant to rule 18, the Attorney General's Chambers, 9 Buckingham Gate, London, SW1E 7JP;

(c)   in the case of a notice or document directed to the National Assembly for Wales pursuant to rule 18, the Counsel General to the National Assembly for Wales, Crown Buildings, Cathays Park, Cardiff, CF10 3NQ;

(d)   in the case of a notice or document directed to a court, the office of the clerk of the court;

(e)   in the case of a notice or document directed to a party—

(i)   the address specified in his originating application or notice of appearance to which notices and documents are to be sent, or in a notice under paragraph (5), or

(ii)   if no such address has been specified, or if a notice sent to such an address has been returned, to any other known address or place of business in the United Kingdom or, if the party is a corporate body, the body's registered or principal office in the United Kingdom, or, in any case, such address or place outside the United Kingdom as the President or a Regional Chairman may allow;

(f)   in the case of a notice or document directed to any person (other than a person specified in the foregoing provisions of this paragraph), his address or place of business in the United Kingdom or, if the person is a corporate body, the body's registered or principal office in the United Kingdom;

and a notice or document sent or given to the authorised representative of a party shall be deemed to have been sent or given to that party.

(5) A party may at any time by notice to the Secretary and to the other party or parties (and, where appropriate, to the appropriate conciliation officer) change the address to which notices and documents are to be sent.

(6) The recorded delivery service shall be used instead of the ordinary post—

(a)   when a second set of notices or documents is sent to a respondent who has not entered an appearance under rule 3(1); and

(b)   for service of an order made under rule 4(5).

(7) The President or a Regional Chairman may direct that there shall be substituted service in such manner as he may deem fit in any case he considers appropriate.

(8) In proceedings brought under the provisions of any enactment providing for conciliation the Secretary shall send copies of all documents and notices to a conciliation officer who in the opinion of the Secretary is an appropriate officer to receive them.

(9) Paragraph (8) does not apply in relation to documents or notices falling within a description of documents or notices in respect of which the Secretary and the Advisory, Conciliation and Arbitration Service have agreed that copies need not be sent.

(10) In proceedings which may involve a payment out of the National Insurance Fund, the Secretary shall, where appropriate, send copies of all documents and notices to the Secretary of State whether or not he is a party.

(11) Copies of every document and copy entry sent to the parties under rules 12(5) or 12(9) shall—

(a)   in the case of proceedings under the 1970 Act, the 1975 Act or the 1986 Act, be sent to the Equal Opportunities Commission;

(b)   in the case of proceedings under the 1976 Act, be sent to the Commission for Racial Equality; and

(c)   in the case of proceedings under the 1995 Act, be sent to the Disability Rights Commission.

INDEX

References are to paragraph numbers and Appendices (App).